Teaching young children
with special needs

Teaching young children with special needs

PHILIP L. SAFFORD, Ph.D.

Professor and Chairman, Department of
Special Education, Kent State University,
Kent, Ohio

with 62 illustrations

THE C. V. MOSBY COMPANY

Saint Louis 1978

Library of Congress Cataloging in Publication Data

Safford, Philip L
  Teaching young children with special needs.

  Bibliography: p.
  Includes index.
  1. Exceptional children—Education. I. Title.
LC3965.S23   371.9   77-14047
ISBN 0-8016-4294-9

CB/CB/B 9 8 7 6 5 4 3 2 1

To
Jane, a very special teacher
Beth
Lynne

FOREWORD

by William C. Morse, Ph.D.

Professor of Education and Psychology,
University of Michigan,
Ann Arbor, Michigan

The very title *Teaching Young Children With Special Needs* invites a wide audience, since there are a great many persons concerned with preschool and young school-aged special children. These are not just "special teachers," although, of course, one assumes the primary interest of teachers in special education. While most children with special needs have always been in regular educational settings, the advent of formal mainstreaming and mandatory federal and state legislation have made regular teachers formally accountable. This accountability requires individualized plans that state reasonable goals related to appropriate education procedures and followed up by periodic reevaluation. Meeting these new legal stipulations calls for considerable expertise. Ignorance is no longer an acceptable excuse.

Since this book covers all areas of special needs, regular and special teachers of young children will recognize its value as a basic reference. Those ancillary personnel both within and outside of the schools who give consultation and participate in planning the interventions will find this book every bit as helpful as will teachers. Psychologists, social workers, administrators, and medical personnel will also find this book essential.

If there is any one thing that characterizes the present approach to special children, particularly young children, it is the recognition that schools cannot function alone. Other community agencies have a part to play. This book will provide information such personnel need to appreciate the nature of a good school program as well as how to contribute to excellence.

But there is another new group of professionals: the parents. The home is the major influence on all children, but especially on young children. In the past we have underestimated the parents' role, concern, and desire to understand the education of their special children. Not only classroom aides or assistants, but also parents, want to read material relevant to their children. Now Dr. Safford has provided a resource for these new "lay professionals." The growing group of articulate parents will find it as useful as will professional educators because this book passes the true test of scholarship for an applied field: the substantive material rests on a firm base, but it is written in plain English. Dr. Safford has provided a careful review and analysis of the fundamental research and theory reported in language that is understandable.

Although a title such as *Teaching Young Children With Special Needs* is engaging, cautious evaluation is required because new areas attract the "quick into print," who wish to capitalize on the desperation of those who find new responsibilities thrust upon them. Many authors come to a complex matter such as this with one of two approaches. The first alternative is to present oversimplified answers that have limited utility. They promise to make the reader an instant success; the children are all made to fit a theory. A second alternative is the compendium method—each chapter written by a different expert with a jumble of theoretical positions put together inside one cover.

How has Dr. Safford avoided these difficulties? He defines the "young child" as from birth to 8 years old, so that the book encompasses not only the usual preschool and first-grade settings but also teaching in the home, through parents. And his viewpoint has evolved from actual cooperative work with experienced teachers; thus it is firmly anchored in reality.

Because of his focus on the child, Dr. Safford is not trapped in any single method or point of view. He sees the value of each approach when it fits a specific situation or a condition confronting a child. But there are two features that help to make this book an integrated synthesis rather than a collection of chapters. First is the constant focus on the whole complex child. It is the nature of the child that dominates all else. The result is a book with an intrinsic humanistic approach. The counterpart helping adult is thus an adult who responds to this whole child. The adult attempts to solve the child's problem—using interventions that reflect various schools of thought. Second, while the volume contains much specific advice, it is no cookbook. The challenge given is to know enough about children's problems to devise relevant strategies. These strategies in turn rest on diverse psychological approaches.

It is clear that we are presented a new image of a teacher, with new roles and across categories. If we are going to be dealing with the child as a whole we must find the wide range of personnel to comprise the "whole" teaching function. There is no illusion that a teacher can do it all alone: collegial relationships are stressed as necessary. In fact Dr. Safford

himself uses his advice in many ways in this volume. He depicts team functioning that includes parents and a wide range of additional experts; often agencies other than the school must help.

Dr. Safford's point of view is an ecological one—the child as an individual interacting with extrinsic conditions in the setting. The child is seen as an activist engaged with the environment in cognitive, affective, and motor ways, not just as a passive responder. What there is to respond to and how this can be rearranged are as important as individual pathology. Thus the procedure is to diagnose and apply specific corrective processes. The teacher no longer works just in a given setting with one set ritual for everything; now the teacher must work with the child in his total life setting.

Each chapter in this book stands by itself, starting with discussions of incidence and identification and carrying through on practice. Yet there are general aspects as well that appear as themes: diagnosis, developmental awareness, and specific remediation. The concreteness of the suggestions to the teacher is most noteworthy. One is not left only with generalizations; there are specific suggestions in every chapter and in the appendices as well.

The final chapters deal with vital issues: the term "least restrictive" is described psychologically rather than by administrative fiat, a view that is most helpful. Individualization is the core of the method summarized. The legal aspects are expanded again to the psychological aspects of attitudes.

This is a prodigious effort, a book that will not be dated. The historical perspective prevents the shallow thinking so common today. The specificity of content and encompassing nature of the coverage will mark it for not only teachers but for all professionals. Dr. Safford deserves our appreciation for this encouraging book in a critical area of education.

FOREWORD

by **Christine F. Branche**, Director
Division of Early Childhood Education,
Cleveland Public Schools,
Cleveland, Ohio

During the mid-1970s the nation suddenly discovered that thousands of youngsters with handicapping conditions were isolated and alienated from the mainstream of educational opportunity. This belated observation and the legislation that followed caused considerable panic among the providers of educational services in schools, day care centers, and hospitals. However, there has been little practical assistance available in remedying the problem. Finally, an experienced scholar and educator has come to the aid of the daily practitioner with *Teaching Young Children With Special Needs*. Dr. Safford's timely, practical, comprehensive volume will be an invaluable resource to all who work with children from birth to 8 years of age. Although focused on the handicapped, the book clearly defines every child as special and recognizes that all children have special needs. The challenge to professionals is the early recognition of specific problems and the provision of appropriate, effective intervention.

For convenience the book is organized around identified areas of exceptionality, including giftedness. It is rare indeed to find theory and practice so well integrated in language that is easily understood and readily applicable. The solutions presented mandate an interdisciplinary *team* approach with support of the entire staff and the maximum involvement of parents. This broadening of the circle of participants is helpful at any age level if each child's best efforts are to be elicited.

Dr. Safford challenges caring professionals to optimize learning by becoming highly skilled in identifying needs and competent in orchestrating solutions in the "least restrictive" environment. Love and good intentions are not enough to get the job done! Children deserve not only a community of supportive adults in a warm, caring environment, but also a clear expectation of success and growth.

Dr. Safford calls repeatedly on all who work in early childhood programs to value and respect the right of children to the individual differences that are a part of the normal developmental process. Individuality must be allowed even as commonalities are preserved. So easily said, so difficult to accomplish.

This is a comprehensive textbook for staff development across many disciplines. Dr. Safford projects insight and humanity in an area that demands our immediate concern and action. His book can help us to move forward in our work on behalf of all young children.

PREFACE

The status of handicapped persons in our society has changed so rapidly within such a brief time that many people may believe that a little complacency is not inappropriate. Teachers know better. A few years ago, I would have specified *special education* teachers, but not today. Every teacher, at every level, from the nursery school through the graduate school, can now be expected to assume responsibility for the education of handicapped students.

This book does not deal with the entire spectrum, however. Its focus is on *young children*—young children who have special needs. Its intent is to provide some basic information concerning handicapping conditions that affect young children and some teaching suggestions that will be of value to those who have, or will have, the responsibility for providing them with *individualized learning opportunities in the "least restrictive" setting.*

It will come as no news to readers that early education now encompasses, not only a broader age range than in the past, but also a broader range of disciplines, services, agencies, and approaches. This is, of course, particularly true when it comes to determining how best to help young children who are exceptional. Consequently, I have attempted in writing this book to address *anyone who teaches or is preparing to teach children of any age from birth through approximately 8 years* (an arbitrary cut-off point, in some ways). This includes teachers in day care, nursery school, kindergarten, and primary grade settings; teachers in specialized settings, such as hospitals; and students in early childhood education. It also includes home visitors, as well as professionals who practice in any of the related services essential to the education of young handicapped children (occupational and physical therapists, speech clinicians, psychologists, social workers, and many others), and it includes parents of young children with special needs.

Students and currently practicing teachers in special education should also find this material valuable. The role of the special educator has been changing rapidly, and several of the organizing themes of this text are intended to reflect and to respond to these changes. Specifically, special educators will probably have increasing need to involve themselves effectively with a broader range both of *forms* and of *degrees* of childhood disabilities than in the past. Their services will be less categorically focused on a specific "kind" of exceptionality. In addition, they will be called on increasingly to function as members of interdisciplinary planning and service delivery teams. This calls for additional competencies beyond those required in the direct teaching of children. A related challenge is that posed by the move toward integration, as much as possible, of handicapped and nonhandicapped children. How can special educators most effectively help their colleagues to *implement a special education program within a regular education setting?*

A major concern involves the responsibility of public education to severely, profoundly, and multiply handicapped children. Here is the new challenge to the special educator! But he or she can certainly not meet it alone. A fifth theme—and, again, a theme related to all of the others—is that of the *parent-teacher team*. This is the basic unit for helping the young child with special needs. Finally, special educators recognize the need to provide early identification of exceptional children and early and appropriate intervention. When we consider the need to provide these as early in a child's life as possible, perhaps beginning at birth, we recognize gaps in our knowledge. The reader may experience some frustration on realizing that the answer to some of his or her most urgent questions must be, at this writing, "We simply don't know—yet."

This book, with the exception of Sections I and VI, is organized around general areas of disability. It can be argued that any kind of organization suggesting a categorical orientation to exceptionality is inappropriate. Nevertheless, a sort of compromise position is taken. The sections are entitled Sensory and Communication Handicaps (speech and language, hearing, and visual impairments), Mild and Moderate Educational Handicaps (mild and moderate mental retardation, learning disabilities, and emotional or behavioral problems), Physical Disabilities and Severe or Multiple Impairments (including physical and neurological impairments and severe, profound, and multiple handicaps), and Gifted and Talented Children.

The text begins with an introductory chapter that, in addition to defining the domains of early education and exceptionality in general terms, has two main goals. The chapter discusses the general rationale for educational intervention early in life for children with special needs, and it introduces what could be considered the basic theoretical orienta-tion that has guided much of the writing. Although one hopes for an informed eclecticism, one's own particular frame of reference can scarcely be cast aside in writing a text of this sort. That I have been heavily influenced by the developmental theories of Jean Piaget and Erik Erikson will probably be apparent to many readers. I have also been affected by Lawrence Kohlberg's point of view that *the goal of education is development.* Our task in considering how education can enhance the development of children with special needs is to *intervene* in ways that can enable these children to experience the child-environment interaction upon which optimal development depends.

The last section elaborates on what are believed to be three basic dimensions of least restrictive alternative education for children with special needs: the dimension of *environment* for early learning, strategies for diagnostic teaching that are focused on the *individual needs* of young children, and the area of *attitude.* Each of these major dimensions is discussed to varying degrees elsewhere in the text with regard to particular forms of exceptionality. However, in this final section the intent is to integrate issues and guidelines that cut across forms of exceptionality.

This book has grown to a great extent out of my own experiences as a teacher, as a teacher-educator, and as a consultant-participant in many early education programs. While at Case Western Reserve University, I was enabled, through a federal grant awarded under the Education Professions Development Act, to work for 3 years with experienced teachers in a number of "front-line" projects with young, high-risk children. Our organizing framework for these efforts was *the prevention of learning and behavior disorders in young children.* From these excellent EPDA Fellows, from the children, teachers, and parents who worked with us, and from the guidance and technical assistance of Malcolm Davis, Edward

Moore, William Smith, Evelyn Deno, Maynard Reynolds, Earl Avery, and other EPDA associates, I learned a great deal about parent and community involvement, providing for handicapped children within regular school settings, and preparation of teachers of children with special needs. Our own project was enriched by the contributions of many people. Their particular contributions were especially meaningful in retrospect as I undertook through this book to translate some of our insights and experiences into guidelines for teachers of young children with special needs; the following individuals are especially acknowledged: Drs. Harriet Alger, John Gehrs, Nancy Klein, and Gloria Small Light; Addie Taylor, Sandra Redmond, and David Wallace (project staff members); Christine F. Branche, Rae Marks, Julia Newman, and many other colleagues in the Early Education Programs of the Cleveland schools; co-workers in community-based programs; Dr. Jane W. Kessler and the clinical staff of the Mental Development Center; faculty colleagues involved with the project, especially Dr. Gerald Jorgenson; and many others, far too numerous to mention.

The other major source of background for this book is my long-standing close relationship with The Society for Crippled Children of Cuyahoga County. To the opportunities I have had to be associated with the programs for young children provided by this outstanding agency, especially Project HEED, I must credit a large share of the inspiration and background required to undertake this book. Specifically, my professional association and collaboration with Dena C. Arbitman has been a rich source of learning for me. The support of William B. Townsend, Director, must also be acknowledged, as must the inspiration and the enrichment of my background stemming from long-standing associations with other professionals at this agency—especially Marguerite Campbell, Laura Gregg Dunne, and my wife, Jane Safford.

For their assistance in the actual preparation of this book, I wish particularly to express my gratitude to Dr. Joanne Hendrick, for her valuable guidance and to several individuals for their expert assistance with specific portions and topics:

Marylou E. Boynton of the University of Rochester, who provided expert collaboration in the treatment of material on blind infants

Muriel Munro of Kent State University, who contributed both constructive criticism and specific guidance concerning hearing-impaired children

Dr. M. Suzanne Hasenstab of the University of Virginia, Charlottesville, who guided me at the beginning in exploring the literature concerning young hearing-impaired children

Dr. Thomas Serwatka of the University of North Florida, who provided guidance and suggestions concerning speech and language problems

Charlotte McQuilkin of the Kent City School District, a master teacher of young mentally retarded children, who provided valuable criticism and guidance in the preparation of that chapter

Dr. Robert Zuckerman of Kent State University, who helped me in many specific ways

Dr. Wilber Simmons of Kent State University, who counseled me concerning gifted and talented children and who contributed material to that chapter

Dr. W. Jean Schindler of the University of Tennessee, Knoxville, who also helped with the chapter on gifted and talented children

Dr. Gloria Small Light, formerly of Case Western Reserve University, who helped me think about environments for learning

And especially Jane Safford of The Society for Crippled Children of Cuyahoga County, who provided specific guidance in the preparation of the chapter concerning young physically handicapped children and who has helped in countless less tangible ways

I must also thank several individuals whose work and association have contributed significantly to my understanding of the severely and profoundly handicapped child: Frances Archer, Phillipa Campbell, Nicholas DeFazio, John Gaus, and Drs. William Bricker and Jeanette Reuter. For the material in the appendices, I am indebted to Ruth Fisher, Director of the United Services for the Handicapped Developmental Preschool in Akron, Ohio; to that agency for permission to include the material; and to Alice Kusmierek for her valuable contributions.

Special appreciation is expressed for the enthusiastic and expert assistance of Gwen Dix, a skilled and sensitive observer of young children, and Lawrence Rubens, Photographic Director, Audio-Visual Services, Kent State University. Their combined talents produced much of the photographic material. Many thanks go also to Gary Reider, Society for Crippled Children, for his willing, expert assistance in the photographic work and to Eugene Maxwell, Association for University Architects, for sharing his superb design of a playground soon to be constructed at The Society for Crippled Children of Cuyahoga County. The cooperation and help of the children, their parents, and the staffs of the centers where the photography was done are particularly appreciated: United Services for the Handicapped Developmental Preschool, The Society for Crippled Children of Cuyahoga County, Akron Children's Hospital Infant Therapy Program, Akron Child Guidance Center Developmental Class, and Kent City Schools.

For her constant, considerate assistance in many forms, including much of the typing of the manuscript, I am very grateful to Adele Marshall, and also to Diane Damicone, Kathryn Copman, and Marge Kenward for their help in typing.

I must also acknowledge with gratitude those from whom I have learned and whose inspiration, as well as tutelage, had much to do with my need to write this book. There are too many to name, but the opportunity to study at The University of Michigan and to learn from William C. Morse, Matthew J. Trippe, James A. Dunn, Melvyn I. Semmel, Calvin O. Dyer, John W. Hagen, and other great teachers imposed on me an obligation that I hope this book will in part repay.

Finally, I gratefully acknowledge both encouragement and assistance, direct and indirect, of colleagues and students at Kent State University.

Philip L. Safford

CONTENTS

Dimensions of the least restrictive alternative

Appendices

Foundations for early intervention

CHAPTER 1

EARLY EDUCATION AND EXCEPTIONAL CHILDREN

EARLY EDUCATION AND SPECIAL NEEDS

"As the twig is bent, so grows the tree." This old saying has taken on new meaning in recent times. We now know that the learning that occurs *before* a child usually enters school, at the age of 5 or 6 years, can have far-reaching consequences on his lifelong patterns of behavior. With such knowledge comes great responsibility, as well as excitement and challenge, for those who teach young children.

In no other dimension of early education is the need for early education seen more sharply than in the teaching of children with special needs. The history of education for these children has been marked by active parent involvement and by lonely and heroic determination on the part of a few pioneers, often against great odds. Today there is a heightened national consciousness and awareness of both the needs and the potential of children whose development may be impaired as a result of handicapping conditions—whether those conditions exist in his early environmental surroundings or within the child himself. Indeed, this distinction is itself difficult to make, as Bettye Caldwell (1973) suggests:

Regardless of the external surroundings, the environment of the young handicapped child is, by definition, depriving. If there is sensory deprivation, he cannot take in the best of the environments that are around him. If he has any kind of motor dysfunction, he cannot get up and move himself to find something better, or at least cannot move himself to a situation where the environment might make a better match with his own current developmental state. It is a clear situation of the old rule of the "haves" and the "have nots." The "have nots" continue to get less. It is very important, as we plan for any kind of environmental design or enrichment, to be aware of this point and to take it almost as a given when we talk about early programs for the handicapped. It is almost impossible to think of a handicapped child who does not have a deprived early environment. (p. 7)

Who are children with special needs?

"Special needs" is a term that has been proposed relatively recently. In the context of education, it refers to children who, because of either *intrinsic* (that is, within the child) or *extrinsic* (environmental) limitations, require some modification or adaptation of their educational program to achieve their maximum potential. Thus the term "children with special needs," in general, encompasses two major groups, which often overlap: children who are termed handicapped and children whose early socialization environments may be described, because of poverty and related factors, as disadvantaged. Terms such as "culturally deprived" and "culturally disadvantaged," which had wide currency in the early days of Project Head Start, have been found unacceptable because they convey a stereotyped and often totally inaccurate conception of family life and parenting patterns among the poor (Cole and Bruner, 1972). However, the child whose family endures severe economic hardship is certainly likely to be disadvantaged in terms of his own access to educational and economic opportunity.

The term "handicapped" must also be defined, since various interpretations of this word are abroad, each suggesting different implications for education. John Cawley (1975) distinguishes *handicap* from *disability*. The latter, he points out, refers to an objective condition, such as blindness, cleft palate, or cerebral palsy; the former, however, implies society's response to a specific disabling condition. With regard to education, one may have a disability without necessarily having a handicap. For example, a disabled child who is confined to a wheelchair may be handicapped in his attempts to attend public school in large part because of obstacles imposed by society, rather than by limitations he himself has. If transportation cannot be provided, if his classroom or lavatory is inaccessible, or if teachers or administrators are unreceptive or fearful, the fact that this child is not hampered intellectually and may be quite capable of learning may be overlooked or ignored. It is not the child alone who "causes" the handicapping condition. The limiting effects of a child's disability may be multiplied greatly if the response of educators is one of fear, prejudice, ignorance, or apathy.

The field of education today is marked by a new sensitivity to the special needs of children—and by a new awareness that all educators share the responsibility for meeting these needs. It does not belong only to a few specialists. Who are children with special needs? The definition is really a circular one. They are children for whom special adaptations in teaching method, administrative arrangement, or learning environment are required for them to learn in the optimal manner.

Why early education?

Together with a new awareness of the needs of handicapped individuals, recent years have witnessed a greatly increased appreciation for early childhood, not merely as a happy and magical time of life, since for many children it is not, but also as a time of great learning.

During the 1960s several trends combined to bring about an altered view of the purpose and promise of early childhood education. Several scholarly works, notably *Intelligence and Experience* by J. McVicker Hunt (1961) and *Stability and Change in Human Characteristics* by Benjamin S. Bloom (1964), gave impetus to a new conception of the possibilities of early childhood education as a social instrument. The suggestion that *external* factors could substantially influence the rate and the course of children's intellectual development, already implied by sociological data, received empirical and theoretical support. This generated renewed interest in the role of *experience* in influencing children. Furthermore, the extensive work of Jean Piaget concerning the development of thinking in young children was "discovered" by American educators.

A new respect was accorded early education, in keeping with its potential to shape lifelong patterns of behavior. Hunt's work implied that early influences played a significant role. From Bloom's analysis could be inferred suggestions concerning *how early* such influences would have impact. It seemed clear that the preschool years were crucial ones. Practicality, however, rather than theory, dictated that the year immediately preceding school entrance would become the target year for intervention through Project Head Start.

The Head Start experience yielded a number of insights. Perhaps age 4 years is too late, or perhaps early intervention can bring about significant gains only when early efforts are sustained and reinforced through programs such as Follow Through. Perhaps, too, home environment exerts such strong influence that school programs cannot hope to counteract it (Jencks et al., 1972). Thus early intervention programs were generated that focused on improving patterns of parenting and enhancing the *teaching-learning* aspect of the parent and child bond (Gray and Klaus, 1969; Gordon, 1967).

Today early childhood education can be seen as encompassing a broad range of programs. The first years in elementary school are generally considered to fall within the early childhood spectrum; however, the years preceding school entrance are particularly emphasized. As the question "How early is early enough?" remains unanswered, programs targeting on infancy are being stressed. That educators must assume responsibility for the educational development of children from birth on has been asserted by some authorities (White, 1975).

A question that remains is what *kinds* of early intervention would be most beneficial and for which children. Early education is characterized by wide divergence concerning teaching approaches and methods. Some criticize the "traditional nursery school" for its lack of attention to factors of intellectual development. Those who advocate a "cognitive" approach differ among themselves as to precisely what this means. (See, for example, Kamii and Radin, 1970; Lavatelli, 1968; Weikart et al., 1970; and Engleman, 1969.) While some writers equate "cognitivists" and "behaviorists" in the field of early education (Pines, 1966), representatives of both these camps find such comparisons quite inaccurate, if not odious! What approach is best for the child with special needs?

EDUCATION AND DEVELOPMENT

At least two broad traditions in the education of young children can be identified. One of these, one that has characterized most nursery school and kindergarten programs in the United States and that now frequently is identified by the term "traditional" or the term "child-centered," has its philosophical roots in the writing of Jean Jacques Rousseau, its pedagogical origins in the work of Friederich Froebel. The basic tenet of this tradition is that education is primarily a process through which the inherent potential of the child can be expressed.

The second major tradition has its roots in the philosophical writings of John Locke, its scientific foundation of empirical support within the mainstream of twentieth century academic psychology. The infant, according to Locke, is a *tabula rasa,* a blank slate, on which experience writes. Internal determinants, whether intraspecific or intraindividual, are less influential than are environmental influences. *Behavioristic learning theory,* the dominant stream in scientific psychology in the United States, tends to emphasize the environmental context in which observable behavior occurs, rather than speculating on internal causes of behavior or internal effects of experience.

The practical consequence of early childhood educators affirming either of these opposite positions is that they will tend to espouse a mode of education quite different from that implied by the other view. In some respects, the "environmentalist"

position can be thought of as the more optimistic of the two. According to this view, the child is not limited by an "internal timing" mechanism that will govern the rate and the manner in which his latent potential will "unfold" nor by his genetic inheritance. Given optimal environmental conditions, what the child becomes can in a real sense be determined by the environmental contingencies that impinge on him. Therefore it is essential that those adults who regulate these contingencies do so effectively and responsibly. Perhaps the most extreme statement of this point of view is found in the following familiar quotation from the writing of John Broadus Watson, the "father of behaviorism":

> Give me the baby and I'll make it climb and use its hands in construction of buildings of stone or wood. . . . I'll make it a thief, a gunman or a dope fiend. The possibilities of shaping it in any direction are almost endless. Even gross anatomical differences limit us far less than you may think. . . . Make him a deaf mute, and I will build you a Helen Keller. Men are built, not born. (1913, p. 233, quoted by Sprinthall and Sprinthall, 1974, p. 48)

One may question the *need* for education if psychological development proceeds mainly in an inwardly determined manner, propelled by internal, rather than external, forces. If, regardless of gross environmental differences, maturational and genetic influences are the major determinants of development, there is an implication that little the early educator or parent does, excluding grossly injurious practices, will be efficacious.

There are actually two lines of empirical evidence in support of what is described here as a single orientation. The first of these can be called *maturationist,* its supportive evidence gathered in highly systematic fashion from the study both of humans from conception through maturity and of other life forms. The biological orientation of the maturationist view is significant, since it has brought into focus both observed and plausible relationships between humans and other species. This perspective consequently gives attention to such phenomena as *instinct,* the evolutionary continuum, and the variety of attributes that human beings have in common with their fellow creatures—both in utero and throughout the early developmental period. The maturationist perspective, as articulated many years ago by G. Stanley Hall in the form of his "Recapitulation Theory" and later through the exhaustive normative studies of development carried out by one of Hall's students, Arnold Gesell, argues for the virtual inevitability of certain developmental events. These events include not only the major milestones of learning to talk and to walk according to a predictable and predetermined time schedule, but all of the many, many less obvious steps and stages on the road to maturity. This *normative* maturationist position tends to emphasize the observed *universality* of behavioral characteristics associated with specific ages and the *commonality* of developmental events.

Individual differences among young children

That differences exist among individuals at any given age, however, is incon-

testable. Among adults, differences in such areas as specific aptitudes and specific interests must be accounted for. These differences can be observed among children as well. Even among infants, pediatricians and mothers are aware of differences in amount or intensity of crying, for example. One baby is "colicky"; another is docile, content, and easily satisfied. Where and how do these differences arise?

This debate, which antedates scientific psychology by many years, is often called the nature vs. nurture controversy. Do people become the unique individuals they are because of their unique genetic endowment? Or is it because of the unique environmental conditions within which each of us is socialized? Since it is obvious that these are both viable possible "causes" of individuality, one may next ask which of the two is *more* influential. Although Anne Anastasi's classic paper, "Heredity, Environment, and the Question: How?" (1958), should presumably have laid to rest that controversy, suggesting instead that the subtle and intricate *interactions* of specific combinations of environmental and organismic influences must be studied, the issue persists, especially in relationship to issues and concerns in early childhood education. For example, Arthur Jensen (1969), based on highly complex analyses of his own research data and of the findings of a great many other investigators, estimates that approximately 80 percent of the variability in one important human characteristic, intelligence, is attributable to heredity, with only 20 percent attributable to environment.

The point of view that tends to attribute human variability more to *intraorganismic* than to environmental factors is commonly associated with the field of genetics. Each of us does, in fact, receive a unique genetic endowment. This inheritance is not expressed directly in overt and observable characteristics, however. A distinction is usually made between *genotype* and *phenotype,* the former denoting potential genetic influences that may

be expressed in certain forms of phenotypic behavior. Even the most radical scientific advocate of genetic explanations for individual differences accepts this distinction, a distinction that assumes that both other organismic influences and a vast array of external influences will color the resultant attribute or trait.

Sequence and stage in early development

There are two remarkable aspects of human development in the early years. On the one hand, it is predictable. There is a remarkable similarity, despite cultural differences and differential exposure to environmental stimuli, in the patterns of development of children throughout the world. When one considers the wide differences in socialization practices that exist, it is truly amazing that the orderly sequential patterns of developmental change described by Arnold Gesell, Jean Piaget, Erik Erikson, and other theorists should be found from one culture to another. Similarly, when one analyzes differences between languages native to specific peoples, it seems incredible that, as David McNeill (1966), Courtney Cazden (1972), and others have reported, children seem to progress through the same stages of language acquisition in the same sequence and generally at about the same rate.

Children are observed to move through these sequential tasks of early childhood with astonishing predictability. "Stranger anxiety" is indeed characteristic of most children beginning in the last half of the first year. First steps are taken at about 1 year of age or soon thereafter. By age 2, children are becoming creatures of language, and they are also becoming somewhat more difficult to get along with and control, by reason of a newfound assertiveness. By age 3, preschoolers seem to bring with them to play a set of skills different from those of 2-year-old toddlers. Three-year-olds talk to themselves and flirt with others, moving on the boundaries of true communication and cooperation. They struggle with the complexities of the universe—time, space, love, and death—yet deal with all of these from a highly subjective frame of reference, lacking real understanding of the principle that each person's reality differs from that of every other. What is *seen* is true, even though it may conflict with what the child is told by adults.

The child as an active agent

What is remarkable about the behavior of young children, then, is its *commonality*—the universality of the tasks of childhood, the manner of progression through stages of development that is shared by children throughout the world and apparently throughout history. But there is an equally fascinating, and apparently contradictory, aspect of the development of young children. That is its *individuality*. It appears to be true that every child must resolve the same crises of development as he learns to interact with his physical and social environment and that these resolutions manifest commonalities, not only within cultures, but from one culture to another.

However, it is the task of each child to construct his *own* universe. Each individual brings to this task a native endowment that is uniquely his own; each child encounters environmental events that are peculiar to him alone. No two children have absolutely identical innate predispositions; no two children experience the same environment. In addition, the environment in which each individual child is socialized is the product not entirely of events beyond his control, but in part of the child himself. The child not only *reacts* to his environment; he helps to *shape* it. The response of parents to a child, reflected in specific ways such as amount of physical contact, affective quality of contact, and vocal interchange, itself depends to some degree on the child's own contribution to the early socialization relationship.

The individuality of infants themselves, as Thomas et al. (1968) have shown, has a

role in the emergence of differential patterns of parenting. Differences among children, although clearly implying different innate predispositions in many instances, may certainly be associated with differential patterns of experience as well. Environmental effects, ranging from prenatal nutrition of the mother, through birth trauma, early experiential deprivation or enrichment, attention and nurturance or rejection, patterns of cognitive stimulation, "teaching to think," independence training, tolerance of autonomy, provision of models, and many other influences appear so evidently capable of causal association with individual differences in childhood that recourse to genetic explanations seems hardly necessary.

One young child seems confident and assured, another fearful and defensive, avoiding encounters with potential threats. A 3-year-old launches into complex fantastic dramatization, given only the stimulus of a pile of sticks, a saucepan, or an object capable of being rolled; another of the same age, supplied even with the most evocative play materials, seems not to know *how* to play.

Developmental-interaction framework for early education

Although eclectic in approach, this book has as its major underlying theoretical framework a theory of psychological development that assigns an active role to the child and that attributes manifest changes in children's behavior over time primarily to the ongoing, reciprocal *interaction* between the child's own mental structures and the environmental milieu in which behavior occurs. As the child actively imposes changes on his environment, the responsive environment similarly evokes changes in the child. Learning is not seen as piecemeal, but in terms of altered structures by which the child is enabled to perceive his world in changing fashion and to act on the basis of his changing view of reality.

Although Jean Piaget is widely recognized as the principal theorist espousing

this *structuralist* and *interactionist* conception of psychological development, other psychologists and educators have expressed related positions, notably John Dewey. Dewey, within a philosophical tradition of American Pragmatism, addressed his attention to the processes of learning and teaching. His analyses of these processes and of the concept of democracy are generally credited with initiating the Progressive movement in education. However, it has been Piaget who, with his co-workers and students, has provided a coherent psychological theory of intellectual development, has identified the major stages through which children pass in their progression toward adult modes of thought, and has described the processes that characterize thinking, or intelligent behavior, at each stage of development.

Edna Shapiro and Barbara Biber (1972) have further elaborated the concept of developmental interactionism in child development, and, in another important article, Lawrence Kohlberg and Rochelle Mayer (1972) have contrasted interactionism with other basic theories of learning and of education.

The developmental-interaction point of view concerning young children and their education assigns a very important role to environment. However, this perspective differs from traditional "behaviorism" in that the child's internal structuring of his experiences is emphasized. In addition to denoting the relationship between child and environment, interactionism also refers to the interrelatedness of *thinking and feeling*—of *cognitive* and *affective* development. Moreover, the individual child must be viewed within a *social* context in which interactions with others, peers and adults, are central to his development.

NORMALCY AND EXCEPTIONALITY IN EARLY CHILDHOOD

Every child is a special child; all education should be special education. To lose sight of the uniqueness of each individual child is to gear one's approach in teaching to a mythical norm that exists only in an abstract sense, rather than to the myriad shades and textures of being that comprise every classroom.

The term "exceptional" should always be used within the framework of an *individual difference* orientation to teaching. Some children exhibit very special needs or manifest behavioral characteristics that deviate from most of their fellows in an extreme manner. It is more helpful, however, to think of such children in terms of a continuum of individual differences. Otherwise, it is easy to fall into a pattern of identifying children (and also adults) as belonging to certain types, or categories. The implication of categorizing people is twofold: (1) that a high degree of homogeneity exists among members of a given category, that is, that they are all pretty much alike, and (2) that a qualitative difference exists between one category and another. When one considers individual children, however, such assumptions are very misleading.

Human beings tend to use this device of categorical thinking as a means of imposing order on what would otherwise be a disorderly universe. It is an extension of one of our most basic and most significant cognitive abilities, developed and nurtured during the early childhood years: *classification*. However, it is important to remember that, as are the preconcepts of young children, our conceptual categories are creations of our own minds; they may or may not correspond with "objective" reality.

This text employs to some extent a categorical perspective in the chapters that follow. Early education considerations for children with special needs are discussed with reference to forms, or types, of exceptionality. However, it is sincerely hoped that the reader will note the emphasis placed on the wide variability among individuals grouped within any single classification of exceptionality. Even more important, attention is repeatedly called to the commonalities among children, handicapped and non-handicapped. It can truly be said that every child is *like* every other child—and every child is *unlike* every other child. These dual themes of *commonality* and *individuality* cut across all systems or methods of classification of children.

What is "normal"?

One of the most difficult tasks facing the teacher of young children is that of determining which among the varying patterns of individual differences among children constitute "problems." A 4-year-old boy seems to be acting out themes of anger and destruction in his play with dolls. A 6-year-old frequently reverses the direction of certain numerals and letters of the alphabet as he learns to copy them from the board. A 3-year-old makes essentially no use of expressive language. Do such patterns of behavior indicate the presence of problems or handicaps, or are they within the bounds of normalcy, given the individuality of children's development?

Perhaps the best principle to remember is not to be primarily concerned with identifying an appropriate label for the child —be it "emotionally disturbed," "learning disabled," "mentally retarded," or "normal"—but rather to attend carefully and sensitively to what each child is communicating about himself through his words and in other ways. A good teacher of young children is first of all a good listener and observer. The relevant diagnostic question is "What does the child *do?*" not "What does the child *have?*"

Concepts of normalcy and deviance

The word "normal" can be defined and used correctly in a variety of ways. In general, however, it implies some statistical norm—that which is most common or most nearly universal, a reference point. We speak of normal child development in terms of the changes that are "normally" observed as children grow and learn. For many people, including many teachers, this usage suggests a commonality among the majority of children that is misleading. It is misleading both in implying that there is a close similarity among the majority of children and in leading us to conceive of deviance in qualitative terms. For example, one might have a concept of *mental retardation* as a category with features distinctively different, in a qualitative sense, from the category called normal. A number of theories have, in fact, been advanced to explain the "differences" between the mentally retarded and the nonretarded, a "difference orientation" concerning retardation that Edward Zigler (1966) has criticized as fallacious and unnecessary.

Intelligence, defined operationally in terms of IQ scores obtained by means of intelligence tests, presents perhaps the best illustration of the relationship between normalcy and deviance. Despite the limitations of such tests in providing fair and meaningful measures of intellectual capability, especially in "culturally different" child populations, the most highly respected among them (such as the Stanford-Binet Intelligence Scale and the Wechsler tests) have been carefully constructed and field-tested through a process called *normatization*. The results of these studies have been compiled in the form of norms. In general, test norms reflect and bear out the theoretical concept of intelligence as a characteristic (or a set of characteristics) that is *normally* distributed in the general population. This is, in turn, reflected in the familiar *normal,* or bell-shaped, curve.

This model makes use of a concept typically related to that of normalcy—the concept of *average*. One speaks of the average child or the child with average intelligence or the child who is within the average range of intelligence. Each of these usages has a unique meaning, and certainly a distinct connotation, although they may frequently be employed interchangeably. When we use the phrase "average intelligence," we certainly do not intend only to encompass those indi-

viduals with scores of exactly 100 on an IQ test. But the upper and lower limits of the average range, or of "normalcy," are subject to interpretation and sometimes arbitrary judgment. For example, some school systems that provide special programs for gifted students specify an IQ of 130 or above as a criterion for participation. Others might use another cutoff point, such as 120. Thus *average* and *normal* are relative terms, rather than absolute ones.

Types of exceptionality in children

Exceptionality is not synonymous with handicap. This term implies deviance from the norm, based on some criterion of what constitutes a significant degree of deviation. If a child is exceptionally bright, his intellectual prowess does not necessarily constitute a handicapping condition, although there are those who say that some facets of American society tend to punish or suppress giftedness (Torrance and Strom, 1967). The intellectual dimension, however, is one on which we can observe quantitative deviation from the norm, in either the direction of superiority or that of subnormality. It is important to remember, however, that the familiar bell-shaped curve is really an ideal schema, one that has been used as a model in the construction of tests of intelligence. These tests have been forced to conform to a theory of intelligence as a general, unitary, monolithic trait that is normally distributed in the population at large. In actual fact, however, obtained test scores are recognized only to *approximate* "true" intelligence for the general population and especially for individuals.

Some theories of intelligence hold that it is a multidimensional, rather than a unidimensional, attribute (Guilford, 1967; Guilford and Hoepfner, 1971). There may not only be various *components* of intelligence, but also various *ways* of being intelligent. Is the intellectually superior individual necessarily superior in all these ways, or possibly only in one or several, such as spatial, verbal, or figural abilities? Is the intellectually impaired individual limited in all intellectual functions, or possibly only in certain areas? It may be more important to determine for an individual child what his particular, unique pattern of strengths and limitations is, rather than that he is "generally" superior, average, or subnormal.

Apart from the issue of unidimensionality vs. multidimensionality—and beyond the well-known limitations of intelligence tests, especially with members of minority groups and with young children—another major question arises. This question pertains to the nature vs. nurture issue and has many implications for education. How *stable* are IQ scores, or to what extent is IQ susceptible to environmental influence? Can education, especially early education, significantly affect children's ability to learn? Resolution of this important issue, which has tended to elicit extreme and emotional positions among both scientists and educational practitioners, has proved difficult. It appears unlikely that mental retardation can be eradicated through education, which has at times seemed to be the position of some associated with what Edward Zigler has called "the environmental mystique" (1970). However, that a child has been labeled as mentally subnormal should not signal hopelessness. First, identification and prediction are, at best, imperfect. Second, all children, even the most profoundly limited, can benefit from educational intervention to a degree that is difficult, if not impossible, to predict.

Whereas the concept of intellectual deviance can be thought of in terms of a continuum, this is not clearly the case with respect to other forms of exceptionality. For example, although sensory impairment (visual and auditory handicaps) does suggest a quantitative dimension of degree of impairment, in each case a number of additional factors enter the picture as important influences. Was the impairment *congenital,* or was it *acquired* after the child had been able to employ the sense modality in interacting with his environment? How old was the child when compensatory measures were introduced, such as hearing aids, glasses, or corrective surgery? Does the child have other handicaps as well?

Samuel Kirk (1972), one of the foremost leaders in the field of special education, has defined the following general forms of exceptionality: *mental deviations* (intellectual giftedness and mental retardation); *sensory handicaps* (visual and auditory handicaps); *communication disorders* (learning disabilities and speech handicaps); *neurological, orthopedic, and other health impairments;* and *behavior disorders.* Other professionals advocate a less "categorical" scheme than even this one. They point out that a child who is handicapped in one area is more likely than not to be handicapped in another area as well. In addition, the specific type or types of handicapping condition may not be the major determinant in planning an appropriate educational program. It may be of more value to distinguish only two general classifications: *mildly handicapped and severely handicapped* (Haring, 1972). Beyond this distinction, it is the particular pattern of individual characteristics of the child, rather than the categorical label that is applied, that determines how he should be taught.

In this text, a compromise position is taken. It is believed that information and suggestions pertinent to particular forms of handicap will be useful, and chapters are organized accordingly. In addition, those areas of handicap with strong associations of commonality in educational practice are grouped together. A separate chapter is devoted to the topic of teaching the severely or multiply handicapped child. Finally, the last section of the book deals with areas that cut across handicapping conditions, focusing rather on alternative modes of programming and service delivery; an individualized, clinical approach to teaching; the physical learn-

ing environment; and helping nonhandicapped children to accept, value, and
benefit from interaction with children who
have special needs.

ROLE OF EDUCATION FOR CHILDREN WITH SPECIAL NEEDS
Education as intervention

The process of education has often been
compared with the practice of medicine,
even though such comparisons may be in
some respects inappropriate. Although
there are many branches of medicine,
these can be subsumed within two general
concerns: treatment and prevention. Education has these concerns also, particularly in regard to children with special
needs. The *treatment* dimension of education includes the concepts of *remediation*
(that is, cure of handicaps in learning or
elimination of deficiencies or disabilities
in learning) and of *compensation* (provision of alternate modes or methods of
learning). *Prevention* of handicapping conditions is a goal of education just as it is a

goal of medicine. What is prevented, however, is not a medical condition, such as
cerebral palsy or impaired hearing, but an
educationally handicapping condition.
Prevention in this educational sense may
be attempted at several levels. Primary
prevention refers to the provision of services *in anticipation* of their need. Essentially therefore, all early childhood education programs can be seen as ventures in
primary prevention of educational handicaps. For children who already manifest
behavioral characteristics suggestive of
potential handicaps in areas important to
school success, attempts to ensure that
these conditions will neither be magnified
nor give rise to problems in additional
areas may be described in terms of secondary prevention. Early education for children with special needs involves both primary and secondary prevention (Cowan
and Zax, 1967).

However, the parallel with medicine
falters when one recognizes that education is not concerned exclusively nor even

most importantly with the prevention of "illness." Rather, the goals of education are directed toward the promotion of the optimal development of the individual learner as an effectively functioning person who can contribute to the well-being of society.

Most educational programming for young children who have special needs has been based on the assumption that early intervention offers greater opportunity to influence development. Programs for young children whose special needs or problems have been identified have attempted to address those needs and problems by providing planned and structured educational experiences. They are explicitly intended to bring about specific *changes* in the children served. Usually this is reflected in statements of goals or objectives, which may include reference to such areas as enhanced mobility, self-feeding, reduction in off-task behavior, and increased vocalization. It is assumed that in most cases these children will not simply outgrow their problems; external intervention to promote the learning of adaptive skills is necessary.

Issues in evaluating effectiveness of intervention

Evaluation of educational effectiveness means comparing a goal statement with an observed result. This implies several important components: (1) goal statements should be appropriate (for example, they should refer to important, rather than trivial, outcomes), (2) they should relate to what is or can be included in an educational program, and (3) they should identify intended outcomes in terms of observable and measurable behavior.

Although it may be possible to measure objectively changes that occur among children served in a program, it may be difficult to ascribe these changes to the program itself. Children do "change" as a function of biological maturation. Skills in areas such as mobility, expressive language, and concept attainment are in-

creased in part by "natural" causes, such as differentiation within the central nervous system and skeletal and muscular growth during the early years. In addition, "nurture"—environmental influences on development—is not at all restricted to the planned educational program. Although a child may participate extensively in a "comprehensive" program, such participation usually accounts for only a small portion of his environmental transactions.

But is it possible to determine that change, growth, skill development, learning, or other forms of developmental progress are a result of the educational program provided? Is it necessary to do so? Relating program impact to observed changes in children is essential for two reasons.

First, since such programs require financial investment, both by society and usually by families of children served—to say nothing of the perhaps more important *personal* investment of time, effort, and hope required of parents—some form of cost-effectiveness is a moral imperative. If involvement, commitment, and support for a program are sought, the program must be demonstrated to be sufficiently effective to justify the demands it places on the individuals served, the community, and society. If the program "makes no difference" (that is, if children could benefit just as much without participating), its continuation cannot be justified (except in terms of other benefits such as provision of custodial child care to provide respite for families). Furthermore, such a program might actually be detrimental, since children might be deprived of taking part in other activities that would be effective, because of discouragement resulting from the unfulfilled hopes and expectations of parents.

Second, evaluation can point to specific benefits attained, identify the program components that are beneficial, and determine what *match* of child characteristics, parent involvement, teacher behavior, instructional strategy, physical environment characteristics, support services, and other program components yields success. Thus effective evaluation does more than determine the total impact of a program on children; it enables educators to modify programs and to develop individualized procedures most beneficial to each child.

Another concern in evaluating programs involves the question of permanence or *stability* of positive effects. The issue is whether the early educational program has impact on the child's subsequent development, rather than affecting him only during the time he participates. This issue is perhaps most clearly demonstrated in the attempt to evaluate the impact of Head Start participation through repeated measurement of IQ and academic achievement as the child progresses through school. Project Head Start lost substantial fiscal support when national studies (Cicerelli et al., 1969) found that gains were not sustained beyond the primary grades in elementary school.

SETTINGS FOR TEACHING YOUNG CHILDREN

Young children are here considered to include children from *birth* through age *8 years*. It is hoped that most of the material discussed in this book will be pertinent to teachers in at least the first three grades of elementary school, as well as kindergarten and nursery school teachers, those in day care settings, and individuals concerned with infant programs and programs in noneducational settings, such as hospitals and community agencies.

As a rule, an attempt is made here to avoid use of the term "preschool." The result may occasionally seem excessively wordy (for example, "teachers of young children" rather than "preschool teachers"). The reason is that I subscribe to the position stated by James Hymes (1974) that "preschool" implies that the nursery program is not really "school," that "real" school begins when the child enters kin-

dergarten. This may seem a mere problem of semantics. However, as we explore areas of exceptionality in children, the reader's attention will be directed time and time again to the important role of the *words* that are employed in both reflecting and influencing the attitudes of professionals, parents, the general public, and the child himself. This book is written with the conviction that educational intervention for young children is very important and that for young children who have special physical, mental, or emotional needs it is extremely important. "Real school" therefore begins long before kindergarten.

The age range of birth through 8 years encompasses more than one period or stage of development. For convenience, however, the terms "early education," "early childhood," and "young children" will frequently be employed with reference to the entire range. Regarding educational levels and program variations, "early education" will be considered here to encompass the following:

1. Developmental day care
2. Hospital programs
3. Parent-child programs
4. Nursery school and Head Start
5. Kindergarten
6. Primary grades (grades 1, 2, and 3)

Developmental day care

Although child care services have long been in demand in the United States, contemporary developments (including the greater prevalence of working mothers) have greatly increased the need at all economic levels. There has been a major national effort to ensure that day care programs meet at least minimal levels of quality standards. This effort has led to the distinction between *custodial* and *developmental* child care and the entry of day care into the field of early childhood education. Day care programs may provide services for children of any age, sometimes on an extended day basis or even around the clock, and may accommodate children during varying parts of the day: before or after school, during lunch periods, or at various times according to parents' work schedules.

Day care programs may be either *home based* or *center based,* and in either case they are often licensed according to minimum standards and codes established by states and local communities. Center-based programs may be established through federal agencies serving the economically disadvantaged or by parent cooperatives; churches; community groups; individuals or businesses on an entrepreneurial basis; industries, businesses, or hospitals (for children of their own employees); or colleges or universities (for children of their own students). The variety is almost infinite, and it has proved difficult to ensure that the quality of care provided is conducive to healthy development of children rather than simply a caretaking operation.

Despite licensing requirements, some child care programs present only minimal service to children and may even operate to the detriment of healthy development, physically as well as psychologically. Since public funding has been slow in coming, vast numbers of parents have had, in desperation, to settle for care that they know is less than optimal but that they must use to maintain employment. Efforts such as Community Coordinated Child Care, some federal and state legislation, the establishment of the national Office of Child Development, and the creation of the role of Child Development Associate (CDA), with standards for certification, have all served to move day care toward a developmental rather than merely a custodial service. Both the number of children served through this means and the level of quality of service they receive continue to increase, and more and more frequently one sees day care centers that resemble good nursery schools. That such a trend is desirable for the handicapped children enrolled, as well as for the nonhandicapped, is obvious.

Hospital programs

Increasingly, hospitals have developed capabilities for fostering the psychological development of children with special needs. Many large hospitals operate programs for infants and young children as a means of conducting research concerning the effects of handicapping conditions on early development, early detection, and multidisciplinary intervention during the early years. Infant stimulation programs or perinatal centers for babies who are *at risk,* clinic services, and provisions for temporarily hospitalized children all have important educational as well as medical facets, and frequently a well-trained teacher is included as a member of an interdisciplinary team. Dmitriev (1974, p. 84) defines a high-risk infant as "one who, for socioeconomic, health, or genetic reasons faces developmental delay." A national organization, the American Association for Children in Hospitals, established in recent years, has already done much to advocate for the hospitalized child and to ensure that his emotional and educational needs, as well as his medical problems, are appropriately served. Many large hospitals now provide a child life education program, through which particularly skilled and sensitive adults work with children in such areas as anticipating surgery, dealing with separation from home and parents, fears associated with hospitalization, transition from home to hospital, the death of another child, liaison with the child's school and teacher, and maintaining school assignments for older children, as well as tutoring (Plank, 1962).

Parent-child programs

Increasingly, since the early days of the War on Poverty during the administration of President Johnson, those who work with young children have recognized the central role played by parents. Few programs provide direct service to the child for more than a few hours each day; by far, most of the child's time is spent with his family. In early analyses of the environment of poverty and its effects on children's development (Deutsch, 1965), the concept of parent as teacher emerged as a significant dimension of the parenting role, and researchers (for example, Hess and Shipman, 1968) began to study what came to be called *maternal teaching style*. The way in which parents interacted with their children was seen as an important factor in influencing many aspects of the child's development, especially his functioning in the areas of language, cognition, and personal-social development. Therefore experimental and demonstration programs (Gray et al., 1966; Shaefer and Aaronson, 1972) were created with a new focus—a focus on the parent-child relationship.

The goal of this parent-child approach was to ensure greater impact on the child by working through his parents, especially his mother. Although *parent education* had long had at least some role in educational programs, its importance now came more sharply into focus as a means of providing comprehensive intervention —both in the sense of extending the time of a child's "educational program" each day and continuing it, hopefully, long after the child and family are no longer directly served.

Like day care, parent-child programs may be either home based or center based. The former, best illustrated by Project Home Start, began to emerge during the late 1960s as a viable way of providing service within the context of the child's "natural environment." This approach has the advantage both of making carryover more likely and of lessening the likelihood of disrupting family patterns. These efforts, based in the homes of families served, rather than in a central location, have been of two types: those in which professionals provide the home guidance and those employing local residents— nonprofessionals—who secure necessary training to serve this function.

Center-based, parent-focused programs,

in the case of economically disadvantaged families, have emerged chiefly in the form of parent and child centers. These federally funded centers are organized nationally and have in common many features; however, each functions in a unique manner. This is primarily because these programs give a high priority to the role of parents, who are involved both in *operating* the program and in determining *policies* for program operation. Thus the parent acts as both client, or consumer, and as the person able to identify and secure the services (within certain constraints) needed. These programs have been generally very successful in demonstrating the ability of parents, including those who are greatly disadvantaged economically, to develop and operate their own program. They have greatly strengthened the argument heard in all areas of education, including education of the handicapped, for greater parent involvement. Parents are seen, not as helpless, passive, ignorant individuals who need to be "changed," but as partners of the highly trained professional—partners who contribute their special, unique knowledge of the individual child to the relationship.

Some specially funded projects have targeted specifically on families of young handicapped children, while many agency programs for the handicapped integrate a family service, casework, home training, outreach, parent group, or other program component with those providing service directly to the child. Parent involvement in the field of special education is traditional, moreover, since so many of the advances in providing educational and other services for children with special needs have come into being chiefly as a result of parent participation and activism. Some special programs for emotionally disturbed children, for example, provide service to the child mainly through work with his parents (Furman and Katan, 1969).

Parent-child projects have addressed

the needs of young handicapped children in a number of ways, including the following:

1. Identifying conditions that contribute to or cause handicapping conditions
2. Identifying children whose special needs are not receiving appropriate service
3. Bringing about the implementation of a home-based program for the child, carried out by his parents
4. Demonstrating techniques that can alleviate stressful home conditions caused by the presence of a handicapped child (for example, feeding problems)
5. Helping parents to promote the child's optimal intellectual, social, and emotional development within the limits imposed by the handicap
6. Providing support to other parents
7. Generating political pressure to obtain funding for necessary services, including special schools

It is particularly important in the case of children who have impaired vision or hearing that home-based intervention be provided very early in life—literally during the first few months of life—and that this take the form primarily of work through and with the child's parents.

Nursery school and Head Start

Although Project Head Start, since its beginning in the summer of 1965, has had a unique identity, the discussion here will not elaborate the distinctions between Head Start (which actually comprises a wide variety of programs) and other distinct program variants, such as Montessori classes, Parent cooperatives, and special focus nursery schools, such as those that emphasize music activities or eurythmics. The term "nursery school," rather, will be used to refer to planned educational programs for children generally 3 and 4 years of age (and "young fives") prior to kindergarten.

In two respects, however, Head Start must be mentioned in a specific sense with reference to the education of children with special needs. First, of course, this program was developed for those children who were believed to be more susceptible to educational handicaps because of environmental handicaps during their early and formative years. By definition, then, Head Start was designed for "children with special needs." Second, since 1973, Head Start programs have been mandated to provide services for handicapped children—those with physical and sensory, mental, and emotional handicaps as well as children with speech, language, and perceptual handicaps. To comply with federal regulations, Head Start programs must demonstrate that no fewer than 10 percent of the children enrolled are handicapped. This particular quota was arrived at on the basis of national estimates of the prevalence of handicapping conditions among children, estimates recognized to be conservative ones. Thus "mainstreaming" in Head Start has been a fact for several years prior to the enactment of federal laws that mandate provision of "least restrictive alternative" programming for all handicapped children.

It is necessary, too, to differentiate those nursery school programs that have been developed specifically for children with some particular form of handicap. Such programs exist for the mentally retarded, the emotionally disturbed, the visually impaired, the hearing impaired, the physically handicapped, and the speech impaired. Much of the discussion of educational practices in the chapters that follow, although intended to be applicable to "regular" as well as to specialized settings, has been based on procedures that have been developed and used in these special settings.

Among nursery school programs other than Head Start and specialized programs for handicapped children, two distinct streams can be identified. The first of these has characterized most privately operated nurseries, parent cooperative nurseries, and university laboratory nursery schools. This stream has been identified by the term "traditional," a term coined during the "cognitive revolution" of the 1960s (Pines, 1966), or by the terms "child centered" and "child development oriented." The course of its history has paralleled that of the kindergarten in that, like the kindergarten, it began as an entity apart from the public educational system. It differs primarily in that prekindergarten programs, at least for the present, continue to function independently of the public schools.

Like the kindergarten, the so-called *traditional* nursery school has been influenced primarily by the early work of Froebel, the MacMillan sisters, and Susan Isaacs. The writings of Isaacs advocated a flexible, child-centered approach, legitimized play as a primary learning mode, and called attention to the child's growth as a social being, to the interwoven nature of all aspects of children's development, and to the child's need to explore and discover. The nursery school was seen as a setting that could provide stimulation for the child's natural inclination to learn and to solve problems, to begin to realize his potential as a unique individual, and to learn to value and contribute to the reciprocal and cooperative social interactions offered within a peer group. The most emphasized aspects of the program were those that were seen to run parallel to the greatest strengths of the young child: his rich imagination, his spontaneity, his propensity for identification with a warm, supportive adult and with his age mates, and his responsiveness to the expanding world around him (Todd and Heffernan, 1970; Landreth, 1972).

The second stream is the Montessori approach (see, for example, Montessori, 1912, 1949). Named for Dr. Maria Montessori, who developed the method through her work with economically disadvantaged and socially and intellectually handicapped children in Rome, this pedagogical approach is really imbedded in a philosophical system. It shares with the tradition of Froebel the element of faith in the child's innate will to learn and to grow and a belief in the integrative nature of learning. It differs in its emphasis on formalized, prescribed materials, structured use of materials, individual rather than group activity, relative deemphasis of language, and comparative lack of emphasis on creative use of art media, musical activity, and sociodramatic play.

The Montessori method is somewhat paradoxical in that it involves a high degree of *structure,* in one sense, while also stressing self-directed activity on the part of the child. The structure, however, is intrinsic to the materials employed and to the learning environment itself. The materials have been designed in such a way that their sequential use was believed to parallel the progressive growth of the child's developing mind. Montessori believed that a child progresses through *sensitive periods* of development and that the key to optimizing his learning is to match the task and the materials with which it is performed to the child. In a sense, but in a different sense than that of the "traditional" child-centered approach, the child directs his own learning. The teacher's role is that of facilitator: "Don't *tell—teach,*" said Montessori.

During her own lifetime, Montessori's approach failed to gain acceptance among leaders of early education in the United States. The 1950s and 1960s, however, saw a revival of interest in and a rediscovery of her approach, and independent Montessori nursery schools (and, in some locations, Montessori programs serving the entire range from infancy through early adolescence) began to appear. Montessori-trained teachers became in demand, as groups of upper-middle income mothers strove to establish their own classes. This development was ironic, in view of the origins of the approach, but seemingly inevitable since public financial support was not available. With the mobilization of efforts to combat effects of poverty leading to the development of early education programs for children of the poor, the approach developed by Maria Montessori became one of the alternative "models," or "planned variations" employed through Project Head Start. However, its effectiveness as an appropriate intervention for low-income children has not been established (Karnes et al., 1970).

The Montessori "sensorial" materials have much in common with instructional materials frequently employed by teachers of mentally retarded children and children with physical, neurological, perceptual, or sensory handicaps: they are manipulable, three-dimensional, and concrete; they are designed to focus the child's attention on salient features and not distract him with irrelevant stimuli; and they are used sequentially. Because of the nature of the materials, the use of a "structured" environment, the emphasis on task analysis and carefully sequenced experience, and the distinct orientation to the individual child and his needs, the Montessori approach would seem to be a particularly fruitful one in teaching children with special needs. Philosophically, Montessori does not emphasize distinctions between children based on categorical "labels"; the method is seen as appropriate to the needs of both the gifted and the very limited child. Although there are many elements of the approach that would seem desirable in fostering the educational development of children with emotional and behavioral difficulties, the Montessori approach in itself may have limitations with regard to the needs of these children since it makes few provisions for adult-child counseling or expressive play with dolls, puppets, and the like.

A variety of alternative prekindergarten programs have been developed that depart both from the "traditional" philosophy and design and from the Montessori method. Some programs, for example, may focus on musical or dramatic activity. One distinctive variation is presented by the eurythmics approach, developed by Eugene Dalcroze. The particular emphasis in Dalcroze eurythmics is on *movement,* an emphasis with many implications for teachers of young children with special needs. In fact, specific approaches involving the use of rhythm and movement and emphasizing physical coordination and integrated motion have been developed for children with handicapping conditions.

Specialized nursery programs have been in operation throughout the United States for years, serving specific groups of young children who have impaired vision or hearing, problems in the development of speech and language, mental retardation, physical or neurological handicaps, or serious emotional problems. Such a program may be operated under the auspices of a hospital, a speech and hearing center, a Society for the Blind agency, a multidisciplinary health agency such as the United Cerebral Palsy Association, a university center, or a private foundation or group. These programs are unique and usually differ from "regular" nursery schools in two major respects: (1) the children (and families) are served by representatives of more than one discipline—in addition to teachers, staff members may represent the disciplines of physical therapy, occupational therapy, speech pathology, audiology, clinical psychology, social work, medicine (including psychiatry), nursing, and others—and (2) these programs are designed specifically for children who have specific forms of handicap.

Although Project Head Start comprises the only prekindergarten educational program not specifically designed for handicapped children that has been mandated to serve these children, two major facets of recent federal legislation have served to bring about a greater degree of integration of the handicapped within "regular" early childhood education. For one thing, federal law now mandates states to provide for the earliest possible identification of all handicapped children.

Second, education of handicapped children is to be guided by the principles of "least restrictive alternative" programming so that the child is integrated as much as possible with nonhandicapped children.

Kindergarten

An outgrowth of the pioneering work of Friederich Froebel, during the eighteenth century, and influenced by the efforts of social reform movements, the American kindergarten has a fascinating history. During the first decades of the twentieth century, the kindergarten was distinct from the public school system. Early leaders, such as the MacMillan sisters, worked to develop standards of practice and of training for teachers. The term "child development specialist," now employed in some programs for young children, would perhaps have been an apt designation for the kindergarten teacher, since she was truly concerned with the development of "the whole child," rather than primarily with readying him for academic learning when he entered the public school. Typically, a kindergarten teacher devoted her mornings to working directly with the children in the manner described by Froebel, her afternoons to visiting with her children and their parents in their homes. Generally, most emphasis was placed on emotional and social development, and play was legitimized as "the child's work," the vehicle children use in developing competence for interacting with their physical and social environments.

Some basic elements of the kindergarten approach were probably sacrificed when the kindergarten became part of the public educational system, and it began a process of change toward a more academic orientation that began to peak during the 1960s (Lazerson, 1972). Kindergarten teachers have had to struggle for recognition of their programs as "educational." One task that has been assigned to the kindergarten teacher is to bring children to a state of "readiness" for the rigors of first-grade work. This idea of kindergar-

ten as mainly an academic readiness program has been criticized by several groups: those who maintain that kindergarten should and does have an important academic program in its own right; those who think that traditional kindergarten goals are valuable in themselves and should not be sacrificed; and those, like James Hymes (1974), who refer to the prevailing view of education at all levels as preparation for the *next* level as "the dribble-down disease."

A wide range of variability, of course, exists in the actual practice of teaching in a kindergarten classroom. Generally, however, at least since Sputnik, a trend toward a greater academic orientation can be seen. This trend has been reflected in new math movement of the late 1950s and early 1960s, which caused 5-year-olds to be introduced to the basic concepts of set theory; in the incorporation of early reading instruction; in recognition that some children are, in fact, "ready" to read when they enter kindergarten and that a few have already begun to read on their own; in adapting Jerome Bruner's concept of "the spiral curriculum" (Bruner, 1960) to curriculum development in the fields of science and social studies for use in the kindergarten; and in the increased use of standardized ability and achievement testing at the kindergarten level. Whereas most teachers continue to offer a child-centered program, give emphasis to the emotional needs and social development of their children, and provide for extensive use by children of their primary learning modality—play—virtually all have experienced increasing pressure (from administrators, colleagues in the higher grades, producers of educational materials, and parents) to develop a more "academic" or "cognitive" program. This pressure often results in a teacher's dealing with *learning* and *play* as though they were dichotomous, rather than integrated.

Because of their characteristic focus on the individual child, awareness of developmental needs of all children and the range of differences one typically sees within in a group of 5- and 6-year-olds, and typically greater contact with parents than is possible for many upper grade teachers, kindergarten teachers have always been in an excellent position to identify children with special needs. Also, since for most children kindergarten represents their first regular participation in a group program with peers, their first continuous separation from home and parents, and the first time they have been required to perform "tasks" and have their performances evaluated, this set of new demands may serve to make apparent, if not to *create,* educational handicapping conditions for the first time. An important role for the kindergarten teacher is therefore within the realm of *screening* and *identification.* The teacher must be on the alert for the child who may have problems in vision and hearing; the child who is fearful or pervasively unhappy; the child who is overly boisterous, inattentive, or difficult to manage; the child who has difficulty concentrating, retaining material in memory, or adapting to new situations; the child who is frequently absent or who otherwise shows possible health problems; and the child whose language or speech development is substantially deviant from that of most of his peers.

Although "mild" educational handicaps may be detected in the kindergarten, resulting in appropriate referral for more careful diagnostic study, such identification and referral rarely lead to differential kindergarten *placement* of children who are ultimately determined to have a learning disability or behavioral problem. These children, along with the mildly mentally handicapped (educable mentally retarded), the speech impaired, and frequently those with sensory or other physical impairments, are today often served within the regular kindergarten classroom. This is in contrast to past practices of *excluding* the child from kindergarten (since compulsory provision of kindergarten was not mandated by state laws). It is still the case, however, that a child's kindergarten entrance may be delayed a year or that a child may repeat kindergarten for a second year. And there are also a variety of special kindergarten programs, sometimes within multidisciplinary agency settings or as continuations of therapeutic or specialized nursery schools. Nevertheless, any kindergarten class today is likely to include several children who present unusual and extreme needs.

Primary grades

In the United States the primary level is generally broken down into specific grades, with children progressing from one grade to the next, and from one teacher to another, on the basis of annual promotion. This is despite a surge of influence from practices that have been developing during the last 30 years in British schools, including the practice of cross-age, vertical, or family grouping. (See, for example, Brown and Precious, 1969, and Mycock, 1970.)

British primary schools generally encompass ages 5 through 7 years in undifferentiated groups. This is partly a matter of convenience, but it mainly reflects recognition that children within this age range follow highly individualized patterns of learning. The educational program consequently is developed not only to *allow* children to learn based on their own, individual levels of readiness and competency and their particular interests, but also to *encourage* such self-directed activity by children. Groups are frequently ad hoc, focusing on specific activities, rather than achievement or maturity levels of the children. No attempt is made to group children *homogeneously,* except on the basis of interest. Variability is considered an advantage, rather than a disadvantage, and the *family grouping* concept is reflected in the phenomenon of younger and older children working and playing together—as one sees in a family or a neighborhood play group setting.

Some American schools have incorporated the *ungraded primary* model within their programs, whether influenced by British practices or independently of such influence. In some schools, *cross-age grouping* is done. This may be intentional, in order to bring about greater articulation between instructional levels and more adequately to recognize individual levels of attainment and maturity within a "grade" or within a specific age group, or it may be a matter of administrative convenience. In these days of limited fiscal capability and rising costs (and, in some communities, changing residential constellations that may affect school enrollment patterns differentially by age) *combined classes* are sometimes found. These may involve various combinations of adjacent grades within the primary level, such as kindergarten and first grade, first and second grades, or second and third grades.

Whatever the organizational framework, the primary level is the period during which children are introduced to and expected to attain proficiency in basic academic skill areas: language arts and communication skills (including listening, speaking, written expression, spelling, and reading) and fundamental computational skills and mathematical concepts. This set of demands frequently results in the emergence of problems for individual children that had previously been undetected or had not been present. In the face of normative expectancies of achievement, children who learn more slowly experience an early disadvantage that tends to become more serious, as do children whose developmental levels at the time of entry are less advanced than are those of the majority of children. Modes of instruction that are appropriate for the majority, common expectations for achievement, and limited availability of alternative approaches within the classroom serve to place at a disadvantage the child who can learn *well* but who learns *differently*. Consequently what may begin as relatively small disparities tend to become progressively greater for the child who is unable to master foundation skills. Deutsch (1965), writing of the problems of the economically disadvantaged child, refers to this phenomenon as a "cumulative deficit."

There have been two general approaches in dealing with the "problem" of individuality of ability levels, achievement levels, learning styles, and learning differences caused by handicapping conditions at the primary grade level: (1) individualizing the instructional program to permit each child to learn at his own pace and in his own way and (2) early educational intervention *prior* to the child's entry into the primary grades to ameliorate individual differences that may lead to educational handicaps. It is the position in this book that both approaches are viable and appropriate, and, further, that both are necessary. Early intervention during the preprimary years probably cannot succeed in "immunizing" most exceptional children to failure in school. However, in the case of most forms of physical, emotional/behavioral, or intellectual deviations, *early and continuing provision* for learning and psychological development of children with special needs is essential to ensure optimal development and educational success (Caldwell, 1973; Dmitriev, 1974).

Alternative approaches and models

In practice, there are probably very few early childhood educators who adhere to a "pure" approach. Most are eclectic, drawing from various theories, adapting what others have found to be successful, and modifying their program on the basis of their own experience. It is useful, however, to examine some of the theoretical and philosophical issues that have in fact given rise to differences in practice and that continue to do so.

In this connection, an important concept is that of structure. However, David Weikart (1971) has described differences between approaches in teaching young children on the basis of not only the *degree* of structure, but also the *source*. In some programs it is mainly the *teacher* who imposes structure; in others, such as Montessori, structure is inherent in the materials used, in the physical environment. In a child-centered program, it is the *child* who structures his own learning.

Diverse children—diverse methods

The fields of special education and early childhood education are simultaneously experiencing rapid expansion and continuous reevaluation. In addition to this commonality, their union has both historical roots and present and future necessities. Both are characterized by wide variation, both in the needs and characteristics of the children they serve and in the techniques and "delivery systems" they have created to provide service.

Theorists have contributed in important ways to the creation of both special education and early childhood programs, as have those who have contributed new knowledge through research. What occurs in a classroom or other educational setting for young children, handicapped and nonhandicapped, is influenced by such knowledge and theory. What takes place, however, emerges from a great number of other influences as well: the particular perspective of the individual teacher, the policies under which he or she must operate, the participation and cooperation of parents, and, most important, the children themselves.

Although practices that are "good" or "sound" or that "make sense" can be identified (as can practices that do not), there is room for and need for a great deal of diversity in the ways in which young children are taught. An "approach" can be effective only to the extent that it suits the child with whom it is employed and that it is personally endorsed by the teacher as being both "right" for the child and "right" for the teacher.

METHODS AND PROBLEMS IN EARLY IDENTIFICATION

If children are more receptive to external influence during the years before school, and if the period from infancy through the early childhood years

is a time of great malleability, it follows that ameliorative efforts instituted during this period would offer the greatest probability of enhancing development. For this reason, recent years have witnessed numerous efforts to institute early intervention programs for children identified as presenting symptoms of handicap. However, some problems have been encountered.

First, there is the fear of mislabeling, and thereby stigmatizing, a child. Given a wide range of variability among infants and young children, identification of exceptional children has at times been problematic. Of course, some handicapping conditions are recognizable at birth, such as Down's syndrome and phenylketonuria (PKU), and increasingly many abnormalities can be identified prior to birth through amniocentesis, a method of testing the amniotic fluid surrounding the fetus. However, positive identification of the vast range of "high incidence" handicaps such as learning disabilities is usually not possible so early, and in many instances problems are not detected until the child begins school.

The rate at which children progress through early periods of physical and psychological development varies greatly from child to child. Some children are conversing at 1 year of age; others do not acquire proficiency in communicative speech until age 3 or later. When can it be determined that one child is gifted, another mentally retarded? Many young children manifest sleep disturbance, feeding problems, negativism, destructiveness, etc. during the early years. In which of these children are such behaviors early indicators of pervasive behavior problems or even serious emotional disturbances? All young children exhibit confused directionality, difficulties in integrating and planning motor acts, and perceptual instability, and many show high distractibility, short attention span, and extremely high activity level. Which of these children will continue to demonstrate these

characteristics in ways that will interfere with academic learning?

Use of a normative perspective

It is imperative that the teacher of young children have some frame of reference to employ in assessing children's behavior and developmental needs and problems. One such reference system is the normative model provided by such writers as Arnold Gesell (Gesell and Amatruda, 1941). Certain patterns of behavior are expectable at certain ages, for example, the well-known "negativism" of 2-year-olds. However, these modes of behavior—greeting each request with "No!" and engaging in mini- (or maxi-!) power struggles with adults—may be seen as developmentally inappropriate in an older child. From a psychodynamic perspective, "passive-aggressive" behavior patterns, a "retentive" personality orientation, "stubbornness," etc. exhibited by latency period–aged children may be indicative of either some degree of *fixation* (on unresolved issues of the anal period) or *regression* (to behavior patterns developmentally appropriate to an early time).

Thus, in a general sense, a normative perspective—that is, awareness of what modes of behavior characterize most children of a given chronological age group—can enable the teacher or parent to determine whether some form of "difficult" behavior is age appropriate or inappropriate. Given the wide range of individual differences in all aspects of development at any age, however, it is important that one not rely completely on this normative orientation. For example, not all 2-year-olds manifest autonomy needs in the same way; some even seem "trusting" (just like 3-year-olds). Differences in specific modes of resolving developmental crises, rate of progression through developmental sequences, underlying and constant individual difference characteristics, and specific experiences to which children are exposed (family breakup, death of a parent, sibship patterns, etc.) make norm-referenced judgments of "normalcy vs. abnormalcy" risky but nevertheless invaluable if used with discretion.

Patterns of developmental deviance cannot always be detected within the first years of life. There are those children who appear to be progressing normally, accomplishing the developmental tasks of infancy and the preschool years without major difficulty. However, when they enter kindergarten and encounter a set of conditions that either impose new stresses or focus attention on some aspect of behavior that had previously gone unnoticed, the children's special needs become suddenly apparent.

Identifying children with special needs

Some of the limitations and problems to be considered in connection with screening procedures are described by William Frankenberg (1973):

Screening out suspected problems has the potential of creating undue anxiety and "labeling" of children. It is therefore of utmost importance that screening tests only be utilized for their indicated purpose—namely, the mass testing of large populations to separate those individuals who have a high likelihood of manifesting a handicap. For this reason, too, it is important to explain to parents that results of a screening test do not make a diagnosis, and the results of screening should not be interpreted to parents as indicating that a child has a particular problem. Likewise, it is irrational to plan treatment solely on the results of a screening test. (p. 33)

Diagnosis is the step that follows identification through screening. It is the diagnostic phase that will lead to the determination of a plan for amelioration that is appropriate to the individual child's specific pattern of needs. *Developmental diagnosis* (Gesell and Amatruda, 1969) is the process of comparing the child's developmental progress and characteristics with norms established by age. Furthermore, diagnosis, unlike screening, is a continuing and ongoing process whereby the child's response to intervention is assessed and his progress continuously charted.

The purpose of identification of handicapped children is to ensure that appropriate measures can be taken to facilitate development and learning. Identification, unless it leads to the provision of ameliorative measures, is of absolutely no value (Bower, 1969).

For many, however, diagnosis continues to mean the assignment of labels. An individual may have a *diagnosis* of cerebral palsy, expressive aphasia, mental retardation, myelodysplasia, or autism, for example. However, the concept of diagnosis when applied to educational practice has a more complex meaning. In education, the purpose of diagnosis is primarily to determine how best to teach the child. Consequently, abstract labels, particularly if such labels themselves lack reference to educationally relevant constructs, are of limited usefulness. Nevertheless, their use may be necessary, to work within the constraints of guidelines supplied by federal and state funding agencies as well as to ensure accountability on the part of schools for the provision of appropriate services (Gallagher and Bradley, 1972).

From the perspective of the classroom teacher, what is most important is the determination of how optimally to teach the child, not which "label" he should have.

What is needed to provide for early identification of young children with special needs is an "early warning system" (Gallagher and Bradley, 1972). The "net" suggested by such a system must be of sufficiently fine mesh that all or nearly all of the children whose symptoms suggest vulnerability to subsequent problems will be caught. And this net must be thrown broadly enough so that significant numbers of these children are not missed.

But what of the children identified through an early warning system who would not in fact develop problems in learning or personal-social development? What of the "false positives"? Are there children for whom the often-criticized advice "He'll outgrow it" is accurate? One must consider any possible adverse consequences of improperly identifying—and labeling—young children as likely candidates for special education services when they reach school age. One such consequence, it has often been suggested, may be a "self-fulfilling prophecy" (Rosenthal and Jacobsen, 1968), which may be the unintentional consequence of genuine concerns and "realistic" expectations of a child's parents, his teachers, or even the child himself.

There is perhaps no reason that early identification of developmental problems —delayed speech, slowness to establish dominance, an inordinately high activity level, sleep or eating disturbances, and the like—need result in an insidious labeling process with the potential of working to the harm of any child, whether or not he is "correctly" labeled. It is reasonable to suppose that there are early educational experiences that are uniquely appropriate to every child and that early education may serve a positive role in primary, as well as secondary, prevention of a greater diversity of difficulties in school, family, and peer group adjustment than that encompassed by the categories of exceptionality.

Some conclude, however, that the basic issue is one of economics. Given limited resources, where should these be invested first? Where is the need greatest, or where can the highest degree of cost-effectiveness be realized? Invoking such terms and considerations may appear crass when applied to small children. However, as has been increasingly established during recent years, those entrusted with public resources (albeit a disproportionately small share) assume a responsibility for accountability to the public. It falls to them to demonstrate convincingly that there are measurable benefits to children, families, and society at large that accrue from their efforts.

Consequently, if early education before age 5 or 6 is desirable or necessary for all children, the task of demonstrating this falls to the educator. In addition to the question of which children should participate or whether all should, there is the basically unresolved question of *when* such experiences should be initiated. Are there children for whom "early intervention" requires the initiation of measures during the first months of *infancy?* Indeed, if participation in appropriately designed programs beginning at age 3 years were universal in the United States, a goal far from realization, might there yet be left insufficiently served a large number of handicapped children? Many authorities believe, especially in the wake of the Head Start movement, that age 3 or 4 years may be too late for the provision of optimally effective intervention efforts for some children. Burton White (1975) identifies the period from *8 months to 3 years* as most critically important in the psychological development of the child.

Strategies for early identification

The concept of identification is inextricably related to that of prevention of problems in development. Recently, the term "children at risk" has been introduced to convey recognition of the susceptibility or vulnerability of certain children to a wide range of problems in physical or psychological development or both. Some signs of risk may seem fairly obvious, while others are less so. Still others are subjects of some controversy, and a massive and continuing research effort is needed if danger signals are to be spotted sufficiently early in the development of the fetus or infant for effective intervention to be provided. Furthermore, the means of such intervention need to be identified—and the means found to make available to the child and family the services that are required.

To appreciate the complexity and difficulty of the vast set of problems associated with the last of these issues, one need only consider the terrible impact of poverty, underemployment, and economic stress in our country; the general problem of providing needed health care for persons of *all* ages and *all* socioeconomic strata; the recency with which any effort at all has been made to consider the need for educating young people for parenting; the impurity of the air in our urban centers; and the unavailability of needed funds for maintenance of local school district programs, to say nothing of new programs for children under 6 and children with special needs and for developmental child care services. Prenatal, perinatal, and postnatal maternal care; homemaker, counseling, and other family services; adequate nutrition; and other services that would seem to be prime requisites of a society that is affluent, advanced technologically, humane and enlightened, and committed to the well-being of its citizens, especially its children, are not available to all. Infant mortality, child abuse, and "crib death" continue to be serious problems.

In recent decades, considerable progress has been made in medical research aimed at identifying causes of birth defects and mental retardation as a necessary step toward prevention. Furthermore, terrible diseases such as poliomyelitis have been virtually conquered, and some causes of handicapping conditions, such as the drug thalidomide, have been identified and eliminated. Today children survive birth and infancy who only a short time ago would not. Not only have risk factors present in the fetus and newborn been identified, but also other signs of risk have been described, especially in the area of maternal health, possible genetic factors, and the environment in which the child will live.

Recently, pursuant to new federal legislation, a national "child-find" effort has been instituted, through which each state has implemented strategies for the identification of all handicapped children and youth in order to provide them with appropriate educational services. Generally, the responsibility for this effort has fallen to state and local public education agencies. However, in view of the need for *early* identification, an increasing degree of cooperative activity involving many professionals, agencies, communications media, the public at large, and, most important, *families* is necessary.

It is obvious that early identification has different meanings, depending on the handicapping condition and the individual child. Some handicaps are not present at birth, for example, handicaps resulting from accidents, the effects of illness, lead poisoning, and the whole range of "environmental causes." In other instances, risk factors can be identified even before a child is conceived.

Prenatal identification. A promising approach, but one that may leave parents with the decision of whether to risk the birth of a child who *may* be handicapped, is *genetic counseling*. Through such counseling, prospective parents may be made aware of possible risk factors indicated by their own genetic histories.

Once conception has occurred, prenatal examination, taking into account both the progress of the fetus and the health of the mother, is carried out. *Amniocentesis* is a relatively safe procedure by which positive identification in utero of developmental problems such as Down's syndrome and Tay-Sachs disease can be accomplished. Again, such identification may place the responsibility on the parents of the unborn child to make extremely difficult decisions.

With regard to prevention, it should be apparent that neither parental decisions not to procreate nor their decisions to terminate pregnancy are easy ones, nor are they clear-cut, and the moral and spiritual dimensions of such decisions are enormous. Furthermore, the limitations in such strategies as approaches in prevention should be equally apparent, in view of the complexity of the problem of etiology, or cause, of handicapping conditions. At least as promising, and more unequivocally indicated from the perspective of personal and societal values, are approaches aimed at eliminating environmental and maternal health causes, through improved nutrition, for example, as well as medical guidance enlightened by current knowledge concerning possibly harmful effects of cigarette smoking during the first trimester or uremic poisoning in later pregnancy.

Identification of handicapping conditions present in the child, however, must be distinguished from identification of *potential* causes, although both are indeed dimensions of prevention.

Perinatal and postnatal identification. The identification of newborns who are "at risk" is based on clinical observation in which important signs may be recognized. Generally, birth weight and length of pregnancy have long been recognized as important indicators of developmental status and prognosis, although in neither case is the relationship a perfect one. A higher proportion of children who were not carried full-term than of those who were is found among handicapped children. Similarly, difficulty in parturition has been associated with a variety of developmental problems, since *anoxia* at birth may result in cortical damage. Also, such consequences have been found to ensue from difficult deliveries requiring surgical instruments.

Some forms of handicap can be recognized immediately at birth, if the condition has not been identified even earlier. For example, the visible symptoms of Down's syndrome, including especially the simian crease in the palms of the hands and the characteristic eyefolds, are usually apparent. Examination at birth and during the first days of life, including reflex testing, can successfully pick up certain abnormalities, and treatment of some conditions can be initiated. Problems with which the child is born are *congenital* problems. These include both those associated with genetic constitution and those incurred during the mother's pregnancy or delivery.

A well-known procedure for rating indicators of well-being at birth was developed by Virginia Apgar. The Apgar test, or "Newborn Scoring System" is " . . . applied to all newborn infants one minute and five minutes after birth to give a quick evaluation of physical condition and to call attention to any need for emergency procedures" (Apgar and Beck, 1972, p. 9).

The neonate is given a rating from 0 to 2 ". . . on each of five vital signs, for which her (Dr. Apgar's) name has become an acronym: Appearance or coloring, Pulse, Grimace or reflex irritability, Activity, and Respiration" (Apgar and Beck, 1972, p. 9). Although attempts have been made to relate Apgar scores to problems appearing later, especially learning disabilities, the procedure has proved most effective in the identification at birth of severe physical and neurological problems. Positive identification of "mild" or "moderate" handicaps is generally not accomplished this early in life; however, early signs are frequently found to have existed through retrospective analysis of birth histories of children later found to be mentally retarded, learning disabled, or behaviorally disordered.

In recent years a great deal of research effort has been initiated in medical centers concerning the early identification of neonates and infants at risk (Brazelton, 1973). This work offers much promise if it leads to the development of effective means of early intervention. At the very least, guidance and support for parents can be provided, for the initial realization that their new baby is handicapped is surely extremely difficult to bear. Increasingly, coordinated services are being developed to ensure that families can secure the forms of help they need when such help can be most beneficial.

Identification during infancy. In sharing their own observations with their child's pediatrician, as well as through participating in the regular pediatric examinations that are essential for every baby, parents can detect signs of health problems of developmental disabilities. Well-baby clinics and multiservice centers have increasingly become available as well, to ensure that careful and expert medical guidance and care are provided children in the first years of life. Tragically, however, such services are not yet available to all. In the case of any health problem during infancy, immediate recognition and provision of appropriate treatment are of paramount importance.

For children with physical or sensory impairment, intervention ideally should begin within the first months of life. It is then that the roots of language, mobility, cognition, and self-concept can be nurtured. Yet serious hearing impairments at times go unnoticed until the child enters school, as do instances of partial sight or other problems in vision or visual perception. Doctors, teachers, other professionals in community service agencies, and parents must work together in the task of identifying problems in infancy so that ameliorative efforts can be provided as early as possible.

Role of the teacher in identification. To be effective in identifying potential handicapping conditions, the teacher of young children should be

1. Familiar with "normal" processes and stages in children's development
2. Aware of symptoms associated with specific handicapping conditions
3. Skilled in observing and recording behavior of individual children
4. Able to employ informal procedures in diagnosing educational problems
5. Familiar with and able to use appropriate resource persons in the school or community
6. Able to maintain effective and continuous communication with the parents of children he or she teaches

Chapters 3 through 10 of this book are intended to provide guidance to the teacher both in identifying specific forms of exceptionality and in providing appropriate and effective assistance to children with special needs within the group's educational program. Chapter 12 provides suggestions for individual educational diagnosis and planning for exceptional children within the classroom. It is hoped that the information presented and the suggested practices for teaching young children with special needs will enable the reader to work effectively with these children, whatever the setting in which they are served.

DISCUSSION QUESTIONS

1. Why is environment a particularly important concept in considering the psychological development of young handicapped children?
2. Explain the issues surrounding differing points of view concerning intelligence in children.
3. How do interactionist theories of psychological development differ from both maturationist and environmentalist theories?
4. Why has so much more attention been given in recent years to early childhood education? To early education programs for handicapped children?
5. Explain the distinction between primary and secondary prevention. What are some approaches to primary prevention of handicapping conditions in children?
6. What are some of the ways in which the setting or type of program in which a teacher of young children works might influence his or her role in helping young children with special needs?
7. What is the basis for the point of view that the earliest possible identification of children's handicapping conditions is desirable? Why is it sometimes difficult to identify handicapping conditions as early as might be desirable?

REFERENCES

Anastasi, A. Heredity, environment and the question: "how?" *Psychology Review,* 1958, *65,* 197-208.

Apgar, V., and Beck, J. *Is my baby all right? A guide to birth defects.* New York: Trident Press, 1972.

Bloom, B. S., *Stability and change in human characteristics.* New York: John Wiley and Sons, Inc., 1964.

Bower, E. M. Slicing the mystique of prevention with Occam's razor. *American Journal of Public Health,* 1969, *59,* 478-484.

Brazelton, T. B. Assessment of the infant at risk. *Clinical Obstetrics and Gynecology,* 1973, *16,* 361.

Brown, M., and Precious, N. *The integrated day in the primary school.* New York: Agathon Press, Inc., 1969.

Bruner, J. S. *The process of education.* New York: Random House, Inc., 1960.

Caldwell, B. M. The importance of beginning early. In J. B. Jordan and R. F. Dailey (Eds.), *Not all little wagons are red: the exceptional child's early years.* Arlington, Va.: Council for Exceptional Children, 1973, pp. 2-9.

Cawley, J. F. Special education: selected issues and innovations. In A. D. Roberts (Ed.), *Educational innovation: alternatives in curriculum and instruction.* Boston: Allyn & Bacon, Inc., 1975, pp. 164-186.

Cazden, C. B. *Child language and education.* New York: Holt, Rinehart & Winston, Inc., 1972.

Cicerelli, V. G., Evans, J. W., and Schiller, J. S. *The impact of Head Start on children's cognitive and affective development: preliminary report.* Washington, D.C.: Office of Economic Opportunity, 1969.

Cole, M., and Bruner, J. S., Preliminaries to a theory of cultural differences. In I. J. Gordon (Ed.), *Early childhood education: the seventy-first yearbook of the National Society for the Study of Education* (Part II). Chicago: University of Chicago Press, 1972, pp. 161-180.

Cowan, E., and Zax, E. The mental health fields today: issues and problems. In E. Cowan (Ed.), *Emergent approaches to mental health.* New York: Appleton-Century-Crofts, 1967, pp. 3-33.

Deutsch, M. The role of social class in language development and cognition. *American Journal of Orthopsychiatry,* 1965, *35,* January, 78-88.

Dmitriev, V. Motor and cognitive development in early education. In N. G. Haring (Ed.), *Behavior of exceptional children: an introduction to special education.* Columbus, Ohio: Charles E. Merrill Publishing Co., 1974.

Engleman, S. *Preventing failure in the primary grades.* Chicago: Science Research Associates, Inc., 1969.

Frankenberg, W. K. Increasing the lead time for the preschool aged handicapped child. In J. B. Jordan and R. F. Dailey (Eds.), *Not all little wagons are red: the exceptional child's early years.* Arlington, Va.: Council for Exceptional Children, 1973, pp. 24-33.

Furman, R. A., and Katan, A. (Eds.). *The therapeutic nursery school: a contribution to the study and treatment of emotional disturbances in young children.* New York: International Universities Press, 1969.

Gallagher, J. J., and Bradley, R. H. Early identification of developmental difficulties. In I. J. Gordon (Ed.), *Early childhood education: the seventy-first yearbook of the National Society for the Study of Education* (Part IV). Chicago: University of Chicago Press, 1971, 87-122.

Gesell, A. L., and Amatruda, C. S. *Developmental diagnosis.* New York: Hoeber, 1941.

Gordon, I. J. *A home learning center approach to early stimulation.* Gainesville, Fla.: University of Florida, 1967.

Gray, S. W., and Klaus, R. A. *The early training project: a seventh year report.* Nashville, Tenn.: John F. Kennedy Center for Research on Education and Human Development, George Peabody College for Teachers, 1969.

Gray, S. W., Klaus, R. A., Miller, J. O., and Forrester, B. J. *Before first grade: the early training project for culturally disadvantaged children.* New York: Teachers College Press, 1966.

Guilford, J. P. *The nature of human intelligence.* New York: McGraw-Hill Book Co., 1967.

Guilford, J. P., and Hoepfner, R. *The analysis of intelligence.* New York: McGraw-Hill Book Co., 1971.

Haring, N. G. *A program report for the investigation and application of procedures of analysis and modification of behavior of handicapped children.* (Final report, grant No. OE6-0070-3916 [607]). Washington, D.C.: U.S. Department of Health, Education, and Welfare, Bureau of Education for the Handicapped, 1972.

Hess, R. D., and Shipman, V. C. Maternal influences upon early learning. In R. D. Hess and R. M. Bear (Eds.), *Early Education.* Chicago: Aldine Publishing Co., 1968.

Hunt, J. Mc.V. *Intelligence and experience.* New York: The Ronald Press Co., 1961.

Hymes, J. L., Jr. *Teaching the child under six* (2nd ed.). Columbus, Ohio: Charles E. Merrill Publishing Co., 1974.

Jencks, C., et al. *Inequality. A reassessment of the effect of family and schooling in America.* New York: Basic Books, Inc., 1972.

Jensen, A. R. How much can we boost IQ and scholastic achievement? *Harvard Educational Review,* 1969, *39,* 1-123.

Kamii, C., and Radin, N. A. A framework for preschool curriculum based on piagetian concepts. In I. J. Athey and D. O. Rubadeau (Eds.), *Educational implications of Piaget's theory.* Waltham, Mass.: Ginn-Blaisdell, 1970, pp. 89-100.

Karnes, M. B., Teska, J. A., and Hodgins, A. S. The effects of four programs of classroom intervention on the intellectual and language development of four year old disadvantaged children. *American Journal of Orthopsychiatry,* 1970, *40,* 58-76.

Kirk, S. A. *Educating exceptional children.* Boston: Houghton Mifflin Co., 1972.

Kohlberg, L., and Mayer, R. Development as the aim of education. *Harvard Educational Review,* 1972, *42,* 449-496.

Landreth, C. *Preschool learning and teaching.* New York: Harper & Row, Inc., 1972.

Lavatelli, C. S. A Piaget-derived model for compensatory preschool education. In J. L. Frost (Ed.), *Early childhood education rediscovered.* New York: Holt, Rinehart, & Winston, Inc., 1968, pp. 530-544.

Lazerson, M. The historical antecedents of early childhood education. In I. J. Gordon (Ed.), *Early* childhood education: the seventy-first yearbook of the National Society for the Study of Education (Part II). Chicago: University of Chicago Press, 1972, pp. 33-54.

McNeill, D. Developmental psycholinguistics. In F. Smith and G. A. Miller (Eds.), *The genesis of language: a psycholinguistic approach.* Cambridge, Mass.: The M.I.T. Press, 1966, pp. 15-84.

Montessori, M. *The Montessori method.* New York: F. A. Stokes, 1912.

Montessori, M. *The absorbent mind.* Madras, India: Theosophical Publishing House, 1949.

Mycock, M. A. Vertical grouping in the primary school. In V. R. Rogers (Ed.), *Teaching in the British primary school.* Toronto: Macmillan Co. of Canada, Ltd., 1970, pp. 34-59.

Pines, M. *Revolution in learning.* New York: Harper & Row, Inc., 1966.

Plank, E. *Working with children in hospitals.* Cleveland: Press of Case Western Reserve University, 1962.

Rosenthal, R., and Jacobsen, L. *Pygmalion in the classroom.* New York: Holt, Rinehart & Winston, Inc., 1968.

Schaefer, E. S., and Aaronson, M. Infant education research project: implementation and implications of a home tutoring program. In R. K. Parker (Ed.), *The preschool in action: exploring early childhood programs.* Boston: Allyn & Bacon, Inc., 1972, pp. 410-434.

Shapiro, E., and Biber, B. The education of young children: a developmental interaction approach. *Teachers College Record,* 1972, *74*(1), 55-79.

Sprinthall, R. C., and Sprinthall, N. A. *Educational psychology: a developmental approach.* Reading, Mass.: Addison-Wesley Publishing Co., Inc., 1974.

Thomas, A., Chess, S., and Birch, H. G. *Temperament and behavior disorders in children.* New York: New York University Press, 1968.

Todd, V. E., and Hefferman, H. *The years before school: guiding preschool children* (2nd ed.). New York: Macmillan Publishing Co., Inc., 1970.

Torrance, E. P., and Strom, R. D. *Mental health and achievement: increasing potential and reducing school dropout.* New York: John Wiley & Sons, Inc., 1967.

Watson, J. B. The behaviorist looks at instincts. *Harper's Magazine,* 1927, *155,* 233.

Weikart, D. P. Early childhood special education for intellectually subnormal and/or culturally different children. Paper presented at symposium, *Cognitive development and the intellectually subnormal,* Conference on Manpower Preparation for Handicapped Young Children, Washington, D.C., December 9-10, 1971.

Weikart, D., Rogers, L., Adcock, C., and McClelland, D. *The cognitively oriented curriculum: a framework for preschool teachers.* Washington, D.C.: National Association for the Education of Young Children, 1970.

White, B. *The first three years of life.* Englewood Cliffs, N.J.: Prentice-Hall, Inc., 1975.

Zigler, E. F. Mental retardation: current issues and approaches. In L. W. Hoffman and M. L. Hoffman (Eds.), *Review of child development research* (Vol. II). New York: Russell Sage Foundation, 1966, pp. 107-168.

Zigler, E. F. The environmental mystique: training the intellect versus development of the child. *Childhood Education,* 1970, *46,* 8.

Sensory and communication handicaps

CHAPTER 2

SPEECH AND LANGUAGE DISORDERS

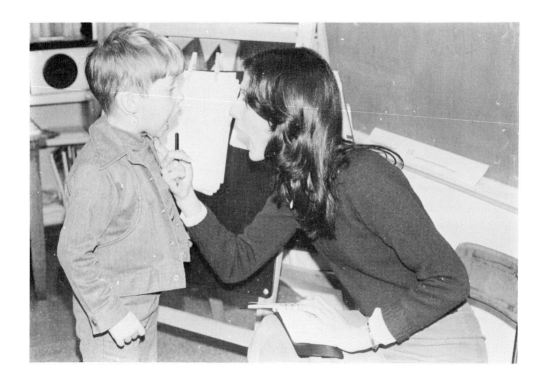

On the continuum of frequency of incidence, no handicap has traditionally been as prevalent among children as have speech disorders. However, depending on which criteria and which incidence reports are used, there is increasingly a trend for learning disabilities to approach the prevalence of speech problems within the school-age population. Some would define specific learning disabilities as disorders in aspects of language functioning (Johnson and Myklebust, 1967). It can certainly be asserted that speech- and language-related problems, coupled with learning disabilities, comprise the vast majority of handicapping conditions of childhood (Kirk, 1972).

In addition, problems in speech or language are very frequently associated with physical and neurological handicapping conditions. Cerebral palsy, in particular, may be accompanied by *perceptual processing disturbances* affecting *receptive* or *expressive* language functioning. That is, the child's ability to interpret sensory data and/or his ability to communicate information to others may be impaired (Cruickshank, 1975). This condition may also cause inability to exercise voluntary control over muscle systems involved in the production of speech (especially control of tongue placement, swallowing, and use of the muscles surrounding the mouth), causing problems of speech. Furthermore, mental subnormality has been seen by some researchers (McLean et al., 1976) as primarily a language handicap, as has the severe form of emotional disturbance known as autism (Hermelin and O'Connor, 1970).

Understanding speech and language disorders in children actually requires at least some familiarity with an exceedingly complex topic: the acquisition of language. It is important for the teacher of young children to become as knowledgeable as he or she can concerning the processes by which children acquire the ability to use language and concerning the dimensions of language functioning. However, to deal comprehensively with this area is beyond the scope of a chapter dealing essentially with strategies available to the teacher for working with young children with special needs in these areas. Consequently, the reader is referred to recent references that provide an extensive treatment of the area, such as the excellent book by Dr. Courtney Cazden (1972), which is addressed directly to teachers, and by Dr. David McNeill (1970), which provides a comprehensive and exceedingly interesting account by one of the foremost scholars on children's language development. Philip S. Dale's *Language Development: Structure and Function* (1976) is also valuable.

DEVELOPMENT OF SPEECH AND LANGUAGE

A distinction is always made between the terms "speech" and "language," for reasons that are obvious. Speech is a particular means of *expression* of language content. Without language, speech would have no "meaning"—and thus would not serve the purpose of enabling the speaker to communicate information to a listener. *Meaning* is determined by the specific words that are spoken, the affect and circumstances that become attached to the symbols that provide true meaning, and the manner in which those words are combined, that is, by the *structure* that characterizes meaningful utterances. *Written expression,* like vocal expression, or speech, consists of words organized according to certain rules. It is a mode of expression normally acquired long after speech proficiency is achieved and that, unlike speech, is usually assumed to require conscious teaching. Speech, on the other hand, is an ability that most children develop in the course of their interactions with others who comprise their social environment. Most children's speech seems to come about "naturally," that is, without conscious teaching. However, as Weiss and Lillywhite (1976) stress, speech abilities, since they are *learned,* in fact do involve teaching. The "naturalness" of the process is deceptive, although innate capability for language is apparently important (McNeill, 1970).

People employ a variety of other modes of expression, most of which meet some but not all the criteria of linguistic expression. Gesture, facial expression, pantomime, and posture ("body language") all convey information and are thus communicative. Some nonverbal communicative behaviors (for example, crying, frowning, and smiling) convey information in a *nonsymbolic* manner. Rather these are *signal* behaviors, or *signs*. Physical communicative behaviors are *symbolic* if they *represent*, or "stand for," a thing, action, person, idea, even for a highly complex thought or action sequence. Obvious examples are provided by the sign communication systems used by many severely hearing-impaired persons, but everyday gestures, such as waving or pointing, may have symbolic as well as sign properties.

Language, however, in the strict sense, is usually thought of as having four major characteristics: (1) *phonology,* a system of rules for combining speech sounds; (2) *morphology,* a system of rules for combining meaningful units, or morphemes, into words; (3) *syntax,* a system of rules for the meaningful combination of words into grammatical structures; and (4) *semantics,* the general dimension of meaningfulness in language as determined by the relationship between linguistic symbols and the items, persons, events, ideas, relationships, etc. to which they refer. Thus speech reflects each of these dimensions of language. However, not all of an individual's linguistic repertoire is conveyed through his speech. This is particularly evident when we reflect on the dimension of vocabulary, since children of any age —and adults as well—understand or respond appropriately to many more words than they may actually utter.

One way of expressing this difference between ability to understand language and ability to use language to communicate meaningfully to others is by means of the terms "receptive language" and "expressive language." The first refers to what is "received" through the senses— vision, hearing, touch, taste, and smell. The second refers to what is expressed, whether through speech or through other motoric means, such as gesture, facial expression, writing, and action, such as running.

If we imagine the human being as a *processor of information,* we have already identified two of the three necessary components of an "information processing system." The third describes what occurs between the stages of "input" (reception) and "output" (expression). We are, of course, referring to *thought.* In a linguistic sense, we can employ the term "inner language" to describe the language processes that facilitate information processing, or thinking (Vygotsky, 1962). Once the child is able to use inner language as a means of thinking, his ability to employ logic and reason, as well as to think creatively, is amplified (Bruner, 1965).

Psycholinguists make an additional distinction. They distinguish language *performance,* as indicated in part by speech, from language *competence.* The surface structure of what the child utters implies a deep structure, or a set of underlying grammatical rules. It is this ability of the child to acquire and to apply language rules that is believed by developmental psycholinguists to account for the extraordinarily rapid rate at which children master language; for the apparent *universality* both of language structure and of the

Table 1. Information processing system

Receptive → language	Inner → language	Expressive language
Sensation → Perception	Cognition (thought)	Motor expression
Hearing, vision, touch, taste, smell	Memory	Speech

language acquisition sequence, regardless of the particular language spoken in a culture: and for the ability of children to "generate" *novel* speech forms, that is, speech forms that they have never heard and have surely never been taught.

The term "generative transformational grammar" is used to explain how a young child presented with a picture and given the nonsense name "wug" forms the plural by adding s ("Here are two *wugs.*") (Berko, 1958). It also explains how a young child comes to employ "erroneous" constructions, such as expressing the past tense form of go as goed or saying, "He *gots* one." In these instances, his response indicates that the child is applying a *rule* in performing a linguistic *transformation.* Many transformations, like these examples, are performed by means of *inflections,* which are "the addition of certain endings to the base of a word to express such meanings as number and tense" (Cazden, 1972, p. 301).

Although many aspects of young children's speech may appear to adults both amusing and incorrect, they may provide important clues to the child's thought and to his increasing ability to apply linguistic rules. An obvious implication for the parent or the teacher is the importance of thinking twice before correcting linguistic "errors" and certainly of avoiding shaming or ridiculing the child for the way he speaks. These "errors" probably represent developmental rules and are developmentally necessary.

Although the basic structures and rules for language are universal, individual languages are culture specific. And within a general culture and its characteristic language, variability exists among subgroups and, of course, among individuals. These differences are reflected mainly in the particular words and combinations of words the child learns to use through what Roger Brown called "the original word game" (Brown, 1958). Whereas children may have an innate capacity for acquiring language according to general rules, the specific labels, etc.—what the child does with language within the boundaries set by those rules—are probably acquired mainly through the two general modes of learning termed reinforcement and modeling. From infancy, the baby's utterances are differentially *reinforced,* or rewarded, by his first and most important teachers—his parents—whose speech he also *imitates.* Therefore it follows that parents' effectiveness in using these teaching tools appropriately is an extremely important determinant of whether the child's speech development will proceed well.

ROLE OF THE TEACHER
Scope of the problem

Problems of speech are the handicapping conditions most frequently encountered by the teacher. They are also among the difficulties children experience that teachers feel least able to correct. Although the language arts comprise one of the major areas of emphasis, if not *the* major area, in the nursery school, kindergarten, and primary curriculum, many teachers feel powerless to serve the needs of those children who manifest problems in the area of vocal communication.

This is most unfortunate, since the early childhood educator is usually in an excellent position to provide positive assistance if he or she is familiar with the characteristics of such problems, referral sources, school and community resources, and appropriate classroom intervention strategies.

Although speech disorders are a high-incidence category of handicap, with estimates of those children involved running as high as 10 percent or more of the school-age population (Kirk, 1972), children who have *severe* speech handicaps are a very small percentage of this number. Furthermore, many minor speech problems are probably amenable to correction through efforts of the classroom teacher in the course of normal attention to needs of individual pupils (Bown,

1971). Problems of this sort are generally in the area of *functional articulation* and may not reflect an underlying neurological anomaly (as in aphasia), serious emotional causative factors (as in some instances of stuttering), hearing impairment, global cognitive deficits (as in mental retardation), or serious problems specific to speech functions (such as voice disorders). When problems of such severity occur, the classroom teacher may work to ameliorate the handicapping condition in four basic ways: (1) identification of and referral to a specialist in speech and language, usually a speech pathologist; (2) working with the specialist to carry out a prescribed program within the classroom, perhaps involving systematic reinforcement of specific speech behaviors to accomplish precise objectives; (3) providing encouragement and support; and (4) ensuring that effective communication is maintained with the child's parents concerning his needs and progress.

However, for the majority of children who suffer from less severe difficulties, or whose speech and language development is proceeding normally, "the classroom teacher is a speech teacher whether he is trained to be or not; indeed, whether he wants to be or not. Both as a speaker and as a listener, he creates an atmosphere either conducive to, or unfavorable to, the development of each child's speech" (Phillips, 1975, p. 13). Of course, this is particularly true of the teacher of young children, who is in a position not only to *remedy* problems, but to *prevent* them, in many cases, from becoming more serious disabilities.

Although it is true that the large number of children for whom a teacher is responsible, as well as the teacher's own lack of specific training in this highly technical field, preclude assuming the role of a speech clinician, there is much that a teacher can do to help the child with special problems in the area of speech. Ideally, a professional who has had specialized training in this area will be available, both to

work directly with the child and to provide guidance to the teacher and the child's parents. This *speech clinician,* the classroom teacher, and the parents can work together effectively as a team to ensure that treatment goals are reinforced in the classroom and at home and also to provide the speech clinician with needed observational data to assist him or her in formulating these goals and determining treatment strategies. For a great many children, the most valuable service the speech clinician can perform is to see a child diagnostically and then to recommend procedures that can be carried out by others on a day-to-day basis. In general, the speech clinician can help the teacher become more aware of indicators of speech problems in children and of habilitative procedures used in speech correction that can be incorporated into the classroom routine.

Identification of speech problems

One of the most valuable skills a teacher of young children can develop is the ability to identify signs of possible speech difficulties. Identification can lead to referral to the speech clinician, following consultation with the child's parents. Thus the identification function of the teacher is a basic and essential link in the chain leading to therapy that can lessen or even eliminate the child's problem. In the area of speech, as in every other aspect of human behavior, diversity is the rule. In the dimensions of pitch, volume, and tone a wide range of variability is encompassed by the term "normal speech." Since speech is learned, since speech capability increases with development through the early years of childhood, and since children vary widely with respect to *rate* of development in all spheres of behavior, many differences in *maturity* of speech among children of the same age may be quite "normal." The teacher must be aware, not only of developmental norms, but of conditions under which deviation from these norms may signal a *problem.*

In the older child or the adult speaker, there are criteria for determining whether an abnormality or disability in speech exists, and under what circumstances therapeutic intervention is indicated:

It is generally accepted that any speech which draws unfavorable attention to itself, whether through unpleasant sound, inappropriateness to the age level, or interference with communication, may be classified as defective. Speech which contributes to feelings of self-consciousness or inadequacy in the speaker himself is also regarded as deviant. For example, the stuttering child may grow so reticent that the casual listener may not be aware of the extent to which the problem has affected him. When speech shows any of these characteristics, its user is in need of speech correction. To be normal, speech should permit the undistracted interchange of verbal language, free from grimaces, phonemic misarticulations, unnatural and unusual voice qualities, speaking rates, and rhythms. Vocabulary and sound usage should be adequate and appropriate for the age level, and speech should be delivered in logical, syntactical order. (p. 74)*

This statement conveys that speech adequacy is important for two major, and closely related, reasons: (1) speech is a primary means of communicating with others, and (2) it is subjectively experienced by the speaker as an *expression of self.*

The other major criterion identified by Kirk for determining whether a problem exists is that of *age appropriateness,* a criterion that is applicable in identifying intellectual deviations and problems in the areas of skill learning and of personal or social development as well. As in these areas, speech proficiency *norms* have been established; they reflect a sequence of development in the acquisition of language and in the mastery of speech skills. As in the case of other dimensions of child development, normative language and speech growth reflects patterns that are

ordinal and *hierarchical;* that is, they follow a generally predictable order, and they are characterized by the acquisition of progressively more complex and diverse behaviors that are built on the foundations of previous behaviors and behavioral capabilities. Given normal variability caused by differential characteristics intrinsic to the child (including differential rates of growth) and differential environmental factors, the steps children follow in speech and language development are not perfectly matched to chronological age. Age norms reflect statistical averages, rather than absolute standards, and it is necessary to determine in any individual instance whether a deviation is sufficiently marked to constitute a problem. If we bear these qualifying statements in mind, it is helpful to refer for general guidance to normative standards, such as those summarized in Table 2.

TYPES OF COMMUNICATION DISORDERS

McLean (1974) proposes three general categories of children with communication disorders: nonverbal children, language-disordered children, and speech-impaired children.

Nonverbal children

The category of nonverbal children includes some (but by no means all) *severely and profoundly* hearing-impaired children who, unable to hear spoken language with ease, have consequently not developed speech. It also includes those children whose lack of verbal behavior has physical causes and children who are autistic. McLean (1974) notes that, whereas in the past institutional programs serving these children have lacked the resources to provide optimal treatment, *community-based* approaches emphasizing *early intervention* are becoming increasingly available.

Language-disordered children

Included in the group of language-disordered children are children with

---

*From Samuel A. Kirk, *Educating exceptional children,* 2nd ed. Copyright © 1972 by Houghton Mifflin Co. Reprinted by permission.

Table 2. Summary of early normal speech and oral language developmental stages*

Age	General characteristics	Usable speaking vocabulary (number of words)	Adequate speech sound production
Months			
1-3	*Undifferentiated crying.* Random vocalizations and cooing.		
4-6	*Babbling.* Specific vocalizations. Verbalizes in response to speech of others. Immediate responses approximate human intonational patterns.		
7-11	Tongue moves with vocalizations (lalling). Vocalizes recognition. Reduplicates sound. Echolalia (automatic repetition of words and phrases).		
12	*First word.*	1-3	All vowels
18	*One-word sentence stage.* Well-established jargon. Uses nouns primarily.	18-22	
Years			
2	*Two-word sentence stage.* Sentences functionally complete. Uses more pronouns and verbs.	270-300	
2.5	*Three-word sentence stage.* Telegraphic speech.	450	h, w, hw
3	Complete simple-active-sentence structure used. Uses sentences to tell stories which are understood by others.	900	p, b, m
3.5	*Expanded grammatical forms.* Concepts expressed with words. Speech disfluency is typical. Sentence length is 4-5 words.	1200	t, d, n
4	Excessive verbalizations. Imaginary speech.	1500	k, g, ng, j
5	*Well-developed and complex syntax.* Uses more complex forms to tell stories. Uses negation and inflexional form of verbs.	2000	f, v
6-8	*Sophisticated speech.* Skilled use of grammatical rules. Learns to read. Acceptable articulation by 8 years for males and females.	2600+	l, r, y, s, z, sh, ch, zh, th, consonant blends

*From Children with Oral Communication Disabilities, by Forrest M. Hull and Mary E. Hull, in *Exceptional Children in the Schools: Special Education in Transition* (2nd ed.), edited by Lloyd M. Dunn. Copyright © 1963, 1973 by Holt, Rinehart & Winston. Reprinted by permission of Holt, Rinehart & Winston.

mild or *moderate* problems, associated with faulty language learning, and those with *severe* language disorders, frequently associated with mental retardation, brain injury, or severe learning disability. Intervention must take into account the complex relationship between language and cognition, and the professional working with these children must attempt to diagnose the needs of the individual child, as McLean (1974) suggests:

. . . somewhere, somehow they have not learned how to map their knowledge about their world linguistically. Why? Is it because they lacked knowledge or because they lacked the resources to learn the linguistic structures necessary to talk about what they know? The person training these children must discover which he is dealing with. If it is only the linguistic structures, he can begin looking at what the child knows and begin to evoke and reinforce the language structures necessary to talk about this knowledge.

. . . if we are to teach language, we must teach the concepts and the linguistic forms which map those nuggets of knowledge. We must help a child to discover the code and the manner in which the code is used. We must help him to mean what he wants to mean. We must do this in the face of many problems the child might have in the area of his or her sensory perception, motor system, and/or cognitive functioning. (p. 486)

It may be that many children with language- and speech-related problems of this sort become identified in school as having a learning disability. Perhaps many specific learning disabilities might actually be considered language disorders.

Speech-impaired children

Speech-impaired children include children who have stuttering problems, voice disorders, and—by far the largest category—articulation problems. In view of the frequency with which this last set of problems is encountered by the teacher of young children, it will be dealt with somewhat more extensively.

Stuttering. Stuttering is usually considered in terms of two general subclassifications: primary and secondary. "Primary stuttering" is the term applied to the less serious manifestations found so frequently among young children between the ages of 3 and 5 as to be considered by many professionals to be within the bounds of normalcy. It is characterized by the repetition of sounds in the absence of nonspeech behaviors found in older stutterers, such as facial grimacing and gasping. Primary stuttering is essentially indicative of nonfluency associated with developing speech abilities.

Secondary stuttering, however, with its concomitant behavioral symptoms of gasping for breath and other apparent manifestations of attempts to avoid stuttering, requires specialized therapy geared to the individual child. Theories accounting for the causes of stuttering suggest emotional or physical explanations and are multitudinous. Treatment should be undertaken by a speech pathologist or a psychologist who is especially knowledgeable concerning this area. However, the possibility that the voice deviation may be associated with an undetected hearing problem must first be thoroughly explored.

Voice disorders. Voice disorders may be associated with voice production or reso-

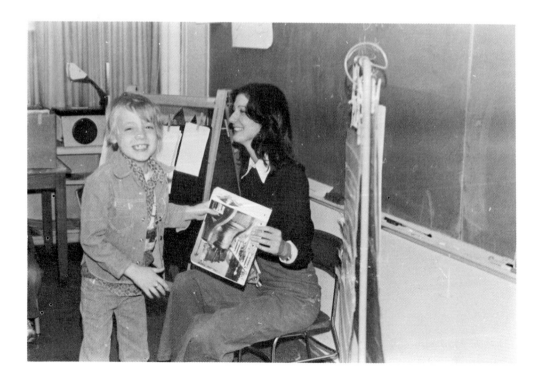

---

nance and usually have physical causes, in which case surgical or prosthetic intervention and speech therapy may be successfully employed. If the child's inappropriate intensity, pitch, or quality of the voice is not found to be associated with malformations of the vocal or auditory mechanism, the speech pathologist's approach is likely to emphasize a learning process in which the child uses feedback to help modify his vocalization.

Articulation problems. By far the greatest number of speech problems are defined as impairments in "functional articulation," as distinguished from *organic* articulation problems, which are associated with motor or sensory defects. These problems, which are least serious (at least in terms of objective standards) and most amenable to correction, comprise an estimated 60 percent of all instances of defective speech in children. Since articulation becomes increasingly more proficient with development, it is probable that at least some such difficulties are virtually self-correcting with time. For many others, however, therapeutic intervention in school, usually by an itinerant speech clinician, is advantageous because it assists many children in learning to develop more mature speech patterns and thus avoid embarrassment or self-consciousness. Without such intervention, articulatory problems experienced by some children would and do persist into adulthood.

Articulation problems are the least serious, most receptive to treatment, and most prevalent of all disorders of speech and language. The fact that their frequency is so much greater among young children just beginning school than among older children is a reflection both of (1) the effectiveness of the work of the itinerant speech clinician and the classroom teacher, and (2) the tendency of these problems to disappear as children develop. Most articulation problems are essentially eliminated in the primary grades. Those still present at the fourth-grade level, however, are very unlikely to improve spontaneously (Kessler, 1966).

These articulation problems take the form of *omission* of sounds, *substitution* of an incorrect sound for one the child has difficulty in forming, or *distortion* of a sound. Among young children of nursery school age, erroneous enunciation is, of course, quite common, particularly of *final* sounds. Vowel sounds are more readily mastered than are consonants, which by definition involve coordinated and controlled activity of diverse parts of the speech mechanism. A consonant can be defined as ". . . a speech sound produced by obstructing the free passage of the breath or voice on its way outwards from the glottis. Lips, teeth, and tongue are the chief obstructive forces" (Miner et al., 1976, p. 2). It is apparent that not only imperfectly developed control of the musculature involved, but also changes in a child's dental structure may account for these characteristic patterns of immature articulation. For this reason, the criterion of *age appropriateness* (always taking into account the normal range of variation) must be applied in determining whether articulatory errors warrant specialized intervention.

CAUSES OF SPEECH PROBLEMS

Physical defects in any of the parts of the physical structures involved in speech production may result in disorders of voice or articulation. In addition to physical causes, however, psychological causes may be involved. A third area of causation has to do with learning processes. Since speech is learned, one may consider the means by which learning occurs as possible sources of difficulty.

Learning and defective speech

Speech and language learning, like other forms of learning, involves at least two general forms of teaching-learning interactive relationships: *reinforcement* and *modeling*. The idea of reinforcement as a major factor in learning means that behavior that persists does so because it is being reinforced by something in the environment. That is, in the case of speech, if a child's utterances "get results," in terms of adult attention and response, the environment is probably providing reinforcement of sufficient strength for these (verbal) behaviors to be maintained. Often a child's infantile or telegraphic speech—reflecting a failure to go beyond simple or immature levels of verbal expression—may be associated with the fact that, if such forms of speech "work," there is little or no incentive to change them.

Modeling (Bandura, 1962) is another important mode of learning in the area of speech development, as in other areas of behavior. Consequently, it suggests a second potential source of difficulty in the child's learning of speech. Speech deficiencies may reflect poor speech models available to the child.

The prevailing view among developmental psycholinguists (that group of scientists concerned with children's acquisition of structured language systems) holds that the *structure* of language is universal; it requires only an "average, expectable environment" to develop. Nevertheless, the particular language that is learned is determined mainly by the *language models* whom the child has an opportunity to imitate. Consequently, specific speech characteristics observed in a child, including articulatory, voice, or other abnormalities, may conceivably reflect similar problems in the adult speech models to which the child has been exposed.

A variety of factors may contribute to speech problems in young children. Since teachers of young children, especially during approximately the first 4 years of life, have the opportunity to intervene *as speech and language are developing,* their role is of great importance. They are in a position to identify possible problems sufficiently early in the child's life so that ameliorative medical procedures can be initiated, including surgery if indicated, and/or specialized therapy can be begun. In addition, with the child's parents, the teacher provides an important source of speech and language learning for the child through (1) encouraging and reinforcing desirable and adaptive speech patterns, (2) providing a good model for speech and language learning, and (3) establishing a language environment that facilitates the child's development in the area of language and speech.

Hearing impairment

If a child's parents or teacher becomes aware of abnormalities in a child's speech behavior of virtually any kind, or even suspects that the child's speech development may not be proceeding optimally, the first possible causal factor that should be explored is impaired hearing. Although a number of other possible causes of problems may be involved, since expressive speech basically reflects the way the child hears language, auditory acuity is central to normal speech.

Teachers, especially in the elementary grades, frequently make the assumption —as do parents—that any possible problems in hearing will be picked up through the routine screening that is done in schools. However, by no means is this the case. Even more detailed checkups conducted by a family physician or pediatrician or in a community health agency may fail to detect some hearing problems. Even the knowledge that a child has had a thorough study to determine the presence of impaired hearing and that no impairment was found does not eliminate the need for continued sensitivity to this possibility. This is true in part because of the possibility of *adventitious* (acquired) hearing loss that may occur following the examination and that may be a result of illness (upper respiratory infection, measles, etc.) or even blockage of sound conduction caused by buildup of wax. For example, a 4-year-old who has been determined to be free of hearing loss may subsequently have an ear infection associated with upper respiratory tract illness that then affects his hearing. In view of the commonness of childhood illness and disease, especially up to about age 7 years, it follows that *regular* and *thorough* hearing evaluations should be conducted during these years for all children. If the child's parents or teacher suspects problems in speech during these years, there may be reason to obtain an even more comprehensive evaluation than can be conducted by the pediatrician in his office. Such an evaluation would include examination by an audiologist as well and may be conducted at a speech and hearing center, where the required room and instruments are available.

Some young children suffer from chronic ear infection. This is especially, but by no means exclusively, true of children who have some form of physical handicap. Among these children are many for whom an annual audiological and audiometric study is insufficient. Since the early years are so crucial for speech and language development and since adequate hearing is basic to such development, almost continuous monitoring is necessary.

Certain voice disorders, such as the *nasality* of speech of many seriously hearing-impaired persons, are particularly associated with hearing impairment. Although certain patterns have been identified as reflecting "deaf speech," it may be quite difficult on the basis of behavioral observation alone to distinguish whether a young child's speech suggests impaired hearing, even if such observation is conducted on a one-to-one basis in a specialized, clinical setting. Nursery school, Head Start, day care, and all other agencies serving young children of prekindergarten age should have regularly established communication linkage, referral procedures, and cooperative relationships with specialized facilities (such as hearing and speech centers) that can provide appropriately trained personnel (such as audiologists) and that use the latest and best audiometric and other equipment.

Within the public or nonpublic school, the classroom teacher's responsibility is to ensure the involvement of the appropriate specialist through standard referral procedures dictated by policies of that school. With regard to determining whether a thorough audiological and audiometric study of the child is indicated, it is far better to err in the direction of caution. So much is at stake during these critical years—the child's health, his learning, his social development, and his feelings of competence—that any indication that impaired hearing may possibly be handicapping his progress in mastering speech and language should be followed up.

Relationship to other handicapping conditions

Speech and language deficiencies may be associated with primary handicapping conditions other than impaired hearing. A neurologically based physical disability such as cerebral palsy is likely to involve difficulties in speech and possibly receptive language as well. The acquisition of language is certainly related to emotional development; consequently distorted, deviant, or delayed speech may also reflect difficulties in personal-social development or even severe emotional disturbance.

Typically the general cognitive retardation of mentally subnormal children is especially reflected in deficient or delayed language functioning. Acquisition of communicative speech by the time the retarded child is about 5 years of age is an extremely important prognostic indicator concerning the level of intellectual performance and adaptive functioning he can attain (Kessler, 1966). Since so much of what is taught in school is dependent on language skills—listening, speaking, reading, and written expression—it is not surprising that *learning ability tests* (that is, intelligence tests) used to predict school performance are so heavily language oriented. Consequently, if mental retardation is defined at least in part on the basis of lower-than-average scores on such tests, the retarded child is almost by definition a language-handicapped child.

It is possible to characterize mental retardation as essentially a *language problem*. General mental retardation is usually, however, distinguished from disabilities that are specific to language functioning (Myklebust, 1968) or to any certain skill or process. Peterson (1974) in fact proposed the term "general learning disability," in contrast to specific learning disability, as a more educationally relevant way of describing mental retardation. Nonetheless, some researchers have noted that retarded children often tend to perform better on concept learning tasks that are relatively "language free" than on those requiring a verbal explanation. It is possible that the deficient expressive capabilities of many retarded children may mask abilities to solve problems and even engage in abstract thinking (Rosenberg, 1963). It is also possible that many of these children may demonstrate greater cognitive abilities in day-to-day living situations than are revealed through usual assessment procedures.

"NONCLINICAL" PROBLEMS OF LANGUAGE AND SPEECH

Many of the communication problems that are of most concern to the teacher of young children are not truly "handicaps" at all, in the sense in which this word is used with reference to exceptional children. To the speech clinician, such problems are "nonclinical." Although in these cases there may be much need for a teacher to implement a carefully individualized program, the child's problem does not require the services of a specialist nor does it "qualify" as a handicap or disability. It goes without saying that close cooperation between the teacher and the child's parents will be the most important ingredient of success. However, it is essential that the teacher present clearly and in a nonthreatening way the goals and the reason for his or her concern. It may be that the child's speech is not at all perceived as a problem by the parents, and they may resent, overreact to, or misunderstand what

is being said. In this area, as in all other facets of parent-teacher communication's, openness, clarity, mutual trust, and respect are the necessary conditions for effective cooperation. It is the teacher's responsibility to establish and maintain with the parents of the children he or she teaches the kind of relationship in which either shares an observation or requests assistance in helping the child.

There are several kinds of problems or concerns relating to speech and language the teacher may have. Brief discussion is provided here concerning two "issues" (as distinguished from "problems," even though the teacher may perceive them as problems): *language differences* and *bilingualism*. Then *speech reticence*, a source of concern in some children's speech behavior, is discussed somewhat more extensively.

Language differences

There has been much discussion in the field of early education concerning the issues presented by language differences among children in language patterns. In its early days, Project Head Start attempted to address what were believed to be language *deficits* among children of the poor. Subsequently, however, a number of researchers began to study language differences among subcultural groups in terms of *linguistic* criteria and found "nonstandard" forms of language essentially equivalent to "standard English" as a communicative system. The work of such sociolinguists as Baratz (Baratz and Baratz, 1970; Baratz and Shuy, 1969) has had considerable impact on such programs as Head Start and other efforts to compensate for "disadvantaged language environments" of young children. Applications of the concept of a *restrictive linguistic code* (Bernstein, 1961) to economically disadvantaged children in the United States have been specifically criticized (Bernstein, 1973).

The main point, from the standpoint of the teacher of young children, is that a range of diversity in speech patterns, as in other domains, is not only acceptable but desirable as well. Teachers should not be quick to criticize or judge nor to impose their own particular standards of what is "correct." This is true not only because of the detriment to a child's self-esteem that may result from criticism of such a basic reflection of himself—and quite probably of patterns he has acquired in his home. It is also true because linguistic constructions and words that may be *different* from those employed by the teacher are by no means necessarily "wrong."

To some teachers, the line may seem a thin one. It seems clear that *poverty* is closely related to difficulties in learning (Deutsch, 1967; Stodolsky and Lesser, 1967; Bereiter and Engleman, 1966) and that language skills comprise one of the most important sources of such difficulties. Yet the principal concern of the teacher of young children should not be with superficial differences of *form,* but rather with the *substance* of language: the child's ability to express his thoughts, to use language flexibly and creatively, to convey complex and subtle symbolic messages, to listen to and understand the messages conveyed by others.

Since assessment is a basic step in identifying and providing special education services to exceptional children, services that may involve labeling the child and placing him in a special class or program, it is obviously important that tests used *should* be corrected or controlled for possible language and cultural bias. However, the *nondiscriminatory testing* mandated by federal law is still an elusive goal, since the most widely used and expertly developed tests are nonetheless "Anglocentric" (Gonzales, 1974). *Multifactored assessment* must include systematic analysis of the child's everyday functioning in real situations, with less reliance than in the past on "ability" test scores.

Joanne Hendrick (1975) summarizes the task of the teacher of young children, with regard to the issue of language "difference" often observed in black children, as follows:

> The best recommendation appears to be that the teacher should respect the black child's dialect just as she respects the Mexican or Puerto Rican child's Spanish, yet, while doing this, also making it possible for him to learn standard English because it is such a valuable tool for the child to possess. It is to be hoped that the child has the opportunity to learn this English in an atmosphere that values and appreciates his already present linguistic strengths rather than in one that smacks of condescension and noblesse oblige. (p. 207)

Bilingualism

A substantial number of children enrolled in early education programs in the United States are members of households in which a language other than English is used. Such children are confronted with the need to develop proficiency, not only in one language, which is accomplished by the majority of American children, but in two. Most frequently, but by no means exclusively, the first language acquired by the child is Spanish. The educational approach employed within our schools, obviously dominated by the English language, has increasingly been to offer a *bilingual* program, especially at the initial levels (prekindergarten, kindergarten, and primary). That is, the child is literally taught both in his native tongue and in English, and he is thereby helped to bridge the gulf created by a school situation in which a language other than his own and that of his family is dominant.

The same principle of *respect* for the child's and his family's language—and for every facet of the culture of which that language is a central dimension—applies. At the same time, it is to the child's advantage that he acquire proficiency in English. Consequently his use of English is conscientiously and systematically encouraged and reinforced. However, this goal is not intended either to have the effect of restricting and eventually eliminating his use of his native language or to deprive initially English-speaking children of the opportunity for enrichment inherent in a school setting that reflects the cultural pluralism within American society.

As Hendrick (1975, p. 208) notes, it is important for the teacher to distinguish between those children who use their native language fluently and effectively—and who in all likelihood can make the transition to English without great difficulty—and those who are not comfortable and expressive in either language. For these children, the goal of learning English is secondary to that of developing the use of expressive language; to accomplish this, the language used depends on the child's apparent preference and ease.

Speech reticence

Hesitance to express oneself vocally is here distinguished from *delayed speech,* which may arise from a number of diverse causes but usually requires specialized professional intervention. A great many young children, however, exhibit a marked lack of communicative speech. They may express themselves poorly, using truncated linguistic structures, and they may be reticent to employ other expressive modes as well. Although such characteristics, strictly speaking, do not fall under the rubric of communication disorders, they are nonetheless areas of concern to the teacher, the child, and his parents. One important reason for the concern is the relationship between expressive speech and the fullest possible realization of the child's potential in learning and success in school.

The task of the teacher in these instances is twofold: (1) to create a learning environment that tends to stimulate not only speech but also expression by means of other modalities, such as sociodramatic play, art, music, eurythmics, and mime, and (2) to implement, when possible with the help of a speech clinician, a planned program of speech and language development based on observation and systematic

diagnosis of the individual child. The former suggests the importance of provisioning the classroom to ensure the availability of appropriate materials and of providing for interaction among the children and creative use of time and space. The latter necessitates a clinical approach geared to the individual needs of the child. Such an approach requires *accurate and systematic observation and recording of the child's behavior; determination of the conditions that tend to elicit desired behavior and to sustain it; mutual sharing of observations with the child's parents;* and *possibly a more thorough study of the child, including consultation with specialists,* such as the speech clinician, psychologist, and social worker. The basic strategy used by the teacher to carry out an individualized program includes the following steps: (1) gaining an accurate picture of the child's language behavior, (2) identifying target behaviors as objectives, and (3) observing and recording the effects of planned modifications in working to bring about the target behaviors. Although it is possible to identify the characteristics of a classroom environment generally conducive to the achievement of language and speech goals, in many situations the teacher must focus specifically on the individual child to enable him to progress at an optimal rate.

REMEDIATION OF SPEECH PROBLEMS IN THE CLASSROOM

It has been noted that serious disabilities in speech and language will require the involvement of highly trained professionals, especially a speech pathologist, and may indeed require concentrated efforts of a whole team of professionals. This team may include a psychologist, social worker, and audiologist as well as the speech clinician, but it may also involve a dentist, occupational therapist, physical therapist, and one or more medical specialists. In these cases, the teacher's role resides first in the realm of *identification* of symptoms of possible communication problems, *parent communication,* and *referral* of the child according to procedures established in the school or center. Subsequently the teacher may have a most important role in carrying out recommendations of the specialists involved, reinforcing their efforts in the classroom, maintaining ongoing communication concerning the child's speech behavior and progress, and generally working with the other professionals and with the child's parents as a full member of the team in carrying out the process of remediation.

A very specific, individualized program may be prescribed, and the specialist may be able to identify goals and even recommend activities for the child to pursue under the teacher's direction. However, it is the teacher's responsibility to determine both how this individualization can be accomplished within the group setting and how an individualized speech and language program can be related to other goals and activities that, from the teacher's perspective, are equally important to the child concerned as well as to the other children.

In the area of *prevention* of communication problems, the teacher establishes a *language environment* that is conducive to the optimal development of young children whose speech and language development is not yet complete. Through encouraging and actively teaching communication, including expression in diverse forms, as well as listening, the teacher of young children can work to enhance language functioning in all aspects of the classroom program. The possibilities are virtually limitless, particularly if the teacher keeps in mind the principle that language is not confined to one aspect of the curriculum. Rather it permeates every facet of what is done.

The suggestions offered here consequently comprise only a very limited sample of the tools, techniques, and activities that can be incorporated in the area of preventive work. Some of the suggested approaches should be used selectively with certain children, determined on the basis of their particular needs, whereas others are offered as general principles and procedures.

Speech modeling

In every area, the importance of the teacher's role as a model should never be underestimated. This is particularly true in the area of speech and language. By giving attention to their own speech patterns (voice modulation, avoidance of elliptical or truncated expressions, appropriate vocabulary, etc.) teachers can be effective in developing effective communication patterns in the children they teach. It is, of course, important for teachers to articulate clearly and to attend to the *rate* of their own speech, not only to ensure that the children understand, but also to increase children's awareness that speech is *intended* to be listened to.

Developing listening skills

By modeling actual *listening* when children speak—communicated by visual attention to the child who is speaking and verbally responding with interest to what he is saying, rather than merely perfunctorily—the teacher can be effective in encouraging listening behavior. *Selective* listening, which many adults take for granted, is a skill that children must learn. Attending to the auditory environment of the classroom can foster the child's ability to *attend* to and *gain meaning from* what is being presented. Too much distracting noise may make it extremely difficult for some children—and perhaps for most *young* children—to learn to listen well. The ability to discriminate and to attend to the important auditory stimuli is developed gradually and may be enhanced through the gradual introduction of distractors, monitored on the basis of determining each child's readiness.

A wide variety of listening games are used in most early childhood classrooms, and traditional activities such as story time can be used effectively *if the teacher is observant of and able to respond to the abilities and needs of individual children.* Choice of the story (or other vehicle) is vital, as is the teacher's flexibility in modifying plans in response to cues from the children. The story may prove to be too long or may be ineffective in capturing the children's interest, or individual children may be unable to stay with it. *How* the teacher reads or tells the story or presents the activity may be the most important determinant of its effectiveness in promoting listening skills.

Some media, the tape recorder in particular, may be especially valuable in working in the area of listening skills. Increasingly, primary-level classrooms include "listening posts" with multiple headsets that permit *social* listening without auditory distraction. The advantage of headsets or individual earphones is, of course, that various listening activities may be going on simultaneously in the classroom in recognition of individual needs of children. Perhaps most important, the teacher can encourage the children to listen to each other. One effective way of accomplishing this goal is through use of designated times for discussion. A circle format in which all participants can face each other may be the only way of providing for true discussion to take place (Glasser, 1969).

Expansion

In language learning, expansion refers to a characteristic of the conversation of adults with children (Cazden, 1970; Bee et al., 1969) in which the child's utterance is not only acknowledged and reinforced, but it is also *expanded* or *extended* by the adult. On a basic level, the toddler may communicate an entire thought by means of a single word: *"Go?"* His mother conveys that she understands his meaning and verbally responds to his question in expanded and complete form: "Yes, we'll go home now." In the classroom, there are many opportunities to *teach* the child in this unobtrusive way, not criticizing or correcting his speech, but rather demonstrating understanding of and interest in what he says.

Encouraging verbalization

The classroom as a language environment implies that there is a great deal of encouragement of and opportunity for children to talk to the teacher and to talk to other children. Expression of ideas, intentions, feelings, etc. *in verbal form* provides an essential avenue for children to learn to appreciate and exploit the power of language. Encouraging verbalization goes hand in hand with encouraging (and *modeling*) listening; speech is used to communicate.

Verbal labeling

Vocabulary recognition and use is, of course, but one facet of language. Sometimes teachers overemphasize the importance of the child's use of a concept *label,* which may or may not actually reflect understanding or mastery of the concept itself. Concept learning may both precede and enhance the acquisition of concept words, and the teacher should be alert to the *"verbal* facade" (Almy, 1966) that some children in our media culture erect. The words children use may mask what they actually understand quite imperfectly. Acquiring the words for things, ideas, emotions, places, and relationships, however, is an important aspect of the language environment. Providing the word for an action or a feeling gives the child additional skills in understanding and coping with the world.

Encouraging symbolic expression

During what Piaget has identified as the *preoperational stage* of cognitive development, that is, from approximately 2 to 7 years of age, the child's basic task, according to David Elkind (1970), is "the conquest of the symbol." Symbolic functioning is integrally related to language development, although Piaget (1928) believes the two are not identical processes.

One author who has been particularly interested in the implications of Piaget's theory for teaching, Hans Furth (1969), has devised a number of classroom activities and approaches for children to develop increased skill in symbolic representation. For example, children can act out in pantomime a shared experience they have had. Furth believes that such activities are important in terms of *symbolic expression,* or *representation abilities,* which underlie speech and which are even more basic to cognition.

• • •

Although the preceding suggestions were offered in the context of prevention, rather than remediation, they are also relevant to the needs of the child who already presents communication problems. In working with this child, however, it is possible for the teacher to draw from a number of sources in attempting to carry out the recommendations of the specialist. A classic text, *Speech Correction: Principles and Methods* by Charles Van Riper (1972), although addressed primarily to speech pathologists, is a useful resource for teachers. *Speech and Hearing Problems in the Classroom* by Phyllis P. Phillips (1975) also enumerates some specific suggestions for teaching the child with problems in speech or language.

Together with much other useful information, *Communicative Disorders: A Handbook for Prevention and Early Intervention* by Curtis E. Weiss and Herold S. Lillywhite (1976) includes one chapter that lists "101 ways to help the child learn to talk" (Chapter 7). These suggestions are valuable both to the child's parents and to his teacher. Although they pertain generally to facilitation of language acquisition of *any* child, whether or not a communication problem is present or suspected, they are particularly applicable to the needs of a child experiencing difficulties in this area.

The following suggested procedures for teachers of young children represent a distillation of suggestions provided in sources such as those just mentioned, the application of principles of learning, and ideas born of personal experience in working with and studying young children whose development in speech and language is delayed or deviant.

Intervention involves assessment

The teacher should first determine the child's current functioning in speech and language. This may involve assessment of communicative functioning in terms of developmental norms, that is, determination of where the child is in relationship to the normative sequence of development in speech and language. Formal testing may or may not be involved. It is essential, however, to undertake a systematic analysis of the child's actual speech behavior. A useful tool in this regard is a tape recorder, which can be used to record speech samples either in the "natural" setting of spontaneous play or in a more controlled, structured setting. The child's utterances can then be analyzed from the standpoint of voice or articulation or of vocabulary and syntactic structure (Lee, 1971).

Target speech behaviors can then be identified, and a procedure for systematic recording and charting of the child's progress can be selected

Whether the behavior in question is one that should be reduced or eliminated or one that should be increased and strengthened, a procedure for quantitative measurement is most efficient. The task is first to establish a *base rate,* that is, to determine the frequency with which the behavior occurs, and then to record changes (increases or decreases) in frequency that are observed.

Progress is best if success is experienced

Encouragement of verbalization is certainly appropriate; however, it is not enough simply to urge the child to talk.

The child's behavior, rather than the adult's expectations, should determine how much encouragement or urging is used. As the child experiences success, rather than failure or frustration, he will be more likely to verbalize. From the teacher's standpoint, success is measured in small steps, but to the child they may be giant ones!

What "works" for each child is specific to that child

For one child, puppet play may elicit speech when all else has failed. For others, the social interaction provided by the opportunity for spontaneous play with evocative dramatic play materials may be effective. For still others, the rhythmic dramatization of singing games or finger plays may induce expression. Some children are especially responsive to the speech model provided by the teacher, whereas others may respond more readily to peer speech models, tape-recorded stories, or the opportunity to hear their own recorded speech. All of these methods are legitimate, valuable, and readily incorporated into classroom routine. In working with any particular individual child, however, the teacher must be ready to recognize a vehicle that seems to be especially effective for him and to adapt that child's program accordingly. Similarly, if desired speech behavior is to be reinforced, what is *reinforcing* or rewarding for a particular child must be found. This is determined not only by what the child "seems" to like, but, more significantly, by what he is observed to do. *Consequences* of a desired behavior are empirically observed to increase the probability that that behavior will occur.

Many individual "remediation" activities can become enjoyable group activities

Some of the specialized techniques used by the speech clinician can be adapted for classroom use with a large group of children. For example, one speech pathologist, together with the nursery school teacher, regularly engaged an entire class of 3- and 4-year-olds in games such as blowing suspended feathers and rhythmically imitating nonverbal utterances. Although the games they devised were particularly targeted on only a few children with problems forming certain sounds, they were helpful and fun for all. Similarly, songs and singing games, group reciting of poetry, choral speaking, open-ended sentences, and teacher-structured dramatic play may all be adapted toward specific objectives for individual children.

• • •

More specific suggestions for remediation of serious individual problems can be found in references such as *Speech and Deafness* (Calvert and Silverman, 1975), especially for working with articulation difficulties. Gray and Ryan (1973) offer specific strategies concerning speech and language problems related to syntax. Children who present serious problems in speech and language areas, however, require the attention of an especially trained professional. If in doubt, referral (following, of course, established procedures) is the best course. Since young children are rapidly progressing through the formative period for language acquisition and mastery, the child's best interests are served through *prompt* attention.

Speech and language problems are related to some degree to virtually every other area of handicap. Our language capability is often taken for granted, yet it is basic to success in learning and social adaptation. The chapters that follow, in which various forms of exceptionality are discussed in relationship to young children's development, underline the importance of speech and language progress as prognostic indicators and as target areas for intervention.

DISCUSSION QUESTIONS

1. In your own words, define the term "language." Explain the relationship between language and speech.

2. How are more serious handicaps of language and speech distinguished from functional articulation problems?
3. How are other forms of handicapping conditions of children often related to language and speech difficulties?
4. Explain the distinction between language difference and language disability. Why is this distinction important to make in identifying children for special education services?
5. Why is knowledge of the sequence of and processes involved in normal language acquisition essential for those who work with children with speech or language problems?
6. What kinds of resource assistance can the speech clinician provide for teachers of young children? How can specialists in speech and language facilitate the integration of children with speech or language problems in regular programs?

REFERENCES

Almy, M., with E. Chittenden and P. Miller. *Young children's thinking: studies of some aspects of Piaget's theory.* New York: Teachers College Press, 1966.

Bandura, A. Social learning through imitation. In M. R. Jones (Ed.), *Nebraska Symposium on Motivation.* Lincoln: University of Nebraska Press, 1962, pp. 211-269.

Baratz, S. S., and Baratz, J. C. Early childhood intervention: the social science base of institutional racism. *Harvard Educational Review,* 1970, *40*(1), 29-50.

Baratz, S. S., and Shuy, R. (Eds.). *Teaching black children to read.* Washington, D.C.: Center for Applied Linguistics, 1969.

Bee, H. L., et al. Social class differences in maternal teaching strategies and speech patterns. *Developmental Psychology,* 1969, *1,* 726-734.

Bereiter, C., and Engleman, S. *Teaching disadvantaged children in the preschool.* Englewood Cliffs, N.J.: Prentice-Hall, Inc., 1966.

Berko, J. The child's learning of English morphology. *Word,* 1958, *14,* 150-177.

Bernstein, B. Social class and linguistic development: a theory of social learning. In A. H. Halsey et al. (Eds.)', *Education, economy and society.* Glencoe, Ill.: Free Press, 1961, pp. 288-314.

Bown, J. C. The expanding responsibilities of the speech and hearing clinician in the public schools. *Journal of Speech and Hearing Disorders,* 1971, *36,* 538-542.

Brown, R. How shall a thing be called? *Psychological Review,* 1958, *65,* 14-21.

Bruner, J. S. The growth of mind. *American Psychologist,* 1965, *20,* 1007-1016.

Calvert, D. R., and Silverman, S. D. *Speech and deafness.* Wasington, D.C.: Alexander Graham Bell Association for the Deaf, Inc., 1975.

Cazden, C. B. Children's questions: their forms, functions, and roles in education. *Young Children,* 1970, *25,* 202-220.

Cazden, C. B. *Child language and education.* New York: Holt, Rinehart &Winston, Inc., 1972.

Cruickshank, W. M. The psychoeducational match. In W. M. Cruickshank and D. P. Hallahan (Eds.), *Perceptual and learning disabilities in children* (Vol. I). Syracuse: Syracuse University Press, 1975. 71-114.

Dale, P. S. *Language development: structure and function.* New York: Holt, Rinehart & Winston, Inc., 1976.

Deutsch, M. *The disadvantaged child.* New York: Basic Books, Inc., 1967.

Dunn, L. M. (Ed.), *Exceptional children in the schools* (2nd ed.). New York: Holt, Rinehart & Winston, Inc., 1973.

Elkind, D. *Children and adolescents: interpretive essays on Jean Piaget.* London: Oxford University Press, 1970.

Furth, H. *Piaget for teachers.* Englewood Cliffs, N.J.: Prentice-Hall, Inc., 1969.

Glasser, W. *Schools without failure.* New York: Harper & Row, Publishers, 1969.

Gonzales, G. Language, culture and exceptional children. *Exceptional Children,* 1974, *40,* 565-570.

Gray, B., and Ryan, B. *A language program for the non-language child.* Champaign, Ill.: Research Press, 1973.

Hendrick, J. *The whole child: new trends in early education.* St. Louis: The C. V. Mosby Co., 1975.

Hermelin, B., and O'Connor, N. *Psychological experiments with autistic children.* Oxford: Pergamon Press, Inc., 1970.

Hull, F. M., and Hull, M. E. Children with oral communication disabilities. In L. M. Dunn (Ed.), *Exceptional children in the schools* (2nd ed.). New York: Holt, Rinehart & Winston, Inc., 1973, pp. 297-348.

Johnson, D. J., and Myklebust, H. R. *Learning disabilities: educational principles and practices.* New York: Grune & Stratton, Inc., 1967.

Kessler, J. W. *Psychopathology of childhood.* Englewood Cliffs, N.J.: Prentice-Hall, Inc., 1966.

Kirk, S. A. *Educating exceptional children.* New York: Houghton Mifflin Co., 1972.

Lee, L. L. A screening test for syntax development. *Journal of Speech and Hearing Disorders,* 1971, *36,* 315-340.

McLean, J. Language development and communication disorders. In N. Haring (Ed.), *Behavior of exceptional children: an introduction to special education.* Columbus, Ohio: Charles E. Merrill Publishing Co., 1974, pp. 449-491.

McLean, J. E., Yoeder, D. E., Schiefelbusch, R. L. *Language intervention with the retarded.* Baltimore: University Park Press, 1976.

McNeill, D. *The acquisition of language: the study of developmental psycholinguistics.* New York: Harper & Row, Publishers, 1970.

Miner, K., et al. *Development of speech skills in hearing impaired children.* Kent, Ohio: Cricket Press, 1976.

Myklebust, H. R. Learning disabilities: definition and overview. In H. R. Myklebust (Ed.), *Progress in learning disabilities* (Vol. I). New York: Grune & Stratton, Inc., 1968.

Peterson, D. Educable mentally retarded. In W. G. Haring (Ed.), *Behavior of exceptional children: an introduction to special educaiton.* Columbus, Ohio: Charles E. Merrill Publishing Co., 1974, pp. 295-374.

Phillips, P. P. *Speech and hearing problems in the classroom.* Lincoln, Nebraska: Cliff Notes, Inc., 1975.

Piaget, J. *The language and thought of the child.* New York: Harcourt Brace Jovanovich, Inc., 1928.

Rosenberg, S. Problem-solving and conceptual behavior, In N. R. Ellis (Ed.), *Handbook of mental deficiency.* New York: McGraw-Hill Book Co., 1963, pp. 439-462.

Stodolsky, S. S., and Lesser, G. Learning patterns in the disadvantaged. *Harvard Educational Review,* 1967, *37,* 546-593.

Van Riper, C. *Speech correction: principles and methods.* Englewood Cliffs, N.J.: Prentice-Hall, Inc., 1972.

Vygotsky, L. S. *Thought and language.* Cambridge, Mass.: The M. I. T. Press, 1962.

Weiss, C. E., and Lillywhite, H. S. *Communicative disorders: a handbook for prevention and early intervention.* St. Louis: The C. V. Mosby Co., 1976.

CHAPTER 3

HEARING IMPAIRMENTS

In no other area of exceptionality is early education more crucial than with the hearing impaired. For the hearing infant, the world of sound helps him to learn to associate objects, persons, and events; to draw inferences; and to make predictions about what will happen. It also provides an excellent means for him to relate to other people. Considering the important role of hearing in the rapid learning that babies accomplish, it is easy to understand the enormity of the impact on child and family that a severe, congenital learning disability can have. In view of the fantastic rate at which young hearing children become proficient in understanding and using their native language, it is apparent that intervention for the child with impaired hearing must begin in the early years.

HEARING IMPAIRMENT, LANGUAGE, AND THOUGHT

The most seriously handicapping aspect of a hearing disability is its impact on language (Kirk, 1972, p. 257). And, since the first years of life are of critical importance for the development of language skills, early detection of hearing impairments is directly related to effective language learning (Lloyd and Dahle, 1976). This, of course, assumes that *detection* leads to *intervention.* There is no question, with this form of disability, of "waiting to see if the child will outgrow it."

That a child is hearing impaired, however, does *not* mean that he "has no language," regardless of how severe the impairment may be. Nor does it mean that he cannot acquire the skills of communicative speech. "There is no evidence that a deaf child is a less capable linguistic agent than a hearing child" (Brennan, 1975, p. 469).

Language is not only unique to human beings, but it is also an extraordinarily complex topic. In the preceding chapter, the various dimensions of language were discussed briefly, including the receptive ("input") and expressive ("output") dimensions, as well as the relationship between language and thought. (This relationship is sometimes identified by the term "inner language" [Vygotsky, 1962].) Precisely *how* thought and language are related is a matter of disagreement among psychological theorists (Piaget, 1928; Bruner, 1965), but it is evident that the relationship is basic to human learning and adaptation.

Does impaired hearing, then, have a handicapping effect on *cognition,* or thinking, as well as on communication? It is true that children whose hearing disability has not been discovered have sometimes first been thought to be "slow." Furthermore, some stereotypes seem to exist regarding "the thinking of the deaf." Joan Laughton (1976), who carried out a study of creative thinking in deaf children, notes that little or no substantiation can be provided for such stereotypes. Nevertheless, they persist.

Although less effective performance on certain kinds of cognitive tasks has been found (see, for example, Myklebust, 1964), in other areas of cognitive functioning, severely and profoundly hearing-impaired children appear to perform at least as well as their hearing peers. In measuring the general intellectual ability of hearing-impaired children by means of IQ tests, accommodations in procedure must obviously be made. According to Vernon (1968), who has researched this issue extensively, when measurement factors that are obviously handicapping to the deaf are controlled, degree of hearing loss has *not* been found to be related to IQ.

Hans Furth (1966, 1970, 1973) has provided especially illuminating insights concerning thinking in children whose hearing is impaired. The question that he addressed is "Does the intellectual development of deaf children progress through the same sequence of stages, and do deaf children learn through the same cognitive *processes* as children who hear?" Applying Jean Piaget's theoretical framework and his *clinical method* (Ginsburg and Opper,

1969), Furth studied the way in which deaf children approached certain tasks, as well as their ability to perform them. These tasks involved reasoning and problem solving, and they required the individual to apply *concepts,* rather than rote learning. He concluded that Piaget's description of children's cognitive development and functioning was applicable to deaf children, as well as to those with intact hearing.

FORMS AND DEGREES OF HEARING IMPAIRMENT

For some time, persons with impaired hearing have been described in terms of two broad categories: the deaf and the hard of hearing. The former term has typically been employed "to describe total loss of hearing or such profound loss that hearing is not usable for practical purposes" (Apgar and Beck, 1972, p. 231). However, deafness has often been erroneously thought of in terms of an "all-or-none" condition (Pollack, 1970). Most of those who are labeled as deaf in fact have some degree of residual hearing. Some professionals insist that *all* "deaf" children have some residual hearing. However, this is difficult to substantiate, and there is strong evidence that at least for a very few children, "... any sort of hearing is totally impossible" (Northern and Downs, 1974, p. 251).

The meaning of deafness

Whereas deafness is considered to be a "low incidence" handicap in the general population, the number of people who have some degree of impaired hearing at some time in their lives, compared to those with other forms of exceptionality, is obviously quite large. Pollack (1970, p. 4) emphasizes the role of the *audiogram* in determining the *extent* of impairment and illustrating the *relative,* rather than *absolute,* meaning of the term "deafness." She quotes O'Connor's definition of deafness: "The deaf, who make up about 4% of the hearing impaired children, are those who are unable to hear spoken language either with or without amplification. They are the children whose impairment is greater than 60 db" (1953, p. 437). This definition makes clear that it is an inability to hear *spoken language* that constitutes deafness, that this handicap must be seen in terms of a *continuum,* and that deafness is characteristic of an extremely small percentage of those children identified as hearing impaired.

In recent years, more attention has been given by professionals in the field to the problem of terminology. "Deafness" implies to many people the total inability to hear. But most children identified as deaf have some degree of residual hearing. It is possible that use of the term "deaf" may result in the failure of some parents and teachers to take into account the usable hearing that the child has. In the past, this term has all too often activated a self-fulfilling prophecy in which "deaf behavior" has been expected and, as a consequence, has been shown by the child. This semantic problem, according to Ross and Calvert (1973), has ramifications affecting the diagnostic process, parent-child interaction and relationship, educational placement decisions, and standards of achievement expected in school.

The statement that hearing impairment may be seen in terms of a continuum means that the degree of loss is determined on the basis of the individual's response to pure-tone audiometric sound varying in *frequency* and *intensity.* Different types of sound produce different frequencies of sound waves, that is, different vibrations. The frequency range for speech is between about 500 and 2,000 vibrations per second. Consequently acuity within this frequency range is important to hear human speech.

The degrees of sound intensity, or loudness, used in interpreting hearing loss are *decibels* (dB) and are scaled in terms of the standards of the International Standard Organization (ISO) or American Standard Association (ASA).

Rather than using only the general distinction of deaf and hard of hearing, specialists may speak of (1) slight hearing loss, referring to decreased hearing ability amounting to a 25 to 40 decibel loss, (2) mild to moderate deafness, a 40 to 55 decibel loss, (3) moderately severe deafness (55 to 70 decibel loss), severe deafness (70 to 90 decibel loss), and profound deafness (essentially no hearing, although the individual may respond to vibrations caused by loud sounds) (Apgar and Beck, 1972, p. 231). Davis and Silverman (1970, p. 255) differentiate six classes in terms of the severity of handicap, the extent of loss, and the functional ability to understand speech:

> *No significant handicap:* not more than 25 dB loss (ISO); no significant difficulty with faint speech
> *Slight handicap:* 25 to 40 dB loss; difficulty only with faint speech
> *Mild handicap:* 40 to 55 dB loss; frequent difficulty with normal speech
> *Marked handicap:* 55 to 70 dB loss; frequent difficulty with loud speech
> *Severe handicap:* 70 to 90 dB loss; can understand only shouted or amplified speech
> *Extreme handicap:* 90 dB loss; usually cannot understand even amplified speech

It should be noted that O'Connor's definition of deafness, cited previously, would encompass marked, severe, and extreme handicaps, according to this classification.

A second way of classifying hearing impairment is according to whether it is *congenital* (that is, present at birth) or *adventitious*. Maternal viral infection and maternal rubella are possible causes of congenital hearing impairment. In addition, premature delivery is frequently associated with this, as it may be with other handicapping conditions. Among other causes are hereditary factors and prenatal injury.

An adventitious hearing loss is one that is acquired, whether in early infancy or at any period of life. In childhood, illness is most often involved, but accidental injury may be responsible, as well as nonpatho-logical factors, that we shall examine presently. Diseases of early childhood are major causes of adventitious hearing loss. These include viral infections associated with upper respiratory illness, measles, and mumps (Northern and Downs, 1974).

If the loss is acquired, *when* it occurs developmentally is very significant. Hearing impairment occurring before language acquisition has been completed would obviously affect language and speech far more than would an adventitious hearing loss in an older child or adult. Congenital impairment or hearing loss suffered very early in life would have the most profound impact, since the baby begins to learn language virtually from the moment he is born.

In addition to the dimensions of *severity* and *age of onset,* a third classification of hearing impairment is based on the type of disability involved. The two general types are *conductive* and *sensory-neural.* A sensory-neural hearing loss is caused by defects either within the inner ear or in the auditory nerve, by means of which sound impulses are transmitted to the brain. This type of impairment is likely to produce the more severe handicap. It may not be amenable to treatment, and amplification through hearing aids may not be as effective. A sensory-neural disability may be reflected in differential hearing acuity, with sounds of higher frequency being more affected.

A conductive hearing loss may be caused by a malformation of the middle ear. However, more frequently a conductive loss results from a buildup of fluid in the eustachian tube, since in young children this is virtually horizontal. Treatment involves draining the fluid. Any impediment to the conduction of sound vibrations can impair hearing. If the problem cannot be corrected medically or surgically, amplification is used.

INCIDENCE OF HEARING IMPAIRMENT IN CHILDREN

Different incidence figures are reported by different investigators. In reviewing incidence studies of hearing impairment in school-age children, Silverman and Lane (1970) found percentages of the general child population ranging from as low as 2 percent to as high as 21 percent, depending on the criteria and the instruments used. Earlier, Silverman (1952) had estimated that approximately 5 percent of the school-age population have impaired hearing and that in anywhere from one tenth to one fifth of this group the disability is sufficiently great to warrant special educational services in some form.

Children in the United States of school age who can be considered deaf were found by Silverman and Lane (1970) to number about 39,000. Nearly half of these were enrolled in public residential schools, according to their findings. Children under the age of 6 were much less likely, as one would expect, to be served in a residential facility:

> In the academic year 1967-68, of 18,926 children enrolled in public residential schools for the deaf in the United States, 1028 were under the age of 6; of 15,370 children in public day schools and classes, 2453 were of preschool age; and of the 3686 children in denominational and private schools, 1646 were under the age of 6. (Silverman and Lane, 1970, p. 385)

In the population of the United States at large, including adults as well as children, there are 1.8 million deaf persons, according to the 1974 National Census of the Deaf Population (cited in Schein and Delk, 1974), compared to 13.4 million with some degree of hearing loss. Although hearing impairment may occur as a single disability, this census revealed that about one third of hearing-impaired persons have additional handicaps.

Secondary learning problems of a serious nature have been found among a great many hearing-impaired students (Fiedler, 1969). In general, persons with impaired hearing are considerably more likely than others to be undereducated in relationship to their ability to learn (Goetzinger and Rousey, 1959). Schein and Delk

(1974) attribute this primarily to the lack of adequate funding and support for education and rehabilitation provided, despite compelling evidence that this group of handicapped persons demonstrates greater benefit from appropriate educative and rehabilitative services than any other. Early education would seem to offer a most promising route to ensure that children with impaired hearing are able to realize their fullest potential to progress educationally and adjust to the mainstream of American education and society.

IDENTIFICATION OF HEARING PROBLEMS

Through neonatal screening in the hospital, some clues may be found that the newborn baby does not have intact hearing. Through *behavioral audiometry* (Lloyd and Dahle, 1976) hearing disabilities can often be detected at birth. Subsequent evaluation may substantiate what is at first suspected. However, even though a serious congenital hearing disability may be detected soon after birth, it is not uncommon for a definite diagnosis to be deferred 8 months or longer (Apgar and Beck, 1972). Frequently, it is the baby's parents or a grandparent who are the first to suspect that their child's hearing may be impaired.

Mild or moderate hearing problems may be undetected, in some cases, until the child enters a preschool or kindergarten program. At this point, it is the teacher who may be the first to suspect a problem. In addition, during the early years (including the first years a child is in school), children are highly susceptible to illnesses that can cause hearing impairment. The vulnerability of children during the early years to hearing problems, although already mentioned, is reiterated here. *Much permanent hearing loss in children, as well as temporary frustration before the problem is identified, can clearly be prevented through vigilance and awareness on the part of parents, teachers, and doctors.*

Role of the teacher

Preschool and annual in-school screening for possible hearing difficulties may not always reveal problems. Just as with school vision screening, if what is being assessed is acuity, the screening procedure may not reveal certain diseases. *What* is being screened for is the major determinant of what is identified (Northern and Downs, 1974). Secondly, problems may develop that had not existed before, not only associated with illness or injury, but also with the accumulation of fluid or wax. Consequently it is extremely important for a nursery school, day care, kindergarten, or primary teacher to be alert for any signs of a possible hearing problem. Ongoing communication with the children's parents regarding these signs is also essential.

As was discussed in the preceding chapter, suspected *abnormalities of voice,* such as speaking very loudly or very softly, and *abnormalities of articulation* are symptoms that should lead to hearing evaluation. In the classroom, *difficulty in sustaining attention* may suggest the presence of a hearing problem, as may occasional or frequent *unresponsiveness when addressed, saying "huh" or "what" when spoken to,* or *careful watching of the speaker's face* (Weiss and Lillywhite, 1976, p. 168). The child may complain that his ear hurts, or his actions and expression may suggest that he is in pain. *Cocking or turning his head* may be a visible attempt to hear better. Since hearing impairment may differentially affect reception of sounds at different frequencies, apparent *preference for low- or high-pitched sounds* may also be symptomatic. *Reticence in speaking* or *apparent shyness* may suggest a possible hearing problem.

In a school setting, a specialist in speech and hearing should not only be available for teachers' referral of children (with parental consent), but also be active in assisting teachers with a systematic, ongoing classroom screening program. Day care, nursery school, Head Start, and special agency programs should ensure that essential audiometric and other specialized services in the community are secured and used.

Since special schools and special programs for hearing-impaired children have been in existence in the United States for many years, how likely is the "regular" teacher in an early childhood setting to come into contact with these children? It is very likely, for four reasons:

1. The vast majority of children with temporary or chronic impairment of hearing, if the disability is mild or moderate, are likely to be served within regular settings as a matter of course. (Nonetheless, their imperfect hearing requires some adaptation on the part of the teacher.)

2. Many children enter nursery school, kindergarten, and even the primary grades whose hearing losses have been undetected previously.

3. The vulnerability of young children to hearing problems associated with disease or with fluid buildup continues throughout the early childhood years. A problem can occur even if the child has had no prior history of hearing difficulties.

4. With the nationwide trend toward integration of all handicapped children within "regular" programs, many hearing-impaired children with even more severe hearing loss will probably be "mainstreamed." This is even more likely with the advent of *early intervention measures* which can lessen the impact of the hearing disability on the very young child's acquisition of speech and language. The intervention primarily includes precise assessment of the infant's problems and needs, early provision of hearing aids, and intensive parent education, support, and guidance (Pollack, 1970).

Northcott (1973) notes that the major trends in the education of hearing-impaired children parallel those in other areas of disability. She observes that emphasis is increasingly seen in the following areas:

1. The rights of the child to an educational diagnosis as soon as the diagnosis of a handicapping condition is established and without cost to the family
2. Identification of the public school as the logical and accountable fiscal agency to coordinate a program for hearing impaired children.
3. Adherence to the principle of normalization throughout the education years, as far as reasonable
4. A shift of emphasis from a medical to an educational model of intervention by the schools
5. A systematic program of sequential auditory training activities offered throughout the school years, based on individually prescriptive behavioral objectives
6. The development of a new classification of specialist in the neighborhood public school—the Consultant, Services for the Hearing Impaired (pp. 3-5)*

In keeping with recent federal legislation, the responsibility for *identification and planning* for hearing-impaired children, as well as for those with other handicaps, belongs primarily to public education. Because of the importance of very early identification and the need for interdisciplinary efforts, it seems obvious that cooperation and communication between schools and other agencies are essential.

INTERVENTION DURING INFANCY

Beginning with the baby's very first vocal utterances and sensory-motor contact with his physical and social environment, language development proceeds rapidly. The normal development of language in a hearing infant begins with sound awareness, which is first demonstrated by responsiveness to loud noises and to the sound of a familiar human voice. Later the baby will turn his head toward the

source of the sound, a kind of auditory *tracking. Talking* to the baby and responding to what he utters make parents their child's first—and most important—language teachers.

As the child develops basic muscle control as well as discriminative abilities, he will turn his head when he hears his name called. By 6 months, the child can usually sit up and follow the sound of his mother's voice. At about 7 or 8 months, possibly earlier, the child begins to produce intonational voice patterns. These vocalizations become a kind of intentional, repetitive *vocal play,* termed *babbling,* as pleasurable sounds are repeated (Van Riper, 1972). There are *imitative* qualities in these sounds, which are significant in terms of the child's cognitive development as well as for speech acquisition. The utterances that are reinforced by the adults in his environment, through expressions, pleasure, attention, and affection, are particularly likely to be repeated. By the time the child is 12 to 18 months of age, identifiable words are used, his repertoire of single-word utterances extends rapidly, and he has begun to produce the rhythm and sounds of the language in his environment.

The infant whose ability to take in information about his world through hearing is limited or essentially nonexistent must rely on other channels to serve this function. However, the baby does not automatically compensate for his loss in establishing communication. The time for him to begin to learn both how maximally to use what hearing he has and how to optimize his use of vision and touch is during the first months of life. His best teachers are his parents.

A relatively new professional role in the education of hearing-impaired children has begun to emerge within recent years: the home trainer. This development parallels trends in the direction of home-based intervention through working with parents in other special needs areas as well, such as visual impairment (Fraiberg,

---

*Reprinted by permission of the publisher, The Alexander Graham Bell Association for the Deaf, Inc., 3417 Volta Place, N.W., Washington, D.C. 20007.

1975). Educational intervention during infancy for hearing-impaired children is primarily carried out through parent guidance and education (Pollack, 1970). Model home training programs for parents of young deaf children have been established (Miller, 1970; McConnell and Horton, 1970).

If the child's handicap has been identified at birth or during infancy, medical intervention may have been initiated, together with at least some guidance for parents in working with their child. But, all too often, this is not the case, despite the apparent importance of very early intervention and the fact that the concept has long been endorsed by educators of the hearing impaired. Davis and Silverman (1970) note that approaches and emphases in parent education programs vary. Because of the parents' own great emotional needs, the emphasis may be primarily on the crucial area of parental response to the child. However, systematic guidance is also needed if parents are to help their child develop optimally. Also, parents need specific information concerning their own child's problem (Northern and Downs, 1974).

A unique service is provided parents of hearing-impaired children by agencies that provide education and guidance through correspondence. Without a doubt the best known of these is The John Tracy Clinic in Los Angeles,* which provides step-by-step lessons and carefully monitors the child's progress through ongoing correspondence with the parents. This agency provides free services to families throughout the world and has been doing so for many years. Davis and Silverman (1970) describe the method as offering ". . . a good psychological approach to the deaf child," which includes lessons emphasizing ". . . the development of visual discrimination by matching colors and

---

*Copies of the program can be obtained at a nominal cost from The John Tracy Clinic, 806 West Adams Boulevard, Los Angeles, California, 90007.

pictures and the comparison of objects varying in size and shape, practice in discriminating odors and tastes, exercise in the imitation of bodily movements, and the use of materials that will aid the child in better muscular coordination." (p. 395)

The audiologist may have a particularly important role in guiding the parents, as well as possibly being the person who interprets diagnostic findings for them (Northern and Downs, 1974; Pollack, 1970). The audiologist, a trained teacher of hearing-impaired children specializing in infancy and early childhood, or another interdisciplinary team member may be able to work directly with the child and parents in their home over a continuous period.

This home-based intervention will help the parents lay a foundation for *speech reading skills,* as parents are encouraged to help their child to attend and respond to visual clues, such as facial expression. The very young child can be helped to coordinate tactual clues with visual ones and to use these aids in enhancing whatever degree of residual hearing ability he may have. Thus not only speech reading abilities, but also sound discrimination skills, can be fostered in terms of receptive language. Even if intervention is initiated during the early years, delayed progress in language development is virtually inevitable (Jarvella and Lubinsky, 1975). However, the possibility of optimizing expressive speech as well as general language functioning is greatly increased through systematic intervention during the period that is so crucial for its development (Davis and Silverman, 1970).

GOALS AND PROCEDURES IN PRESCHOOL AND PRIMARY SETTINGS

Kirk (1972) identifies the following major purposes for severely hearing-impaired children in the nursery school or kindergarten setting:

(1) to give the child experiences with other children in sharing, playing, and taking turns

(a socialization process); (2) to develop language, speech, and speech reading ability; (3) to help the child take advantage of his residual hearing through the use of hearing aids and amplified sounds; (4) to develop in the child elementary number concepts; (5) to develop a readiness for reading words and phrases; and (6) to provide parent education (p. 283).

Beyond these general purposes, divergent thinking, generalizing to new experiences, and proficiency in useful language are emphasized (Grammatico and Miller, 1974).

Developing speech and language skills

Since very young children can now be fitted with hearing aids, there is the op-portunity to capitalize on the early years as the optimal time for developing language abilities. The development of both receptive and expressive language skills, important goals of the nursery and kindergarten curriculum for *all* children, since these skills develop rapidly in the early years and are so crucial to all subsequent learning, is even more important for the child with impaired hearing. Auditory discrimination and vocal communication can be systematically fostered through a sequential approach based on monitoring the child's progress. Pollack and Ernst (1973) identify four levels: *attending and orienting, localizing and identifying sounds, discriminating and*

classifying, and *learning appropriate responses to sounds.*

The teacher's use of *verbalization* in working with the young hearing-impaired child fosters receptive and expressive language in several ways. Primarily, talking to the child enables him to gain awareness and appreciation of the role of speech in communication. Although visual clues are valuable in enabling him to derive meaning from what is said, overuse of gesture by the teacher may divert his attention from listening. By verbalizing what the child is experiencing, the teacher helps him not only to acquire labels but to integrate his experience in a meaningful way. The encouragement of speech is one of the most important dimensions in teaching the young child with a hearing disability. The *kinds* of questions the teacher asks can determine the extent, complexity, and quality of the verbal responses they elicit. For example, questions that can be answered with a single word (yes, no, fine, nothing, etc.) are less effective than those that require of the child a more complex and elaborate verbalization. Conversationally pursuing a topic with a single child can lead to the child's playing an increasingly major role in the discussion, with "teacher talk" becoming less dominant and more facilitating.

A classroom atmosphere in which this sort of *dialogue* is possible is one in which more and more verbal participation on the part of the hearing-impaired child can be elicited. The child can feel that what he has to say is meaningful and interesting to the teacher—which is shown by the teacher's sustained participation with him in conversation, direct verbal expressions of interest, building new questions on his responses, and possibly asking him to share with other children what he has told the teacher. This evidence that he is succeeding in expressing himself verbally can encourage him to talk more and motivate him to develop greater conversational skills, both as a listener and as a speaker.

Activities that help the hearing-impaired child to broaden his span of *auditory memory* are valuable, including listening to stories and participating in discussions. Auditory sequencing skills can be enhanced through activities such as *finger plays, sharing nursery rhymes,* and *songs.* Much repetition may be necessary.

Directions for active games, as well as other activities, should not be overly complex and should be given in simple sentences. This will facilitate the child's ability to focus attention on important points, discriminate separate steps to be followed, retain them in memory, and translate them into action.

Repetition of word or digit sequences in itself is a meaningless activity from the standpoint of the child's learning or understanding. Such tasks are often included in psycholinguistic ability and intelligence tests. Tasks involving rote memorization or mechanical repetition can be useful components of a much more comprehensive assessment approach. However, as teaching activities, such tasks are of dubious value at best, since they do not contribute to *meaningful learning* (Ausubel, 1968).

A helpful resource for teachers in working with young hearing-impaired children in the area of language is *Language and the Preschool Deaf Child* by Grace M. Harris (1971), as is Mildred Groht's *Natural Language for Deaf Children* (1958).

The auditory environment

It is possible to employ the standard features and activities of the nursery school or kindergarten program in working with the special problems and needs of the hearing-impaired child. For example, techniques of storytelling have been developed (McDermott, 1971) that provide an effective and intrinsically enjoyable approach to fostering lipreading skills as well as leading to reading readiness.

Pollack and Ernst (1973) provide ten recommendations for structuring the "auditory environment" of the nursery school:

1. *Develop an attitude of readiness to listen* (through such methods as reminding the child to sit quietly in anticipation encouraging him to say, "I'm ready," use of pauses and contrasting auditory patterns to indicate introduction of the next activity, and vocal inflection, for example in storytelling).
2. *Use auditory signals.*
3. *Use the voice to get attention* (by, for example, speaking the child's name rather than touching him).
4. *Allow sufficient time for auditory processing.*
5. *Keep within close range when speaking* (sitting beside the child when giving individualized instructions, attempting to speak at ear level).
6. *Use normal conversational tone of voice* (speaking in short sentences and providing context clues which are appropriate to the activity).
7. *Provide good speech models* (through inflection and the use of short, clear phrases, without overuse of gesture).
8. *Use frequent repetitions* (talking more, rather than less to the hearing impaired child and expanding what he expresses).
9. *Orient the child to the activity or discussion.*
10. *Encourage the parents to expand the*

work of the nursery school. (pp. 160-162)*

Rather than being primarily concerned about clarity of the child's speech, the teacher should give greater emphasis to helping the child build greater comprehension of language, including developing listening skills and acquiring a repertoire of receptive vocabulary. Most important, his experiences with language enable him to develop the structural rules by means of which he will be able to generate sentences (Cazden, 1972). Language teaching approaches for young hearing-impaired children, as for other young children, have been substantially influenced by discoveries concerning *generative transformational grammar* in children's language development (McConnell, 1971).

By commenting on, interpreting, and explaining environmental sounds, the teacher helps the child to sort out these experiences in meaningful ways. By speaking to the child—and giving him the opportunity to respond, to *do* something—the teacher is fostering an awareness of the role of language in communication. That the child is progressing in the area of listening can be determined, despite his limited expressive language, by observing that his span of auditory attention is increasing. Progress is also seen in evidence of more interest in visual clues, such as the speaker's eyes and facial expression (Northcott, 1970).

Expressive language can be encouraged through *reinforcing* the child's efforts verbally and by *expanding* his utterances. Prolonged participation may be difficult in activities that are primarily oriented to listening, such as story time (as would be the case for virtually all young children!). However, the young hearing-impaired child can participate productively in all facets of the classroom routine, including story time, and definitely in music activ-

------

*Reprinted by permission of the publisher, The Alexander Graham Bell Association for the Deaf, Inc., 3417 Volta Place, N.W., Washington, D.C. 20007.

ities (Allen, 1975). Although repetition is generally helpful, varying the form for stories, songs, and routines makes them more interesting and appropriately challenging. *Dramatizations* are good follow-ups to story time (Hart, 1963).

Introducing the child to reading

Since hearing-impaired children learn to rely heavily on their visual modality in learning, it is not surprising that reading readiness activities are introduced in the nursery school setting (Kirk, 1972). However, the emphasis is not on early reading of "the printed page." Objects in the room may be labeled with the identifying word printed on a card, as is often done in the nursery, kindergarten, or primary classroom for hearing children. *Experience stories* are written in short sentences, which may be illustrated with drawings or pictures. A basic sight word vocabulary, an introduction to the printed word, and a favorable attitude are sought, but formal instruction in reading of printed materials is generally not initiated earlier than for hearing children (Hart, 1963).

The introduction of reading for severely hearing-impaired children is complicated by the lack of proficiency in language that they bring to reading (Hart, 1975). For hearing children, learning to read involves extending their competence in a representational system of symbols to another dimension.

A hearing child approaches his reading having already acquired a sizable vocabulary, great facility with oral language and a wide range of concepts. The written words met by the hearing child represent ideas he has already met before. He simply has to learn to recognize the word; the idea is already familiar to him.

This is not true with most deaf children. The usual deaf child approaches reading with a limited vocabulary, fairly limited concepts, and a lack of facility with oral language. Many of the words met in printed form are totally new to him. Even if he attempts to attack reading of the word, he may still be unable to comprehend the idea behind it. It is as though one were reading a text which contained many foreign words in every paragraph. Though these words could be phonetically sounded out, the reader could only guess at their meaning. If there were a sufficient number of such words, or if these words happened to be key words, the meaning of the paragraph might be completely elusive. For the deaf child, the teacher must constantly provide direct experience so that the "foreign" words come within comprehension. (Hart, 1963, pp. 5-6)*

---

*Reprinted by permission of the publisher, The Alexander Graham Bell Association for the Deaf, Inc., 3417 Volta Place, N.W., Washington, D.C. 20007.

The basic principle involves relating words directly to the child's personal experience and thus introducing reading as a personally *meaningful* activity. This principle is essential to the *Language Experience Approach* (Allen and Allen, 1970) and is underlined by Sylvia Ashton-Warner's (1963) discoveries of how the children she taught found learning to read and write motivating and meaningful. The individual child, rather than a preordained set of materials, provides the best guide—whether or not the child has a hearing impairment. Such individualization of reading experiences is based on ob-

servation and on sensitive awareness of what each child is ready to approach.

In working with reading at the primary level (approximately ages 6 through 9), Beatrice Hart (1963) has identified seven major skill areas to be developed:

1. Enriching the background of experience so that concepts and verbal meanings are fostered
2. Acquiring a sight vocabulary
3. Developing word recognition techniques
4. Reading in thought units
5. Preparing for reading in longer units
6. Beginning use of the dictionary
7. Stimulating interest in and comprehension of stories (p. 37)

Instructional materials

Although the most important ingredient in the learning environment for any young child is the human interaction component (*peer* as well as adult), technology has presented many new contributions. This is certainly a promising area in work with young hearing-impaired children. Prescott (1971), for example, has described an application of teaching machine technology called the *"acoustic puzzle."* Children are presented familiar sounds, such as a ringing telephone, which they match to appropriate pictured objects by pressing a button; if the answer is correct, a light comes on. Such technology has the advantage of allowing the child to work on his own and the related advantage of allowing him to experience feedback from his own actions. Such "autotelic" approaches help to create a "responsive environment" (Nimnicht, 1972), that is, an environment that responds to the child's actions, thus contributing to his sense of competence. Montessori materials are similarly "self-correcting." The child can work on his own, interpret sensory clues to monitor his own performance, and gain the feeling of competence from independent mastery of tasks.

Montessori and similar materials are valuable in another way. They can foster concept learning and mastery in cognitive areas such as classification and seriation. These cognitive areas underlie "academic skills" in arithmetic, science, and other curriculum areas, including language arts.

Visual arrays, labeled objects and parts of the room, experience charts, etc. are all of potentially great use in teaching young hearing-impaired children. It is important that their use be meaningful. The visual environment of the classroom can greatly contribute to learning. It can be rich and evocative without being cluttered or chaotic.

Hearing aids

An important area of progress in the education of hearing-impaired children has been that of improved technology in amplification. Highly advanced systems, such as the *phonic ear,* are now sometimes found in classrooms for the hearing impaired. Of greater significance, however, is the increased capacity provided by the phonic ear for amplification of the hearing of the very young child.

More "traditional" types of hearing aids are also being continuously improved as well. Specific types vary, and it is necessary for the teacher to know how a particular child's hearing aid operates. To teachers who have not had this experience, helping a young child with his hearing aid may be at first difficult. Some guidelines are provided by Pollack and Ernst (1973):

Worn either behind the ear or in a special harness on the chest, the modern hearing aid is easy to handle. The parent should test the battery or batteries for power before the child leaves home, and it is helpful to leave a spare at school in case the aid stops working. A small wheel on the hearing aid controls the volume: a slight turn and the sound is amplified for the child, just as the volume of a radio is increased with a turn of the dial. Sometimes, there is a separate on-off switch, too. The sound is conducted into the ear from the aid through a cord or tube attached to an earmold which must fit snugly into the ear. If the mold slips out a little, a squealing or whistling sound will be heard, but it is easy to push the mold back without hurting the ear. The aids should be worn at all times. During water or sandbox play, the aids can be covered with a piece of plastic. If, because of a change in the child's responses to sound, the teacher suspects that the aids are not working, she should alert the parent as soon as possible. (p. 157)*

There is good reason for a teacher of young children to be encouraged, rather than alarmed, finding that a child wears hearing aids. As Stassen (1973) observes,

Of all handicapped pupils, those with amplifiable hearing losses are among the most potentially teachable. Yet, this group historically has been among the most undereducated. Too often the poor academic standing of the hearing impaired pupil begins with the stultifying alarm that fills the teacher when hearing aids in the classroom are discovered. (p. 3)

Teachers must bear in mind, however, that amplification does not totally "correct" the impairment as eyeglasses may do for imperfect vision. There is invariably some degree of distortion in what the child takes in. Seeing that he wears hearing aids should not lead the teacher to infer that he is able to sit anywhere in the classroom and hear without difficulty or that he has no need to rely on visual and contextual clues. It is important to remember, too, that hearing aids do not selectively amplify speech sounds—they amplify *all* sounds, including extraneous ones. This means that the child is not necessarily better able to distinguish *speech* sounds but actually experiences more environmental *noise* from which speech sounds still must be discriminated.

Usually young hearing classmates readily accept a child's hearing aids without undue alarm and in most instances without even a great deal of curiosity. Discussion of hearing aids and what they are for is usually desirable, however, both for the intrinsic benefits of the learning

and human understanding experience provided the hearing child and to ensure the well-being of the handicapped child. The children should be aware that pulling the cord may break it and that a bump on the earmold may hurt their friend's ears, and they need to know, through the teacher's guidance and example, how to modulate their voices in talking to him (Pollack and Ernst, 1973). Although comparing aids to glasses is, strictly speaking, not exactly accurate, it is usually an effective analogy.

For teachers inexperienced with hearing aids, there may be concerns about how to help the child make the best use of his amplified hearing, as well as about the mechanical aspects of amplification, how it helps, and what are its limitations. Since hearing impairment is now detected earlier in life and amplification is provided at younger ages than in the past, the teacher in a regular nursery school or day care center is very likely at some time to have in his or her group a child who wears hearing aids. Raymond Stassen (1973) provides some guidelines that are especially relevant for teachers at the nursery school and kindergarten levels:

. . . even though a child may be using a hearing aid full time, before the age of three years, he may not have the manual dexterity to manipulate the instrument. To complicate matters, the young child may not have mastered the clarity of speech or the expressive language necessary to alert his teacher to the fact that his aids are not working and are consequently acting as plugs in his impaired ears. Therefore, teachers of a very young hearing impaired child should develop some expertise in manipulating the controls of the particular model of hearing aid worn by that child, learn the technique of inserting the earmold, and master the soap and hot water approach to removing ear wax from the opening of the earmold. They must also know how to replace a spent hearing aid battery and should have spare batteries available as needed. (p. 29)*

*Reprinted by permission of the publisher, The Alexander Graham Bell Association for the Deaf, Inc., 3417 Volta Place, N.W., Washington, D.C. 20007.

*Reprinted by permission of the publisher, The Alexander Graham Bell Association for the Deaf, Inc., 3417 Volta Place, N.W., Washington, D.C. 20007.

The teacher and the child's parents can work together in this as in other areas, going over instructions in the use of the hearing aid and ensuring that the spare batteries of the appropriate type are on hand in the classroom. A teacher should know how to check for breaks in the cord as well, since young children often chew the cord or play with it. This can break the fine wires inside.

Mainstreaming: participation in educational settings with hearing children

Northcott (1973) has observed that children successfully integrated in regular classroom settings may range in degree of hearing loss from moderate to profound. However, she suggests that these children have several characteristics in common:

1. Active utilization of residual hearing and full-time hearing-aid usage, if prescribed
2. Demonstrated social, academic cognitive, and communicative (auditory and oral) skills *within the normal range of behaviors* of hearing classmates at a particular grade level
3. Intelligible speech and the ability to comprehend and exchange ideas with others through spoken, written, and read language
4. Increased confidence and independence in giving self-direction to the tasks at hand (p. 3)*

Are some young children with impaired hearing unlikely to make a good adjustment when integrated with hearing children in a nursery school or kindergarten program? And, if so, is this a question mainly of degree of severity of the hearing handicap? Most writers concur that degree of severity alone is not the most crucial determinant of ability to develop cognitively and linguistically. The presence of at least some communicative speech,

however, may be essential for successful intergration (Brackett and Henniges, 1976). Northcott (1970) believes that parent-child and home environment factors are of great significance in terms of the readiness to develop communicative abilities and to ensure carry-over. She thinks that integration into a regular nursery program is *not* appropriate if

1. The hearing loss was recently diagnosed and there has been no parent guidance to ensure transfer and maintenance of educational gains through home stimulation, and
2. The child is not yet aware that his hearing aid brings in meaningful environmental sounds, including speech, or that he must look at faces to gain understanding from moving lips and facial expression. (p. 368)*

Therefore home-school cooperation and communication, rather than severity of hearing loss, is the most important criterion for admission into a regular program. What has gone *before*, in terms of work with both the child and his parents, is even more crucial, however (Garrett and Stovall, 1972).

Although there should not be a certain "quota" of children with hearing handicaps in a hearing preschool setting, it may be, as Northcott (1970) suggests, that a ratio of about four hearing children to each hearing-impaired child provides optimal benefits for all and is most manageable.

Not all nursery schools have had experience with severely hearing-impaired children, although with the implementation of new federal mandates many undoubtedly will. Rather than simply to call on the telephone and ask whether the nursery school will take a child with a hearing impairment, parents would be

*Reprinted by permission of the publisher, The Alexander Graham Bell Association for the Deaf, Inc., 3417 Volta Place, N.W., Washington, D.C. 20007.

*Reprinted by permission from *Young Children*, Vol. 25, No. 6 (September, 1970), p. 368. Copyright © 1970, National Association for the Education of Young Children, 1834 Connecticut Ave., N.W., Washington, D.C. 20009.

better advised to visit the school, observe, and discuss the whole question of matching the child's needs with the program's resources with the teachers.

Dorene Pollack (1970) argues against a "specialized environment" for young hearing-impaired children:

The child can be placed, almost without exception, in a normal hearing nursery program if the object is socialization. This is just as beneficial to the normal hearing children, for they develop understanding and friendship with a handicapped child at an early age. (p. 24)

Although Pollack notes that there is a need for specially prepared teachers of young hearing-impaired children, especially if parents are not able to carry out the necessary home training program, wherever possible ". . . special grouping with other 'deaf' children should be postponed until it becomes necessary for formal education, if ever" (Pollack, 1970, p. 24).

Beyond the nursery school level, Pollack identifies readiness of the child, attitude of the teacher, and availability of resource persons as "factors for successful integration." A specialized *resource room,* for support and supplementary tutoring on an "as-needed" basis, can be created (Bowman, 1973).

Regarding the child himself Pollack (1970) has this to say:

A child must be placed educationally where he will reach his potential without unnecessary emotional disturbance. His health, personality, home background, and so on must be taken into consideration. Intelligence is not a major factor. In many elementary classrooms today there is a spread of 50 I.Q. points and children are grouped according to ability. The *degree* of hearing loss is not a criterion, because it is what the child has accomplished with his usable hearing that is of major importance, and this cannot be predicted from an audiogram.*

*From Pollack, D. *Educational audiology for the limited hearing infant.* Springfield, Ill.: Charles C Thomas, Publisher, 1970, p. 24.

General principles for teaching the hearing-impaired child

Ideally, the young child with impaired hearing should be "just like everyone else" in terms of the way he feels about himself in the educational setting. However, there are some special principles and practices that, if observed by the teacher, can make his experience much more successful and happy. Interestingly, many of these are applicable also to non–hearing-impaired children.

Make visual clues available to the child. The best set of clues in the context of conversation is provided by the speaker's face. "Speech reading" involves more than interpretation of the speaker's lip movements; it also includes interpretation of facial expression in combination with whatever auditory clues are available. Thus the teacher should attempt to look at the child when speaking to him and to try, when possible, to speak to him at eye level. A teacher of young children generally develops the habit of kneeling or stooping in order to speak to *all* children at their eye level. It is also important to avoid pacing or turning away in the midst of speaking, to be sure that the child is close enough to allow him to speech-read comfortably, and in whatever ways possible to support the child's efforts to *integrate* visual and auditory information.

Be sure the child's position is optimal. It is difficult for anyone to gaze directly and intently into light; therefore avoid speaking to the child from a position between him and the windows so that he is not forced to look directly at the glare of sunlight. It is helpful if the speaker's face is well lighted and if both sunlight and artificial light illuminate the person or object to which he is attending, rather than cast a glare that makes visual concentration both difficult and fatiguing. If the impairment involves only one ear or if it is greater in one ear than the other, placement of the child in relation to the source of sound so that he can make maximal use of his better ear is desirable.

Remember that listening activities are hard work. The teacher should be sensitive to signs of flagging attention. In view of the extra effort involved in the child's attention to such activities as listening to a story, it should not be surprising that his span of attention may not be as great as that of a hearing child. A good rule in this area, as in all other aspects of teaching, is not to expect more of a child than he can produce; rather, ensure that he will be successful in successively more demanding situations—and stop before he experiences the frustration and despair brought on by fatigue.

Speak in clear, well-modulated tones. Clarity, rather than loudness, is the guiding principle. It is easier for the child to interpret relatively brief statements than long, circuitous ones. In addition to facilitating the hearing-impaired child's ability to listen to and respond to communication, the teacher is also serving as a speech model—both for his nonhandicapped classmates and for the child himself. However, unnatural and exaggerated patterns of speech are unnecessary and inappropriate. It is not desirable to speak differently to the child with impaired hearing than to other children, for this tends to single him out, in his own mind and the minds of his classmates, as a handicapped child. Exaggerated speech is also difficult to speech-read. Rather, clear and distinct patterns of speech are desirable to inculcate in all children, while simultaneously encouraging focused attention in listening.

Regarding the attitude of the teacher who is working with a hearing-impaired child, perhaps the best summarizing statement has been provided by Gearhart and Weishahn (1976):

Above all other suggestions or techniques, the overriding factor is the attitude of the teacher. The teacher is the single most important variable. She must be understanding, but not sympathetic. She should treat the hearing impaired child as near as possible like any other child in the classroom, being fair and truthful, not lenient, in reporting his progress. *The handicapped child should be treated as a*

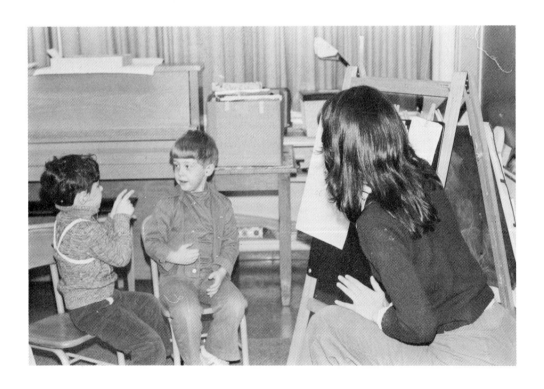

child who is able, who is an individual, and who, incidentally, has impaired hearing. (p. 43)

Oralism vs. manualism controversy

For more than a century an argument has been raging in the field of education of the hearing impaired as to whether manual communication (sign language or finger spelling, often referred to popularly as the "natural language of the deaf'") or an oral-aural approach is the better method. Why is this issue so emotionally debated? It is an issue of such deep concern because so much is at stake. To the oralist, the individual's ability to develop communicative speech and hence to become integrated within a hearing world is of primary importance. Most members of our hearing society do not know how to communicate via sign language. The strong advocate of an oral-aural approach (so called because it advocates maximizing whatever residual hearing the individual may possess and helping him learn to communicate via speech) wishes the hearing-impaired person to take his place within "normal" society, to compensate for his handicap (Croft, 1974).

Few workers in the field argue for a purely manual approach for all deaf children because of the recognized value of learning to communicate vocally, if possible. The point of view that argues for the legitimacy of alternative communication modes, rather than relying on speech alone, is represented primarily today by the advocates of total communication. This approach emphasizes the use of whatever vehicles for communication, or combination thereof, will work for the individual. In practice, oral and manual communication may be carried on simultaneously, as in the Rochester Method (Scouten, 1964). This can be difficult for the young child, since he must attend to *two* sets of visual stimuli: the speaker's face and his hand (Northern and Downs, 1974). However, Brill and Fahey (1971) reported good results.

Total communication would seem to represent a compromise position. However, to some oralists there is no compromise. Maximization of residual hearing through early amplification and early and continuous intervention in the areas of language and speech can determine whether an individual is enabled to achieve his educational, vocational, and social potential or whether he is forever relegated to an isolated subculture, cut off from the broader society.

There is a great need for research concerning the issue of methodology. The goal should be to determine which procedures are effective with which children and under which circumstances.

WORKING WITH PARENTS

According to Thomas Watson (1973), many British authorities favor part-time rather than full-day school programs for young hearing-impaired children. This is primarily to ensure that parents retain responsibility for working with their child in carrying over the school's program and that there will be time for them to do so. As is the case for children in the United States, however, there are instances when the child's interests are better served through full-day participation: if the mother is ". . . overworked, under great stress, or expecting another child" (Watson, 1973, p. 154). In any case, however, programs in England emphasize continued parental involvement and regard home environmental factors as the best prognostic indicators of whether integration in regular school programs will be successful. Integration of the child with a hearing handicap into "regular" programs is considered one of several options available in England, albeit one that has been widely used only within the last 20 years (Watson, 1973).

Parents have been found an invaluable resource to optimize the progress of young hearing-impaired children (Shepherd, 1973; Reynolds and de Reynolds, 1972). The professional has a crucial task of determining precisely how to work most effectively with individual parents, who present their own particular needs and characteristics, as do the children (Connor, 1976).

Parent activism in seeking greater support for programs for young children with impaired hearing was reported as an outcome of a project emphasizing parent participation by Luterman (1970). The major modes of involving parents were through their serving as tutors and participating in group discussions as their 18-month-through 3-year-old children participated in an integrated nursery school program.

McConnell and Horton (1970) also described a home teaching program for preschool children that featured a high degree of parent involvement. Parents were shown how to encourage the children to use their residual hearing and were guided in how to talk to them. The average age of the children was 2 years 4 months, and the project continued over a 3-year period, involving a total of 94 children. Gains in language age were demonstrated, and these were found by repeated testing to be stable. Children also improved in their ability to make optimal use of amplification. An additional outcome, the authors noted, and one that was directly attributable to the parent-involvement focus of the project, was the mobilization of these parents to find ways to continue the project under community auspices when the external funding was no longer available.

Parent participation in the nursery or kindergarten means more than simply visiting from time to time, if meaningful carryover is to occur. There should be specific goals for classroom visitation, as well as using such visits as a means of demonstrating interest and maintaining good public relations. A parent observing the classroom usually tends to get a global impression of the program and of the child's adjustment (Parker, 1973). He seems to be happy, he is a bit withdrawn, or he likes block play best. A visiting parent can be provided with a checklist and asked to record his or her observations of specific aspects of the child's behavior. This helps the parent focus on important facets of child development, to gain a sense of the structure and purpose of the program, and to identify areas that can be followed up at home. Just as a teacher can profitably use a structured checklist in conferring with the parent, the child's mother or father can employ a parental observational instrument in ensuring that important questions are asked in parent-teacher conferences.

Educating the young child with a hearing disability will optimally involve a real partnership between the child's teacher and parents. This partnership is built on mutual trust and respect, sharing, and continuous effort on the part of the teacher to ensure that lines of communication are open. As in other areas, it is not just the mother who has an important role to play. That of the child's father is just as significant.

A FINAL WORD

Those who have always moved comfortably within a world of meaningful sound, who are part of "hearing society," have difficulty appreciating the enormity of the task facing the individual with a serious hearing loss. From the onset of the disability, the hearing-impaired person's experiences have been substantially different from those of persons who are not handicapped. If the loss was congenital or sustained during early childhood, the development of speech is inevitably difficult. What occurs "naturally" for the hearing child requires *teaching*. The ability to use language to communicate, so taken for granted by most people, yet so basic to human experience, represents the greatest single challenge to the hearing-impaired child, his family, and those who teach him.

These facts may sometimes cause us to lose sight of the basic ways in which the needs of the severely hearing-impaired child are identical to those of non-

handicapped children. Through adapting classroom programs as necessary, consulting available resource persons, and working in partnership with the child's parents, a teacher of young children *can* provide for successful learning and social development of many severely hearing-impaired children within a nonspecialized setting.

DISCUSSION QUESTIONS

1. If you, as a classroom teacher, learn that "a deaf child" may be entering your class, what are some of the important questions you might ask concerning the child's handicap?
2. Why is the earliest possible identification of a congenital hearing loss of such crucial importance?
3. Describe an early childhood education classroom environment in which a young child with a serious hearing disability might achieve optimal adjustment and success.
4. Why have stereotypes about hearing-impaired persons persisted? What harm may be done by these prejudices and stereotypes?
5. List and describe the functions of school, program, and community resources providing services that might be needed by young hearing-impaired children in your setting.
6. Why have hearing-impaired children so frequently been prevented from achieving a maximum level of accomplishment and productivity? What role do teachers of young children have in correcting this situation?

REFERENCES

Allen, M. Teacher's forum: education through music—an innovative program for hearing impaired children. *Volta Review*, 1975, *77*, 381-385.

Allen, R., and Allen, C. *Language experiences in reading*. Chicago: Encyclopedia Britannica, Inc., 1970.

Apgar, V., and Beck, J. *Is my baby all right? A guide to birth defects*. New York: Trident Press, 1972.

Ashton-Warner, S. *Teacher*. New York: Bantam Books, Inc., 1963.

Ausubel, D. P. *Educational psychology: a cognitive view*. New york: Holt, Rinehart & Winston, Inc., 1968.

Bowman, E. A resource room program for hearing impaired students. *Volta Review*, 1973, *75*, 208-213.

Brennan, M. Can deaf children acquire language? An evaluation of linguistic principles in deaf education. *American Annals for the Deaf*, 1975, *1*, 469-470.

Brill, R. G., and Fahey, J. A combination that works in a preschool program for deaf children. *Hearing and Speech News*, 1971, *39*(4), 17-19.

Bruner, J. S. The growth of mind. *American Psychologist*, 1965, *20*, 1007-1016.

Cazden, C. B. *Child language and education*. New York: Holt, Rinehart & Winston, Inc., 1972.

Connor, L. E. New directions in infant programs for the deaf. *Volta Review*, 1976, *78*, 8-15.

Croft, J. C. A look at the future for the hearing impaired child of today. *Volta Review*, 1974, *76*, 115-122.

Davis, H., and Silverman, S. R. *Hearing and deafness* (3rd ed.). New York: Holt, Rinehart & Winston, Inc., 1970.

Fiedler, M. *Developmental studies of deaf children*. Washington, D.C.: American Speech and Hearing Association, 1969.

Fraiberg, S. Intervention in infancy: a program for blind infants. In B. Z. Friedlander, G. M. Sterritt, and G. E. Kirk (Eds.), *Exceptional infant: assessment and intervention* (Vol. III.) New York: Brunner/Mazel, Inc., 1975, 40-62.

Furth, H. G. *Thinking without language: psychological implications of deafness*. New York, The Free Press, 1966.

Furth, H. G. A review and perspective on the thinking of deaf people. In J. Hellmuth (Ed.), *Cognitive studies* (Vol. I). New York: Brunner/Mazel, Inc., 1970, pp. 291-338.

Furth, H. G. *Deafness and hearing: a psychosocial approach*. Belmont, Calif.: Wadsworth Publishing Co., Inc., 1973.

Garrett, C., and Stovall, E. M. A parent's views on integration. *Volta Review*, 1972, *74*, 338-344.

Gearheart, B. R., and Weishahn, M. W. *The handicapped child in the regular classroom*. St. Louis: The C. V. Mosby Co., 1976.

Ginsburg, H., and Opper, S. *Piaget's theory of intellectual development: an introduction*. Englewood Cliffs, N.J.: Prentice-Hall, Inc., 1969.

Goetzinger, C., and Rousey, C. Educational achievement of deaf children. *American Annals of the Deaf*, 1959, *104*, 221-231.

Grammatico, L. F., and Miller, S. D. Curriculum for the preschool deaf child. *Volta Review*, 1974, *76*, 280-289.

Groht, M. *Natural language for deaf children*. Washington, D.C.: Alexander Graham Bell Association for the Deaf, Inc., 1958.

Harris, G. M. *Language for the preschool deaf child* (3rd ed.). Washington, D.C.: Alexander Graham Bell Association for the Deaf, Inc., 1971.

Hart, B. D. *Teaching reading to deaf children*. Washington, D.C.: Alexander Graham Bell Association for the Deaf, Inc., 1963.

Hart, B. D. Learning to read begins at birth. *Volta Review*, 1975, *77*, 168-172.

Jarvella, R. J., and Lubinsky, J. Deaf and hearing children's use of language describing temporal order. *Journal of Speech and Hearing Research*, March, 1975, 58-73.

Kirk, S. A. *Educating exceptional children*. Boston: Houghton Mifflin Co., 1972.

Laughton, J. *Non-verbal creative thinking abilities as predictors of linguistic abilities of hearing impaired children*. Unpublished doctoral dissertation, Kent State University, 1976.

Lloyd, L. L., and Dahle, A. J. Detection and diagnosis of a hearing impairment in the child. In R. Frisina (Ed.), *A bicentennial monograph on hearing impairment*. Washington, D.C.: Alexander Graham Bell Association for the Deaf, Inc., 1976, pp. 13-17.

Luterman, D. M. *A parent-centered nursery program for pre-school deaf children: final report*. Boston: Emerson College, 1970.

McConnell, F. The psychology of communication. In L. E. Connor (Ed.), *Speech for the deaf child: knowledge and use*. Washington, D.C.: Alexander Graham Bell Association for the Deaf, Inc., 1971.

McConnell, F., and Horton, K. B. *A home teaching program for parents of very young deaf children: final report*. Nashville, Tenn.: Vanderbilt University, School of Medicine, 1970.

McDermott, E. F. Storytelling—a relaxed and natural path to lipreading, language, and reading. *Volta Review*, 1971, *73*(1), 54-57.

Miller, J. B. *A demonstration home training program for parents of preschool deaf children: final report*. Kansas City: Kansas University Medical Center, 1970.

Myklebust, H. R. *The psychology of deafness*. New York: Grune & Stratton, Inc., 1964.

Nimnicht, G. P. A model program for young children that responds to the child. In R. K. Parker (Ed.), *The preschool in action: exploring early childhood programs*. Boston: Allyn & Bacon, Inc., 1972, 245-267.

Northcott, W. M. Candidate for integration: a hearing impaired child in a regular nursery school. *Young Children,* September, 1970, *25,* 367-380.

Northcott, W. H. (Ed.). *The hearing impaired child in a regular classroom: preschool, elementary, and secondary years.* Washington, D. C.: Alexander Graham Bell Association for the Deaf, Inc., 1973.

Northern, J. L., and Downs, M. P. *Hearing in children.* Baltimore: The Williams & Wilkins Co., 1974.

O'Connor, C. Children with impaired hearing. *Volta Review,* 1953, *56,* 437.

Parker, S. G. Observation by parents: the pre-primary hearing impaired child. In W. H. Northcott (Ed.), *The hearing impaired child in a regular classroom: preschool, elementary, and secondary years.* Washington, D.C.: Alexander Graham Bell Association for the Deaf, Inc., 1973.

Piaget, J. *The language and thought of the child.* New York: Harcourt Brace Jovanovich, 1928.

Pollack, D. *Educational audiology for the limited hearing infant.* Springfield, Ill.: Charles C Thomas, Publisher, 1970.

Pollack, D., and Ernst, M. Don't set limits: expectations for preschool children. In W. H. Northcott (Ed.), *The hearing impaired child in a regular classroom: preschool, primary, and secondary years.* Washington, D.C.: Alexander Graham Bell Association for the Deaf, Inc., 1973, pp. 156-162.

Prescott, R. Acoustic puzzles: training games. *Volta Review,* 1971, *73*(1), 51-53.

Reynolds, J. A., and de Reynolds, L. R. A parent's approach to language: the daily journal. *Volta Review,* 1972, *74,* 345-351.

Ross, C., and Calvert, D. R. The semantics of deafness. In W. H. Northcott (Ed.), *The hearing impaired child in a regular classroom: preschool, elementary, and secondary years.* Washington, D.C.: Alexander Graham Bell Association for the Deaf, Inc., 1973, pp. 13-17.

Schein, J. D., and Delk, M. T. *The deaf population of the United States.* Silver Springs, Md.: The National Association of the Deaf, 1974.

Scouten, E. L. The place of the Rochester method in American education of the deaf. *Report of the Proceedings of the International Congress on the Education of the Deaf,* 1964, pp. 429-433.

Shepherd, B. D. Parent potential. *Volta Review,* 1973, *75,* 220-224.

Silverman, R. Education of the deaf. In L. E. Travis (Ed.), *Handbook of speech pathology.* New York: Appleton-Century-Crofts, 1952.

Silverman, S. R., and Lane, H. S. Deaf children. In H. Davis and S. R. Silverman (Eds.), *Hearing and deafness* (3rd ed.). New York: Holt, Rinehart & Winston, Inc., 1970, 384-425.

Stassen, R. A. I have one in my class who's wearing hearing aids! In W. H. Northcott (Ed.), *The hearing impaired child in a regular classroom: preschool, elementary, and secondary years.* Washington, D.C.: Alexander Graham Bell Association for the Deaf, Inc., 1973.

Van Riper, C. *Speech correction: principles and methods.* Englewood Cliffs, N.J.: Prentice-Hall, Inc., 1972.

Vernon, McC. Fifty years of research on the intelligence of deaf and hard of hearing children: a review of literature and discussion of implications. *Journal of Rehabilitation of the Deaf,* 1968, *1,* 1-12.

Vygotsky, L. S. *Thought and language.* Cambridge, Mass.: The M.I.T. Press, 1962.

Watson, T. J. Integration of hearing impaired children in nursery schools. In W. H. Northcott (Ed.), *The hearing impaired child in a regular classroom: preschool, elementary, and secondary years.* Washington, D.C.: Alexander Graham Bell Association for the Deaf, Inc., 1973.

Weiss, C. E., and Lillywhite, H. S. *Communicative disorders: a handbook for prevention and early intervention.* St. Louis: The C. V. Mosby Co., 1976.

CHAPTER 4

VISUAL IMPAIRMENTS

with the assistance of
Marylou E. Boynton

DEFINITIONS AND INCIDENCE

As must other handicapping conditions, visual impairment must be seen on a continuum, rather than as an all-or-none phenomenon. This will seem obvious to those readers whose vision is corrected for near- or far-vision difficulties or other visual acuity problems. Clearly, however, relatively common visual disabilities shared by such a great number of individuals need to be distinguished from severe visual deficits or disabilities resulting in an inability to distinguish printed forms in order to read.

Traditionally the distinctions between blindness, partial sightedness, and essentially normal visual acuity have been represented numerically:

Blindness is generally defined in the United States as visual acuity for distance vision of 20/200 or less in the better eye, with best correction; or visual acuity of more than 20/200 if the widest diameter of field of vision subtends an angle no greater than 20 degrees.

The *partially seeing* are defined as persons with a visual acuity greater than 20/200 but not greater than 20/70 in the better eye with correction. (National Society for the Prevention of Blindness, 1966, p. 10)

The paired numbers correspond to *Snellen Chart* symbols. For example, 20/70 communicates that the individual can identify at a distance of 20 feet what a normally sighted individual can distinguish at 70 feet.

However, this index of visual acuity, together with the operational definition of legal blindness it provides, has not proved sufficient for the purpose of educational classification. In a study of more than 14,000 children who were classified as legally blind, Jones (1961) found that 76 percent had some degree of residual vision—that is, approximately one-fourth were *totally* blind—and a substantial number of those with some vision were able to read print. For educational purposes, a classification based on a more functional definition is needed (Kirk, 1972):

1. The visually impaired, which refers to those who can learn to read print;
2. The blind, who cannot learn print, but who need instruction in braille. (p. 293)

Visual impairment that is sufficiently serious to warrant special educational provisions constitutes a low-incidence handicapping condition, a condition that afflicts approximately 0.1 percent of all school-age children. According to Ashcroft (1963), 1 in 3,000 persons is legally blind, while approximately 1 in 500 persons is partially sighted.

IDENTIFICATION BY THE TEACHER

Whereas total blindness is usually identified during the first year of life, less severe visual handicaps may often not be recognized during the early childhood years. It is sometimes the case that visual impairment is not picked up even at the time of school entrance. The Snellen procedure is useful only in identifying acuity problems, whereas detection of other forms of visual disability, such as poor peripheral vision, requires careful observation on a day-to-day basis. Gearhart and Weishahn (1976) provide a list of characteristics and behaviors that may signal the presence of a visual problem in a school-age child:

Observable signs
1. Red eyelids
2. Crusts on lids among the lashes
3. Recurring sties or swollen lids
4. Watery eyes or discharge
5. Reddened or watery eyes
6. Crossed eyes or eyes that do not appear to be straight
7. Pupils of uneven size
8. Eyes that move excessively
9. Drooping eyelids

Visual behavior
1. Rubs eyes excessively
2. Shuts or covers one eye; tilts head or thrusts head forward
3. Sensitivity to light
4. Difficulty with reading or other work requiring close use of the eyes
5. Squinting, blinking, frowning, facial distortions while reading or doing other close work

6. Holds reading material too close or too far or frequently changes the distance from near to far or far to near
7. Complains of pain or aches in the eyes, headaches, dizziness, or nausea following close eye work
8. Difficulty in seeing distant objects (preference for reading or other academic tasks rather than playground or gross motor activities)
9. Tendency to reverse letters, syllables, or words
10. Tendency to confuse letters of similar shape (*o* and *a, c* and *e, n* and *m, h* and *n,* and *f* and *t*) (p. 53)

Generally and with some obvious exceptions, these signs and behaviors are applicable in nursery school, Head Start, kindergarten, and day care settings as well. Although the child's mode of response when confronted with the printed page may provide the clearest demonstration of certain forms of visual problems, observation of his behavior in a free play situation, in performing manipulative tasks, in drawing or painting, in using large equipment in gross motor activity, and in many other areas may provide the alert adult with cues suggesting the possibility of a vision problem.

A child with a visual problem may observably *avoid* certain types of activities, such as looking at books or engaging in fine motor tasks requiring eye-hand coordination, such as peg boards or puzzles. Sometimes the child who is having difficulty seeing will seek to be physically close to the teacher a great deal. If he is unable to, his interest may seem to totally flag. This particular behavior, however, may be symptomatic of any of a number of problems or needs—not only a visual problem.

The teacher of young children can provide a valuable service by alerting children's parents to signs of possible visual difficulty and by sharing with them his or her observations.

Obviously, the diagnosis of a visual handicap and the determination of whether and when correction should be initiated should be made by a specialist, based on his own intensive examination and on the information reported to him by the child's parents. Two kinds of specialists may have a particularly important role: an *ophthalmologist,* a medical doctor specializing in diagnosis and treatment of diseases of the eye; and an *optometrist,* a highly trained specialist who does not have a medical degree. Consequently, although glasses may be prescribed and fitted by either, if disease of the eye is suspected, it is the ophthalmologist to whom the child is referred.

Every educational program, including prekindergarten-level programs, should carry on systematic screening procedures that include, but are not limited to, individual Snellen-type examinations of all children. Teachers should be prepared to check for possible visual problems in a variety of ways, including following up any suggestive signs promptly and completely. In spite of the screening processes employed at the elementary school level, a great many children experiencing visual difficulties escape detection. Extra vigilance on the part of prekindergarten and kindergarten teachers and close communication with parents might serve to prevent unnecessary hardships for the child during that crucial period of initial exposure to academic demands.

In recent years, a nationwide attack on *amblyopia,* or "lazy eye," has been implemented. This involves community-based screening programs directed by local public schools; children are screened for this condition prior to kindergarten entrance. As in so many other areas, the success of this program has been to a great extent a result of the efforts of parent volunteers working in partnership with educators. Screening efforts are generally very successful; however, the teacher should also be observant of mannerisms, such as cocking the head to one side in order to focus, that may suggest amblyopia. Early detection and treatment of amblyopia are absolutely essential to its cure.

In addition to public schools, vision screening is also carried out by community health and multiservice agencies and is a routine part of pediatric examinations. Nevertheless, in a great many instances, it is the teacher who remains in the best position to notice and follow up vision problems that have gone undetected. It is not unknown for a child to progress several years in school, to be identified as learning disabled when a marked disparity between ability and performance becomes evident, and to belatedly reveal a previously unnoticed visual problem.

BLINDNESS AND EARLY DEVELOPMENT

So much important research has been carried out in very recent years concerning the psychological development of blind children during infancy and the early childhood years that discussion in detail of some of the findings is warranted. As in the case of psychological research concerning other areas of exceptionality, these studies have been valuable in two major ways: (1) they have pointed to effective strategies of intervention to help the handicapped child realize his maximum potential and (2) they have contributed greatly to our understanding of psychological processes of development in *all* children.

In the case of visual impairment, nearly all of the studies of psychological processes of development have focused on the blind. Later in this chapter, recommended educational strategies to accommodate the needs of young children with less severe visual disorders are presented and discussed. The present discussion, however, focuses primarily on the effects on psychological development of congenital blindness or blindness acquired perinatally or early in life, as well as on intervention during infancy.

The important role of efforts to help the young blind child achieve *orientation of his own body in space* and to acquire *mo-bility* is generally recognized. However, even more basic questions can be raised concerning the blind child's route to proficiency in *cognitive functions, awareness of self and others,* and use of various means (especially, but not exclusively, the auditory and tactile senses) to *compensate* for his inability to take in information about his world through his visual sense. There is often a tendency on the part of parents and other adults to assume that the blind child "naturally" learns to compensate for his handicap. Thus they offer too little direct help to the child or fail to approach this need in a planned and systematic way—as something to be taught. On the other hand, as in the case of other handicapping conditions, some parents or teachers may tend to overprotect, fearing so for the child's physical safety that they unduly restrict the physical activity and exploration so necessary for learning during the early years.

What additional ramifications of the young child's inability to see are of potential importance? Reading Jean Piaget's accounts (Piaget, 1952; Inhelder and Piaget, 1969) of the acquisition of the sensory-motor "building blocks" of intelligence during the first 2 years of life, one is struck by the enormity of the handicap constituted by blindness during this period. As evidence that he has acquired the concept of the *permanent object,* for example, which Piaget has identified as one of the most critically important foundations for conceptual development, the very young child is seen to *pursue* an object removed from his *visual field.* How can a blind infant acquire an awareness of objects themselves and of the fact that they continue to exist even though removed from view? How can he become aware of their attributes without being able to see them? Would not the cognitive developmental processes, and thus the *thinking,* of blind children necessarily be qualitatively different from those of sighted children?

Frequent statements can in fact be

found in the literature to the effect that blind persons have difficulty in abstraction (Axelrod, 1959; Tilman, 1967). Zeibelson and Barg (1967) found evidence that the blind individual's ability to store and to organize mental representations is imparied.

Higgins (1973) also found that, on ten manipulative classification tasks, congenitally blind children mastered all preoperational tasks before they mastered operational tasks, suggesting that the Piagetian description of the sequential development of classification is applicable to them. On a verbal class inclusion test composed of five subtests of question categories, each representing a different combination of criteria relating to degree of abstractness of class content, ranging from concrete to abstract, "as predicted, the blind subjects answered correctly more class inclusion questions relating to concrete content than logically comparable questions involving abstract content" (pp. 24-25). Sighted subjects, however, performed equally across categories. These results supported a hypothesis of "developmental asynchrony," according to which a blind child could perform logical operations with concrete elements but could not perform the same logical operation with abstract elements. Higgins concluded that the

> . . . totally blind child is not necessarily handicapped in developing the intellectual structures underlying classification. He may be handicapped in exercising these capabilities because he cannot obtain the prerequisite data from his surroundings. It may be the case, therefore, that the problem facing the educator is not so much how to compensate for a deficiency in the blind child's classificatory structuring, but how to help him derive maximum benefit from his available senses so that the information flow is sufficient to support the thought of which the child is capable. (p. 37)

In considering the cognition of the blind it is apparently important to distinguish between *qualitatively different thinking* and *restricted representational abilities re-* *sulting from restricted experience*. Kephart et al. (1974) suggested that a blind child may live in a psychological environment that is less *differentiated*. Based on verbal descriptions of an imaginary child, they found blind children across all ages to have a constricted body image. Witkin et al. (1971) postulated a more "global" style of thinking when they found blind children's clay modelings of the human figure to be less differentiated than the drawings of sighted peers. This is not surprising since fewer cues are available to them than to sighted children. The blind child has not had the opportunity to compare visual impressions of other humans with information gained through his tactile explorations.

In addition, a sighted child has had far greater experience with representations of his body in the form of mirror reflections, dolls, pictures, and the like. Selma Fraiberg's research (Fraiberg et al., 1969) has demonstrated that external representations, that is, those not created by the child's activity, are so far from the experiences of blind infants of 15 to 18 months that a doll is an incomprehensible toy to them. Two- and three-year-old blind children who are able to name their facial parts and those of their parents usually cannot transfer this skill in naming when dolls are employed.

The delay caused by the absence of vision in the development of the Piagetian object concept alters the timing of investment in an *affectional* "object" as well. Blind babies achieve awareness of a single "significant other" between 6 and 12 months of age; however, they may not master the concept of object permanence until much later (Fraiberg, 1968). This may have the effect of leaving them vulnerable to separation anxiety for an unusually long time, an emotional vulnerability that may be reflected in less effective styles of cognitive functioning. Witkin et al. (1971) have related difficulties children have in separating from their mothers to a global style of thinking. This cognitive-affective handicap would surely offer implications for the teacher of a young severely visually impaired child.

It has been argued that the restricted perceptual and motor experience early in life of the congenitally blind must seriously impede the growth of what Piaget (1952) has called *operational structures.* However, investigations of blind, school-age children of normal intelligence indicate that their performance on Piagetian tasks is similar to that of sighted peers if they have had prior experience with the objects involved in the experimental tasks. For example, in studies by Witkin et al. (1971) and Gottesman (1971), on tasks requiring the manipulation of a form with subsequent selection of an identical form, congenitally blind persons performed as well as sighted individuals who were blindfolded. Gottesman (1971) found that both his blind and sighted subjects, across age groups (2 to 4, 4 to 6, and 6 to 8 years), organized their exploratory manipulative movements in the manner described by Piaget.

Apparently, children who are congenitally blind follow a different developmental route, but one that nevertheless leads to cognitive functioning that is essentially equivalent to that of sighted children. Developmental differences during the first 3 years in motor, affective, cognitive, and representational areas are apparent. However, with appropriate stimulation during the first years of life, by 5 years of age the blind child apparently can approach behavioral norms for sighted children in these areas (Fraiberg, 1968; Ashcroft and Harley, 1966; Lowenfeld, 1964).

Much of the research points to the importance of early intervention, especially in the form of assisting parents to help their blind infant by becoming more aware of the tasks the child must accomplish and more skillful in their efforts to facilitate his mastery of those tasks. This implies a particularly valuable form of educational intervention—based in the home, accomplished by the child's parents with aid from professionals, and *initiated during the first months of life.*

AREAS FOR INTERVENTION DURING INFANCY AND THE TODDLER PERIOD

With severely visually impaired children, the importance of early educational intervention is paramount. The position is taken here that programs for congenitally blind children should begin in the first weeks or months of life and should be continuous throughout the early years. The role of the professional is that of *home visitor* and *parent educator.* This may involve functions such as the following:

1. Individual parent counseling
2. Parent group counseling
3. Demonstration of procedures to parents
4. Observing and recording the child's progress
5. Providing materials for use at home

It may be that these and other functions are performed by an interdisciplinary team. In some cases, however, they will be coordinated or actually carried out by a single professional. Not only sensory stimulation, but the parent-child interaction, as well, will be the focus of concern (Carolan, 1973).

The approaches and procedures suggested in the following pages are, for the most part, equally applicable to blind infants and blind toddlers who are participating in a center-based developmental child care program.

Mother-infant communication

A baby's emotional investment in its human partners is a major step toward becoming a social being. In view of the high rate of autistic-like behavior observed among infants who are congenitally blind (Fraiberg, 1975), the work of Brazelton (1973) concerning early mother-child interaction is a particularly important resource in the area of intervention strategies for blind infants. The relevance of this research concerning the development of normal infants is indicated (1) by the important role attributed to vision in mother-infant interaction, (2) by the infant's use of vision as a means of self-regulation of external stimulation, and consequently of internal state, and (3) by indications that blind infants characteristically show less initiative in interaction than do sighted infants (Fraiberg, 1975).

These studies of interaction of sighted infants with their mothers document that, even when the focus of attention is shifted to another object, the mother is retained peripherally in view. A mother of a blind infant might help her child to be secure in the knowledge of her presence by, for example, *holding, talking, lightly blowing, humming, maintaining touch contact,* and in diverse other small ways.

The general mode for mother-infant interaction is one in which the infant regulates the interaction by *rewarding* the mother with his attention and the intensity of his response through eye contact, smiles, giggles, squeals, and excited movement. The mother will follow her baby's lead in regard to the intensity of interaction, and she will be rewarded with longer periods of attention. If she is not able to interpret his responses, the infant may avert his head and even fall asleep, thus terminating contact (Brazelton, 1973).

Because so much of normal "dialogue" is mediated through vision, the blind infant and his mother may have difficulty in developing a system for communication. Before the infant can engage his mother in a dialogue, *he must in a sense teach her a form of "sign language."* The mother must learn to disregard postures and expressions, such as the averted head and muted smile, that are typical and do not signify "no interest." She must do without such maternal favorites as eye contact, bright automatic smiles, arms extended in greeting, and imitative gestures and expressions, attending instead to fine hand movements and to differential levels of motor arousal. This suggests the great

need a mother of a blind infant may have for guidance. The parents can become aware that tactile-kinesthetic contact—bouncing, jiggling, tickling, and swinging—can produce a smiling response. Hand language conveys more subtle meanings: a scanning with the hand may denote interest; hand activity that continues after cessation of interaction or removal of an object may mean "more"; pantomime actions or grasping and ungrasping activity indicates recognition. A selective smile in response to the mother's voice occurs at about 4 weeks of age, but it will not be automatic and will seem muted. Blind babies, like those who see, indicate tactile recognition of the mother by protesting being held by strangers, beginning at about 7 months. Turning the head toward the sound of mother's approach does not occur until sound begins to be associated with objects near the end of the first year, in contrast to the earlier orientation to sound observed in seeing infants. At approximately 5 to 8 months, manual scanning of the mother's face becomes deft and organized and conveys a sense of expecting what is found (Fraiberg et al., 1966).

If the mother does not learn the "sign language," she will only be able to decipher basic need states (hunger, pain, etc.) that produce a wail. What she must do is learn to attend to, and communicate by means of, tactile, kinesthetic, and auditory signals. To accomplish this, she might be encouraged to initiate *interactive cycles* with her baby through such techniques as the following:

1. Swinging or rocking the baby, noting whether he adopts a posture that corresponds to a cradling position, and stopping periodically, sitting the baby up, and seeing if he tries to fall back into the cradling posture or begins to imitate swinging motion—in which case, continuing the motion

2. Blowing gently against the baby's face at midline, stopping when the

face is averted and continuing when the midline is presented

3. Imitating the baby's rate and range of cooing sounds

4. Doing "patty-cake" with feet and hands, stopping periodically to see if the baby brings his hands or feet together and continuing if he does

5. Engaging in an activity involving two modalities, such as cooing and tickling, then stopping one activity and continuing the other to see if the baby reacts

6. *Talking* to the baby—and responding to his utterances!

A blind baby may search for interpersonal stimulation in such ways as the following:

1. Rooting and nuzzling

2. Discriminating through smell and enjoying the smell

3. Postural adjustment and anticipation

4. Continuing part of an activity

5. Vocalizing (However, Fraiberg et al. [1966] report that blind babies are typically very quiet and vocalization for self-amusement is infrequent. Vocalizing must be stimulated.)

6. Mouthing, which in a well-stimulated blind infant is as normal as it is for a sighted one

7. Hand scanning

The mother can become alert to these and other messages conveyed by her baby and respond to them accordingly. A variety of forms of reinforcement, acknowledgement, and expansion are possible to establish communication cycles and patterns.

Developing compensatory strategies

Parents' hopes for innate compensatory abilities can be damaging to a blind infant who needs help learning to use his remaining sense modalities efficiently. Parents may, for example, provide monotonous or inappropriate stimulation rather than employing it meaningfully. Music played too frequently, specifically the ra-

dio and television, may obscure the sound of daily life from which the child can learn. Simply waiting for compensation to occur automatically may cause parents to fail to provide appropriate stimulation needed to facilitate development.

The first 18 months of life apparently are a crucial period for the congenitally blind infant (Fraiberg et al., 1969). During this period, the crucial accomplishments are as follows:

1. Establishment of human object relations

2. Development of a bimanual exploratory manipulative skill

3. Development of the concept of the permanent object (at least as manifested by reach on sound cues alone)

4. Gross motor mobility

To accomplish these and other tasks in the absence of vision, the remaining exploratory modes available are *grasping, smelling, sucking,* and *hearing.* All of these involve reflexive patterns as tools in learning and enable the infant to focus attention (Piaget, 1952); none, however, substitutes for vision in facilitating adaptation.

Mouthing patterns of a well-stimulated blind baby are similar to those of a normal baby. Hand-mouth coordination is a basic organization of sensory-motor activity through which "the baby is introduced to himself, so to speak" (Adelson and Fraiberg, 1972, p. 423).

The difficulty with hand-mouth coordination as a learning modality is that it is fundamentally body centered. For the hand to develop the ability to make fine discriminations, it must be involved in manipulating a variety of objects, not just in holding objects to the mouth for oral satisfaction. Among normal children the sight of objects stimulates eye-hand activity that becomes the dominant exploratory mode in the second half of the first year. Lacking the motivation supplied by vision, a blind child may fail to develop beyond hand-mouth coordination. Inducing the hands to meet at midline is a first step in facilitating the development of manipulation. A mother can be helped to facilitate her blind infant's learning of this task in such ways as the following:

1. Holding the bottle at midline and placing the infant's hands on it
2. Playing hand games, such as patty-cake
3. Placing toys on the infant's stomach
4. Hanging a cradle gym and placing the infant so that graspable parts, possibly including a bell, are at midline
5. Inducing the infant to grasp the mother's finger, then finger-walking on his stomach

Coordination of schemas is facilitated if the baby's hands are placed on a spoon and bottle so that the objects are experienced manually and orally at the same time. Finger feeding as early as possible likewise facilitates schema coordination.

Because of the limited mobility of blind babies, there is a need for more mature hand-mouth activity (Fraiberg, 1972) as the baby develops the abilities to grasp and release, to extend a single exploratory finger, and to achieve the pincer grasp.

FACILITATING DEVELOPMENT OF MANIPULATION IN HAND-MOUTH COORDINATION

1. Playing emptying games: Place small foods suitable for pincer grasp in a variety of containers. It may be necessary to show the baby where the food is to be found. For containers use a small bottle with some neck to encourage extension of a single finger; containers with lids, such as a sugar bowl; a container the baby may first shake and hear rattling; and a container with a handle, such as a cup. Small containers keep contents close together and easier to find. Suitable foods include raisins, pieces of cookies, grapes, squares of cheese, M & M's, and dry cereal.
2. Passing a variety of objects to the child in sequence. The child will have to pass one from one hand to another and may use mouth as a third receptacle.
3. Letting the child mouth a variety of object that will feel different: different sizes and shapes, different textures, dangly objects that change as they are handled or mouthed. A string of beads of different sizes, shapes, and, if possible, textures so the child can go from one to the other and compare.
4. Finger feeding.

The hand that is busy supplying the mouth is moved toward the body frequently. To develop manipulations independent of the mouth, the parent can encourage movement of the hand away from the body.

ACTIVITIES TO FACILITATE HAND MOVEMENT AWAY FROM THE BODY

1. Using a suction cup, fix a plastic or metal cup to the baby's tray. Induce the baby to bang the cup with a spoon.
2. Play a patty-cake game in which the baby claps hands against the adult's hands.
3. Place different textured coverings over the baby's tray or play space (a swatch of rug, a wet sponge, sandpaper, a silk scarf). Fix the covering so that it stays on the tray.
4. A Busy-Box can be fixed to the side of crib or play pen.
5. Cradle gyms can be used.

As mobility develops, the hand must assume new postures for crawling, climbing, and walking.

Development of grasping and reaching. The absence of vision delays reaching on sound cue until the development of the object concept. "The coordination of prehension and hearing is achieved by the blind infant late in the first year and correlates with a stage in the development of the 'object concept,' the beginning attribution of permanence to objects" (Fraiberg et al., 1966, p. 329). The stage sequence in the development of reaching relates to the object concept.

STAGES IN DEVELOPMENT OF REACHING

I. The hand usually remains motionless after an object is removed. Sometimes the baby will pantomime briefly the action previously involving the object.
   A. Initially it is tactile contact that activates the hand.

B. No hand response to sound is evident.

C. No head orientation to sound is observed.

D. On the conceptual level the object is determined by the child's activity and has no independent existence.

II. Loss of object results in a global search. The child does not take into account the location in which the object was lost. The search is brief and random. It is a differentiation of activity, but there is no use of cues that relate to the object.

A. A sound cue immediately after object loss will activate grasping but not search.

B. Sound alone brings attentiveness but no directional orientation—no head turning, no hand activity.

C. Hand activity in response to the sound of the object immediately after object loss suggests sound is just beginning to be associated with the tactile schema.

III. Response to cues: "The radial, global exploration of the table surface or space gives way to intentional reaching when there are cues for locating the object or following its trajectory." (Fraiberg et al., 1966, p. 3)

A. A sound cue alone activates grasping pantomime.

B. A tactile clue alone becomes associated with position in space when the child resists the removal of the object. As he holds onto the object, his arm is drawn forward and his trunk is extended, two motor patterns important to crawling. The child will recover an object held in the spot where lost.

C. The object is beginning to be differentiated from a motor scheme that involves it as it is additionally associated with a position in space.

D. A sound cue after a tactile experience is ignored. The child searches in the place where he last had contact with the object, despite hearing it in new location.

E. That sound is vaguely associated with tactile events is indicated by the grasping and motor excitement in response to a sound cue alone.

IV. Following tactile contact with an object, the child searches for it where he hears sound.

A. The child is beginning to construct trajectories.

V. The child reaches for an object on a sound cue alone.

A. By this time the child's manipulative exploratory gestures are organized and explicit and indicate belief in the object's quality.

B. Even after reaching on sound cue alone is achieved, search behavior will remain limited to stage IV in the development of the object concept.

ACTIVITIES TO FACILITATE GRASPING AND REACHING

I. During stage I

A. Provide manipulative experience with a variety of toys that make a variety of sounds: rattles, cradle gyms, squeak toys, bean bags.

B. From day 1 associate all human interactions with talk.

II. During stage II

A. To maximize the chance of contact during the brief searches, create play spaces for child. Have several that utilize different postures, for example, cradle gyms for supine position and a play table with an edge for sitting.

B. Announce an object by making it sound so that the sound may acquire signal value.

C. Greet the baby vocally before tactile contact. (This also avoids startling the baby and builds trust.)

D. Remove the object the baby is playing with, sound it, and return it (to reinforce grasping schema).

III. During stage III

A. To encourage the gesture of reaching and trunk extension, play tug-of-war games.

B. See activities to develop reaching.

C. Remove the object from the child. Hold it in a variety of positions, permitting him to retrieve it. Do this with the child in many postures.

D. Tie a ball to each end of a cord. Hold one end and give one to the baby. Shake it; then wait for him to shake it, etc.

IV. During stage IV: Provide activities to facilitate the construction of trajectories.

A. Along the body

1. Roll balls, gently stroke brushes, tap rattles, etc., along the baby's body to give the tactile experience of the object's path. Frequently terminate the path in the baby's hand and allow him to manipulate the object.
2. Use warm and cold things similarly.

B. Use vibrating toys to give a clue intermediate between sound and touch.
   1. Wind-up toys: put the baby's hand on the toy as it moves along the table top. After this tactile-kinesthetic experience, remove the toy and direct it at the baby's hands.
   2. Provide toys like the Fisher-Price basset hound that move with a rhythmical thump.
   3. Seat the child at the play table. Prop a thin metal cookie sheet on some books. Roll a variety of objects toward the child. Announce them verbally and place one hand of the child on the cookie sheet to feel it rattle. Position the other hand to receive the object.

C. Use bimanual activity to construct trajectories:
   1. Roll a ball from one hand to another.
   2. Place one hand on the water faucet and the other lower down to feel stream of water. Bring one hand up and down.
   3. Open and close hinged objects.

D. With a musical ball or top that the child can track in a play space, play with the baby, remove the object, sound it, and allow him to find it.

"In order to place an object on sound cue alone, in order to reach for and recover an object on sound cue, [the blind baby] will need a concept of the object in space" (Fraiberg et al., 1966, p. 348). Before the blind baby develops this, he will have to construct the *trajectory* of an object without ever having seen movement. The baby's experience with movement has always been with his own; therefore constructing a trajectory is a difficult problem for a congenitally blind child. The activities listed for stage IV (particularly activities along the body) should be begun early as general stimulation.

Probably because without vision he does not see objects at a distance in a variety of locations, the blind baby seems to closely associate objects and specific places. Multiple play spaces are important to keep up the expectation of finding objects and to keep the baby's exploratory habits flexible. Fraiberg et al. (1966, p. 350) note that a child who searches well in a given posture and place will not utilize his search patterns in an unmapped space. Play spaces need to be of a variety of sizes, geared to a variety of postures, and in a variety of locations about the house.

Developing mobility

Norris et al. found that 4- and 5-year-old blind children who achieved mobility were those provided with an optimum environment very early. She also concluded, "According to our findings, skill in orientation seems to bear little or no relationship to intellectual capacity as measured by the psychological tests or degree of vision" (Norris et al., 1957, p. 128). Adelson and Fraiberg (1972), reporting on gross motor development in blind infants, found a consistent pattern:

(1) Postural items testifying to neuromuscular maturation in control of head and trunk appeared within the age range for sighted children. (2) The mobility items which normally follow each postural achievement were considerably delayed. (3) The onset of self-initiated mobility was related to the demonstration of each child's ability to reach out and attain an object by sound cue alone. (p. 114)

No child in our sample demonstrated a form of prone progression or upright progression before he had first demonstrated . . . "reach on sound cue alone," that is, the coordination of ear and hand which enabled pursuit by hand and extension of the trunk toward an external lure. (p. 115)*

---

*From Adelson, E., and Fraiberg, S. Mouth and hand in the early development of blind infants. In J. Bosma (Ed.), *Third symposium on oral sensation and perception.* Springfield, Ill.: Charles C Thomas, Publisher, 1972, pp. 114 and 115.

The findings of Norris et al. and of Adelson and Fraiberg strongly suggest that it is *cognitive readiness,* accomplished through adequate stimulation (sensory-motor experience), that is the critical factor in the development of mobility among the congenitally blind.

Because convergence of auditory and tactile schema eventually will provide the rudimentary object concept that motivates the child to reach out and map space, associating sound and touch with gratifying experience is the first step in facilitating later gross motor development. Cuddling and talking are natural ways to begin. Incubator babies may resist (Brazelton, 1973), and the mother should gradually accustom the baby to being held.

As the baby begins to incorporate objects into play patterns, sounds including words should be associated with the objects. Musical toys, such as rattles, music boxes, tops, and musical balls, are useful to the extent that they are motivating and pleasurable. However, their sounds fail to tell anything distinctive about the object and may therefore not be as effective as objects made of materials that make distinctive sounds: for example, a set of aluminum measuring spoons and a tin cup for light sounds, wooden spoons and rolling pins, pots and pans for "heavy" ones. Tactile auditory experience with objects used about the house will help the child interpret household sounds, which may facilitate mapping, which would in turn facilitate reaching and crawling.

The periods of motor lag in the very young child's development probably represent periods of risk. Since a certain amount of cognitive growth is required to utilize a new posture, inertia is dangerous. Fraiberg's research indicates that the motor lags are reduced by intervention, but they are not eliminated (1974). It is important to remember that a lag is to be expected and that too much pressure toward movement for which a blind baby is cognitively or emotionally unready may produce regression.

As the blind baby progresses toward walking he loses his full-length tactile contact with the floor. Loss of perceptual surface is likely to produce anxiety. It is interesting that rolling from supine to prone (in which there is no loss of perceptual surface) is the one mobility item blind infants accomplish within the same range as nonhandicapped infants (Fraiberg, 1974). In attempting to motivate the blind child toward movement, the adult needs to be sensitive to the anxiety of the child, since the resulting disorientation can be frightening. Mannerisms such as tics or swayings and clinging are common before a child embarks on independent walking (Fraiberg, 1974).

The following activities can be effective in encouraging mobility in a blind baby. As the child accomplishes these tasks, the adult responds with pleased affection; this is as important as the activity itself.

ACTIVITIES TO FACILITATE GROSS MOTOR DEVELOPMENT

I. Use of prone position: To facilitate raising on the arms in the prone position, place the baby on his stomach and then engage in a pleasurable activity to keep him there. Do not just hold or return the baby to the prone position; blind babies typically dislike it. If they are unaccustomed to it their heads may feel heavy and they may experience difficulty breathing with their weight against their chest. However, since they need to develop postural flexibility, since they will have a better chance of retrieving objects, and since crawling begins with the prone position, the baby should become accustomed to this position.

   A. Play response games that reward turning the face upwards.
      1. Blow on the baby's face when it is upturned.
      2. Rub a finger beneath the baby's chin.
      3. Try to induce lateral tracking by using the rooting reflex. Rub a finger against the center of the baby's mouth, then against a corner of the

mouth. If the baby follows so that the finger is again in the center of the mouth, move the finger laterally.

B. Offer smells to reward raising the head and to motivate lateral tracking.
  1. Soak a piece of cotton with a variety of strong scents such as vanilla, peppermint, vinegar, perfume.
  2. Orange rind, lemon rind, onion skins, and oregano can be used. Don't limit activities to sweet soft smells; babies frequently like strong pungent odors.

II. Rolling from supine to prone position: This item occurs close to the timetable for sighted infants. Frequently it is little used because the baby dislikes the prone position. The point is to reward movement with contact and interest.
  A. Place the baby between objects of different textures. Bolsters or rolled towels may be covered with fake fur, crinkly vinyl, nylon stocking, sponge.
  B. Place the baby between objects of different temperatures wrapped in a towel. Watch the temperatures closely. Do not leave a baby to lie on a hot or cold object.
  C. Various objects interesting to manipulate may be tied to the crib bars so the baby can lie on his side and touch them.

III. Move the baby from a sitting position to supine and back, letting the baby hold your fingers while being raised up and down.

IV. Crawling: This will follow the baby's ability to reach on a sound cue alone. Since it begins with a continuation of a motor pattern for reaching, the activities to develop reach away from the body would be applicable here.

V. Pulling to standing position
  A. Practice with the baby holding his hands, accompanying with short songs and chants, such as "Up and down" or "So big!"
  B. Provide the baby with a small ladder securely fastened in a favorite play space. If he uses it, put similar ones in other spaces.
  C. Let him practice climbing up an adult's leg.

D. Put the desired object up on chair or other place where he can touch it and must rise to get it.

VI. Independent walking: These activities are begun after the child can support his own weight and makes stepping movements when his hands are held.
  A. Stand the baby on an adult's feet and, holding his hand, walk with him. A blind baby does not have models for walking. This activity lets the baby (1) practice walking, (2) maintain tactile contact along length of body, (3) share adult activity.
  B. Verbalize the goal and then go directly to it to make walking purposeful and rewarding. "Let's walk to Daddy." (Using a person as a goal permits the "goal" to call to the child.) "Let's walk to the refrigerator." "Your toy is in the chair. Let's get it."
  C. Allow plenty of opportunity for cruising: inside the playpen, outside the playpen, around low tables, along window ledges. Arrange chairs to make interesting and different spaces bounded by familiar objects. Leave very small gaps between objects so they may be easily bridged.
  D. Practice cruising with a gradually reduced series of supports.
    1. Hold one of the baby's hands and let the other hand maintain contact with familiar cruising territory (to get the body facing front, away from object and facing space).
    2. Hold one hand and go across open spaces, short distances at first, from one known thing to another.
    3. Use a favorite toy as a "transitional object," the adult holding one end of the toy and the child holding the other.

Forward motion poses problems for the blind toddler. Confusions in directionality may persist unusually long. Normal children frequently move backwards when they begin to crawl and walk. This is even more common in the blind toddler, who does not have the visual incentive for head-first movement. And, as Lowenfeld (1964) points out, a bump on the fanny is easier to take than a bump on the head. A blind child may walk with both hands outstretched; a more efficient posture is one arm bent across the chest and the other free to touch lateral and low objects. It is best to avoid attempting to modify a blind child's walking until the child develops confidence in his ability to get around independently in at least some places, with gradual extension of the territory within which he can move.

THE VISUALLY IMPAIRED CHILD IN THE NURSERY, KINDERGARTEN, OR PRIMARY CLASSROOM

There are two major areas in which the education of severely visually impaired children may be primarily the responsibility of a specialist with unique skills and training: *orientation and mobility training* (also termed *peripatology*) and *braille*. However, braille instruction may be quite

unnecessary and inappropriate if the child has the ability to read print. Some forms of mobility training, such as use of a guide dog, are undertaken when the individual is older and, again, are generally for persons with essentially no vision. In these areas, the direct services of one or more specialists (itinerant or resource teacher and mobility trainer) may be required, although the services of the latter specialist are sometimes performed by the more readily available itinerant teacher.

The two points to be emphasized here are (1) most visually impaired children have *some residual vision* that can be employed in learning and (2) regardless of the severity of the visual handicap, the young child who is visually impaired is more like nonhandicapped children in his needs than he is different. Specialized services may be provided by an itinerant

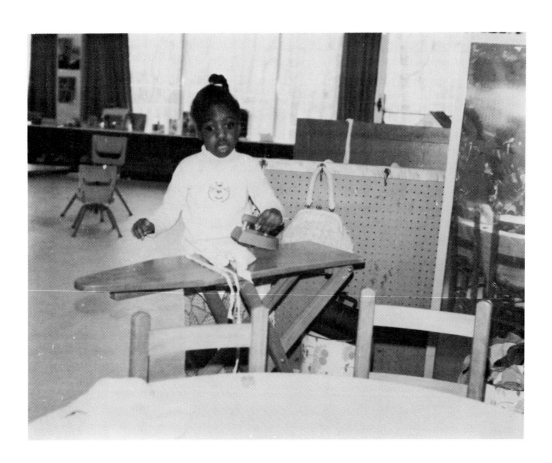

teacher to visually impaired children participating in regular programs.

Guidelines in teaching

There are, however, a number of special principles and suggested practices with which the teacher of young children can facilitate the learning and personal-social development of visually handicapped children, whether in a "specialized" or a "regular" setting. The following guidelines for the teacher in working with visually impaired children have been suggested by Rose C. Engel (1973):

1. The sense of touch helps to round out what the child hears.
2. "Puppy" is only a word until experiences of its wiggling, tail-wagging, cold nose, and wet tongue add meaning.
3. Listen and refuse a request if you need to but do not ignore it by not responding.
4. Many of the child's concepts are built and clarified by what he hears. Tell him where and why he is going before moving him. Talk about the type of flooring the child is crossing, such as "Now, you are on the grass (cement, asphalt, tile, wooden floors)."
5. Thoughtfully arrange the environment for free movement with safety. Encourage independence.
6. Tell him what is going on. When you touch him, tell him who you are. Teach other children to identify themselves when touching him.
7. Let him make as many movements as possible by himself. Tell him to "come to your voice." Let him open doors with his own effort, when possible.
8. Hearing is the child's main channel for learning. Don't be afraid of a sensory overload on this channel for the visually impaired.
9. Give him opportunities to help others. He is so often on the receiving end.
10. Expect the standards of courtesy and waiting expected of others. A handicap is not to be used to take advantage of the rights of others.
11. Care for him rather than always taking care of him.
12. Adapt the environment or situation so that each child can be part of the activities enjoyed by others in the group.
13. Work for communication and praise the child for each success, remembering that receptive language always precedes expressive language.
14. Use a multisensory approach in teaching.
15. Be a good language model.
16. Use many kinesthetic experiences and sensory art activities to encourage manual dexterity and manipulation.
17. Physically take the child through what is expected before asking him to do it alone.
18. Encourage the child to verbalize his needs rather than anticipating them. In a situation where there is some problem in relation to another child, help him use a verbal rather than a physical approach.
19. Work with the child's parents and therapists. Parents are the prime educators of their children.
20. Listen! Give him time to talk by waiting for his response and try not to answer for him.
21. Respect the contribution and opinion of each child, including the visually handicapped child.
22. Use concrete experiences.
23. Repeat, but *vary,* the situation to keep the child interested.
24. Encourage free physical movement. (pp. 10-11)

Role of play

Play is particularly important as an area of emphasis in its own right, not only for the blind child, but for all young children. In addition to encouragement, the child with a severe visual impairment will, at times, need active guidance and help. Not only in the classroom or center program, but also through guidance of the child's parents, the teacher can help the child use play as a principal vehicle for learning. Barry (1973), among others, has presented a number of specific enjoyable activities with which parents of partially sighted preschool children can help their child at home. Prescriptive use of activities, however, is not intended. Parents are encouraged to create enjoyable situations and to try to match activities with the child's developmental readiness as well as his interests.

The visually impaired child should not be deprived, at home or in school, of the joy of exploring, taking risks, discovering, and feeling a sense of mastery. It is the child who must structure experience in his own way; adults, activities, and materials can help. The teacher's and the parent's task is to sense when assistance is needed and when it is not, when "structure" will help and when it will interfere. These important adults, on whom the young child depends, must be able to *respond to him*. Their ability to respond can determine the child's growth in the ability to *initiate*. From a basis in *trust* we can help the visually impaired child move toward *autonomy, initiative,* and *industry*.

Blind mannerisms

The hand movements, rocking, bodily movements, and noises often observed in blind children have been termed "blindisms." Not all blind children employ such behaviors, however, and the teacher should not lose sight either of the fact that many nonhandicapped children may do these same things or of the possible adaptive significance of such behaviors (Halliday, 1970). The child may be seeking stimulation through his own body because of momentary frustration, boredom, or temporary inability to engage in meaningful environmental contact.

Sometimes the child may be using his own *sounds* as a means of orienting himself to objects in his physical environment. To the blind child, object perception may be associated with sensing a change in facial sensation. The sense of pressure on the face is probably the result of high-frequency echoes created by the blind person's movement (Lowenfeld, 1964). Since leather-soled shoes produce high-frequency sound waves, they may aid a child in developing object perception. Blind persons use echoes to determine how large

a room is and whether it is filled with objects or people. Blind children frequently use explosive sounds, such as lip smacking, popping or clicking their tongues, and finger snapping as navigational aids (Lowenfeld, 1964).

Nonhandicapped children frequently discharge tension through running. Because horizontal movement may seem hazardous to a blind child, he may resort to vertical movement for relief. Hopping in place and rocking are common. "Blindisms" may develop as vehicles for muscular release of tension (Smith et al., 1969). Age-appropriate play equipment may help a blind child discharge muscular tension and get exercise without resorting to regressive or stereotyped motor patterns: bouncers for active babies and swings, small slides, and gym bars across doorways for older children. *Developmental swings* are commercially available, for example, a two-seat swing that can be moved by the pumping of just one child. A small slide may be especially valuable since it demands a sequence of different motor patterns rather than the repetition of one. In addition, of course, a small indoor slide is less overwhelming initially and may help the child to overcome a fear of height.

Developing self-awareness and body image

The importance of increasing the child's awareness of his own physical self, through body-image training, has been stressed as paramount during the early childhood period (Cratty and Sams, 1968). Such awareness is basic to other areas of concept learning, personal-social development, and mobility. According to Cratty and Sams (summarized in Lydon and McGraw, 1973, p. 12), body image includes the following components:

Body planes: location of self in relation to body planes, that is, sides, front, and back
Body parts: ability to name and locate various parts of the body

Body movements: gross motor movement and various limb movement

Laterality: identification of left and right sidedness in addition to knowing left and right body parts

Directionality: projection out, away from the self, in terms of left-right, front-back, up-down; positioning oneself so that the left-right, etc. are nearest to the object's movement in relation to left-right, etc.; knowledge of objects in terms of left-right, etc. and relating objects to self in terms of left-right, etc.

Developing self-care skills

Self-help skills, including eating and dressing, are basic goals in working with young children who have severely impaired vision. Surprisingly, effective work in helping the child to achieve mastery of these skills is not always carried out as it could be, even in specialized programs (*Proceedings of National Seminar,* 1969, p. 71).

Helping the young child to master feeding, dressing, and undressing himself can be integrated with other goals, such as enabling the child to gain confidence in his ability to move safely and efficiently within his environment. A teacher in a nursery school serving primarily sighted children who have orthopedic or other physical handicaps has described this sort of integrated approach with "Jeannie," a blind 3-year-old girl who also had an orthopedic handicap:

Jeannie comes down the hall each morning accompanied by an adult for support, and proceeds to the locker room. Like all the other children in the group, Jeannie has her own locker in which to keep her belongings. Her locker is kept at the end of the row and is closest to the door to make it easy for her to find. She is encouraged to reach outward as she walks to feel for the objects that she passes on the way to the locker room. Teachers reinforce in words what she feels as she moves, "Now we're going to pass the rack of smocks . . . now you're feeling the door . . . can you feel how hard it is? . . . it's not soft like the smocks, is it?" Once she has located her locker she grabs with one hand to keep her balance and reaches

to unhook her coat with the other hand. Through verbalization and the sense of touch Jeannie now has learned to be independent in putting on and taking off her coat. She is also learning spatial relationships in regards to her school environment. (Taichnar, 1974, p. 26)

Similarly, helping Jeannie to gain confidence and skill in eating and in drinking from a cup was correlated with her learning to identify sounds, textures, and other attributes:

Teaching Jeannie to eat cookies came easier than getting her to drink milk or juice. Because paper cups are used at school, we felt that perhaps the unfamiliarity might be the problem. A cup that Jeannie was comfortable with at home was sent to be used at school. Jeannie was encouraged verbally to use her napkin and chew with her mouth closed. Teachers talked about the texture of foods and how they tasted. Discriminating between sounds that different foods made, how they differed in touch, and which smelled better were things that Jeannie picked up quickly and she was eager to report that the ice cream was cold and that the pretzel was salty. We also listened to the sound of cookies crunching and juice being swallowed. (Taichnar, 1974, p. 25)

Encouraging expression and communication

Although the child who has no vision is not able to see the results of creative art activity, he can nevertheless gain the same sense of accomplishment as can a sighted child, both in the product and the process of artistic expression (Dorward and Barraga, 1968; Granato, 1972). The teacher must be sensitive to a child's initial reservations or fears concerning use of art media, however, while at the same time supporting the child's efforts. Laurel Taichnar (1974) describes how Jeannie was helped to overcome her hesitance and thereby gain access to what became for her an important medium for expression:

Getting Jeannie to even become involved in the experience was difficult. Jeannie was still fearful of extending her hand to touch new objects or art materials. To further complicate the process, she had the tendency to rub her eyes after touching paste or paint.

For the experience to be meaningful, the art media would have to be something that was both tactile and kinesthetic. Hopefully, the process would be more important than the product. Equally important when choosing an activity for Jeannie to participate in was gearing the project to her level so that she could complete it independently. Therefore, a teacher would sit by her to encourage her and perhaps guide her hands in the beginning, but it ultimately was to be her work, not an adult's.

The first creative activities that were chosen to acquaint Jeannie with materials were fingerpaint, playdough, and paste. Teachers presented playdough as her first experience. It had to be presented several days in a row before any meaningful exploration of the medium was actually tried. Teachers explained verbally to Jeannie just what she would be feeling and just how it would feel.

To take a blind child's hand and pull it toward an object without any explanation can be very harmful to a fearful child and can cause regression. Jeannie talked about the playdough, repeating the teacher's words, "It's cold, it's soft," many times before actually making contact with it. Once she touched it, she withdrew her hand quickly. The day after her initial contact, however, she talked repeatedly about the playdough, using the words the teachers had used to describe it. Playdough was brought to her and she had greater success with it each day until she was comfortably able to explore and experiment with it (Taichnar, 1974, pp. 27-28).

Fostering conceptual development

Not only is vision basic to so much of young children's focused learning—the *mediator* of all other impressions gained through the senses (Dorward and Barraga, 1968)—it is the key to the tremen-

dous amount of *incidental* learning with which young children gain cognitive mastery over their environments. In the absence of full use of the visual modality, the visually impaired child relies more extensively on *touch* and *sound* in learning to identify and classify objects, discriminate differences, and understand functions and relationships.

Classroom materials selected for their tactual appeal are desirable. Beyond the level of experiencing different textures and tactile attributes and learning the names by which these can be described (soft, hard, fuzzy, scratchy, smooth, rough, cold, warm, etc.), similarities and contrasts can be noted. Concept learning can proceed to *differentiation* of an unlike object or material and ultimately to classification based on tactile attributes. Materials such as a *texture-matching puzzle* or *texture-matching board* (Dorward and Barraga, 1968) are commercially available, or these can be developed by the teacher. With such activities, it is important that the child be provided sufficient verbal cues and instructions. Generally the teacher helps the child learn to describe what he is touching. However, it is possible to confuse him with too much verbalization (Dorward and Barraga, 1968).

Helping visually impaired children with multiple handicaps

As with all other handicapping conditions, severe visual impairment becomes much more debilitating if it carries with it other problems. Whereas most visually impaired children can readily be integrated within a sighted educational setting, a blind child with severe emotional disturbance will probably require a highly specialized approach, one required by this *combination* of problems. A report of a symposium concerning the severely disturbed blind child, sponsored in the early 1960s by the American Foundation for the Blind (Gruber and Moor, 1963), described curricular, administrative, family casework, and other concerns to be addressed in educational planning for these children.

Children with a severe dual sensory handicap—deafness and blindness, frequently associated with maternal rubella —present very special problems. Discussion of their needs and of approaches in teaching these children is provided in Chapter 9. Children affected by rubella, as well as some others who have severe visual impairments, may be mentally retarded. A child with cerebral palsy may also have a visual handicap, as is discussed in Chapter 8.

Although multiple handicapping conditions obviously increase the challenge, it is possible that even a child with a severe visual impairment in combination with other handicaps may be appropriately and effectively served within a "regular" setting. Whether in a specialized or a regular day care, nursery, kindergarten, or primary grade program, the educational approach for the multihandicapped visually impaired child should be an individualized one. Citing other work on educational curriculums for multihandicapped children (Best and Winn, 1968; Rogow, 1973; Talkington, 1972), Natalie Barraga, (1976, p. 39) has identified the following major curriculum areas for the multihandicapped visually impaired:

Human interactions and relationships: pleasurable personal contact; acceptance and trust of teachers, peers, and others; recognition of self and others as human beings

Sensory awareness and stimulation: exposure to sounds, odors, taste, textures, and visual stimuli (if appropriate); discrimination and recognition of differences and likenesses

Physical movement and activity: body awareness and control (coactive movement with teachers); object manipulation and manual dexterity; exploratory movement in environment

Self-care and daily living skills: self-care skills dressing, and so forth; handling tools and materials; social play and interaction with others

Language development and communication: expression of personal needs and response to language (gesture, vocal, sign); word-object or word-action association; psychodrama, storytelling, and role playing (records and tapes); following basic commands and instructions; meaningful language expression

Work attitudes and habits development: assigned work duties; personal and group responsibility; field trips on bus and public transportation

Physical education and recreation: tumbling, running, jumping, swimming, adapted games, arts, and crafts

For the teacher who is responsible for one or more seriously visually impaired children, the most important resource is likely to be an itinerant teacher who has special training in this area. There are many possible modifications a teacher might make; however, these are specific to each child. The goal is for the child to be provided what he needs, by both the classroom teacher and the specialist, without calling undue attention to the child's handicap or providing a program that is more special than is necessary.

DISCUSSION QUESTIONS

1. What very important accomplishments in psychological development are associated with the first 2 years of life in which the visual sense plays a basic role? What kinds of early intervention can be provided infants and very young children with serious visual disabilities during this period?
2. What kinds of services might be provided a visually impaired child by an itinerant-consultant teacher? How might these services facilitate a visually impaired child's success in a regular education program?
3. What is mobility training? What is its role in the education of seriously visually impaired children?
4. Discuss some of the problems and complications in attempting to define the term "blindness."
5. What is the role of the teacher of young children in the identification of visual problems?

REFERENCES

Adelson, E., and Fraiberg, S. Mouth and hand in the early development of blind infants. In J. Bosma (Ed.), *Third symposium on oral sensation and perception*. Springfield, Ill.: Charles C Thomas, Publisher, 1972.

Ashcroft, S. Blind and partially seeing children. In L. M. Dunn (Ed.), *Exceptional children in the schools*. New York: Holt, Rinehart & Winston, Inc., 1963, pp. 413-461.

Ashcroft, S. C., and Harley, R. K. The visually handicapped. *Review of Educational Research,* 1966, *36,* 75-92.

Axelrod, S. *Effects of early blindness performance of blind and sighted children on tactile and auditory tasks.* New York: American Foundation for the Blind, 1959.

Barraga, N. C. *Visual handicaps and learning: A developmental approach.* Belmont, Calif.: Wadsworth Publishing Co., 1976.

Barry, M. A. How to play with your partially sighted preschool child: suggestions for early sensory and educational activities. *New Outlook for the Blind,* 1973, *67,* 457-467.

Best, J. T., and Winn, R. J. A place to go in Texas. *International Journal for the Education of the Blind,* 1968, *18,* 2-9.

Brazelton, T. B. Assessment of the infant at risk. *Clinical Obstetrics and Gynecology,* 1973, *16,* 361.

Carolan, R. H. Sensory stimulation and the blind infant. *New Outlook for the Blind,* March, 1973, *67,* 119-126.

Cratty, B. J., and Sams, T. *Body image of blind children.* New York: American Foundation for the Blind, 1968.

Dorward, B., and Barraga, N. *Teaching aids for blind and visually limited children.* New York: American Foundation for the Blind, 1968.

Engel, R. C. *Language motivating experiences for young children.* Van Nuys, Calif.: DFA Publishers, 1973.

Fraiberg, S. Parallel and divergent patterns in blind and sighted infants. *Psychoanalytic Study of the Child,* 1968, *23,* 264-300.

Fraiberg, S., Smith, M., and Adelson, E. An educational program for blind infants. *Journal of Special Education,* 1969, *3,* 121-139.

Fraiberg, S. Intervention in infancy: a program for blind infants. In B. Z. Friedlander, G. M. Sterritt, and G. E. Kirk (Eds.), *Exceptional infant* (Vol. 3). New York: Brunner/Mazel, Inc., 1974, pp. 40-62.

Fraiberg, S., Siegel, B. L., and Gibson, R. The role of sound in the search behavior of a blind infant. *Psychoanalytic Study of the Child,* 1966, *21,* 327-357.

Gearheart, B. R., and Weishahn, M. W. *The handicapped child in the regular classroom.* St. Louis: The C. V. Mosby Co., 1976.

Gottesman, M. A. A comparative study of Piaget's developmental schema of sighted children with that of a group of blind children. *Child Development,* 1971, *42,* 573-580.

Granato, S. *Day care: serving children with special needs* (No. 73-1063). Washington, D.C.: U.S. Department of Health, Education, and Welfare, Office of Child Development, 1972.

Gruber, K. F., and Moor, P. M. (Eds.). *No place to go.* New York: American Foundation for the Blind. 1963.

Halliday, C. *The visually impaired child—growth, learning, development—infancy to school age.* Louisville, Ky.: American Printing House for the Blind, 1970.

Higgins, L. C. *Classification in congenitally blind children.* New York: American Foundation for the Blind, 1973.

Inhelder, B., and Piaget, J. *The psychology of the child.* New York: Basic Books, Inc., 1969.

Jones, J. W. *Blind children, degree of vision, mode of reading* (Bulletin 24). Washington, D.C.: U.S. Office of Education, 1961.

Kephart, J., Kephart, C., and Schwarz, G. A journey into the world of the blind child. *Exceptional children,* 1974, *40,* 6.

Kirk, S. A. *Educating exceptional children.* Boston: Houghton Mifflin Co., 1972.

Lowenfeld, B. *Our blind children: growing and living with them.* (2nd ed.). Springfield, Ill.: Charles C Thomas, Publisher, 1964.

Lowenfeld, B. Psychological problems of children with impaired vision. In Cruickshank, W. M. (Ed.). *Psychology of exceptional children and youth.* Englewood Cliffs, N.J.: Prentice-Hall, Inc., 1971.

Lydon, W. T., and McGraw, M. L. *Concept development for visually handicapped children.* New York: American Foundation for the Blind, 1973.

National Society for the Prevention of Blindness. *N. S. P. B. fact book: estimated statistics on blind-ness and visual problmes.* New York: The Society, 1966.

Norris, M., Spaulding, P., and Brodie, F. H. *Blindness in children.* Chicago: University of Chicago Press, 1957.

Piaget, J. *The origins of intelligence in children.* New York: W. W. Norton & Co., Inc., 1952.

Piaget, J. Quantification, conservation, and nativism. *Science,* 1968, *162,* 976-979.

Proceedings of the National Seminar on Services to Young Children With Visual Impairment. New York: American Foundation for the Blind, 1969.

Rogow, S. M. Speech development and the blind multi-impaired child. *Education of The Visually Handicapped,* 1973, *4,* 105-109.

Smith, M. A., Chethik, M., and Adelson, E. Differential assessments of blindisms. *American Journal of Orthopsychiatry,* 1969, *39,* 807-817.

Taichnar, L. R. A blind child in a sighted program. *CAEYC Review,* Spring, 1974, pp. 24-30.

Talkington, L. W. An exploratory program for blind-retarded. *Education of the Visually Handicapped,* 1972, *2,* 33-35.

Tilman, M. H. The performance of blind and sighted children on the Wechsler Intelligence Scale for Children. *International Journal for the Education of the Blind,* 1967, *16,* 65-74, 106-112.

Witkin, H. A., Oltman, P. K., Chase, J. B., and Friedman, F. Cognitive patterning in the blind. In J. Hellmuth (Ed.), *Cognitive studies, II: deficits in cognition,* New York: Brunner/Mazel, Inc., 1971, pp. 16-46.

Zeibelson, I., and Barg, C. F. Concept development of blind children. *The New Outlook for the Blind,* 1967, *61,* 7.

Mild and moderate educational handicaps

CHAPTER 5

MENTAL RETARDATION

DEFINITION AND CLASSIFICATION

The concept of mental deficiency or subnormality has been with us for a long time. However, only in very recent times have educational programs been provided on a broad scale and under the auspices of public education. Before the mid-1970s, the public schools' statutory responsibility for the education of many mentally retarded children was not universally established.

Problems and concerns in classification for education

Many definitions and classification systems have been proposed concerning mental retardation. This diversity is probably in large part a result of the fact that many professional groups are involved in this field: educators, doctors, psychologists, sociologists, and lawyers, to name a few (Gearheart and Litton, 1975). Part of the problem inherent in definition and classification involves *relevance* and *function;* terminology that is meaningful and useful in one field is not necessarily of value in another.

"Mental deficiency," "subnormality," and "retardation" are probably substantial improvements over such terms as "feeblemindedness." And yet, for the educator, these terms are not directly related to instructional issues and concerns. Perhaps a concept such as *general learning disability* (Peterson, 1974), in contrast to *specific* learning disabilities, is more functional and relevant to the teacher.

Beyond definition of the general phenomenon of subnormal intellectual functioning, there have been attempts to classify according to degree of subnormality. Earlier systems used such terms as "moron," "imbecile," and "idiot," in descending order of ability level, to denote degrees of "feeblemindedness." It is hard to determine when or how such terms took on the distinctly derogatory connotation they now have. However, their use as technical terms today is rare and is professionally condemned, at least within the

Table 3. AAMD classification of measured intelligence*

Level	Intelligent quotient scores	
	Stanford-Binet	Wechsler Intelligence Scale for Children
Mild	68-52	69-55
Moderate	51-36	54-40
Severe	35-20	39-25
Profound	<20	<25

*From Gearheart, B. R., and Litton, F. W. *The trainable retarded: a foundations approach.* St. Louis: The C. V. Mosby Co., 1975, p. 23; modified from Grossman, H. J. (Ed.). *Manual on terminology and classification.* Washington, D.C.: American Association on Mental Deficiency, 1973, p. 18.

United States. They are examples of *labels* that are probably harmful. In any case, such classificatory labels as these bear no relationship to the work of the teacher—except, perhaps, to imply a high degree of hopelessness, of permanence of the condition, and of inability to benefit from education.

Two significant improvements on this terminology are reflected in a four-part classification indicating degree of retardation and another system reflecting the level of educational attainment and independence believed possible. The first of these systems, proposed by the American Association of Mental Deficiency, is summarized in Table 3.

It should be noted that this system is based entirely on *measured levels of intellectual functioning* using the two most widely accepted *individually administered* tests of general intelligence. They do not take into account assessment of the ability of the individual to function on a day-to-day basis. That is, they do not measure his observed ability to *adapt* to the demands of living. Social competence (Doll, 1953) has become an important index in the assessment of ability.

Measured intelligence levels have also been used for educational purposes. Although there are internal, statistical

Table 4. Educational classifications of mental retardation

Level	IQ range	Definition (Kirk, 1972, pp. 164-166)
Educable mentally retarded (EMR)	50-75/80	"Unable to profit sufficiently from a regular program but has potentialities in (1) academic subjects, (2) social adjustment, and (3) minimal occupational adequacies."
Trainable mentally retarded (TMR)	25/30-49	"Not educable in the traditional sense but has potentialities for training in (1) self-help skills, (2) social adjustment in the family, and (3) economic usefulness."
Totally dependent	Below 25/30	"Unable to be trained in total self-care, socialization or economic usefulness and requires almost complete care and supervision throughout life."

differences among standardized tests (reflected in the AAMD classification), the standard educational classification system does not reflect these differences (Table 4).

Recently, attempts to assess the individual's ability to function in society and to deal adequately with social and environmental demands have resulted in the development of measurement tools, such as the revised *AAMD Adaptive Behavior Scale* (Fogelman, 1975).

Limitations in measurement of intelligence

Although the definitions given in Table 4 refer to presumed potential level of educational, social, and occupational attainment, the traditional criteria for classification are nevertheless based on a test of intelligence, rather than on *adaptive behavior* in life experiences. Because formal intelligence tests are imperfect in their ability to measure potential to adapt to the demands of day-to-day living, among other limitations, federal regulations now require that educational placement decisions can no longer be made on the basis of a single test. A *multifactored assessment* is required.

Beside their limited scope, at least three other problems can be identified with the practice of classifying children for educational purposes on the basis of measured intelligence alone:

1. The *instability* of test scores, especially for young children (Sattler, 1974)
2. The *inaccuracy* of test scores, a result of inherent inadequacies of the tests, especially for minority group children (Dunn, 1968; Johnson, 1969), which often results in erroneous labeling and placement
3. The failure of a classification system based on test scores to denote *individual differences* in learning characteristics and abilities within a classification

All of these problems, which revolve around the measurement concepts of *validity* and *reliability,* involve highly complex issues. Even a cursory reading of the detailed analyses of the measurement of intelligence that have been provided makes clear the principle that intelligence tests, though useful, are imperfect. (See, for example, Guilford and Hoepfner, 1971, for a comprehensive treatment of intelligence and its measurement.)

For practical purposes, the teacher of young children should bear in mind at least the following guidelines:

1. An "IQ" is an indication of what the child *has already learned,* which may or may not, for a given child, also predict well what he *can* learn in the future.
2. Fluctuations in IQ scores are "normal" and expectable.
3. The older the child, the greater the likelihood that an IQ score can pre-

dict reasonably well what IQ will be if measured at adulthood. *Measured IQs of young children are highly unstable, compared to those of older children* (Bloom, 1964).

4. IQ tests (for children older than 3 years) place great emphasis on certain language skills.
5. Children with similar measured IQs do not necessarily learn at the same rate or in the same way.
6. IQ tests may, in subtle as well as in obvious ways, discriminate against minority group children and children with "different" prior experiences from those on whom the test was standardized.

Much more could be said. The limitations and flaws of IQ tests for the identification and classification of children for educational purposes have been well documented. Yet, such tests, *if used appropriately, interpreted conservatively, and regarded as but one aspect of a multifactored assessment approach,* may be of educational value. Are IQ tests "dangerous?" Do teachers base their *expectancies* of what a child can do on their knowledge of his "IQ," teach him accordingly, and therefore get the very results they expect —a self-fulfilling prophecy (Rosenthal and Jacobson, 1968)? Although some teachers may do this, there is evidence that many more do not (Fleming and Anttonen, 1970).

Summary: the concept of mental retardation

Attempts to define and to explain mental retardation have paralleled, in many ways, the study of human intelligence itself. Many issues concerning mental retardation are inseparably related to important questions about intelligence?

1. Is intelligence a *general* trait (Spearman, 1904; Terman and Merrill, 1960), or does it comprise many separate abilities: "primary mental abilities" (Thurstone, 1938) or multifactored dimensions (Guilford, 1959; Guilford and Hoepfner, 1971)?

2. To what extent is intelligence predetermined by hereditary influences, and to what extent can it be modified by environmental factors such as child-rearing or teaching practices?
3. How important is "intelligence" to a person's ability to adapt adequately to his or her physical and social environment? What are the minimum competencies a person needs?
4. What do intelligence tests measure? What are their capabilities and their limitations in assessing the adaptive competence of children and in predicting future levels of adaptive competence?

Differences in the functional ability of children to reason and solve problems, function independently, and adapt to the environment undeniably exist in any case. In using the term "mental retardation" in this chapter and elsewhere throughout this book, we are recognizing such individual differences. Because of the danger of *incorrectly* identifying young children as retarded, some researchers and educators (for example, Weikart, 1971) have proposed abandoning the concept as a diagnostic classification for childhood problems in learning and adaptation. The position is taken here, however, that, like intelligence tests, the concept of mental retardation is useful and meaningful for purposes of education. However, like the tests with which it has been so closely identified in the past, this concept has very often been misused and misinterpreted.

Causes of mental retardation

General points of view regarding mental retardation and its causes are of two types (Haring, 1974):

1. *Defect theories:* theories that attribute retarded development and behavior mainly to *problems within the individual,* such as genetic influences, brain damage, and chromosomal and endocrinal anomalies. (Certain syndromes, such as phenyl-

ketonuria [PKU] and Down's syndrome, are known to be associated with *intra-organismic* factors.)

2. *Deficit theories:* theories that emphasize *environmental,* rather than intra-organismic (or constitutional), factors. Such influences include inadequate socialization practices and sensory or affectional deprivation (Spitz, 1945; Bowlby, 1966).

It is readily apparent that these two emphases parallel differences in views concerning intelligence itself (Hunt, 1961; Guilford and Hoepfner, 1971). As in the case of intelligence, influential factors underlying retardation are apparently multiple and interactive.

One major dichotomy which has often been emphasized is the distinction between *exogenous* retardation (associated with brain injury) and *endogenous, or familial,* retardation (including all retarded individuals whose subnormality is not associated with known, presumed, or suspected brain damage). Such a distinction would be useful to the extent that brain-injured and non-brain-injured children manifest different characteristics and needs and that different approaches in education, management, or treatment are effective. However, research has not totally borne out the view that such differences are consistently found, nor the belief that differential educational approaches would be effective for brain-injured and non-brain-injured retarded children. On the contrary, Gallagher's classic study indicated the greater educational significance of differences among individuals, as compared to differences between the two groups (Gallagher, 1957).

Phenomenon of pseudoretardation

The term "pseudoretardation" has been applied to two general types of children: (1) those whose retarded behavior is actually a *defense* erected in response to emotional conflict, and (2) those whose failure to develop optimally is a result of extreme sensory, affectional, or experien-

tial *deprivation* during the early years of life (Kessler, 1966). This term has been criticized because of its implication that a distinction between "real" and secondary retardation can be reliably made, or that differential education and treatment approaches are indicated. Jane Kessler (1966) summarizes the issue in these words:

The diagnostic differentiation between primary and secondary, or innate and psychogenic, retardation is not easy to make, nor is it as important as commonly believed, *provided the diagnosis is an ongoing process combined with a remedial program.* A child who exhibits both mental and emotional problems needs treatment of both, no matter which came first. (p. 179)

In a related sense, there are children whose performance on ability or other language tests (and often on other types of measures as well) is *depressed* by limited or harmful early experiences. The *behavioral repertoire* or experiential readiness of these children may appear quite restricted. However, with effective intervention, there is the potential that future learning and positive development can proceed unimpeded by handicaps. Such children might be thought of as pseudo-retarded (Hendrick, 1975) in the sense that they do not appear as intellectually capable as they actually are. It is, of course, necessary to distinguish *limited* experiences from *different* experiences (Cole and Bruner, 1972).

SCOPE OF THIS CHAPTER

As a pragmatic matter, we shall be concerned in this chapter with the teaching of young children who might be classified as mildly and moderately mentally retarded. It should be noted that this will encompass not only the range designated by educable mental retardation, but also much of the trainable mental retardation range as well. Implicitly therefore, we are rejecting this *categorical* distinction while affirming the greater significance of individual differences regardless of "category." The position is presented that knowledge of individual differences among young mentally retarded children is more important to the teacher than is knowledge of collective characteristics.

In the sections that follow, principles and practices are recommended for teachers who work with mentally retarded children in a preschool or primary program, whether "regular" or specialized. Five major themes are predominant:

1. The need for an individualized approach
2. The importance of emphasis on language development
3. The importance of a cognitive developmental approach
4. The importance of fostering positive emotional and social development
5. The value of meaningful parent involvement and teacher-parent teamwork

The final section of this chapter presents a brief discussion of an extraordinarily promising "new frontier": programming for infants and toddlers. In that discussion, each of the five themes will be again apparent. However, as in all infant intervention, it is the parent-child dimension that is particularly emphasized, together with the roles this dimension implies for professionals.

Theme of individual differences

The most unfortunate error in thinking—and in practice—among those concerned with the mentally retarded child is the *assumption of homogeneity* among these children. This means assuming that what retarded children have in common simultaneously marks them as qualitatively different from "normal" children and outweighs in importance the differences that exist within the retarded group. Edward Zigler (1966) has criticized the "difference orientation," the point of view that the retarded are fundamentally different, in a qualitative sense, from the rest of us. This tendency to assume a degree of similarity among retarded children that does not exist has to some extent

characterized many educational programs for mentally retarded youngsters. The "difference orientation," while implying that retardates are qualitatively different from nonretardates in some way, simultaneously implies that retardates are like each other with respect to that characteristic. For example, retarded children might be seen as having difficulty with memory functions (Ellis, 1963), perception processing or discrimination (Spivack, 1963), attention (Zeaman and House, 1963), or other psychological processes. Some psychological theories of mental retardation emphasize the differences between the concrete approach to learning and problem solving observed in retarded persons, stressing the difference between concrete and abstract thought (Goldstein and Scheerer, 1941).

That "differences" between the retarded and the nonretarded child can be found is undeniable. Zigler (1966) and other researchers (for example, Cromwell, 1961), however, note that the *life experiences* a retarded child has, which may have included institutional living, may play a large role in accounting for some of these characteristics. An example is the child's often-noticed great desire to please adults.

Not only *interindividual* differences (differences between children), but also *intraindividual* differences (Kirk, 1972), are found among retarded children. Each retarded child, like a child of normal or superior intelligence, manifests a pattern of strengths and weaknesses, as well as unique past experiences, interests, desires, fears, and all the other characteristics that combine to produce individuality. Children identified as having learning disabilities are generally recognized to have individual learning profiles and therefore to require individualized teaching approaches based on educational diagnosis. However, frequently neither the diversity among the mentally retarded nor the diversity of learning characteristics within an individual child is reflected in the way these children are taught.

The first requisite in teaching young mentally retarded children is thus the development and use of a diagnostic approach. This does not necessarily imply that the teacher should make extensive use of standardized tests. Such tests may be part of the teacher's diagnostic approach, but educational diagnosis is likely to rely even more heavily on observation and task analysis or on other informal procedures.

Diagnosis, then, is used for educational purposes in a different sense than that of determining what condition a child "has" or what "type" of child he is, although this is frequently an important aspect of the diagnostic process. For example, certain types of medical treatment or specialized therapy may be indicated, depending on the particular anomaly. However, the most useful purpose of diagnosis in teaching the child effectively is to reveal individual patterns of strengths and limitations, or deficits, of specific skills and disabilities.

ATTRIBUTES OF EFFECTIVE INSTRUCTIONAL APPROACHES

In general, the suggestions that follow are applicable to children within an age range of approximately 3 years through 8 years and who are functioning within the range of mild to moderate mental retardation. It will be readily apparent, however, that the general instructional strategies discussed are applicable to all young children, including those of normal and even superior intelligence. This fact illustrates that modes of learning in early childhood are, to some extent, universal. However, whereas many children are able to create for themselves the optimal conditions for learning, for a great many, including those we characterize as mentally subnormal or as lagging in intellectual development, it is necessary to structure the learning situation to ensure that the desired conditions are met. This suggests a more active, and a more directive, role for the teacher. Nevertheless, among the mentally retarded, as with all young children, it is the child himself who ultimately provides the "structure" by means of which learning can occur.

Teaching should be based on diagnostic assessment of the individual child

That the teacher should be a diagnostician does not mean necessarily that he or she should administer formal tests, although these have a legitimate role. Basically, this principle implies that each child's "program" is based on a determination of his unique profile of strengths and weaknesses, preferences, and learning styles, rather than exclusively on some predetermined "curriculum." It was the need felt by professionals to identify precisely a child's learning difficulty that led to the development of tests, such as the Illinois Test of Psycholinguistic Abilities (ITPA) (Kirk et al., 1968). Tests such as the ITPA enable the teacher to prescribe specific tasks and activities that match a child's level of readiness in certain aspects of learning, address a particular area of difficulty, or capitalize on specific strengths. The ITPA is specifically noted here not because it is necessarily endorsed as a means teachers should employ, but because of the concept of an intra-individual difference profile it illustrates.

Whatever the approach that is used, the teacher's task of carrying out an individualized program implies the need for systematic, ongoing assessment. *Meaningful assessment is the key to individualized prescriptive teaching.* A variety of tests and scales for young children can aid in implementing diagnostic-prescriptive teaching. One of the best sources of information concerning various kinds of tests for young children is *Tests and Measurements in Child Development,* a two-volume compilation prepared by Orval G. Johnson (1976).

A systematic diagnostic and assessment approach enables the teacher to establish appropriate objectives and implement appropriate teaching procedures. For example, Morrison and Potheir (1972) found that task selection based on a detailed developmental analysis resulted in significantly greater gains in language, motor, and social development by 4-year-old retarded children than when the activities were randomly provided, even if accompanied by praise and encouragement.

Although there may exist some set of skills or competencies that are determined to be within the reach of and appropriate for all children in a group, the road to attainment of each of these is unique to the individual. The teacher must first assess "where the child is"—that is, determine what his *entry-level* competencies are—to decide what opportunities should next be presented. Hunt (1961) has termed this educational problem—determining what learning experience will present just the right level of difficulty (neither too easy nor beyond his capabilities to achieve success)—the *problem of the match*. The task should present an optimal level of incongruity or dissonance, just sufficient to arouse curiosity and elicit the desire "to find out," but not so difficult as to frustrate and impede exploration.

Solving the problem of the match is especially important in teaching young children of low measured learning ability, since so many stereotypes exist concerning their learning characteristics. Furthermore, it is easy to be deluded by *apparent* behaviors, so that what the child actually *can* do (or cannot do) may be overlooked. It is necessary to delve beneath the surface and to present tasks that provide the opportunity to observe the child in the process of problem solving. How does he approach the task? What expectancies does he appear to have? Does he test hypotheses? What features of the stimulus situation capture his attention?

The problem of the match refers also to a motivational match. The diagnostic process involves determination of the strength for the child of alternative sources of motivation, both extrinsic and intrinsic. Is the child able to pursue a task primarily to gratify his curiosity, to find out the solution, or to achieve the satisfaction of accomplishment (intrinsic motivation)? If such sources do not provide sufficient motivation, is the child at a developmental level at which social rewards (teacher or peer group approval) will be influential and can provide the impetus for him to perform? Or is some more immediate and tangible reinforcer needed? It is a mistake to assume that all children are "self-powered" learners, especially those who have already experienced a history of failure. It is equally wrong to assume that some external reward is automatically needed if the child is functioning at a lower developmental level than most others of his age. What is needed is a systematic assessment of the individual child's motivational profile, together with his unique pattern of strengths and weaknesses, a compilation of his prior accomplishments, and a determination of his preferred learning style or approach.

Generally, *criterion-referenced* rather than *norm-referenced* tests are more useful to the teacher in assessing the child's progress and in determining objectives (Hammill and Bartel, 1975). I had the privilege of working with teams of teachers of educable mentally retarded children in designing and field testing an assessment procedure known as the *Developmental Learning Profile* (1975). The profile is made up of sequentially ordered accomplishments, called *instructional objectives*, and divided into the following curriculum areas at four major instructional levels (primary, intermediate, junior high, and senior high):

1. Physical and perceptual development
2. Language arts
3. Mathematics
4. Science
5. Social studies

6. Career development
7. Personal-social development

The teacher notes for each specific objective (that is, each task, skill, or other accomplishment) whether the behavior in question is *consistently present, emerging,* or *not present.* Using a system such as this one, a teacher can maintain an ongoing record of each individual child's progress in terms of skills that are directly relevant to his classroom learning. This record can be used in setting objectives, selecting tasks, and conferring with the child, parents, or other professionals.

The next two "principles" to be discussed relate directly to, and follow from, the principle of individualization through a diagnostic-prescriptive approach. These principles involve *task analysis* and *successive approximations,* or steps, in working with a child toward his eventual mastery of a major skill.

Teaching should follow a plan based on task analysis

Assessment of a child's current level of functioning serves to indicate what goals are appropriate and a time within which each is capable of accomplishment, as well as the alternative routes through which

these goals may be attained. Learning goals, in most instances, can be analyzed in terms of their components to suggest a sequence of *enroute objectives,* that is, specific bits leading to the attainment of the general, or terminal, objective. Each instructional activity can be analyzed in terms of the *child performance* behaviors required (for example, grasp pencil, mark with pencil, mark within indicated space). It is thus possible for the teacher to determine which specific component of a learning task is currently difficult for the child and which ones he performs consistently well. Through such analysis, the teacher can provide the opportunity for the child to progress at an appropriate pace through an ordered sequence of steps that lead to the ability to perform a complex act. Marc Gold, among others, has demonstrated the effectiveness of task analysis in accomplishing a wide variety of teaching objectives with retarded children and adults (Gold and Scott, 1971).

Teaching should proceed by means of successive steps

Frank Hewett (1968) points out that many of our educational failures may be due to the "bucketful" approach we often employ, whereas a "thimbleful" approach would be more likely to bring success. By this he means that global goals are difficult to achieve; these must be broken down into the successive steps required to achieve them. "Yard by yard, life is hard; inch by inch, it's a cinch!" goes the old adage. This, incidentally, applies both to the child and to the teacher.

Teaching should be success oriented and provide reinforcement

The Skinnerian phrases "the principle of errorless training" and "successive approximations" suggest a scientific basis for that other old saying, "Nothing succeeds like success." As the child masters each small accomplishment, not only is his skill repertoire successfully expanded, but he also enjoys the satisfaction of experiencing success.

Learning materials should be familiar and meaningful to the child

If the child can relate his past experiences to the task, both his interest in it and his confidence in his ability to succeed stand to be increased, unless, of course, the associations that it evokes are unpleasant or painful. Klein and Safford (1977) found that trainable mentally retarded pupils (IQ range from 30 to 50) both acquired and retained classification concepts of size and color when experience and training were provided with meaningful play materials illustrating these attributes.

We sometimes are unaware of the *abstract* quality of many of the materials and learning tasks provided for young children. The test of a child's mastery of a concept is indeed his ability to apply it when confronted with novel situations (Sigel, 1964). Experiences at home, on trips to a store with his parents, etc. provide unending opportunities for meaningful learning.

In describing a concept teaching approach for preschool-age mentally retarded children, Bellamy and Bellamy (1974, p. 115) cite the following definition of the goal of concept teaching:

A concept has been taught when any or all members of the concept set are correctly identified (responded to in the same way), even though some were not in the teaching set, and any or all not members of the concept set are responded to in a different way. (Becker et al., 1971, p. 238)

Conceptual behavior involves the child's ability to *abstract* a principle and to *apply* that principle in an appropriate way (Rosenberg, 1963). However, the steps required for a mentally retarded child to be able to acquire and use concepts may be many. Working from the familiar to the novel may substantially facilitate this process from the standpoint of motivation as well as understanding.

Learning begins with attention

In Frank Hewett's (1968) hierarchy of developmental levels of learning readiness, the first level is that of attention. Hewett points out the fallacy of expecting complex learning to occur in the absence of this basic condition. Attention cannot be assumed; it must be planned for and ensured by the structuring of the learning environment, provision of appropriate materials, and close monitoring of the child's response. Both visual and auditory distractors may tend to reduce attention, and the child may have great difficulty in avoiding responding to extraneous stimuli (distracting sounds, an array of seductive objects, interesting events) that have more potency than the task at hand. Some materials, particularly those employed in the Montessori approach, are especially designed to focus the child's at-tention on relevant features. Care should be given to the overall physical design of the classroom (as is discussed in Chapter 11), the placement of learning materials within it, the characteristics of the materials themselves, and the establishment of routines and expectations. All of these factors can support or interfere with the child's efforts to attend to the task.

Learning is enhanced through the child's active involvement

The advantages of manipulable, three-dimensional learning materials have been so well established and described that there is little need to recite them here. The wisdom of an ancient Chinese proverb is borne out in the writings of

Friedrich Froebel, John Dewey, Maria Montessori, Susan Isaacs, Jean Piaget, and many other observers of the learning processes of children. To *touch* objects or to smell and taste them enables children to experience their properties. To pour or stack or combine items enables the child to obtain direct sensory and kinesthetic feedback from his own actions and from materials with which and on which he acts.

Multisensory experiences enhance learning

Years ago, Grace Fernald (1943) described a teaching approach that incorporated simultaneous involvement of four modalities: *visual, auditory, kinesthetic,* and *tactile*. Her method was developed primarily as a means of working with children who had particular problems in mastering reading skills, and it represented a significant departure from practices used at that time (and, regrettably, today as well!). Traditionally, methods of teaching reading have tended to emphasize either visual properties or auditory properties. However, Fernald advocated a method by which "input" is provided simultaneously through four modalities. The child *sees* a word, he *hears* it said, he *forms* it, and he *touches* it.

A significant aspect of Fernald's approach was her insight that we do not employ our senses in isolation. Rather, they enhance and support each other. Young children characteristically approach their world in a sensory-dominated manner (Bruner et al., 1966) and are generally able to construct for themselves a great many associations of sounds, sights, smells, tastes, and notions of the way things feel. A child whose vision or hearing is impaired requires external assistance in associating impressions and events. In fact, to some extent virtually every early childhood classroom consciously incorporates experiences (and lessons) intended to assist children in *integrating* the data they receive through

their senses. *Words* for the way things feel or look or sound or smell or taste and for relationships between things (bigger, heavy, dark) provide keys in this process of association and integration. Young mentally retarded children are also engaged in the process of making meaningful the myriad sensations and experiences they encounter in the course of any single day. Planned inclusion of learning experiences via all the senses, with much opportunity for talking about what is experienced, is an important element in their learning.

Learning is expressive as well as receptive

A major area of emphasis in teaching young children of presumed mental subnormality is that of language development. We speak of language *development* rather than merely language *skills* for good reason. Language is an evolving system, incorporating several interdependent processes that expand as the child learns. To teach specific skills in isolation is to lose sight of this interdependence.

A teacher can first assess the linguistic functioning of the young retarded child through unobtrusive observation of his play. Play has been called the child's work, that is, the principal means he uses to structure his world. It has also been referred to as the universal language of childhood. To an observant teacher, what the child does with play materials such as dolls, a housekeeping corner, wheeled vehicles, or blocks provides clues not only to what he is thinking *about* but to the *way* in which he thinks. When a young child "feeds the baby" or dons an apron, he is acting out his mental interpretation of events he has observed and experienced.

We sometimes concentrate so much on what we want to get into the child that we overlook the principle that learning proceeds "from the inside out" as well as "from the outside in." In the area of language, for example, contemporary psycholinguistics posits an innate predisposition for language acquisition—a "language acquisition device" (Lenneberg, 1967; Chomsky, 1965, 1968). Psycholinguists note with what ease and in what predictable, universal fashion children throughout the world, regardless of specific language differences, acquire in succession the set of syntactic structures that enable them to use language.

Piaget describes the progression from innate reflexive *schemas,* as the child interacts with his physical and social environment, into *cognitive structures.* Hans Furth (1969), who has attempted to translate Piaget's theories into educational applications, advocates placing the emphasis on *representational expression* through all means available. These means include such areas as expressive or dramatic play, recounting or narrating events in words, mime, and art media. Finger painting or brush painting, singing, and building are valid means of expression.

In the area of reading instruction, two influential systems—Sylvia Ashton-Warner's (1963) and Roach Van Allen's "language experience approach" (Allen and Allen, 1970)—are based on the principle of beginning with what the child *produces,* or *expresses,* what is "inside" him. Reading is thus seen as an advanced phase of the development of language, a process that extends language into a new but related area of experience. It should be noted that some leaders in the field of mental retardation (White, 1976) believe that the value of reading in teaching many of these children may be overemphasized. Reading is seen as one dimension of language and communication, rather than as an end in iteself.

Practice and "overlearning" are essential

The psychological principle of "overlearning" has long been believed to be especially applicable in teaching the mentally retarded. The difficulties of retarded youngsters in holding or retaining newly acquired skills and knowledge has been a major source of concern to their teachers, and several theories have been advanced to account for these apparent "memory deficits" (see, for example, Ellis, 1963; Kessler, 1970; Moss and Mayer, 1975). Mere repetition, however, is insufficient for any child. If the child has truly mastered the skill or concept or idea, like the familiar example of riding a bicycle, it is "there," in his repertoire. Sometimes, even though "criterion behavior" has been demonstrated by the child, the achievement may be spurious. He may have been performing randomly or may be unable to duplicate the correct performance after a time interval. It needs to be determined that he can perform the task *consistently.*

With young children, the child's own inclinations may sometimes provide an important guide as to how much more exposure to an activity will be valuable or *endurable.* As Piaget has observed (Piaget, 1954; Piaget and Inhelder, 1969) young children typically employ *repetitive play* as a means of *assimilating* an experience, that is, truly internalizing it so that it becomes a part of cognitive structure. The child should be encouraged and certainly allowed to *rehearse* events, to repeat, to retell, to do over and over, if he wishes, for this is his most effective way of understanding and internalizing his understanding.

Teacher creativity in providing opportunities for transfer and generalization are preferable to drill. Excessive repetition of the same task leads to perseveration, rather than learning.

CONTENT AREAS FOR A COGNITIVE DEVELOPMENTAL CURRICULUM

The intent here is not to design a "curriculum" per se, but rather to identify some of the key dimensions of cognitive functioning within the early childhood years as appropriate targets for educational intervention with young mentally retarded children. The goal of cognitively oriented teaching is not to "cure" mental

SOME SUGGESTED OBJECTIVES FOR PRESCHOOL RETARDATES IN SIX BROAD AREAS OF DEVELOPMENT*

Perceptual-motor development and physical fitness

Preschool retarded children should be able to:
1. Attend to visual stimuli and discriminate among sizes by selecting the larger(est) and smaller(est); among colors; and among shapes, triangles, squares and circles
2. Control, associate, and coordinate various body parts in visual-motor activities
   a. Maintain proper postural adjustment in general body balance and locomotion, such as actions involved in walking, jumping, hopping, skipping, and galloping
   b. Integrate various muscle systems involved in throwing, pushing, pulling, and swinging
   c. Coordinate arms and legs in movements which involve unilateral, bilateral, and crosslateral activities
   d. Locate objects in space and be able to translate from spatial to temporal dimensions, such as actions involved in batting a ball, hitting a punching clown, or catching a floating balloon
3. Respond to stimuli in a motoric way or through gesture
   a. Locomote about the environment (same as in 2a above)
   b. Express some skill in using both sides of the body in activities involving regular and irregular patterns of rhythm
   c. Express a concept or process (such as in fishing or driving a car) by using gestures
   d. Begin using small muscle groups especially in activities which involve prehension, grasping, manipulation, and other finger movements
   e. Become involved in the use of the total body in vigorous types of activities
4. Become relatively more physically fit
   a. Develop an interest in participating in activities which will help to develop speed, strength, body flexibility, and power
   b. Relax at appropriate times with less manifest tension, fatigue, and hyperactivity

Verbal communication

Preschool retarded children should be able to:
1. Attend to, listen for, and discriminate among various auditory stimuli
   a. Differentiate between high and low sounds, loud and soft sounds, and combinations of these
   b. Identify similarities and differences in the sounds of various parts of words
   c. Listen for familiar words and use them as clues to gain meaning from a story
   d. Listen for words that express various types of action and activities
2. Develop an increasingly more elaborate speaking vocabulary:
   a. Use different synonyms to express a concept or meaning
   b. Distinguish among the temporal meanings of certain words, e.g., as in today, tomorrow, yesterday, not yet, now, and never
   c. Connect the meaning between a concrete object and an abstract intention, e.g., as in hug and affection, hit and unkind, book and learn, or ladder and climb
3. Express ideas in an increasingly more effective way
   a. Organize their expression of an idea, story, or thought in a logical order
   b. Use proper words to express an idea
   c. Speak with increasing levels of fluency, pertinence, and elaboration of ideas
   d. Willingly engage in meaningful discussions with peers, parents, teachers, and other adults

---

*From Smith, R. M. *An introduction to mental retardation.* New York: McGraw-Hill Book Co., 1971, pp. 110-112. Used with permission of McGraw-Hill Book Co.

4. Develop increasingly more precision in speaking with clarity, comprehensible enunciation, and with satisfactory voice quality

Cognitive skills
Preschool retarded children should be able to:
1. Develop positive attitudes toward activities which involve school work, learning new facts and information, solving problems by using new knowledge and past experiences
2. Become increasingly more sensitive toward their surroundings and initiate more complex contacts with them and with those individuals, situations, and components of their environment which foster inquiry, interest, and curiosity
3. Profit, in terms of demonstrating increasingly higher level skills for solving problems, by widened experiences, explanation, intentional instruction, suggestions, and evaluation of performances
4. Value independent thinking and the contribution of one's own ideas to group situations
5. Widen and increase their repertoire of general information, performance in associating and remembering, the comprehension and meaning of ideas, the basic components involved in quantitative thinking, and the evaluation of alternative solutions to problems

Self-care and emotional development

Preschool retarded children should be able to:
1. Develop positive attitudes and feelings toward self-care including areas such as feeding, toileting, and grooming
2. Establish routine patterns and a satisfactory level of skill in routine health habits including such areas as brushing teeth, washing hands, toileting, blowing and wiping nose, and resting when fatigued
3. Understand why safety is essential in work and play and employ a cautious approach in activities which are potentially unsafe for himself or for others
4. Exercise some control over their emotions
   a. Tolerate and profit from constructive assistance from adults with whom they are familiar
   b. Increase in self-control and in tolerance for frustration
   c. Decrease in the incidence of the use of defense mechanisms as reactions to problems and increase in the incidence of attempting to deal with problems in a more emotionally healthy manner.

Social skills

Preschool retarded children should be able to:
1. Show respect for the personal and property rights of others
   a. Distinguish between one's own rights and belongings and those of others
   b. Understand that rules are helpful to everyone
   c. Defend their rights in socially appropriate ways
2. Increase the quantity and quality of interpersonal interactions with other children
   a. Engage in cooperative play, mutual activities, and participate in group projects
   b. Assume responsibilities as a leader within a group and willingly allow other children to become leaders without opposition or conflict
3. Increase spontaneous contacts with adults and exhibit interest in interacting with the teacher and other authority figures
   a. Maintain a balance between independence from and dependence on adults for solution of problems, issues, or controversies
   b. Develop a comfortable style in interacting with adults

Continued.

SOME SUGGESTED OBJECTIVES FOR PRESCHOOL RETARDATES IN SIX BROAD AREAS OF DEVELOPMENT—cont'd

Social skills—cont'd

Preschool retarded children should be able to:
  c. Show respect for authority figures and adults
  d. Exhibit basic social skills involving the proper use of manners in usual social situations in which preschool children might be exposed
  e. Be thoughtful and considerate of others

Aesthetic and creative development

Preschool retarded children should be able to:
  1. Willingly participate in numerous and various experiences and activities in areas involving opportunities for artistic expression, e.g., as in painting, singing, clay work, acting, playing instruments, finger plays, and so on
  2. Feel free from all evaluations which are externally imposed and recognize that one is free to express himself artistically in any fashion he desires, so long as it is socially acceptable
  3. Develop any specific skills or competencies as fully as possible within limits of personal preference

---

retardation; it is to enhance cognitive functioning. The level of highest attainment may differ, as does the rate of progression through the sequential stages of cognitive growth (Stephens et al., 1971). However, young mentally retarded children appear to proceed through the same developmental progression as do nonretarded youngsters (Inhelder, 1944/1968; Robinson and Robinson, 1965). In a review of research studies in which Piagetian tasks and concepts were applied to mentally retarded children, general consensus was found on these points (Klein and Safford, 1977).

The essence of a cognitive developmental approach can be described through three general principles:

1. The child plays an active role in "structuring" his own learning.
2. There are conceptual dimensions—pivotal concepts and ways of understanding and of knowing—that underlie specific skills and items of knowledge.
3. Observation of what the child *does*, how he proceeds, and the questions he asks provide the best insights concerning what he knows and how he thinks.

The following areas are intended to serve as examples of appropriate areas of a cognitive developmental approach in teaching young children. It is assumed that the young child who has been identified as mentally retarded or developmentally slow may need *more time, more explicit adult guidance,* and *more systematic arrangement and sequencing of learning experiences* to master such areas as these. However, these are areas that are essential to his cognitive growth as they are to that of all children.

Differentiation and discrimination

The infant's earliest learnings involve discrimination between entities, especially discrimination between *self* and *other*. His mastery of the concept of the *permanent object*—that is, his understanding that a thing continues to exist even when it disappears from view—provides the first indication that he differentiates objects in his environment as something more than extensions of himself. The baby's "strange" reaction (or stranger anxiety) in response to the appearance of someone other than his principal caregivers provides a basis for determining that he has learned to distinguish from among other people the significant, familiar "other." Cognitive development throughout the period of infancy and the early childhood years has been described, in fact, as fundamentally a continuing process of increasing differentiation (Wohlwill, 1962).

Before being able to generalize, to apply some overarching principle (such as bigness, redness, loudness, "peopleness") to separate features of his experiential world, the young child must learn to discriminate differences. In other words, the concept of difference precedes that of sameness (in the sense of having some dimension of commonality) (Sigel, 1964).

"Oddity problems" have long been used in experimental research designed to assess children's ability to attend to salient stimulus features. Basically, learning tasks enabling the child to focus attention on common characteristics or attributes or functions can be sequenced in the same manner. The child is first asked to "find the one that is different." Later, through such procedures, he can be helped to discern elements of commonality among objects in an array. Mastering the "different," however, can provide a very useful tool for the child when he later attempts to understand "sameness." But the word need not precede the concept, nor is it synonymous with the concept (Blank, 1973).

Association and similarity

The cognitive point of view with respect to children's learning is usually distinguished from the "associationist" tradition in psychology, usually thought of in terms of stimulus and response. Basically, the distinction is based on the view that the child is doing more as he learns than simply *associating* discrete impressions

and events; he is building internal structures that enable him to apply rules to new experiences. (The stimulus-response, or behaviorist, term for this is "transfer.")

Dimensions of relatedness or similarity are many: things that can be eaten, things that are cold, and things that are round suggest only a few of the kinds of experiences usually provided in an early childhood classroom. However, before children become able to *categorize*—to extract a unifying principle and apply it to diverse members of a set—they must first grasp the idea that objects are *alike* in some way. This can be experienced across a variety of situations, proceeding gradually to the realization that two things can be alike and also different. Two round objects that roll are called balls, although one is large and the other small, or the teacher is a lady and so is Mama, or the small, short-haired family pet is a dog and so is Lassie on television. The experience of identifying and learning to label dimensions of similarity is perhaps one of the most fundamental and important, as well as continuous and gradual, aspects of the early learning program. Basically, the child's task is to make sense out of the confusion of his world, to impose order on the diversity of his experience, to develop *structures* for understanding reality.

Grouping and classification

Classificatory concepts are essential tools by which the young child structures his environment. The ability to classify depends on the prior ability to identify features of commonality and of differences among objects in an array. The child must be able to determine that things are like each other in some respect and that other objects lacking this specific feature are not members of the set described by a concept word. Children may, however, recognize a conceptual basis for classifying objects and sort them accordingly into categories without being able to provide verbally the basis for sorting. That mentally retarded children, in particular, are likely to be disparate in their ability to produce conceptual classifications and their ability to identify in words the conceptual basis has been implied by research findings (Safford, 1967). Retarded children can and do demonstrate abstract thought in the sense of applying a generalized rule in problem solving, although they are at a disadvantage when such tasks depend on verbal explanations (Rosenberg, 1963).

Very young children develop classificatory skills in a predictable sequence, beginning with random groupings, proceeding through associative chaining (in which the basis for determining similarity shifts with each association), and arriving ultimately at the ability to assign objects to categories on a conceptual basis (Vygotsky, 1962). Opportunities to *experience* through the senses attributes of physical objects in the child's environment, with adult guidance toward accommodating successively more subtle or complex features, provide the means by which the child can develop classificatory structures. Such structures help him to interpret and predict events in his environment.

Ordering and seriation

Ordinal relationships parallel in importance relationships based on similarity and differences that lead to the ability to classify. In Piaget's theory, early understandings of ordinality form the groundwork for the child's concept of numeration and his comprehension of ideas of quantity, comparativity, and relativity. Whereas to the young child the world may be dichotomous—everything is either big or it is small, soft or hard, high or low, pretty or ugly, loud or soft—this mode of conceptualizing phenomena soon proves inadequate. The child discovers a need to order elements along a continuum, that is, to formulate *ordinal* relationships. In terms of temporal relationships, similar discoveries are made; children can learn to *scale* temporal events on the basis of their recency or their imminence.

The classroom activities that can be employed to provide experiences in recognizing relative relationships of objects or events along a continuum are virtually limitless, including enabling the children to discover that they themselves can form an "ordinal scale" based on height, for example. Assignment of numerical values to items ranked on some basis can serve to promote an understanding of the role of ordinal number concepts, indeed of the nature of *number* itself. Prior experiences with simple objects and events also provide a background foundation for more ambitious work in the areas of sequencing and sequential memory, areas believed to be typically difficult for mentally retarded children to master. Maria Montessori gave particular emphasis to seriation and ordinal number concepts, and some of the Montessori materials are particularly useful in these areas. *Teaching Montessori in the Home,* by Elizabeth Hainstook (1968), is a useful guide for both parents and teachers.

Cause-effect relationships

As is the case with other areas of concept development emerging as "pre-concepts" during what Piaget has called the preoperational stage, *causality* has its roots in the action schemas of infancy. Causal thinking in the early childhood years is characterized by the child's ability to retain an image in his mind of a relationship between events that is not only a *temporal* one but one of *contingency* as well: Event A occurs, followed by event B; event B occurs whenever event A first occurs; event A *causes* event B. Obviously, such reasoning is quite susceptible to error. Among the fallacies in logic of this type is that of inferring *causation from correlation;* that is, that two events are associated with each other does not necessarily imply that one causes the other to happen. As Piaget (1967) says, the reasoning of children during the preoperational period is neither deductive nor inductive, but rather *trans*ductive.

That is, the child reasons from the particular to the particular—from one specific instance to another, rather than either deducing on the basis of general principles or inducing such general principles from specific instances.

Like classification and seriation, concepts of causality enable us to make sense out of events occurring in our environment and in our own personal "life space." Specifically, a sense of causal relationships enables us to predict events and to anticipate consequences, an ability that is essential to ensuring our own physical safety. Until the young child is able to understand what consequences might occur, it is difficult to get him voluntarily to refrain from running into the street or yanking the fur of a pet dog or cat. As a matter of fact, toddlers are exceedingly *experimental* in their explorations, seeming to approach new situations with great curiosity, reflecting excitement in discoveries, and replicating them endlessly as though testing and confirming hypotheses.

An additional feature of young children's thinking with respect to understandings of causality is its "magical" quality. *Anything* can happen, not only events that could be anticipated and explained on a naturalistic basis (in the adult sense). Selma Fraiberg (1959) has provided a vivid description of this aspect of the thought of young children in her book, *The Magic Years.* Cognitive development involves, among other trends, a trend toward increasing reliance on naturalistic explanations, rather than what we would call "fantastic" ones, in the prediction of consequences and the interpretation of causes. In Piaget's terms (Piaget, 1962), the child becomes less *egocentric* and less prone to explain physical phenomena in animistic or anthropomorphic terms.

One consequence of delay or lag in mental development is the child's persistence in "primitive" modes of thought for a more extended period. The mentally retarded or mentally handicapped child may find it difficult to move beyond the constraints placed on his ability to predict and explain by his egocentrism and transductive reasoning. In distinguishing three "kinds" of knowledge—physical, social, and logicomathematical—Piaget (Kamii, 1971) makes the point that, whereas some information can be conveyed to the child verbally by adults (social knowledge, such as the name of a person, a place, or a thing) cognitive growth depends more on the child's ability to develop cognitive structures. This *structuring* of thought comes about through continuous "transactions" between the child's mind and his environment. It is dependent neither exclusively on "maturation" nor alone on "experience." Rather, the child's ability to form, expand, and modify cognitive structures—that is, his conceptual development—occurs through a reciprocal relationship between internal and external factors. It is an *interactive* process.

It is important for the teacher to remember that simply *explaining* relationships of cause and effect, whether in the physical world or the interpersonal sphere, is insufficient to affect the way the child thinks or his understanding of such relationships. However, this does not imply that the child should be left to discover for himself "what will happen if. . . ." The teacher's role can best be described as *facilitator,* rather than *explainer.* Selection of materials and structuring of the classroom environment are two major ways in which the teacher can facilitate children's concept acquisition. A third is *demonstrating* the use of materials, in the manner advocated by Maria Montessori (see, for example, Montessori, 1912). A fourth component of teaching that facilitates cognitive growth is *questioning* (Taba, 1962), or *dialogue* (Blank, 1973), in a manner that guides thinking toward a problem-solving orientation. As Montessori said, *"Don't tell. Teach!"*

Association of related events

It is important to help the child distinguish between relationships of cause and effect and relationships of other kinds. As Susan Isaacs (1971) once noted, our language itself often makes this distinction a difficult one for the child to figure out. Experience with causal relationships can be highly pragmatic and part of the child's everyday experience with light switches, water faucets, and toys.

Relational concepts

An important set of relationships is that denoted linguistically by the term "preposition." By definition, words we call prep-

ositions are always used in conjunction with names of persons, places, things, (or conditions, ideas, or abstractions, as in the phrase "in love"), or pronouns used in place of these names. Classroom activities abound that can assist children in understanding physical relationships implied by these words:

Put the ball *in* the cup.
Put the ball *behind* the boy.
Put the bead *under* the cup.
Put the dish *on* the table.
Jump *over* the stick.
Crawl *under* the stick.
Come *down* the sliding board.

As this brief list of examples indirectly suggests, opportunities for guided, first-hand discoveries of these relationships can be found in both fine motor activities and large motor activities, such as games or an obstacle course. Painting and other graphic representational media also provide opportunities to help the child understand relationships of relative position.

In terms of temporal relationships, the ideas of before and after are difficult to understand and are dependent also on guided experience and observation.

It should be obvious that the child is not expected to understand or be able to define the idea of prepositions as a class of relationships. Knowledge of the words used to denote specific kinds of relationships is similarly not an end in itself. Rather, the words may assist the child in mastering the concepts they suggest.

Expression and representation

During the preoperational period of cognitive development, the child, whether of average or lower than average intelligence, is accomplishing a number of "developmental tasks" that have been identified by the term "representation." What is meant by this term is the child's ability to possess a mental image of something or some relationship that exists or might exist in the external world. Various modes of *expression,* including speaking, drawing, block play, sociodramatic play, mime, and still others, are avenues through which the child can communicate an image, or idea that exists in his mind. Consequently, such activities as these provide excellent opportunities for the teacher to assess what understandings or impressions the child has, how he interprets various aspects of reality, how things appear to him, how sophisticated or detailed is his interpretation, etc. Apart from their diagnostic utility to the teacher, however, these expressive modes perform an essential function for the child by enabling him to attempt consciously to formulate a representation and to communicate it. He is thereby able to obtain responses from others to a product of his own thinking, as well as responses to his expressive ability (which vary according to the expressive medium being used).

Some writers who have attempted to apply the insights of Piaget and others to education assign an important role to expressive functions, especially during the preschool and early school years. Hans Furth (1969), for example, advocates placing far more emphasis on representational activities that can be carried out *independently of spoken language,* such as mime and movement, than on either *reception* or *language-bound expression.*

Decoding

The preceding was not intended to suggest that language is unimportant either in furthering cognitive development or as a critical area in its own right. This is certainly not the case. Language-saturated classroom activities, however, sometimes both serve to place undue emphasis on performance at the expense of learning and place at a disadvantage the mentally retarded child whose language deficits may mask emerging cognitive capabilities. As one scholar (Almy, 1966) has noted, the teacher should attempt to move beyond the "verbal facade" that young children frequently erect. This advice is applicable whether the facade implies a higher level of sophistication than in reality exists or whether it fails to convey a complete picture of what the child is actually capable of accomplishing cognitively.

An aspect of language that is important both in its own right and as a prelude to reading is the child's ability to interpret signs and symbols. Classroom activities intended to encourage the child to associate verbal or other symbolic designations with particular places or conditions have long been valuable components of the preschool and kindergarten program for all children and continue to be emphasized throughout the educational program for children diagnosed as mentally handicappped. One important example of this type of activity is the use of safety signs; others include means of enabling the child to use public transportation, to locate buildings, and to obtain assistance in finding his way. All interpretation of signs and symbols involves a process of decoding, that is, of associating particular meaning to some intentional representation of that meaning. Children decode not only visual signs and symbols, but auditory ones as well, in addition to clues provided by means of all other sense modalities.

The decoding involved in reading is primarily visual in integration with auditory interpretation of visual images. Activities commonly designated as "reading readiness" include a great many diverse opportunities to *discriminate* among visual and auditory data, to associate visual and auditory clues, and to extend the developmental process of symbol interpretation. Generally, understanding the distinction between the word for something and the thing itself precedes the ability to associate a *printed representation*—a visual configuration, consisting of lines—with a *word*.

Self-awareness

The area of self-awareness subsumes a great many kinds of knowledge, as well as a substantial *affective*, or *attitude*, component. On one level, we are concerned that the child gains an awareness of the parts of his body, knows their names, and understands their functions. Even more basically, however, he must gain an understanding that he is a *self*, different from all others and yet like others, a unique individual and yet having many things in common with other children.

The child's ability to name body parts, to respond to questions such as "Why do we have ears?" to add missing body parts to a human figure by drawing, and to draw a person have long been used as

means to assess children's mental maturity and to predict intellectual potential. (See, for example, Harris, 1963, for a complete discussion of the rationale for the use of human figure drawing in assessment of intelligence as well as for other clinical purposes.)

PERSONAL AND SOCIAL DEVELOPMENT

There is no clear line between "cognitive" and "emotional," or *affective*, development (Kessler, 1966; Piaget, 1967) in the mentally retarded child or the child of average or above-average intellectual ability. The child's feelings about himself, however, comprise an area deserving of special emphasis, along with his ability to cope with frustration, to resolve emotional conflicts, and to relate well to others. Like every child, the boy or girl of lower-than-average intellectual ability has two basic psychological needs that contribute to his *identity:* to feel loved and valued and to feel competent and capable (Glasser, 1969).

The child's experience of success is an important contribution to his sense that he is a worthwhile and effective person (White, 1959; Glasser, 1969). Similarly, experiencing the satisfaction of coping successfully with difficult and frustrating demands strengthens the child's confidence in his ability to undertake new and difficult tasks. Some specific practices that can help the young mentally retarded child to develop personally and socially include the following:

1. *Listening* to the child when he talks
2. *Responding* to the child's questions and statements by encouraging him to extend and elaborate them and *engaging the child in conversation*
3. *Respecting* the child's needs for stability, repetition, and routine, rather than pushing him to move on before he is ready
4. *Avoiding comparisons* with others or a competitive climate

5. *Creating opportunities for cooperative activity*
6. *Providing recognition* for his achievements, verbally and otherwise
7. *Encouraging* the child's attempts at independent activity while assuring him of support when it is needed
8. *Recognizing and acknowledging* what is important to the child
9. *Highlighting* the child's achievements
10. *Helping* him to talk about feelings and to use the words that convey how he feels

CONSIDERATIONS IN DEVELOPING A TEACHING PROGRAM

Extensive work has been done in the area of curriculum for mentally retarded children, particularly those in educable mentally retarded (EMR) programs in the public schools. Generally, goals and recommended methods for mildly and moderately retarded children have focused on developing practical skills needed to cope with "persisting life problems" (*Ohio Curriculum Guide,* 1977). Teaching the retarded child in skill areas has always been closely related to fostering his fullest development as a person, and has been aimed toward promoting maximum possible independence and social competence. Consequently, classroom activities and goals are ideally intertwined with emotional and social development, family concerns, prevocational experiences, and recreational development.

Educational program development for young mentally retarded children has given particular stress to the reciprocal needs of the child and his family. Helping the child in the family setting is the primary emphasis. A particularly useful resource to the teacher attempting to implement a sequential approach based on developmental assessment is *An Experimental Curriculum for Young Mentally Retarded Children* by F. P. Conner and M. E. Talba (1970). Still another valuable guide for individualized, focused teaching to ensure skill development in very young retarded children is provided by T. F. Lind and T. Kopp (1973) in a book entitled *Training Retarded Babies and Preschoolers.* The sequential approach associated with the Montessori method has also been advocated as appropriate for young retarded children.

Vicki M. Johnson and Roberta A. Werner (1975), in *A Step-by-Step Learning Guide for Retarded Infants and Children,* describe an approach based on sequential task analysis and criterion-referenced assessment. A total of 240 specific teaching-learning tasks are related to nine areas of functioning: (1) gross motor; (2) self-care: eating; (3) self-care: dressing; (4) self-care: toilet training; (5) self-care: grooming; (6) receptive language; (7) expressive language (speech); (8) fine motor grasping and manipulation; and (9) perception.

In the last analysis, regardless of the "curriculum" or "approach" that is being employed, it is the individual teacher who primarily determines what is done and how effective it will be. Although he or she cannot "control" what the child brings to the learning situation, there are many important determinants that are indeed under the control of the teacher. Gearhart and Litton (1975) list six of these dimensions:

1. *Space*—the physical setting or work area. A nondistracting environment may be necessary for certain students.
2. *Time*—the length of lessons. For a child with a very short attention span, concise, short lessons may be desirable.
3. *Multiplicity variables*—the number of factors a child must manipulate in a task. Included are the number of pieces of work, extraneous material, and modality channel (visual-auditory, and so forth).
4. *Difficulty*—of the tasks involved. The key here is to present challenging tasks but within present ability level.
5. *Language*—on the part of the teacher. Communication by the teacher should be direct, simple, and meaningful. It may be helpful for some children to touch or maintain visual contact when talking.

6. *The interpersonal relationship factor*—between child and teacher. This is of great importance to learning and teachers must establish this rapport. (p. 101)

The key to an effective educational program for young mentally retarded children is the teacher's ability to regulate these and other important dimensions, such as reinforcement, *differentially* for individual children, based on continuous, ongoing assessment of each child's progress and needs: an *individualized approach applied within a heterogeneous group setting.*

PROGRAMS FOR INFANTS

A mentally retarded infant who is not identified at birth may possibly be identified during the first months of life. As with all forms of handicap, an excellent case can be made for initiating intervention as early as possible. Earliest possible identification of developmentally delayed infants requires the coordinated efforts of professionals, employing home-based as well as hospital-based child study (Weintraub, 1973). Identification should lead to the provision of appropriate services, initiated as early as possible.

In addition to newborns who can be positively diagnosed as having a specific anomaly that is likely or certain to involve retardation, such as Down's or Hurler's syndrome, there are infants who show signs of *risk* of retardation. This is sometimes referred to as *failure-to-thrive* (Brazelton, 1973).

Developmental milestones (Gesell and Amatruda, 1941) provide useful guidelines, since delay in accomplishing important early skills and demonstrating key behavioral responses, smiling, for example, *may* be predictive of retardation. It is essential to note, however, that failure to stand, develop speech, or accomplish other tasks precisely "on schedule" does not, by any means, positively denote retardation. There is wide variation within the range of normalcy, and significant deviations may be caused by factors other than mental subnormality.

Infant stimulation programs that are instituted by many agencies serving mentally retarded children employ a variety of approaches. By working directly with the child through an interdisciplinary team approach and by helping parents to learn how to stimulate development, these programs intend to maximize the young child's learning through gross and fine motor activities and language stimulation (Hayden and Dmitriev, 1975).

Questions have been raised concerning whether it is sufficient simply to provide "stimulation" early in life and let nature take its course. Most workers in the field who have compared a generalized enrichment or stimulation approach with young retarded children to one that incorporates systematic diagnostic evaluation of the child's functioning in gross and fine motor skills, self-care, auditory and visual perception, speech, and concept acquisition endorse the superiority of the latter approach (Connor and Talba, 1970). In the case of infant programs, scales such as The Cattell Infant Intelligence Scale (Cattell, 1947), The Bayley Scales of Infant Development (Bayley, 1969) and the Piaget-type ordinal scales developed by Uzgiris and Hunt (1966) are useful in identifying precisely an infant's current functional level in sensory-motor intellectual development. Procedures such as those described by Gesell and Amatruda (1941) are well established guides for conducting *developmental diagnosis*. Developmental assessment can point to specific intervention procedures for individual children at particular points in their development.

From Piaget's theories (see especially Hunt, 1961; Robinson and Robinson, 1965), we are made aware of the continuity of children's development, from the primarily sensory-motor "schemas" of infants, which form the "building blocks" of thought and intelligence. It is reasonable to suppose, since thinking is indeed built on activity and early sensory-motor learning lays the groundwork for symbolic and logical thought, that infant stimulation should emphasize sensory and motor learning.

Similarly, in the area of early language stimulation, models for intervention can be provided based on research findings with normal infants (Simeonsson and Weigerink, 1974). Systematic language training programs for developmentally delayed infants and toddlers have been developed to assess and build on *prelinguistic* behaviors in promoting receptive and expressive language (Bricker and Bricker, 1970).

The hope of enhancing the intellectual capabilities of children through early intervention has been expressed most dramatically in research with the mentally retarded. Actually, the major "programs" of research involving young mentally retarded children are among the most suggestive concerning the whole issue of the effects of modifications in early environment on children's subsequent mental development. These include the work of Samuel Kirk (1958), that of Blatt and Garfunkle (1965), a particularly dramatic report by Skeels (1966), and a current effort that is the subject of much interest and of some controversy (Heber and Garber, 1975).

PARENT AND TEACHER

In working with young mentally retarded children, the teacher's best resource is likely to be the children's parents. All of the instructional program, unless it is extended beyond the "school day" and into the child's total life space, can be quite limited in its impact and ability to help the child. At the same time, unless the teacher is able to relate what is done to the child's daily life experiences, to people, events, and things with which he is familiar, the opportunity is lost to maximize his learning and social adaptation.

Many vehicles for communication between parents and teacher are possible, such as parent groups, regular conferences, home visits, school visits by parents, and special parent-child events. What particular means a teacher and his or her children's parents evolve will probably depend on their own preferences and style. Fathers as well as mothers have much to gain from and much to contribute to both individual communications and group meetings.

For the young child who is mentally retarded, continuity of experience, based on cooperation, mutual respect, and ongoing communication between his teacher and his family, can be a most important factor in his success and happiness, both at home and at school.

DISCUSSION QUESTIONS

1. Why and how has the terminology applied to mental retardation changed over the years?
2. How might the mandate to provide a *multifaceted assessment* that employs *nondiscriminatory testing* change special education placement and programming?
3. What is the basis for early intervention for very young mildly and moderately retarded children?
4. In what ways can a teacher of young children ensure that a mildly or moderately retarded child can be effectively provided for in his or her program?
5. How can experiences gained through participation in early education experiences positively affect the self-esteem of mentally retarded children?
6. What is the basis for adopting a *cognitive developmental* approach in teaching young mentally retarded children?

REFERENCES

Allen, R., and Allen, C. *Language experiences in reading.* Chicago: Encyclopedia Britannica, Inc., 1970.

Almy, M., with E. Chittenden and P. Miller. *Young children's thinking: studies of some aspects of Piaget's theory.* New York: Teacher's College Press, 1966.

Ashton-Warner, S. *Teacher,* New York: Bantam Books, Inc., 1963.

Bayley, N. *Bayley Scales of Infant Development: birth to two years.* New York: The Psychological Corp., 1969.

Becker, W., Engleman, S., and Thomas, D. *Teaching: a course in applied psychology.* Chicago: Science Research Associates, Inc., 1971.

Bellamy, G. T., and Bellamy, T. T. Descriptive concepts for preschool retarded children. *Education and Training of the Mentally Retarded,* 1974, *9*(3), 115-122.

Blank, M. *Teaching learning in the preschool: a dialogue approach.* Columbus: Charles E. Merrill Publishing Co., 1973.

Blatt, B., and Garfunkle, F. *A field demonstration of the effects of nonautomated responsive environments on the intellectual and social competence of educable mentally retarded children.* Boston: Boston University, 1965.

Bloom, B. S. *Stability and change in human characteristics.* New York: John Wiley & Sons, Inc., 1964.

Bowlby, J. *Maternal care and mental health.* New York: Schocken Books, Inc., 1966.

Brazelton, T. B. Assessment of the infant at risk. *Clinical Obstetrics and Gynecology,* 1973, *16*, 361.

Bricker, W., and Bricker, D. A. A program of language training for the severely language handicapped child. *Exceptional Children,* 1970, *37*, 101-111.

Bruner, J. S., Olver, R., and Greenfield, P. M. *Studies in cognitive growth.* New York: John Wiley & Sons, Inc., 1966.

Cattell, P. *The measurement of intelligence of infants and young children.* New York: The Psychological Corp., 1947.

Chomsky, N. *Aspects of the theory of syntax.* Cambridge, Mass.: The M.I.T. Press, 1965.

Chomsky, N. *Language and mind.* New York: Harcourt Brace Jovanovich, Inc., 1968.

Cole, M., and Bruner, J. S. Preliminaries to a theory of cultural differences. In I. J. Gordon (Ed.), *Early childhood education: the seventy-first yearbook of The National Society for the Study of Education* (Part II). Chicago: University of Chicago Press, 1972, pp. 161-180.

Connor, F. P., and Talba, M. E. *An experimental curriculum for young mentally retarded children.* New York: Teacher's College Press, 1970.

Cromwell, R. L. Selected aspects of personality development in mentally retarded children. *Exceptional Children,* 1961, *28*, 44-51.

Developmental learning profile (Prepublication draft). Cleveland: Cuyahoga Special Education Service Center, May, 1975.

Doll, E. A. *The measurement of social competence.* Minneapolis: American Guidance Service, 1953.

Dunn, L. M. Special education for the mildly retarded—is much of it justified? *Exceptional Children,* 1968, *35,* 5-24.

Ellis, N. R. The stimulus trace and behavioral inadequacy. In N. R. Ellis (Ed.), *Handbook of mental deficiency: psychological theory and research.* New York: McGraw-Hill Book Co., 1963, pp. 134-158.

Fernald, G. *Remedial techniques in basic school subjects.* New York: McGraw-Hill Book Co., 1943.

Fleming, E., and Anttonnen, R. G. *Testing practices project: final report, Cleveland Associated Foundations.* Cleveland: Press of Case Western Reserve University, 1970.

Fogelman, C. J. (Ed.). *AAMD adaptive behavior scale* (Rev.). Washington, D.C.: American Association on Mental Deficiency, 1975.

Fraiberg, S. *The magic years.* New York: Charles Scribner & Sons, 1959.

Furth, H. *Piaget for teachers.* Englewood Cliffs, N.J.: Prentice-Hall, Inc., 1969.

Gallagher, J. J. A comparison of brain-injured and non-brain-injured mentally retarded children on several psychological variables. *Monographs of the Society for Disorders in Child Development,* 1957, *22*(2, Whole No. 65).

Gearheart, B. R., and Litton, F. W. *The trainable retarded: a foundations approach.* St. Louis: The C. V. Mosby Co., 1975.

Gesell, A. L., and Amatruda, C. S. *Developmental diagnosis.* New York: Paul B. Hoeber, Inc., 1941.

Glasser, W. *Schools without failure.* New York: Harper & Row, Publishers, 1969.

Gold, M. W., and Scott, K. G. Discrimination learning. In W. B. Stephens (Ed.), *Training the developmentally young.* New York: The John Day Co., 1971.

Goldstein, K., and Scheerer, M. Abstracts and concrete behavior: an experimental study with special tests. *Psychological Monographs,* 1941, *53, 2.*

Grossman, H. J. (Ed.). *Manual on terminology and classification.* Washington, D.C.: American Association on Mental Deficiency, 1973.

Guilford, J. P. Three faces of intellect. *American Psychologist,* 1959, *14*(8), 469-479.

Guilford, J. P., and Hoepfner, R. *The analysis of intelligence.* New York: McGraw-Hill Book Co., 1971.

Hainstook, E. *Teaching Montessori in the home.* New York: Random House, Inc., 1968.

Hammill, D. D., and Bartel, N. R. *Teaching children with learning and behavior problems.* Boston: Allyn & Bacon, Inc., 1975.

Haring, N. G. Perspectives in special education. In N. G. Haring (Ed.), *Behavior of exceptional children: an introduction to special education.* Columbus, Ohio: Charles E. Merrill Publishing Co., 1974, pp. 3-33.

Harris, D. B. *Children's drawings as measures of intellectual maturity.* New York: Harcourt, Brace & World, Inc., 1963.

Hayden, A. H., and Dmitriev, V. The multidisciplinary preschool program for Down's syndrome children at the University of Washington model preschool center. In B. Z. Friedlander, G. M. Sterritt, and G. E. Kirk (Eds.), *Exceptional infant: assessment and intervention* (Vol. 3). New York: Brunner/Mazel, Inc., 1975, pp. 193-221.

Heber, R., and Garber, H. The Milwaukee Project: a study of the use of family intervention to prevent cultural-familial mental retardation. In B. Z. Friedlander, G. M. Sterritt, and G. E. Kirk (Eds.), *Exceptional infant: assessment and intervention* (Vol. 3). New York: Brunner/Mazel, Inc., 1975, pp. 399-433.

Hendrick, J. *The whole child: new trends in early education.* St. Louis: The C. V. Mosby Co., 1975.

Hewett, F. M. *The emotionally disturbed child in the classroom.* Boston: Allyn & Bacon, Inc., 1968.

Hunt, J. McV. *Intelligence and experience.* New York: The Ronald Press Co., 1961.

Inhelder, B. *The diagnosis of reasoning in the mentally retarded.* New York: The John Day Co., 1968. (Originally published, 1944).

Isaacs, S. *Intellectual growth in young children.* New York: Schocken Books, Inc., 1971.

Johnson, J. L. Special education and the inner city: a challenge for the future or another means for cooling the mark out? *Journal of Special Education,* 1969, *3,* 241-251.

Johnson, O. G. *Tests and measurements in child development: Handbook II* (Vols. 1 and 2). San Francisco: Jossey-Bass, Inc., Publishers, 1976.

Johnson, V. M., and Werner, R. A. *A step-by-step learning guide for retarded infants and children.* Syracuse: Syracuse University Press, 1975.

Kamii, C. K. Evaluation of learning in preschool education: socio-emotional, perceptual-motor, and cognitive development. In B. S. Bloom, J. T. Hastings, and G. F. Madaus (Eds.), *Handbook on formative and summative evaluation of student learning.* New York: McGraw-Hill Book Co., 1971, pp. 281-344.

Kessler, J. W. *Psychopathology of childhood.* Englewood Cliffs, N.J.: Prentice-Hall, Inc., 1966.

Kessler, J. W. Contribution of the mentally retarded toward a theory of cognitive development. In J. Hellmuth (Ed.), *Cognitive studies* (Vol. 1). New York: Brunner/Mazel, Inc., 1970.

Kirk, S. A. *Early identification of the mentally retarded.* Urbana, Ill.: University of Illinois Press, 1958.

Kirk, S. A. *Educating exceptional children.* Boston: Houghton Mifflin Co., 1972.

Kirk, S. A., McCarthy, J. J., and Kirk, W. D. *The Illinois Test of Psycholinguistic Abilities* (Rev. ed.). Urbana, Ill.: University of Illinois Press, 1968.

Klein, N. K., and Safford, P. L. Application of Piaget's theory to the study of thinking of the mentally retarded: a review of research. *Journal of Special Education,* 1977, *11*(2), 201-216.

Lenneberg, E. H. *Biological foundations of language.* New York: John Wiley & Sons, Inc., 1967.

Lind, T. F., and Kopp, T. *Training retarded babies and preschoolers.* Springfield, Ill., Charles C Thomas, 1973.

Montessori, M. *The Montessori method.* New York: F. A. Stokes, 1912.

Morrison, D., and Potheir, P. Two different remedial motor training programs and the development of the mentally retarded pre-schooler. *American Journal of Mental Deficiency,* 1972, 77(3), 251-258.

Moss, J. W., and Mayer, D. L. Children with intellectual subnormality. In J. J. Gallagher (Ed.), *The application of child development research to exceptional children.* Reston, Va.: Council for Exceptional Children, 1975, pp. 262-298.

Ohio curriculum´ guide for moderately mentally retarded learners. Columbus: Ohio Department of Mental Health and Mental Retardation, 1977.

Peterson, D. Educable mentally retarded. In N. G. Haring (Ed.), *Behavior of exceptional children: an introduction to special education.* Columbus, Ohio: Charles E. Merrill Publishing Co., 1974.

Piaget, J. *The construction of reality in the child.* New York: Basic Books, Inc., 1954.

Piaget, J. *Play, dreams, and imitation in childhood.* New York: W. W. Norton & Co., Inc., 1962.

Piaget, J. *Six psychological studies.* New York: Random House, Inc., 1967.

Piaget, J., and Inhelder, B. *The psychology of the child.* New York: Basic Books, Inc., 1969.

Robinson, H., and Robinson, N. *The mentally retarded child: a psychological approach.* New York: McGraw-Hill Book Co., 1965.

Rosenberg, S. Problem-solving and conceptual behavior. In N. R. Ellis (Ed.), *Handbook of mental deficiency: psychological theory and research.* New York: McGraw-Hill Book Co., 1963, pp. 439-462.

Rosenthal, R., and Jacobson, L. *Pygmalion in the classroom.* New York: Holt, Rinehart & Winston, Inc., 1968.

Safford, P. L. *Differences in the cognitive functioning of normal, mentally retarded, and emotionally disturbed subjects: implications for school-relevant differential diagnosis* (Research monograph No. 5, IRCOPPS Midwest Research Center for Pupil Personnel Services). Ann Arbor: University of Michigan, 1967. (ERIC)

Sattler, J. M. *Assessment of children's intelligence.* Philadelphia: W. B. Saunders Co., 1974.

Sigel, I. E. The attainment of concepts. In M. L. Hoffman and L. W. Hoffman (Eds.), *Review of child development research* (Vol. 1). New York: Russell Sage Foundation, 1964, pp. 209-248.

Simeonsson, R. J., and Weigerink, R. Early language intervention: a contingent stimulation model. *Mental Retardation,* 1974, *12*(2), 7-11.

Skeels, H. M. Adult status of children with contrasting early life experiences: a follow-up study. *Monographs of the Society for Research in Child Development,* 1966, *32,* 2.

Smith, R. M. *An introduction to mental retardation.* New York: McGraw-Hill Book Co., 1971.

Spearman, C. General intelligence objectively determined and measured. *American Journal of Psychology,* 1904, *15,* 201-293.

Spitz, R. A. Hospitalism: an inquiry into the genesis of psychiatric conditions in early childhood. *Psychoanalytic Study of the Child,* 1945, *1,* 53-74.

Spivack, G. Perceptual processes. In N. R. Ellis (Ed.), *Handbook of mental deficiency: psychological theory and research.* New York: McGraw-Hill Book Co., 1963, pp. 480-511.

Stephens, B., McLaughlin, J., and Mahaney, E. Ages at which Piagetian concepts are achieved. *Proceedings of the Annual Convention of the American Psychological Association,* 1971, *6,* 203-204.

Taba, H. *Curriculum development: theory and practice.* New York: Harcourt, Brace & World, Inc., 1962.

Terman, L. M., and Merrill, M. A. *Stanford-Binet Intelligence Scale: manual for the third revision, form L-M.* Boston: Houghton Mifflin Co., 1960.

Thurstone, L. L. *Primary mental abilities.* Chicago: University of Chicago Press, 1938.

Uzgiris, I. C., and Hunt, J. McV. *Scale of infant psychological development.* Urbana: University of Illinois, 1966. (Mimeographed.)

Vigotsky, L. S. *Thought and Language.* Cambridge, Mass.: The M.I.T. Press, 1962.

Weikart, D. P. *Early childhood special education for intellectually subnormal and/or culturally different children.* Paper presented at National Conference on Manpower Preparation for Handicapped Young Children, Washington, D.C., December 9-10, 1971.

Weintraub, D. A program is born. *Mental Retardation,* 1973, *11*(3), 5.

White, R. W. Motivation reconsidered: the concept of competence. *Psychological Review,* 1959, *66,* 297-333.

White, R. Education of the retarded: a point of view. *Education and Training of the Mentally Retarded,* 1976, *11*(4), 295.

Wohlwill, J. From perception to inference. In W. Kessen and C. Kuhlman (Eds.), Thought in the young child. *Monographs of Society for Research in Child Development,* 1962, *27,* 87-112.

Zeaman, D., and House, B. J. The role of attention in retardate discrimination learning. In N. R. Ellis (Ed.), *Handbook of mental deficiency: psychological theory and research.* New York: McGraw-Hill Book Co., 1963, pp. 159-223.

Zigler, E. F. Mental retardation: current issues and approaches. In L. W. Hoffman and M. L. Hoffman (Eds.), *Review of child development research* (Vol. 2). New York: Russell Sage Foundation, 1966, pp. 107-168.

CHAPTER 6

SPECIFIC LEARNING DISABILITIES

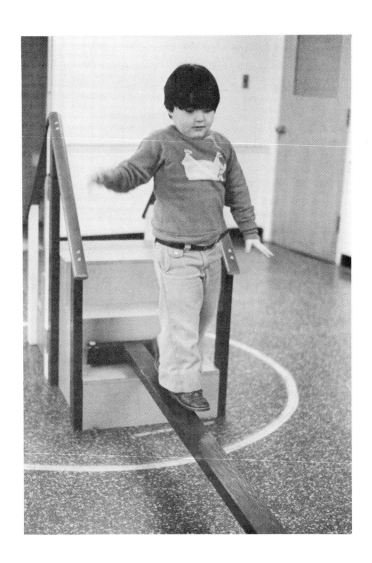

The "discovery" of learning disabilities in children has had a profound impact on all aspects of special and regular education. Parent activism, both nationally and in local communities, through the Association for Children with Learning Disabilities, has been instrumental in bringing about the enactment of laws and the creation of programs that potentially will assist all teachers and benefit all handicapped children. This assertion is based on a recurrent theme—a theme that is now being related to all other areas of exceptionality in addition to learning disabilities:

The child with a learning disability is essentially like all other children. He does, however, have specific educational needs. It is the educator's responsibility to determine those needs precisely and to provide for them by means of an individual instructional program.

It is, of course, a truism that *every* child has "specific educational needs." The goal of individualized instruction that is truly tailored to the needs of all children has probably been furthered by the realization that some children *must* have an individualized program if they are to avoid failure and to achieve in proportion to their ability.

This chapter concerns children who, in the past, had incorrectly been described as "slow learners" or sometimes as "lazy," "uncooperative," "unmotivated," or "clumsy." It concerns the misunderstood child.

DEFINITION, INCIDENCE, AND ETIOLOGY

Throughout its rather short history, the field of learning disabilities has been fraught with problems of definition. Most generally accepted definitions are characterized by their emphasis on *exclusion*. That is, a child with a learning disability is one whose problem is *not* primarily a result of such causes as mental retardation, emotional disturbance, environmental disadvantage, or a physically handicapping condition (Wallace and McLoughlin, 1975). On this basis therefore, a child may be identified as having a learning disability when all other possible diagnoses have been excluded.

Many professionals are dissatisfied with the definitions of learning disabilities that have been generally used. With their lack of operationalism, these definitions lead to disagreement in estimating the number of children and youth who have learning disabilities. Whether one estimates the incidence of learning disabilities to be 1 percent, 3 percent, 10 percent, or 30 percent of the school-age population clearly depends on the inclusiveness of the definition (Bryan and Bryan, 1975).

In addition, however, learning disabilities are generally described in terms of a *discrepancy* between the ability to achieve and the actual demonstrated achievement in some academic or developmental skill area or areas. These include the curriculum areas of school learning, such as reading, writing, and mathematics, and the more general underlying psychological processes of language and perception.

In the case of young school-age children—within the age range of approximately 5 to 8 years—the usual convention in definitions of specifying a discrepancy of approximately 2 years between ability scores and scores of demonstrated performance in some areas of achievement is difficult to apply. For example, if the norm for reading achievement in grade 1 is proficiency with first-level basal reader and related materials by the end of the school year, it is not possible to specify the level of reading achievement that would be 2 years lower. We speak of reading *readiness* levels, so it is somewhat possible to determine the prereading level of a child. However, at grade 1 it is quite difficult to ascertain that a child's reading achievement is *significantly discrepant* from the norm.

What causes learning disabilities?

When one observes a child of 10 or 11 years who encounters failure in school, it is apparent that many interrelated causes could be involved. A child may find it difficult to master fourth- or fifth-grade–level reading materials because he may lack the foundations of basic sight word recognition, word attack skills, and the like, which should have been acquired during the early grades. Another child may be unable to handle multiplication because he has not mastered the prerequisite number concepts, understanding of place value, or fundamental addition facts. Furthermore, after several years of academic failure experiences, he may have an expectancy of failure, resulting in motivational deficits, lack of concentration, acting out behavior, or other affective consequences.

In terms of identifying original, or primary, causal factors, one of the major definitional controversies relates once more to the question of exclusion. Should those children who fail in some aspect of school learning because of less than optimal environmental or experiential preparation during the years before school be counted as children with learning disabilities? Or should this term be reserved for those children whose learning difficulties are based on characteristics *intrinsic* to the child?

Obviously, this is a significant problem only if it is important for different interventions to be selected for different etiologies. That is, it must be determined whether a child whose problems are *organic* (not necessarily congenital, but within the child himself) requires different instructional approaches than one whose problems are related to *environmental* factors. Since these categories of causal factors are unquestionably intertwined, especially as the child grows older, it is very difficult to sort them out. Attempts to do so have sometimes given rise to the suspicion that learning disabilities comprise a handicap of middle-class children—that the children of economically disadvantaged backgrounds are often excluded from the services (and

federal and state funding) available under the rubric of learning disabilities.

There are many reasons why one might expect disadvantaged children to be more vulnerable to problems in learning: A greater incidence of premature birth, health and nutritional inadequacies, and environmental handicaps can all contribute to problems in the neurological development of young children (Grotberg, 1970). Moreover, psychological stress on the part of the pregnant mother has been found to affect birth weight and fetal development (Meyers, 1976). However, special programs for children with learning disabilities appear to have fewer poor and minority children than one would expect and seem to be underrepresented in urban and poverty areas. Having to "label" children on the basis of a "definition by exclusion" may interfere with a child's receiving the specific assistance he needs (Moss, 1973).

The prevalence of "definitions by exclusion" in the field of learning disabilities, however, represents an attempt to accomplish three goals: (1) to focus the attention of educators, lawmakers, and the general public on those children who have what has been called an "invisible handicap" and who would otherwise continue to be misunderstood, subjected to failure experiences in school, and misclassified as mentally retarded or behavior problems; (2) to develop instructional approaches that help these children overcome or compensate for their disabilities without suffering possible harmful effects of labeling and segregation from "normal" children; and (3) to make available necessary funding from limited resources to provide appropriate services for these children. Considering the question of etiology may not be essential to achieving these goals. However, it continues to be a controversial issue.

One leader in the field summarizes the current status of our knowledge of the many possible causes of learning disabilities in the following way:

As far as I can see, we probably have six causes of nonlearning in children. First, genetic variations in the function of the central nervous system. Second, chemical or physical trauma or infection in utero, as in the case of rubella, blood incompatibilities, ingestion of drugs by the mother, and so forth. Third, trauma during the birth process. Fourth, trauma after birth, including trauma or infections during childhood (encephalitis, meningitis, galactosemia, and all the other things that happen). Fifth, delayed maturation of the functions of the nervous system perhaps due to inadequate sensory stimulation and resulting biochemical imbalances. And then sixth, none of the above. I think every one of us has to throw that in if we're going to be realistic and accurate. Teachers need to know that they should not hesitate to say they don't know. Too often teachers feel that someone else knows all the answers and they don't, so they feel embarrassed to say "I don't know." (McCarthy, 1972, pp. 162-163)

Medical considerations in etiology

The field of learning disabilities had its origins in work with adult stroke patients and veterans with neurological injuries. The early work of Werner and Strauss (1941) and later of Strauss and Lehtinen (1947) led to attempts to identify characteristic forms of perceptual dysfunction in children who had difficulty in performing academic and social tasks in school. Similarities between these characteristics and those of neurologically impaired adults were observed; it was assumed that the child with learning problems was *brain injured.*

Early attempts to define and understand what are now called learning disabilities were based mainly on a sensory neurological model (Haring and Phillips, 1962). Terms such as "minimal cerebral dysfunction" and "the brain-injured child" (Cruickshank et al.,1961) suggested fundamentally that severe problems in learning had their origins in some form or degree of brain damage. The "Strauss syndrome" represented an attempt to identify commonalities among children who had organic brain injury. These children were

believed to demonstrate the following characteristics: *distractibility, perseveration, figure-ground disturbance, motor disinhibition, hyperactivity* and *poor body image.*

There proved to be two major problems in this initial conception of a brain injury syndrome reflected in various difficulties in school performance: (1) not all children manifesting one or several of the characteristics had difficulties in the other areas identified and (2) positive diagnosis of brain injury proved particularly difficult to establish and not always relevant to educational planning.

As the field of learning disabilities began to assume the proportions of a movement during the 1960s and 1970s (a movement whose leadership was shared by professionals of various disciplines and parents, and whose activist arm was clearly parent dominated), the problem of etiology, or cause, became less important and the pragmatic issue of *how to help the child* grew in prominence.

However, continuing medical research can contribute in important ways to early, accurate identification and effective treatment (McElgunn, 1976). It has been stressed by neurologists that cortical tissue, once destroyed, cannot regenerate. Consequently, surgery has not seemed a promising approach to treatment. Nonetheless, attempts by neurological researchers, for example, Ralph Reitan (Reitan and Boll, 1973), offer promise for more precise diagnosis. This may in turn lead to more effective intervention.

In addition to research on the effects of brain injury, other medical areas have recently been emphasized. It is by now well known that neurological processes and brain development are affected by diet. Nutritional deficiency has been advanced as a causal agent in problems of intersensory integration and general central nervous system development (Raman, 1975). Many individuals have asserted, perhaps often going somewhat beyond the actual data available, that many nutritional inadequacies, including such modern "improvements" as artificial food coloring and other additives, account for a substantial proportion of learning disabilities and behavioral problems in children. Consequently, treatment would involve diet control and possibly megavitamin therapy (see, for example, Cott, 1972). The relatively recent discovery of hypoglycemia and allergies as etiological factors has similarly focused the attention of many professionals on new avenues of cure and prevention through attention to nutritional factors. A particularly influential and respected contributor in this area of diagnosis and treatment of learning and behavioral problems is B. F. Feingold, whose book, *Why Your Child Is Hyperactive* (1975), has been widely read by parents and teachers.

Nevertheless, for the present, the opinion of most medical and educational professionals is that learning disabilities are primarily *educational* problems, and it is the educator who must find ways to ameliorate them. Generally, the educational strategy, following identification and diagnosis, is twofold: (1) to capitalize on the individual's strengths and (2) to attempt to strengthen the areas in which deficiencies exist as much as possible. Usually, this means helping the child to *compensate* for a limitation or deficiency in order that he may both become competent in important areas in school learning and experience a personal *sense of competence* necessary in the development and maintenance of a positive self-image. This has brought to the attention of all educators the realization that, not only is there no one "royal road" to learning, but that individuals can achieve mastery of basic skills such as reading, writing, computation, and mathematical reasoning in diverse ways.

It is a fundamental premise of this book that children do learn in different ways, that common approaches to instruction will doom some children, perhaps as many as one third of any learning group (Bloom

et al., 1971), to failure. Those children who have *severe* impairments in one or more of the psychological processes involved in learning, however, require more significant modifications of the instructional program than those that are required to accommodate the *normal range of individual differences* that exists within any learning group. However, qualitative as well as quantitative adjustments in teaching method, materials utilization, and the like should characterize every teacher's approach to "regular education." If such adaptation to differential learning needs and styles were made, it is likely that the extent of school failure could be substantially reduced. This suggests the need to fit instruction to the child, rather than attempting to fit each child to some hypothetical norm.

EARLY IDENTIFICATION OF LEARNING DISABILITIES
The case for early identification

It is generally thought to be desirable to intervene as early as possible for children who seem to be at risk for learning problems. Since there are dangers in false identification (labeling, stigmatization, and the self-fulfilling prophecy), it may certainly be *safer* to avoid this type of error by deferring identification until it is clearly established that, for example, a 2-year discrepancy exists between expectation and performance. However, by that time good opportunities to intervene during a period of presumed greater receptiveness to external intervention may have been missed.

Even more significantly, the child who suffers from impaired functioning in some aspect of learning will have been subjected to experiences of frustration and failure during that period of waiting. This child is aware that his classmates are performing better than he, that what is difficult for him—or indeed seemingly impossible—other children accomplish with ease. This inability to make reasonable progress is observed by the teacher as well, who all too often mistakes his problem for laziness or lack of motivation. Tensions can ensue between teacher and child, within the child himself, and even by extension, between the child and his family as teacher-parent conferences, written reports from the teacher, papers sent home from school, or the child's apparent unhappiness with school arouse anxiety on the part of his parents.

Can learning disabilities be prevented through early identification? At present, little is definitely known about the potentialities and the limits of educational intervention early in life. If the possibility exists that remediation of physical and psychological dysfunctions associated with later problems in academic learning *might* be effective during the early childhood years (*might,* because this possibility still has not adequately been researched and remains a "testable hypothesis"), the problem is one of early identification. Do children who will ultimately have problems in learning manifest deficiencies or dysfunctions in *underlying physical and psychological processes* during the years before school? If so, how can they be identified, at what age should intervention be undertaken and what intervention procedures will prove to be effective? Will one of the learning disabilities specialists of the future be an *infant program specialist,* as is the case with visually and hearing impaired, physically handicapped, and mentally retarded children?

How early can learning disabilities be identified?

The rule of thumb in medical diagnosis of central nervous system dysfunction has been that the earlier (younger) an infant's disability is able to be conclusively diagnosed, the more severe it will be. Children with serious central nervous system dysfunction are relatively easily identifiable within the first years or even days of life. Children with subtle central nervous system deficits, or those who will demonstrate problems in learning (mild retar-

dation or specific learning disability), are more difficult to identify accurately and reliably in the early years of life.

It is probably the case that at least a sizable minority of children who are later identified as having learning disabilities acquire their "disability" as a result of inappropriate or inadequate instruction. If it is true that children learn in different ways within the limits of "normalcy," many teachers have been insufficiently prepared to accommodate this degree of diversity. Use by a school or school district of a single, uniform method of reading instruction for all children, for example, will place at a disadvantage some children who could learn better with an alternative approach. Some children begin with a "difference" that becomes a *disability* only if instruction is not appropriate. Learning disabilities of this sort may be thought of as *educationally caused* (Wallace and MacLoughlin, 1975). The learning disability may not *exist* until the child reaches school age.

On the other hand, some infants identified at birth as being at risk are also likely to develop problems in learning. Research has not conclusively established a definite relationship between stress factors at birth and evidence of neurologic impairment (Colligan, 1974). However, it seems clear that factors such as prematurity and difficult delivery are early indicators of potential problems (Denhoff, 1972; Rubin, 1973). *Failure-to-thrive* babies may be susceptible to a variety of problems (Brazelton, 1973). Some authors have attempted to relate problems in reading or other skills directly to abnormalities in areas that can be diagnosed soon after birth. These include reflex patterns (Mayberry, 1974) and vestibular abnormalities (deQuiros, 1976), among others. Failure of an infant or toddler to achieve developmental milestones on schedule may be indicative of problems, possibly including mild, specific learning difficulties (Francis-Williams, 1970).

Identification of potential learning problems in young school-aged children

Identification by the nursery school teacher of children who present a high risk for learning disabilities can be an effective preventative measure, according to Barbara Keogh and Lawrence Becker (1973). At this level, they suggest, identification actually means *hypothesizing about future development from present behavior*. Although children needing special attention and assistance may be identified in the early childhood classroom, it is frequently difficult to distinguish children who are neurologically impaired from those who are "immature" (Eaves et al., 1972).

Identification of learning-disabled children at the nursery, kindergarten, or primary level may involve a variety of methods. Medical examinations may continue to provide an important component, as well as school observation and assessment. One physician (Uyeda, 1972) has advised pediatricians to assess the following areas as part of routine physical examinations of young school-age children:

1. Family and child's history and general appraisal

2. Physiological examination
3. Speech and language testing
4. Neurological appraisal (including evaluation of gait, posture, muscle tone, and reflexes)
5. Coordination (both gross and fine motor, as well as balance)
6. Handedness
7. Right-left orientation
8. Ability to cross midline of body
9. Figure drawing (assessing auditory comprehension, intermodal functioning, and fine motor control)

Regular day care or nursery school, kindergarten, or primary teachers are generally agreed to have a most important role in early identification of learning disabilities (Keogh and Smith, 1970). Some recommend that the regular teacher should be *principally* responsible, with assistance by resource personnel to develop and implement whatever specialized provisions are indicated within the classroom rather than considering special placement (for example, Schaer and Crump, 1976). Precise, specific, and systematic observation and rating of the child's behavior by the teacher is considered essential (Cowgill et al., 1973; Novack et al., 1973; Hiltbrunner and Vasa, 1974). However, classroom observation, even if conducted systematically and objectively, does not always appear to be totally successful in identifying young children who may require specialized assistance for learning problems (Forness and Esveldt, 1975), nor does testing (McKnab and Fine, 1972).

Generally, early identification of young children with potential learning disabilities involves an interdisciplinary approach. In addition to the teacher (and, of course, the child's parents), other professionals usually involved include a psychologist and speech clinician. Depending on the school or agency's resources and composition, and, most important, on the possible problems a child may have, a number of other professionals may be involved. These may include a pediatrician, neurologist (possibly a pediatric neurol-

ogist), nurse, social worker, audiologist, and reading specialist. An emerging new role is that of a special educator skilled in the use of formal and informal educational diagnostic techniques and in designing prescriptive instructional programs (McKenzie, 1972).

In recent years, there have been attempts in many communities to carry out large-scale screening programs at the point of kindergarten entrance. Traditionally, the "kindergarten roundup" has included attempts to gain gross assessment of the child's readiness for kindergarten via informal activities such as drawing a human figure. If early kindergarten entrance is sought by the parents for their child, school districts usually require more comprehensive and detailed psychological assessment as a condition. Kindergarten screening has increasingly come to include, with vision and hearing assessment, a variety of measures of motor, perceptual, and language functioning. In some schools, these children who are identified through this means as showing some evidence of developmental delay or problems in one or more specific aspects of functioning are provided an *enrichment* program complementary to or incorporated within the kindergarten program.

Kindergarten screening programs for learning disabilities have tended to emphasize certain aspects of gross motor coordination, visual perception, and visual-motor coordination with relatively less emphasis on auditory perceptual skills and syntactic and semantic aspects of language development. Accordingly, the enrichment or remedial programs provided for children at this level have tended to place most stress on large motor skill activities and activities intended to improve skills in perceptual-motor integration emphasizing the visual modality—what Newell Kephart (1971, 1975) called the *perceptual-motor match*.

Studies that have attempted to determine the effectiveness of perceptual-motor training in alleviating learning disabilities have been at best inconclusive; in general, it has *not* been demonstrated that such forms of remediation have been effective in enhancing academic skill learning (Hammill, 1975). However, there is reason to believe that this approach to intervention can improve general physical coordination and readiness skills that might certainly be a desirable outcome in itself. It should be noted that many of the "efficacy" studies have been with children of school age. Therefore they have involved to some extent the attempt to help a child develop skills that were perhaps "missed" or inadequately developed *earlier in life*. Generally, there has been insufficient opportunity to measure the effectiveness of perceptual-motor training during the years when growth in these areas is most rapid and pronounced and of such central importance to all aspects of the child's development—that is, during infancy itself and the years preceding kindergarten entrance (Adkins and Walker, 1972).

PROBLEMS ASSOCIATED WITH EARLY IDENTIFICATION

This discussion will describe some of the characteristics often associated with learning disabilities. It will also suggest some of the difficulties inherent in using these characteristics as criteria for identifying learning disabilities in young children. The general characteristics discussed are:

1. Problems in directionality and laterality
2. Channel and modality deficiencies
3. Hyperactivity, distractibility, and attention deficits

It is notoriously difficult to predict on the basis of observation or formal testing prior to school entrance which children are likely to encounter significant problems once they begin formal schooling. The purpose of early screening is to identify any possible problems or impairments of one or more of the psychological processes involved in learning. The difficulty

is due in part to the fact that a child is an "incomplete organism"; he is *changing* (Saphier, 1973; Shipe and Miezitis, 1969). Unfortunately, it is precisely those behaviors that are indicators of learning problems in school-age children that characterize, to some degree, *all* children during the early years. Let us consider some examples.

Problems in directionality and laterality

Many children with learning problems carry over into the processes of reading and writing more basic confusions of handedness, eyedness, and footedness (Kephart, 1971). A child who reverses figural images, such as numerals or letters of the alphabet or even words or word arrangements in sentences, may actually perceive them in that manner. Among children 6 or 7 years old it is not at all uncommon to observe a cavalier disregard for whether the "loop" on the "stick" protrudes to the left or to the right. For such reversal patterns to be regarded as evidence of problems in visual perception, generally three conditions should be met:

1. The reversal is relatively consistent, indicating that the child actually sees the figure "backward" or has a mirror image.
2. Reversed perceptions of figures are observed across many kinds of stimulus situations rather than only when letter or numerical code symbols are involved.
3. The pattern persists over time, even when instructional procedures targeted specifically on the problem are employed.

With regard to the establishment of *dominance* (handedness, eyedness, footedness) it is often the case that constant, habitual patterns are as yet unformed in the preschool child. Therefore failure to demonstrate clear and consistent preference is not necessarily a danger signal in a nursery school child. However, should a child continue to manifest confused dominance, there is reason to believe (Kephart,

1971) that acquisition of basic academic skills, such as reading and writing, will be hampered. Two abnormal handwriting orientations, *mirror writing* and *inversion,* have been related to problems in handedness (Benson, 1970).

In general, laterality and directionality, although reflecting innate capabilities and constitutional preferences in children, emerge at varying rates in response to varying internal and external (environmental, or experiential) influences. It is desirable within the early education setting to provide opportunities and direct guidance for children in these areas. The dangers of too much concern about rate differences, periods or episodes of regression, or behavioral inconsistencies in demonstrating laterality and directionality are twofold: (1) the child may become anxious and self-doubting as he perceives the anxious mood of significant adults (parents or teachers) and (2) an inappropriate label may be assigned to the child, one that may evoke "excep-

tional" behavior in a "normal" child, or that may continue to be applied long after "spontaneous remission," that is, changes during the normal course of development, has caused the problem behavior to disappear.

Channel and modality deficiencies

The notion of pronounced *channel deficiencies* (that there are visual learners and auditory learners) has not been demonstrated to be strongly related to learning in young school-age children (Waugh, 1973). Young children are in a constant state of change with regard to their ability to employ receptive and expressive modalities in learning and in communicating. As Piaget's observations have demonstrated, young children not only depend inordinately on what they see, they are easily misled by the appearance of things. One reason for this can be found in Piaget's concept of *centration,* a tendency to attend to one perceptual feature of an object or situation to the exclusion of all others. Thus the *preoperational* child, when shown the familiar identical containers, each full to the same level with water, thinks that if the contents of one are poured into another container of different *shape* (say, shorter and wider) there is now less water in this container than in the first. Perception dominates cognition: the child does not grasp that, since nothing had been added or taken away, the quantity is unchanged. Nor does he reason that the process could be reversed, that the water could be poured back into its original container and would appear at the same level as before. Furthermore, for him, height may be the salient dimension in this specific situation, making him blind to the difference in width and thus unable to compensate mentally for the decrease in the former dimension by considering the increase in the latter.

With respect to both visual and auditory perception, based on a number of experiments, Gibson (1965) has concluded that development can be thought of in part as a progression in the ability to attend to *distinctive features*. It is the inability to distinguish the important from the extraneous in solving a task, the tendency to be inordinately distracted by irrelevant aspects of the stimulus situation or to be unable to separate figure from background, that is frequently associated with certain manifestations of learning disability. Again, inability to discriminate, to attend to, and to respond to distinctive features may be indicative of problems in older children but quite common and indicative of normal patterns of development among younger children. It has been proposed (Cohen, 1974) that young children are in transition from reliance on other senses to increasing refinement of the visual modality by approximately age 6. The question to be asked is "Is there evidence that the child's development in visual perceptual areas is *not* moving forward, regardless of pace, in the anticipated direction?"

Problems in the coordination of motor

"output" with either visual or auditory "input" are similarly quite the norm in the years before school and during the early school years. Not only are variable rates of long bone and muscle growth responsible for motor coordination difficulties, but also the important developmental tasks relating to purposeful linking of movement to visual or auditory signals are being mastered at variable rates and in variable ways. In terms of vocal expression and its relationships to the rapid emergence of new language capabilities, it is clear that at age 3 years this is a modality very much in a state of change, and it is by no means stabilized in most children prior to the age of school entrance or soon thereafter.

In sum, specific learning disabilities are often thought of as involving a problem in one or more of the functions within visual or auditory perception (such as discrimination), or relating to motor or vocal expression, or specific to one of the reception-expression channels: auditory-motor, auditory-vocal, visual-motor, visual-vocal. And each of the specific functions relating to each of these is a developing or emerging line in the preschool, kindergarten, and even primary grade child. That *deficiencies* or *weaknesses* are present and are stable and pervasive characteristics of the child's learning processes is difficult to establish conclusively. This is not to imply, however, that early warnings are impossible to detect—only that it is quite possible for a teacher who is insufficiently knowledgeable concerning "normal" developmental patterns to be misled.

Hyperactivity, distractibility, and attention deficits

The term "hyperactivity" is probably among the most overused and misused words in the lexicon of educators. It implies an inordinately high level of activity. This leaves a great deal of room for individual interpretation. When is a child's activity level inordinately high? If young children are inclined by their very nature to employ active modes of exploring their environment and to be "physical" in their approach, and if they often seem to draw from boundless reservoirs of energy, how can one determine that a given child, compared to the normal expectancy for children of his developmental level, is *hyperactive?*

Most young children are more active in some situations than in others. There are environmental influences that seem to draw out impulsive or especially assertive behavior. Probably every teacher has experienced in his or her classroom the uncomfortable sense of developing chaos and has felt compelled to intervene. At these times, noise levels rise with heightened levels of physical activity, and it becomes clear that it is time for the adult, as "auxiliary ego," to step in. Contagion affects very young group members, as well as elementary school age youngsters—and adults! We all respond to the vectors impinging on our "life space" from without as well as to internal stimuli.

It is undoubtedly true that some youngsters are more readily seduced in this fashion than are others, just as is the case with older children, adolescents, and adults. However, by hyperactivity what is usually implied is a *disposition within a given child to exhibit a high degree of physical activity under varying environmental conditions.* Needless to say, it is very difficult to make a judgment that a 4-year-old is a "hyperactive child."

Although many children may at times be highly or even unduly active, there are undoubtedly some children who should be properly labeled as hyperactive. This, too, is misleading. In recent years, it has become increasingly evident that hyperactivity is an unsatisfactory catch-all word and is surely not appropriate as a diagnostic category. Whereas in earlier literature (for example, Strauss and Lehtinen, 1947) the term implied organic impairment of the central nervous system (brain injury), William Cruickshank et al. (1961) and subsequent researchers have found it

extremely difficult to identify positively an organic etiological factor in many instances. Recently, some researchers and clinical practitioners have identified several additional etiological factors, each of which requires a particular mode of treatment. These include hypoglycemia (low blood sugar), allergic reactions, other dietary deficiencies or problems (Cott, 1972), and more mundane factors, including even ill-fitting underwear.

Some writers prefer to distinguish between *hyperkinecity* and hyperactivity. The former term is reserved for those cases in which some evidence of organic brain damage is present, and the latter is used when it is determined that cortical lesions may not be present. Such a judgment may be based on "hard signs," (that is, positive diagnostic indications) but in most instances "soft signs" such as performance patterns in drawing or on certain psychological tests are relied on.

Unfortunately, the concept of hyperactivity in children has produced a great deal of panic, irrationality, and faddishness in adults. In keeping with what has seemed to some observers to represent a characteristic American solution, *chemotherapy* has been seen as an appropriate route. Some of the dangers inherent in the approach of "drugging America's children" have been amply described elsewhere (for example, Grinspoon and Singer, 1973); the "Ritalin controversy" will not again be rehearsed here. It suffices to state some cautions concerning the use of amphetamine-like chemicals, such as methylphenidate hydrochloride (Ritalin), especially with young children:

1. Educators *cannot* prescribe drugs, nor should they under any circumstances suggest drugs to parents (Bosco, 1975).
2. For a teacher to label a child as hyperactive or hyperkinetic may be tantamount, in some cases (hopefully isolated ones), to "prescribing" drug treatment, since doctors' prescriptions are often based on second-

hand information (Neisworth et al., 1976).

3. Some adults, including teachers and parents, have inordinate control needs, and "control" may be made easier by psychotropic drugs.

4. Little is known about possibly deleterious side effects and long-term consequences of such drugs, *especially* with young children.

Distractibility and *short attention span* are twin symptoms usually associated with hyperactivity. Again, it is almost in the nature of young children to be distractible, to be readily seduced by an attractive sight or sound. Most young children, however, are also able to exhibit a truly amazing degree of concentration and continuous attention, as Maria Montessori observed (see especially Montessori, 1949). Montessori thought that teachers mistakenly suspend "work" in the classroom at the first sign of restlessness—what she called "false fatigue." She insisted that if the child were allowed to continue (as is the case in most orthodox Montessori classrooms), he would enter his "period of great work," his most productive time. She believed that teachers, including those who teach very young children, do their pupils a grave injustice by *depriving* them of this opportunity and urged that we attend to factors in the classroom environment (especially the characteristics of learning materials) that can enhance interest, maintain attention, arouse innate curiosity and perseverance, and provide feedback for the child.

Attentional deficits comprise one of the most extensively investigated problems among children with learning disabilities. Attention is considered by some (Hewett, 1969) the most basic prerequisite for learning, although some investigators (for example, Harris, 1976) think that mere *attending behavior* has been overrated. Attention, however, is probably a complex multilevel process reflected in different ways in all aspects of learning. Keogh and Margolis (1976), for example, have distin-

guished three distinct phases: (1) coming to attention, (2) decision making, and (3) maintaining attention. There is ample evidence that many learning-disabled children have more difficulties in various aspects of focusing and maintaining attention and resisting distraction than do their peers (Tarver and Hallahan, 1974).

PROGRAMMING IN THE EARLY CHILDHOOD CLASSROOM

There are increasing efforts to identify children with possible learning problems during the early childhood years and to provide special programs if appropriate. Whether in such a special program or in a "regular" nursery, Head Start, day care center, kindergarten, or primary classroom, some general guides can be provided for programming. This section will discuss four general aspects of planning and carrying out a teaching approach that is appropriate for children of ages 3 through 8 who may have specific learning problems:

1. An individualized diagnostic approach
2. Provision for planned motor activity
3. Use of an intersensory approach
4. Importance of the physical environment

Developing an individualized diagnostic approach

The teaching of children and youth with specific learning problems, at all age levels, is notable mainly for its highly individualized focus. Although group activities may be employed, each decision concerning an individual student's activity is based on an assessment of that student's current situation. Although differences exist among practitioners concerning the *how* of diagnosis and remediation, there is virtually universal agreement that teaching of children and youth with learning disabilities must be based on a diagnosis of the learner's characteristics and needs.

The purpose of diagnosis, in education as in medicine, is to point to the appropriate "treatment." Diagnostic teaching is carried out to ensure that what is provided for the learner is congruent with his needs at that moment. The aim, to use the phrase of Hunt (1961), is to solve "the problem of the match." Although not all educators like to pursue the medical analogy this far, some identify the step that follows diagnosis as the *prescription* phase.

Philosophical differences have existed among educators for many years as to whether education is or should be *prescriptive* in nature. In early education, the *Integrated Day* model that characterizes the English Infant School (see, for example, Brown and Precious, 1969) and the nursery school approach that emerges from Kamii's (1971) interpretation of piagetian theory would seem to point toward a nonprescriptive, child-directed orientation to teaching. On the other hand, Hodges et al. (1971) described an objective data-based prescriptive approach.

The most crucial and fundamental tenet of the diagnostic approach to teaching is that children differ, not only from each other (*interindividual* differences), but also within themselves (*intraindividual* differences) (Kirk, 1972). Although it is sometimes necessary to group children by type or category, based on commonality of some general characteristic such as age or IQ range, it is known to every teacher— and every parent and child as well—that wide differences exist within such categories. In addition to these differences within groups, however, an individual's own abilities may differ. Basic to the concept of *specific learning disabilities* is the assumption that a child has special needs for assistance and specialized programming in one or more areas, but not in all.

Basically, the idea of intraindividual differences rests on the assumption that for every child it is possible to plot a profile of strengths and weaknesses, areas of above average, average, and below average functioning (compared to age norms), that can be of use in instructional planning. It is possible, and probably most useful, to construct an actual graphic profile, rather than to use the term in a metaphoric sense.

The key to diagnostic/prescriptive teaching is assessment. Initial assessment enables the teacher to identify the child's current levels of functioning in the various areas, which leads in turn to the establishment of instructional objectives. Both formal, standardized tests and informal procedures such as observation and teacher-constructed measures may be used.

One way of using diagnostic information is to determine whether a child seems to learn better in one modality (mainly visual or auditory) and then to teach him accordingly. A diagnostic profile may suggest strengths to be exploited, as well as weaknesses to be remedied. The notion that "visual learners" respond best to visually oriented methods and materials, whereas "auditory learners" need emphasis on sound, rather than sight, is an appealing one. Probably much informal, subjective evidence can be gathered in its support. Unfortunately, research has not conclusively demonstrated the value of differential teaching based on diagnosed *modality preferences* for young children. Waugh (1973) found that "auditory learning" second graders exceeded "visual learners" on both auditory *and* visual tasks, and Newcomer and Goodman (1976) found that fourth-grade "visual learners" learned meaningful tasks equally well regardless of how they were presented.

Language skills comprise an area of particular concern in diagnostic teaching of young children. The diagnostic focus concerns *receptive* abilities, *expressive* abilities, and *association* of receptive and expressive processes. Since it is so basic to all aspects of school learning, language has been especially analyzed as an appropriate area for early intervention. Among the useful references concerning this area is *Language and Learning Disorders of the*

Pre-Academic Child by Tina E. Bangs (1968).

One test that has been extensively used to plot profiles of pupils' strengths and weaknesses is the *Illinois Test of Psycholinguistic Abilities* (ITPA) (Kirk et al., 1968). This test is administered individually to children between 2 and 9 years of age by persons competent and experienced in individual testing and specifically trained in the use of this test; these may be psychologists, special education teachers, or speech-language specialists.

Remedial teaching based on diagnostic assessment with the ITPA focuses on underlying psycholinguistic process measured by the various subtests. There are three basic questions that must be addressed concerning the validity of this approach:

1. Do the subtests actually measure the specific psycholinguistic abilities they purport to measure?
2. If so, are these abilities relevant to learning of academic skills and subjects?
3. If they are related to academic skills, will remediation of psycholinguistic process deficiencies improve the child's ability to learn the related academic skills?

Several remedial programs have been developed as systems for psycholinguistic training (Minskoff et al., 1973; Kirk and Kirk, 1971). In a publication titled *ITPA Remediation Materials,* Marion L. Peacock (1974) lists, by subtest area, some 375 commercially available materials to be used in remediation of psycholinguistic skill deficiencies.

How effective is psycholinguistic training? Hammill and Larsen (1974), in reviewing 38 studies, concluded that there is insufficient validation to support the psycholinguistic skill training approach. They endorse direct remediation of deficient academic skills, rather than indirect efforts intended to strengthen "underlying" processes (auditory or visual sequential memory, discrimination of figure from background, etc.). In a rebuttal, however, Minskoff (1975) noted flaws in the training studies reported. In particular she stresses their failure to provide for the *individuality* of children's learning characteristics and needs.

Psycholinguistic training based on any particular formal testing program is certainly not the only possible method of diagnostic teaching. Formal, standardized tests play a role, but informal, *criterion-referenced* assessment may be more important. Using a variety of methods, the teacher continually assesses the child's progress. Every activity and every task provides an opportunity for diagnosis. Diagnostic *checklists* or *profiles,* such as that developed by Robert Valett (1969), can enable the teacher to maintain an ongoing record of each child's accomplishments while also making it possible to identify next steps.

Provision for planned motor activity

Kephart (1971) described four major *motor generalizations* as underlying subsequent learning: (1) balance and maintenance of posture, (2) locomotion, (3) contact (including grasping and releasing), and (4) receipt and propulsion. Each of these areas can be translated into a wide variety of activities for the early childhood classroom beneficial to all children as well as to the child with special problems in any of these areas.

Eurythmics and movement-to-music activities are pleasurable while also helpful to all children in gaining greater muscle control and coordination. A variety of games that involve imitative movement, including alternately paced walking, running, hopping, skipping, jumping in place, etc., can be introduced as well as movement routines to exercise records such as "Chicken Fat." Obstacle courses are also fun and challenging for all and can involve an almost infinite variety of positions, locomotion attitudes, and muscle combinations. Balance beams and individual balance boards can also be used,

both to identify children who show problems in equilibrium and coordination and to assist all children in these areas. Motor skills and perceptual-motor training have long been stressed in remedial work with young children who may have or may develop specific learning problems. One of the earliest guides for teachers' use in remediation, *The Slow Learner in the Classroom*, by Kephart (1971) is still widely used (first edition published in 1960).

Games such as "Bear Hunt" and "Simon Says" provide good opportunities to observe children who have difficulties imitating movement, translating visual clues into motor acts, or inhibiting motor acts. Similarly, they are helpful in developing and improving the abilities of attending, inhibiting, and imitating. Wheeled vehicles (tricycles, cars, etc.) have a legitimate place, and special wheeled equipment, such as scooter boards, is also appropriate.

Balls of all kinds can be profitably used in working on receipt and propulsion, using both unilateral (one hand) and bilateral (both hands) modes and alternating positions for both kinds of acts and with balls of varying sizes and textures. Beanbags and balls of spongy material combine contact with receipt and propulsion. Rhythmic ball bouncing (as in some traditional children's games) can have a wide variety of applications, for example, in combining motor coordination with awareness of linguistic rhythms. Suspension of a Marsden ball (Kephart, 1971) from the ceiling permits one, two, or more children to gain experience in visual-motor coordination by batting the ball with a stick held alternately in the right and left hands and in both hands (so that the ball is met in front of the body).

In addition to the many implications the teacher of young children may draw from the activities recommended by Kephart (1968, 1971), at least two other individuals have been particularly active in generating recommended educational practices that involve motor activity and that are based on theories emphasizing the role of motor development. Like Kephart, these authors have focused more on the children of school age, who are more likely to have been identified as having learning disabilities, than on children less than 5 years of age. However, their work can readily be translated into activities appropriate for young children. R. H. Barsch (1965, 1967) has developed educational procedures based on a "movigenic" theory concerning the relationship between motor patterns and learning.

Getman et al. (1968) have formulated a "visuomotor model" that, although it places major emphasis on visual perception, approaches this objective (as does Kephart) through building earlier patterns of motor functioning that are subsequently coordinated with visual perceptual processes.

Professionals in the fields of physical education and occupational therapy have become increasingly interested in early identification and amelioration of learning disabilities through motor activities. Frequently, early childhood educational programs are able to call on members of these professions who have secured special training to provide guidance. In recent years, a number of publications, including several books, have appeared in which a great many suggestions for promoting learning through movement are contributed. These include *Motor Development in Early Childhood: A Guide for Movement Education With Ages Two to Six* by Dr. Betty M. Flinchum (1975) and *Education of Children Through Motor Activity* by Dr. James H. Humphrey (1975). Cratty, in particular, has done extensive work in the area of motor activity and its relationship to learning and intelligence (Cratty, 1970).

Although positive ties between motoric approaches to intervention and amelioration of problems in academic skill areas have not been demonstrated conclusively (their relationship is certainly a *theoretically* reasonable hypothesis), there are undoubtedly values in motor experience for its own sake. The desirability of incorporating a great many provisions for physical activity, including large muscle exercise and coordination, in educational programs for young children had long been maintained and is therefore nothing new. It is surprising, however, to what extent these avenues are neglected, especially in kindergarten and primary grade programs, which may make little provision for appropriate equipment, space, or time for active learning, especially that involving large muscle activity.

Use of an intersensory approach

One area that has been especially stressed in educational intervention for young children with possible learning problems is that of *visual perception*. The work of Marianne Frostig (1970; Frostig et al., 1964; Frostig and Horne, 1964) has been particularly influential. However, both Kephart's and Getman's recommended diagnostic and remedial strategies emphasize visual perception at least as much as motor functioning.

One obvious explanation for this stress has been the apparent relationship between visual perception and reading. A child who perceives images inaccurately or in distorted fashion, or who has difficulty in distinguishing figure from background, would presumably be especially handicapped in learning to read. A child who cannot coordinate visual and motor skills would be expected to have a difficult time in learning to write.

As in the case of psycholinguistic skill training, perceptual training based on diagnostic testing is fraught with controversy. The problem is twofold:

1. The relationship between reading skills and a child's performance on diagnostic tests of visual perception has not been clearly established by research (Sabatino, 1974).
2. The effectiveness of training in visual perception skills as a means of improving reading has not been demonstrated by research (Hammill and Wiederholt, 1972; Sabatino, 1974).

Nevertheless, although reading is a multifactored skill, visual perception is clearly involved (Spache, 1972). In teaching young children, guided perceptual experiences may be particularly appropriate, however, almost irrespective of their relationship to reading.

Furthermore, there are reports in the literature that individualized remediation based on diagnosis can be effective in correcting some perceptual problems, such as reversals (Greenspan, 1975). To aid in identifying specific problems in visual perception, a great many tests and procedures are available, each with its own particular merits and limitations (Colarusso and Gill, 1975). Probably selective diagnosis and remedial procedures that are specific to the individual child, rather than global visual perceptual *programs,* will enable the teacher of young children to give appropriate emphasis to this area.

Importance of the physical environment

Since services first began to be provided for children with learning disabilities, the learning environment has been considered of the utmost importance. Dr. William Cruickshank, in particular, has contributed specific guidelines and rationale for the design of classrooms for children with learning problems (Cruickshank et al., 1961). He has continued to stress the importance of helping the child to monitor and filter environmental input through his senses, rather than overwhelming him with distracting stimuli. Cruickshank notes (1975) that insufficient and inadequate research has addressed the area of environmental considerations for children with learning disabilities.

These children are sometimes described as *overly* responsive to stimulation from their environment. They have difficulty in focusing attention, in discriminating central from peripheral features in visual or auditory stimuli, and in the ability to *inhibit* response (Cruickshank et al., 1961).

Some general guidelines for early childhood classroom arrangement suggested by children's problems in screening out irrelevant stimuli and in refraining from responding would be the following:

1. The actual size of the classroom itself is significant. If the room is too large, the child may feel overwhelmed by sheer space, in which it is difficult to establish a sense of location and orientation. Should the available space be inappropriately large, the teacher can use furniture skillfully to divide it or even to reduce it. It is important to be sure that partitions or furniture are sturdy, resistant to stress, and that they achieve the desired reduction in psychological space, rather than merely restrict movement.

2. Areas of the room used as learning centers should be clearly designated and employed consistently in the intended manner. In one area, large muscle activity may be appropriate (where, for example, the balance beam is located, physical exercise takes place, and patterned bouncing of rubber balls is guided); another area calls forth different behavior—quiet play or sitting at a table, for example.

3. Visual displays should be simple and sharply focused, emphasizing planned use

of color and dimension to highlight the central feature.

4. Each child may have his own identifiable "area" or "place" in the classroom. In some self-contained special classes or resource rooms for children with learning disabilities, each child has his own "office," that is, an individual partitioned cubicle. The sides of the cubicle serve to provide "psychological blinders" of a sort by enabling the child to concentrate on his own task without distraction. Within the cubicle is a writing surface, which may simply be a school desk. Either in this space or in another definite, specified location, the teacher leaves for each child assigned work, instructions, special communications, etc. In many learning disabilities classrooms, each child enters the room and goes directly to his own shelf, drawer, or bin to see what communications are there for him. In this way, he is able to begin immediately during those crucial first few minutes to structure his activity in a purposeful way.

5. Instructional or other materials that are not being used are stored in such a way that they do not distract the children from their work. Closed cabinets may be preferable to open shelves for this purpose.

6. The watchword of the classroom is *structure*. It is a *controlled environment* in which the child can become better able to structure his own behavior.

A number of ideas and guidelines suggested and developed by Strauss and Lehtinen (1947), Cruickshank et al. (1961), Haring and Phillips (1962), and Hewett (1969) have been incorporated in many classroom programs for children with learning disabilities. In particular, the concept of *structure* itself has been effectively defined by these leaders in terms of the classroom situation. Other models and designs for the learning environment have been developed specifically for young children or considered particularly appropriate, in particular, the Montessori method (Montesorri, 1949), the Respon-

sive Environment (Nimnicht and Johnson, 1973) and the informal or integrated day approach. These various designs for the physical environment are discussed and compared in Chapter 11.

TEACHER AND PARENT TEAMWORK AND COMMUNICATION

It may be that a learning-disabled child's parents have been unaware of any developmental problems before the child is identified in school. If this is the case, such news from public school personnel can be received with shock, possibly disbelief. The new laws make it essential that a child's parents participate in any consideration of special diagnostic evaluation, programming, or special school placement. The teacher has an extremely important role in establishing effective communication and genuine understanding concerning the child's needs, as he or she sees them. It is imperative that the teacher be able to describe *specifically* that a child has certain special learning needs or problems. This is, of course, true in every area of handicap.

The parents of a child with a learning problem will continue to play an important part in terms of his educational needs, even beyond the necessary involvement in planning and placement decision making. Sometimes an actual *home program* to be carried out by the parents may be difficult to implement (Neifert and Gayton, 1973) or may be inappropriate. However, generally there will be some attempt to insure carry-over and consistency. Parent's attitudes toward their learning-disabled child are extremely important to the child's ability to improve his skills and to maintain positive feelings about himself and learning (Wetter, 1972). With young children, parents may need guidance in the area of child management to sustain optimal interaction between parents, child, and other family members (Doleys et al., 1976). In all these areas, the importance of ongoing, open home-school communication cannot be emphasized enough.

Education of children with specific learning disabilities is virtually a brand new field. There is great need for research to identify the most effective means of teaching children who present such a wide variety of still enigmatic problems. The ultimate goal is to be able to match teaching method precisely to the accurately diagnosed needs and learning characteristics of each individual child—to accomplish the *psychoeducational match* (Cruickshank, 1975). The area of learning disabilities still sustains the belief that, through appropriate and effective early intervention, serious problems in academic learning and personal-social adjustment *can* be prevented. Teachers of young children, working together with parents, may be the most crucial persons in determining the success or failure of children with manifest or potential learning problems throughout their educational career.

DISCUSSION QUESTIONS

1. What are the most important elements of official definitions of learning disabilities?
2. What is the basis for perceptual-motor training in the remediation of learning disabilities? Why is the effectiveness of this sort of approach controversial?
3. What are some of the issues and problems in early identification of learning disabilities (prior to age 5 or 6 years)? How, in your opinion, could some of these problems be overcome?
4. Discuss the role of early childhood education in *primary prevention* of learning disabilities.
5. How can various specialists and the "regular" early childhood education teacher work together to provide for young children with specific learning problems?
6. What are some of the issues involved in the controversy concerning the use of drugs with hyperactive and learning-disabled children?
7. Many special educators believe that altering the *learning environment* is more appropriate and effective than "altering the child" through the use of drugs, diet therapy, etc. Why? What kinds of environmental factors can be modified, and how?

REFERENCES

Adkins, P. G., and Walker, C. A call for early learning centers. *Academic Therapy*, 1972, 7, 447-451.

Bangs, T. E. *Language and learning disorders of the pre-academic child.* New York: Appleton-Century-Crofts, 1968.

Barsch, R. A. *A movigenics curriculum.* Madison, Wis.: State Department of Public Instruction, 1965.

Barsch, R. A. *Achieving perceptual-motor efficiency.* Seattle: Special Child Publications, 1967.

Benson, D. F. Graphic orientation disorders of left handed children. *Journal of Learning Disabilities*, 1970, 3(3), 6-11.

Bloom, B. S., Hastings, J. T., and Madans, G. F. *Handbook on formative and summerative evaluation of student learning,* New York: McGraw-Hill Book Co., 1972, pp. 43-60.

Bosco, J. Behavior modification, drugs, and the schools: the case of Ritalin. *Phi Delta Kappan,* 1975, 7, 489-492.

Brazelton, T. B. Assessment of the infant at risk. *Clinical Obstetrics and Gynecology,* 1973, 16, 361.

Brown, M., and Precious, N. *The integrated day in the primary school.* New York: Agathon Press, Inc., 1969.

Bryan, T. H., and Bryan, J. H. *Understanding learning disabilities.* Port Washington, N.Y., Alfred Publishing Co., Inc., 1975.

Cohen, M. E. *Betz wishz doc.* New York: Penguin Books, 1974.

Colarusso, R. P., and Gill, S. Selecting a test of visual perception. *Academic Therapy,* 1975, 11(2), 157-167.

Colligan, R. C. Psychometric deficits related to perinatal stress. *Journal of Learning Disabilities,* 1974, 7(3), 36-42.

Cott, A. Megavitamins: the orthomolecular approach to behavioral disorders and learning disabilities. *Academic Therapy,* 1972, 7, 245-257.

Cowgill, M. L., et al. Predicting learning disabilities from kindergarten reports. *Journal of Learning Disabilities,* 1973, 6(9), 577-582.

Cratty, B. Perceptual and motor development in infants and children, New York: Macmillan Publishing Co., Inc., 1970.

Cruickshank, W. M. The psychoeducational match. In W. M. Cruickshank and D. P. Hallahan (Eds.). *Perceptual and learning disabilities in children: psychoeducational practices* (Vol. 1). Syracuse: Syracuse University Press, 1975, 71-114.

Cruickshank, W., Bentzen, F., Ratzeburg, F., and Tannhauser, M. A teaching methodology for brain-injured and hyperactive children. Syracuse: Syracuse University Press, 1961.

Denhoff, E. Precursive factors to early and later identified learning disabilities. *Slow Learning Child,* 1972, 19(2), 79-85.

deQuiros, J. B. Diagnosis of vestibular disorders in the learning disabled. *Journal of Learning Disabilities,* 1976, 9, 1.

Doleys, D., Cartelli, L. M., and Doster, J. Comparison of patterns of mother-child interaction. *Journal of Learning Disabilities,* 1976, 9(6), 42-46.

Eaves, L. C., et al. The early detection of minimal

brain dysfunction. *Journal of Learning Disabilities,* 1972, *5,* 454-462.

Feingold, B. F. *Why your child is hyperactive.* New York: Random House, Inc., 1975.

Flinchum, B. M. *Motor development in early childhood: a guide for movement education with ages two to six.* St. Louis: The C. V. Mosby Co., 1975.

Forness, S., and Esveldt, K. Prediction of high-risk kindergarten children through classroom observation. *Journal of Special Education,* 1975, *9,* 375-386.

Francis-Williams, J. *Children with specific learning disabilities.* New York: Pergamon Press, Inc., 1970.

Frostig, M. *Movement education: theory and practice.* Chicago: Follett Publishing Co., 1970.

Frostig, M., and Horne, D. *The Frostig program for the development of visual perception.* Chicago: Follett Publishing Co., 1964.

Frostig, M., Maslow, P., Lefever, D. W., and Whittlesey, J. R. B. *The Marianne Frostig Developmental Test of Visual Perception.* Palo Alto, Calif.: Consulting Psychologists Press, 1964.

Getman, G. N., Kane, E. R., Halgren, M. R., and McKee, G. W. *Developing learning readiness.* New York: Webster Division, McGraw-Hill Book Co., 1968.

Gibson, E. Learning to read. *Science,* 1965, *148,* 1066-1072.

Greenspan, S. B. Effectiveness of therapy for children's reversal confusions. *Academic Therapy,* 1975, *11*(2), 169-178.

Grinspoon, L., and Singer, S. Amphetamines in the treatment of hyperkinetic children. *Harvard Educational Review,* 1973, *43,* 515-555.

Grotberg, E. H. Neurological aspects of learning disabilities: a case for the disadvantaged. *Journal of Learning Disabilities,* 1970, *3,* 25-31.

Hammill, D. Assessing and training perceptual-motor processes. In *Teaching children with learning and behavior problems.* Boston: Allyn & Bacon, Inc., 1975, pp. 203-274.

Hammill, D. D., and Larsen, S. The effectiveness of psycholinguistic training. *Exceptional Children,* 1974, *41,* 5-14.

Hammill, D. D., and Wiederholt, J. L. Review of the Frostig Visual Perception Test and the related training program. In L. Mann and D. Sabatino (Eds.). *First review of special education* (Vol. 1). Philadelphia: Journal of Special Education Press, 1972.

Haring, N. G. and Phillips, E. L. *Educating emotionally disturbed children.* New York: McGraw-Hill Book Co., 1962.

Harris, L. P. Attention and learning disordered children: a review of theory and remediation. *Journal of Learning Disabilities,* 1976, *9*(2), 100-110.

Hewett, F. *The emotionally disturbed child in the classroom.* Boston: Allyn & Bacon, Inc., 1969.

Hiltbrunner, C. L., and Vasa, S. F. Watch the children: precision referring. *Academic Therapy,* 1974-1975, Winter, 167-172.

Hodges, W. L., McCandless, B. R., and Spicker, H. H. *Diagnostic teaching for preschool children,* Arlington, Va.: Council for Exceptional Children, 1971.

Humphrey, J. H. *Education of children through motor activity.* Springfield, Ill.: Charles C Thomas, Publisher, 1975.

Hunt, J. McV. *Intelligence and experience.* New York: The Ronald Press Co., 1961.

Kamii, C. K. Evaluation of learning in preschool education: socio-emotional, perceptual-motor, and cognitive development. In B. S. Bloom, J. T. Hastings, and G. F. Madaus (Eds.), *Handbook on formative and summative evaluation of student learning.* New York: McGraw-Hill Book Co., 1971, pp. 281-344.

Keogh, B. K., and Becker, L. D. Early detection of learning problems: questions, cautions, and guidelines. *Exceptional Child,* 1973, *40,* 5-11.

Keogh, B., and Margolis, J. Learn to labor and to wait: attentional problems of children with learning disorders. *Journal of Learning Disorders,* 1976, *9,* 276-284.

Keogh, B. K., and Smith, C. E. Early identification of educationally high potential and high risk children. *Journal of School Psychology,* 1970, *8,* 285-290.

Kephart, N. C. Teaching the child with a perceptual-motor handicap. In M. Bortner (Ed.), *Evaluation and education of children with brain damage.* Springfield, Ill.: Charles C Thomas, Publisher, pp. 147-192.

Kephart, N. C. *The slow learner in the classroom* (2nd ed.). Columbus, Ohio: Charles E. Merrill Publishing Co., 1971.

Kephart, N. C. The perceptual-motor match. In W. M. Cruickshank and D. P. Hallahan (Eds.), *Perceptual and learning disabilities in children: psychoeducational practices* (Vol. 1). Syracuse: Syracuse University Press, 1975, 63-70.

Kirk, S. A. *Educating exceptional children.* Boston: Houghton Mifflin Co., 1972.

Kirk, S. A., and Kirk, W. D. *Psycholinguistic learning disabilities: diagnosis and remediation.* Urbana, Ill.: University of Illinois Press, 1971.

Kirk, S. A., McCarthy, J. J., and Kirk, W. D. *Illinois Test of Psycholinguistic Abilities* (Rev. ed.). Urbana, Ill.: University of Illinois Press, 1968.

Mayberry, W. Developing infant predictors for sensory-integrative dysfunction. *American Journal of Occupational Therapy,* 1974, *28,* 141-143.

McCarthy, J. Input lecture by Jeanne McCarthy. In N. D. Bryant and C. Kass (Eds.), *Final report: LTI in learning disabilities* (Vol. 2). (U.S.O.E. Grant No. OEG-0-71-4425-604, project No. 127145.). Tucson: University of Arizona, 1972, pp. 162-163.

McElgunn, B. Learning disability: the need for medical research. *Journal of Learning Disabilities,* 1976, *9,* 393-395.

McKenzie, H. S. Special education and consulting teachers. In F. Clarke, D. Evans, and L. Hammerlynk (Eds.), *Implementing behavioral programs for schools.* Champaign, Ill.: Research Press Co., 1972, 103-125.

McKnab, P. A., and Fine, M. J. The Vane kindergarten test as a predictor of first grade achievement. *Journal of Learning Disabilities,* 1972, *5,* 503-505.

Minskoff, E. Research on psycholinguistic training: critique and guidelines. *Exceptional Children,* 1975, *42,* 136-143.

Minskoff, E., Wiseman, D., and Minskoff, J. *The MWM program for developing language abilities.* Ridgefield, N.J.: Educational Performance Associates, 1973.

Montessori, M. *The absorbent mind.* Madras, India: Theosophical Publishing House, 1949.

Moss, J. W. Disabled or disadvantaged: there is a difference! *Journal of Special Education,* 1973, *7,* 387-391.

Myers, R. E. Fetal trauma—psychological stress. *Journal of Learning Disabilities,* 1976, *9,* 33-34.

Neifert, J., and Gayton, W. Parents and the home program approach in the remediation of learning disabilities. *Journal of Learning Disabilities,* 1973, *6,* 31-35.

Neisworth, J., et al. Naturalistic assessment of neurological diagnoses and pharmacological intervention. *Journal of Learning Disabilities,* 1976, *9,* 149-152.

Newcomer, P., and Goodman, M. Effect of modality of instruction on the learning of meaningful and non-meaningful tasks by auditory and visual learners. *Journal of Learning Disabilities,* 1976, *9*(3), 261-268.

Nimnicht, G. P., and Johnson, J. A., Jr. *Beyond "compensatory education". A new approach to educating children.* San Francisco: Far West Laboratory for Educational Research and Development, 1973.

Novack, H. S., Bonaventura, E., and Merenda, P. F. A scale for early detection of children with learning problems. *Exceptional Children,* 1973, *39,* 98-100.

Peacock, M. L. *ITPA remediation materials.* Clarksville, Fla.: Carr School, 1974.

Raman, S. P. Role of nutrition in the actualization of the potentialities of the child: an anise perspective. *Young Children,* 1975, *30*(1), 24-32.

Reitan, R. M., and Boll, T. J. Psychological correlates of minimal brain dysfunction. *Annals of the New York Academy of Sciences,* 1973, *205,* 65-88.

Rubin, R., et al. Psychological and educational sequence of prematurity. *Pediatrics,* 1973, *52,* 352-363.

Sabatino, D. P. What does the Frostig DTVP measure? *Exceptional Children,* 1974, *40,* 453-454.

Saphier, D. The relation of perceptual-motor skills to learning and school success. *Journal of Learning Disabilities,* 1973, *6,* 583-592.

Schaer, H., and Crump, D. Teacher involvement and early identification of children with learning disabilities. *Journal of Learning Disabilities,* 1976, *9*(2), 91-95.

Shipe, D., and Miezitis, S. A pilot study in the diagnosis and remediation of special learning disabilities in preschool children. *Journal of Learning Disabilities,* 1969, *2,* 579-592.

Spache, E. B. *Reading activities for school involvement.* Boston: Allyn & Bacon, Inc., 1972.

Strauss, A. A., and Lehtinen, L. E. *Psychopathology and education of the brain-injured child.* New York: Grune & Stratton, Inc., 1947.

Tarver, S. G., and Hallahan, D. P. Attention deficits in children with learning disabilities. *Journal of Learning Disabilities,* 1974, *7,* 36-45.

Uyeda, F. F. The detection of learning disabilities in the early school age child. *Journal of School Health,* 1972, *42,* 214-217.

Valett, R. *Developmental survey of basic learning abilities.* Belmont, Calif.: Fearon Publishers, 1969.

Wallace, G., and McLoughlin, J. A. *Learning disabilities: concepts and characteristics.* Columbus, Ohio: Charles E. Merrill Publishing Co., 1975.

Waugh, R. P. Relationship between modality preference and performance. *Exceptional Children,* 1973, *39,* 465-469.

Werner, H., and Strauss, A. Pathology of figure-background relationship in the child. *Journal of Abnormal and Social Psychology,* 1941, *36,* 236-248.

Wetter, J. Parent attitudes toward learning disability. *Exceptional Children,* 1972, *38,* 490-491.

CHAPTER 7

EMOTIONAL AND BEHAVIORAL DISORDERS

CONCEPTUAL AND SOCIAL ISSUES
What does it mean to teach emotionally disturbed children?

Emotional disturbance is a condition experienced by everyone at various times during our lives. Therefore it is possible for us to empathize with a chronically or acutely disturbed individual, for that person's suffering is something that has been experienced, to some degree and in some way, by each of us. Perhaps the reaction of fear generated by the thought of contact with someone who is seriously emotionally ill is based not only on the belief that the person might bring harm to us, but also on the subliminal awareness that the individual may be acting out impulses that exist within ourselves.

Who is emotionally disturbed? Is there, indeed, such a phenomenon as "mental illness" (Szasz, 1970)? During the last two decades a resistance has developed within the field of education, as well as other "mental health" disciplines—psychiatry, clinical psychology, and social work—to use of a medical model in studying the origins of impaired personal and social functioning and in providing treatment. "Traditional" approaches, involving a *psychodynamic* framework, have been abandoned by many professionals in favor of perspectives that emphasize the *environmental context* in which a person's behavior occurs rather than hypothesizing conflicting forces that operate *within* the individual.

Divergent etiological explanations may or may not imply different treatment approaches. Teachers who interact with children on a day-to-day basis may be primarily interested in discovering what "works" in guiding children's social behavior. This is understandable and quite appropriate. However, teaching is by no means entirely a matter of engineering, even though we have progressed in developing a "technology of teaching" (Skinner, 1968; Haring, 1974). Differences of opinion exist concerning the validity of various methods, and there is also limited knowledge concerning the long-range effects of specific interventions. There are unresolved value questions, as well as an underlying value dimension that cuts across every facet of teaching. A teacher must ask himself or herself questions such as these: *What is important for the children I teach? What are my goals as a teacher? What do I wish to help children to do and to become? What ways of interacting with my children will be an authentic representation of me as a person and of my values?*

Discipline, control, and the difficult child

Such questions as these become readily recognized as important when one considers the issue of the school's response to deviance in children's behavior. Charles Silberman (1970), for example, found in his study of American schools, at all levels, two predominant problems: a pervasive *mindlessness* and a *preoccupation with control*. Do we wish to employ strategies of behavior management that will most efficiently ensure our control over the individual child and the group? If so, there are highly effective and efficient methods of doing this that depend on external control. However, most teachers accept the principle that the aim of classroom discipline is the *internalization* of control by the child (Morse and Wingo, 1969). If we agree with this premise then we must ask what strategies of behavior management will be most congruent with this goal, rather than merely choosing a method that ensures compliance with the teacher's demands. As William Glasser (1969) has observed, children too often feel no personal responsibility for their behavior if it is the adult teacher who controls and manages, rewards and punishes.

Some observers fear that educators' responses to behavioral deviance in children are likely to reflect primary concern with considerations other than what will benefit the child whose behavior is discordant. A child may engage in behavior that disrupts the classroom, for example, and interferes with the learning of others. As a consequence, many people have been outspoken concerning the need for special class programs for these children. Dealing with a child who does not respond well to the teacher's usual classroom management and motivational strategies is perplexing and difficult as well as exhausting. Many believe that a "different" type of classroom structure with a specialist in charge is necessary. That *every* teacher should be equally effective in serving *all* children, no matter how complex their needs, is certainly an unreasonable expectation—an "omnicompetence demand" (Redl and Wattenberg, 1959).

Another side of the question, however, is suggested by the following observations:

1. Many teachers who are very effective in the area of positive discipline and classroom management with children who do not present pronounced emotional and behavioral deviance are also very effective with those children who do (Kounin et al., 1966).
2. With very few exceptions (for example, Vacc, 1968), most of the research studies undertaken to measure the efficacy of the special class vs. the regular class integration mode of educating behaviorally deviant children have failed to demonstrate the superiority of the special class approach.
3. There is evidence that regular class teachers, even those lacking prior ability to cope with the difficult child, can be helped to acquire the "competencies" necessary to do so (Lilly, 1974).

The problem of exclusion

Another pressing issue is posed by the children and youth for whom schools currently fail to provide *any* educational services. A Children's Defense Fund study (1974) revealed that, across the United States, an incredible number of children are "out of school," often because of deviant social behavior with which the schools have been unable to cope. A further observation is that this group, as well as the population of children referred for special class placement for behavioral deviance, includes disproportionately large percentages of children of minority groups —Black, American Indian, Mexican-American, Puerto Rican–American, and others. This provides substantiation for the accusation by many of these groups that institutional racism permeates the American educational system.

It is the position here that *exclusion* is an inappropriate, unconstitutional, and immoral response to deviance. It is the educator's responsibility to develop and to make available for each child an educational opportunity appropriate to his needs and from which he will derive optimal benefit. That this goal is difficult to accomplish is obvious; that it is essential to pursue has been unequivocally established and is now reflected in federal law.

The foregoing is intended to suggest neither that all children benefit equally from the same mode of instruction, nor that "behaviorally deviant" is merely a code word for culturally different. Perhaps more than ever before in our history, many children and young people—as well as adults—experience conflicts that are crippling in their effects. It is essential, then, that we as teachers seek helping solutions to the problems of individual children, rather than contribute to their problems through adding to their sense of alienation, inadequacy, rejection, or failure.

The child as victim

It is a tragic truism that, in time of conflict or catastrophe, it is children who suffer most. What is less generally faced is the widespread neglect and cruelty with which children still must contend. Physical and psychological abuse of infants, children, and youth has only recently been addressed as a national concern.

Child malnutrition persists to an appalling extent in the midst of plenty. Neglect, abandonment, sexual violation, and exploitation of children continue.

In fact, concern for the *emotional* well-being of children is a very recent phenomenon (Despert, 1965). The idea of *childhood* as we think of it today has apparently itself been "discovered" quite recently (Aries, 1962). It was not so long ago that small children were subjected to brutal labor in coal mines. The French author Emile Zola, in his great novel *Germinal,* portrayed vividly the horrors of long childhood days spent in cramped, airless, underground tunnels.

Beginning during the nineteenth century, services began to be provided in America for dependent children. The social reforms that followed in the wake of the industrial revolution reflected some awareness of the plight of the chief victim of industrialization and "progress"—the child.

During the twentieth century, a series of White House conferences reflected a growing commitment to ensure the physical and emotional well-being of the nation's children. Although this has been called "the century of the child" the goals and national priorities set on behalf of children with "behavior disorders" must take into account those social conditions, in America and throughout the world, that continue to make growing up in a healthy manner exceedingly difficult for a great many youngsters (Joint Commission on Mental Health, 1970).

Impact of early school experiences

Although the challenge to all educators presented by children with special social and emotional needs is great, it is perhaps greatest for those who teach in kindergarten, primary grade, and Head Start or nursery school classrooms. It is here that long-term patterns may be established, both in a child's response to formal learning situations and in the response of teachers to the child. Labeling can occur, possibly with the effect of stigmatizing the child, setting into motion a self-fulfilling prophecy of maladaptive behavior and failure reinforced by teachers and parents alike (Hobbs, 1975). William Glasser (1969) asserts that it is at the time of school entrance that a child establishes a *success* or a *failure identity*.

Teachers of young children have always perceived the significance of these initial encounters with formal achievement demands, the need for conformity to a group social code, an element of competition, and a variety of stresses, including separation from the protective and supportive structure of home and family. Certainly, in a great many instances, the child's previous experiences have been of a sort not likely to prepare him well to adapt to a group learning situation. What has gone before is indeed of critical importance. However, the teacher of young children senses that a great deal of malleability yet exists; consequently, the learning and growth experiences the teacher helps to make possible for a child, whatever his previous experience has been, can have profound effect on the course of his subsequent personal and social development.

Changing conceptions of deviance

Historically, society's response to the mentally ill individual has been to incarcerate him, and we may not have progressed as far from this level as we would like to believe. The work of leaders such as Pinel, however, did begin to bring about a change in these practices and a realization that an enlightened civilization could not continue to perpetuate the mistreatment of the mentally ill reflected in the custodial institutions of Europe and the United States.

Further advances came about with the insights of Sigmund Freud concerning the origins of mental disturbance. Freud's "discovery of the unconscious" constituted what a present-day pioneer in providing services for disturbed children, Nicholas Hobbs, has called the "second revolution" in the field of mental health (Hobbs, 1964). The full extent of Freud's contribution can probably not yet fully be weighed.

However, it is clear that his theories have had profound and far-ranging effects on nearly every facet of modern life—including family life and child-rearing practices, education, the arts, and sexual relationships and behavior, as well as the clinical treatment of disturbed persons.

No brief summary of Freud's views concerning the origins of disturbance could do justice to the brilliance of his insights and the monumental labors of study, thought, and clinical experience out of which they grew. What Freud was able to grasp and to communicate was a sense of the continuity of human experience throughout history, of the universal themes of human conflict portrayed by the great dramatists, poets, and artists of the past, and of relationships of these themes to the mental suffering he encountered in his clinical practice. He saw that a person's motive for a particular course of behavior, or the specific reason for an "irrational" fear, was often masked or only hinted at by the symbolic language of dreams, in an overuse of inexplicable behavior, or by momentarily breaking through one's defensive structure in the form of a "slip of the tongue."

Freud's most brilliant—and at the time, most controversial—observations concerned the first years of life. He thought that during the periods of infancy and early childhood, fundamental aspects of adult personality structure and consequently the origins of psychic stress and conflict in the adult were formed.

Freud emphasized the inherent conflict between *impulse* and *reality demands* and the difficulties a child experiences in both gratifying and restraining desire. A pervasive concern of the developing personality is "the problem of anxiety" (Freud, 1936), which Freud saw as being at the root of all neurotic conflict. Throughout life, the individual must employ various means to defend against anxiety (A.

Freud, 1964). Some of these *defense mechanisms* are in themselves debilitating, and the process of therapy might involve helping the client to become aware of wishes or fears that he has *repressed,* that he *projects* onto another or *denies,* or that he otherwise handles in a maladaptive manner.

In discussing children, Freud tended to emphasize the dimension of personality that he termed libido. Later psychoanalytic writers, however, placed greater emphasis on the "regulatory agency" of the personality: the *ego* (A. Freud, 1965; Hartmann, 1951; Erikson, 1963). These theorists are often identified as *ego psychologists.*

A number of theories have been formulated, each offering constructs to account for the formation of personality characteristics and the problems of continuity and change in human experience and behavior. In analyzing the various ways in which emotional disturbance among children has been viewed, William Rhodes et al. (Rhodes and Tracy, 1972) summarized five general conceptual models:

1. Biophysical model
2. Sociological model
3. Behavioral model
4. Ecological model
5. Psychodynamic model

In addition, a sixth position, identified by the term "countertheory," was analyzed. These diverse conceptions of deviance reflect the disagreement among authorities concerning the meaning, as well as the causes, of behavior disorders in children. One general issue relates to the *locus* of the problem: Is it within the child or within the environment? What are the interactive aspects of the problem, and how can they be modified?

EMOTIONAL AND BEHAVIORAL PROBLEMS IN YOUNG CHILDREN

Although adult mental and emotional illness may perhaps be defined on the basis of generally accepted criteria, such as *freedom from crippling internal stress, ability to relate effectively with other people, and ability to function independently as a contributing member of society* (Jahoda, 1958), the issue is not as clearcut in childhood. A child's personality is not yet completed; it is in progress. (It should be noted that some personality theories emphasize the continuous capacity for change and growth in adults as well as children. A good example is Erik Erikson's theory depicting the growth of *ego-identity,* in successive stages, throughout the entire life cycle.)

To determine whether a child has a serious problem in the social-emotional sphere of development, just as in other areas such as physical and intellectual development, *normative scales* are useful. That is, a child whose behavior is *inappropriate to his chronological age* may be manifesting a problem. It is very important to note that many behaviors often thought of by adults as problems, such as swearing, lying, "talking back," and thumbsucking, are in fact quite normal at certain ages (MacFarlane et al., 1954). That is, a large percentage of children of a certain age are observed to engage in a particular behavior pattern that, at another age, is considered unacceptable. This kind of insight is particularly important for teachers of young children for two major reasons:

1. The teacher's own reaction to a child's behavior can have profound impact. Emotional overreactions to quite normal, expectable instances of hitting, "stealing," use of "nasty words," and "making-up" things that are presented as fact can be counterproductive or possibly devastating.
2. The teacher is in a good position to help parents understand and avoid over-reacting to such behaviors.

Obviously, not all behavior is "normal and expectable." A teacher must be alert to the things that may signal the possible beginnings of more serious problems, for he or she is in an excellent position to provide help for the child and parents at what may be a critical point.

What is a problem?

Charlotte Buhler (1965) anticipated this crucial question, which is asked at some time by everyone who teaches young children, as well as by parents. It should be stressed that determining that a problem exists does not necessarily mean that the child must be *labeled* (as emotionally disturbed, emotionally handicapped, educationally handicapped, or behaviorally disordered). It does mean that whatever help is appropriate to the needs of that child should be provided and that it should be provided without delay.

A basic criterion for determining whether a child (or an adult) is emotionally disturbed, in psychological distress, or in need of psychiatric* help is *the quality of his adaptive functioning in a social environment,* involving interpersonal relationships, perception of the environment, and learning. The problems in adaptation that can be experienced by children are, of course, numerous, and not all of these are primarily related to mental health and emotional well-being. To varying degrees all children suffer from transient problems, experience stressful events, or exhibit patterns of behavior that could not be described as optimally adaptive.

In general, a child may be thought of as having a serious problem in the area of psychological well-being or personal-social adaptiveness if his difficulty is persistent. A second criterion for determining the existence of a problem relates to the age appropriateness or inappropriateness of some of the child's behavior (Buhler, 1965).

According to one definition,

. . . emotionally disturbed children behave in ways their teachers consider undesirable or inappropriate, and their behavior differs from that of normal children along several crucial dimensions: (a) *severity*—the extreme to which their behavior goes; (b) *chronicity*—the period

---

*"Psychiatric" is used here in its general sense rather than referring exclusively to the branch of the medical profession called psychiatry.

of time over which they exhibit inappropriate behavior; and (c) *context*—when and where they do certain things. (Payne et al., 1974, p. 22)

Identification of emotionally handicapped children in school

Eli M. Bower (1964, 1969) has long been especially concerned with the early identification of emotionally disturbed or emotionally handicapped children in order that effective approaches to prevention of more serious and of continued problems can be instituted. With Nadine M. Lambert, he has developed an approach to screening in school that combines three sources of information: the *teacher's observations* of the child, *peers' perceptions* of the child, and the *child's perceptions of himself*. Bower and Lambert (1961) categorize symptoms of emotional handicaps that may be apparent in school into five general characteristics:

1. Inability to achieve in school that cannot be explained by sensory or health factors
2. Inability to establish and maintain satisfactory interpersonal relations with peers and adults
3. Demonstration of inappropriate feelings or affect under normal conditions, for example, laughing when someone is hurt
4. Pervasive mood of unhappiness or depression
5. A tendency to develop physical symptoms, such as pains or fears, associated with the problems

Emotional problems may be reflected in *excessive* or *situationally inappropriate* behaviors that are otherwise quite normal and acceptable, such as seeking physical contact, masturbating, or expressing fantasy in verbalization or play. Confusion of wishes or fears with reality is developmentally normal in young children, and one of the tasks of early childhood is to learn to differentiate fantasy from reality. Fearfulness of injury to himself or a parent, although also generally healthy, is similarly indicative of problems if it is *extreme* and *persistent*. Physically aggres-

sive play, impulsivity, and speech or drawing that is full of aggressive imagery may likewise be developmentally normal; the determination that a problem exists must be decided on the basis of *chronicity* and *severity,* as well as assessment of the child's ability to develop internal controls to regulate these impulses and channel them in constructive ways.

Abnormal persistence of age-inappropriate behaviors, remnants of what was normal at an earlier age, must be distinguished from occasional temporary regressive lapses. Such behaviors as crying, thumb sucking, having toilet accidents, reversion to immature speech patterns, and demonstrating inexplicable or inappropriate fearfulness may signify a "problem" only if they continue. Nevertheless, the teacher needs to be alert to such signs and to observe and possibly support the child's ability to cope, even in transitory episodes.

A variety of speech and language problems may also signal an underlying emotional cause, especially stuttering and delayed speech (Chapter 2). Speech disabilities may be results of any of a variety of factors, however, and do not necessarily reflect emotional conflicts. Since speech is for the child both an expression of self and an important means of adaptation, problems in that area may indeed *contribute to* emotional difficulties. So may other handicapping conditions, whether physical or mental.

Sex differences and behavioral deviance

It is common knowledge among special educators that far more boys than girls are *identified* as having learning or behavior problems in school. This should not be construed to mean necessarily that so many more boys than girls *actually have* these problems (although that is certainly possible). Since special classes have been provided for emotionally handicapped children, boys have substantially outnumbered girls in their membership.

A possibly related phenomenon is the

greater incidence of *acting-out* problems among children referred for special education services and assignment to special class programs (Morse et al., 1964). In general, many more boys than girls are identified in school as emotionally handicapped, and many more acting-out problems, as compared to extreme withdrawal or other patterns, are served in special education programs for emotionally handicapped.

A study carried out by Kohn and Rosman (1973) sheds additional light on these two observations. Using ratings by teachers to identify emotional problems in 3- to 7-year-old children in various settings, they identified two major factors: *factor I, interaction-participation vs. apathy-withdrawal,* and *factor II, cooperation-compliance vs. anger-defiance.*

Generally speaking, a factor I problem would be reflected in a child's inability to become involved in group activity, or lack of interest in tasks, play, etc. This child might be preoccupied with his own thoughts or might seem to hang back from shyness or fear of rejection or failure. A factor II problem would be presented by the child who resisted adult controls or direction, was angry or belligerent, bullied other children, or tended to be a destructive influence on group activity. Other children might fear this child.

That many more factor II–type problems were identified by teachers is congruent with a long history of "identification" studies, beginning with that of Wickman (1928), as was the finding that boys were much more frequently identified than girls. However, those girls who were identified as emotionally disturbed more frequently had problems of the factor I apathy-withdrawal type.

It is unwarranted to conclude, on the basis of such research findings, either that there are more emotionally disturbed boys than girls or that boys and girls generally manifest emotional problems in different ways. Noting that elementary school–aged girls were more likely than

boys to express anxieties, worries, concerns, and fears about a *self-report* scale, Seymour Sarason et al. (1960) suggested that social norms may make it more likely that girls will state such feelings on a questionnaire. For a boy to express that he is afraid or worried may not be congruent with the "male image" to which boys aspire as a result of cultural and parental socialization influences.

On the other side of the coin, girls do indeed manifest "acting-out" problems. If these are extremely deviant, they are more likely to be manifest, or at least identified, at puberty or during the adolescent years; such behaviors may include status offenses, such as running away, truancy, and promiscuity, as well as belligerence, vandalism, and theft. Some clinicians (such as William Glasser, 1965) observe that acting-out adolescent girls who ultimately are seen in institutional placement are far more difficult to manage and treat than boys in the same or similar settings.

Recognizing symptomatic behavior in the early education setting

Several specific problem areas are particularly familiar to the teacher of young children. In each case, the difficulty may be a temporary one, or it may reveal a potentially more serious problem. The teacher should attempt to be an objective observer of the child and should record specific accounts of *what happens,* before attempting to interpret the child's behavior. A plan of action for dealing with the problem will follow from an accurate record of what the child does, and may be evolved in consultation with supervisory and supportive staff, as well as the child's parents.

These familiar problem areas, which may or may not indicate a "problem," include the following:

1. Great difficulty in separating from parent (The teacher should be aware of the essential *normalcy* of difficulty in initial separation—for both child

and parent—and be willing to suggest and support a *gradual* withdrawal of the child's parent over many sessions if necessary.)

2. Extreme withdrawal (The teacher should be willing to respect the child's needs and "style," attempting to support his involvement in activities but not pushing too hard or demanding.)

3. Extreme aggressive behavior ("Aggression" probably means something very different for young children than for older youngsters, as is discussed later in this chapter. The teacher should make clear *expectations,* and analyze *objectively* what the child actually does. However, attempts to *punish* aggression will very likely backfire.)

4. Infantile patterns of behavior (Regression to earlier modes is not uncommon under stress, even for adults. The teacher should support, encourage, and reward behavior that is age appropriate rather than shame the child by emphasizing immature things that he does, such as baby talk, thumb-sucking, toilet accidents, clinging, and unnecessarily seeking the teacher's help.)

DEVIANT BEHAVIOR AS A DEVELOPMENTAL PROBLEM

Behavioral deviance has both an *objective* and a *subjective* component. It involves overt manifestations in the form of inappropriate interactions with others, undesirable habit patterns, and the like. These may, however, be reflections of what is basically an internal state—pervasive unhappiness, fears of rejection, impulses to injure, or feelings of unworthiness. To focus exclusively on the "behavior" may be to ignore the subjective meaning or function for the child of his actions.

In interpreting behavioral deviance in young children, it is necessary to consider it within a developmental frame of reference. Patterns of personal and social behavioral characteristics are always reflections of general developmental trends and needs, as well as of influences (constitutional and experiential) that are unique to the individual child.

Personality development and behavioral deviance

From a psychoanalytic, or Freudian, perspective, many problems of personality development are viewed as manifestations of either of two factors: *fixation* or *regression.* The first, fixation, implies a stunting of personality growth. The child has been as yet unable to resolve conflicts associated with earlier events and so remains "stuck" at that level. His development is said to be fixated at the point where conflicts occurred that he has not as yet been able to work through satisfactorily. The levels referred to correspond to the general stages of psychosexual development postulated by Freud. Each of these stages is distinguished by both physical and social phenomena; that is, the modes of social interaction observed at each level reflect in large part physiological and neurological changes occurring within the child. Each stage, according to Freud, is characterized by the investment of libidinal energy in a specific erogenous zone of the body. Thus during the oral stage of development, the tissues of and surrounding the mouth and the pharyngeal tract are particularly sensitive to stimulation. This general zone, focused around the mouth, is of central importance.

This "oral period" continues throughout at least the first year of life, during which time the child's mode of responding is basically a process of "taking in"—nourishment, sensory stimulation, love. There is a change in the way this mode of interaction is observed, however, which corresponds to the eruption of teeth. From a passive, receiving posture, the baby moves to a more active and aggressive style of "getting" and "holding."

The anal stage is called thus because the focal area shifts to this zone as the child strives to master excretory functions. With maturation of the sphincter muscles, the child gains the physical capability to retain and to release feces. With the corresponding increase in sensitivity of the anal region, his awareness of the process is heightened. These two gains—in muscular control and in awareness—enable him to learn to regulate defecation, to be "toilet trained." However, these same gains correspond with a more generalized push on the child's part toward autonomy and self-direction, assertions of will, and independence. Growth in muscular control and strength is reflected in the child's increased mobility, as well. Freud felt that at this point in the child's development there was inherent conflict between instinctual needs and the demands of civilized society. It is necessary for the child to regulate defecation and to do so in privacy.

Erikson (1963) has emphasized the personal and social dimensions of these early events. He has described the process by which individuals build a sense of ego identity in terms of a series of developmental crises. In infancy (Freud's oral stage), the crisis has to do with the growth of a sense of *trust,* that is, security, feelings of safety, or confidence in the basic goodness of things and people. Freud referred to oral *optimism,* noting that one form of the "oral personality" is reflected in naive, childlike faith. For the individual whose efforts to seek oral gratification during infancy were frustrated, "orality" continues to be reflected either in the pursuit of gratification (for example, compulsive overeating, sexual promiscuity, possessiveness in friendships and love relationships), or in extreme pessimism, fearfulness, paranoiac delusions, fear of "external" forces, etc. Erikson has described the developmental task of infancy as involving the resolution of a crisis of trust: basic trust vs. mistrust.

The second crisis point in the development of the ego identity, Erikson notes, parallels Freud's description of an anal period. The child's struggle to assert self-control, while at the same time regulating his instinctual needs and impulses in accordance with society's constraints—that is, to be "socialized"—is the pervasive theme of the toddler years. Erikson notes that, although the conflict is epitomized by the issue of toilet training, it is reflected in many other areas as well. With his newly gained powers of ambulation and his needs to exercise and use large muscle systems, the toddler is an adventurer. Since he is lacking in experience and in ability to anticipate consequences and exercise critical judgment, his parents are required to set limits and restraints on his self-assertion, often in direct conflict with the child's own desires. Freud (1908/1955) described the consequences of inadequate resolution of issues surrounding the young child's need to be self-regulating in view of the reality of his continuing dependence on the parent for guidance, protection, and control in terms of certain characteristics observed in adults—a preoccupation with neatness and orderliness, unreasonable stubbornness, compulsive adherence to certain forms and rituals, stinginess or miserliness with money (which Freud showed to be symbolically equated with feces), an ungenerous or "withholding" attitude in diverse areas of social relationship, etc.

To Erikson, the crisis to be resolved during the toddler years has to do with *autonomy vs. shame and doubt.* Erikson believes that in both of these successive developmental crises, an "ideal" resolution involves some compromise between the individual's needs and social constraints and realities. Too much "trust" produces an "oral" individual, ill equipped to deal with the realities of life as an autonomous person. Too much "autonomy" is not desirable in view of the realities of life in a social environment, where one's own needs must be regulated in accord with cultural mores and the wishes and rights of others. The "ideal" resolution to each enables the individual to view himself as valued by others, to feel basically safe, and to be generally competent.

The third major psychosexual phase is marked by the child's beginning awareness of his own identity as a boy or a girl. Part of this awareness is due to discovery by the boy of his penis or by the girl of her vagina and clitoris and, according to Freud, increased sensitivity to this part of the body. Freud believed that this period is characterized by "discoveries" concerning sexuality, discoveries that may be thwarted, suppressed, or distorted. The "oedipal conflicts" associated with this period have to do with resolving an unattainable desire in a way that is both *acceptable* and *satisfying*. The child is beset with impulses and emotions that are powerful and deeply disturbing. The resolution comes about through *identifying* with the (potentially) punishing parent: the father for a boy and the mother for a girl.

This type of identification is termed *defensive identification,* or identification with the aggressor. Through internalizing the parent of the same sex, the child acquires not only an "internal parent" (a superego, or conscience), but also reflects the wish to be *like* that parent. "Being like" one's father or mother includes attempting to adopt or imitate the mannerisms, attitudes, and characteristics that this *model* of masculinity or femininity conveys as related to the child's sex role.

Whether Freud's portrayal of these psychological events is accurate is certainly open to question, as is the universality of the Oedipus complex. In attributing so much importance to sexual motives, Freud may have neglected other factors of possibly even greater significance. There is certainly question of the extent to which characteristics linked to male or female sex roles are biologically determined ("intrusiveness" for boys, "receptiveness" for girls). Many contemporary researchers would see in Freud's interpretation more than a little "male chauvinism."

Whether Freud was right or wrong about this conceptualization, young children during the preschool years can be observed to show some striking changes in emotional development and social behavior. Evidence of sex role identification (Mischel, 1970) is present, and the child shows evidence of a developing conscience. Along with this capacity of having an internalized awareness of right and wrong, there is a new ability to experience guilt. This places the child in a conflict between his desire to learn, to explore, to try new things, to interact effectively with the world around him, and his desire to avoid disapproval or punishment. To Erikson, the ego identity problem is represented by the phrase *initiative vs. guilt.*

Freud did not say a great deal about personality development during the school years prior to the onset of puberty. He believed that earlier psychic events were the most important determinants. Erikson, however, notes that children move increasingly into cooperative, constructive interaction with peers during these years and suggests that the child has yet another ego identity crisis to resolve: *industry vs. inferiority.*

From an educational perspective, Frank Hewett (1968) has observed that children's readiness for learning can be viewed along a developmental continuum comprising several sequential and hierarchical levels. As in Erikson's conception, each successive stage is dependent on the satisfactory resolution of the ones that precede it. An interesting parallel has been drawn between the views of Erikson and Hewett by Susan Swap (1974), who combines them in identifying several successive educational stages for teaching children with behavioral problems:

1. *Basic trust and attention stage:* At this level mistrust prevents the child from focusing on educational tasks,

so encouragement must be given to the child's interest. He must feel safe before he can attend.

2. *Basic trust and response stage:* Mistrust of self and others inhibits the child from responding. Therefore situations should guarantee success, allow retreat, and provide consistency of routine.

3. *Autonomy and order stage:* Low frustration level is caused by self-doubt and fear of exposure of the child's inadequacies. Therefore structured situations are provided to ensure success and make clear that finished products are expected.

4. *Initiative and exploratory stage:* Fear of failure in attempts to take initiative causes dependency. Multisensory and meaningful experiences that emphasize reality should be provided.

5. *Industry, social mastery, and achievement stage:* The child works with others, and learning is its own reward.

Regression

The concept of regression is a very important one to understand in attempting to distinguish between normalcy and deviance. Since a major criterion to be applied in making this distinction is that of age appropriateness, there is the implication that it is "not normal" for a child not to "act his age." However, reversions to earlier modes of behavior are not only expected in the course of normal development, they serve constructive purposes. Anna Freud has used the term "regression in the service of the ego" (1965) to suggest the adaptive significance of this concept. For example, children of all ages frequently delight in returning temporarily to modes of play that have been "outgrown."

It is not unusual for a child to "regress" as a means of defense against anxieties brought on by some significant occurrence or period in his life—birth of a sibling, move to a new home, family disruption or conflict, death of someone close to the child. Night fears may bring about sleep disturbances and the child may revert to behavioral patterns long since abandoned, such as eneuresis, thumb sucking, and unwillingness to sleep in his own bed or to be alone in a room. Often parents are not able to identify any objective change that might constitute a "cause" for such behavior; it may reside within the child's own mind. However, it is therefore no less real.

Both very brief regressive episodes and even more extended periods during which the child employs behavior usually associated with earlier developmental periods legitimately fall within the range of "normalcy" for most children. However, even for a very healthy child these may provide clues of special emotional needs that the child is manifesting *at that time* and signal the need for sensitive and supportive guidance by the teacher and parent.

Problems in ego development

The term "ego" has a highly specific meaning in psychoanalytic theory, but it may have a somewhat different meaning in other conceptions of human personality. Most people use "ego" nearly synonymously with "self" in everyday speech, usually with specific reference to positive feelings about the self or gratification of needs for self-esteem. A person enjoying the adulation of others, who is in the spotlight, is on an "ego trip" if he becomes convinced of his own importance.

Personality theorists, however, usually differentiate between ego and self and describe the former as a part of the personality that directs, regulates, and mediates conflicting forces and *synthesizes* diverse aspects of personality. It is sometimes likened to a "general" or "manager." *Ego strength* may reflect self-confidence, but this concept implies something larger; it implies abilities *to defer gratification, to learn and to adapt, to maintain some degree of balance of mood, to resolve conflicting needs or wishes,* and *to defend against anxiety.* According to Freud's original formulations, the ego is developed out of conflict. The young child was seen as dominated by impulse, that is, by instinctual forces, or id. "Conscience," the internalized guide to right and wrong, results through the *internalization* of standards through a process called *identification.* In identifying with a parent, the child does more than simply learn to be like or to imitate the parent; he actually incorporates within himself elements of the parent *(introjection),* including some elements that he himself has attributed to the parent *(projection).* Among the consequences of this process of identification, which Freud believed marked the resolution of oedipal conflicts, is the development of a *superego,* an *internalized parent,* which is the source of the child's ability to experience guilt.

The language may sound as if these components of personality actually exist in a physical sense—as though the ego is a homunculus, or "inner man," residing within the person's brain and with a personality all its own. In actuality these terms describe psychological *constructs* that provide useful ways of explaining what kinds of forces operate within an individual to determine behavior. In another perspective, that of Eric Berne (1961), these internal determinants are conceptualized in terms of a three-part ego structure: *parent, child,* and *adult.* Both intraindividual conflicts and, most particularly, interpersonal communication processes and dynamics are explained in part on the basis of these three aspects of adult personality in a system called Transactional Analysis.

Another way of looking at the role of the ego in helping the child to learn and to adapt to his physical and social environment in an optimal manner has been provided by Eli Bower. Bower (1967) employed the term "ego processes" to include also the means by which we learn to use language and other symbolic functions to

deal effectively with the complexities of our world. Ego processes provide a range of *options* from which an individual may choose to confront a difficult situation, to express wants and needs, and to relate to others. Elsewhere, he used the phrase "degrees of freedom" (Bower, 1961) to reflect the individual's ability to choose from among alternatives, noting that some school-age children, like infants, have a very restricted range from which they can choose. Lois Murphy (1961) has conveyed a similar idea in describing the range of coping mechanisms that young children employ as an index of healthy personality development.

In some instances, behavioral deviance may be conceived as a kind of distortion or stunting of ego development. It may reflect the inability of a partially or imperfectly developed ego to cope effectively with environmental stress—whether such stress is objectively great (as in the case of death of a parent, parental separation, serious illness or hospitalization, natural disasters, serious accident, etc.) or is only perceived by the child as great. As with all psychological phenomena, it is not so much the "objective reality" as the subjective experience and perception of the situation that is critical.

EDUCATIONAL APPROACHES

The relationship between origins of psychological problems of childhood (whether of a transient, situational nature or quite serious in their impact) and *treatment* of those problems represents an area of substantial disagreement among psychologists, child psychiatrists, and others concerned with childhood psychopathology. To some clinical workers, questions of etiology are really far less important than is treatment, and the origin of the problem is not necessarily considered relevant to intervention. What is believed to be important is the accurate identification of the *behavior* to be changed, rather than the analysis of its underlying causes and the early events that might have brought it about (Ullman and Krasner, 1965). Among the viewpoints presented have been two that are diametrically opposed with regard to the teacher's role in working with young children who are emotionally handicapped:

1. Treatment of the underlying psychological condition requires the specialized abilities and training of a child analyst or child therapist. Treatment must involve a basic restructuring of personality, which can come about only by sophisticated use of therapeutic tools. It may also involve intensive therapeutic involvement with the child's parents. The teacher can contribute to this long and complex process in important ways, but teaching and therapy are not the same.

2. "Treatment" really means arranging conditions in the child's environment in such a way as to differentially reinforce observable behaviors. It is *current behavior* with which one works, rather than inferred internal processes or historical antecedents. The teacher or parent may be in an excellent position to provide the necessary treatment—that is, through identifying target behaviors and associated environmental contingencies, to bring about the *extinction* of a maladaptive behavior, the *substitution* of a desired behavior for one with which it is incompatible, or the *acquisition* of an adaptive behavior.

The issue is an extraordinarily complex one and a great many points of view have been expressed in the professional literature. The preceding two statements represent extreme positions and oversimplifications. In actual practice, most teachers, psychologists, etc. are to some degree *eclectic,* drawing on a number of conceptualizations and techniques. The following principles are ones that are generally agreed on by those engaged in therapeutic work with young children:

1. Adult "categories" of psychiatric illness do not, for the most part, fit children well, especially young children. This is perhaps because the child is "an incomplete organism" and also because the needs and experiences of childhood are unique.

2. The child does not exist in a social vacuum; family, peer group, and classroom social influences interact with and influence his internal state, as well as his overt behavior.

3. Children are actively involved in learning, a process that reflects not only the acquisition of specific behaviors, skills, and items of knowledge but also the continuous restructuring of what is learned in some organized fashion.

4. Cognition (thinking and learning) is inseparable from affect (emotions, fears, wishes, attitudes, and fantasies).

5. "Reality" has different meanings, both in children as compared to adults, and in children at different levels of development.

6. Children have strong needs to experience a sense of being both loved and valued by significant adults in their lives, as well as to experience "a sense of competence" (White, 1959).

Concept of therapeutic education

Psychodynamically based psychotherapy is by definition a learning process (Pearson, 1954), although the goals and methods of the therapist may differ from those of the teacher. The other major system applied in working with disturbed children, sometimes referred to generally as *behavior modification,* explicitly applies principles of learning. In this approach, there is no sharp distinction made between *education* and *therapy.*

The idea of *education as therapy* is not entirely new. George Devereaux (1956) has traced the essential relatedness of education and therapy in terms of the relationship between both school and society and the individual and society. A. S. Neill (1960) developed Summerhill in part on the basis of psychoanalytic insights. Neill's influence (as well as that of

Count Leo Tolstoy, an educational vision-
ary and literary genius) is reflected in the
First Street School created by George
Dennison (1969) as a "learning community" for troubled children. In *Manchild
in the Promised Land,* Claude Brown
(1965) recounts the influence of his experience in New York's Wiltwyck School
in enabling him to redirect his life.

In residential treatment programs—
that is, treatment settings in which children live while participating in individual
and group therapeutic activity—a school
program is usually an important part of
the total treatment approach. School,
recreation, and living experiences together comprise what is often called
milieu therapy (Redl, 1959), as opposed
to individual psychotherapy.

Residential programs are by no means
necessary or appropriate for all emotionally disturbed children. They may be
extremely costly and they really involve
placing the child in an artificial environment—that is, one that is especially structured to provide for the child what he may
need for a short time, possibly including
some assurance of protecting him from
himself. As with other handicapping conditions, we can view educational placement provisions for emotionally handicapped children in terms of a continuum,
ranging from maximum participation in a
"regular" setting for the vast majority, to
possible institutional programs. The point
to be emphasized is that educational
placement is not an either-or matter:
there is a wide range of alternatives
through which the specific needs of an
individual child may be served:

1. Regular education program with no
   special support services
2. Regular education program with
   support services such as consultation
   to the teacher by specialists
3. Regular education program with
   support services provided directly to
   the child and family (such as individual or family therapy, tutoring, or
   supportive relationship program)

4. Regular education program with
   some time spent in a special program
   (such as resource room or school-
   based group counseling)
5. Regular education program with
   substantial time in a specialized
   class
6. Primarily special class with some
   time in a regular program
7. Special day school program including supportive therapy, psychotherapy, and other services as needed
8. Residential setting (A range of possibilities exists, including group
   homes, residential treatment, and
   psychiatric hospitals. Although temporarily residing in a setting other
   than his home to secure needed specialized treatment, the child may attend a public school with the specific
   programming determined by his
   educational needs, rather than his
   diagnostic label or status.)

Therapeutic education for children with
emotional and behavioral problems is not
offered only in specialized psychiatric
settings; it can and should be available in
the school, including *individualized programming for children within a regular
class.* Therapeutic education is a means of
helping the child to work through emotional conflict, to develop more adaptive
modes of interacting with others, to develop a more realistic and positive self-
concept, to learn to channel impulses, to
develop a more accurate orientation to
reality, and to gain a better understanding of causal relationships and consequences of behavior. Its basic components
include the following:

1. *The curriculum* (Rhodes, 1963): all
that is done and how it is done, including
the subdimensions of goals, tasks, time,
space, rules, expectations, rewards, and
responsibilities. The curriculum is the
structure for activity and the *vehicle* for
accomplishment.

2. *The group:* the social system of the
classroom, including all "messages,"
roles, interactions, friendships, collective

motives or goals, and all observable and invisible communications and peer influences.

3. *The teacher:* the most important component, since he or she determines the curriculum, sets the tone for the group, and monitors both. The teacher is authority symbol, representative of adult values, model, identification figure, relationship figure, auxiliary ego, group leader, maker and enforcer of rules, assurer of physical and psychological safety, valuer, and sometime evaluator.

Educational therapy for young children

Although "talking" psychotherapy may be useful with many children, a medium or vehicle through which a child may more easily express conflicts, wishes, fears, and fantasies is often employed by especially trained persons—child psychiatrists, child psychoanalysts (who have undergone extensive preparation, but need not be medically trained psychiatrists), or other child therapists. *Play therapy* (Axline, 1947; Moustakas, 1953)

is an especially appropriate technique in work with young children, but it is also employed with children of school age. *Art therapy, music therapy, dance therapy,* and still other specialized forms may be employed by practitioners of these disciplines. *Psychodrama,* a technique of acting out themes, situations, etc. was developed by J. L. Moreno (1943) and is often used with adolescents and adults as well as children and is applicable with young children in the form of *dramatic play* (Strain and Wiegerink, 1976). *Puppetry* is a particularly effective application of dramatic play (Woltman, 1951).

What these approaches have in common is that they permit and encourage the child to express his feelings, wishes, fears, etc. safely and acceptably. They may enable the child to act out and thereby communicate what is bothering him, as well as to test both reality factors and his ability to cope with them. Play provides the young child a vehicle through which he can practice, test his observations, and structure his experiences.

A specialized therapeutic nursery school program (Furman and Katan, 1969) not only provides the child opportunities for expression through block play, art, music, etc., but also helps him learn to use *language* as an integrative mode for mastering inner needs and coping with external reality demands. In such a program, learning is seen not only in terms of preparing the child for eventual success in academic skills but, more important, in terms of fostering basically healthy development of a well-integrated personality. The young child who is experiencing inner conflict with which it is difficult for him to cope may also be treated on a one-to-one basis, complementary to his participation in the group program.

In the psychoanalytic treatment of young emotionally disturbed children, an approach that may be employed is that of *treatment of the child via the parents* (Furman and Katan, 1969). The child may be involved in the therapeutic nursery program and, as is normally the case in any specialized program, parents receive supportive assistance and guidance in child management and other areas. However, what is distinctive is the enrollment of parents, in effect, as therapists for their child. In view of the relationship existing already, the likelihood that the child's problem is closely related to parent-child matters, and the key importance of fostering this relationship, parents are guided in understanding the child's problem and in carrying through therapeutic procedures. The classic model for this approach is provided by Freud himself in his report of the treatment of "little Hans" who had a phobia of horses (Freud, 1909/1955). It is substantiated by subsequent discoveries in the psychoanalytic treatment of children's emotional disorders.

It is true that close and continuing parent involvement is basic to any early childhood education program. However, in the early education of young children with special emotional problems the parent-educator relationship and continuous communication between home and school (or center) take on a special significance and meaning, regardless of the theoretical orientation or specific approach which is used.

A particularly helpful guide to teachers who work with young children with emotional and behavioral problems is *Developmental Therapy: A Textbook for Teachers As Therapists for Emotionally Disturbed Young Children,* edited by Mary M. Wood (1975). In this book, Dr. Wood and her co-workers provide a comprehensive system for teaching young disturbed children that can be adapted to various settings. The objectives, recommended teaching procedures, and methods for observing and recording children's progress emerged out of their own extensive experience and the writings of others and indicate a sound blend of psychodynamic and behavioral principles. The most important dimension of the system is its *developmental* orientation, according to which objectives are sequentially ordered and change on the part of individual children is charted.

The program is organized around four basic curriculum areas: (1) behavior, (2) communication, (3) socialization, and (4) (pre)academics.

In each area five sequential levels, or stages, of functioning are identified corresponding to "key milestones" (Wood, 1975, p. 6), and ongoing educational/developmental diagnosis of the progress made by each child indicates not only where he is currently functioning in each of the four areas, but what next steps are indicated. The book includes highly specific elaboration of what is done at each stage and makes clear the relationship observed for children in this program between social-emotional development and educational progress in this therapeutic setting. Their direct work with children is supported by other specialists and consultants, but it is the teacher who diagnoses, prescribes, implements, and evaluates. *The therapy is teaching—the therapists, teachers!*

THE ECOLOGICAL PERSPECTIVE: ANOTHER WAY OF VIEWING MISBEHAVIOR

Undesirable or nonconstructive behavior on the part of the young child may be a product of many interacting influences, some of these residing within the child himself, others within his environment. Behavior does not occur in a vacuum. Whether a specific behavioral act is "purposeful" in the sense of conscious intention or is not rationally determined, it has some relationship to the acts of others, the physical environment, or both. Basically the ecological point of view concerning the concept of childhood behavioral deviance attempts to take into account the interdependence of individuals and of vectors of influence within a specific "ecosystem" (Hobbs, 1966; Rhodes, 1967). Ecosystems may involve such groupings of persons as occur within a family network, a classroom, or a play group. As anyone who is attuned to and experienced with group process is aware, any such group tends to take on characteristics of its own, beyond the characteristics of each of its component members (Newman, 1971). There are communication patterns and phenomena unique to groups, such as "contagion" (Redl, 1966). There are aspects of the situation in which the group is formed that tend to determine some features of its behavior *as a group*. Some of these situational determinants include mores, conventions, and expectations concerning modes of behavior that are appropriate in a specific setting, for example, in a classroom.

But ecological determinants of behavior go beyond the pattern of group dynamics found within a collection of interacting individuals. The physical dimensions of the setting, the size and physical arrangement of the room, the temperature, the time of day, the range of activity

modes explicitly or implicitly sanctioned, to name just a few broad kinds of influence, also exert influence. In general, the ecological perspective asserts the interactive and transactional nature of the behavior of individuals within a social setting and the interactive and transactional character of the individual's relationship to his immediate physical environment.

Some ecosystems, such as some classrooms, contain sets of forces that by their very nature are more likely than others to contribute to the production of discordant behavior among individual children. Obviously, the adult group leader, the teacher, is quite influential in regulating such influences as group social codes relating to inclusion or exclusion, tolerance of deviance, rivalry, noise levels and excitement level, predictability of events, sequencing of activity modes, "visual clutter," presence of seductive influences, and many others. Classroom *structure*—in the sense of preplanned use of time and space and clearly defined and understood systems of rules, expectation, and rewards —is largely the responsibility of the teacher (Cruickshank et al., 1961; Haring and Phillips, 1962; Hewett, 1968).

DIMENSIONS OF BEHAVIOR MANAGEMENT
The meaning of management

In the role of "manager," it is the teacher who, as Hewett (1968) says, *controls* the learning environment, sets the tasks, and determines the rewards. But perhaps in a more important sense, *we help the child to manage*. It is the child who has the task of regulating his impulses, of balancing his own needs for gratification against the restrictions and demands of his classroom society and against his own desire to be valued and liked. We help the child most when we enable him to gain increased control over both his external environment and his internal impulses.

Young children have a sense of what it means to be "in control," to *control oneself*.

Management practices that enhance the growth of inner controls contribute most to the child's long-range growth as an individual and group member, as a citizen, and as a moral and ethical being (Morse and Wingo, 1969).

Management directed toward internalization of control can appeal to the best impulses in the child: his desire to be "like the teacher," helpful to others, resourceful, and respectful; his need to feel self-sufficient and competent, able to deal with his environment on his own terms; and his ability to make decisions as to the best course of action, weighing the consequences of various alternatives. Management directed toward internalization, however, does injury to the child's growth of self if it plays on *guilt* too intensely and attempts to create a self-punitive orientation on the child's part or if control is achieved by *shaming* the child into regulating his own behavior. It is not whether the child wishes to "be a baby" that should be capitalized on; rather, it is the wish to "be a big boy or girl."

An important tool in the young child's ability to gain mastery over himself, his fantasies and fears, and events in his environment is *language*. Knowing the *word* for a subjective state that the child experiences can make it less overpowering or frightening. The teacher can help significantly, often through supplying the word: "It made us *sad* when the goldfish died"; "sometimes we feel *angry* when someone takes our things." The child is able to see that these feelings are not things that exist only within himself; others experience them, too. Talking about them provides reassurance as well as emotional relief.

It is necessary to sense what the child may be *feeling,* as well as to note what he is *doing,* and to respond empathetically. Thus the teacher hears what the child is saying, whether through his solitary play or through his interactions with peers in the classroom, and reflects it back to him in words.

This is not to say, however, that a child's antisocial behavior—destroying another child's block tower, throwing something at another, hitting, etc.—is tolerated. The way he *feels* is accepted, and certainly *he* is accepted. Destructive or hurtful behavior, however, is *not* acceptable. There are more suitable and more effective ways of expressing how we feel.

Young children need a sense of order, structure, and dependableness. Also, young children's boisterousness may mask a genuine fear of physical harm and of unbridled or unrestrained impulse. For the nursery school or kindergarten child, the teacher is a surrogate mother (or father) on whom he depends as a "auxiliary ego," which can support his still-developing one. The child whose emotional growth is "at risk" or in special conflict will need more of this sort of external support.

Guidelines for behavior management

Some general management practices and principles may be summarized as follows:

Verbalization. Having a name for the way one feels makes it less frightening or overwhelming, thereby permitting the child to experience a degree of mastery over his fears, emotions, and fantasies. Being able to respond *with words* ("Don't take my car, John!") increases the "degrees of freedom" (Bower, 1961) a child has, his whole repertoire of ways of *coping* with his world. Verbal responses to conflict and frustration are more socially acceptable than physical ones and less likely to result in even more frustration. Whereas withdrawal from the source of conflict with no overt means of expression does not bring about resolution, verbal coping can involve others.

Recognizing the teacher's role as model and identification figure. The teacher is a "significant other," whose response to the child and whose moods, values, and human qualities the child may be ready to internalize. As models, how teachers deal with their own frustration is influential, as well as how they use their greater size and strength and authority. Do they teach that "might makes right," thereby reinforcing the child's own primitive concepts of right and wrong, of reward and punishment? Teachers also set the tone for the level of excitement in their classrooms through their own behavior and style. Some teachers provide chaotic or noisy models. Teachers who themselves employ social amenities (please and thank you), who listen well, and who are respectful of children's feelings and property send effective messages concerning how the children respond to others.

Establishing short-range, achievable goals. Whether one is attempting to promote more purposefulness in play, more attentive behavior, sharing with peers, or willingness to separate from mother, a "thimbleful" approach works better than does a "bucketful" one (Hewett, 1968). Expecting the child to accomplish immediately some achievement, such as "being able to play cooperatively with other children," may doom him to failure. However, attacking this long-range goal by means of small, successive steps, beginning wherever the child is currently functioning, may make ultimate success possible. In the meantime, both child and teacher can experience *immediate* success, which helps to establish both a pattern of attainment and the expectation of accomplishment.

Communicating expectations. Both through the model presented and through his or her own actions, the teacher conveys to the children what is expected. One of the great strengths of the Montessori approach is the establishment of clear expectations regarding the care of materials, together with a *valuation* of materials. They are treated carefully, even reverentially. They are valued as means by which children learn, as important things that should be cared for. Similarly, the kinds of individual behavior expected are also communicated by the teacher, not so much in the form of inviolable rules written on tablets of stone (although a very few rules may be desirable) as in the form of well-established guidelines of conduct and consistent messages. These messages include the whole array of means, verbal and nonverbal, by which an adult conveys to a child what he or she believes the child is capable of doing.

Avoiding the tendency to overreact to extreme behavior. One facet of young children's behavior to which adults—parents and teachers—may tend to overreact is wordplay. Young children are inclined to believe that words have magical properties and this belief is reinforced by adults who panic if a small child uses a "street" word he has picked up from older siblings. The words may be used specifically to see what reaction they will get, and it is important to be able to judge whether the expression should be ignored or discussed with the child in a neutral manner. To the child, "pooh-pooh head" may be a much worse epithet than some of the "really bad words" he may pick up and try out. It may be sufficient to say, "No Billy, you may not call your friend a pooh-pooh head in nursery school."

Other forms of behavior to which some adults may react in an inappropriately extreme manner include the familiar "phallic play," through which children sometimes transparently convey aggressive impulses; other dramatic or representational play behaviors, which may not convey aggression but which may express other fantasies, such as sexual fantasies; overt masturbation; and toilet accidents (some of which, one suspects, may not be entirely accidental). To all of these, an extreme or emotional reaction on the part of the adult is counterproductive. The intense reaction may serve to reinforce the very behavior that is considered undesirable. The child may feel that the teacher attaches great importance to these words, an impression that offers interesting possibilities and plays into the young child's tendency to attribute almost magical properties to words.

Contingency management. The point of view expressed throughout much of this chapter is often seen as diametrically opposed to a more *behavioral* orientation. It has been suggested that, not just what a child *does,* but what that behavior might *mean* should be attended to. However, clearly the actual act is important too. The child learns that certain consequences follow alternative courses of action. These consequences are not artificial or contrived, imposed at the whim of a powerful adult. They are reality constraints. Certain forms of behavior meet with the approval of the teacher and of the other children, for example. Others do not. Teacher praise may be a powerful and appropriate reinforcer for one child, but not for another. *A reinforcing consequence is an event that is observed to increase the likelihood of a behavior.* The basic principle underlying behavior modification approaches is applicable, not only to children with behavioral problems, but to everyone: *Our behavior is dependent on the reinforcement it receives.* This implies that the fact that a behavior persists indicates that it is being reinforced. When the individual "emits" a particular behavior, it is rewarded either consistently or with sufficient predictability that it remains strong (that is, likely to occur) in the *response repertoire* of the individual. If this basic assumption is granted, it follows that the most effective way to change someone's behavior is to alter the pattern of reinforcement following either that particular response or some response that is incompatible with it—or to do both simultaneously.

Young children (like older children and adults) can and do alter their behavior patterns in response to events occurring in their environments. In essence, behavior modification represents a set of procedures that can be employed to capitalize on this tendency in a systematic and planned manner. The first task is to specify the *target behavior,* that is, to identify the behavior that is to be altered. It is important that this be done in a highly specific manner and that the behavior be defined in observable and measurable terms. Thus behavioral problems described by terms such as "sloppiness," "hyperactivity," and "aggressiveness" are inappropriate since they do not specify a particular behavior that can be observed. Rather, the clearer goals of "keeping his nose wiped," "sitting and finishing a nine-piece puzzle," or "asking instead of snatching" can be substituted.

Once the target behavior is identified, it is determined what events presently occur as its consequences. Obviously, this is easier said than done, since one can seldom judge with any degree of certainty that, for example, it is the teacher's attention that is encouraging continued dependence. However, it is possible that, by applying observation techniques, one can identify the source of the payoff, or gratification.

From this, one can generate a reasonable hypothesis that can then be tested. If the intent is to eliminate the behavior, several alternatives are possible. It may be possible to eliminate the reinforcing consequences, thus *extinguishing* the behavior. Also, the behavior can be punished. In technical language, an *aversive stimulus* is supplied. As a matter of fact, this method is seldom advocated by proponents of the behavioral approach, although it may prove necessary under certain circumstances. For example, Lovaas and his co-workers (Lovaas and Simmons, 1969; Lovaas et al., 1965) have described their use of such aversive methods as shock to halt dangerously self-destructive behavior in seriously limited children.

Usually what is desired is that the child learn to acquire some new behavior, to act in a way more congruent with the needs of others and with his own long-range well-being. This involves attempting either to bring about a mode of behavior not presently part of the child's repertoire or to increase the likelihood of occurrence of a behavior that he presently demonstrates at times (smiling or sitting in his seat). It may be that the objective is simultaneously to reduce an undesirable behavior and to increase a desirable one, the latter of which is *incompatible* with the former. For example, the child cannot be speaking quietly while at the same time yelling. In this case, the task is to make speaking quietly more rewarding for the child than yelling.

One method of attempting to increase the likelihood that a "low-probability" behavior will occur is to reinforce its occurrence by means of a "high probability" behavior. This means, simply stated, that the child's ability to engage in some activity that he (apparently) enjoys or finds rewarding is made *contingent* on his first performing a low-probability behavior that we wish to increase in frequency. This scientifically sound application of traditional wisdom is termed the Premack principle (Premack, 1965) and has the advantage of relying on reinforcers already available in the child's environment, rather than injecting new ones that might be artificial or contrived. This tends to increase the frequency of the desired behavior, formerly low in probability, in effect making it "stronger" in the child's "response hierarchy." The reinforcer may be to allow the child to play in the block corner (if that is a high-probability behavior) after he has completed a puzzle.

Some research undertaken to study the applicability of the Premack principle in teaching has demonstrated that it is possible to increase the criterion required for reinforcement gradually (for example, the child works at his seat for longer periods of time before he is permitted to play with blocks). One often-cited example of such research is a study conducted by Lloyd Homme et al. (1963), who undertook to reduce hyperactive and disruptive behavior in 3-year-old nursery school children by using opportunities to engage in these kinds of behavior, in appropriately designated areas, as rewards for quiet, task-oriented conduct (which was very low in probability). This had the effect of rapidly increasing the time children spent quietly working on tasks, behavior that continued to increase as requirements were gradually made greater.

A method used to bring about a behavior that is not part of the child's repertoire, or is very low in strength, is to provide reinforcement for *successive approximation* to the desired result. This approach is called *shaping,* and involves determining what small (even infinitesimal) steps lie between what the child presently does and the long-range goal. Thus the child is brought gradually toward the goal, one small step at a time, as each successive achievement is reinforced. This principle relates to the observation made earlier concerning short-range, attainable tasks through which the child may move successively toward an ultimate *terminal objective.*

Managing the classroom

The adult's role in helping young children with special emotional needs is multifaceted. In a classroom setting, a teacher influences behavior both directly and indirectly. At times it may be necessary to apply direct, external controls, although the aim is to further the child's ability to regulate himself using inner resources rather than outer constraints. The teacher is thus an "auxiliary ego" to provide support, when needed, for the young child's developing one; he or she is also a source of indirect influence through the physical environment and temporal structure of events in the classroom. As a powerful, admired, and perhaps also loved figure who is a source of reinforcing consequences, the teacher is a potent model whose overt behavioral modes and style are likely to be imitated by the children (Bandura, 1965), including such aspects of behavior as voice modulation and verbal expressions.

On a deeper level, as a potential

surrogate figure of identification, the teacher's unconsciously espoused beliefs, values, fears, and attitudes may possibly be internalized, as well as overt behavior (Miller and Hutt, 1949).

Teachers of young children with special emotional needs have such great potential power of influence that they need to be as self-aware as possible, recognizing their own inevitably ambivalent attitudes toward some children, their own natural inclinations to identify more closely with some children than with others, and the real possibility of conveying messages of rejection to some children or, because of feelings of guilt, to respond to some children in ways that fail to help the child to assume responsibility for his own behavior.

Teachers of young emotionally disturbed children, however, need not conform to a single pattern or style. In fact, a degree of diversity and individuality is not only inevitable, if teachers are to be authentic in their modes of interaction with children, it is desirable from the child's standpoint as well. Not only does the child need to learn to live with and to value differences among his peers, he must also learn to relate to adults as individual human beings.

A broad range of teaching styles and strategies are evolved as adults, as unique individuals, translate therapeutic goals for individual children into instructional and management practices. These are further influenced by the responses of individual children and of the group as a distinct entity. Although in general a degree of consistency is desirable, teachers must recognize that each specific transaction between teacher and child will be to some extent shaped by a set of dynamics unique to that situation.

Developing a clinical child study orientation to teaching

As in other areas of special education, working with a child with special emotional or behavioral needs requires a plan,

and this must be developed on the basis of careful study of the child. The mere label "emotionally disturbed" does not help a teacher know how to work with a child. It is necessary to observe and analyze samples of the child's behavior in response to diverse situations. This process of systematic observation leading to identification of specific needs and formulation of objectives is really what is meant by the term "diagnosis" in education.

The most valuable tool a teacher can have in conducting a diagnostic study of a child is the ability to observe. Observation of children is, unfortunately, something that many teachers have little opportunity to do. Others, however, structure their classroom in such a way as to provide substantial opportunity to observe children engaged in activities of all kinds. If classroom activities are consistently teacher dominated and whole-group directed, there are obviously few occasions to step back and see what an individual child is able to initiate for himself, how he spends his time, how he is received by his peers, what peer contacts he initiates and how, what behavioral mannerisms he demonstrates, whether he seems happy or sad, and what conditions in the environment impinge on his attention and his affective state.

Some teachers are less comfortable with an "open" or "informal" classroom format than are others. It is possible to conduct an *individualized* program that is at the same time tightly structured and teacher dominated, of course. Although the informal classroom structure has distinct advantages in terms of the teacher's ability to observe children under relatively more "natural" conditions, it is not the only valid approach for a teacher to gain a good picture of how a child functions in the classroom. There are many misunderstandings concerning what really happens in an "informal" classroom, as well as misunderstandings about the concept of structure. Rather than *open vs. structured,* the issue is really *individualization,* a goal that can be reached in a variety of ways. This point is discussed more fully in Chapter 12.

Special educators experienced in work with emotionally disturbed children or children who manifest *discordant* or *maladaptive* behaviors have developed a number of strategies for conducting systematic child study. To gain a thorough understanding of the child, reliance on a single strategy may be inadequate. Conversely, however, if the objective is to help a child deal more constructively with his environment and the expectations it places on him, focusing on a single, discrete *behavior* by means of a more specific technique may be more appropriate.

Responding to aggression

Aggression has many facets. In a very illuminating article, Bettye Caldwell (1977) provides some clarification of this pervasive concern for those who teach young children. An important consideration, she notes, is the matter of *intent:* whether a child wishes to inflict harm on someone else (*hostile* aggression) or whether an aggressive act is simply a means of obtaining a desired goal, such as securing a toy or protecting one's territory (*instrumental* aggression). She cites Hartup's (1974) evidence that young children's aggression is much more frequently of the latter type, rather than being intentionally harmful to someone else.

How does one deal with aggressive behavior in the young child? What teachers have often been counseled to do is to ignore the behavior. Caldwell rejects this as both impractical and tacitly approving. On the other hand, a physically punitive response conveys a "might makes right" principle. In addition, the adult serves the role of an *aggressive model* (Bandura et al., 1963). Physical punishment is certainly inappropriate.

She also cites Berkowitz' (1973) observation that the notion that children's aggression should be permitted in the interests of "release of tension" or "catharsis" is not supported by scientific evidence. Berkowitz regards this as an outmoded idea and possibly a dangerous one. Instead of any of these three alternatives, Caldwell offers the following recommendations:

1. *In order to minimize aggression, we need parent cooperation.*
2. *In order to control aggression, we must strengthen altruism.*
3. *Non-permissiveness in our attitudes towards aggression may be as important as punishment for aggression.* [This suggests the importance of conveying clearly what sorts of behavior are *expected* and what is not *permitted.*]
4. *We must help children de-escalate their aggressive behavior.*
5. *Children need to learn different alternatives to problem situations.*
6. *We need to be more willing to play with children and to help them learn to play.*

NEEDS OF THE TEACHER

Teaching emotionally disturbed and behaviorally disordered children can be, at times, physically exhausting and emotionally draining. Outstanding teachers of these children cannot help but become emotionally involved, but nevertheless they must retain their objectivity and maintain their own lives. Particularly helpful accounts of what it is to be a teacher of troubled children have been provided in such books as *Nine Rotten Lousy Kids* by Herb Grossman (1972), *The Lives of Children* by George Dennison (1969), and *P.S., You're Not Listening* by Eleanor Craig (1972).

How can the teacher release some of the intense emotional pressure he or she may live with and gain the support needed to carry on in such a way that one's *own* needs never take precedence over those of the child? Some suggestions from personal experience and that of others are offered here:

1. Be objective, about yourself and what you do, as well as about the child and what he or she does.

2. Share problems and experiences regularly with colleagues formally (through case conferences) and informally.
3. Ask colleagues to observe your class; then discuss openly with them your concerns and invite their suggestions.
4. Maintain dialogue with the child's parents for mutual support as well as for consistency of approach.
5. Consult with the psychologist. Raise your questions and request his or her supportive involvement.
6. Be willing to agree to or even recommend that the child spend part of his day with another teacher.
7. Be willing to recommend a shortened school day for a child if you think it is indicated.
8. Have a colleague, the psychologist, or another person conduct an objective analysis of a child's behavior and/or of your own interaction with him. Behavior Counting, Flanders' Interaction Analysis, or another objective recording system may provide you with valuable insights.
9. Maintain your own identity, including interests, relationships, and out-of-school life.
10. Literature, theater, good films, music, and art may somehow become more meaningful to you when you work with disturbed children. Why this is so often the case is speculative, but it probably has something to do with a heightened sensitivity to the universal language of human experience and receptiveness to the integrative and communicative functions of art.
11. Maintain a sense of humor.
12. Above all, maintain a sense of who you are, legitimate confidence in both your professional and personal "credentials," and trust in your own ability and worth. *Do not expect or seek reinforcement and assurance from the children you teach. It is your task to provide these for them.*

DISCUSSION QUESTIONS

1. What is meant by an ecological approach to understanding and dealing with discordant behavior?
2. What are the origins of the children's rights movement? How does the concept of the rights of the child relate to society's, and education's, response to emotionally disturbed or behaviorally deviant children?
3. What is the teacher's role in identification and referral of young children who may have serious emotional problems?
4. Why is an understanding of normal development essential to understanding special emotional needs and problems in social adaptation?
5. Take a position, and be prepared to defend it, on the issue of whether the teacher's role must be distinguished from that of a therapist.
6. Many psychological theorists emphasize that children's development cannot be "compartmentalized"; that is, that physical, cognitive, social, and emotional development always interact. What implications might this interactive relationship have for understanding and dealing with emotional or behavioral difficulties?
7. For a teacher to implement a systematic contingency management approach in the classroom, what steps and procedures are necessary?

REFERENCES

Aries, P. *Centuries of childhood.* New York: Alfred A. Knopf, Inc., 1962.
Axline, V. M. *Play therapy.* Boston: Houghton Mifflin Co., 1947.
Bandura, A. Behavioral modification through modeling procedures. In L. Krosner and L. P. Ullman (Eds.), *Research in behavior modification: new developments and implications.* New York: Holt, Rinehart & Winston, Inc., 1965, pp. 310-340.
Bandura, A., Ross, D., and Ross, S. Imitation of film-mediated aggressive models. *Journal of Abnormal and Social Psychology,* 1963, *66,* 3-11.
Berkowitz, L. Control of aggression. In B. Caldwell and H. Ricciuti (Eds.), *Review of child development research* (Vol. 3). Chicago: University of Chicago Press, 1973, pp. 95-140.
Berne, E. *Transactional analysis in psychotherapy.* New York: Grove Press, Inc., 1961.
Bower, E. M. Primary prevention in a school setting. In G. Caplan (Ed.), *Prevention of mental disorders in children.* New York: Basic Books, Inc., 1961, pp. 353-378.
Bower, E. M. The modification, mediation, and utilization of stress during the school years. *American Journal of Orthopsychiatry,* 1964, *34,* 667-674.

Bower, E. M. *Early identification of emotionally disturbed children in school* (2nd ed.). Springfield, Ill.: Charles C Thomas, Publisher, 1969.

Bower, E. M. Three rivers of significance to education. In E. M. Bower and W. G. Hollister (Eds.), *Behavioral science frontiers in education*. New York: John Wiley & Sons, Inc., 1967.

Bower, E. M., and Lambert, N. M. *Teacher's manual for in-school screening of emotionally handicapped children*. Princeton, N.J.: Educational Testing Service, 1961.

Brown, C. *Manchild in the promised land*. New York: Macmillan Publishing Co., Inc., 1965.

Buhler, C. What is a problem? In N. Long, W. C. Morse, and R. L. Newman (Eds.), *Conflict in the classroom. The education of emotionally disturbed children*. Belmont, Calif.: Wadsworth Publishing Co., Inc., 1965.

Caldwell, B. Aggression and hostility in young children. *Young Children*, 1977, *32*(2), 4-13.

Children's Defense Fund of the Washington Research Project, Inc. *Children out of school in America*. Cambridge, Mass.: Children's Defense Fund, 1974.

Craig, E. *P.S., you're not listening*. New York: Richard W. Baron Publishing Co., Inc., 1972.

Cruickshank, W. M., Bentzen, F. A., Ratzeburg, F. H., and Tannhauser, M. T. *A teaching method for brain-injured and hyperactive children*. Syracuse: Syracuse University Press, 1961.

Dennison, G. *The lives of children: the story of the First Street School*. New York: Random House, Inc., 1969.

Despert, J. L. *The emotionally disturbed child—then and now*. New York: Robert Brunner, 1965.

Devereaux, G. *Therapeutic education: its theoretical bases and practice*. New York: Harper & Row, Publishers, 1956.

Erikson, E. H. *Childhood and society* (2nd ed.). New York: W. W. Norton & Co., Inc., 1963.

Freud, A. *The ego and the mechanisms of defense* (2nd ed.). New York: International Universities Press, 1964. (Originally published 1946.)

Freud, A. *Normality and pathology in childhood: assessments of development*. New York: International Universities Press, 1965.

Freud, S. *The problem of anxiety*. New York: The Psychoanalytic Quarterly Press and W. W. Norton & Co., Inc., 1936.

Freud, S. *Character and anal eroticism,* (Standard ed., Vol. 10; J. Strachey, Ed.). London: Hogarth Press, 1955. (Originally published 1908.)

Freud, S. *Analysis of a phobia in a five-year-old boy* (Standard ed., Vol. 10; J. Strachey, Ed.). London: Hogarth Press, 1955, pp. 5-149. (Originally published 1909.)

Furman, R. A., and Katan, A. *The therapeutic nursery school*. New York: International Universities Press, 1969.

Glasser, W. *Reality therapy*. New York: Harper & Row, Publishers, 1965.

Glasser, W. *Schools without failure*. New York: Harper & Row, Publishers, 1969.

Grossman, H. *Nine rotten, lousy kids*. New York: Holt, Rinehart & Winston, Inc., 1972.

Haring, N. G. Perspectives in special education. In N. G. Haring (Ed.), *Behavior of exceptional children: an introduction to special education*. Columbus, Ohio: Charles E. Merrill Publishing Co., 1974, pp. 3-33.

Haring, N. G., and Phillips, E. L. *Educating emotionally disturbed children*. New York: McGraw-Hill Book Co., 1962.

Hartmann, H. Ego psychology and the problem of adaptation. In D. Rapaport (Ed.), *Organization and pathology of thought*. New York: Columbia University Press, 1951.

Hartup, W. W. Aggression in childhood: developmental perspectives. *American Psychologist*, 1974, 336-341.

Hewett, F. M. *The emotionally disturbed child in the classroom*. Boston: Allyn & Bacon, Inc., 1968.

Hobbs, N. Mental health's third revolution. *American Journal of Orthopsychiatry*. 1964, *34*, 822-833.

Hobbs, N. Helping disturbed children: psychological and ecological strategies. *American Psychologist*, 1966, *21*(12), 1105-1115.

Hobbs, N. *The futures of children*. San Francisco: Jossey-Bass, Inc., Publishers, 1975.

Homme, L. E., DeBaca, P. C., DeVine, J. V., Steinhorst, R., and Rickert, E. J. Use of the Premack principle in controlling the behavior of nursery school children. *Journal of the Experimental Analysis of Behavior*, 1963, *6*, 544.

Jahoda, M. *Current concepts of positive mental health*. New York: Basic Books, Inc., 1958.

Joint Commission on Mental Health of Children. *Crisis in child mental health: challenge for the 1970's*. New York: Harper & Row, Publishers, 1970.

Kohn, M., and Rosman, B. L. A two-factor model of emotional disturbance in the young child: validity and screening efficiency. *Journal of Child Psychology and Psychiatry*, 1973, *14*(1), 31-56.

Kounin, J., Friesen, W., and Norton, A. Managing emotionally disturbed children in regular classrooms. *Journal of Teacher Education*, 1966, *57*, 1-13.

Lilly, M. S. Special education in transition: a competency base for classroom teachers. Urbana, Ill.: University of Illinois, 1974. (Mimeographed.)

Lovaas, O. I., Schaeffer, B., and Simmons, J. Building social behavior in autistic children by use of shock. *Journal of Experimental Research in Personality*, 1965, *1*, 99-109.

Lovaas, O. I., and Simmons, J. Manipulation of self destruction in three retarded children. *Journal of Applied Behavior Analysis*, 1969, *2*, 40-53.

MacFarlane, J. W., Allen, L., and Honzik, M. *A developmental study of the behavior problems of normal children between twenty-one months and fourteen years.* Berkeley, Calif.: University of California Press, 1954.

Miller, D. R., and Hutt, M. Value interiorization and personality development. *Journal of Social Issues,* 1949, *5,* 2-30.

Mischel, W. Sex-typing and socialization. In P. A. Mussen (Ed.), *Carmichael's manual of child psychology* (Vol. 2, 3rd. ed.). New York: John Wiley & Sons, Inc., 1970.

Moreno, J. F. Sociometry in the classroom. *Sociometry,* 1943, *6,* 425-428.

Morse, W. C., Cutler, R. L., and Fink, A. H. *Public school classes for the emotionally handicapped: a research analysis.* Washington, D.C.: Council for Exceptional Children, National Education Association, 1964.

Morse, W. C., and Wingo, G. M. *Psychology and teaching* (3rd ed.). Glenview, Ill.: Scott, Foresman & Co., 1969.

Moustakas, C. *Children in play therapy.* New York: McGraw-Hill Book Co., 1953.

Murphy, L. B. Preventive implications of development in the pre-school years. In G. Caplan (Ed.), *Prevention of mental disorders in children.* New York: Basic Books, Inc., 1961. pp. 218-248.

Neill, A. S. *Summerhill: a radical approach to child rearing.* New York: 1960.

Newman, R. G. Groups: how they grew and what they're all about. In N. Long, W. C. Morse, and R. G. Newman (Eds.), *Conflict in the classroom: the education of children with problems.* Belmont, Calif.: Wadsworth Publishing Co., Inc., 1971, pp. 231-235.

Payne, J. S., Kaufman, J. M., Brown, G. B., and Demott, R. M. *Exceptional children in focus: incidents, concepts, and issues in special education.* Columbus, Ohio: Charles E. Merrill Publishing Co., 1974.

Pearson, G. *Psychoanalysis and the education of the child.* New York: W. W. Norton & Co., Inc., 1954.

Premack, D. Reinforcement therapy. In D. Levine (Ed.), *Nebraska Symposium on Motivation, 1965.* Lincoln: University of Nebraska Press, 1965.

Redl, F. The concept of a therapeutic milieu. *American Journal of Orthopsychiatry,* 1959, *29,* 721-734.

Redl, F. *When we deal with children.* New York: The Free Press, 1966.

Redl, F., and Wattenberg, W. W. *Mental hygiene in*

teaching. New York: Harcourt, Brace & World, 1959.

Rhodes, W. C. Curriculum and disordered behavior. *Exceptional Children,* October, 1963, *30,* 61-68.

Rhodes, W. C. The disturbing child: a problem in ecological management. *Exceptional Children,* 1967, *34,* 499-455.

Rhodes, W. C., and Tracy, M. L. *A study of child variance: conceptual models* (Vol. 1). Ann Arbor: University of Michigan, Institute for the Study of Mental Retardation and Related Disabilities, 1972.

Sarason, S. B. et al. *Anxiety in elementary school children.* New York: John Wiley & Sons, Inc., 1960.

Silberman, C. E. *Crisis in the classroom.* New York: Random House, Inc., 1970.

Skinner, B. F. *The technology of teaching.* New York: Appleton-Century-Crofts, 1968.

Strain, P., and Weigerink, R. The effects of sociodramatic activities on social interaction among behaviorally disordered pre-school children. *Journal of Special Education,* 1976, *10*(1), 71-76.

Swap, S. Disturbing classroom behaviors: a developmental and ecological view. *Exceptional Children,* 1974, *41,* 163-171.

Szasz, T. *The manufacture of madness.* New York: Harper & Row, Publishers, 1970.

Ullman, L., and Krasver, L. *Case studies in behavior modification.* New York: Holt, Rinehart & Winston, Inc., 1965.

Vacc, N. A. A study of emotionally disturbed children in regular and special classes. *Exceptional Children,* 1968, *35*(3), 197-206.

White, R. W. The concept of competence. *Psychological Review,* 1959, *66,* 297-333.

Wickman, E. K. *Children's behavior and teacher's attitudes.* New York: Common Wealth Fund, 1928.

Woltmann, A. G. The use of puppetry as a projective method in therapy. In H. H. Anderson and G. L. Anderson (Eds.), *An introduction to projective techniques and other devices for understanding the dynamics of human behavior.* Englewood Cliffs, N.J.: Prentice-Hall, Inc., 1951.

Wood, M. W. *Developmental therapy: a textbook for teachers as therapists for emotionally disturbed young children.* Baltimore: University Park Press, 1975.

Physical disabilities and severe or multiple impairments

CHAPTER **8**

PHYSICAL AND NEUROLOGICAL HANDICAPS

Children with physical handicaps have been labeled with such terms as "crippled," "orthopedically handicapped," "physically disabled," and "physically impaired." Not all physical problems involve orthopedic impairments or limitations, however, and the term "crippled" is clearly inadequate as a catch-all designation. The child who suffers from a chronic disease such as hemophilia or from allergy may not be impaired in mobility, general intellectual functioning, or communication. However, this child has special needs as well, many of which will be reflected in the context of the classroom.

Overall, physical handicapping conditions in children, including crippling conditions and all other chronic health impairments, are a low-incidence category, when compared to learning disabilities, mental retardation, or behavior disorders. That is, their numbers are relatively few, compared to other forms of handicap. This fact, perhaps, has resulted in a slowness on the part of schools and other public facilities to incorporate in their physical design the provisions that are often necessary to accommodate these children—and handicapped adults as well.

Incidence figures are misleading for several reasons. For one thing, categories of exceptionality in children overlap. Some physically handicapped children may have sensory impairments, for instance. In addition, there remains in the United States a great number of children —in *absolute* terms—who are receiving inadequate medical attention and habilitative therapy, although badly needed, and whose educational needs are *unserved*. Many handicapped children have not been identified as in need of special educational services. Although the recent history of federal legislation concerning handicapped children shows a progressive trend toward recognizing and serving their medical, habilitative, and educational needs, it has only been since 1974 that schools have been explicitly mandated by the federal government to iden-

tify and serve *all* children. Now for the first time all state departments of education must implement a state plan in compliance with federal mandates for identification and provision of appropriate educational programming for all handicapped children, across all handicapping conditions, and regardless of severity. Therefore it is difficult to accurately establish the actual incidence of physically handicapping conditions at the present time.

THE YOUNG PHYSICALLY HANDICAPPED CHILD AND THE SCHOOL

In the past, physically handicapped children have participated in educational program of various types, depending on such factors as the severity of the handicap; the extent to which the child's mobility was impaired; whether surgical, medical, and habilitative therapy intervention could successfully be employed or was necessary on a continuing basis; and whether the child presented secondary or related handicapping conditions, such as mental retardation or sensory impairments. Conditions with a neurological basis, such as cerebral palsy, are more likely to involve multiple associated disabilities. In contrast, a specifically orthopedic problem, such as club-foot or tibial torsion, is usually both amenable to orthopedic treatment supplemented by gait training through physical therapy and unlikely to be associated with central nervous system dysfunction and consequent learning disorders.

For those children whose physical disabilities represent but one facet of an interrelated pattern of severe and multiple impairment, including severe or profound mental retardation, residential institutional placement has often been provided. However, in recent times new points of view have been expressed (Wolfensberger et al., 1972; Blatt and Kaplan, 1966) concerning the appropriateness, necessity, and humaneness of institutionalization as it continues to be practiced in the United States. (This topic is discussed in Chapter 9.)

During the twentieth century, public schools have become increasingly involved in taking the place of residential care. School districts in heavily populated areas have provided services through special schools and special classes for those children whose needs were believed incapable of being met within the regular school program. In addition, homebound instruction has been provided for children too handicapped to participate even in these programs and in areas where appropriate schools or classes were not available (Connor et al., 1970). Often transportation has been a determining element for children, for example, a child whose wheelchair must be lifted onto a special van. With the recent heightened social awareness and mandate to educators to provide *least restrictive alternative* programming for all exceptional children, there is a new charge to assess carefully for each child, with the child's parents, what type of educational experience would be least restrictive for each individual child. If architectural barriers such as second-floor classrooms, high curbs, inaccessible toilet facilities, and stairs constitute impediments to integration of the child within the educational mainstream, federal regulations have required that *these barriers must be removed.* The child's *educational* needs, rather than his medical diagnosis, are the determinants of where, how, and by whom he is to be educated. And it is the responsibility of the public school to provide both the *mode* and the *setting* for instruction that least restrict and most enhance his development.

A child with a physical *disability* may or may not have a *handicapping condition* so far as successful adjustment and achievement in schools are concerned (Cawley, 1975). Whether such a child is *educationally handicapped* may depend at least as much on the response of the school personnel to him as on his own physical limitation or problem.

The actual architectural arrangement and design of preschool and day care centers and schools eloquently expresses the attitude of the planners and staff toward the physically disabled child. In the past, many such sites seem to have been selected or constructed without any awareness whatsoever that some children are confined to wheelchairs or can move about on a scooter board or require a support bar to use the toilet. For public buildings, this is no longer possible, if it could ever have been deemed defensible. Often relatively simple physical arrangements are all that may be required to accommodate a physically disabled child. Without such adjustments, the degree of a child's *handicap* is greatly increased and may be rendered so severe as to preclude his participation in an educational program from which he could derive great benefit.

Beyond modifications in *space* utilization, teachers may be able to implement modifications in the use of another dimension—time. Many nursery school personnel have recognized for years that children's needs to rest (or even sleep) and to use the bathroom vary widely and accordingly make appropriate provisions. This may mean the elimination of an afternoon nap period, as such, while still providing opportunities for individual children to rest as needed. Not only do children (as do adults!) require opportunities to use the bathroom as individual needs dictate, some children handle excretory functions differently. Not only is regimentation of bathrooming unnatural (although admittedly much easier for the teacher), it calls undue attention to the exceptional child.

EARLY EDUCATION APPROACHES

Through the work of organizations such as The United Cerebral Palsy Association (UCPA) and Societies for Crippled Children, nursery school programs have been developed within multidisciplinary agency settings, primarily within the last three decades. These settings may provide, concomitantly with the nursery program, physical, occupational, and speech therapy as needed and prescribed by a physician as well as psychological evaluation and social work counseling for parents. In some, medical services are also provided within the agency; others work closely with medical facilities in the community. In recent years there has been much more attention devoted to the learning needs of young physically handicapped children. Under the sponsorship of the National Task Force of United Cerebral Palsy Association, a two-volume annotated bibliography concerning early intervention with young cerebral palsied children has been compiled; it contains more than 1,000 entries (Rembolt and Roth, 1972).

The nursery school is typically an integral part of the habilitative program, which may involve one or more special therapies. Teachers participate with other members of the interdisciplinary professional staff in formulating goals and evaluating the progress of individual children. In addition, they attempt to facilitate the child's transition into an appropriate public school or other program, whether "regular" or specialized, usually by age 5 or 6 years. Although the child may have been seen by therapists as an outpatient prior to nursery school entrance, he may have entered the nursery school program at age 3 or 4. Increasingly, however, pilot programs for even younger children with physical handicapping conditions have been developed (Safford and Arbitman, 1975).

In light of the child's medical needs and the emotional stress these often involve, too early imposition of academic demands in a formal school situation has not generally been advocated (Cruickshank, 1965). Basically, the increasing trend toward *early* educational programming for these children reflects an awareness that the whole child, not only his physical disability, needs to be served. Because of his handicap, the child's ability to learn through spontaneous interaction with his physical environment may be limited; consequently, guided and facilitated exposure to the world of object, symbol, and sensation is beneficial, as is guidance in the area of social interaction and social play. If preschool participation serves to promote socialization, cognitive learning, language skills, and feelings of competence and self-worth among children generally, these areas are especially important to the young child with a physical disability. For this reason, it is especially desirable to involve him in a nursery school program as early as is reasonably possible to do so.

Each of the special therapy areas, whether these are conducted independently or are integrated through an interdisciplinary team approach, is in large measure a *teaching-learning process* as well. The child must learn how to walk in braces or with crutches or a walker; how to position himself while playing on the floor; how to increase his limb and body mobility; how to handle self-care functions, such as dressing or undressing; how to compensate for involuntary muscle activity in walking, eating, or speaking; or how to compensate for unresponsive muscles, or strengthen others in learning to produce sounds leading to speech. In all of these areas, the nursery teacher attempts to carry out the prescribed program suggested by the physical, occupational, or speech therapist and to institute recommended activities within the classroom. The teacher also communicates to the special therapists suggestions concerning the child's emotional needs, motivational readiness, and cognitive functioning, as well as observations that relate to the child's educational progress. Ideally, all of these adults working with a child avoid fragmenting him, confusing him with conflicting or contradictory approaches, and frustrating him by imposing demands that are physically and psychologically too great. However, this can only be accomplished if the adults who are responsible for a child's well-being remain consistently in touch and work together.

Although approaches in the field of physical therapy for developmentally disabled children vary, there is increasing emphasis on *facilitation* approaches (B. Bobath, 1971; K. Bobath, 1971). The therapist especially trained in a system such as neurodevelopmental training (NDT) can often apply his or her techniques under more or less "natural" circumstances. Relaxation of spastic muscle impulses and responses and promotion of greater volitional control of movement are emphasized, and there is a de-emphasis on use of specialized equipment. This often enables the therapist and teacher to work side by side in a classroom setting.

In an excellent book, *Handling the Young Cerebral Palsied Child at Home,* Nancie Finnie (1968), an English occupational therapist, describes and illustrates for parents ways in which they can best help the child. This book is a valuable resource for teachers as well, since they will need guidance in positioning and working with the child in the areas of self-care, mobility, and motor integration.

TYPES OF PHYSICAL HANDICAPPING CONDITIONS

In general it is of more value for the teacher to know a great deal about the strengths, potential, limitations, and special needs of the individual child, regardless of what his medical diagnosis may be, than to know about the *condition* he has. However, at least some basic knowledge concerning medical aspects of the handicap is essential. In addition, if functioning as a member of an interdisciplinary team, the teacher must be able to integrate to some degree the perspectives of other disciplines within his or her own program and certainly must comprehend the goals and methods being employed with a child by the physical therapist or other profes-

sionals. Obvious examples include speech and self-care skills, such as dressing. But appropriate *positioning* of the child for learning activities can be guided by the physical and occupational therapist, and enhanced mobility and independent movement are equally important.

Especially for the teacher working within an agency setting for physically handicapped children, but for the "regular" teacher as well, a single chapter simply cannot suffice to provide the background of required knowledge about specific forms of handicap. To grasp the many and variegated dimensions of cerebral palsy, for example, the reader should consult a volume such as *Cerebral Palsy: A Developmental Disability,* edited by William Cruickshank (1976), for a comprehensive treatment. *Physically Handicapped Children—A Medical Atlas for Teachers,* edited by Eugene E. Bleck and Donald A. Nagel (1975), provides an illustrated and straightforward guide to understanding the forms of physical and neurological handicap most commonly observed, as well as many suggestions for the educator working with a child who has a specific medical problem.

Provided here are general descriptions of some of the physical disabilities most commonly seen by teachers of young children. This summary is necessarily incomplete, since there are a great many medical syndromes, diseases, and other health problems with which young children may be afflicted.

Cerebral palsy

Cerebral palsy is a nonprogressive condition characterized primarily by inability to control muscle reflexes voluntarily (Keats, 1973). By definition, cerebral palsy implies damage to the brain. Although in most instances a result of any of a number of prenatal or perinatal causes, such as infection to the mother during pregnancy, insufficient oxygen during birth, Rh incompatibility, birth trauma, or (rarely) heredity (Bleck, 1975a), cerebral palsy can also result from brain infection, tumor, or head injury during the developmental years.

Cerebral palsy can be classified as to *type* (spasticity, athetosis, rigidity, ataxia, tremor, or mixed) and according to limbs affected: hemiplegia, involvement of one side of the body; paraplegia, involvement of legs but not arms; diplegia, major leg involvement and minor arm involvement; triplegia, involvement of three limbs; quadriplegia or tetraplegia, major involvement of all four limbs; and double hemiplegia, more arm than leg involvement (Minear, 1956).

Spasticity comprises about half the cases of cerebral palsy, especially in young children, who may with development acquire athetoid patterns as well (Keats, 1973). Spasticity results from the inability to control or suppress reflexes and impulses and a consequent tension in antagonistic muscles. Movements are jerky and uncontrolled, subject to spontaneous muscle contraction, and the child may have insufficient voluntary control over the involved area to sit or walk unaided or to reach or grasp. It is also the most likely to be associated with concomitant impairments to learning. Mental subnormality is more common among children with the spastic type of cerebral palsy, and these children are also more likely to have impaired perceptual functioning (Bleck, 1975a). However, problems in speech and language and in gross and fine motor control often make it difficult to ascertain intellectual potential or limitations (Freedheim, 1966; Sattler and Anderson, 1973). A single test—especially with young children—should never be used as the sole basis of judgment of a cerebral palsied child's intellectual potential, and test results should be integrated with day-to-day data in judging current levels of functioning (Cruickshank et al., 1976).

Individuals with athetoid cerebral palsy comprise the next largest group of cerebral palsied individuals. They present a different, usually more optimistic, clinical picture, since impairment of intellectual and perceptual functioning is less common. Involuntary, sometimes wavelike movements and a lurching, stumbling gait are commonly observed, as are facial grimacing and inarticulate speech in more severe cases. These involuntary movements are subject to the emotional state of the individual, becoming more apparent in periods of upset or excitation, less so when the individual is relaxed, and not present at all during sleep.

Ataxia is associated with damage to the cerebellum; consequently, balance and muscle coordination are primarily affected. Ataxia is less likely than spasticity or athetosis to be detected at birth. The ataxic child walks with unsteady gait, is subject to falling, and lacks accurate sense of his position in space.

The type of cerebral palsy is determined by clinical observations of the child and his reflex patterns. Although each form or type is known to be associated with damage to a particular area of the brain (Keats, 1973), such knowledge is less important than is clinical study of the individual child, since surgery is not effective in restoring damaged tissue or neurological functions.

Orthopedic surgery may be employed as the child grows in order to ameliorate skeletal deformity or joint separation due to muscle stress; however, there is no cure of the basic neurological problem. Drugs are used to control seizures and, although generally such treatment has been only somewhat successful in other areas such as muscle relaxation, new developments in drug treatment may have promise (Bleck, 1975a), especially for older children and adults. Since convulsive disorders, characterized by seizures, are exceedingly common among individuals, with the spastic type of cerebral palsy (much less so among those with the athetoid type) (Perlstein et al., 1947), a teacher will need to be aware if a child is receiving medication for seizure control and may be asked by physician or parent to observe the child's responses to varying drug programs.

Epilepsy (convulsive disorder)

Epilepsy, or convulsive disorder, is a symptomatic condition, rather than a disease in the strict sense, that often coexists with a known neurological disability, such as cerebral palsy. The presence of seizures indicates some basic, underlying dysfunction of the central nervous system. Continued seizures in young children may be instrumental in causing more extensive and serious neurological damage; hence seizure control through medication is implemented as early as feasible in the child's life once the condition is known, and it is an important aspect of the child's maintenance. The amount and type of anticonvulsant medication is, of course, a matter of medical supervision, and the child's program of medication is subject to modification as his needs dictate. Naturally, close coordination between doctor, parent, and teacher is essential, with the child learning to willingly assume responsibility as well.

The incidence of epilepsy is difficult to determine, and statistics vary with age. It is most common among children under 5 years of age, however, with studies suggesting an incidence of 152 cases in 100,000 individuals (Lennox and Lennox, 1960, cited in Berg, 1975). There are several classifications of epilepsy, or convulsive disorder, but there are three general types of seizure patterns most important for the educator to be aware of: grand mal, petit mal, and psychomotor, or temporal lobe. The following descriptions of each of these three general types are provided by Bruce O. Berg in *Physically Handicapped Children: A Medical Atlas for Teachers.*

Grand mal

The grand mal, or generalized fit, is a very dramatic awe-inspiring event. The patient may be aware that a seizure is about to occur because of some unusual sensory perception

(the aura) moments before the convulsion. That perception may include abdominal cramping, a feeling of nausea, an unpleasant odor such as burning rubber, or some pervading nondirected fear. Often the patient can only say "it just feels funny." The patient may suddenly appear strange or bewildered, stop all activity and then lose consciousness. The arms are extended or flexed, the legs are extended with generalized body stiffening, and the patient falls to the ground. As the muscles contract, air may be forced from the lungs through the vocal cords, resulting in a peculiar eerie, sometimes frightening cry, and there may also be a loss of bowel and/or bladder control. This is the *tonic* (stiff) phase that usually progresses to the *clonic* (jerking) phase.

Commonly the patient becomes less rigid, quivers or becomes tremulous and then the arms and/or legs will jerk synchronously. The jerking decreases in frequency and severity and then suddenly stops and the entire episode, including both tonic and clonic phases, lasts less than two minutes, and commonly less than one.

During the fit the patient's pupils may constrict and then dilate, and because of inefficient swallowing of saliva and movement of the lips and mouth there may be a "froth" or bubbling about the lips. Regular respiration ceases and the patient often becomes cyanotic, but at the termination of the spell and the beginning of regular respiration the color soon returns to normal. Following the spells, the patient has postictal confusion, headache, or may fall into a deep sleep that lasts from minutes to hours.

Petit mal

Three different types of seizures are considered under that category of petit mal epilepsy: the typical variety, or staring spell, and two forms of atypical or petit mal variants. The typical petit mal spell is the momentary suspension of all activity, a staring spell, or as some have called them, lapses or absence attacks. They are commonly overlooked initially as if the child were daydreaming and, indeed, it may well appear to be so. Minor movement of the eyes or slight fluttering of the eyelids have been observed to accompany some of the staring spells, and the entire episode lasts less than 5-10 seconds. The posture of the child is usually maintained.

The atypical or petit mal variant may take

one or two forms: the myoclonic or akinetic attack. Myoclonic epilepsy is a disorder in which the patient has paroxysmal brief contractions of part of a muscle or group of muscles. There may be a brief sudden neck flexion or extension in which the head suddenly drops forward or backward; other muscles or muscle groups may be involved causing the arms to jerk upward or the trunk to bend sharply upon itself.

The akinetic attack is also known as "astatic" or "inhibition" epilepsy. These spells are characterized by sudden drop attacks during which time the patient suddenly loses muscle tone and plummets to the ground, only to rise again shortly thereafter. Some patients appear to have an aborted akinetic attack as if they have "caught themselves" before falling to the ground, and look as if they are nodding or having a sudden momentary jolt.

Psychomotor

Some convulsive phenomena, consistently related to one area of the brain, have been named for that cerebral location, as in the case of temporal lobe (or psychomotor) epilepsy. Temporal lobe fits are characterized by their semipurposeful, automatic nature. The patient appears to have an altered conscious state but at the same time is able to carry out complex, coordinated acts. The variability of temporal lobe fits is great and the patient may later recount vivid ictal visual, auditory, or gustatory hallucinations. During the spells he may perform such complex acts as walking about, or undressing and repeating a phrase or sentence over and over. If one attempts to restrain the patient during the spell, the patient may vigorously resist and/or become obstreporous.*

Conflicting and erroneous beliefs concerning the management of a grand mal seizure are widespread, despite efforts to prepare teachers and other adults with the information to respond to these appropriately and effectively. The following steps have been recommended by The Epilepsy Foundation of America:

---

*From Berg, B. O. Convulsive disorders. In E. E. Bleck and D. A. Nagel (Eds.), *Physically handicapped children—a medical atlas for teachers.* New York: Grune & Stratton, Inc., 1975, pp. 103-104. Used by permission.

1. Remain calm. Students will assume the same emotional reaction as their teacher. *The seizure itself is painless to the child.*
2. Do not try to restrain the child. Nothing can be done to stop a seizure once it has begun. It must run its course.
3. Clear the area around the student so that he does not injure himself on hard objects. Try not to interfere with his movements in any way.
4. Do not force anything between his teeth. If his mouth is already open, a soft object like a handkerchief may be placed between his side teeth.
5. It generally is not necessary to call a doctor unless the attack is immediately followed by another major seizure or if the seizure lasts more than ten minutes.
6. When the seizure is over, let the child rest if he needs to.
7. The child's parents and physician should be informed of the seizure.
8. Turn the incident into a learning experience for the entire class. Explain what a seizure is, that it is not contagious, and that it is nothing to be afraid of. Teach the class understanding toward the child— not pity, so that his classmates will continue to accept him as "one of the gang." (Gearheart and Weishann, 1976, p. 81)

Myelodysplasia or spina bifida

Myelodysplasia is an abnormality of the spinal cord caused by malformation and failure of the vertebrae to close in the embryo at the end of the first trimester of pregnancy. Myelomeningocele, meningocele, and spina bifida occulta are all "open defects in the spinal canal" (Bleck, 1975b, p. 181). Although the terms "myelodysplasia" and "spina bifida" are often used (incorrectly) interchangeably to refer to any such deformity, the three terms cited above more precisely communicate the degree of seriousness. A *myelomeningocele* is a cystlike formation on the spinal column containing part of the spinal cord, whereas in a *meningocele* only the covering tissue (meninges), rather than the spinal cord, is contained in the protruding sac. In *spina bifida occulta,* the vertebral malformation is present but there is no protrusion of either spinal cord or meninges. Although the protrusion may be surgically removed and the malformation closed soon after birth, its removal may not eliminate the effects. Such effects vary widely among individuals and depend greatly on the location of the lesion; however, paralysis of the legs and incontinence frequently result.

Although similar to other handicapping conditions that impair mobility, this disability most frequently carries with it an additional complication of great significance in terms of the child's personal and social adjustment and ability to master self-care: lack of voluntary control of bowels and bladder.

Since *hydrocephalus,* the retention of intracranial fluid around the brain, is also likely to ensue, mental retardation and death were formerly common consequences of this congenital disorder. However, with the development of a procedure called *shunting,* by means of which the fluid is drained off through a plastic tube inserted into a ventricle, many, many more—indeed most—of these children now survive and develop intellectually in a normal manner.

The meningocele may be surgically removed and the malformation closed. The procedure for insertion of a shunt may or may not be necessary, possible, or desirable. If done, it is only the first episode in an extended sequence of shunt revisions as the child grows. A third surgical procedure (iliostomy) may also be performed. It involves removal of the bladder and diversion of the ureters to a collecting bag for urine that the child wears and that is filled continuously. Although this procedure may eliminate many problems of self-management for the child, as well as embarrassment caused by odor, it is by no means universally regarded as necessary or desirable. If this ileal surgery is not performed, the child may be able to learn to manage and to regulate his fluid intake and, within limits, his voiding. Teachers of young children can anticipate the need

to assist actively in this process, including changing of clothing (in some cases, diapers). Conscientious care is essential, not only to facilitate the child's social acceptance and adjustment, but also to prevent infection.

Positioning of the child is important not only to insure maximal mobility and participation but also to guard against pressure sores and, most important, bone deformities such as dislocated hips. Bracing may be but is not always employed to assist the child in standing and walking, as well as crutches and/or a walking frame. In addition to paralysis, the child's ability to experience sensation below the lesion is absent. This makes it particularly difficult for him to learn to walk, even with the aid of braces and crutches, for he cannot feel the floor beneath his feet. It also makes him vulnerable to possibly serious effects of skin or pressure sores, since he may not be aware of them.

Congenital or surgical amputation

Loss of a limb may be caused by trauma, a limb may be electively (surgically) removed, or it may be congenitally absent. A *prosthesis,* or artificial limb, is most often supplied, and a young child who is fitted early for a prosthesis finds adjustment to its use easier and more natural than if it is delayed until he is older. A condition related to that of congenital amputation is *phocomelia,* which rarely involves the use of a prosthesis since the hand or foot of the affected limb or limbs are unimpaired. The limb itself, however, is reduced in size so that the hand or foot is abnormally near the trunk.

A properly fitting prosthesis is obviously very important, both in terms of the child's comfort and in terms of his ability to master its use. Since the young child is steadily growing, frequent adjustment and replacement of the prosthesis should be anticipated, and the teacher should carefully observe the child's functioning to ensure that it is fitting well. Teachers should also have an understanding of the mechanics of the artificial limb and be able to provide activities that require its use. The child's personal acceptance of his handicap is extremely important and can be fostered by a supportive teacher who helps him to use the prosthesis as a part of him—*not* refer to it as "my *bad* arm" (or leg).

As is the case with other physical handicaps, attention to physical positioning is important to ensure that postural problems do not develop through habits the child is forming. From this standpoint particularly, intervention very early in the child's life is important before abnormal postures and motor patterns develop (Fiorentino, 1973). Physical activity is a particularly valuable component of the educational program, especially activity exercising the joints around the amputation. With proper attention to the mechanical aspects of use of the prosthesis, and with support at home and in school, the prognosis for the child to live a full and normal life can be very good.

Osteogenesis imperfecta

Osteogenesis imperfecta is commonly referred to as "brittle bone disease," since susceptibility of the bones to fracture is one of its most notable features. The other major characteristic, deformed skeletal growth, is a consequence of the continual fracturing and rehealing of bones. Since fractures may even have occurred before birth, the infant may be born with visibly malformed bones. Spine and chest deformities are observed in more severe cases. However, in milder forms of the disability the effects may be scarcely observable, and brittleness of the bones may cease once the child enters puberty.

Osteogenesis imperfecta is not associated with impaired intellectual functioning, although visual and auditory impairments sometimes occur. Bone malformations are amenable to surgical treatment in which the bone is actually "rethreaded" in sections onto a rod (Bleck, 1975c). The educational need is to en-

courage as much activity as is safely possible and to develop social skills with the expectation that the child will be able to function well within a nonsegregated school setting as his condition stabilizes and his vulnerability to fracture decreases.

Arthrogryposis

Arthrogryposis is a congential stiffness of the joints with defective development of muscle tissue. There is an inward rotation of the arms and an outward rotation of the thighs; clubfeet are usually present. The wrists and fingers are flexed, and dimples often appear in the skin at the joints. In severe cases the child may be confined to a wheelchair; in less severe cases bracing, orthopedic surgery, and intensive physical therapy may be helpful in facilitating ambulation (Safford and Arbitman, 1975, pp. 12-13). The child's ability to carry out many self-care skills may be impaired to some extent, depending on the severity of the condition, and many fine motor tasks may be difficult for him.

Temporary orthopedic disabilities

There are several types of disabilities that may be included in the category of temporary orthopedic disabilities. In general, they have in common two elements of particular educational significance:

1. They do not in themselves constitute *educationally* handicapping conditions, since ability to learn is in no way impaired.
2. They are generally amenable to treatment through such means as orthopedic surgery, bracing, and physical therapy.

Within this group of disabilities, bowleg and knock-knees "are considered developmental variants which are usually corrected by growth" (Safford and Arbitman, 1975, p. 14), with bracing employed not to correct the existing deformity but to facilitate further growth.

Clubfoot usually involves orthopedic treatment with cast and splint, together with stretching. Surgery may be required if the disability is not responsive to more conservative treatment.

Legg-Calvé-Perthes disease is characterized by degeneration of tissues at the head of the femur that, if untreated, would result in flattening and consequently improper fit into the socket joint of the hip. Treatment today typically involves immobilization of the involved hip by means of casts or braces to avoid placement of the child's weight on it. If such treatment is undertaken promptly, the prognosis is favorable, although dependent on severity as well. The child's response to this restriction of his movement, however, can be one of anger and frustration.

Other health impairments

A teacher of young children may also have occasion to work with children who suffer from seriously debilitating and degenerative diseases, such as muscular dystrophy, cystic fibrosis, Tay-Sachs disease, and sickle cell anemia. In view of the complexity and seriousness of problems such as these—and in light of the emotional demands inherent in working with a child who has a progressive, incurable, and terminal disease—the reader is both advised to refer to more detailed discussions (for example, Bleck and Nagel, 1975) and to seek consultation concerning both the medical and psychological ramifications of these illnesses for children.

Similarly, problems such as allergies, asthmatic conditions, congenital heart defects and diabetes frequently have a serious impact on the child's physical and psychological functioning. Like the illnesses mentioned above, these problems in many cases warrant both more detailed study and medical consultation. In such instances, the teacher, with the parents, does have a role in medical management, and it is necessary to determine what, if any, limitations on physical activity may be necessary and what special modifications may be required in the program.

INTAKE AND PREPARATION

If the nursery school program is within an interdisciplinary community agency setting, there are undoubtedly well-established procedures for intake. Depending on state laws and agency policies, a doctor's referral may be required for a child to be admitted. This may come from the child's pediatrician or family physician or, as is often the case, from a medical facility, such as a hospital clinic concerned with the particular form of disability the child has. In any case, in addition to some specific information pertaining to medical history, there may be accompanying reports by one or more medical specialists, such as an orthopedist or pediatric neurologist, or by a physical or occupational therapist, speech pathologist, audiologist, or other specialist. In a multidisciplinary agency setting, it is likely that this information will be sent to an individual designated as being in charge of intake, such as a social worker. A sequence of parent interviews, possibly including preliminary visits by the child to various activities in the agency, including nursery school, usually ensues.

If the setting is primarily an educational one—a "regular" nursery school, Head Start or day care center, or public school program—the intake process should parallel that of the multidisciplinary rehabilitative agency. Specialists in the various special therapies may be available to assist in this process and in implementing a program for the child, and specialists such as psychologist, social worker, and speech clinician may be involved or at least available for consultation by the educational personnel. In either case, however, whether the child will participate in a school program within a multidisciplinary agency or exclusively in a school program, teaching staff have an important role from the first contact, through the decision process, and in facilitating an optimal entry and initial experience. Although in some cases a case worker or home visitor may be the individual with principal responsibility for parental contact in a particular setting, this does not lessen the need for direct and effective communication between teacher and parent.

Among the special information teachers need from parents are suggestions concerning how to handle specific areas with their child. Are any special precautions taken or procedures suggested in the areas of feeding and toileting? Does the child have a special "word" for toileting? From the parents, also, the teaching staff can ascertain if the child has any special fears or worries of which they should be aware. They can learn what the parents' hopes and expectations are for their child in the school experience. No less important, they can convey to the parents that they have a special interest in their child and wish to undertake a partnership with them in helping the child, that they will be in regular communication, and that parents are urged to visit, to observe the program, and to take part at any time they wish.

Some medical information that is necessary in working effectively with the child in a "regular" as well as in a specialized setting may not be forthcoming from the parent but is obtained instead, with parental consent, from medical referral reports and communications from the referring physician or agency. For administrative purposes, if for no other reasons, it is desirable to have on record the child's medical diagnosis. This in itself may tell little about the child's actual current level of physical and psychological functioning or about what the child's future capabilities will be as he progresses through childhood and adolescence; however, for purposes of working with the child, information such as the degree to which a child can actually employ an involved hand or arm is needed. What are reasonable expectations and goals as far as mobility is concerned? Should the child be provided special safety devices to prevent injury from falling?

Guidance of physical therapists, whether they are part of the staff or consultants, is invaluable in suggesting to teachers ways of positioning specific children for floor and table play, eating, and toileting. Teaching staff should be aware, if the child is simultaneously participating in a program of therapy of any sort, what the goals of the program are for the child and how the therapist is working to attain those goals.

If the child is participating in a specialized agency or clinic program, it is desirable for the teacher and others who will be working with him to visit prior to his transfer into their setting. Thus the nursery or kindergarten teacher may talk directly with those professionals concerning their approach with the child, as well as their methods and the child's response. Such contact immeasurably enhances the teacher's preparedness for insuring an important supplement to the necessary exchange of written information. Ideally, the professionals involved in both the "sending" and "receiving" settings handle this transition in close dialogue and cooperation with the child's parents. The investment of time, energy, and personal concern required to effect a smooth transition from one setting to another invariably pays ample dividends.

Multidisciplinary agencies, in which a child and his parents will be participating in several program facets and interacting with various staff members, hold staff conferences periodically to review habilitative and educational goals and procedures for each child and to assess the child's progress. The first of these is the intake conference, in which all of the referral information is reviewed, summarized, and translated into a treatment plan if the child will be entering the program. A social worker or other designated case manager leads the discussion and takes responsibility for facilitating decision making. In addition to the child's needs, those of the family are also considered, especially those of the parents (or other "principal caregivers"), as they will affect work with the child. An interdisciplinary program serves the family as well as the child through direct casework counseling, referral for other needed services (sometimes marital counseling, help for a sibling, provision of a homemaker, or assistance concerning financial burdens) guidance in working with the child at home, coordinating clinic appointments, and the like.

The school or child care setting will also require this initial opportunity to review and synthesize referral information, determine plans for work with the child and family, and establish procedures for periodic review and communication with other professionals and medical or social agencies also serving the child and family. It may be desirable, if the child is coming from another agency program, for one or more of the persons who have worked with him there to be present at this meeting.

The nursery or kindergarten teacher, or child development specialist in a day care program, will want to prepare the other children prior to the entrance of a child with special needs. The teacher does not wish to create fears, and certainly not to convey any anxieties he or she may feel. The children will hopefully be accustomed to knowing in advance when any new classmate is to join them. If the teacher has established a practice of letting the children know something about the child who will be joining them, doing so in the case of a handicapped child will not seem like a "special case." In the course of talking with the children, the teacher can find a way of noting that each of them has some individual characteristics and of describing the new child, including reference to his handicap if appropriate.

The teacher will probably be well advised to inform the parents of the other children directly. For a teacher who normally works closely with parents, this is not difficult to do by means of individual telephone calls, in the context of a parent group meeting, or even in "gateside chats"

when parents bring or pick up their children. The parents can be told that their children have discussed in class that they will have a new classmate who, for example, uses crutches and wears metal leg braces, and that they may have further questions to discuss with their parents.

THE EDUCATIONAL PROGRAM

Much of the present chapter is devoted to young physically handicapped children served within either a specialized or "regular" nursery, day care, or kindergarten classroom, whether in a public or private school, hospital or clinic, or community developmental child care program. In summarizing the general purposes of early education for these children, whatever the setting, some general guidelines can be stated. According to Kirk, a preschool program for physically handicapped children is intended to do the following:

1. Develop motor abilities in the child through special materials, special aids and supports for mobility, and through special methods provided by the physiotherapist, the occupational therapist, the recreational therapist, and the special teacher. In the school situation the teacher is the coordinator of the program even though specific prescriptions are given by the attending pediatrician or orthopedic specialist.

2. Develop language and speech, especially in the cerebral-palsied child, since this is one area where the majority are retarded or defective. This includes the ability to perceive oral language and to express it, to perceive visual stimuli and interpret them, and to express oneself in motor terms. The latter includes both speech and gestures. This phase of the child's development is assisted by a speech correctionist, the parents, and the special teacher.

3. Develop in the child the psychological factors of visual and auditory perception, discrimination, memory, and other factors considered intellectual. These functions are best developed through the school program which includes language usage, listening, planning, problem solving, dramatization, imagination and creative expression (through art and mu-

sic media), creative rhythms, visual and auditory memory and discrimination, and perception. At this age level an environment with toys, sand tables, doll corners, and so forth, is provided so that the children will learn to respond to the attractions of the environment both physically and mentally. Through the addition of materials and the verbal and manual suggestions of the special teacher the children are helped to progress from one developmental stage to the next.

4. Develop social and emotional adequacy in the child at home and in the school by providing him with opportunities for acquiring emotional security, belongingness, and independence. The school situation is probably superior to the home in not overprotecting the child and in giving him opportunities to do things himself. The environment of the school which includes other children of the same age gives the child an opportunity to learn to interact with others, to share, and to cooperate. It offers him examples of activities which he can imitate, and at the same time the protection and help which he needs when he really needs it.*

Promoting conceptual development

Intellectual development during the first two years of life has been described by Piaget (Piaget, 1952; Piaget, 1954; Piaget and Inhelder, 1969) as primarily a matter of integrating and extending *sensory-motor schemas*. These schemas are built on innate reflexive capabilities: looking, sucking, extending and flexing, grasping, etc. Action patterns form the basis for subsequent development of thought, according to Piaget. Similarly, Jerome Bruner (Bruner, 1964; Bruner et al., 1966) has used the term "enactive representation" to describe one of three main modes of thinking (the others being iconic, or perceptual, and symbolic, or abstract and language based). In both points of view, and important relationship is believed to exist between *motor activity* and thought.

---

*Reprinted from *Educating Exceptional Children* (2nd edition) by Samuel A. Kirk. Copyright © 1972 by Houghton Mifflin Co. Used by permission of the publisher.

Just as the blind or the deaf child's lack of an ability basic to the development of cognition constitutes at least a *potential* handicap in conceptual development, the mobility-impaired child's disability suggests the need for early educational intervention. It has been proposed that such early intervention during infancy and the toddler period may be particularly important for the child with a motor impairment, as it is for the visually or hearing impaired child (Safford and Arbitman, 1975). Those working with very young physically handicapped children can focus simultaneously on enhancing the child's motor and cognitive functioning, in view of the interactive relationship between these areas. The physical therapy goals of developing greater head and trunk stability, facilitating movement, and increasing voluntary control of motor acts can be coordinated with promoting the child's progression through the substages of sensory-motor development (Campbell, 1974). Goals suggested by Piaget's observations—such as *awareness of the permanent object,* development of functional *means-to-end behavior* and *awareness of causality,* and *imitation* are reflected in scales used to assess infants' intellectual functioning, such as those developed by Ina C. Uzgiris and J. Mc. V. Hunt (1966) and by Nancy Bayley (1969).

The basis for a "cognitive curriculum" for physically handicapped children within the age range of approximately 18 months to 3 years has been presented elsewhere (Safford and Arbitman, 1975). Object-awareness, the concept of object permanence, imitation of self and others, demonstrating an understanding of physical causality (through performing acts intended to bring about certain results), discriminating sensory phenomena, and awareness of self and of objects in space are among the major areas addressed. Because of a child's physical disability, he may require direct, programmatic intervention to master these important steps, whereas nonhandicapped children appear to move through the sensory-motor period "naturally," given only a "normal" environment with which to interact. A theoretical framework such as Piaget's and the *normative* stages it suggests, enable the interventionist to assess the individual handicapped child's current functioning and to establish next objectives (Bricker, 1976).

Piaget's second major stage, the *preoperational period,* begins when the child demonstrates the ability to retain in his mind a *representation* of external reality. According to Piaget (Piaget, 1967; Ginsburg and Opper, 1969), this ability *transcends* language; it may be reflected in deferred imitation, that is, repeating an act some time after he has observed it. Further, from knowledge that objects have an independent existence (object permanence), the child moves to concepts about objects. That is, the child becomes aware of the *attributes* of objects, able to *discriminate* differences among objects based on their attributes, and eventually able to perceive similarities and relationships between objects (classification) and to order them along some dimension (seriation).

David Elkind (1970) has stated that the major task of preoperational development, during the period that extends approximately from 18 months or 2 years to 7 years of age, is the *conquest of the symbol.* That is, through his overt play and through his language, the child functions symbolically: he is able to distinguish between a symbol (a word, for example, or a play sequence) and the thing, event, or person to which it refers. With the ability to represent reality internally, and to organize and structure it, he becomes a creature of thought.

The child's thinking during this period is logical, but in a sense different from adult logic. He reasons, but his reasoning is *transductive* (Ginsburg and Opper, 1969), rather than truly deductive or inductive. That is, he reasons from the specific to the specific, rather than abstracting general rules or principles.

Some of the major emphases in the nursery school and kindergarten program, then, would be enabling the young child to have opportunities to transfer learning from a specific experience to new ones, to note differences, to perceive similarities, and to infer relationships and rules.

A child whose mobility is impaired, or whose ability to manipulate with both hands is limited, may require specific individual attention in regard to these areas of concept acquisition. For example, the *materials* used may have to be especially designed or adapted so that he can grasp them, or he may need to be especially *positioned* so that he can explore with water or sand or complete a puzzle or shape-matching task. In the area of representational play, the child may need not only encouragement, but possibly specific guidance or demonstration. And, as with all young children in a nursery program, major emphasis on *language* is basic to the child's understanding of himself and of the world around him.

Piagetian tasks, such as classifying objects and arranging them ordinally, and tasks involving *conservation* can be readily adapted for use with physically handicapped children in the classroom setting, both for assessment, and for instructional purposes (Wolinsky, 1970). These activities, because they enable a teacher to determine the child's understanding as it is demonstrated in action, rather than only suggested by his ability to express in words, may provide more accurate and trustworthy methods than exclusively verbal procedures (Almy et al., 1966; Weissman and Safford, 1971).

More basically, what Piaget has termed his *methode clinique,* or clinical method, can become a useful approach in individualized teaching of young children, whether handicapped or nonhandicapped. This method can involve a sequence such as (1) presenting to the child a physical phenomenon, problem, or situation; (2) asking him what he thinks about it or predicts will occur; (3) enabling him to

test his own hypothesis himself (observing carefully what he does as he does it); and (4) noting what he has to say about it if (a) his hypothesis is confirmed or (b) there is a discrepancy between what he expected and what he now observes. It is a child-centered and open-ended method, one that does not impose an artificial situation on the child but capitalizes on opportunities that arise naturally.

Providing emotional support

For the young physically handicapped child, entrance into a nursery program may represent his first exposure to a peer group. Although it may not be his first separation from his mother, since he may have experienced separations during hospitalizations, this removal from home and mother may be all the more frightening because of such prior experiences. Some children with congenital orthopedic, neurological, or other health impairments may have spent many of their early months in and out of hospitals. If the school program they are entering is

housed in an agency setting, the therapy equipment and procedures they see and experience there may well be difficult for them to disassociate from the hospital experience, at least at first.

Provision for gradual separation from mother is very important in effecting a smooth entry for an apprehensive child. Sensitivity on the part of staff to what the child is experiencing in a new world of strange adults and many children can be conveyed in many ways. Encouraging the mother to stay with her child may be appreciated by both mother and child. In lieu of that, a little extra warmth, physical closeness, and tolerance on the teacher's part will help.

The teacher should also be aware that, although the child may have had experience with younger or older siblings, his experience with children his own age is likely to have been very limited. Perhaps this, too, has been confined to a children's floor of a hospital, which he may associate with frightening and painful memories. Children's hospitalization practices have been improved immeasurably in recent years by the institution of live-in provisions for parents and child life programs (Plank, 1962, 1963). A national organization devoted to providing for the psychological well-being of children in hospitals has been established, and good child life programs have transformed the hospitalization experience from the nightmare of psychological trauma it had been all too often (Spitz, 1945; Provence and Lipton, 1961). In spite of these advances, however, hospitalization for a young child (indeed for any of us, child or adult) is inevitably a difficult time. Teachers should respond, not with pity, but with empathetic understanding to the hesitance with which a handicapped child approaches his first experience in a nursery or child care program. Although he has visited and his parents and the teacher have talked to him about what school will be like and what he can do there, it is nevertheless difficult for him to know exactly what to expect and perhaps impossible to overcome his fears except through patient working through of his anxieties during the early days of his participation in the program.

It is also important for teachers to recognize any possible conflicts or unusual emotional reactions they may have to particular physical disabilities. One may react with unexpected aversion to a tracheotomy, for example, if it evokes deep-seated fears of asphyxiation. A teacher may be able to deal with nearly all sorts of physical disabilities in children and yet, to his or her shock, react with disgust to a particular child's problem. Obviously, such feelings can be communicated to children even though they may be rigidly repressed. Therefore it is valuable for staff members working with handicapped children to feel free to describe their emotional reactions and to share such feelings. Not only is this a necessary safety valve in terms of staff members themselves, but it can ensure that the children are not subjected to messages of rejection. A sense of personal martyrdom is likely to be a destructive, rather than a helping, motivation in working with children. Teachers and other staff members should be aware of and sensitive both to their own and to each others' emotional responses and possible conflicts if these are expressed in work with the children. A mature and professional response is not one of guilt, which may demand expiation perhaps at the *expense* of the child's psychological well-being; rather, it is one of honest self-knowledge, open sharing with colleagues, and seeking ways of ensuring that the child's needs are being met and best interests are being served.

It is not surprising that many young physically handicapped children may manifest unusual emotional sensitivity and reactiveness, although even in children who are quite young strong defenses against anxiety and fears may already have begun to be erected. The defense mechanism of *denial* is frequently employed concerning the handicap; some children seem to have rejected or to deny the existence of an involved limb.

Beyond traumatic experiences, the frustration of not having a sense of control of one's own body, and the pain and restrictions of braces, there may be family conflicts and frustrations that also affect the child's emotional growth and self-concept. The incidence of divorce and marital disharmony is higher among parents of handicapped children (Segal, 1976), and many of the families have multiple problems. A large percentage have more than one handicapped child. A sibling who does not have a physical disability may express his or her own emotional reactions to the handicapped child's experience in a variety of ways or may suffer quietly from guilt as a result of ambivalent feelings toward the handicapped brother or sister (Farber, 1976). The mother may have conflicting feelings, which may be expressed in guilt, emotional rejection, or withholding of emotional investment.

False hopes, overcompensatory emotional involvement with the child, and fears for the child's physical safety may further contribute to the child's emotional vulnerability. These factors may also result in a strong need on the child's part to defend against fears of loss of love, guilt, and frustration or to resist emotional investment in others. Many young children with physical disabilities present emotional problems to which teachers need to respond sensitively and supportively (Cruickshank, 1949). This is an area that is extremely important to recognize and deal with effectively, both in work with children individually and through group experience. Meeting the child's emotional needs is as crucial as is providing for his physical ones. However, teachers often observe that it may be difficult to get nursery school children with physical handicaps to talk about their feelings or fears in group discussions. It is an area that should be approached with sensitivity, planning, and with an awareness of what each child is ready to handle.

Fostering socialization

An important, if not central, aspect of most early education programs, social development is a particularly crucial area in work with young handicapped children (Cruickshank, 1948). Many may have had very little or no prior experience with age-mates. The developmental progression in patterns of social play, from solitary, through parallel, and ultimately to true cooperative, task-oriented, sociodramatic play may be delayed or distorted. Play may be the "natural" language and learning vehicle of childhood (Piaget, 1952; Axline, 1947); however, some children require adult guidance and intervention to *learn how to play,* particularly in a social context (Smilansky, 1968). The young handicapped child in particular may need to be helped to get started in this area, as well as to be given time to experiment in social interactive play. A teacher can help by observing and, with sensitivity to the child's readiness, determining when and how to intervene as well as when to withdraw. If every minute of the school session is structured in advance, children will have little opportunity to engage in the experimentation necessary to approach this important area of social cooperation confidently and at their own pace.

Managing braces and toileting

The child whose limbs do not work for him may trust neither his own body nor the ability of a new adult to help him manage it. He does not know whether the teacher will lock and unlock his braces properly so that they will not pinch his flesh. He is not sure that the teacher will understand how his *body* works, or about his braces and crutches. The teacher must be skillful in gauging when a touch of firmness will convey to him that he can place confidence in the teacher and when it may be better to hold back or to proceed gently. For a teacher and mother together to help a child on or off with coat or boots, to lock or unlock leg braces, etc. may provide reassurance to the child, as well as to both mother and teacher. Such procedures should involve a minimum of stress for all concerned and should provide an opportunity for child and adult to talk with one another as they work together.

Although there are various types of leg braces, some bracing the lower torso as well as the leg, generally they are of two types: long leg and short leg braces. Since the latter rise to below the knee, there is not the need to unlock them to provide flexibility as in the case with the long leg braces. With some handicaps, such as tibial torsion, the braces may be kept locked at all times, whereas other children's braces may be unlocked for the child to sit in a chair to use the toilet. Depending on the type of brace, it may be unlocked at the knee or at the hip.

A teacher should know how to take the braces off and put them on if, for example, the children are bathing in a plastic pool in good weather. It may also be necessary to remove braces if a child has had a toilet accident. Basically, the goal is to help the child do this as much as possible for himself.

Among the equipment needs required with very young handicapped children may be a long changing table and a supply of disposable pads and gloves. Both the pad and plastic gloves worn during changing and cleaning should be disposed of after use to guard against infection as part of normal sanitary procedures. While the child is being changed it is important for him to be involved and alert, certainly not to be only a passive participant in the process. The teacher should talk to him while changing him, telling him what he or she is doing, both to reassure him and to point out names of clothing items and body parts. The teacher may say, "Now, we'll put your *arm* in your *sleeve*," encouraging him to participate actively.

A child with a minimal handicap may be capable of being toilet trained, and the teacher should know what, if any, medical limitations there are before embarking on such a program. With a handicapped child, the parents may in some instances be lax and entertain lower expectations concerning toilet training, as well as in other areas. They may need encouragement from staff and assurance that they will work with the parents in helping the child to master this area, which is so important to his own sense of competence and self-esteem. Unrealistic goals may be frustrating to the parent, however, and harsh demands are potentially injurious to the child.

Mechanically, some special physical provisions are needed for many handicapped individuals to use bathroom facilities. Such provisions as diagonal bars next to urinals and toilets are now increasingly found as a matter of course in public buildings and should be routinely installed in school facilities. Such adaptations may be crucial to the accomplishment of integration with nonhandicapped individuals in educational programs for many handicapped children, and usually only minimal modification of facilities is required.

For young handicapped children, learning to stand at the sink to wash hands is an important accomplishment, one that yields major satisfaction to the child while also increasing his ability to care for himself independently. He needs to learn how to lean his crutches or place his walker, if these are used, next to the sink so that they can be reached when he is through. Nonslip strips on the floor of the room can facilitate the child's management of toileting and washing and protect his safety.

PROMOTING AWARENESS OF BODY AND OF SELF

For the handicapped child, the important developmental task of attaining body concept and a sense of himself in relationship with his physical environment is at least as important as for every child. However, it is likely to be far more difficult to accomplish. The child who lacks feeling in the lower part of his body, who cannot make a limb move, who is able to move about only with very great difficulty, or who wears a prosthesis experiences his own body very differently as a consequence. It is not unusual for a child to reject an involved arm by refraining from using it as a "helping arm" or by acting as though it did not exist.

For handicapped children, activities to promote awareness and understanding of body parts and of the body as a unified entity are especially important. Even very young children, prior to the age of usual entrance into a nursery school program, are receptive to games that emphasize parts of their bodies. According to Piaget (1967), the concept of self is basic to all other concepts that children acquire. It begins to be established in infancy, during which the child learns to differentiate himself from his mother and from the environment. A child who lacks volitional control over parts of his own body requires special and continuing guidance in this area to sustain his cognitive growth, as well as his development of feelings of autonomy and independence.

In the early childhood classroom, group activities such as songs and finger plays are useful and enjoyable vehicles for achieving this. A great many such activities have been developed, and the possibilities for improvization are endless. For example:

Head and shoulders,
Knees and toes—
Head and shoulders,
Knees and toes—
And it's eyes and ears
And mouth and nose,
Head and shoulders, knees and toes

This finger play involves repetitive rhythmic patterns and rhyming, accompanied by the teacher's and children's pointing to the parts named.

Or the teacher asks, "Where are your ears? What do ears help us to do? Why do we have a mouth? Why do we have a nose?" The children are encouraged to suggest many ways in which we use each part, to listen to the suggestions made by others, and to discuss how the body part is used in that way.

The teacher asks, "What parts of our bodies *bend?*" Children point to and name joints, such as knees and elbows and actually bend them.

Using round shapes on butcher paper for those children who need this guide, the children may draw faces. This provides an opportunity to talk about facial features and also about articles that some children use to help them see and hear—glasses and hearing aids—and how these help. They also note at this time characteristics that all have, as well as characteristics that differ, such as skin color. Discussion of helps used by some children such as glasses can lead to talk about prosthetic devices that some of the children have and how they are used to help, as well. For one child, the braces help him to walk. For another, to help his bones grow straight. Such times provide a good opportunity for

the teacher to observe and take note of a child's reaction to his handicap, his understanding of it, and how it is affecting him emotionally.

An excellent activity, and one frequently used in early childhood programs, whether specialized or integrating handicapped and nonhandicapped children, is that of outlining each other's bodies on larger butcher paper. The products, fastened to the wall and labeled with names of the children, add a colorful and meaningful contribution to their awareness of themselves as individuals and as members of a group. The teachers also participate, and with the handicapped children it is often best for the adults to be drawn first, to demonstrate that it is safe and fun. Some children will need guidance in doing their tracing, such as pointing out how the legs and arms can be traced. As each part is traced, its name is mentioned.

Fostering motor skill development and mastery of activities of daily living

Another area of central importance in every facet of the early childhood education program for physically handicapped children is that of self-help and independence in daily routines. Although the areas in which these skills are involved are numerous, three major aspects are of particular importance: dressing and undressing, eating, and toileting. Specific goals for each child are identified through a combination of diagnostic assessment, informal observation, and parent consultation, and these should be regularly reviewed and progress assessed both by professional staff and parents. Sometimes, because of the difficulty in working with a child in these areas, it seems easier to "do it for him"; it is also less disruptive of family routine, less messy, or less time-consuming. Unnecessary patterns of dependency may be developing, and the child may be deprived of experiencing the autonomy and feeling of competence his growing personality needs. At the same time, these are often difficult and emotion-laden areas for the child and the parents, as well as siblings, and progress may be frustratingly slow.

It is important to determine first what the child's actual level of functioning is with respect to each task, not only with reference to age norms, but in terms of specific accomplishments. Such assessment suggests appropriate objectives. A child may not be able to unzip his pants but may have learned to pull them down when undressing or preparing to go to the toilet. The child is encouraged to do those things that he can do and gradually to add to his repertoire of self-help skills, one step at a time. "Successive approximations," with the child experiencing a sense of successive accomplishment with each new skill, mark the way toward independence and self-esteem.

Whether or not the child is seen individually by special therapists, specialized nursery programs for children with physical disabilities integrate gross and fine motor activities, perceptual development, and self-care skills within the classroom routine in a variety of ways. Careful attention is given to the provisioning of the classroom with respect to the special needs of the children. Large equipment items, such as an elevated house-play area that children must ascend stairs to reach are valuable to include, if possible. Scooter boards provide, for many children, an excellent means of promoting mobility in an enjoyable manner, one that tends to encourage socialization and to enhance feelings of competence and independence. A great deal of space—not so much as to overwhelm the children, but sufficient to provide room for scooter board locomotion and movement activity—should be provided.

Movement on wheeled vehicles, especially tricycles, is popular. Some children can operate these if long leg braces are unlocked and their feet are strapped to the pedals. Generally, some means of allowing every child to participate in riding activities in some manner can be found. For some, this may be restricted to being pulled about in wagons or carts. It is important to ensure that no one is left out and that all children are enabled to participate in ways that provide meaningful and pleasurable experiences.

A teacher cannot make assumptions about what a child can do based on the medical diagnosis. In a multidisciplinary agency, a teacher and physical therapist can work together to find some means of adapting equipment for each child, so that despite severe physical limitations he may experience the pleasure and satisfaction of joining others in boisterous and exuberant physical activity. On the other hand, the teacher cannot assume that if a child is physically capable of, for example, riding a tricycle that he will immediately be able to do so. Such experiences may be very unfamiliar and the child may approach them fearfully and awkwardly. There is risk that, if he is initially pushed too fast, he will experience a sense of failure and his fears will be exacerbated. His readiness must be assessed and sufficient psychological support provided by the teacher, as he is allowed to progress in these areas at his own pace with guidance and encouragement from the adult.

In learning to play ball, a child may not reflexively put out his hands to catch. It is helpful first to allow the child to feel and manipulate the ball, to roll it around the floor and experience its roundness and to find out how it can be grasped. Soft cloth balls, such as the Nerf ball, are better than rubber balls at first, since these can be more readily grasped and will not hurt if the child misses a catch. Such items can be manipulated even by children with significant hand involvement, that is, whose use of their hands is impaired because of neurological problems.

For a child with cerebral palsy who has hand involvement, the teacher, with the assistance of an occupational therapist, if available, should determine the size and shape of certain items, such as pegs, that he will be able to grasp. Generally, inlay puzzles with a small, wooden knob on each piece are easier to use. Adult help may still be needed, but the teacher should avoid doing more for the child than is necessary, in this area of the educational program as in all others. As much as possible, the child should be encouraged to complete tasks on his own.

In group activities involving the use of manipulative materials, the teacher can always find some way to enable each child to participate. For example, if a child is unable to stand at the water table—or is at first afraid to do so—a tray of water can be brought to him and placed in such a way that he can splash in it, fill and pour, bathe a doll, or whatever the other children are doing. If special equipment is available in the center, a standing table can be used to enable a child to stand for table play with the other children.

At snack time, when children may alternate responsibility to pass the wastebasket for clean up, a handicapped child who can walk by pushing a small weighted grocery cart can carry the basket in his cart and take his turn. Similarly, at "clean-up time" every child participates in some way in putting away play items. To be able to contribute to the group and to execute a task—to *work* (Hendrick, 1967)—is a most important avenue for developing self-esteem.

Physical activity is an integral facet of every good preschool and kindergarten program—not just as release, but for its intrinsic value in every aspect of physical and psychological development. As Humphrey (1975), Cratty (1969), and others have demonstrated, motor activity can be profitably incorporated as a means of enhancing virtually every aspect of learning, including academic skill areas.

There are obviously particular and specialized benefits of activities involving movement for young children who have physical disabilities, and yet, in terms of integrating such children within regular child care, nursery, and public school programs, this area may present the greatest single impediment as well.

In a multidisciplinary agency setting, each child's program of guidance and learning in the area of movement and body may be coordinated and overseen by a physical therapist. For each child, there are specific goals. The therapist may prescribe or recommend specific procedures to be used consistently in helping the child to increase voluntary control over the large and small muscles of his body, to increase range of motion, to compensate for severely involved portions of his body, to learn to use braces or a prosthesis, to walk with crutches or in a walker, etc. There may be specific procedures prescribed for positioning a child for feeding or toileting, or important principles to be adhered to when a child is seated on the floor at play—for example, that he is to be reminded to "fix his feet," rather than be allowed to sit between his legs in a W fashion.

An occupational therapist, in addition to working directly with the child on a one-to-one basis, may provide guidelines and suggest specific activities for working with him in the classroom, especially concerning activities of daily living (ADL), fine motor control (grasping, etc.), and perceptual-motor coordination.

In these areas, suggestions of an occupational therapist can be valuable to the teacher as well as the parent. The therapist can demonstrate techniques of helping a hand-involved child get his coat on, for example; ways of positioning both the child and oneself to facilitate each part of dressing and undressing can be demonstrated. Optimal positions for the child in toileting and in feeding can be employed. To facilitate learning to drink from a cup, some children progress more satisfactorily if allowed to use a weighted cup at the beginning. For some, cutting a semicircular notch in the edge of the cup enables the child to drink from it more readily and reduces spillage. Spoons are available with special handles, or adaptations can be made with utensils available. For snacks, different *kinds* of food can be introduced, rather than relying always on cookies and milk. This is desirable not only for the nutritional benefits but also to enable the child to gain experience with foods of varying textures. Out of eating experiences with puddings, raw vegetables, and a variety of other foods, specific guidelines may emerge for use in advising parents concerning this important aspect of family life. Cooking and other food preparation experiences in which each child participates in every phase of the preparation and then enjoys the final product are full of exciting discoveries and personally satisfying for young handicapped children, as they are for the nonhandicapped child.

Teaching the whole child

As with any other handicapped child, the child with a medical, orthopedic, health, or other physical problem or disability is first of all a *child*. The *visibility* of some handicapping conditions should not cloud the educator's awareness, nor the awareness of specialized medical and therapy personnel, that a child who has a physical problem, however serious or disabling, is more *like* nonhandicapped children than different. Pity will not help him learn or adapt to his environment or work effectively with others or develop self-esteem. Protecting him will not foster the independence he might attain and the

feeling of independence that he, like every child, needs—protecting him will not help him achieve *competence* and the *sense of competence* (White, 1959).

We teach *children*—not "conditions." A physical disability is one of the great many characteristics an individual child may present. Teaching him effectively may require some specialized knowledge and some program adaptations to accommodate his special needs. However, it mainly requires the teacher to know what a teacher must know about any child: what this individual child *can* do, what he is *ready* to do, and how he as an individual is most likely to accomplish the next step, and what experiences will contribute best to his developing awareness of himself as a competent and valued person.

DISCUSSION QUESTIONS

1. How have society's attitudes toward physically handicapped persons changed through the years? What evidences do you see that there is yet some residual fear, misunderstanding, or aversion?
2. What are the basic arguments for early educational intervention for physically handicapped children, even though such intervention may not "cure" the physical problem?
3. Do young children who have non–mobility-limiting physical problems, such as certain diseases or health problems, sometimes present special needs from an educational point of view? Why?
4. Discuss the roles of specialists such as the physical therapist, occupational therapist, and speech pathologist in relation to that of the teacher.
5. If you learn that a physically handicapped child will be entering your class or program, what information will you wish to have?
6. What agencies are there in your community that provide services to physically handicapped children and their families? What specialized hospital or agency clinics are provided? How do their functions relate to public school, day care, and nursery school programs?
7. What resource persons and services are available in your community, and what referral processes must be followed for your school or program to use these resources?

REFERENCES

Almy, M., with Chittendon, E., and Miller, P. *Young children's thinking: studies of some aspects of Piaget's theory.* New York: Teachers' College Press, 1966.

Axline, V. *Play therapy.* Boston: Houghton Mifflin Co., 1947.

Bayley, N. *Bayley Scales of Infant Development: birth to two years.* New York: Psychological Corp., 1969.

Berg, B. O. Convulsive disorders. In E. E. Bleck and D. A. Nagel (Eds.), *Physically handicapped children—a medical atlas for teachers.* New York: Grune & Stratton, Inc., 1975, pp. 101-108.

Blatt, B., and Kaplan, F. *Christmas in purgatory: a photographic essay on mental retardation.* Boston: Allyn & Bacon, Inc., 1966.

Bleck, E. E. Cerebral palsy. In E. E. Bleck and D. A. Nagel (Eds.), *Physically handicapped children —a medical atlas for teachers.* New York: Grune & Stratton, Inc., 1975, pp. 37-90. (a)

Bleck, E. E. Myelomeningocele, meningocele, spina bifida. In E. E. Bleck and D. A. Nagel (Eds.), *Physically handicapped children—a medical atlas for teachers.* New York: Grune & Stratton, Inc., 1975, pp. 181-192. (b)

Bleck, E. E. Osteogenesis imperfecta. In E. E. Bleck and D. A. Nagel (Eds.), *Physically handicapped children—a medical atlas for teachers.* New York: Grune & Stratton, Inc., 1975, pp. 205-208. (c)

Bleck, E. E., and Nagel, D. A. (Eds.), *Physically handicapped children—a medical atlas for teachers.* New York: Grune & Stratton, Inc., 1975.

Bobath, B. Motor development: its effects on general development and application to the treatment of cerebral palsy. *Physiotherapy,* 1971, *49*(11), 1286-1293.

Bobath, K. The normal postural reflex mechanism and its deviation in children with cerebral palsy. Physiotherapy, 1971, *49*(11), 1294-1299.

Bricker, W. Service of research. In M. A. Thomas (Ed.). *Hey, don't forget about me! Educations' investment in the severely, profoundly, and multiply handicapped child.* Reston, Va.: Council for Exceptional Children, 1976, pp. 162-179.

Bruner, J. S. The course of cognitive growth. *American Psychologist,* 1964, *19,* 1-16.

Bruner, J. S., Olver, R. R., and Greenfield, P. *Studies in cognitive growth.* New York: John Wiley & Sons, Inc., 1966.

Campbell, S. K. Facilitation of cognitive and motor development in infants with central nervous system dysfunction. *Physical Therapy,* 1974, *54*(4), 346-353.

Cawley, J. F. Special education; selected issues and innovations. In A. D. Roberts (Ed.), *Educational innovation: alternatives in curriculum and instruction.* Boston: Allyn & Bacon, Inc., 1975, pp. 164-186.

Connor, F. P., Wald, J. R., and Cohen, M. J. *Professional preparation for educators of crippled children: report of a special study institute.* New York: Teachers College Press, 1970.

Cratty, B. J. *Perceptual-motor behavior and educational process.* Springfield, Ill.: Charles C Thomas, Publisher, 1969.

Cruickshank, W. M. The impact of physical disability on social adjustment. *Journal of Social Issues,* 1948, *4,* 78-83.

Cruickshank, W. M. The emotional needs of crippled and non-crippled children. *Exceptional Children,* 1949, *16,* 33-40.

Cruickshank, W. M. Educational planning for the cerebral palsied. In W. M. Cruickshank (Ed.), *Cerebral palsy: its individual and community problems.* (Rev. ed.). Syracuse: Syracuse University Press, 1965, pp. 459-497.

Cruickshank, W. M. (Ed.). *Cerebral palsy: a developmental disability.* Syracuse: Syracuse University Press, 1976.

Cruickshank, W. M., and Hallahan, D. P., with Bice, H. V. Personality and behavioral characteristics. In W. M. Cruickshank (Ed.), *Cerebral palsy: a developmental disability* (3rd ed.). Syracuse: Syracuse University Press, 1976.

Elkind, D. *Children and adolescents: interpretive essays on Jean Piaget,* London: Oxford University Press, 1970.

Farber, B. Family process. In W.M. Cruickshank (Ed.), *Cerebral palsy: a developmental disability,* Syracuse:Syracuse University Press, 1976, pp. 459-476.

Finnie, N. *Handling the young cerebral palsied child at home.* New York: E. P. Dutton & Co., Inc., 1968.

Fiorentino, M.R. *Reflex testing method for evaluating central nervous system development.* Springfield, Ill.: Charles C Thomas, Publisher, 1973.

Freedheim, D. K. Individuality of intellectual development. *Journal of the American Physical Therapy Association,* 1966, *46,* 149.

Gearheart, B. R., and Weishahn, M. W. *The handicapped child in the regular classroom,* St. Louis: The C. V. Mosby Co., 1976.

Ginsburg, H., and Opper, S. *Piaget's theory of intellectual development.* Englewood Cliffs, N.J.: Prentice-Hall, Inc., 1969.

Hendrick, J. The pleasures of meaningful work. *Young Children,* 1967, *22,* 373-380.

Humphrey, J. H. *Education of children through motor activity,* Springfield, Ill.: Charles C Thomas, Publisher, 1975.

Keats, S. *Cerebral palsy.* Springfield, Ill. Charles C Thomas, Publisher, 1973.

Kirk, S. A. *Educating exceptional children* (2nd ed.). Boston: Houghton Mifflin Co., 1972.

Lennox, W. G., and Lennox, M. *Epilepsy and related disorders.* Boston: Little, Brown & Co., 1960.

Minear, W. L. A classification of cerebral palsy. *Pediatrics,* 1956, *18,* 841.

Perlstein, M. A., Gibbs, E. L., and Gibbs, F. A. The EEG in infantile cerebral palsy. *Proceedings of the Association for Research in Nervous and Mental Disorders,* 1947, *26,* 377.

Piaget, J. *The origins of intelligence in children.* New York: W. W. Norton & Co., Inc., 1952.

Piaget, J. *The construction of reality in the child.* New York: Basic Books, Inc., 1954.

Piaget, J. *Six psychological studies.* New York: Random House, Inc., 1967.

Piaget, J., and Inhelder, B. *The psychology of the child.* New York: Basic Books, Inc., 1969.

Plank, E. *Working with children in hospitals.* Cleveland: Press of Case Western Reserve University, 1962.

Plank, E. Preparing children for surgery. *Ohio State Medical Journal,* 1963, *59,* 809.

Provence, S., and Lipton, R. *Infants in institutions.* New York: International Universities Press, 1961.

Remboldt, R. R., and Roth, B. *Cerebral palsy and related disorders, prevention and early care: an annotated bibliography.* Washington, D.C.: U.S. Office of Education, Bureau of Education for the Handicapped, 1972.

Safford, P. L., and Arbitman, D. C. *Developmental intervention with young physically handicapped children.* Springfield, Ill.: Charles C Thomas, Publisher, 1975.

Sattler, J. M., and Anderson, N. E. Peabody Picture Vocabulary Test, Stanford-Binet, and modified Stanford-Binet with normal and cerebral palsied preschool children. *Journal of Special Education,* 1973, *7,* 119.

Segal, R. M. Social work. In W. M. Cruickshank (Ed.), *Cerebral palsy: a developmental disability.* Syracuse: Syracuse University Press, 1976, pp. 477-506.

Smilansky, S. *The effects of sociodramatic play on disadvantaged preschool children.* New York: John Wiley & Sons, Inc., 1968.

Spitz, R. A. Hospitalism: an inquiry into the genesis of psychiatric conditions in early childhood. In *The psychoanalytic study of the child,* (Vol. 1). New York: International Universities Press, 1945.

Uzgiris, I. C., and Hunt, J. McV. *A scale of infant psychological development.* Urbana: University of Illinois, 1966. (Mimeographed.)

Weisman, L. I., and Safford, P. L. Piagetian tasks as classroom evaluative tools. *Elementary School Journal,* 1971, *71,* 329-338.

White, R. W. Motivation reconsidered: the concept of competence. *Psychological Review,* 1959, *66,* 297.

Wolfensberger, W., et al. *The principle of normalization in human services.* Toronto: National Institute of Mental Retardation, 1972.

Wolinsky, G. The application of some of J. Piaget's observations to the instruction of children. *Teaching Exceptional Children,* Summer, 1970, 190-196.

CHAPTER 9

SEVERE, PROFOUND, OR MULTIPLE HANDICAPS

THE NEW CHALLENGE FOR EDUCATION

It has only been very recently that educators have begun a concerted effort to meet the needs of the most severely impaired children. Traditionally, we have spoken of the "back wards" of the institutions; there has been an attitude of hopelessness. Tragically, for great numbers of children and adults we have failed even to provide good custodial care. Reflected in this failure are remnants, even in our advanced, enlightened, and humane civilization, of the ignorance, apathy, and cruelty associated with earlier historical periods.

The responsibility of educational institutions and agencies to children who are very handicapped had not been clear until new federal laws, court litigations, and an enlightened profession and public clarified this responsibility unequivocally. *Every* child—including every handicapped child—is entitled to a free and appropriate education, and it is the responsibility of the state and local educational agencies, with federal support, to provide for every child all the components of an optimal education for that child. Our new laws make no exceptions; they make mandatory a "zero reject model" (Lilley, 1971) whereby schools must serve all children and exclude no one.

What does this mean for those of us working in the public schools? Obviously, it means that we can no longer rationalize our exclusion of any handicapped children from public school programs regardless of the severity of their handicap. It means that we can no longer exclude children because "we don't know how to teach them" or "do not have adequate facilities" for teaching them. Rather, it is implied that we should be using all the information available to us to program for them in the most efficient manner possible. (Jens et al., 1976, p. 2)

In no way does this suggest that all children have the same educational needs. Rather, each child's needs must be individually determined and provided for. The concept of a *cascade* of services conveys the notion that various levels of specialization of program are potentially available (Deno, 1970). The setting in which a child is educated depends, not on the "category" of handicap he has, but rather on an individualized educational plan designed specifically for him.

Previous definitions of levels of mental deficiency had distinguished between those children capable of benefiting from an education and those who could not benefit from an education. Such a distinction reflected a very narrow conception of education. In the times when education was thought of mainly in terms of grounding in the classics, such preparation was seen as appropriate for only a few. As the concept of universal schooling became accepted in the United States during the latter half of the nineteenth century, and indeed well before the spread of universal public education, ideas of the purposes of schooling underwent basic change. *Education for all* is a meaningful goal if education is viewed in terms of the optimal development of the potentialities of each individual. If education, seen in these terms, is a basic right of each child, then to fail to provide educational opportunities uniquely suited to the needs of any child, including a handicapped child, is to deprive that child of an inherent right.

It is not surprising that recent landmark legislation is described in such terms as "right to education mandate," "education for all handicapped act," and "a bill of rights for the handicapped child." Reference is made in Public Law 94-142 to the more than 1 million American children not served by educational agencies at all. Among those children who have been unserved by public education, or who have been inadequately or inappropriately served, are those children whose extreme disabilities mark them as visibly different from the nonhandicapped majority.

The need to provide appropriate education for severely, profoundly, and multiply handicapped children now poses perhaps the greatest challenge to public education in the United States (Sontag et al., 1973; Luckey and Addison, 1974).

Who are severely, profoundly, and multiply handicapped children?

This chapter, unlike others in this book, does not deal with *one* form of exceptionality. What the children with these kinds of handicaps have in common is the need for a highly *individualized, precise,* and *specialized* teaching approach. But the diagnostic labels and the etiologies included are many and varied. Collectively, these children constitute the greatest challenge to educators today (Sontag, 1976b; Luckey and Addison, 1974).

Not all multiple handicapping conditions are by any means equivalent in their impact on psychological development or in their implications for education. Keeping in mind the artificiality inherent in all category systems and the pronounced individuality of all children's educational needs—*especially* the severely handicapped—we can nevertheless identify some broad differences among *severely, profoundly,* and *multiply* handicapped children.

Regarding *multiple* handicapping conditions it must be immediately noted that this term encompasses many children whose intellectual functioning is not impaired and may even be superior. It has been asserted that every handicapped child is multiply handicapped. For a child with a learning problem, to confront failure in school is likely to affect negatively his personal and social well-being and development, for example, whereas for other children emotional conflict may impair academic learning. Here, however, we are using the term "multiply handicapped" to refer to three broad groups: (1) children in whom both the visual and auditory senses are significantly impaired; (2) children whose physical disability is neurologically based and who consequently have associated impairments in one or more of the areas of visual acuity or visual per-

ception, auditory acuity or auditory perception, speech or language processes, or cognitive processes; (3) profoundly mentally retarded children whose physical development and physical health is such as to require ongoing or even constant medical supervision and care.

Children with anything beyond a mild degree or highly localized form of cerebral palsy are almost by definition multiply handicapped. This impairment to central nervous system functioning may have ramifications in impaired visual or auditory acuity, perceptual processes, and speech. Thus children with cerebral palsy are more likely than children in general to be hearing impaired, visually impaired, learning disabled, or handicapped in communication skills. In some instances as an artifact of perceptual or linguistic impairments, sometimes as a result of limited opportunities to explore their environment, and certainly in some cases because of actual retardation, a large proportion of cerebral palsied children score below the average range on measures of intellectual ability. This is especially true of those with the spastic type of cerebral palsy. Finally, with a combination of impairments affecting mobility, self-care and independent functioning, social interaction through speech and language, and perceptual-motor coordination, a high incidence of problems in the socioemotional sphere would certainly be anticipated among these children.

The term "severely and profoundly handicapped" is seen as an overlapping category encompassing (1) the severely and profoundly mentally retarded, (2) the severely physically handicapped, and (3) the severely emotionally disturbed, including autistic children. Programs and services have frequently been provided for these children on the basis of the following categorical designations:

1. Trainable mental retardation (TMR) (This group includes many severely retarded children who have physical disabilities as well. Many of these

children would, by definition, be classified as *moderately,* rather than severely, retarded, however.)

2. Profound mental retardation (This group includes many profoundly retarded children who have physical disabilities as well.)
3. Cerebral palsy and other physical disabilities (in combination with associated secondary handicaps)
4. Deaf-blind
5. Severe emotional disturbance (including autism)

Since the third of these categories, cerebral palsy, was dealt with in the preceding chapter and much of the chapter on mental retardation is intended to be applicable to many children within the so-called trainable category, the present discussion will focus primarily on three general areas: deaf-blind children, seriously disturbed or autistic children, and profoundly limited children.

DEAF-BLIND CHILDREN

Deaf-blind children are defined, for educational purposes, as those who cannot be adequately served in a program for either the visually impaired or hearing impaired. In view of their dual handicap in these important areas, even more specialized programming is needed.

Curtis et al. (1970) identify several causes of this form of multiple handicap, including retrolental blindness, retinitis pigmentosa, and others caused by infectious diseases in the children themselves. The largest number of cases, however, are associated with maternal infectious diseases, especially rubella, but also Asian flu and toxoplasmosis. Frequently such causes also produce additional handicapping conditions, such as respiratory or digestive problems, and sometimes mental retardation. However, all levels of cognitive ability are represented within the deaf-blind population.

Teaching children who are significantly handicapped in both the auditory and the visual sensory modalities is clearly complicated by an obvious reality: the education of hearing-impaired children generally emphasizes a visual approach, whereas auditory cues are basic to the education of severely visually impaired children. In the case of those children who are handicapped in both modalities, two basic principles are applicable:

1. Whatever residual abilities are available in either sight or hearing —or both—are fostered.
2. The child is helped to use his intact senses—especially tactile and kinesthetic cues—optimally.

Although *relatively* few in number, these children pose one of education's greatest challenges. A disability in either vision or hearing is a formidable obstacle for the young child. The dual handicap suggests general goals. However, each child's program must be individually prescribed and his progress systematically monitored.

Some basic educational needs include those relating to self-concept and body image; the differentiation of self from others and from the environment; the differentiation of facets of the environment; body orientation in physical space; gaining understanding of sequence and cause-consequence relationships to gain a sense of safety and security; mobility; self-help skills; and, of course, language as a communicative and representational system.

In view of the extreme difficulty a young child would be expected to encounter in each of these areas, it would seem obvious that the expertise of diverse professional disciplines would be required. In addition to appropriate medical specialists, an interdisciplinary team might include specially trained teachers, a mobility trainer, an occupational therapist, a psychologist, a speech pathologist, an audiologist, and possibly a physical therapist. Baseline and continuing evaluation of the child's functional abilities by this interdisciplinary team contributes to the establishment of long-term and short-term educational objectives and to decisions about how these objectives can be attained.

A basic need for all human beings is to be able to *communicate* with others—to have some way of at least expressing needs, of conveying whether one is in pain or hungry or uncomfortable. Beyond such basic, necessary communication needs there is the need for human interaction. With any sensory-impaired child, it is imperative to enable the child to find some way of establishing such communication with others. For the child who is significantly handicapped in the use of both his visual and aural sensory modalities, the problem is substantially greater. And if the child is also severely physically handicapped, by cerebral palsy, for example, it is extreme. Using a variety of mechanical aids, including sophisticated electronic means, communication devices have been created whereby a severely and multiply handicapped individual can learn to communicate through the touch of a button on a panel containing as many alternative signals as are appropriate and feasible. If even this is impossible, *visual focusing* on any of various alternative signals can enable communication to take place.

A variety of communicative systems, employing varying degrees of oral-aural, manual gesture, and tactile means, have been developed. (See especially Dinsmore, 1959, for descriptions and graphic presentations of the basic approaches used to communicate with deaf-blind persons.) For each individual, some means of communication can be found that not only permits him to express needs and wants but also provides access to the most essential vehicle for human learning: *language*. The dramatic discovery made by the young Helen Keller through the work of her teacher, Annie Sullivan, described so vividly in her autobiography (Keller, 1961), can be and is replicated by other deaf-blind children, including those less gifted than Miss Keller: the discovery that *things have names*.

Children who have severe impairments in both vision and hearing need specialized early and continuing educational intervention. With appropriate and timely educational and related services, however, they can and do learn.

Behavior modification procedures, using differential reinforcement that is contingent on the child's approximating the desired response, have been successfully employed with young deaf-blind children (Calvert et al., 1972). Some workers (for example, Tweedie, 1974) have employed the technique of analyzing videotape recordings of children's behavior and movement over an extended time period to objectively assess progress.

Curtis et al. (1974) emphasize the importance of teachers of deaf-blind children focusing on each of three fundamental areas: adjustment, communication, and learning systems. The first of these areas, adjustment, is defined in terms of bringing the child into contact and interaction with his physical and social environment. Consequently, this area would seem basic to the goals of promoting learning and communication. Curtis et al. observed, through analysis of videotape recordings, that the children they studied preferred self-stimulation to environmental stimuli and tended to avoid contact with others.

Mira and Hoffman (1974) have offered brief guidelines for educational programming for multihandicapped deaf-blind children. Their suggestions focus on strategies for pinpointing educational targets, methods for modifying stereotyped behavior patterns, and procedures for bringing about behavior changes.

A number of materials concerning the education of deaf-blind children are available through the Perkins School for the Blind, in Watertown, Massachusetts. The newsletter *Children of the Silent Night*, published by the Perkins School, is a good source of current information concerning legislation, organizational activities, and reports from training programs that focus on the deaf-blind child.

SEVERELY DISTURBED AND AUTISTIC CHILDREN

Not all severely emotionally disturbed children are autistic. In fact, severe emotional disturbance is difficult to define. The distinction between the terms "psychosis" and "neurosis," borrowed from adult psychiatry, is not entirely applicable to very young children.

Chapter 7 is devoted to a more comprehensive discussion of emotional disturbance and behavioral problems in young children. Although the focus of that discussion is the mildly disturbed child, no sharp line is drawn separating mild and severe problems.

Although other psychiatric syndromes unique to infancy and early childhood have been identified, such as *symbiosis* (Mahler, 1965), the problem known as autism is probably the most widely discussed among educators. This is perhaps because of the unique challenges the autistic child presents to the educator.

Definitions of autism and autistic-like behavior vary. Although the former term exists as a label for a diagnostic entity, the word "autistic" can also be used descriptively, as a way of describing certain kinds of behaviors. It was to avoid labeling children with a term identified in the professional literature with a psychotic condition that the term "autistic-like" came into being.

First described by Leo Kanner (1944) and subsequently also by Eisenberg (Eisenberg and Kanner, 1956) as a syndrome, autism is described differently by various writers. It is usually differentiated from childhood schizophrenia. However, several of Kanner's original criteria are generally applied: *a profound inability to relate to other people, an insistence on the preservation of sameness and an inability to tolerate change, abnormalities in language development,* and, often, *stereotyped mannerisms.*

Problems in relating to others take the form of a sort of aloofness and apparent absence of awareness of the other person as a human. Indeed, the autistic child is often described as showing more interest in objects than in people, or as not differentiating between things and persons, and frequently able to manipulate and control objects with great facility (Kessler, 1966, p. 265). He seems not to exhibit emotion (although he will reveal agitation or distress), appreciate humor, or have the capacity for empathy or sympathy with others (Rutter, 1966). His interest in things, however, is sometimes deceptive. Jane Kessler describes it as

more restricted than that of the normal child. Things that spin, puzzles, reflections of light and shadow, for example, have been known to engross an autistic child for months on end. For him, everything is form. If he likes to look at books, it is for the form of the letters and words, not for the accompanying pictures (Kessler, 1966, p. 265-266).

This inability to relate to others has been attributed by some (Eisenberg, 1957; Bettelheim, 1967) to parental rejection, aloofness, or coldness. Such a view can be questioned, however, on several bases: (1) the same parents may and often do have other children who are neither autistic nor otherwise deviant; (2) many "rejecting," detached parents do not have autistic or autistic-like children; (3) it is possible that the child's abnormalities—specifically, his inability to relate and his tendency to reject cuddling—may play an important role in bringing about parental detachment and ambivalence. It has been proposed that infants with constitutional "unusual sensitivities" to sensory stimuli (Bergman and Escalona, 1949) may erect a psychological barrier, a wall against the world, to protect themselves. In addition, it must be borne in mind that many parents perceive professionals as hostile toward them and inclined to attribute "blame" for the child's problems to his parents, especially in the case of severe emotional disturbance and autism (Sullivan, 1976).

Inability to tolerate change in routine or in physical arrangements is reflected in the child's evidence of distress when something is altered, in his apparent preoccupation with certain special objects, and in his tendency to engage in endlessly repetitive manipulations of objects. The child's play repertoire is extraordinarily limited. Rimland (1964) remarks on his apparent inability to relate new experiences to remembered ones and to integrate them symbolically and conceptually. Perhaps this inability, which suggests a *cognitive* impairment, might account for the child's abnormal patterns of social and emotional behavior.

Abnormal language development may take the form of *mutism*—the absence of speech altogether—or of delayed or deviant patterns of speech, such as reversal of pronouns, echolalic speech, or the tendency not to use certain language forms that convey awareness of self-identity (Bettelheim, 1967). Speech abnormalities, in fact, are often the first symptoms to be observed (Rutter, 1966). In addition to deviancies in expressive language, receptive language problems have also been identified. First, the autistic child is often observed to be profoundly unresponsive to sounds, not to exhibit a startle response, and to be undistracted by sounds. For these reasons, perhaps, he has often been suspected of deafness. Hermelin (1967) suggests that the child's failure to develop normal speech can be related to a basic impairment in language. However, others see in autism an emotional defense—a "psychic deafness" (Myklebust, 1954)—rather than a primary defect in the comprehension and use of language.

Stereotyped mannerisms exhibited by many children diagnosed as autistic, especially hand flapping and similar behaviors, resemble the mannerisms of some severely retarded children. That they are stereotyped means that these behaviors occur in a standard, repetitive manner, and they apparently reveal no intent to communicate, to express meaning, or interact in any way with the physical or social environment. They are, in a sense,

a way the child has discovered to experience sensation from his own body and that he consequently repeats. Woodward (1959; 1963) has described similar behaviors among severely and profoundly mentally retarded individuals and compared these to Piaget's descriptions of primary and secondary circular reactions during the sensory-motor period of normal development. This would seem to suggest that stereotyped mannerisms might be considered to represent a pronounced *delay* in development or perhaps a *fixation* at a much earlier level. The autistic child's hand flapping or similar behavior might be emitted in lieu of a desired speech response or as a way of avoiding a stimulus. Consequently these overt behaviors might be among the first targets for behavior change strategies.

Whatever the causes of autistic patterns in young children, the most promising intervention approaches seem to be those based on systematic analysis of the child's behavior in relationship to environmental consequences (Wolf et al., 1964). There may be immediate and urgent needs to eliminate maladaptive behavior patterns. Some children actually demonstrate behaviors that are self-injurious. Interfering with patterns that are obviously injurious to the child, such as eye gouging and head banging, may involve aversive procedures (Lovaas et al., 1974, 1965).

Strengthening, or *accelerating*, desired responses is accomplished through *reinforcement*. This essentially involves *increasing the likelihood* that a desired behavior will occur by arranging events in the environment in such a way that the behavior results in reinforcing consequences. When the behavior is emitted, a reward is given. The following general guidelines are applied:

1. *Approximations* to the end goal are reinforced; thus, the behavior is *shaped* through *successive approximations,* or small steps, rather than attained in a single great leap (Skinner, 1966).

2. The *reinforcer,* or reinforcing consequence or reward for a particular behavior, for a particular child, and at a particular time is found through empirical analysis: the "consequence," whether it is a certain kind of cereal or candy, a "social reinforcer" (for example, "Good girl!"), is the event that increases the frequency, or probability, of the behavior.

3. A *schedule* of reinforcement is followed. *Continuous* reinforcement means rewarding the desired behavior whenever it occurs and is an effective way to shape the response rapidly. *Intermittent* reinforcement provides for the gradual removal of an artificial or contrived consequence (fading) and for guarding against the possibility that the response will be *extinguished* when the reward is ultimately removed. Intermittent schedules of reinforcement are *fixed* or *variable* and are based on either *time intervals* or *ratio* of the target to other behaviors (Krumboltz and Krumboltz, 1972).

The basic principle underlying the teaching of children whose behavioral patterns are autistic-like from a behavior modification orientation, is that *intervention is based on systematic analysis of the child's overt behavior.* Specific target behaviors are identified, recorded as they occur, and quantified. The teacher is, in effect, in control of the reinforcing contingencies in the child's environment. The approach involves the use of a technology (Haring, 1974) known as the applied analysis of behavior.

CHILDREN WITH VERY LIMITED BEHAVIORAL REPERTOIRES

Children who function within the range of severe and profound mental retardation present many needs that are basically similar to those of children identified as autistic, even though etiological (causal) factors may differ. There is a need to build the child's *repertoire* of adaptive behaviors, starting with what the child can do. There may also be a need to decrease the probability of responses that are undesir-able because (1) they are injurious to the child, such as head banging and grinding teeth, or (2) they interfere with the desired response (rocking may make maintenance of eye contact impossible).

No sharp distinction is drawn here between approaches in teaching autistic and very limited children. Two points should be remembered, however: (1) some workers (for example, Bettelheim, 1967) advocate very different methods of teaching for autistic children and (2) by no means are all severely emotionally disturbed children autistic or manifest autistic-like behavior.

The need for care: a dilemma

Children whose intellectual functioning is profoundly limited may present a variety of physical and health problems as well. Almost by definition, central nervous system integrity is lacking in these children so that sensory and motoric functioning are likely to be significantly impaired. The child's physical condition may be so vulnerable that, in extreme cases, life cannot be sustained without constantly available external life-support measures. Some children cannot swallow food. Digestion or respiration may be impaired, and the child may be extremely vulnerable to infection and illness. For these reasons, constant medical supervision and available medical and nursing attention may be required, factors probably dictating the need for a residential medical facility.

The need for such care may, however, be temporary or occasional. At those times when continuous medical care is not required and for those profoundly limited children not requiring such care, a living situation in home and community would generally represent the least restrictive environment. In the past, however, many parents of such children have been presented with painful and difficult decisions. The child could be "placed," but those facilities available and within the economic means of all but a very few were frequently undesirable, often appallingly inadequate. "Good" institutional care, if it could be found anywhere, was prohibitively costly. Furthermore, even though a family could consider placing their child in a satisfactory institutional setting, the decision has been an agonizing one for many, and frequently "good" programs will not accept a child younger than a certain age or older than a certain age. Mainly, however, although supportive counseling is provided by professionals, the burden of responsibility is placed by society solely on the parents. The choice, for the most part, has been between institutional placement and caring for the child at home. The latter alternative may require a degree of self-sacrifice on the part of the parents that is extreme in its almost inevitable impact on family relationships and family life.

What then is the role of public education for children who are severely and profoundly limited in learning and adaptive abilities? Edward Sontag (1976a) has described evidence of a marked change in attitudes concerning these children on the part of special educators within the early 1970s and corresponding evidences of successful programs—especially those involving early intervention during the first years of life. The "zero reject" or "zero exclusion" models proposed by some leaders have been mandated by federal and state law (Sontag, 1976b). Whereas in the past "custodial" care has been the norm, in some areas today extremely handicapped and limited children are transported daily to *public schools* where they participate in special programs tailored to their needs (Brown et al., 1975).

A basic goal is to help the child achieve as much independence as possible. This includes independence of movement as well as the ability to care for himself in areas such as feeding, dressing and undressing, and toileting. It necessarily includes also the ability to communicate his needs and wants to others in some way. Whatever type of program is provided

to strive toward these goals, and whatever the setting in which it is provided, educating severely and profoundly handicapped children is now clearly the responsibility of public education.

The challenge to the traditional pessimism regarding the potentialities of severely and profoundly retarded persons and the traditional belief in the inevitability of "custodial," rather than developmental, programs is relatively new (for example, see Menolascino and Pearson, 1974). As Allen (1976) has observed, those who have advocated for the rights and basic human worth of the retarded have had consistently to struggle against the "doom-sayers," those "authorities" who have described the severely retarded as hopeless and, almost incredibly, as "parasitic," and "subhuman."

Recent years have seen the development of exciting new projects involving the severely handicapped, especially the very young handicapped child. The necessity of beginning intervention *as early as possible* in the child's life is consistently stressed (Haring et al., 1976). As Norris Haring (1976) states, "Educators must recognize that for the severely handicapped child, programs that begin in infancy are very nearly the main hope: they should be our first priority from today onward" (p. 19). According to Allen (1976), "the more handicapped the child the more important it is that he or she have access to preschool education and enter into it as young as possible" (p. 48).

General goals and approaches in teaching

The severely or profoundly retarded child may be thought of as having, comparatively speaking, a quite limited *behavioral repertoire*. Given this, the first task is to determine precisely what the child *does*—that is, *what behaviors does he use?* For example, one would wish to know whether the child attends visually to a stimulus, tracks with his eyes a moving object, smiles or shows some other affective response to changing stimulus presentations. Regarding motor development, it can be discerned whether the child is in control of flexor and extensor movements of his limbs, whether he grasps objects and in what manner, and whether he releases them. His degree of head and trunk stability and control is assessed, since these are prerequisites for his performance of many tasks. Using developmental observation approaches or instruments, one can assess the child to determine what *reflexive patterns* that normally disappear in the first weeks or months of life are yet present.

The purpose of such assessment, however, is not merely to compare his global developmental progress with that of the normal child. Rather, since physical and mental development proceeds in a sequential, predictable fashion (Gesell and Amatruda, 1941; Knobloch et al., 1966; Piaget, 1952), determining what behaviors a child can perform implies the next steps that can be attempted.

Intervention will be directed either toward *acceleration* of a behavioral pattern —that is, increasing its probability of occurrence—or toward *deceleration* of a behavior that is maladaptive or interferes with the child's progress. The goal of the former is to strengthen and gradually extend present behavioral responses. Effective means of accomplishing this, beyond general environmental stimulation, include planned, systematic provision of *reinforcing consequences* for the child in response to target behaviors that he emits.

Obviously, progress in attaining major milestones will not be as rapid as the progress of a less handicapped child. With the application of at least two basic principles, however, observable and measurable progress can and does occur. these principles are *task analysis* and *successive approximations*. The first principle calls for the analysis into its component steps of any task to be learned; the second calls for procedures by which the requisite behaviors for performing the task can be shaped

through systematic reinforcement of steps in the direction of the goal.

Helping the child to learn some means of communicating his wants and needs, at a minimum, is one of the central tasks in work with many severely and profoundly or multiply handicapped children. A variety of techniques, some of which were mentioned in an earlier chapter, have been developed to help the child who is not able to develop a vocal communication system. Whether an alternative *language* system—that is, a communication system that is symbolic in nature—can be acquired depends to some extent on the degree of retardation, rather than the degree of physical involvement.

Vanderheiden and Harris-Vanderheiden (1976) describe a symbol system used in work with nonvocal severely handicapped individuals, called *Bliss symbols,* as "unique, ideographic symbols that represent concepts (as opposed to words only) through simple line drawings" (p. 635). These symbols represent individual *ideas,* including concepts such as "happy" or "like," through *pictographic* representations.

Vanderheiden and Harris-Vanderheiden note that this symbol system can be used with young children, including moderately and severely retarded and multiply handicapped children (severe retardation coupled with cerebral palsy). With regard to the specific symbols and the manner in which the approach is used, they summarize as follows:

Bliss symbols often visually resemble the concept or ideas that they are portraying. It is important to note that the Bliss symbols always appear with a word describing the basic meaning of the symbol printed directly beneath them. Thus, the system can be used with total strangers, and there is no need to "learn" the system to be able to communicate with someone who uses Bliss symbols." (p. 636)

This system is one exceptionally promising option among others designed for use with children who cannot use vocal communication systems. For applications with young severely or multiply handicapped children, individual needs and capabilities would dictate feasibility. Because of its symbolic nature, requiring a certain requisite level of cognitive functioning, the Bliss symbol system would probably be unusable with young children who are profoundly limited intellectually.

Role of environmental stimulation

One general strategy applied in teaching young severely and profoundly handicapped children is that of *sensory stimulation* (Mattei, 1974). Sensory modalities provide the avenues by which the developing infant takes in his environment and consequently the basis for his learning. However, many profoundly impaired children seem unable to relate to their environment through the senses. Nonetheless, "bombardment" with stimulation from the environment may be ineffective or even counterproductive, for the child may be easily overwhelmed. In some children, the "shutting off" from auditory, visual, and even tactile stimulation seems to represent a *defensive* strategy (Ayres, 1972). Intervention is a matter of programming and monitoring sensory input, rather than general stimulation. The required stimulation is focused, rather than diffuse, and gradually increased as the child demonstrates that he is able to tolerate and respond to it. One sensory-oriented program for 18- through 36-month-old multihandicapped children (Safford et al., 1976) employed a routine that alternated *relaxation* procedures; individually programmed and monitored sensory stimulation, involving experiences with touching objects and surfaces of gradually modified texture; and feeding, providing gradual introduction of different textures and tastes.

A general goal may be to bring about longer periods of time when the child is involved with his environment, rather than relying on stimulation exclusively from his own body. The first level of involvement could be thought of as *attention* (Hewett, 1968). Beyond attending, the *response* level involves some purposeful action performed by the child in response to a stimulus situation.

Development involves the reciprocal interaction of *assimilation* of environmental experience and *accommodation* to those experiences that are too novel or unique to be directly assimilated (Piaget, 1967; Flavell, 1963; Hunt, 1961). The very limited child can be thought of as needing to move toward an *interactive* relationship with his environment (Hunt, 1961). This child is *experientially deprived,* not because of any inherent inadequacies of the environment in which he lives, but because of his *inability to become engaged in interaction with it.*

Limited to responding to internal stimuli and lacking awareness of the environment around him, this child is often preoccupied with stimulating his own body and may often mutilate it. Some of these children seem to have an extraordinarily high pain threshold and thus will inflict great abuse on their own bodies unless prevented (Lovaas et al., 1965).

The aim is to increase the child's responsiveness to the events outside the limits of his own body, to increase his awareness of the environment. This would seem a necessary first step before building of *attention* to specific environmental features can be developed. The ability to attend would, similarly, be prerequisite to the more complex task of *discriminating* between or among specific stimuli, an ability that, once developed, signals a readiness on the part of the child to move toward concept formation.

EDUCATIONAL APPROACH

Clearly, the challenge presented to teachers by young children who have severe and complex handicapping conditions is great. Furthermore, few teachers have until recently been directly trained to teach such children. There have recently been significant attempts to iden-

Table 5. Behavioral procedures for use in teaching*†

Procedure	Definition	Example/use	
1. Reinforcement (positive)	1. The process of increasing or maintaining behavior through the presentation of a stimulus contingent upon the emission of the behavior	Use: 1.	Positive reinforcement may be used whenever the teacher desires to teach a new behavior, to increase a behavior already in the child's repertoire, or to maintain a behavior.
		Ex: 1.	To determine appropriate positive reinforcer, teacher may present an assortment and observe child in a free-choice situation.
a. Primary	2. Primary reinforcement has the effect of maintaining or perpetuating life	Use: 2.	Primary reinforcement should be used in the early stages of teaching and for children who do not respond to other forms of reinforcement.
		Ex: 2.	When child emits desired sound, teacher delivers food (candy, cereal, etc.).
b. Secondary	3. Secondary reinforcement has effectiveness because of prior systematic association with primary reinforcement	Use: 3.	Secondary reinforcement may be used with many children for whom primary reinforcement is not necessary. Praise, or physical approval (hug, pat), should always be given when primary reinforcement is used in order to establish these as secondary reinforcers.
		Ex: 3.	When child emits desired phoneme, teacher delivers pat on back and verbal praise.
2. Modeling/ imitation	4. A procedure which occurs when the desired behavior is demonstrated, then copied by the student	Use: 4.	Imitation may be used when the child does not have the desired behavior in his repertoire but does have the skills necessary to perform the behavior, or some approximation of it.
		Ex: 4.	Teacher emits desired response and reinforces the child for repeating it.
3. Shaping	5. A procedure through which new behaviors are developed. The systematic reinforcement of successive approximations toward the behavioral goal.	Use: 5.	Shaping is used when the child does not have the skills to perform the desired terminal behavior.
		Ex: 5.	Teacher reinforces "b," "ba," "ball," in sequence when teaching the word "ball."
4. Prompting	6. A procedure through which extra discriminative stimuli are provided during the learning of a new behavior	Use: 6a.	Prompting is used when a child needs additional cues. In the case of a child who has no language, physical prompts may be necessary.
		Ex: 6a.	Teacher holds child's lips together to facilitate emission of "buh" sound.

*This is a minimal list of procedures which teachers should be able to use.

†From Jens, K. G., Belmore, K., and Belmore, J. Language programming for the severely handicapped. *Focus on Exceptional Children*, 1976, *8*(3), 4. *Continued.*

Table 5. Behavioral procedures for use in teaching—cont'd

Procedure	Definition	Example/use		
4. Prompting—cont'd		Use:	6b.	For a child who has language, verbal prompts may be used.
		Ex:	6b.	Teacher shows ball and says, "It's a ball. Tell me what it is."
5. Fading	7. The gradual removal of discriminiative stimuli such as cues and prompts	Use:	7.	Fading is used when a teacher perceives that prompts are no longer necessary.
		Ex:	7.	Teacher puts fingers increasingly gently on child's lips while child emits "buh" sound or teacher shows ball and says, "Tell me what it is."
6. Stimulus control	8. A procedure for discrimination training during which reinforcement is provided for responses to the presence of a certain stimulus and not for responses in the presence of other stimuli	Use:	8.	Stimulus control is used when the teacher wishes to be sure that the child will apply his words only under appropriate circumstances.
		Ex:	8.	Teacher reinforces the word "ball" only when a ball is presented to the child.
7. Generalization	9. A process which occurs when the student responds to different stimuli in a similar manner	Use:	9.	The teacher programs for generalization when she wants to be sure that the word the child has learned will be used appropriately for all members of a class of stimuli.
		Ex:	9.	Child says "ball" when various balls or pictures of balls are presented.
8. Extinction	10. The reduction or elimination of a conditioned response by withholding reinforcement for that response	Use:	10.	Extinction may be used when the child makes sounds other than those desired—for example, babbling, mumbling, screaming.
		Ex:	10.	Teacher does not reinforce the emission of extraneous sounds.

tify the *competencies* required by teachers (Certo and York, 1976). Once these have been agreed on, *competency-based* programs of preservice and in-service teacher preparation can be provided.

There appears to be a virtual consensus that teaching strategies oriented toward child behaviors—that is, *behavioral approaches*—are needed. Jens et al. (1976) have outlined what they consider a "minimal list" of behavioral teaching procedures that teachers of severely handicapped children should be able to employ with specific reference to *language* behaviors (Table 5).

A systematic approach to teaching is especially necessary in working with severely and profoundly handicapped children. Haring et al. (1976) identify the essential elements of such an approach as follows:

1. Measure entering behavior (developmental level).
2. Specify terminal behavior (the particular skill or set of skills to be learned).
3. Require an active response by the pupil.
4. Arrange small, sequential steps to achieve the terminal behavior in order to maximize the opportunities for success.
5. Build in periodic review of skills already

learned (for instance, through drill and practice).

6. Withdraw discriminative stimulus systematically by shaping generalization and differential discrimination skills.
7. Systematically measure progress throughout program (precise data collection). (p. 2)

Developmental assessment

An essential component of effective instruction for severely and profoundly handicapped children is an effective assessment system. Haring et al. (1976) identify the characteristics of a good assessment system as follows:

It can be administered by personnel with developmental expertise (such as a pediatrician, neurologist, or practitioner) who are readily available in most communities.

It is amenable to *quantified* scoring, with high interrater reliability.

It is keyed to a fine focus of development, so that items are not mere repetitions.

Week by week it will show the examiner an *evolving* picture of developmental status.

In addition it leads directly to remediation or intervention efforts (implies a programming sequence). (pp. 22-23)

However, it is important for the teacher of very handicapped children to be able to simultaneously apply two general conceptions of learning: the *developmental* and the *behavioristic* perspective (Scheuerman, 1976). Developmental theories and schedules provide a framework within which the teacher operates and that enable the teacher both to identify entering behavior and to specify objectives. What is then applied has been called (Bricker, 1976) a test-teach approach, incorporating the two basic types of testing: *norm-referenced tests,* in this case derived either from normative schedules of development or from theories such as that of Piaget (1952, 1967), and *criterion-referenced tests,* which are specific to the child and represent the results of task analysis of developmental milestones or accomplishments.

An assumption is made of underlying universality of developmental sequences and processes. What is different for the severely handicapped child is the necessity to intervene in what for nonhandicapped children appears to occur "naturally." This is illustrated in Allen's observation concerning the role of play in development and its relevance to the structured curriculum required for work with very handicapped children:

The nonhandicapped child often seems to move through such a play-oriented learning environment on his own momentum, self-propelled as it were, acquiring new skills and practicing previously learned skills in the course of his spontaneously initiated play activities, his ready participation in group activities, and his eager attention to the teacher directed play type tasks. But this is not so for the severely retarded child. He needs what might be called a "double barreled" program—a sound developmental curriculum upon which is imposed an exceedingly detailed program that breaks every developmental task in every area of development into carefully detailed and sequenced subtasks, or to put it another way, into discrete behavioral components. (1976, p. 55)

Some approaches, often assumed to be essential in teaching severely handicapped children, have been challenged as being intrinsically self-limiting: a one-to-one approach, homogeneous groups, and repeated practice instructional strategies (Brown et al., 1976). Brown et al. (1976) suggest that such practices, in their inherent artificiality, may be counterproductive when measured against *the criterion of ultimate functioning.* This criterion, which is an essential one from the standpoint of long-range planning for the handicapped individual,

. . . refers to the ever changing, expanding, localized, and personalized cluster of factors that each person must possess in order to function as productively and independently as possible in socially, vocationally, and domestically integrated adult community environments. Since severely handicapped citizens will ultimately function in settings which contain less handicapped and nonhandicapped citizens, the majority of the developmental environments to which most severely handicapped citizens are now exposed will require substantial changes. Longitudinal segregation, whether manifested in residential institutions of self-contained schools, homes or classes will not culminate in the realization of the criterion or ultimate functioning. (p. 8)

The alternative proposed is a "naturalized" curriculum involving increasingly complex environments and varieties of tasks, opportunities for social interaction, and substitution of "the logic of heterogeneity" for "the logic of homogeneity."

Curriculum areas

What constitutes the curriculum for severely and profoundly handicapped children? Generally, the areas of *motor functioning, language and communication, perceptual and cognitive development, self-care,* and *personal and social development* are priority areas included in most curricula for them, as for all young children, to which Allen (1976) adds an area equally central to most early childhood education programs: *arts and crafts skills.* She notes the value of art media as a mode of expression and release, as well as a means of enabling the child to gain both flexibility and a sense of control over his environment.

Wehman (1976), in noting the importance of play in children's development, suggests the need for a means of *classifying* toys and play materials, based on developmental levels and educational goals. (See Table 6.) Although severely and profoundly handicapped infants and young children do not respond to play materials in the manner in which nonhandicapped or less severely impaired children do, he recommends the use of developmental norms:

A general rule for programming play for severely and profoundly handicapped infants and preschoolers can be stated as follows: Whenever possible, program exploratory play activity that is consistent with the develop-

Table 6. A taxonomy of play materials*

Group 1 Toys for the infant
Purpose: to increase sensory awareness and exploratory activity
Examples: rattles, spoons, or any bright colored objects with multiple sounds

Group 2 Toys for the development of strength
Purpose: promote physical development and growth
Examples: push-pull toys, wagons, balls, jump ropes, skates

Group 3 Toys for constructive and creative play
Purpose: develop low level creative abilities
Examples: building logs, paper construction, Tinker Toys

Group 4 Toys for dramatic and imitative play
Purpose: promote cooperative behavior, sharing, and socialization skills
Examples: table games, group games

Group 6 Toys for artistic development
Purpose: provide introduction to music and the arts
Examples: musical instruments, weaving looms, sewing boards

Group 7 Toys that stimulate knowledge and aid in school activity
Purpose: to serve as a facilitator of academic skills and to provide novel tasks
Examples: simple puzzles, object Lotto games, spelling boards

Group 8 Hobbies and special interests
Purpose: promote self-initiated activity which may be of educational value
Examples: wood carving, photography, animal care

*From Wehman, P. Selection of play materials for the severely handicapped: a continuing dilemma. *Education and training of the mentally retarded,* 1976, *11*(1), 48.

mental norm. However, objects can be presented more frequently and social or tangible reinforcers may be required initially to encourage such activity. (Wehman, 1976, p. 48)

Exploratory play, which is *spontaneous* in nonhandicapped infants and young children, must often be *taught*. Mere exposure to materials is probably insufficient in most instances. But involvement of the child with a very limited behavioral repertoire with his environment through the use of play objects would be an important goal. As in other areas, precise monitoring of the child's response to specific items is important to effect a gradual, step-by-step expansion of his play repertoire.

Objectives for these children will be specific to the child, determined by his present functioning and what he can next accomplish. Some curriculum approaches that have been developed, such as the Portage Project (Shearer and Shearer, 1972), feature prescriptive activities that can be carried out with the child by his or her parents or teacher.

Basic target areas in working with a child may include such skills as the following:

Head and trunk stability
Visual focusing and attending
Mobility in prone position
Purposeful reaching
Grasping and releasing
Visual tracking
Visual search for the source of a sound
Visual pursuit of object removed from view
Spontaneous vocalization
Imitative vocalization
Exploratory manipulation of objects
Responding to environmental changes
Mouthing, sucking, swallowing

Any of these accomplishments might be, for a given child, extraordinarily difficult. They are requisite for more advanced and complex behaviors involved in *mobility* (creeping, pulling to stand, walking), *self-care* (especially self-feeding), *communication,* and *purposeful and preconceptual behavior.* Pip Campbell (1976) has provided a practical, systematic approach to *feeding,* one of the primary areas of concern. Once specific sources of difficulty have been identified, such as tongue protrusion, inability to coordinate mastication, or inability to swallow, these problems can be dealt with systematically. Often the first need is to discover facilitating positions for feeding.

Role of the teacher

The teacher's role as a member of an interdisciplinary team, or as a professional functioning separately from those in medicine, special therapy, and other fields, is that of a *synthesizer* (Bricker, 1976). Much may be known about the child and his current functioning and needs, all of which is applicable in teaching him. However, the language of the medical specialist is ordinarily not that of the educator. An ability to function as an *educational synthesizer* is needed, that is, as one who

1. Seeks appropriate information or techniques from professionals in other disciplines.
2. Applies such information or techniques to develop effective intervention strategies.
3. Implements such strategies in order to remediate problems (e.g., insuring special diets for children with allergies, monitoring seizure activity) or to facilitate the acquisition of new skills (e.g., implementing muscle relaxing activities or special language training procedures).

The educational synthesizer needs skills in acquiring, organizing, evaluating, and implementing (in a practical sense) inputs from disciplines that either are not or cannot be included as daily, integral parts of an intervention program. The educational synthesizer becomes the pivotal force in the overall educational program by seeking and coordinating the necessary resources to produce growth and change in the severely impaired child. (Bricker, 1976, p. 88)

The teacher can be viewed as a *manager* (Baldwin, 1976). He or she is responsible for selecting from a range of materials, techniques, and resources and coordinating the group program such that individualized programming is accomplished. In addition to physical resources, the teacher also coordinates the work of aides, parent volunteers, and students in training who are directly involved with the children. In a sense, the classroom environment and all of the ways in which it affects each child at any particular moment are under control of the teacher.

Clearly, one of the most important dimensions of the teacher's role in working with severely and profoundly handicapped children is his or her ability to work effectively with the parents of these children (Sontag et al., 1973). This is related to the synthesizer function described by Diane Bricker, in that parents are one of the most important sources of information concerning the needs and abilities of their child. There is a great need for teachers and other professionals to learn to become better able and more willing to *listen* to parents as well as to advise them (Sullivan, 1976). Not only must teachers be sympathetic to the needs and problems of the parents with whom they work, they must be able to function in *partnership* with a child's parents (or other caregivers) to ensure the consistency and continuity that may be necessary in slowly, sequentially building and extending basic skills.

Information is now rapidly accumulating concerning the area of the severely and profoundly handicapped, which had been neglected by educators in the past, but there is a great need for further curriculum research (Meyer and Altman, 1976). Applying the word "education" to work with severely and profoundly retarded children is itself a new development. Concerns persist, necessarily, with the needs of many of these children in areas relating to medical care and attention and life maintenance. But we can anticipate eliminating the adjective "custodial" when we speak of their care. Educators now are assuming an important role and must weigh their efforts in teaching severely and profoundly handicapped children against "the criterion of ultimate functioning" (Brown et al., 1976). Aided by resources of many disciplines, teachers of severely and profoundly handicapped children are contributing toward major breakthroughs in human knowledge. They are evolving methods for teaching children who had been thought "incapable" of learning and helping to make "zero reject" a reality.

DISCUSSION QUESTIONS

1. Why have severely and profoundly handicapped children not benefitted in the past from public educational services? What has happened to change this situation? Why?
2. In your opinion, what special skills are required to teach severely and profoundly handicapped children?
3. What is meant by "zero exclusion?"
4. Why is self-stimulation often observed in profoundly and some multiply handicapped children?
5. What special problems in assessment are presented in working with seriously and multiply handicapped children? What modifications in assessment procedures and in the purposes of assessment do such problems suggest?
6. What is meant by the concept of normalization as proposed by Wolfensberger?

REFERENCES

Allen, K. I. Early intervention. In M. A. Thomas (Ed.), *Hey, don't forget about me: education's investment in the severely, profoundly, and multiply handicapped.* Reston, Va.: Council for Exceptional Children, 1976, pp. 46-63.

Ayres, J. *Sensory integration and learning disorders.* Los Angeles: Western Psychological Services, 1972.

Baldwin, V. L. Curriculum concerns. In M. A. Thomas (Ed.), *Hey, don't forget about me: education's investment in the severely, profoundly, and multiply handicapped.* Reston, Va.: Council for Exceptional Children, 1976, pp. 64-73.

Bergman, P., and Escalona, S. K. Unusual sensitivities in very young children. In *The Psychoanalytic Study of the Child* (Vol. 3). New York: International Universities Press, 1949, pp. 333-352.

Bettelheim, B. *The empty fortress: infantile autism and the birth of the self.* New York-London: Collier Macmillan, Ltd., 1967.

Bricker, D. Educational synthesizer. In M. A. Thomas (Ed.), *Hey, don't forget about me: education's investment in the severely, profoundly, and multiply handicapped.* Reston, Va.: Council for Exceptional Children, 1976, pp. 84-97.

Brown, L., Crowner, T., Williams, W., and York, R. (Eds.). *Madison's alternative for zero exclusion: a book of readings* (Vol. 5). Madison, Wis.: Madison Public Schools, 1975.

Brown, L., Nietupski, J., and Hamre-Nietupski, S. Criterion of ultimate functioning. In M. A. Thomas (Ed.), *Hey, don't forget about me: education's investment in the severely, profoundly, and multiply handicapped.* Reston, Va.: Council for Exceptional Children, 1976, pp. 2-15.

Calvert, D. R., Reddell, R. C., Jacobs, U., and Baltzer, S. Experiences with preschool deaf-blind children. *Exceptional Children,* January, 1972, *38,* 415-421.

Campbell, P. *Problem-oriented approaches to feeding the handicapped child* (First draft copy). Akron, Ohio: The Children's Hospital of Akron, 1976.

Certo, N., and York, R. Proposed competencies for teachers of severely and profoundly handicapped students (Working draft). Task Force on Teacher Competencies, American Association for the Education of the Severely and Profoundly Handicapped, 1976.

Curtis, W. S., Donlon, E. T., and Wagner, E. (Eds.). *Deaf-blind children: evaluating their multiple handicaps.* New York: Arner Foundation for the Blind, 1970.

Curtis, W. S., Donlon, E. T., and Tweedie, D. An examination procedure for behavior characteristics. *Education of the Visually Handicapped,* October, 1974, 67-71.

Deno, E. P. Special education as developmental capital. *Exceptional Children,* November, 1970, 229-237.

Dinsmore, A. B. *Methods of communicating with deaf-blind people* (Rev. ed.). New York: Arner Foundation for the Blind, 1959.

Eisenberg, L. The father of autistic children. *American Journal of Orthopsychiatry,* 1957, *27,* 715-724.

Eisenberg, L., and Kanner, L. Early infantile autism: 1943-1955. *American Journal of Orthopsychiatry,* 1956, *26,* 556-566.

Gesell, A. L., and Amatruda, C. S. *Developmental diagnosis.* New York: Paul B. Hoeber, Inc., 1941.

Haring, N. G. Perspectives in special education. In N. G. Haring (Ed.), *Behavior of exceptional children: an introduction to special education.* Columbus, Ohio: Charles E. Merrill Publishing Co., 1974.

Haring, N. G. Infant identification. In M. A. Thomas (Ed.), *Hey, don't forget about me! Education's investment in the severely, profoundly and multiply handicapped.* Reston, Va.: Council for Exceptional Children, 1976, pp. 16-35.

Haring, N. G., Hayden, A. A., and Beck, G. R. General principles and guidelines in programming for severely handicapped children and young adults. *Focus on Exceptional Children,* 1976, *8*(2), 1-14.

Hermelin, E. Coding and immediate recall in autistic children. *Proceedings of the Royal Society of Medicine,* 1967, *60,* 553-564.

Hewett, F. M. *The emotionally disturbed child in the classroom: a developmental strategy for educating children with maladaptive behaviors,* Boston: Allyn & Bacon, Inc., 1968.

Hunt, J. McV. *Intelligence and experience.* New York: The Ronald Press Co., 1961.

Jens, K. G., Belmore, K., and Belmore, J. Language programming for the severely handicapped. *Focus on Exceptional Children,* 1976, *8*(3), 1-15.

Kanner, L. Early infantile autism. *Journal of Pediatrics,* 1944, *25,* 211.

Keller, H. *The story of my life.* New York: Dell Publishing Co., Inc., 1961.

Kessler, J. W. *Psychopathology of childhood.* Englewood Cliffs, N.J.: Prentice-Hall, Inc., 1966.

Knobloch, H., Pasamanick, B., and Sherard, E. A developmental screening inventory for infants. *Pediatrics,* 1966, *38,* 1095-1104.

Krumboltz, J. D., and Krumboltz, H. B. *Changing children's behavior.* Englewood Cliffs, N.J.: Prentice-Hall, Inc., 1972.

Lilly, M. S. A training based model for special education. *Exceptional Children,* 1971, *37,* 745-746.

Lovaas, O. I., Schreibman, L., and Koegel, R. L. A behavior modification approach to the treatment of autistic children. *Journal of Autism and Childhood Schizophrenia,* 1974, *4,* 111-129.

Lovaas, O. I., Schaeffer, B., and Simmons, J. D., Building social behavior in autistic children by use of electric shock. *Journal of Experimental Research in Personality,* 1965, *1,* 99-109.

Luckey, R. E., and Addison, M. R. The profoundly retarded: a new challenge for public education. *Education and Training of the Mentally Retarded,* 1974, *9*(3), 123-130.

Mahler, M. S. On early infantile psychoses: the symbiotic and autistic syndromes. *Journal of Academic Child Psychiatry,* 1965, *4,* 554.

Mattei, A. M. *Stimulation procedures for the extremely low-functioning, cerebral palsied and other health impaired child: practical guidelines.* New Brighton, Pa.: The McGuire Home, 1974.

Menolascino, F. J., and Pearson, P. H. (Eds.). *Beyond the limits: innovations in services for the severely and profoundly handicapped.* Seattle: Special Child Publications, 1974.

Meyer, E. L., and Altman, R. Public school programming for the severely/profoundly handicapped: some researchable problems. *Education and Training of the Mentally Retarded,* 1976, *11*(1), 40-50.

Mira, M., and Hoffman, S. Educational programming for multi-handicapped deaf-blind children. *Exceptional Children,* April, 1974, 513-514.

Myklebust, H. *Auditory disorders in children: a manual for differential diagnosis,* New York: Grune & Stratton, Inc., 1954.

Piaget, J. *The origins of intelligence in children.* New York: W. W. Norton & Co., Inc., 1952.

Piaget, J. *Six psychological studies.* New York: Random House, Inc., 1967.

Rimland, B. *Infantile autism.* New York: Appleton-Century-Crofts, 1964.

Rutter, M. Behavioral and cognitive characteristics of a series of psychotic children. In J. K. Wing (Ed.), *Childhood autism: clinical educational, and social aspects.* London: Pergamon Press, 1966.

Safford, P. L., Gregg, L. A., Schneider, G., and Sewell, J. M. A stimulation program for young sensory-impaired multi-handicapped children. *Education and Training of the Mentally Retarded,* 1976, *2*(1), 12-17.

Scheuerman, N. A teacher's perspective. In M. A. Thomas (Ed.), *Hey, don't forget about me: education's investment in the severely, profoundly, and multiply handicapped.* Reston, Va.: Council for Exceptional Children, 1976, pp. 74-83.

Shearer, M. S., and Shearer, D. E. *The Portage Project: a model for early childhood education.* Exceptional Children, 1972, *39,* 210-217.

Skinner, B. F. What is the experimental analysis of behavior? *Journal of the Experimental Analysis of Behavior,* 1966, *9,* 213-218.

Sontag, E. Federal leadership. In M. A. Thomas (Ed.), *Hey, don't forget about me: education's investment in the severely, profoundly, and multiply handicapped.* Reston, Va.: Council for Exceptional Children, 1976, pp. 146-161. (a)

Sontag, E. Zero exclusion: no longer rhetoric. *Apropos* (Columbus, Ohio, National Center for Educational Media and Materials for the Handicapped), Spring-Summer, 1976. (b)

Sontag, E., Burke, P., and York, R. Considerations for serving the severely handicapped. *Education and Training of the Mentally Retarded,* 1973, *8*(2), 20-26.

Sullivan, R. C. The role of the parent. In M. A. Thomas (Ed.), *Hey, don't forget about me: education's investment in the severely, profoundly, and multiply handicapped child.* Reston, Va., Council for Exceptional Children, 1976, pp. 36-46.

Tweedie, D. Demonstrating behavioral changes of deaf-blind children. *Exceptional children,* April, 1974, 510-512.

Vanderheiden, G. C., and Harris-Vanderheiden, D. H. Communication techniques and aids for the nonvocal severely handicapped. In L. L. Lloyd (Ed.), *Communication assessment and intervention strategies.* Baltimore: University Park Press, 1976, pp. 607-652.

Wehman, P. Selection of play materials for the severely handicapped: a continuing dilemma. *Education and Training of the Mentally Retarded,* 1976, *11*(1), 46-50.

Wolf, M. M., Risley, T., and Mees, H. Application of operant conditioning procedures to the behavior problems of an autistic child. *Behavior Research and Therapy,* 1964, *1,* 305-312.

Wolfensberger, W., et al. *The principle of normalization in human services:* Toronto: National Institute of Mental Retardation, 1972.

Woodward, M. The behavior of idiots—interpreted by Piaget's theory of sensori-motor development. *British Journal of Educational Psychology,* 1959, *29,* 60-71.

Woodward, M. The application of Piaget's theory to research in mental deficiency. In N. R. Ellis (Ed.), *Handbook of mental deficiency: psychological theory and research.* New York: McGraw-Hill Book Co., 1963, pp. 297-324.

Gifted and talented children

CHAPTER 10

FOSTERING CREATIVITY
AND GIFTEDNESS

MEANINGS OF GIFTEDNESS

Giftedness means different things to different people. It is difficult to establish agreement on criteria for the identification of gifted children, much less on the educational provisions that should be made for them. Indeed, in the minds of some there is probably doubt that gifted children are legitimate candidates for special education. On the other hand, when some hear the expression "exceptional children," the immediate association this term suggests is with the exceptionally *capable*.

Perhaps some educators and citizens see a basic conflict between the idea of giftedness and the role of education in a democratic society. A number of critics of American education have castigated the schools for encouraging mediocrity and discouraging the expression of special gifts and talents (Conant, 1959; Pressey, 1955; Thistlethwaite, 1958). Nevertheless, there have been periods in recent American history when some degree of national attention has been focused on the need to identify gifted and talented students.

In general, however, the idea of providing special educational services and opportunities for gifted children at the elementary and secondary school level has not received a great deal of national support. There have been other priorities, and the prevailing assumption seems to have been that very bright and highly motivated children can and will learn under almost any circumstances (Martinson, 1973). When this assumption has been questioned and large-scale efforts have been initiated, as occurred after the Soviet Sputnik success in the 1950s, the concern has been mainly that American scientific and technological resources were underdeveloped. Discovery and nurture of *scientific talent* has been stressed.

IQ as a criterion

Specialized educational programs designed for gifted children have relied primarily on the intelligence quotient (IQ) for determining eligibility (Pegnato and Birch, 1959; Payne, 1974). This index is also important in estimating the number of gifted individuals one would expect to find in the general population. According to the standard employed by Terman and Merrill (1960) for interpretation of the Revised Stanford-Binet Intelligence Scale, Form L-M, the IQ range 110 to 119 is designated high average, 120 to 139 is designated superior, and 140 and above is very superior. Based on the *normal curve,* 4½ percent of the general population would be expected to have an IQ of 130 or higher.

Everyday speech, however, reflects awareness that there are various kinds and forms of giftedness. Obvious examples are in the area of the arts, but we also speak of gifted athletes, politicians, military leaders, and certainly teachers. These examples underline the question of whether those who achieve great success in some field of endeavor have "inborn" gifts and the logical next question of whether, or to what extent such gifts may be hereditary. Sir Francis Galton (1869) in his studies of genius became convinced that greatness runs in families and drew the not necessarily logical inference that this is caused by biological inheritance. There is certainly ample support for the view that unusual capability can be traced from generation to generation. However, such evidence in itself does not establish that giftedness is transmitted genetically, since bright parents might be expected to be more likely than less capable ones to provide stimulating and enriching environmental opportunities and experiences for their children. From the standpoint of the educator, resolving this particular issue of the origins of giftedness is clearly far less important than the questions of how best to teach the gifted child and how best to nurture the abilities of all children.

Another fundamental theoretical issue concerning the nature of intelligence, however, *is* relevant to the teacher. That is the question of whether intelligence is a unitary, global trait or has many dimensions. The conception of intelligence that underlies most attempts to measure it implies that there is an *ability to learn and adapt* (Spearman, 1927; Terman and Merrill, 1960; Wechsler, 1944) that may be reflected in specific ways but is general and pervasive. However, beginning with the early efforts of Thurstone (1926, 1935) to identify *primary mental abilities,* multidimensional viewpoints have been offered. J. P. Guilford and his associates (Guilford, 1959, 1967; Guilford and Hoepfner, 1971), in particular, have developed an argument that there may be a number of different *kinds* of intelligence. The Structure of Intellect model proposed by Guilford differentiates a total of 120 conceivable components, each one reflecting an interactive relationship between a specific *process,* certain *content,* and a type of *product.*

Creativity and intelligence

Guilford's conception of human abilities permits the inference that a person could be highly capable in certain areas but not necessarily in all. One of the most intriguing distinctions in the Structure of Intellect is that between two different kinds of "intellectual operations": convergent and divergent. Convergent thinking is defined essentially in terms of logical reasoning ability: the ability to learn the "correct answer." Divergent thinking, on the other hand, is thinking that may pursue many possible courses and conceivably reach any number of *different* answers. It is this capacity to generate many ideas *(fluency)* of many kinds *(flexibility),* some of which may be highly uncommon *(originality),* that has been identified by some researchers as the hallmark of creativity. E. Paul Torrance (1966), in particular, has attempted to measure these abilities, both in the sphere of verbal creativity and in creative responses to figural tasks or problems.

In a sense, highly creative children *continue* to show, throughout their development, some of the attributes of thought and attitude of children during the early childhood years, especially ages 3 through 5. They continue to see the world in a way that is fresh and novel (Haney, 1961), and they retain the ability to employ fantasy to balance their increasing objectivity and rationality (Kubie, 1958). There persists a kind of *egocentrism* in the thought processes of highly creative persons that is reminiscent of the highly subjective orientation of the preschool-aged, preoperational child. Whereas, according to Piaget (1951), this early egocentrism subsequently gives way to *socially adapted* thought, some children seem to retain the capability of seeing the world from a perspective uniquely their own. It may be this capability that, more than any other, distinguishes the highly creative individual (Rogers, 1959).

If creativity is, in a sense, a *childlike* quality, it surely does not reflect "stunted development" in the personal and social sphere. Creative children and adults can adjust to the demands of their peer society and its institutions, but they are also able, at will, to return to earlier ways of seeing the world (Rogers, 1959). The psychoanalytic concept of *regression in the service of the ego* (A. Freud, 1965) conveys the notion of intentional, willed indulgence of the childlike part of the personality. Creative adults are "in touch with" the "child" within them, the child they once were (Jersild, 1952). They have not totally renounced this part of themselves but are able to channel "childlike" modes of thought in constructive directions.

It should be noted that not all highly intelligent children are necessarily highly creative (Getzels and Jackson, 1962). Americans also were made intensely aware during the early 1970s that a high degree of moral and ethical responsibility does not necessarily go hand in hand with unusual capabilities for achievement and leadership. That issue (probably the most important one of all) suggests that what one *does* with one's gifts is the basic concern, to society as well as to the individual.

General types of giftedness

For convenience, although they overlap, we can identify at least four general forms of giftedness that are relevant to the education of young children*:

1. *Academic talent:* Some children demonstrate unusual abilities primarily in the learning of academic skills. These children may be particularly proficient in a specific area, such as reading or mathematics, and may show readiness earlier than other children to move ahead in one or more areas. Language skills may be particularly advanced. The child may show great interest in "how things work."

2. *Special talent:* Some children demonstrate unusual ability in a special area, such as music, art, dramatics, or creative writing. Such an ability or abilities may begin to be manifest quite early in life in some children, while in others they may go unrecognized during the early years.

3. *Social abilities:* Some children show special "gifts" in the sphere of social relationships, adaptation, or leadership. Although it is likely that the child who relates unusually well with both adults and his peers, and who is often in a leadership role, will also be very successful in academic learning, this is not always the case.

4. *Creative thinking:* Most definitions of creativity (for example, Beitteld and Lowenfeld, 1959) associate this characteristic with productivity of one kind or another. However, the creativity may not necessarily be expressed in any of the three ways mentioned previously. Some children may show a high degree of divergent thinking in play or in conversation.

---

*I am indebted to Dr. Jean Schindler for this classification scheme.

Summary

We sometimes use words such as "high intelligence," "giftedness," and "talent" to mean pretty much the same thing. Nevertheless, everyday experience indicates that this is not necessarily the case. It is probably true that educational programs and provisions for gifted children have tended to place major emphasis on academic skill areas, often neglecting those children with unusual abilities in the arts or other fields. Particularly, highly original or inventive thinking has not necessarily been emphasized in special programs for very capable youngsters.

NEEDS OF GIFTED AND TALENTED CHILDREN

Although folklore and common stereotypes paint a picture of the very bright individual as at best a bit of a "queer duck" and at worst physically puny, sickly, unhappy, and unpopular, research has shown this image to be far from accurate. The gifted tend to exceed their peers in early physical development and generally to maintain some advantage in this sphere. They are typically well liked by other children, and as adults achieve a higher degree of career success and marital and family stability than is seen in the general population (Terman, 1925; Terman and Oden, 1947).

Like all children, the gifted do not present a unitary set of characteristics and needs, however. The unique characteristics and interests of the individual child, rather than the fact that he is gifted, are most important in determining his educational needs. At the same time, this principle itself implies the importance of helping the child to cultivate and to value his special abilities.

Is specialized early education desirable?

Should children identified early in life as unusually capable be enrolled in special prekindergarten programs? What possibilities are there and what is known about the effectiveness of specialized early education for young children who are very bright? One partial answer to these questions is provided by the autobiographical account of the nineteenth century genius John Stuart Mill. Kept at home and systematically educated by his father from infancy, young Mill could read Greek at age 3 and at age 6½ wrote a history of Rome. However, wrote Mill, ". . . the education which my father gave me, was in itself much more fitted for training me to *know* than to *do*" (1924, p. 26).

Rather than such an intensified, didactic approach carried out by the child's own parents, other options more appropriate to the needs of the *whole child* are available.

One of these that should be mentioned is that of *no* particular conscious intervention; another is represented by the parents' (and other family members') attempts to ensure that the developing child's experiences are as rich as possible, that there are interested responses to his questions, and that his curiosity is stimulated and challenged in a variety of ways through everyday experience.

Prekindergarten experiences of a more formal instructional variety have been available, particularly in specific areas: dramatics and theater, art, music (for example, the Suzuki violin method), movement (for example, Dalcroze eurythmics), and dance. There has also been a tendency to identify erroneously (Elkind, 1967) the Montessori method as an early education program best suited to young children who show indications of giftedness.

Finally, an option frequently proposed and more frequently sought by parents is that of early school entrance. Many school districts allow early entrance (that is, entrance in kindergarten or first grade of children whose birthdate falls after that prescribed by state law). However, this practice does not seem to be generally encouraged by school officials and is usually permitted only on the basis of unusual performance on ability tests administered by a psychologist.

Perhaps because early childhood educators have for so long resisted attempts to infuse their programs with expectations creating greater pressures for young children (Hendrick, 1975), one hears very little about the need to provide for gifted children in preschool programs. To do so, however, need not entail making the early childhood classroom more "academic." Not to do so may be to fail to challenge and stimulate young children who possess unusual abilities.

The approaches to *enrichment* that a teacher of young children may employ are many and varied, determined both by his or her own resources and imagination and by the interests and readiness of the children. The teacher will recognize that individual children differ in the maturity of their interests, in their ability to handle complexity (for example, in a story), and in the intensity of their curiosity. He or she will endeavor to provide for this range of differences, rather than to impose uniform expectations and tasks for all.

The early childhood classroom offers a wealth of resources for responding to and encouraging curiosity and exploration in highly capable young children. The teacher should be ever on the alert for new items and activities that present challenges to children who wish to find out "how things work" or to gain the satisfaction of advanced levels of accomplishment. Much of the remainder of this chapter is devoted to suggestions for teaching young children who seem to be unusually capable.

EARLY IDENTIFICATION OF GIFTED CHILDREN

Although there is now a fairly sizable body of professional literature concerning the education of gifted children, surprisingly very little of it concerns the young child. Even the newest edition of one of the most highly regarded books of readings on educating the gifted, *Psychology and Education of the Gifted* by Walter B. Barbe and Joseph S. Renzulli (1975), contains virtually no references to teaching the gifted child at the nursery or kindergarten level. The same observation can be made concerning both other texts specific to this field (for example, Barbe, 1965; Gallagher, 1964) and general texts dealing with all exceptionalities (for example, Kirk, 1972; Payne, 1974; Martinson, 1973).

Does the relative absence of literature concerning early education of gifted children reflect an unfortunate omission, or is this lack appropriate? The latter would imply either of two things: either it is not possible to identify truly gifted children early in life, or no specialized attention should be given by educators at this level.

In writing about the importance of identifying and encouraging exceptional talent, Lewis Terman (1954) noted that such talent, according to his research findings, seems characteristically to be manifest early in life. Giftedness, he asserted, can be identified in childhood, although the specific direction it would take might not yet be crystallized. However, Terman was discussing identification during childhood essentially in terms of the elementary school years.

Nonetheless, at least in retrospective analysis, children later identified as gifted often showed advanced or possibly precocious development in the early years. This is certainly not always the case, however; striking examples of apparent exceptions, like Albert Einstein, can readily be found. Furthermore, children who reach early developmental milestones "ahead of schedule" or who are "early readers" do not necessarily maintain their advantage. Similarly, formal measures of intelligence administered during infancy or the preschool period do not predict subsequent IQ scores very accurately (Bloom, 1964). It is probably easier to detect significant indications of slowness in development early in life than significant indications of superiority, and these early signs are more predictively significant in the former case than the latter (Gesell and Amatruda, 1941).

Teacher identification

Relying on selection by teachers has generally proved unsatisfactory as a means of identifying gifted children. One study (Pegnato and Birch, 1959) found nearly one third of the children identified by their teachers as gifted to be inappropriately selected, while more than one half of the actually gifted children were not picked. Winifred Kirk (1966) found that the much worse record of kindergarten teachers in her study was associated with the teachers' tendency to select *older* children. These teachers apparently did not take into account age differences in making their selections. More than two thirds of the children *not identified* by the teachers in this study had an IQ higher than 116, while most of those thought to be "gifted" tended, in fact, to cluster within the average range.

Jacobs (1971) found kindergarten teachers only 10 percent effective in identifying gifted children, compared to 50 percent effectiveness of secondary-level teachers. These findings led Jacobs to question the value of kindergarten screening as a means of identifying gifted children. At this age level, at least, parent judgment seemed more accurate, and individual assessment, rather than whole-group screening, also seemed to be indicated.

In addition to relatively younger age, at least at the kindergarten level, a number of other factors may interfere with teachers' ability to recognize giftedness. These include *unevenness in development,* especially in the perceptual-motor sphere; *cultural and language differences; underachievement caused by any number of motivational or other factors; shyness or reticence;* and *discordant or difficult behavior.*

If identifying gifted children in the early childhood classroom is so difficult, why should it be attempted? If kindergarten teachers are actually "wrong" more often than they are "right" in identifying gifted children, shouldn't they avoid even trying to make judgments about which children may show signs of being unusually capable? The danger is that if teachers fail to recognize the special abilities and talents of at least some children, these abilities and talents may not receive the special encouragement they may need.

There is not a great deal of conclusive evidence to support this position, at least in the form of "hard data." However, individual and subjective reports abound. One does not have to talk to many people to find at least one who feels that a teacher's recognition and encouragement could have made a great difference in his or her life. In *The Autobiography of Malcolm X* (Haley, 1964), this deeply sensitive and gifted leader recalls how a teacher explicitly guided him away from academic pursuits and preparation for a professional career.

Some empirical evidence that *early* identification of giftedness by teachers is important is provided by one research study (Jacobs, 1970). In this study, gifted children whose abilities were not recognized by their kindergarten teachers actually showed a *decline in measured IQ*. That teachers' "expectancies" regarding the capabilities of children in their classes somehow influence those capabilities, as measured by intelligence tests, was found by Rosenthal and Jacobsen (1968). This expectancy, or *self-fulfilling prophecy* (also called a "Pygmalion" effect), may or may not be a crucial determinant for many children. However, there is certainly more than a suggestion that *what teachers expect of children has some relationship to what children accomplish*. Whether identification of very capable children actually leads to placing them in specialized programs may not be as important as the encouragement, support, and opportunities a teacher provides within his or her own classroom.

Finally, as was suggested earlier in this chapter, children may be gifted in different ways. This implies that a teacher who values and encourages *diversity,* rather than imposing uniform standards, may be better able to recognize various *kinds* of gifts, talents, special abilities, and strong interests.

Giftedness and creativity in young economically disadvantaged and culturally different children

Despite the early pioneering work of leaders such as Maria Montessori, serious recognition of and respect for creativity and giftedness among the children of the poor were not reflected in American education until very recently. Some efforts to identify gifted children and youth within low socioeconomic level communities (Renzulli, 1973) have demonstrated both the need for such programs and the difficulties they face. It has long been established that giftedness is no respecter of race or privilege. However, the problem of *expectations* of substandard pupil performance in low-income communities has been effectively documented in several firsthand accounts, such as *Death At An Early Age* by Jonathan Kozol (1967) and *The Way It Spoze To Be* by James Herndon (1966).

Giftedness and creativity in young handicapped children

Superior intellectual ability is found among children who are physically handicapped, visually or hearing impaired, speech impaired, learning disabled, and emotionally disturbed. High intellectual ability in a child who is handicapped is a definite advantage in helping the child to compensate for his disability. In general, intellectual proficiency is positively associated with abilities to achieve social, academic, and occupational success. The brighter the child, other factors being equal, the better the prognosis.

However, by the very nature of some handicapping conditions and as a result of the inequalities of educational opportunity accorded the handicapped in the past, special abilities and talents among these children have tragically often gone unrecognized and undeveloped. The example of Helen Keller stands as perhaps the most inspiring example of the greatness that can be achieved by even a severely handicapped person. And that of her teacher, Annie Sullivan, is perhaps the most inspiring example of what a teacher can accomplish. Nevertheless, only recently have there been concerted efforts to recognize the potential and to foster excellence and talent in handicapped children and youth. Old prejudices persist, and, generally, the expectations of both educators and the society at large regarding the achievement potential of handicapped persons fail to reflect awareness of the contributions that could be realized.

EDUCATIONAL PROVISIONS

Despite the increasing awareness of limitations of IQ tests (especially for young children) and of the diverse ways in which unusual abilities and talents may be expressed, the IQ has continued to be the major criterion used for assignment of pupils to special educational programs for the gifted. Special provisions for intellectually superior children fall within three general categories: acceleration, special classes or programs, and enrichment. (Payne, 1974; Martinson, 1973).

Acceleration

Acceleration includes a variety of procedures for hastening an unusually capable child's progress through the "steps" of formal schooling. In general, there are two major forms of acceleration: *early school entrance* and *grade skipping*. The latter method is probably less frequently employel, except in the form of early graduation from high school through accelerating the secondary-level program for a student. This may be accomplished through summer study, "overload," or combining high school and college work. Basically, all students must complete a requisite number of credit hours to graduate from high school, but there are various ways in which this can be "telescoped" into a shorter time span than the traditional 4-year period.

Early entrance remains somewhat controversial and is probably not widely endorsed by public school officials. Despite widespread beliefs by educators, however, early kindergarten entrance or entrance directly into the first grade is apparently advantageous far more often than otherwise (Braga, 1972). There is concern that the child will be unduly pressured, not really as "ready" as he seems, and more likely to suffer failure if entrance is effected sooner than the particular state's starting age policy dictates. However, the extensive research that has addressed this question has demonstrated no ill effects on the child who begins school early, if early entrance is well planned (see, for example, Payne, 1974; Martinson, 1973; Reynolds, 1962). Effective home-school communication and individualized assessment and planning are essential. But, with these components, it would seem that enabling a young child to begin schooling when he is ready for it is more reasonable and educationally sound than assuming that all children whose birthdates fall within a specified range have matured equally by a given calendar date.

Special classes and programs

With a few striking exceptions, the special class approach has not been widely employed in educating unusually capable children. *Tracking* systems for differentiating broad levels of apparent ability, however, have been employed. Generally, there is not impressive evidence to support ability grouping or tracking at the elementary school level (Borg, 1964) without differentiating the instructional approach as well. The idea of segregating more capable students from less capable ones and vice versa has been criticized as a form of elitism (Bettelheim, 1958). However, ability grouping is regularly done, at least within a classroom. Many teachers differentiate levels of ability and performance, especially in reading, and create smaller, relatively homogeneous groups. As a means of carrying out reading instruction at the primary and intermediate levels, this practice has also been criticized by some educators (for example, Hall, 1970).

Specialized programs for children identified as gifted are not very common. However, one such approach, the Major Work Program offered by the Cleveland Public Schools, was begun in the 1920s and has operated continuously ever since. It is thus the oldest continuous program for gifted children in the United States. Major Work enrolls students with a measured IQ of 125 or higher and provides continuous participation throughout the student's elementary and secondary school career (Jordan, 1976).

Enrichment

By far the most widely educational provision for gifted children in the United States is enrichment. This means that a child is enrolled in a "regular" program with others his age, but within the regular class or grade he enjoys special opportunities for learning. These may be in the form of specially selected activities, differential assignments, or individualized programming. Such special provisions may be made on a structured, programmatic basis or may be carried out less formally. It may or may not be the case that a child is formally "identified" or selected on the basis of standardized test criteria to participate in an enriched program.

The basis for providing enrichment opportunities for very capable children is twofold:

1. To capitalize on the child's interest in learning and his motivation, opportunities that challenge and stimulate learning must be available. Material and activities that are overly familiar, redundant and repetitive, and already well known by the child may be boring and may cause the child to lose interest, possibly become a behavior problem, become "turned off," and lose his enthusiasm and intense interest in learning.

2. If a child is deprived of the opportunity to learn what he is ready to learn, he is being unnecessarily held back. The child is forced to crawl when he could fly. Apart from the impact of this deprivation on the child's incentive and attitude, it is wasteful for society as well. Enrichment may permit the capable child to continue to stretch beyond the limits of the norm.

The suggestions that follow could be incorporated either within a segregated, specialized instructional program or as enrichment provisions within a "regular" program. Since they pertain to the nursery school, kindergarten, or primary grades, it is assumed that the latter approach would generally be more likely to be used. At the nursery school level, those specialized programs that are available generally emphasize one or more areas of the arts and are not as a rule established specifically for children who are believed to be gifted or to have special talents. Also, since intellectual superiority in young children is difficult to establish either through test data or through identification by teachers, it is assumed that enrichment in "regular" nursery or kindergarten will much more commonly be employed. Beginning in the primary grades, specialized programs may be developed; however, such programs are few and far between. Generally, the young child who is unusually bright, highly creative, or specially gifted or talented is provided for within a regular early childhood classroom or program.

EMPHASES AND PRACTICES FOR TEACHING YOUNG GIFTED AND CREATIVE CHILDREN

Should there be a certain type of curriculum or teaching methodology for young children who are unusually capable? If so, self-contained classes or homogeneous grouping might be effective or even necessary if such a curriculum and methodology are not appropriate to the needs of other children. However, although there are many opinions concerning this issue, there is not conclusive evidence supporting the necessity or desirability of such specialization.

Let us assume a prekindergarten, kindergarten, or primary grade classroom setting in which a broad range and variety of ability levels, characteristics, learning styles, and interests are represented by the children. Given such a setting, the following approaches are suggested as particularly appropriate for highly capable, highly motivated, and very creative young children. They are offered as areas that are not always emphasized but that may be effective avenues *for fostering the creativity and for enhancing the cognitive growth of all young children,* as well as those who are exceptionally capable.

Supporting intrinsic motivation

Although programmed learning approaches have been employed with gifted children (Rice, 1970), there seems to be greater enthusiasm in the field of education of the gifted for more "open-ended"

methods (Torrance, 1965). Such methods emphasize challenging the child's curiosity, inherent desire to learn, and ability to structure knowledge in his own way. Motivation to learn comes primarily from within the child, rather than being artificially imposed in the form of external rewards and punishments.

Jerome Bruner (1966) has described four general forms of intrinsic motivation that may be essential to the development of a "lifelong love of learning" but that are not always recognized or encouraged:

1. The child's curiosity, his need to explore, his will to know and understand, and his desire to resolve incongruity or "dissonance" created when what he observes differs from what he expects. Piaget's theory suggests a kind of intrinsic motivation that could be called epistemic curiosity: a desire to obtain knowledge (Furth, 1969).
2. The child's need to experience a sense of mastery over his environment, to be *competent* and to have a *sense of competence* (White, 1959).
3. The child's desire to imitate and to be like *models* presented by admired and loved adults (Bandura and Walters, 1963).
4. The child's responsiveness to his peers and his ability to gain satisfaction from cooperative activity with others "in pursuit of a common goal" (Sherif and Sherif, 1964).

According to William Glasser (1969), the child's *involvement* in taking responsibility for his own behavior and learning accomplishments is important to his self-esteem, effective participation as a member of a group, and favorable attitudes toward learning. In terms of intellectual development, according to Piaget's theory (Piaget, 1967; Piaget and Inhelder, 1969), the growth of logical thought requires the individual child to *actively structure knowledge* in his own way. The "informal" approach associated with the British primary school stresses the need to *trust* the child to direct his own learning (Brown and Precious, 1969; Weber, 1971; V. Rogers, 1970). The teacher's role is primarily to maintain an environment conducive to learning and to *facilitate,* rather than to direct, learning (C. Rogers, 1969).

Encouraging discovery learning

A mode of teaching that has been presented as congruent with the way in which children seem to learn emphasizes the encouragement of *inquiry* or *discovery* (Suchman, 1961; Bruner, 1961; Shulman and Keislar, 1966). According to those who advocate discovery learning, the child's intrinsic motivation to learn will best be aroused if the learning environment is rich with problems to be solved. Typically, such problem solving takes place through an inductive, rather than a deductive, process of reasoning. This implies that through the resolution of specific problems the child may discover the underlying or basic principle reflected in the specific instance.

Such a view of learning—and teaching—is diametrically opposed to that espoused by David Ausubel (1968). Ausubel's theory of instruction emphasizes the parallels between an individual's "cognitive structure" and the structure of a discipline of knowledge. The learner's understanding of "material to be learned" is enhanced, Ausubel believes, through a deductive process of reasoning, facilitated by the teacher's initial presentation of *advance organizers*—organizing, general principles to which the specific information can be related. This conception of learning is often termed learning by reception, as opposed to learning by discovery. Ausubel notes that meaningful reception learning is more characteristic of *academic* learning than that most often employed by young children.

Both views of learning are considered relevant, by their advocates, to the teaching of most children, not just the gifted. Both make a common assumption: *that the child is motivated to learn.* Neither approach has been demonstrated to be superior in all areas of learning and for all children. One tends to hear more about the advantages of discovery learning in teaching exceptionally capable young children, however, because of the close relationship between this approach and those teaching techniques that have been advocated as conducive to the development of creative thinking of children (see, for example, Torrance and Myers, 1970).

As Hilda Taba (1963) has pointed out, discovery learning is really not a totally new idea. Especially regarding the teaching of young children, conceptions closely paralleling present-day views can be found in both of the two streams, different though they are, associated with Friedrich Froebel and Maria Montessori.

A discovery learning approach in the early childhood classroom would be one in which children are confronted with problems to be solved. Intriguing items of all kinds provide unlimited opportunities for problem solving and discovery. Generating questions through novel experiences, challenging situations, and curiosity-provoking objects is perhaps even more important than discovering answers and solutions. Above all, *divergent* approaches are accepted, encouraged, and valued.

Piaget's theories have been most readily applied by educators in the sequencing and mode of presentation of mathematical principles and in development of science curriculum. This is appropriate, in view of the kind of knowledge with which Piaget and his co-workers have been most concerned: *logicomathematical knowledge.* Basically, Piaget's theory of knowledge and how it is acquired by young children posits an interactive relationship between mental "structures" and objective reality, developed through transactions between the active child and a responsive environment. *Concepts* concerning relationships between objects and events are extensions of structures that in turn have evolved from the sensory-motor "building blocks"

of infancy. And these in turn form the basis of the *formal* reasoning abilities of adult thought.

Emphases derived from Piaget's formulation include: (1) recognition of the value of *physical activity* in learning, (2) recognition of the child's active role in *constructing* knowledge, (3) recognition of the importance of conceptual *development,* in contrast to specific skill learning, and (4) recognition of the inherent motivational properties of tasks that present an optimal level of incongruity or "dissonance," together with the need to solve "the problem of the match" (Hunt, 1961).

Encouraging and supporting creativity

Much has been written about the nature of creativity in young children and ways it can be cultivated through education (for example, Torrance and Myers, 1970). This brief discussion will only summarize a few of the areas to which teachers of young children can attend. The areas suggested here do not comprise a comprehensive list, nor are the suggestions prescriptive. They are introduced only with the observation that young children's creativity is closely related to that of the teacher.

A great many diverse teaching methods have been developed for the purpose of stimulating creativity in children. Treffinger and Gowan (1971) list 49 separate instructional programs or types of approaches, including variants of the familiar *brainstorming* technique, *affectively-oriented* methods, *problem-solving projects,* and others. Many of these are targeted toward the older learner, including the adult. Business concerns, for example, have extensively adopted brainstorming, sensitivity training, imaginative or futuristic problem solving and ideation, and psychodrama, role-playing, and simulation games in attempting to enhance the effectiveness of executives and sales personnel. However, a great many of these procedures can be readily adapted for use with young children, and

some have been explicitly designed for use at the elementary school level.

Use of time and space. An important dimension of creative thinking identified by Guilford (1959) is *flexibility*. A willingness on the part of the teacher to modify plans based on awareness of what is important for the child at any given moment, to rearrange space, and to accept a degree of unevenness in children's learning— these are certainly all manifestations of flexibility. A flexible stance regarding scheduling of activity does not eliminate the need for planning. On the contrary, it makes all the more necessary instruc- tional planning that anticipates the need for a range of alternatives.

Provisioning of the classroom. Much of the writing concerning the English infant school (see, for example, Brown and Precious, 1969; V. Rogers, 1970; Weber, 1971) emphasizes the importance of the physical learning environment. An environment for learning is a *rich* environment, full of things with the potential to provide organizing centers for children's learning. Rich, however, is not synonymous with cluttered, and all items in a classroom must be selected with an eye to both their inherent motivational properties and

their potential to be organized by a child within a coherent scheme. The arrangement of materials, as well as selection of the materials themselves, is an important determinant of their teaching potential.

Valuing creativity. Teachers convey the extent to which imagination and creativity are valued in their classrooms through the model they provide, through what they allow and what they reward, through the way they structure the environment, and through what they say and ask. Teachers who value creativity value *diversity* as well and are able to share the excitement of young children engaged in making fresh discoveries. Unfortunately, there is evidence that not all teachers respond favorably to highly creative children (Getzels and Jackson, 1962; Yamamoto, 1963).

Fostering peer learning. In addition to placing their faith in the child and his ability to structure his own learning, teachers must have confidence in the value of *children teaching children.* This does not mean making individual needs subservient to the group. It does mean respecting children's desires to work together and recognizing the inherent value of cooperative activity. In Erik Erikson's theory, *making things with others* is a central aspect of the young child's ego identity development during the early years of school in resolving the developmental conflict of industry vs. inferiority (Erikson, 1963). Individual creativity may be encouraged and supported through cooperative activity with one or more peers.

Encouraging language

The dimensions of "language arts" particularly emphasized here are those of questioning and discussing. The importance of children's questions, as sources of clues to their thought as well as means of seeking information, has been amply documented, as has the importance of the teacher's ability to ask questions that promote children's growth (Taba, 1964). A questioning mode is probably the central feature of discovery learning (Suchman, 1961), and guided discovery (Gagné, 1966) can be thought of as a kind of "dialogue of questioning" involving children and teacher.

Discussion places equal emphasis on verbal expression and on genuine listening. William Glasser (1969) has contributed the insight that real discussion rarely takes place in school, as well as suggesting steps in developing and using a mode of discussion that he calls the "class meeting." At least some of the prerequisites for real discussion to take place, according to Glasser, are (1) inherent meaningfulness of what is discussed to the children, which contributes to their *involvement,* (2) valuing (but not evaluating) what is said, (3) modeling and valuing listening, (4) a nonjudgmental and facilitating role for the adult, and (5) a *circle* format, so that all participants face each other.

The language young children employ may often be deceptively sophisticated, especially in its saturation in our media culture, with scientific terms and adult-sounding words to which young children are exposed. It is necessary for the teacher to attempt to move behind the "visual facade" that may often mask the child's quite imperfect understanding of concepts (Almy et al., 1966). Some of the tasks that Piaget has employed to determine whether children bring to bear certain mental *operations* in solving problems can be readily adapted to classroom use by the teacher, however (Weissman and Safford, 1971). Because he was aware that the child's words alone might prove undependable guides to determine his knowledge, Piaget revised his methode clinique (clinical method) of interviewing children so that the way in which the child goes about solving a problem could be analyzed (Ginsburg and Opper, 1969). Basically, this *revised clinical method* consists of an open-ended interview procedure in which the child is observed as he approaches a problem to be solved, he is asked what he thinks will occur, his actions are noted, and his explanations solicited if the outcome is not what he had predicted. It is to some extent a *nondirective* procedure, and it is totally a *child-centered* approach, rather than requiring strict adherence to a prescribed format of adult questioning.

Not all young gifted children are fluent "talkers" and not all those who are are gifted. However, young children who are unusually capable as far as intellectual proficiency is concerned are likely to be advanced in their language development, to enjoy conversing with others, and to be fascinated by words and their meanings. Encouraging such interests and skills implies a significant emphasis on conversing with individual children, as well as encouraging discussion among the children. The need to develop expressive language as well as listening skills is certainly not unique to young gifted children. It is noted here primarily to point out that the value of listening, responding, conversing, and discussing should not be minimized in working with children who are proficient in these skills.

Encouraging expression through nonverbal activity

Nonverbal activities and media offer many opportunities for the child to grow in expressive abilities and creativity. Work with gifted children often tends to center around verbal language, however. Consequently, brief mention is made here of several vehicles for the child to develop expressively in an early childhood program: play and creative dramatics, art media, movement, and music.

Play and creative dramatics. Play is the young child's way of internalizing experience, of rehearsing, of expressing, and of communicating. Whereas socialized, shared, or cooperative play is an advanced mode, it is built on prior experience with play as a *representational* or *symbolic* activity, a kind of *language system*. Representational or thematic play that is shared by more than one child is termed *sociodramatic play* (Smilansky, 1968). Examples, which often appear spontaneously in classroom or other play group, include the familiar and traditional scenes of "playing house," but also a great many other diverse forms of play that is thematic or symbolic or representational. These spontaneous modes constitute the original and prototypic form of creative dramatics. The value of such activity, including forms in which an adult may provide stimulus, guidance, or structure, is almost universally recognized by those who teach 3- and 4-year-old children. However, kindergartens have shown some tendency to overlook the value of "play" as "the child's work" (Hymes, 1974). A distinction is all too often made between play and "work."

Hans Furth (1969b) has presented a convincing argument for "reordering priorities" in the primary grade curriculum, resulting in greater emphasis on *symbolic expression* as a means of promoting cognitive development, with less emphasis on getting information *into* the child. Furth suggests, for example, that activities in which children can recount experiences through mime or other means may be more valuable in promoting cognitive growth than language arts activities that are generally stressed.

Art media. The term "creative project" is sometimes misused in the nursery classroom when task constraints for an art activity are so rigidly imposed by the teacher that little or none of the child's imagination is involved. There is clearly a need, especially for many children with physical or other handicaps, for activities in which children must draw within lines, cut following a designated pattern, and so forth. However, *art* is something very different. It includes a limitless variety of ways of experiencing and ways of "saying."

In addition to the familiar easels for brush and finger painting and, of course, clay, any number of kinds of art media can become vehicles for expression. Although it is not frequently found in American primary or preschool classrooms, *carpentry* is an excellent area to develop as a regular component. Building in all forms, as well as molding, drawing, painting, etc., allow the child to experiment, test hypotheses, discover relationships, and express his individuality.

Movement. It has been said that Americans have never really resolved the "mind-body problem," that Americans regard their bodies as things to adorn but things that are really functional only in the areas of sex and sports. Dance, until recently, has not occupied a central place in American cultural life. Gymnastics have not been as prominent as in many other countries. The body is a vehicle for communication that is rarely exploited in our culture.

Piaget has stressed the motoric roots of logical thought, and Jerome Bruner (1964) has described enactive representation, along with the iconic and symbolic modes, as a way of knowing that we use throughout life. Particularly for young children, physical movement—through mime, dance, rhythmic or interpretive motion or gesture, as well as in the countless other forms—should be a "way of life" in the early childhood classroom. Often one sees a striking demarcation between nursery school and primary classroom in this respect, with the latter involving very little opportunity for movement and then only for "exercise" and specific motor tasks in physical education. When one considers the developmental needs of young children, however, such a distinction is quite inappropriate. Physical expression can relate to every aspect of learning.

Music. Musical activity, including some aspects of movement, has long been recognized as a central component of the nursery and kindergarten program. Traditionally, there has been a separation of music from the "academic" program in the elementary school, a separation that contributes to two unfortunate, if not tragic, consequences: (1) music comes to be regarded as the province of the talented few

—"special teachers" and those individuals who "have musical ability"—and (2) music is relegated to a decidedly secondary niche in the educational program and in the culture, as a "frill." The centrality of musical experience to a young child's life is only rarely sustained as fully as possible through the years of schooling.

Emphasizing the "fantasy and feeling" dimension of children's literature

A few years ago a psychoanalyst, Richard Jones, in a book called *Fantasy and Feeling in Education* (Jones, 1968), reflected on an unacknowledged dimension of much curriculum development work. Although his analysis was inspired by his work with the upper elementary interdisciplinary curriculum project called Man: A Course of Study, it related to many areas of children's learning. Fears, internal and repressed conflicts, impulses, love, concerns about death, and all dimensions of children's emotional life are intimately involved in "cognitive" learning. This generalization is certainly true—as every early childhood teacher knows—of young children, but it is true of older children as well. "Inner life" is inextricably interwoven with all learning and certainly with all manifestations of creativity (Kubie, 1958). Perhaps the best criterion in the choice of children's literature is its responsiveness to the psychic needs of children. In *Uses of Enchantment*, another great child psychoanalyst, Bruno Bettelheim (1976), presents a provocative analysis of children's stories and traditional fairy tales in terms of their relatedness to pervasive themes in children's psychic development. Literature for children, and for adults, provides personal and at the same time shared experiences that nurture that which is most human: the ability to *feel*.

Fostering social awareness and interpersonal relations

Giftedness involves the social sphere as well as the areas of intellectual proficiency and creative and artistic expression. The basic task of the young child in this area is to relate his own perspective to that of others—to move outward from self, to identify with the feelings and needs of others, and to experience a sense of community. The "curriculum area" is social studies, but the vehicles for per-

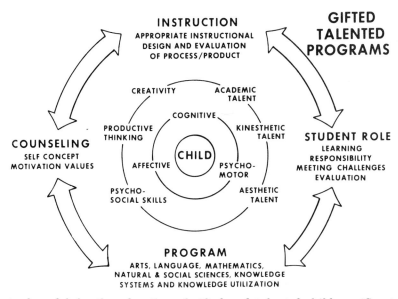

Conceptual model for the education of gifted and talented children. (Courtesy Dr. Wilber Simmons, Kent State University.)

sonal and social development transcend any single part of the curriculum or school day.

• • •

Teaching young children with unusual capabilities requires attention to all aspects of the child. Just as there are probably many different forms of giftedness, there are many dimensions of a child's learning and living. A comprehensive approach to teaching gifted children would take all of these into account, as the model on p. 245 suggests.

Wilber Simmons (1977) describes this conceptualization as follows:

Gifted and talented programs should focus primarily on the child. To develop an appropriate program, a series of dynamic factors must be considered and utilized. The first set would be the behavioral areas—cognitive, affective, and psychomotor dynamics—since they provide indices as to basic abilities. The second set of factors look at six performance capabilities in the areas of academic, kinesthetic, and esthetic talents through psychosocial skills (leadership), productive thinking, and creativity. The final set in the figure represents the major elements of the gifted program—instruction, student role, program component, and counseling—which are interdependent. Program development for gifted and talented children must consider all of these interrelated factors if the needs and interests of such children are to be met with relevant and stimulating educational services.

THE CHALLENGE OF THE GIFTED CHILD

If creativity and giftedness are expressed in many forms, teachers of young children must be receptive to diversity. Early educational experiences can be crucial in influencing what a child is able to do with the special gifts he may possess. Programs that stress rigid conformity to uniform expectations leave little room for the child who "marches to a different drummer" or who is ready before his peers to move on into new territory. The teacher who recognizes and accommodates individual needs of the handicapped child should be no less attentive to those of the especially capable child.

DISCUSSION QUESTIONS

1. How would you describe gifted children?
2. In your opinion, should gifted and talented children be identified early in life? Why?
3. What educational provisions are made in your community and in your state for especially capable children?
4. What is creativity? Why, and in what ways, are children creative? Can creativity be taught?
5. What kinds of teaching techniques do you think are most likely to encourage creativity?
6. What are the relative advantages and possible difficulties associated with each of the three major educational approaches to providing for gifted children?

REFERENCES

Almy, M., with E. Chittenden and P. Miller. *Young children's thinking: studies of some aspects of Piaget's theory.* New York: Teacher's College Press, 1966.

Ausubel, D. P. *Educational psychology: a cognitive view.* New York: Holt, Rinehart & Winston, Inc., 1968.

Bandura, A., and Walters, R. H. *Social learning and personality development.* New York: Holt, Rinehart & Winston, Inc., 1963.

Barbe, W. B. *Psychology and education of the gifted.* Englewood Cliffs, N.J.: Prentice-Hall, Inc., 1965.

Barbe, W. B., and Renzulli, J. S. *Psychology and education of the gifted* (2 ed.). New York: John Wiley & Sons, Inc., 1975.

Beitteld, K., and Lowenfeld, V. Interdisciplinary criteria of creativity in the arts and sciences. In *Research yearbook of the National Art Association.* Washington, D.C.: National Art Association, 1959.

Bettelheim, B. Segregation: new style. *School Review,* 1958, *66,* 251-272.

Bettelheim, B. *Uses of Enchantment.* New York: Alfred A. Knopf, Inc., 1976.

Bloom, B. S. *Stability and change in human characteristics.* New York: John Wiley & Sons, Inc., 1964.

Borg, W. R. *An evaluation of ability grouping* (Cooperative Research Project No. 577). Washington, D.C.: U.S. Office of Education, 1964.

Braga, J. L. Early admission: opinion vs. evidence. *Elementary School Journal,* 1972, *72*(1), 35-46.

Bronfenbrenner, U. The split-level American family. *Saturday Review,* 1967, *50,* 60-66.

Brown, M., and Precious, N. *The integrated day in the primary school.* New York: Agathon Press, Inc., 1969.

Bruner, J. S. The act of discovery. *Harvard Educational Review,* 1961, *31,* 21-32.

Bruner, J. S. The course of cognitive growth. *American Psychologist,* 1964, *19,* 1-16.

Bruner, J. S. *Toward a theory of instruction.* Cambridge, Mass.: Harvard University Press, 1966.

Conant, J. B. *The American high school today.* New York: McGraw-Hill Book Co., 1959.

Elkind, D. Piaget and Montessori. *Harvard Educational Review,* 1967, *37,* 535-545.

Erikson, E. H. *Childhood and society* (2nd ed.). New York: W. W. Norton & Co., Inc., 1963.

Freud, A. *Normality and pathology in childhood: assessments of development.* New York: International Universities Press, 1965.

Furth, H. *Piaget and knowledge: theoretical foundations.* Englewood Cliffs, N.J.: Prentice-Hall, Inc., 1969. (a)

Furth, H. *Piaget for teachers.* Englewood Cliffs, N.J.: Prentice-Hall, Inc., 1969. (b)

Gagné, R. M. Varieties of learning and the concept of discovery. In L. S. Struhnan and E. R. Keislar (Eds.), *Learning by discovery: a critical appraisal.* Chicago: Rand McNally & Co., 1966, pp. 135-150.

Gallagher, J. J. *Teaching the gifted child.* Boston: Allyn & Bacon, Inc., 1964.

Galton, F. *Hereditary genius: an inquiry into its laws and consequences.* London: Macmillan, 1869.

Gesell, A., and Amatruda, C. S. *Developmental diagnosis.* New York: Paul B. Hoeber, Inc., 1941.

Getzels, J., and Jackson, P. *Creativity and intelligence.* New York: John Wiley & Sons, Inc., 1962.

Ginsburg, H., and Opper, S. *Piaget's theory of intellectual development.* Englewood Cliffs, N.J.: Prentice-Hall, Inc., 1969.

Glasser, W. *Schools without failure.* New York: Harper & Row, Publishers, 1969.

Guilford, J. P. Three faces of intellect. *American Psychologist,* 1959, *14*(8), 469-479.

Guilford, J. P. *The native of human intelligence.* New York: McGraw-Hill Book Co., 1967.

Guilford, J. P., and Hoepfner, R. *The analysis of intelligence.* New York: McGraw-Hill Book Co., 1971.

Haley, A. *The autobiography of Malcolm X.* Detroit: Grove Press, Inc., 1964.

Hall, M. A. *Teaching reading as a language experience.* Columbus, Ohio: Charles E. Merrill Publishing Co., 1970.

Haney, T. Creativity in a summer arts center. *NEA Journal,* March, 1961, 26-27.

Haring, N. G. (Ed.). *Behavior of exceptional children: an introduction to special education.* Columbus, Ohio: Charles E. Merrill Publishing Co., 1974.

Hendrick, J. *The whole child: new trends in early education.* St. Louis: The C. V. Mosby Co., 1975.

Herndon, J. *The way it spoze to be.* New York: Simon & Schuster, Inc., 1966.

Hunt, J. McV. *Intelligence and experience.* New York: The Ronald Press Co., 1961.

Hymes, J. R., Jr. *Teaching the child under six* (2nd ed.). Columbus, Ohio: Charles E. Merrill Publishing Co., 1974.

Jacobs, J. C. Are we being misled by fifty years of research on our gifted children? *Gifted Child Quarterly,* 1970, *14*(2), 120-133.

Jacobs, J. C. Effectiveness of teacher and parent identification of gifted children as a function of school label. *Psychology in the Schools,* 1971, *8*(2), 140-142.

Jersild, A. T. *In search of self.* New York: Teacher's College Press, 1952.

Jones, R. *Fantasy and feeling in education.* New York: New York University Press, 1968.

Jordan, C. Personal communication, 1976.

Kirk, S. A. *Educating exceptional children.* Boston: Houghton Mifflin Co., 1972.

Kirk, W. D. A tentative screening procedure for selecting bright and slow children in kindergarten. *Exceptional Children,* 1966, *33,* 235-241.

Kozol, J. *Death at an early age.* Boston: Houghton Mifflin Co., 1967.

Kubie, L. S. *Neurotic distortion of the creative process.* Lawrence, Kans.: University of Kansas Press, 1958.

Martinson, R. A. Children with superior cognitive abilities. In L. M. Dunn (Ed.), *Exceptional children in the schools: special education in transition* (2nd ed.). New York: Holt, Rinehart & Winston, Inc., 1973.

Mill, J. S. *Autobiography.* New York: Columbia University Press, 1924.

Payne, J. The gifted. In N. G. Haring (Ed.), *Behavior of exceptional children: an introduction to special education.* Columbus, Ohio: Charles E. Merrill Publishing Co., 1974, pp. 189-213.

Pegnato, C. W., and Birch, J. W. Locating gifted children in junior high schools: a comparison of methods. *Exceptional Children,* 1959, *25*(7), 300-304.

Piaget, J. *Play, dreams, and imitation in childhood.* New York: W. W. Norton & Co., Inc., 1951.

Piaget, J. *Six psychological studies.* New York: Random House, Inc., 1967.

Piaget, J., and Inhelder, B. *The psychology of the child.* New York: Basic Books, Inc., 1969.

Pressey, S. L. Concerning the nature and nurture of genius. *Scientific Monthly,* 1955, *81*(3), 123-129.

Renzulli, J. S. Talent potential in minority group students. *Exceptional Children,* 1973, *39*(6), 437-444.

Reynolds, M. C. A framework for considering some issues in special education. *Exceptional Children,* 1962, *29,* 367-370.

Rice, J. P. *The gifted: developing total talent.* Springfield, Ill.: Charles C Thomas, Publisher, 1970.

Rogers, C. Toward a theory of creativity. In H. H. Anderson (Ed.), *Creativity and its cultivation.* New York: Hayden & Brothers, 1959.

Rogers, C. *Freedom to learn.* Columbus, Ohio: Charles E. Merrill Publishing Co., 1969.

Rogers, V. R. *The English primary school.* New York: Macmillan Publishing Co., Inc., 1970.

Rosenthal, R., and Jacobson, L. *Pygmalion in the classroom.* New York: Holt, Rinehart & Winston, Inc., 1968.

Sherif, M., and Sherif, C. W. Reference groups. New York: Harper & Row, Publishers, 1964.

Shulman, L. S., and Keisler, E. R. (Eds.). *Learning by discovery: a critical appraisal.* Chicago: Rand McNally & Co., 1966.

Simmons, W. Personal communication, 1977.

Smilansky, S. *The effects of sociodramatic play on disadvantaged preschool children.* New York: John Wiley & Sons, Inc., 1968.

Spearman, C. *The abilities of man.* New York: Macmillan Publishing Co., Inc., 1927.

Suchman, J. R. Inquiry training: building skills for autonomous discovery. *Merrill-Palmer Quarterly of Behavioral Development,* 1961, *7,* 147-169.

Taba, H. Learning by discovery: psychological and educational rationale. *Elementary School Journal,* 1963, *63,* 308-316.

Taba, H. Teaching strategies and thought processes. *Teachers College Record,* 1964, *65,* 524-534.

Terman, L. M. Mental and physical traits of a thousand gifted children. In *Genetic studies of genius* (Vol. 1). Stanford, Calif.: Stanford University Press, 1925.

Terman, L. M. The discovery and encouragement of exceptional talent. *American Psychologist,* 1954, *9*(6), 221-230.

Terman, L. M., and Merrill, M. A. *Stanford-Binet intelligence scale: manual for the third revision—form L-M.* Boston: Houghton Mifflin Co., 1960.

Terman, L. M., and Oden, M. H. The gifted child grows up. In *Genetic studies of genius* (Vol. 4). Stanford, Calif.: Stanford University Press, 1947.

Thistlethwaite, D. L. The conservation of intellectual talent. *Science,* 1958, *128:* 822-826.

Thurstone, L. L. *The nature of intelligence,* New York: Harcourt, Brace & World, 1926.

Thurstone, L. L. *The vectors of the mind.* Chicago: University of Chicago Press, 1935.

Torrance, E. P. *Rewarding creative behavior: experiments in classroom creativity.* Englewood Cliffs, N.J.: Prentice-Hall, Inc., 1965.

Torrance, E. P. *Torrance tests of creative thinking.* Lexington, Mass.: Personnel Press, 1966.

Torrance, E. P., and Myers, R. E. *Creative learning and teaching.* New York: Dodd, Mead & Co., 1970.

Treffinger, D. J., and Gowan, J. C. An updated representative list of methods and education programs for stimulating creativity. *Journal of Creative Behavior,* 1971, *5*(2), 127-139.

Weber, L. *The English infant school and informal education.* Englewood Cliffs, N.J.: Prentice-Hall, Inc., 1971.

Wechsler, D. *The measurement of adult intelligence* (3rd ed.). Baltimore: The Williams & Wilkins Co., 1944.

Weissman, L. I., and Safford, P. L. Piagetian tasks as classroom evaluative tools. *Elementary School Journal,* 1971, *71,* 329-338.

White, R. W. Motivation reconsidered: the concept of competence. *Psychological Review,* 1959, *66,* 293.

Yamamoto, K. Relationships between creative thinking abilities of teachers and achievement and adjustment of pupils. *Journal of Experimental Education,* 1963, *32*(1), 3-25.

Dimensions of the least restrictive alternative

CHAPTER 11

LEAST RESTRICTIVE ENVIRONMENTS

ENVIRONMENT AND DEVELOPMENT

Descriptions of normal developmental sequence, such as that provided by Piaget, make a fundamental assumption: *Given an intact organism interacting with a normal environment, development progresses in a predictable fashion.* If these conditions are present, educational experiences facilitate development, but education need not be interventive. However, if either condition is not met, intervention is required to enable the effective child-environment relationship, on which development depends, to occur.

The child's environment may be limiting because of the absence of opportunities to explore, discover, experience, and solve problems; poor or ineffective language models; sensory deprivation; or an inadequate affectional base on which to build a sense of trust and competence and the ability to love.

On the other hand, the objective environment may be adequate but a handicapping condition may impair or limit the child's ability to experience it. Obvious examples of conditions that impede sensory-motor learning are severe visual and auditory handicaps and limited mobility caused by a physical disability. Speech and language disabilities, perceptual problems, and emotional disturbance also impose limits of distortions on these environmental interactions, which are essential to development.

Intervention may take the form of attempts to *change the child* directly. Examples include the use of prosthetic devices, surgery, diet or vitamin therapy, and psychotropic drugs. Educational approaches, however, always involve attempts to modify the *environment* with which the child interacts. Education is used here generically to include specialized therapies, parent and/or child counseling or psychotherapy, adaptive physical education, and so forth as well as the work of the teacher in the classroom.

A basic premise is that, without accommodations to the specific needs of the individual child with a handicapping condition, the environment that he experiences is restrictive. Therefore the discussion that follows focuses on the theme of *least restrictive environments* for young children with special needs.

In a broader sense, this entire book is an attempt to elaborate this very theme. Teaching young handicapped children always, almost by definition, implies planned environmental modifications. The goal is to enable the child to interact with an environment that is conducive to the realization of his fullest potential. The focus of this particular chapter, however, is primarily on what has been called the physicosocial environment (Wohlwill, 1970). We shall here examine some of the dimensions of physical and social settings in which young children are taught and consider some elements of these settings that may make them least restrictive.

USE OF SPACE AS A DIMENSION OF TEACHING

One of the most important dimensions of the teacher's role is that involving the use of space. In a real sense, the teacher creates the environment in which learning occurs. It is therefore useful to have in mind some general guidelines for environmental space planning, even though the specific environment itself cannot be prescribed. How these guidelines are applied by the teacher in designing a learning environment may vary greatly.

The basic principle is that the teacher can *use* physical space to create opportunities for the kinds of child-environment transactions that stimulate learning. It is helpful for the teacher to approach this part of his or her role in the same way an environmental designer or design engineer might, identifying first the desired outcomes and then the means by which these can be facilitated (Small, 1973). Such a planning mode can suggest a much wider variety of options than are usually attempted for design of an early childhood classroom. Relative locations of areas within a room become important. So do both the manner in which these are provisioned and the guidelines established for their use by children.

The dimensions of light, sound, traffic patterns, and visual impact should be considered from the perspective of the children in arranging the environment. Furniture and play equipment and materials, as Montessori stressed, should be child sized. Beyond the basic and essential consideration of providing for physical safety of the children, most classrooms suggest a multitude of alternative arrangements of learning areas, equipment, storage, etc. Decisions of what should go where should not be made arbitrarily, but with a specific plan in mind.

ATTRIBUTES OF LEAST RESTRICTIVE ENVIRONMENTS

In view of the important role ascribed to environment in early learning (Hunt, 1961, 1969) and the evidence of harmful effects of restricted, barren, or depriving environments on young children (Spitz, 1945; Dennis and Najarian, 1957; Yarrow, 1961), the environment is an area of early education worthy of intensive analysis and study. Consequently, major comprehensive texts dealing with early education emphasize the significance of an environment that is as conducive to learning as possible (for example, Todd and Heffernan, 1970; Hendrick, 1976; Leeper et al., 1968; Hess and Croft, 1972).

Scientific analysis of the relationship between influences in the physical and social environment and human behavior has been reflected in the development of a distinct branch of psychological inquiry (Wohlwill, 1966, 1970). An approach known as ecological psychology (Barker and Wright, 1949; Barker, 1965; Wright, 1967) emphasizes the *naturalistic* study of children's development and behavior within an environmental context, rather than assuming that children function independently of continuous, ongoing environmental influences.

In recent years, early childhood educators have increasingly focused attention on the characteristics of good learning environments for young children. A young handicapped child, whatever his disability, presents unique needs calling for specific environmental modifications. The observations presented here cannot serve as a prescription. However, if handicapped children *by definition* experience deprived environments (Caldwell, 1973), teaching these children requires particular attention to environmental considerations. These dimensions of learning environments for young children do not in themselves necessarily imply specific modifications for children with certain forms of handicap. However, working with environments from these perspectives can serve to make them "least restrictive" for young handicapped and gifted children.

Learning environments for young children with special needs are here considered in terms of the following general dimensions or characteristics:
1. Accessibility
2. Safety
3. Flexibility or adaptability
4. Aesthetic appeal and evocativeness
5. Responsiveness
6. Normalcy

Accessibility: the first requisite

Transportation. The most basic consideration in terms of environmental suitability is the program's accessibility to the child. This dimension is first of all reflected in the provisions that are made for transportation. Children whose mobility is limited require assistance entering and exiting from a bus. Wheelchair-bound children need to be helped out of and into their chairs, or the chair itself is lifted. Some vehicles are especially equipped to accommodate children in wheelchairs, having both the necessary space on board and a lift platform that automatically raises the handicapped individual in a wheelchair to a level with the vehicle door and lowers him to the ground. On board, means of securing the chairs are provided. Young physically handicapped children need to be accompanied by adult riders on the vehicle to ensure their safety. Special adapted seats may be needed.

A recurring problem has been presented when a public school has been willing to accommodate a handicapped child and he could be picked up and returned home via regular school bus services. However, the child must be lifted onto and off the bus, a task that the driver may be unwilling to do or may be prevented from doing, possibly by union regulations. Usually, it is extremely difficult for a member either of the school staff or the child's family to ride along to handle this responsibility. In many instances, the child's attendance and participation in a "least restrictive" environment have been possible only because the building principal or a teacher has been willing, day after day, regardless of whatever conflicting responsibilities might threaten to interfere, to meet the bus in the morning to help the child off and to help him back on at the end of the day, with the parent handling it at the other end.

Special transportation needs may be presented by children with forms of handicap other than physical ones as well; however, transporting physically handicapped children presents the greatest challenge in view of the expense that may be involved if specially designed vehicles must be used. Since difficulties in transporting a child are not justifiable reasons for a school's inability to enroll him, it is incumbent upon school personnel to arrange for safe and suitable transportation, for the handicapped child as for any other.

In nonpublic school programs, such as day care centers or private or cooperative nursery schools, greater responsibility may fall to the parents of all children for transporting. Whatever the setting, and whether or not outside funding is involved, a spirit of cooperative problem solving among the parents and staff members will prove the most valuable resource in resolving difficulties concerning transporting the children as well as other issues. A variety of community resources can be brought to bear, and in every community there is a latent, if not very visible, wealth of volunteer resources that can be enlisted.

Removing physical barriers. In addition to transportation, another dimension of the issue of accessibility relates to architectural barriers. Great strides have been made in recent years in modifying public buildings and in constructing new buildings to accommodate, rather than exclude—and thereby discriminate against—handicapped persons. Such features as the width of doorways, ease with which doors can be opened from a wheelchair, provision of ramps, etc. are important considerations in the early childhood education setting as in any other. Location of the classroom has historically been a source of difficulty in many instances, with children having been excluded from an otherwise appropriate program by its location on an upper floor and the lack of elevators. Such exclusion is no longer justifiable, if it ever was. Whether through relocation of the classroom or installation of elevators, the child must be served, and without compromise in the area of safety considerations. When the program involves use of more than one facility within a building—other classrooms, playground, gymnasium, lunchroom, special activity areas, an auditorium, etc.—similar provisions must be made to ensure that the handicapped child can participate in all activities from which he is capable of deriving benefit without restriction by physical barriers or limitations.

In the area of physical barriers, a special set of problems and needs concerns bathroom facilities. In all early childhood programs, a lavatory should, of course, be adjacent to the classroom or contained within it. In some older public school buildings, lavatories located in the basement have presented seemingly insoluble problems (which now, of course, must be solved). The lavatory itself should be designed and arranged in such a way as to facilitate its use by a child who uses crutches or a walker or who is confined to a wheelchair. This requires appropriate placement of bars, attention to stall doors, and a variety of other concerns of which planners of new buildings are increasingly aware. As a general principle, directors, supervisors, and teachers in any setting serving children should seek assistance and consultation from appropriate specialists to ensure that lavatory facilities, and other aspects of the physical arrangement, are suitable. *It is the school's responsibility to accommodate the child.*

Safety

Excessive concern for the special safety needs of handicapped children sometimes leads us to protect them from experiences they need. This concern may cause a teacher or parent to "protect" the child when what he needs is the opportunity to set out on his own. Like all young children, the handicapped child needs to experience mastery and a sense of competence.

The child with a handicapping condition may also have a particular need for assurance that adult support or assistance will be provided when and if they are needed. Beyond that, safety considerations are basically identical to those for the nonhandicapped child. Some key areas include the following:

1. *Toys and other materials.* Recently, we have been made more aware of the positively dangerous features of some play materials. Toxic substances, easily breakable items, and things that can cut or pinch are not usually appropriate for any small child, whether handicapped or not. Every year, many children are maimed because of the continued marketing of dangerous toys.
2. *Equipment.* Unsturdy play equip-

ment can be dangerous for non-handicapped children, as well as those who have special needs.
3. *Placement of areas and equipment.* One obvious example of an unsafe arrangement, and one that is often seen in children's play areas, is placement of play space too near a swing. Attention should be given to traffic patterns (Small, 1973), and designated areas need to be made safe for active play.

Flexibility or adaptability

For a teacher to be able to adapt the learning environment to the specific needs of individual children, it must have the property of adaptability or flexibility. This means different things in different classrooms or centers. Although some rooms may have some inherent adaptive properties (such as discrete areas defined by the shape of the room, the existence of "nooks and crannies"), the problem is more commonly one of transforming a basically unpromising space into an area appropriate for young children. The flexibility is usually not built in; it is *designed* by the teacher through the way the room is divided, arranged, and provisioned. Needs may change, and probably should, as the teacher continues to study the children's individual patterns of interaction with their learning environment.

Whether a learning environment is flexible and adaptive really depends on how it is used. As Hewett (1968) has pointed out, the teacher *controls* the environment of the classroom. It is not an oversimplification to state that *flexible teachers create flexible environments.*

Esthetic appeal and evocativeness

Regardless of how a school environment may be judged from a *functional* standpoint, it is unusual to find one that is a place of beauty. Here is one particularly searing indictment:

Most schools give their students a powerful and effective esthetic education: they teach them that interest in the arts is effeminate or effete, that study of the arts is a frill, and that music, art, beauty, and sensitivity are specialized phenomena that bear no relationship to life. The schools teach these lessons in a variety of ways. The most important, perhaps, is the lesson that is taught by the ugliness of the buildings themselves: the barrenness of the walls, the absence of flowers, paintings, sculpture, and music; in short, the esthetic sterility of the entire environment. (Silberman, 1970, pp. 183-184)

An important idea conveyed in Silberman's criticism of the ugliness of many learning environments is that the appreciation of beauty should not be regarded as important only to the few; it is of value to all. Young handicapped children have esthetic needs to be nurtured, as do all young children. Too often, however, almost exclusive attention is devoted to their problem, disability, or deficiency. Unfortunately, providing for the child's esthetic development and encouraging him to experience the richness of beauty frequently ranks low on the list of educational priorities for handicapped children.

Among the dimensions, or characteristics, of learning environments for young children is one that has been called "softness" (Prescott et al., 1971). This concept has been applied by Elizabeth Prescott and her associates at Pacific Oaks College to the development of a scale for assessing preschool environments—called, of course, a softness scale. Using this scale, as summarized by Gloria Small (1973), the "softness" of the environment is determined on the basis of the relative presence or absence of the following:

1. Child/adult cozy furniture: rockers, couches, lawn swings, etc.
2. Large rug or full carpeting indoors
3. Grass that children can be on
4. Sand that children can be in, either in a box or other area
5. Dirt to dig in
6. Animals that can be held (usually guinea pigs)
7. Single sling swings

8. Play dough
9. Water as an activity
10. Very messy materials such as finger-paint, clay, mud
11. "Laps"—teachers holding children (p. 111)

Beauty and "softness" are two aspects of the evocativeness of an early learning environment. Whether a center or classroom, an area, or an item is evocative for young children cannot be judged on the basis of its apparent or intrinsic merits. Children tell us by what they do—by whether their imagination and industry are called forth.

Responsiveness

The idea of a responsive environment for young children (Nimnicht, 1972) is based in part on Robert White's (1959) concept of *effectance motivation*. The young child has a need to be *competent* in interacting with his environment, to observe the *effects* of his own actions, and to have a *sense of competence* or of being effective. Responsive environments contain objects and materials that respond to the child's actions—that give him *feedback*. This feedback contributes both to his learning and to positive feelings about himself.

It is recognized that children respond to stimuli in their environment and that environmental influences can bring about changes in behavior. However, development is interactive. The child is not simply a passive "responder," but an active *agent* (Gordon, 1966) who affects the physical things with which he interacts.

Responsive environments emphasize opportunities for children to act and to gain feedback from their own activity. Consequently, materials that are autotelic or self-correcting may be valuable. These include manipulable materials of the sort developed by Maria Montessori and possibly technological innovations such as the Language Master, "listening posts," O. K. Moore's "talking typewriter" (Moore and Anderson, 1968), and so forth.

There are special reasons for attention to the responsiveness of the learning environment in teaching young children with special needs. A young handicapped child may have been limited in his ability to experience a sense of competence gained through mastery and accomplishment. A responsive early learning environment can help to provide opportunities for the child to grow in autonomy, independence, and feelings that he is an effective person.

Normalcy

Learning environments for young children with special needs should be as normal as possible. Wolf Wolfensberger (1972) advocates having as few "special" articles and features in an environment for handicapped persons as possible. Specialized equipment identifies the users as *deviant* and therefore as *devalued*. Whenever possible, this should be avoided. The task is to adapt the environment as much

as is necessary, while avoiding stigmatizing the handicapped child through inordinate use of equipment, materials, or other physical features or modes of use that mark the child as "different." There may be some needs for specialized adaptive furniture and equipment. However, their use should not exceed what is essential. Whether in classroom or play or recreational setting, achieving an atmosphere of normalcy is a desirable end in itself.

LEARNING CENTERS: VEHICLES FOR INDIVIDUALIZED TEACHING

All behavior occurs in an environmental context and is influenced in important ways by some aspects of the physical setting and the social setting. It is not only the *objective* environment to which we respond; our actions are related to our *perceptions* of physical factors and those involving people with whom we interact. It is a *psychological* environment, Kurt

Lewin (1935) theorized, that influences what we do.

This insight can be of great value to the teacher. It clarifies why individual children respond so differently to particular features of the classroom, and it emphasizes the importance of attempting to consider the matter of space utilization from the vantage point of the child, rather than the adult teacher.

Attempting to accomplish the latter, Gloria Small (1973) assisted Head Start and day care teachers to view room arrangements quite literally from the standpoint of the 3-, 4-, and 5-year-old children who used them. Photographs of activity centers, taken at children's eye level, revealed in some instances confusion, impediments, and "visual clutter" in equipment arrangements, displays, and access patterns; at adult eye level, these appeared orderly, systematically planned, and convenient. Resulting rearrangements of rooms were carried out using specific design criteria, consideration of curricular purposes and objectives, and informal assessment of the characteristics and responses. Basically, the teachers who participated in this project added to their repertoire of teaching skills some of the insights and techniques of the environmental designer.

As individualization is the key to successful integration in a "regular" classroom setting of a child with special needs, as well as being desirable for all children, organization of the physical environment is a basic and essential component of individualization. Although there are alternative approaches to individualization, these approaches have in common a provision for *simultaneous operation of diverse activities*. Decentralization of the classroom, as John Thomas (1975) has termed it, implies the need for learning space divisible into as many discrete subenvironments as are needed, each one explicitly designed in such a way as to facilitate the sort of activity intended to take place within it. In early education classrooms, these subenvironments are often called learning centers, and they may include such centers as the following:

Sociodramatic play area, which may include the "housekeeping" center

Area including sand and water table, possibly combined with other quiet constructive or discovery materials

Group listening center ("story and music" area)

Sufficiently large and open area for large muscle (gross motor) activity, possibly combining exercise (for example, a balance beam), dance and movement, and wheeled vehicles

Carpentry area

Block area

Fine motor area, including tables and accessible shelves on which are kept appropriate materials (for perceptual and fine motor tasks, order and sequencing tasks, experiment and discovery, cognitive tasks involving classification, etc.)

Reading "corner" for simultaneous individual use of several children

Some considerations that are necessary in making effective use of such learning center classroom design—which are important for all children, but especially so for children with special needs—are the following:

1. Boundaries between centers should be sufficiently clearly established to prevent undue spillover, yet sufficiently flexible to allow for desirable variations in activity.

2. Boundaries between centers should not be fragile or insufficiently secure, for safety as well as learning value reasons.

3. Care must be given to the location of centers in relation to each other, to minimize distraction, both visual and auditory.

4. Floor covering is an important component of the environment of each center; block play, some gross motor activities, and other activities may require an uncarpeted surface.

5. Center design and location should take into account needs for direct adult oversight and participation, where appropriate.

6. Accessibility to centers within a room is just as important as accessibility of the room and building themselves.

Although what comprises the actual physical setting of the classroom is certainly very important, the use of space must be planned in relationship to the use of time. For example, the actual number of children who use a particular area of the room at any given time is based on planning and scheduling for individual children and for the group. Once these considerations are addressed, the physical setting of a specific area may be designed to facilitate, rather than interfere with, the intended use. This principle has implications, not only for the actual size of each activity area, but for the equipment and materials it contains as well. The physical setting, as well as the purposes, objectives, and planned activities that constitute the curriculum, should be developed and adapted to fit the children served, rather than the reverse.

In developing learning centers or activity areas, the teacher can consider questions such as the following:

What is the organizing principle of the center?

What sorts of child activities are consistent with this organizing principle?

How many children should be able to engage in these activities at any given time?

How much actual space is needed?

How should the center be provisioned to facilitate these activities?

How should materials be placed, displayed, or stored to arouse interest and curiosity and be accessible, but not overstimulating?

Where should the center be located in relationship to other areas to provide for physical safety, accessibility, appropriate light and temperature, etc., and to minimize distraction?

One useful approach in developing a center is to follow a principle of gradual expansion. For example, rather than suddenly creating a "rich environment" for order tasks involving fine motor skills (for example, puzzles, pegboards, formboards), such materials may be introduced one by one and children can be initially guided in their use, one item at a time. As more items and activities become available, a gradually increasing number of children can be involved at the same time. This approach can serve to minimize confusion, nonpurposeful activity, inappropriate use of materials and loss of parts, conflict between children, and the difficulty some children may have in experiencing a sense of competence when they are simply "exposed" to the materials, no matter how much intrinsic merit the materials may have. Teachers who have attempted to introduce a new set of games all at once to their first-grade pupils are well aware of the frustrations that may ensue for both the adult and the children.

The needs of handicapped children in such areas as these are essentially no different from those of all children, although they may be more pronounced. Auditory distraction in the form of extraneous noise is difficult for most young children to tolerate, but for a child with impaired hearing it may be disastrous. Ensuring that children can move about safely and comfortably is universally necessary, but for a visually impaired, blind, or orthopedically handicapped child it becomes a consideration of paramount importance. Providing opportunities for gradual mastery of specific tasks is important for all, but for the child who is mentally retarded it is particularly essential. Minimizing visual and auditory distraction facilitates all young children's ability to structure their own activity in a purposeful and satisfying way; it is particularly helpful for those who may have minimal or severe perceptual processing disturbances.

ALTERNATIVE ENVIRONMENTAL MODELS

It is likely that a teacher's consideration of the special learning needs of a child with a handicap will lead him or her to discover materials, organizational patterns, procedures for observing and recording behavior, and strategies for ensuring motivation that are applicable to and beneficial for all or most of the children he or she teaches. With respect to the physical environment itself, approaches such as Hewett's engineered classroom (Hewett, 1968) and materials developed originally out of experiences with youngsters with special needs by Séguin (1866), Montessori (1966), Kephart (1971), Frostig and Horne (1964), and other pioneers have been widely incorporated into "regular" early education programs.

Some models for early childhood education programs, conversely, offer different kinds of advantages for young children with handicapping conditions. Although rarely is any one of these models found in "pure" form—that is, most teachers of young children create an environment that draws from many sources and that bears their own, unique stamp—it may be instructive to consider several distinctly different approaches in relationship to the child with special needs. The particular approaches selected here differ from each other in an especially pronounced way in terms of the sort of learning environment implied by each. Many variants and combinations of each of these are possible.

Structured classroom

In the field of special education, the importance of *structure* has been emphasized particularly by William Cruickshank et al. (1961), Norris G. Haring and E. Lakin Phillips (1962), and Frank Hewett (1968). Cruickshank (1975) has maintained that, for a child with neurological impairment, the ordering of experience, maintenance of attention, ability to screen out irrelevant and distracting stimuli, and other prerequisites for meaningful learning are especially difficult. Neurological involvement resulting in such difficulties may be found in a great many mentally retarded children (those to whom the term "exogenous retardation" has been applied), children with cerebral palsy (especially spasticity), children with "minimal" or specific learning disabilities, and children identified as behavior disordered whose activity is characterized by impulsivity, short attention span, and various forms of acting out. Cruickshank therefore prescribed that visual, auditory, and even tactile and kinesthetic stimulation be minimized and focused, each child's activity be carefully planned and monitored, and classroom and program arrangements be designed to increase gradually the child's tolerance for distraction and complexity, rather than to overwhelm the child. In the "Syracuse study," Cruickshank et al. (1961) concluded that these principles were appropriate for *hyperactive* children whether or not brain damage could be conclusively established.

Building on Cruickshank's work, Haring and Phillips (1962) extended it in three important ways. In an experimental program comparing a structured approach with alternative modes of classroom design and organization, they found the structured approach superior as reflected in both achievement and personal-social adjustment for a group of children identified as *emotionally disturbed,* including some who were neither hyperactive nor inclined to engage in acting-out behavior of any kind. Their method also emphasized the application of behavior modification through the use of planned contingency control—that is, differential *reinforcement* of desired and inappropriate behaviors by means of a systematic observation procedure and reward schedule. This technique is based on the assumption that behavior persists if it is rewarded. Simply put, environmental events that are contingent on the specific behaviors we emit are the conditions that motivate us to change those behaviors. Change can take the form of increased or decreased frequency, elimination *(extinction)*, or gradual extension *(shaping through successive approximations)*.

The third area in which Haring and Phillips extended the structured environment was to extend its scope. Consistency in child management from classroom to home and neighborhood is assumed to be advantageous, but to ensure maximal impact of the structured learning approach and contingency management system it was thought to be particularly important. For example, a rewarding consequence of parental *attention* in response to excessive dependency behavior might be counterproductive if classroom procedures involved planned ignoring such behavior but reinforcement of independent activity, self-reliance, and autonomy.

It is in Frank Hewett's (1968) further refinement of these concepts that the relationship between classroom structure and developmental sequence is made most explicit. Although writing specifically about the emotionally disturbed child, Hewett made clear that the principles of a hierarchy of developmental levels, planned task selection, systematic reward, and structure were applicable in teaching the educationally handicapped child, regardless of the origins of his problems in learning or personal and social development.

Open classroom

During the late 1960s, along with revolutionary stirrings on many fronts, there seemed to be the potential for a major reform of the American educational system—a total rethinking and restructuring. The "lockstep" age-grade structure, "egg crate" school buildings, and "preoccupation with control" (Silberman, 1970) were attacked, and students everywhere across the nation, including eventually even those of elementary school level, began to be to some degree politi-

cized, at least with respect to their own life in school.

Four of the most vigorous and outspoken critics of American schools, John Holt (1964), Jonathan Kozol (1967), Herbert Kohl (1969), and James Herndon (1966), began to describe not only what was wrong with schools but the way schools *could be.* Through their efforts and those of a great many other deeply concerned and committed parents, students, and professionals, an American version of the *child-centered learning community* began to emerge.

Parallel to these events, and influencing them in significant ways, were the continuing evolution and spread of the informal education, or *integrated day,* approach in British primary schools (Featherstone, 1967; Brown and Precious, 1970; Blackie, 1967; Rogers, 1970). The term "integrated day" implies awareness that it is the child himself who structures his daily learning experiences. In a sense a sort of historical accident—having been born almost out of necessity during World War II—this set of ideas about learning and teaching increasingly attracted the attention of American educators, such as Lillian Weber (1971), who then set up pilot programs in the United States. Weber's work in particular directly addressed the issue of the applicability of informal, child-centered methods in the education of American children of low socioeconomic level. Although the famous Plowden Report (Central Advisory Council, 1967) revealed that these informal integrated day schools could be found in low income communities as well as among the more privileged, the concern persisted that English children might be "different" with regard to socialization influences. It was thought that perhaps this system was appropriate in England because of a respect for adult authority and for learning that transcended social class.

Applications of the British primary school approach through Project Head Start and Project Follow Through, as well as the creation of "free schools," "pride schools," and alternative school variations for economically disadvantaged children would seem to have demonstrated its value. However, there is strong feeling among some parents that children of low income families and cultural minority backgrounds have particular needs to acquire academic, linguistic, and social skills through their schooling in order to ultimately become successful. There probably continues to be a lack of confidence in educational methods that do not appear to be directly bringing about these skills through direct, structured teaching.

Finally, "open classroom" is a deceptively difficult concept about which to communicate. It means radically different things to different teachers. To some, it conjures up images of chaotic and purposeless activity of "play, play, play" (Hymes, 1974), of the absence of rules and constraints, of rampant permissiveness. Some teachers describe their approach as "open" when to other observers it appears teacher directed, prescriptive, and externally structured in the extreme. Descriptions of more specific aspects of the approach would seem more fruitful, particularly to judge its applicability for handicapped children. Environmental features are related directly to conceptions of how children learn, in this approach (or cluster of approaches) as in any other. Therefore the notions about children's learning and motivation on which informal learning environments are predicated will be briefly mentioned.

Advocates of the British primary school approach claim support for their methods in the theories of Jean Piaget (for example, Inhelder and Piaget, 1969) and in the work of Susan Isaacs (1929/1968, 1971), rather than "stimulus-response" theories. The child is believed to be naturally inclined to learn and, given a rich environment with which to interact, he will learn. The child structures his own learning, and each child consequently must to a large extent pursue his own individual course.

Learning does not determine development; rather development encompasses both environmental transactions and internal changes in the child's thought (Piaget, 1967). Thinking is inherently based on activity by the child, whether overt and physical or covert and "mental." The child's mind is not a container into which knowledge is poured nor a sponge nor a telephone switchboard. His manner of learning is more accurately described by the Chinese proverb that states that only *doing,* rather than seeing or hearing, can bring about true understanding—by John Dewey's maxim, "learning by doing."

According to this view, children do not need to be rewarded by others for them to be encouraged to continue to learn. Their efforts are elicited in response to *intrinsic* motives, rather than *extrinsic* rewards. Briefly, these intrinsic sources of motivation include a natural curiosity and consequent need to discover, to resolve uncertainty, to *find out,* as well as a need to master the environment and achieve a sense of mastery, competence, and autonomy.

The British system and most of the "free school" or "alternative school" variations also place great emphasis on the value of children's cooperative activity. The concept of *family grouping* (Brown and Precious, 1970) suggests that learning groups ideally should span several ages, rather than be homogeneously assigned by age.

There is little information available concerning the appropriateness of the "open classroom" concept as such, for young handicapped children. However, Rose Engle and Beatrice Gold (1974) describe an application of this approach with 3- through 7-year-old orthopedically handicapped, trainable mentally retarded, and "educationally handicapped" children. They report that an informal, open, and age-integrated style seems effective in facilitating growth in communication through children's interaction as well as in promoting greater individual independence.

The ideas of integrated curriculum, learning experiences, family grouping, learning centers, and active learning would seem to suggest valuable ways of teaching young children with special needs.

Montessori approach

The system and specific methods of education developed by Maria Montessori are distinctive in many respects. One of the most striking features of the Montessori method (Montessori, 1912) is the learning environment it involves. In the Montessori approach, one can readily observe the interplay of physical and human factors in the evoution of an *environment* that is really indivisible into these two broad elements.

The Montessori classroom is characterized, perhaps most of all, by a high degree of *respect*. This respect is reflected in the way teachers guide children, the way children interact with each other, and the way all, adults and children, handle the physical materials. The Montessori approach can be termed a "materials-centered" approach, but this is in fact an oversimplification. The materials themselves and the way they are used are integrally interrelated with the central role of the child in his own learning and with the extremely important role of the teacher—the adult—as guide and model. Incongruously, the Montessori approach is regarded by some as a highly (perhaps overly) structured system, whereas others see in it close similarity to the British "informal" approach. On visiting a Montessori classroom, one is in fact likely to be struck by two first impressions: the impression of orderly, purposeful activity being carried on in a very quiet manner and an impression that individual learning pace, interest, and preference are respected and the ability to work independently and autonomously is valued and cultivated.

Maria Montessori's pedagogical contributions have been related to the theories of Piaget, whose contributions to education have been, perhaps, less direct (Elkind, 1970), since her system is predicated on observation and beliefs concerning the growth of children's minds. Her concept of *sensitive periods* emphasizes the importance of the match between a child's cognitive and personality developmental readiness and the tasks he undertakes. For Montessori, the child is by his very nature curious and thirsty for knowledge (Montessori, 1967) and capable of persistent and diligent effort. Her analyses of children's work patterns pointed up what she considered the fallacy in attributing to children a "short attention span," suggesting instead that children will demonstrate *false fatigue,* but if the adult erroneously believes that interest is waning and productivity is near an end, the child will be deprived of the opportunity to enter his *period of great work.*

Like Piaget, Montessori emphasized the importance of *activity* in learning and the interrelatedness of all dimensions of children's development—sensory and motor, intellectual, personal, social, and, Montessori would add, spiritual. Learning in the Montessori classroom is determined far more by the child's interaction with his physical environment than with either his peers or with the adult teacher. Teaching becomes a matter of enabling the child to use properly and effectively the materials that can enable his mind to grow. She would accept Piaget's distinction between social knowledge and the kind of knowledge that is determined by the interaction of evolving mental structures with an environment that encourages and stimulates growth. *Teaching is not telling.*

Although the most important dimension of the Montessori classroom environment is the kind of "climate" described above, the specific materials themselves have a very significant role. Her sensorial materials, for example, are painstakingly designed to be virtually self-correcting and to take into account the process by which perceptual and motor processes interact and contribute to the acquisition of concepts. Consequently, single-concept tasks precede those that require the simultaneous handling of two or more concepts (for example, form, color, and size). Puzzles, cylinder blocks, and other items have small knobs designed to develop finger-thumb opposition while also avoiding interference caused by difficulties in manipulation. The materials follow a definite sequence. Although a child may work with specific items for as long as he wishes, before he uses any of the materials he must be guided, through demonstration, in their proper use. He must also be sure that they are returned to their proper location, intact, when he is finished.

Disadvantages or possible shortcomings of the Montessori classroom as a learning environment have been identified by some critics in at least five basic areas: (1) Not all Montessori settings adhere equally well to the tenets of the approach, and it is possible, in fact, to find some Montessori programs that are rigid, authoritarian, and punitive and others that are even disorderly. (2) It is a doctrinaire system, at least as practiced by some of its adherents, and consequently risks "fitting the child to the program, rather than the program to the child." There is, furthermore, a rift among Montessorians as to what constitutes the "true" Montessori approach. (3) It does not encourage fantasy or imaginative creation through spontaneous individual or social play, movement, construction, or the arts; in fact, it deemphasizes the importance of play itself. (4) It places little emphasis on children's application of spoken language skills and tends to minimize the value of direct, overt, social interaction in learning. (5) The materials prescribed are quite costly, and well-equipped programs run by appropriately trained teachers are expensive to operate.

Some would say that the more "authentic" the class, the more truly congruent with Maria Montessori's educational philosophy and method, the more likely it will be that these potential limitations and problems will be mitigated. Others would affirm exactly the opposite position: that Montessori has contributed important dimensions to early childhood education, but Montessori programs that are at least somewhat eclectic, drawing from other sources as well, are better for children. The reader is strongly urged to make a careful study, both of Montessori's ideas as contained in her writing and of a *number* of Montessori classrooms before making a judgment. Her rejection out of hand by the American educational establishment in the early years of this century seems tragic indeed, in light of the magnitude of her work and the sensitivity of her observations of children. The persistent relative ignorance concerning her work on the part of the majority of early childhood educators today is no less tragic.

Since Maria Montessori developed her system through her efforts with children of the poor and children thought to be of limited ability, it is surprising that most American children enrolled today seem to be of more affluent families and, excluding isolated special programs, are not likely to be slow to learn. In fact, many parents regard the Montessori approach as best suited to gifted children and perhaps as something of a status symbol. Although it has not been well established that the Montessori system, with its perceptual learning emphasis, is effective in remedying (or preventing) learning disabilities, there is certainly a strong basis for undertaking research to determine its effectiveness. Regarding behavioral disorders, it may be that a Montessori climate is "just right" for some children with such problems, but for others fails to provide sufficiently for specialized emotional and behavioral needs.

Whether the Montessori approach

would be appropriate as part of an educational prescription for a handicapped child—that is, whether the child should or should not be placed in a Montessori setting—is an important issue and one that has really not been sufficiently well studied. Limiting problems include the cost of Montessori programs (traditionally and still usually borne entirely by parents) and the wide variability among both Montessori programs and handicapped children. However, many aspects of the Montessori environment can be replicated in a manner that lends itself well to the effort to indiviualize for all children, including those with special needs. Some of the most important of these aspects relate to materials and equipment considerations, others to method. Most basically, however, there is a less readily definable *quality* found in the Montessori environment, which is compounded of respect, trust, faith, love, and industry. It is this quality that would seem most valuable in teaching young children with special needs.

PLAYGROUNDS

Outdoor play is an important component of an educational program for young children, and principles and techniques of design can guide the development of areas for such activity in addition to the classroom. A design expert might first ask questions such as "Who are the users?" "What are their characteristics and their needs?" "What are the purposes and objectives to be achieved through the use of this space?" and "What special considerations concerning the use of this space must be borne in mind?"

Some "special considerations" affecting playground design, with which a great many early childhood educators are quite familiar, include the following:

1. It is necessary to ensure the physical safety of the children.
2. Outdoor playground equipment is likely to be used at times when no adult supervision is available and by children other than those enrolled in the program.

3. Destruction and theft of equipment are often a serious problem.

Ideally, an outdoor play area is an extension of the classroom, so that fluid movement in and out at certain times is possible. Some activities, such as carpentry, may require such fluidity (see, for example, descriptions of the integrated day approach used in British Infant Schools, as described in Blackie, 1967, and Brown and Precious, 1970). Often, however, this inside-outside "flow" is difficult, if not impossible, to attain because of inherent limitations in location, budget, or both.

Generally, playground design can be considered from the standpoint of the criteria for environments mentioned previously:

1. *Accessibility:* Can the equipment be readily used by the child in as independent a fashion as possible?

2. *Safety:* Has due regard been given to each child's safety in access and in operation of equipment and use of play space?

3. *Flexibility or adaptability:* Can equipment and areas be adapted to various uses? Can things be rearranged, moved, or altered to suit changing needs?

4. *Aesthetic appeal and evocativeness:* Outdoor play space can be arranged in such a way as to stimulate exploration and imagination. Things to climb or enter or crawl under can evoke imaginative individual and group play. Uneven terrain with hills and valleys makes for a more intriguing play area than does a flat surface. To create a perfect blend of play apparatus and material with natural surroundings—shrubs, trees, running water, grass, flowers, an herb garden, etc.—may require an architect's or designer's talents. However, this kind of blend can be inexpensively achieved, to some degree, in almost any outdoor play space.

5. *Responsiveness:* Young children's outdoor play can be genuinely adventurous. The child's imagination can be aroused through fantasy play, and he can experience exhilarating movement—and risk taking. Activities and equipment that the child can control contribute to his

sense of competence. As much as possible, the play space should permit self-initiated physical activity in which the child is enabled to experience mastery and control of his body and the environment.

6. *Normalcy:* Is the handicapped child's use of the playground essentially like his nonhandicapped age-mates' use? This may depend far more on the teacher and his or her attitude and sensitivity to the need for normalcy than on the child's own limitations.

ENVIRONMENTAL DIMENSIONS OF PREVENTION
Attacking environmental causes

Some environmental causes of handicapping conditions can be readily identified; others are less obvious. Through attention to nutritional needs of both expectant mothers and young children, perhaps an untold number of children who would otherwise be handicapped can be healthy and enabled to function optimally. That the area of nutrition is included under the broad heading of environmental influences is perhaps surprising. However, nutrition and, of course, general health care are integrally related to economic well-being, community awareness and concern, and indeed the national "environment."

For young children to experience the kind of early socialization environment that contributes most positively to their healthy psychological and physical development, parent education and education for parenting are extremely important considerations. If many forms of handicap have their origins in factors and influences that exist in the environment with which young children interact, efforts to prevent these forms of handicapping conditions must focus on the elimination of these factors (Wallace and McLoughlin, 1975). Accidents, especially suffocation, falls, burns, and injuries sustained in automobile or bicycle accidents, are now a major cause of death and disability in children.

The same reasoning can be applied to

early childhood education programs and facilities. It had been proposed (E. Bruner, 1971) that some educational handicapping conditions represent the result of poor or inappropriate teaching. To assert that *any* program is better than none at all for young children is simply unwarranted. It may well be that there have been children who have been *damaged* by the very programs designed to help them. The position has been widely held in fact that the child's earliest exposure to school is very possibly a significant factor in his acquiring problems in the areas of academic learning and personal-social development (see, for example, Glasser, 1969).

Preventing handicapping conditions through modifying the environments in which young children live, grow, and learn requires first the identification of environmental causes of handicapping conditions. Some of these causal factors come immediately to mind; they are fairly obvious. Others, however, are less obvious and may exert a more subtle influence. In some respects, environmental cause of educationally handicapping conditions is the subject of considerable dispute, especially in the case of children who live in areas of urban or rural poverty or near poverty, or who are to some degree economically disadvantaged. We no longer believe that there is a direct relationship between a parent's being *poor* and being an ineffective or harmful socializing influence on his or her child. At the same time, it is clear that, although there may not be a uniform *culture of poverty,* the environmental factors associated with economic stress are to some extent predictable and they are harmful. These include, in the urban situation, such conditions as the following:

1. Greater exposure and susceptibility to illness or disease because of less effective and less available medical protection and care.
2. Greater susceptibility to accidental injury or other physical harm caused by the stress and dangers of urban life, community apathy and neglect

by government and privileged interests, and inadequate police and fire protection.
3. Greater susceptibility to neurological damage associated with the factors previously mentioned, including febrile convulsive childhood illness, lead poisoning, and inadequate diet.
4. Greater susceptibility to learning problems in school as a result of appropriate or ineffective teaching, which itself may be a result of economic stresses on the schools that often cause (a) inordinately large class sizes, (b) a tendency to employ beginning inexperienced teachers, since veterans with advanced training draw higher salaries, and (c) insufficient quantity of support services and personnel, such as reading, speech, and other specialists; supplementary tutors; psychologists; and school social workers.

At the base of such presumed, known, or possible environmental causes of handicapping conditions lies a complex set of sociological and economic factors. Many of the children who are most likely to be at risk with respect to etiological factors associated with living in cities are minority children. They are black, or Mexican-American, or Puerto Rican–American, or American Indian, or children whose families have roots in the Appalachian traditions and regions of our country. Some of these same groups are heavily represented within the population of the migrant workers who must follow the crops to sustain a livelihood. In less heavily populated sections of the United States—the West, Southwest, and South —health-related and educational causal factors associated with learning handicaps differ in specific ways from those associated with urban life, but inordinately large numbers of the victims are members of the same minority groups.

In some respects, handicapping conditions in childhood are no respecters of socioeconomic status or ethnicity. At the same time, it is clear that environment contributes in significant ways and that a great many handicapped children—particularly those of minority groups and whose families endure great economic stress—would not be handicapped under more favorable environmental conditions. These children are included among the physically handicapped population, the emotionally disturbed or behaviorally disordered, and those who are incorrectly labeled educable mentally retarded (Dunn, 1968). That minority children do not swell the ranks of those identified as having learning disabilities is more a reflection of political conditions (one should note the *exclusion* cause in official definitions of learning disabilities) than of actual fact (Wallace and McLoughlin, 1975).

Based on these observations, environmental approaches to prevention would focus on such avenues as the following:

Adequate nutrition, for both potential or expectant mother and child

Guarantee of physical safety from violence or accidental harm

Optimal educational conditions

Needed day care services

Optimal health services

Changes in welfare provisions that adversely affect family stability

Elimination of environmental hazards such as air and water pollution, toxic paints, and abandoned buildings

Removal of psychic stresses associated with acute economic insecurity, the struggle to survive, and fear

School as a preventive environment

Environment is clearly a word with many meanings. In terms of children and their development, however, all these definitions and shades of meaning come together in the form of a single theme: *environment consists of those factors external to the child with which his developing mind and self interact in order to grow.* It includes a set of forces that impinge on the child and influence his behavior and, at the same time, respond to his activity.

The environment of the school must be viewed in terms of physical space and the way in which it is used, the children and adults who populate it and what they do and say, and—most important—how the environment is *experienced* by the individual child. It is a *psychological environment* (Lewin, 1935).

Other terms have been used to express the social context in which an individual's behavior occurs and that both influences and is influenced by that behavior. We may speak of the *climate* of the classroom or school. By that we usually mean to imply that certain expectations, values, attitudes, and feelings are inherent in the setting. Ideally one finds in a school or classroom a climate of acceptance, of mutual respect, of success.

One may also speak of the psychological environment of an educational setting as an *economy*—an economy of want or of plenty.* The medium of exchange in this economy may be positive regard, recognition for successful performance, or the attention of a caring adult to one's needs. Some special education settings are actually structured as "token economies" in which the conditions and the nature of reinforcement contingencies are clearly specified (Ferster and De Myer, 1962).

The classroom environment is also a *milieu* (Redl, 1959)—a social context to which an individual contributes, as a member of a group, and that exerts influence on his behavior.

In these senses a classroom environment for young children that assists in preventing education handicaps in young children might be one in which

Each child is recognized and valued as an individual.

Each child is able to employ means of need gratification that neither are in conflict with group well-being nor are in conflict with values the child himself recognizes or is in the process of internalizing.

---

*I am indebted to Dr. William C. Morse for this apt phrase.

Each child regularly experiences success in acquiring skills.

Each child regularly experiences success in physical and emotional self-control.

Each child is able to express, verbally or through other representational modes, his fears and concerns.

Early education may prove to be the most important and most effective means of preventing learning and behavior problems. However, without appropriate and positive educational programming on a *continuous* basis, even the best early childhood education programs may be limited in their potential as a preventive influence. The key concepts would seem to be *begin early, program comprehensively* (for child and family), *program continuously,* and *focus on the individual child.*

DISCUSSION QUESTIONS

1. What are the requirements for physical design and environmental provisions of public schools with respect to handicapped persons? How have and how will these requirements affect the schools in your community?
2. Discuss the approach you would use in establishing and using learning centers in your classroom, in light of the special needs of children you teach.
3. What provisions must be made to ensure that young children who have impaired hearing or vision experience a least restrictive environment in terms of their education?
4. What are the distinctive elements, from the standpoint of the learning environment, associated with the Montessori approach? Compare and contrast this approach with the structured classroom and with the informal approaches.
5. Discuss the teacher's role in establishing and using the classroom environment to facilitate the learning of young children with special needs.
6. What is meant by the concept of a "responsive environment"? Why is this a particularly important aspect of learning environments for young children with special needs?

REFERENCES

Barker, R., and Wright, H. Psychological ecology and the problem of psychosocial development. *Child Development,* 1949, *20*(3), 131-143.

Barker, R. Explorations in environmental psychology. *American Psychologist,* 1965, *20*(1), 1-14.

Blackie, J. *Inside the primary school.* London: Her Majesty's Stationery Office, 1967.

Brown, M., and Precious, N. *The integrated day in the primary school.* New York: Agathon Press, 1970.

Bruner, E. Teaching disorders. In B. Bateman (Ed.), *Learning Disorders,* (Vol. 4). Seattle: Special Child Publications, 1971, pp. 17-44.

Caldwell, B. M. The importance of beginning early. In J. B. Jordan and R. F. Dailey (Eds.), *Not all little wagons are red: the exceptional child's early years.* Arlington, Va.: Council for Exceptional Children, 1973, pp. 2-9.

Central Advisory Council for Education in England. *The Plowden report: children and their primary schools.* London: Her Majesty's Stationery Office, 1967.

Cruickshank, W. M. The psychoeducational match. In W. M. Cruickshank and D. P. Hallahan, (Eds.), *Perceptual and learning disabilities in children. Psychoeducational practices* (Vol. 1). Syracuse: Syracuse University Press, 1975, pp. 71-114.

Cruickshank, W. M., Bentzen, F. A., Ratzeburg, F. H., and Tannhauser, M. A. *A teaching method for brain-injured and hyperactive children.* Syracuse: Syracuse University Press, 1961.

Dennis, W., and Najarian, P. Infant development under environmental handicaps. *Psychological Monographs,* 1957, *71,* 436.

Dunn, L. M. Special education for the mildly retarded—is much of it justified? *Exceptional Children,* 1968, *35,* 5-22.

Elkind, D. Piaget and Montessori. *Children and adolescence: interpretive essays on Jean Piaget.* London: Oxford University Press, 1970.

Engle, R. C., and Gold, B. The early childhood unit —a lot of room for children to grow. *Teaching Exceptional Children,* 1974, *6*(2), 58-67.

Featherstone, J. The primary school revolution in Britain. *The new republic reprint.* New York: Pitman Publishing Corp., 1967.

Ferster, C., and De Myer, M. A method for the experimental analysis of the behavior of autistic children. *American Journal of Orthopsychiatry,* 1962, *32,* 89-98.

Frostig, M., and Horne, D. *The Frostig program for the development of visual perception.* Chicago: Follett, 1964.

Glasser, W. *Schools without failure.* New York: Harper & Row, Publishers, 1969.

Gordon, I. J. *Studying the child in school.* New York: John Wiley & Sons, Inc., 1966.

Haring, N., and Phillips, E. L. *Educating emotionally disturbed children.* New York: McGraw-Hill Book Co., 1962.

Hendrick, J. *The whole child: new trends in early education.* St. Louis: The C. V. Mosby Co., 1976.

Herndon, J. *The way it spoze to be.* New York: Simon & Schuster, Inc., 1966.

Hess, R. D., and Croft, D. J. *Teachers of young children.* Boston: Houghton Mifflin Co., 1972.

Hewett, F. M. *The emotionally disturbed child in the classroom.* Boston: Allyn & Bacon, Inc., 1968.

Holt, J. *How children fail.* New York: Pitman Publishing Corp., 1964.

Hunt, J. McV. *Intelligence and experience.* New York: Ronald, 1961.

Hunt, J. McV. *The challenge of incompetence and poverty: papers on the role of early education.* Urbana: University of Illinois Press, 1969.

Hymes, J. L., Jr. *Teaching the child under six* (2nd ed.). Columbus, Ohio: Charles E. Merrill Publishing Co., 1974.

Inhelder, B., and Piaget, J. *The psychology of the child.* New York: Basic Books, Inc., 1969.

Isaacs, S. *The nursery years: the mind of the child from birth to six years.* New York: Schocken Books, Inc., 1968. (Originally published, 1929).

Isaacs, S. *Intellectual growth in young children.* New York: Schocken Books, Inc., 1971. (Originally published 1960.)

Kephart, N. C. *The slow learner in the classroom* (2nd ed.). Columbus, Ohio: Charles E. Merrill Publishing Co., 1971.

Kohl, H. R. *The open classroom: a practical guide to a new way of teaching.* New York: New York Review, 1969.

Kozol, J. *Death at an early age.* New York: Houghton Mifflin Co., 1967.

Leeper, S., Dales, R., Skipper, P., and Witherspoon, R. *Good schools for young children: a guide for working with three, four, and five year old children.* New York: Macmillan, 1968.

Lewin, K. *A dynamic theory of personality: selected papers of Kurt Lewin.* New York: McGraw-Hill Book Co., 1935.

Montessori, M. *The Montessori method.* Philadelphia: F. A. Stoker, 1912.

Montessori, M. *A Montessori handbook: Dr. Montessori's own handbook with additional new material on current Montessori theory and practice.* New York: Capricorn Books, 1966.

Moore, O. K., and Anderson, A. R. The responsive environments project. In R. C. Hess and R. M. Bear (Eds.), *Early education.* Chicago: Aldine Publishing Co., 1968.

Nimnicht, G. P. A model program for young children that responds to the child. In R. K. Parker (Ed.), *The preschool in action: exploring early childhood programs.* Boston: Allyn & Bacon, Inc., 1972, pp. 245-267.

Piaget, J. *Six psychological studies.* New York: Random House, Inc., 1967.

Prescott, E., Jones, C., and Kirtchevsky, S. *Assessment of child-rearing environments: an ecological approach* Pasadena, Calif.: Pacific Oaks College, June, 1971. (Mimeographed.)

Redl, F. The concept of a therapeutic milieu. *American Journal of Orthopsychiatry,* 1959, *29,* 721-734.

Rogers, V. (Ed.). *Teaching in the British primary school.* New York: Macmillan Publishing Co., Inc., 1970.

Séguin, E. *Idiocy: its treatment by the physiological method.* New York: William Wood, 1866.

Silberman, C. *Crisis in the classroom: the remaking of American education.* New York: Random House, Inc., 1970.

Small, G. *Environment and early education: an experimental course* (Research Monograph, Education Professions Development Act [EPDA] Program). Cleveland: Case Western Reserve University, 1973.

Spitz, R. A. Hospitalism: an inquiry into the genesis of psychiatric conditions in early childhood. In *The psychoanalytic study of the child* (Vol. 1). New York: International Universities Press, 1945.

Thomas, J. *Learning centers: opening up the classroom.* Boston: Holbrook Press, 1975.

Todd, V. E., and Hefferman, H. *The years before school: guiding preschool children.* New York: Macmillan, 1970.

Wallace, G., and McLoughlin, J. A. *Learning disabilities: concepts and characteristics.* Columbus, Ohio: Charles E. Merrill Publishing Co., 1975, Chapter 14, pp. 284-307.

Weber, L. *The English infant school and informal education.* Englewood Cliffs, N.J.: Prentice-Hall, Inc., 1971.

White, R. W. Motivation reconsidered: the concept of competence. *Psychological Review,* 1959, *66,* 297-333.

Wolfensberger, W. *The principle of normalization in human services.* Toronto: National Institute on Mental Retardation, 1972.

Wohlwill, J. F. The physical environment: a problem for a psychology of stimulation. *Journal of Social Issues,* 1966, *22*(4), 29-37.

Wohlwill, J. F. The emerging discipline of environmental psychology. *American Psychologist,* 1970, *25,* 303-312.

Wright, H. F. *Recording and analyzing child behavior.* New York: Harper & Row, Publishers, 1967.

Yarrow, L. J. Maternal deprivation: toward an empirical and conceptual re-evaluation. *Psychological Bulletin,* 1961, *58,* 459-490.

CHAPTER 12

INDIVIDUALIZED TEACHING AS THE LEAST RESTRICTIVE ALTERNATIVE

TEACHING THE INDIVIDUAL CHILD

The word "mainstreaming" can easily be misunderstood. To some, it may mean reverting to the approach that characterized the education of most handicappped children before special education gained acceptance and before the special needs of handicapped and gifted children began to be recognized and addressed. Some special educators fear that great numbers of children now receiving specialized services may simply be "dumped" back into regular classes and will not receive needed services. Some administrators and officials may see in the mainstreaming movement a means of reducing the relatively greater cost of educating children with special needs. Special education is expensive! Some will see nothing new in the concept of "regular" placement for handicapped children.

However, such perceptions are inaccurate. The new laws call for a new approach, one that is in fact revolutionary. They constitute a "bill of rights" for the handicapped child (Weintraub and Abeson, 1974) and require every individual, organization, and agency involved in the education of handicapped children in every community and state to implement major changes.

On one level, the concept of mainstreaming can be seen as the educational parallel to *normalization* (Wolfensberger, 1972). Both trends emphasize extension of basic human rights and rights under law guaranteed by the constitution to every individual. Both stress the primacy of the individual and reject assumptions of homogeneity based on categories and labels. Both imply broader assumption of responsibility for the handicapped within communities.

The federal legislation implies three basic principles regarding mainstreaming: (1) The specific educational needs of the individual child, rather than the "type" of handicap he has, should determine what educational provisions are made for him; (2) there are not just two forms of education, "regular" and "special," but a variety of alternatives; and (3) the handicapped child should be integrated as much as possible with his non-handicapped peers. The superordinate principle, providing the basis not only for the educational programming provisions of the federal laws, but for all of their provisions, is that *every child, including every handicapped child, must be provided a free, appropriate education.*

It is assumed that these changes affect not only special education but general education as well. Teachers, supervisors, and administrators heretofore concerned mainly with a range of individual differences within specified limits—the range of "normalcy"—will now be charged with responsibilities that they have for the most part not had to face in the past.

However, since the 1960s there has been a movement for change in general education, as well, a movement that in many ways parallels the recent revolutionary changes in special education. This movement has had many dimensions, but several distinct themes can be discerned. These might be summarized as follows:

1. The theme of valuing *diversity* and *pluralism* in a democratic society
2. The theme of recognition of the *individuality* of children's learning needs and styles
3. The theme of *accountability* of educators to the individual child, his parents, and society for the quality and effectiveness of his educational experience
4. The theme of recognition of the importance of *affective aspects of learning:* attitudes, values, personal responsibility, motivation, and healthy self-concept

These themes have been reflected in a wide variety of innovations, including "open classrooms," individually prescribed instruction, cross-age grouping, affective education in various forms, performance contracting, greater involvement of parents and paraprofessionals in the classroom, peer teaching, new approaches to assessment and evaluation, new technology, new curricula, and new instructional methods and materials. Such developments as these make more reasonable the possibility of accommodating children with special learning needs within the regular instructional program (Charles, 1976). Indeed, the presence of exceptional children can serve to make regular educators even more sensitive to the individuality of need and wide range of differences among *nonhandicapped* children. A "whole group" approach to teaching will indeed make difficult the accommodation of children with special needs, but it is also inappropriate for the nonhandicapped.

PATHS TO INDIVIDUALIZATION

Two general approaches have been advocated by which individualization of instruction can be implemented. These could be described by the terms "informal child directed" and "diagnostic prescriptive." It is possible, however, to integrate these two general strategies in a single classroom. To fulfill legal requirements for an *individualized educational program* (IEP) for children identified as handicapped, there must be prescriptive planning based on educational diagnosis. Although the basic approach employed by the teacher may emphasize an "open" or informal teaching style, this does not preclude prescriptive planning where it is indicated. Regardless of the degree or the source (Weikart, 1971) of classroom structure, working with young handicapped children requires that the teacher assume a clinical attitude. This attitude is the core element of individualized teaching.

The clinical attitude

A clinical attitude is, first of all, a questioning attitude. A teacher with such an attitude has a need to *inquire* about children through observation, to formulate and test hypotheses, to gather relevant data, and to substitute documentation for

supposition. But such inquiry is not pursued as an end in itself, although it may be intrinsically rewarding. It is undertaken to increase the potentialities in a teaching-learning situation so that a child can benefit maximally and realize his highest potential. The clinical attitude therefore reflects both the desire to optimize learning for each child and a faith in the child's ability to benefit from instruction that is appropriately matched to his specific and unique learning characteristics.

Early childhood education programs can be, for convenience, categorized as being of three general types: *teacher centered, material centered, or child centered* (Weikart, 1971). Of course assignment of a particular teaching style or program to any of these three categories usually is a vast oversimplification. In some respects the term "child-centered teaching" suggests some of the characteristics of the clinical approach. Basically, child-centeredness suggests an awareness that it is the learner who must be the focal concern of instruction. Schools exist, not to provide employment for great numbers of adults nor to permit the marketing of great quantities of materials, but as *places where individual children may learn*.

Diagnosis

A diagnostic approach to teaching assumes that it is possible to determine accurately and objectively the characteristics and needs of an individual child to design and implement a program of instruction directed toward specific objectives for that child (Blanco, 1972). In educational diagnosis, the major purpose is to determine these objectives and the strategies which can insure their attainment. This implies a somewhat different conception of diagnosis than the term may suggest in other contexts. In medical usage, diagnosis usually means the identification of a malady. A doctor's prescription is to some extent (but not entirely) based on specification of the illness from which the individual is suffering. Penicillin (barring contraindications specific to the patient) is the treatment of choice for a streptococcal infection, but probably not for a viral infection. A broken bone requires one approach, a muscular sprain another. Thus identification of the malady implies identification of its *cause,* as well as specification of the treatment.

The educational counterpart of this aspect of the diagnostic process is *differential diagnosis:* identification of the *kind* of handicapping condition the child has. Many special educators believe, however, that this aspect of diagnosis has serious limitations and may often be unnecessary for educational purposes. (However, it is absolutely essential with respect to visual or auditory problems and all conditions requiring medical or surgical treatment. Serious emotional disturbance also might be included within this group.) To determine that a child is functioning within the range of mental retardation, is learning disabled, behaviorally disordered, orthopedically handicapped, cerebral palsied, partially sighted, or severely hearing impaired, however, is insufficiently specific. It does not specify how he learns as an individual and how he should be taught. This is true for several reasons:

1. Wide variability exists within all of these categories.
2. The categories themselves are not necessarily educationally relevant.
3. Learning characteristics of children within a category overlap with those of children within another category —and also children who are not handicapped.

Although to some extent past special education practices had implied that knowledge of the kind of disability that a child had was sufficient to determine how (in what setting, by whom, with what materials, and by what methods) he should be taught, this view is no longer considered tenable. Furthermore, it is explicitly countermanded by federal law. *For every individual child identified as handicapped, there must be an individual educational plan.*

To label a child as mentally retarded does not indicate what his present competencies are, what his experiences have been, what he is ready to learn, how he learns, what interests him, and what factors are powerful motivators for him to learn. And to determine that the child is mentally retarded as a result of genetic causes, brain injury resulting from encephalitis, or experiential deprivation may add little or nothing to the planning enterprise (Gallagher, 1957). In educational diagnosis the diagnostician is primarily the teacher, working as a member of an interdisciplinary diagnostic team. It is essential to identify specifically the child's present functional level in all areas that are relevant to his learning.

Developing an individualized educational plan

The diagnostic process leads to the formulation of an individual educational plan (a plan for the provision of services and the evaluation of progress) and, within this, an individual instructional plan. Undertaking this planning based on diagnosis requires asking questions such as the following:

1. What does the child *do?*
2. What are the child's apparent strengths, and what specific difficulties does he have?
3. What are the long-range educational objectives for this child?
4. What are immediate, or short-term, objectives that are *important, attainable,* and *measurable?*
5. What strategies will be employed to bring about the achievement of these objectives, or "target behaviors"?
6. In what sort of educational placement can these strategies best be implemented and these objectives attained?
7. Within this placement, what specific educational and related services must be provided to implement these

strategies and attain these objectives?

8. For what period of time will these special services be required?

9. Specifically how will the child's progress be evaluated?

It should be noted that the foregoing makes no reference to determination of a disease entity, syndrome, or classification. That may be necessary for reasons that have nothing whatsoever to do with teaching the child, but the position is taken here that diagnosing educational needs does not require classification or identification of etiology. Diagnosis is rather *an inquiry process by which instructional goals are identified, instructional procedures selected, and a plan for the evaluation of instructional effectiveness is determined.*

This position is based on the assumption that there is not one correct manner of teaching children labeled as educable mentally retarded, one for children who have learning disabilities, or one for children who are emotionally handicapped. There may be one best or most effective way of teaching *one child.* More often, however, there is a variety of strategies, involving various combinations of alternative materials, modes of utilizing them, selection of reinforcers, and uses of the time dimension. The goal of educational diagnosis is to *match* the strategy with the individual child's characteristics, readiness levels, and preferred modes of interaction with the environment.

Diagnostic/prescriptive instructional materials are available that provide guidance and tools for a systematic and programmatic approach to individualization. Karnes and Zehrbach (1973) have described such a program based on the Illinois Test of Psycholinguistic Abilities (ITPA). Schortinghuis and Frohman (1974) found that not only teachers, but paraprofessional personnel as well, could implement a precision diagnostic teaching approach, with training in the use of Portage Project materials. In both cases,

the method is to select specific target behaviors and intervention methods based on precise diagnosis in areas related to learning.

ASSESSMENT AND INDIVIDUALIZED TEACHING

For a teacher to describe what he or she has "presented," what material has been "covered," or what he or she has "had the children do," does not serve, of course, to identify what a particular child has *learned.* Given the individuality both of prior experiences and of modes of responding to instruction, children in any learning group will benefit both to different degrees and in diverse ways to a particular "lesson" or activity. The child-centered teacher therefore recognizes the need to *observe, assess,* and *record* how and what individual children learn. This information can be gained through an integration of several techniques.

Assessment may suggest immediately the notion of giving tests. Tests are indeed a way of assessing children's learning and other characteristics and needs. In the past, however, special education planning and placement may have relied excessively on formal test procedures—especially on the use of IQ measures. There are many ways of assessing children's needs, characteristics, and progress. This section will stress three major themes of educational assessment:

1. *Assessment for individualized planning must be multifactored.* It is now mandated by law that a single test cannot be the sole criterion for determining special education placement.

2. *Criterion-referenced educational assessment specifies objectives and permits evaluation of children's progress.*

3. *Informal assessment permits the teacher and others working with the child to assess continuously and unobtrusively all areas related to the child's needs and progress.*

Multifactored assessment

Traditionally, tests of ability, or intelligence, have been extremely important in making placement decisions for children. Since the relative superiority of individual tests (such as the Stanford-Binet Intelligence Scale and Wechsler tests) to *group* measures (that is, ability tests administered simultaneously to a group of students) has long been recognized, individual testing has usually been required. These individual tests, especially when administered by a skilled psychologist, are capable of tapping diverse aspects of intellectual functioning. However, placement decisions have typically been made on the basis of a single score—the IQ. Special education programs have often been identified, based on state legal requirements, in terms of an IQ cut-off score or range score (for example, the definition of educable mental retardation as an IQ range from 50 to 70 or 80).

However, the IQ score in itself conveys no information concerning how an individual child learns, what concepts and skills he has mastered, how he responds to the demands of a social situation, what factors influence his social behavior and learning and in what ways, and so on. A skilled and sensitive psychological examiner is able to gain clinical impressions and insights concerning such areas in the course of a diagnostic evaluation. The score or scores on the test, although important, are generally of far less significance than the behavioral characteristics, the pattern of apparent strengths and weaknesses, and social responsiveness observed by the psychologist in the testing situation. The psychological examiner's study of the child within this controlled situation provides valuable contributions to educational planning.

Nevertheless, the testing situation is a limited and to some extent an artificial one. Most psychologists would prefer to relate test findings to day-to-day observations of the child within a classroom, and some insist on having this opportunity. Although an evaluation by a psychologist or psychometrist (an individual qualified to administer psychological tests) does, at least potentially, provide information concerning diverse facets of the child's functioning, the concept of multifactored assessment requires that still other forms of assessment be used to contribute to educational planning decisions. The following are some of the most important principles.

1. Assessment must deal with *adaptive functioning* in life situations, including home and school.
2. Assessment must be conducted by representatives of more than just one professional discipline.
3. Assessment must be related directly to the development of an educational plan designed specifically for the individual child.
4. Assessment, in the form of evaluation of the child's progress and the efficacy or appropriateness of the plan, must be repeated at least annually. (This may not necessarily require annual readministration of formal tests.)

Criterion-referenced assessment

Measures that yield scores in the form of quotients or age- or grade-equivalent scores are *norm referenced*. This means that the child's performance on the test is compared to the average performance of others. Tests that permit interpretation in these terms have been *standardized*. A major dimension of standardization is the development of norms, which are based on actual administration of the test to sufficiently large and appropriately representative groups of people. In effect, the individual's performance is interpreted on the basis of comparison with others. Criterion-referenced testing, however, evaluates an individual's performance on the basis of objectives that have been established for that individual. This form of assessment is thus more useful for purposes of individual educational planning.

Some concepts important in connection with criterion-referenced testing are *task analysis* and *behavioral objectives*. The former refers to the identification of the specific *components* of a more complex concept or skill that is to be learned and the *sequence* in which those components must be acquired. Behavioral objectives specify what is to be learned in terms of *learner behaviors* that will be accepted as evidence that the learning has taken place. Educational planning based on criterion-referenced assessment involves study both of the tasks to be mastered and of the learner's functioning as it relates to those tasks.

Informal assessment

In the educational planning process, some purposes in assessment can be achieved through the use of formal tests, that is, tests that are published and commercially available and that are administered according to a standardized format. Some of these tests may be administered by the classroom teacher, whereas others are generally given by professionals specifically trained in their use. For example, individual intelligence tests are usually administered by a psychologist or psychometrist; certain testing procedures concerning speech and language functioning are done by a speech clinician; physical

reflex testing according to a standardized scale may be done by a trained physical therapist. However, representatives of all those disciplines engaged in child assessment rely as well on informal procedures to ascertain a child's needs and to formulate a treatment plan. The classroom teacher, in particular, relies extensively on informal assessment in all areas relating to individual educational planning. Informal procedures are equally useful in areas relating to skill and concept learning and the many dimensions of social interaction, motivational determinants, emotional needs, and behavioral characteristics.

Among the general strategies used by the teacher to assess informally a child's specific accomplishments, readiness for new experiences, interests, and social-emotional needs are behavioral observation, individual or group interviewing, sociometric techniques, semiprojective procedures, and teacher-made tests or tasks.

Behavioral observation. There are two general modes of recording behavioral observations (in addition, of course, to electronic or other mechanical means): *narrative/descriptive* and *quantitative*. In addition, there are two general strategies for conducting either of these: *time sampling* and *event sampling*. The regular maintenance of a *log* of comprehensive observations is extremely valuable but may be unwieldy. *Anecdotal records* are relied on by many teachers and may be extremely useful in planning and evaluation. The *critical incident technique* implies the need for the observer to select an event of possible significance and to describe it thoroughly, including antecedent conditions and occurrences, the setting in which the event took place, and the consequences of the event. In these forms of documentation it is particularly important to distinguish between description of what occurs and interpretation of the event. For example, the statement "John cried silently for 2 minutes" is a state-

ment of what occurred, whereas "John was very unhappy because . . ." is an interpretation both of John's feeling state and of why he felt the way he did. *Developing Observation Skills* (Cartwright and Cartwright, 1974) is an excellent guide for teachers attempting to develop a data-based system for individualized teaching.

Quantitative recording is particularly helpful in attempting to provide an objective measure of the frequency with which a particular behavior occurs. This is generally for the purpose of attempting to bring about some changes in the behavior, such as increasing or reducing its frequency through differential reinforcement. As K. Eileen Allen (1972) has noted, teachers of young children can acquire and use the skills that are required by this scientific approach in their classroom.

The steps are (1) a behavior is identified; (2) a system for recording its occurrence is determined (that is, noting whenever it occurs or noting the number of occurrences within designated time intervals); and (3) an observational chart, or graph, is constructed. Changes in the frequency with which a behavior occurs can then be measured as new conditions are introduced, especially as planned attempts to provide or withhold reinforcement for the behavior—or to reinforce some *incompatible* behavior—are implemented. The behavior may be reported in terms of the absolute number of times it occurs within a specified time period or its comparative frequency, in terms of percentages or proportions, in relation to other behaviors. Sometimes a general distinction of *on-task* vs. *off-task* behaviors is made. However, usually it is important to identify a specific behavior, such as "maintains visual attention," "sucks thumb," or "taps foot on floor."

Individual or group interviewing. One distinction often made in the field of counseling is that between *directive* and *nondirective* interviewing (Rogers, 1951).

When applied diagnostically directive interviewing refers to such techniques as direct questioning and giving advice. The nondirective approach provides a means of encouraging the child or adult to express what is on his mind by attempting to *reflect* the way he seems to feel, rather than guiding what he says along predetermined lines. Some approaches that represent combinations of the two modes are (1) questioning, (2) life-space interviewing, (3) Piaget's *methode clinique,* or clinical method, and (4) class meetings.

Techniques of *questioning* as a means both of determining what the learner knows or at what level of understanding he is functioning in a particular area and of guiding his thought toward new understandings have been described by many educational psychologists and instructional theorists (see, for example, Taba, 1964). *Socratic* questioning is based on the dialogues described by Plato in which the great teacher and philosopher Socrates enabled those with whom he conversed to discover truth themselves. Inquiry training (Shulman and Keislar, 1966) is a teaching approach whereby teacher and pupils employ a questioning approach in various aspects of classroom activity. Adaptations for young children of the technique known as *brainstorming* are also possible, as are simulation or gaming strategies and problem-solving experiences.

Life-space interviewing (Redl, 1959; Morse, 1971; Newman and Keith, 1967) is a clinical procedure particularly applicable to the goal of helping the child or young person to gain understanding of and assume responsibility for his own behavior, especially in a crisis situation. The adult facilitates this process by focusing the child's attention on the realities of the immediate situation and helping the child to identify possible consequences of alternative courses of action. Observing the child's response to a stressful situation and his ability to cope constructively with it is facilitated by this technique, which is

at the same time a therapeutic management procedure available to the teacher.

Piaget's *methode clinique* consisted originally of a questioning procedure concerning the child's understanding of natural phenonema, such as dreams, wind, and the moon, developed by Piaget to ascertain the way in which the child structured reality (Piaget, 1962). Subsequently, however, he modified the technique to take into account the fact that the child's words might only imperfectly reflect what he actually thought. The revised clinical method (Ginsburg and Opper, 1969) consists of observing the child's response to a situation requiring problem-solving activity after first questioning the child concerning what he "thinks will happen if . . ." and then inquiring further as the child's hypotheses are or are not confirmed. A fundamental principle of Piagetian questioning is that the adult follows the child's lead, rather than attempting to direct the child's responses along certain lines.

Among those who have described discussion procedures applicable with groups of children, William Glasser (1969) has been most explicit concerning the techniques of effective discussions as applied in what he calls *class meetings.* Glasser insists on the necessity that the children (and adult) be seated in a circle so that all are facing each other. The adult does not evaluate; rather he encourages and models genuine listening. Everyone's contribution is valued.

Sociometric procedures. Beyond simply observing and recording instances of children's response to social situations—including friendship pairings, role in initiating group play, level of development reflected in parallel or cooperative play, etc.—sociometric procedures include a wide range of techniques for the systematic study of the group as a social constellation. Methods such as *A Class Play* (Bower and Lambert, 1961) provide insights concerning how group members are seen by their peers. The *sociogram* is a graphic representation of patterns of social choice within the peer group based on children's responses to questions like: "What three children in the class would you like to have go to the circus with you?" Children frequently selected are "stars," those seldom or never selected are "isolates," and specific friendship pairs or triads become evident.

Semiprojective procedures. Through observation of children's sociodramatic play, play with puppets, and use of art media the teacher may derive insights concerning the child's emotional needs, fears, wishes, feelings about himself, aspirations to be like others, particular likes or dislikes, or internal conflicts that might otherwise be masked. Much care should be taken in undertaking any kind of interpretation of a child's play behavior, painting, self-drawing, and the like. The distinction between factual reporting of what the child actually does and interpretation of what the child "seems to be saying" must be kept firmly in mind. Although some aspects of inner concern are characteristically represented by young children symbolically in these expressive modes, excessive use in painting of the color red does not necessarily mean the child is obsessed with fears of being hurt, black need not signify pervasive unhappiness, and placement and size of human figures or body parts may or may not have symbolic significance.

Human figure drawing, in particular, has long been established as an effective means of estimating the child's developmental progress (Harris, 1963; Di Leo, 1970, 1973; Kellogg, 1967). This technique may have additional diagnostic utility (Di Leo, 1973), but caution must be exercised in drawing inferences about possible neurological or emotional problems (Harris, 1963).

Teacher-made tests or tasks. Teachers at the primary level (and beyond) often compile their own criterion-referenced assessment system. This may take the form of a kit consisting of specific test items,

pages taken from workbooks, and other materials. "Home-made" tasks are often incorporated. The teacher may routinely assess the learning characteristics and needs of all children with an entire battery of tasks, or specific items may be used selectively with individual children.

Some published materials, such as *The Psychoeducational Inventory of Basic Learning Abilities* developed by Robert Valett (1968), are also useful in criterion-referenced assessment. This inventory represents a combination of items drawn from standardized tests and other sources, grouped within the following categories:

1. Gross motor development
2. Sensory-motor integration
3. Perceptual-motor skills
4. Language development
5. Conceptual skills
6. Social skills

This inventory is not intended to serve as a norm-referenced measure or as a basis for determining special placement. The purpose of such instruments as these is to assist the teacher in working with an individual child.

Check-sheets, teacher-made rating scales and profiles, or any of a variety of recording methods can be used by the teacher to code observations (Smith, 1969). Anecdotal records kept in brief, well-organized narrative form may also be used (Almy, 1974).

ROLE OF OBJECTIVES IN TEACHING AND EVALUATION

A great deal has been written recently about the role of objectives in education, as well as in other fields such as business and government. The idea of *management by objective* (MBO) has become basic to administrative science. This idea implies that the effectiveness of any operation can be assessed in terms of the degree to which stated objectives are attained. Consequently, much care must be given to the objectives themselves, from the standpoint of their appropriateness, their feasibility, and their measurability. The language in which the objectives are stated is particularly important; it must be *precise*.

In teaching, effectiveness must be measured on the basis of children's progress. This implies that an objective is a statement of *what the child will be able to do*. *Behavioral objectives* (Mager, 1962) are statements of intended outcomes for a child that are expressed in behavioral language. To determine that a given objective has been attained for a child, the child must demonstrate some specified, observable behavior.

Long-range objectives are sometimes called *terminal objectives*. At the instructional level, short-term or immediate objectives are seen as steps in a sequence of enroute objectives. Individualized educational planning for handicapped children requires the specification of both, determined on the basis of multifactored assessment.

Well-stated objectives are statements of the criteria for evaluating a child's progress. Each objective is actually a criterion behavior, rather than just a vague ambiguous goal.

STRATEGIES FOR INDIVIDUALIZATION IN REGULAR EARLY EDUCATION PROGRAMS

Jenny Klein (1975) estimated that in 1975 there were 29,000 handicapped children enrolled in Head Start programs, in response to the 1972 amendment to federal law requiring that 10 percent of Head Start children be handicapped. She further estimated that about *one half* of these children required a great deal of special assistance, often involving the need for additional personnel. Subsequent analysis (Nazzaro, 1974; Ensher et al., 1977) confirmed that many handicapped children have been served in Head Start. However, the dangers in labeling children at this level were noted.

Materials as well as personnel can provide valuable resources for working with children with special needs in early childhood programs. For example, Elizabeth

Meyers et al. (1973) have published a comprehensive guide for individualization in kindergarten classrooms, entitled *The Kindergarten Teacher's Handbook*. This resource presents suggestions for identification of children with special needs, including the gifted, for assessment, and for individualized teaching.

Teaching young children with special needs, whatever the setting, requires particular planning in relating curriculum experiences to interactive developmental processes (Wolinsky, 1972). The processes of cognitive, linguistic, perceptual, physical, social, and emotional development in fact *are* the curriculum areas around which teaching is organized. This *developmental orientation* is appropriate in teaching all young children; for those with special needs, it is essential.

Barbara Keogh and Marc L. Levitt (1976) have outlined some of the specific needs and challenges posed by the move to accommodate handicapped pupils in regular classrooms. They stress the need for in-service training of regular teachers on the basis of analysis of research and evaluation of the effectiveness of mainstreaming programs (see, for example Lilly, 1971). One study (McGinty and Keogh, 1975) found elementary teachers willing to accept handicapped pupils and in agreement about what knowledge and skills would be needed by a teacher to work effectively with these children. The teachers sampled, however, were almost unanimous in expressing their own limitations in most of these areas:

1. What are the characteristics and needs of exceptional children?
2. How does one plan and carry out a specialized remedial program?
3. How can one meet learning needs in a broad range of curriculum areas?
4. What resource and supportive services are available in the school and community?
5. How can one deal effectively with the social and attitudinal issues of mainstreaming, involving the inter-

action of handicapped and nonhandicapped children?

Accommodation within a "regular" educational setting of a child whose special needs require that he follow an individually determined program is greatly facilitated if the total classroom program is individualized (Charles, 1976). Mainstreaming, in an important sense, requires modifications in classroom procedures in the direction of a total individualized program. The child with pronounced special needs only makes more obvious what has always been known: *in any classroom group each child learns in his own way and at his own pace.* The only difference is that most children are able to "adjust" to expectations of homogeneity, at least superficially. Although they might not learn and grow as well as they might otherwise, most can at least "get along" (Bloom, 1968). The presence in a classroom of a child who cannot conform to a rigid format requiring lockstep progress requires the teacher to carry out with him a plan that has been developed in light of his unique needs. Is such an approach any the less appropriate for his classmates whose deviations from the "norm" are simply less extreme?

Individualization is easy to talk about; it is less easy to implement, particularly given the age-grade form of organization in which our schools are generally operated. Whether the general approach to individualization of instruction is one of individually prescribed activity (Hodges et al., 1971) or one of "open" learning based heavily on self-selection and self-pacing (Hammerman and Morse, 1972), the teacher's task is much more difficult and time consuming than in the traditional, group-oriented classroom. Great expectations are placed on the teacher to record and monitor what individual children are learning on a day-to-day basis. However, if the teacher is able to maintain careful individual records and to guide the children on the basis of intimate knowledge of where they are functioning and how they

are progressing, the instructional possibilities are multiplied.

At least in principle, if not always in practice, such a mode of instruction has been standard practice in the field of special education. Individualized teaching is an area in which special education techniques and methods can greatly enrich the learning opportunities of all children, whether handicapped or not.

Some components of an individualized approach that have been described in the literature and used successfully by many teachers of young children include the following:

Learning centers
Diagnostic profiles
Learning contracts
Self-instructional materials
Provisions for peer learning
Teaching assistants

These are diverse strategies, and they comprise only a partial list of those that are possible. It is the teacher's task to draw from available resources ideas that might prove useful and to design a classroom program on the basis of considerations such as (1) the characteristics and needs of the particular children in the class, (2) curriculum and program objectives he or she is expected to follow and meet, (3) the resources available in a particular school and community, including especially parent resources, and (4) his or her own individual teaching style and philosophy.

Learning centers

The terms "learning center," "interest center," and "activity area" all reflect dimensions of a larger aspect of the teaching-learning process: use of the physical environment. Whether in an "engineered" classroom (Hewett, 1968) or an "open" classroom, the idea of *centers* reflects the design of the physical classroom environment so that specific areas lend themselves as ideally as possible to specific kinds of activity. They may correspond to hierarchical levels of learning readiness, as in Hewett's "order center," which includes varieties of patterning tasks, puzzles, etc.; to academic skill areas, as in the "maths center" of the British primary school; or to forms of physical activity intended to be elicited, as in a "gross motor," "fine motor," and "story and music" distinction.

Diagnostic profiles

There are a multitude of checklists, inventories, and profiles available commercially with which individual pupils' progress can be charted. Basically, general areas of learning are identified such as gross motor skills, fine motor and adaptive skills, cognitive and language skills, personal and social skills, and, if appropriate, areas corresponding to academic skill areas, such as mathematics and social studies. Then within each area appropriate objectives are listed, as much as possible in the sequential order corresponding to their level of difficulty and complexity. These objectives are in the form of child behaviors—that is, statements of what the child does, such as "drinks from a cup unassisted," "counts to 10," "repeats four digits in correct sequence," and "sorts objects by color."

Performance criteria can be specified to ensure that ratings are reliable—that is, that different observers would agree in their ratings. For example, the conditions of task performance can be specified, levels of performance consistency or facility can be differentiated, or a quantitative criterion, such as "80 percent of the time" or "with 90 percent accuracy," can be specified. It may be useful at the very least to differentiate skills or behaviors that clearly reflect *mastery* or that are *consistently* present from those that are *emerging.* Ratings can be done informally, through observation of the child's daily activities, or more formally, through administering certain prescribed tasks to the child.

A diagnostic profile can provide an effective, ongoing assessment of the child's progress in all curricular areas and consequently a useful means of determining specific instructional objectives and strategies. It can also be useful in coordinating the teacher's observations effectively with those of other members of the interdisciplinary team, such as the psychologist and speech clinician. Finally, and perhaps most important, a profile provides an effective vehicle for communicating with the child's parents about his progress in parent conferences and possibly with the child himself.

Learning contracts

It is helpful for the child to have a clear idea of what his teacher believes are important goals for him. This gives the child, too, something for which he can strive and, with successful accomplishment, a sense of pride and satisfaction. The idea of a contract enables the child to explicitly endorse and commit himself to a course of action (Glasser, 1969). Use of a contract approach provides a further means of carrying out an individualized approach. Barbara Colorosa (1976) provides some excellent examples of learning contracts. Although the specific content and format used would depend on the preference and

style of the teacher and his or her perception of the needs of the child, the following components are generally included:

1. A statement of the task
2. A statement of the *consequences* of completion of the task
3. The signatures of the individuals making the agreement—the child and the teacher

Self-instructional materials

Some electronic equipment, such as cassette tape recorders and the Language Master, can be used by the children themselves. In a "responsive" classroom environment (Meier et al., 1968), great care is given to provisioning the classroom with materials that can be used independently by children, that are autotelic or self-correcting, and that actually *teach,* in the manner of the Montessori materials. Availability of such materials eliminates many of the logistical barriers to individualization. Materials as well as the environment within which they are used and the planning for their systematic use have been described (Armstrong, 1976) as a most important component of planning for mainstreaming.

Provisions for peer learning

Learning from peers is a daily fact of life for children, especially as peer influences become more potent as the child leaves the toddler period and becomes increasingly a social being. Whereas a high priority has traditionally been placed in the nursery school setting on cooperative play and other vehicles for encouraging peer interaction, some teachers of primary level children work to minimize such interaction in the belief that it is exclusively the adult's role to teach. An individualized approach, however, can be greatly enhanced through the planned use of peer teaching and learning. A child's age-mates can have great constructive influence, whether in a highly structured "tutoring" relationship or in less formal, everyday cooperative projects, tasks, and play activity. The significant influence of peer models in particular should be recognized and respected.

Teaching assistants

Many teachers are fortunate to be able to work with paid paraprofessional assistants or aides. All, however, have a potentially vast resource of volunteer persons available who can assist them, including the following:

Parents

Members of service organizations in the community

College students preparing not only for careers in education but in other fields as well

High school students undertaking a "senior project" or other field-based experiential activity

Individuals registered through a community agency coordinating volunteer services

Some teachers find it difficult to supervise adult and student volunteers, particularly if there are many involved and their times of availability are infrequent and brief (for example, 2 hours, one day each week) or sporadic. However, those who have learned to make effective use of volunteers find them an extremely valuable resource and essential to an individualized program. Effective use of volunteers, however, requires that careful attention be given to these areas:

Recruitment, selection, and orientation

Planning of volunteers' responsibilities and specific assignments

Provision for ongoing communication between the teacher and each volunteer

COORDINATION OF RESOURCES FOR INDIVIDUALIZED EDUCATIONAL PLANNING

Communication between school and community agencies

A community, particularly if it is a large, densely populated, urban center, may have a multiplicity of individuals, organizations, and agencies who are concerned with the welfare of young children. In the past, communication and coordination of services have not always been accomplished with ease and efficiency. There has often been duplication of some services, while other needs have gone essentially unmet. In recent years, many communities have made strong efforts to bring about communication among agencies, and certain aspects of the new federal legislation—particularly the provision for identification of all handicapped children so that appropriate comprehensive services can be provided—have had the effect of encouraging improved communication.

Hospitals and community health and rehabilitation agencies serving young children have not been identified primarily as educational programs. However, increasingly the need has been felt within these settings for an "education component," whether in the form of a specialized nursery school, services of child life educators, or other services. As young children have entered and left these programs to enter a nonspecialized nursery school or developmental day care or to begin formal schooling, the need for continuity has been apparent. The former dichotomy between "school" and "other setting" has proved increasingly unworkable, and the definition of educational services has been quantitatively extended and qualitatively changed to encompass a variety of activities and goals.

Young children with special needs are taught in many settings. But state and local educational agencies—that is, public schools—have the responsibility of identifying *all* handicapped children and of ensuring that each child receives an appropriate education. This means that, whatever the setting in which the child is served, public education's responsibility is to ensure that each child has an individualized educational plan and program and that he is educated as much as possible with nonhandicapped children.

The regular teacher and the specialist

Working with a young handicapped child in a day care, nursery, kindergarten, or primary classroom inevitably requires interdisciplinary communication and teamwork. The teacher must be able to *synthesize* information from a variety of professionals: doctors, psychologists, speech clinicians, special therapists, and others (Bricker, 1976). Although other professionals may work directly with the child, usually none is involved as continuously and extensively as the teacher. To avoid conflicting and confusing methods and approaches, the teacher needs to be able to maintain the perspective of the whole child. To a great extent, the teacher must carry out recommendations and suggestions of other professionals, integrating these with the goals and procedures that he or she thinks should be stressed. A planning team evolves the individualized educational plan, but the child, his parents, and his teacher comprise the team that carries it out on a day-to-day basis.

Even if the child will be taught primarily or exclusively in a "regular" classroom setting, a special education teacher can contribute substantially to each phase: diagnosis, planning, intervention, and evaluation. This specialist may be designated as a *diagnostic/prescriptive teacher, consultant teacher* (McKenzie, 1972; McKenzie et al., 1970), *or resource teacher.* The child's plan may call for part-time placement in a *resource room* (Reger, 1973; Hammill and Wiederholt, 1972) or a self-contained special class setting. Whatever the arrangement may be, communication and effective cooperation between the regular teacher and the specialist are essential. They share the responsibility for teaching the exceptional child.

Parents as team members

In the past, many parents of handicapped children have frequently not found educators and other professionals either responsive to their needs or able to work effectively with them in helping the child (Sullivan, 1976). In both special education and early childhood education, however, the importance of the parents' role has long been recognized. Nonetheless, work with parents has been an area that has not received due emphasis in the training of teachers.

Today, parents are recognized as the first and most influential teachers of their children. Parents must give informed consent for diagnostic evaluation of children and have the right to question the recommendations of educators for special services in school. Legal procedures have been established for resolving disagreements to ensure that the child's best interests are served. However, the intent of recent legislation is that parents will be actively involved in educational planning for children with special needs. This intent identifies the child's parents as genuine partners of the professionals who work with the child in school.

Most teachers in early childhood programs, whether or not they primarily serve exceptional children, will see nothing unfamiliar, threatening, or inappropriate in the idea of teacher-parent teamwork or the idea of the centrality of the parents' role. Infant and toddler programs typically emphasize facilitating the child's development through parent training and guidance. Many nursery and day care programs are parent cooperatives, in which parents govern the program, establish policies and procedures, employ the teacher, and assist in working with the children on a rotating basis. From its beginnings, Project Head Start has stressed parent involvement at all levels. By tradition, teacher-parent cooperation has always been basic to the kindergarten program.

Parental involvement has even greater importance in specialized efforts with young handicapped children. The following are some dimensions of the educator's work with parents of children with special needs:

1. Ongoing *exchange of information*

concerning the child's behavior, needs, and accomplishments

2. *Guidance of parents* in working with their child at home, possibly through a specific home program

3. *Consultation with parents* concerning all aspects of educational planning for the child

4. *Leadership of parent groups,* which may focus on discussion of child development and management, as well as other areas related to the needs of group members

Parents of exceptional children have special needs, too. Sensing the validity of these needs and the severity of the problems many parents face, the teacher may feel unable to provide the help that is needed. Dealing with deep and complex emotional problems and marital difficulties, family dynamics, or serious problems experienced by siblings is beyond the scope of the teacher's role. He or she may be able to identify professionals or agencies that can help, however. Possibly troubled parents or a multiproblem family can be guided to these sources.

It seems clear that to help young children with special needs develop their fullest potential requires an approach to intervention that emphasizes meaningful parent involvement and parent-teacher partnership. Parents of handicapped children have demonstrated their concern that full rights and effective educational opportunities should be available for their children. They have also demonstrated their effectiveness in working toward the accomplishment of these goals through litigation, community action, and lobbying for the sweeping legislative reforms we have recently experienced. Both on this broad scale and on the level of helping the individual child, parent participation is an indispensable element in helping children with special needs.

DISCUSSION QUESTIONS

1. What is diagnostic/prescriptive teaching? What do recent laws require be included in individual educational plans prepared for every handicapped child?

2. What do the legal requirements for multifactored assessment, nondiscriminatory testing, and due process imply for you as a teacher of young children?

3. Distinguish between time sampling and event sampling as methods in observing and recording children's behavior. What are the advantages of a systematic approach?

4. For an individualized educational plan for a handicapped child to be carried out within a "regular" classroom program, what is required of the classroom teacher? What information or assistance may he or she need, and how can this be obtained?

5. What should the relationship between "regular" and "special" education be to ensure that each handicapped child will be provided the least restrictive alternative and the most effective and appropriate education?

REFERENCES

Allen, K. E. Behavior modification: what teachers of young exceptional children can do. *Teaching Exceptional Children,* 1972, *4,* 119-127.

Almy, M. *Ways of studying children: a manual for teachers.* New York: Teachers College Press, 1974.

Armstrong, J. R. Individually guided education (IGE): one model for mainstreaming. *Focus on Exceptional Children,* 1976, *8*(7), 1-11.

Blanco, R. *Prescriptions for children with learning and adjustive problems.* Springfield, Ill.: Charles C. Thomas, Publisher, 1972.

Bloom, B. S. Learning for mastery. *Evaluation Comment* (Vol. 1) Los Angeles: University of California, Los Angeles, Center for the Study of Evaluation of Instructional Programs, May, 1968.

Bower, E. M., and Lambert, N. M. *Teacher's manual for in-school screening of emotionally handicapped children.* Princeton, N.J.: Educational Testing Service, 1961.

Bricker, D. Educational synthesizer. In M. A. Thomas (Ed.), *Hey, don't forget about me! Education's investment in the severely, profoundly and multiply handicapped.* Reston, Va.: Council for Exceptional Children, 1976, pp. 84-97.

Cartwright, C. A., and Cartwright, G. P. *Developing observation skills.* New York: McGraw-Hill Book Co., 1974.

Charles, C. M. *Individualizing instruction.* St. Louis: The C. V. Mosby Co., 1976.

Coloroso, B. Strategies for working with troubled students. In B. R. Gearhart and M. W. Weishahn, *The handicapped child in the regular classroom.* St. Louis: The C. V. Mosby Co., 1976.

Di Leo, J. H. *Young children and their drawings.* New York: Brunner/Mazel, Inc., 1970.

Di Leo, J. H. *Children's drawings as diagnostic aids:* New york: Bruner/Mazel, Inc., 1973.

Ensher, G. L., Blatt, B., Winschel, J. F. Head Start for the handicapped; an audit of the congressional mandate. *Exceptional Children,* 1977, *43,* 202-210.

Gallagher, J. J. A comparison of brain-injured and non-brain-injured mentally retarded children on several psychological variables. *Monographs of the Society for Research in Child Development,* 1957, *22*(2, Whole No. 65).

Ginsburg, H., and Opper, S. *Piaget's theory of intellectual development: an introduction.* Englewood Cliffs, N.J.: Prentice-Hall, Inc., 1969.

Glasser, W. *Schools without failure.* New York: Harper & Row, Publishers, 1969.

Hammerman, A., and Morse, S. Open teaching: Piaget in the classroom. *Young Children,* October, 1972, 41-54.

Hammill, D., and Wiederholt, J. L. *The resource room: rationale and implementation.* Philadelphia: Buttonwood Farms, Inc., 1972.

Harris, D. B. *Children's drawings as measures of intellectual maturity.* New York: Harcourt Brace Jovanovich, Inc., 1963.

Hewett, F. M. *The emotionally disturbed child in the classroom.* Boston: Allyn & Bacon, Inc., 1968.

Hodges, W. L., McCandless, B. R., and Spicker, H. H. *Diagnostic teaching for preschool children.* Arlington, Va.: Council for Exceptional Children, 1971.

Karnes, M. B., and Zehrbach, R. R. Curriculum and methods in early childhood special education: one approach. *Focus on Exceptional Children,* 1973, *5*(1), 1-11.

Kellogg, R. *The psychology of children's art.* New York: Random House, Inc., 1967.

Keogh, B., and Levitt, M. L. Special education in the mainstream: a confrontation of limitations. *Focus on Exceptional Children,* 1976, *8*(1), 1-11.

Klein, J. W. Mainstreaming the preschooler. *Young Children.* 1975, *30,* 317-326.

Lilly, M. S. A training based model for special education. *Exceptional Children,* 1971, *37,* 745-749.

Mager, R. F. *Preparing instructional objectives.* Palo Alto, Calif.: Fearon Publishers, 1962.

McGinty, A. M., and Keogh, B. K. Needs assessment for inservice training: a first step for mainstreaming exceptional children into regular education (Technical report). Los Angeles: University of California, 1975.

McKenzie, H. A. Special education and consulting teachers. In F. Clark, D. Evans, and L. Hammerlynk (Eds.), *Implementing behavioral programs for schools.* Champaign, Ill.: Research Press Co., 1972, pp. 103-125.

McKenzie, H. S., Egner, A., Knight, M., Perelman, P., Schneider, B., and Garvin, J. Training consulting teachers to assist elementary teachers in the management and education of handicapped children. *Exceptional Children,* 1970, *37,* 137-143.

Meier, J. H., Nimnicht, G., and McAfee, O. An autotelic responsive environment nursery school for deprived children. In J. Hellmuth (Ed.), *Disadvantaged child: Head Start and early intervention* (Vol. 2). New York: Brunner/Mazel, Inc., 1968, pp. 299-398.

Meyers, E., et al., *The kindergarten teacher's handbook.* Los Angeles: Gramercy Press, 1973.

Morse, W. C. Crisis intervention in school mental health and special classes for the disturbed. In N. Long, W. C. Morse, and R. G. Newman (Eds.), *Conflict in the classroom: The education of children with problems* (2nd ed.). Belmont, Calif.: Wadsworth Publishing Co., Inc., 1971, pp. 459-465.

Nazzaro, J. Head Start for the handicapped—what's been accomplished? *Exceptional Children,* 1974, *41,* 103-106.

Newman, R. G., and Keith, M. M. *The school-centered life space interview.* Washington, D. C.: School Research Program, Washington School of Psychiatry, 1967.

Piaget, J. *Play, dreams, and imitation in childhood.* New York: W. W. Norton & Co., Inc., 1962.

Redl, F. The life space interview. *American Journal of Orthopsychiatry,* January, 1959, *29,* 1-18.

Reger, R. What is a resource-room program? *Journal of Learning Disabilities,* 1973, *6*(10), 15-21.

Rogers, C. R. *Client-centered therapy.* Boston: Houghton Mifflin Co., 1951.

Schortinghuis, N. E., and Frohman, A. A comparison of paraprofessional and professional success with preschool children. *Journal of Learning Disabilities,* 1974, *7,* 245-247.

Shulman, L., and Keislar, E. R. (Eds.), *Learning by discovery: a critical appraisal.* Chicago: Rand McNally & Co., 1966.

Smith, R. M. (Ed.), *Teacher diagnosis of educational difficulties.* Columbus, Ohio: Charles E. Merrill Publishing Co., 1969.

Sullivan, R. Parent. In M. A. Thomas (Ed.), *Hey, don't forget about me! Education's investment in the severely, profoundly, and multiply handicapped.* Reston, Va.: Council for Exceptional Children, 1976.

Taba, H. Teaching strategies and thought processes. *Teachers College Record,* 1964, *65,* 524-534.

Valett, R. A. *A psychoeducational inventory of basic learning abilities.* Belmont, Calif.: Fearson Publishers, 1968.

Weikart, D. P. Early childhood special education for intellectually subnormal and/or culturally different children. In *Cognitive development and the intellectually subnormal.* Symposium presented at Conference on Manpower Preparation for Handicapped Young Children. Washington, D.C., December 9-10, 1971.

Weintraub, F. J., and Abeson, A. New education policies for the handicapped: the quiet revolution. *Phi Delta Kappan.* April, 1974, *55,* 525-529.

Wolfensberger, W. *The principle of normalization in human services.* Toronto: National Institute for Mental Retardation, 1972.

Wolinsky, G. F Some thoughts on curriculum development for very young handicapped children. *Education of the Visually Handicapped,* 1972, *4*(4), 112-119.

CHAPTER 13

DEVELOPING LEAST RESTRICTIVE ATTITUDES*

*Some of the material in this chapter is adapted from an address, with the same title, presented by the author as part of the conference on Least Restrictive Alternatives in the Education of Handicapped Children of the Mideastern Ohio Special Education Regional Resource Center, Akron, Ohio, April 12-13, 1976.

ORIGINS AND EFFECTS OF ATTITUDES TOWARD THE HANDICAPPED

Probably the most pervasive concern relating to teaching children with special needs in least restrictive settings is with the issue of attitude. A major basis for seeking to integrate handicapped children with those who are not handicapped is the belief that segregation can stigmatize the child (Ross et al., 1971; Hobbs, 1975).

The *affective* consequences of educational segregation of handicapped children are believed to be potentially two-fold:

1. Negative attitudes of others toward the stigmatized child can be created or can become more negative; these can restrict and hurt the child in many ways (Jones, 1972).
2. Both awareness of "differences" and awareness of being segregated from those who are not "different" can negatively affect the child's attitude toward himself: his self-concept and self-esteem (Meyerowitz, 1962).

At the same time, there is a great concern that mere contact or integration cannot change negative, devaluing attitudes that may already exist toward handicapped people. If the child is not accepted by his classmates, or possibly even not accepted well by his teacher, there is fear that he will suffer even greater emotional harm. The argument that the opportunity to know and to interact with this child with special needs will benefit nonhandicapped children suggests to some that the handicapped child is being exploited. Frequently, but certainly not always, the parents of some handicapped children may have this fear. This may lead them to resist integrated placement for their child even though he is capable of meeting the educational demands of a regular program.

Attitudes toward handicapped persons have been of concern to professionals for a long time. However, only recently have these attitudes begun to be comprehensively analyzed. Furthermore, the handicapped have recently emerged, along with other minorities, as a vocal political force —no longer willing to be "done to" and not satisfied with being "done for." A national coalition of handicapped persons now speaks tellingly of the nonhandicapped population as the "temporarily able bodied" (Abeson, 1977).

Not all handicapped persons, however, have been able to act as advocates on their own behalf. Certainly young children have not been able to speak for themselves and to demand their rights. They have been regarded as unfortunate victims, as objects of pity, rather than as individuals who have been guaranteed rights under the law (Ogg, 1973).

Difference, discomfort, and devaluation

Throughout most of the history of the human race, handicapped persons have been regarded and treated, at best, as "different." From the primitive custom of destroying the defective child, societies progressed to the point that residential institutions were provided. It can be argued that institutions were probably created less to serve the handicapped than to protect the "normal" from having to associate with them.

If there is aversion or fear toward the handicapped, why should these exist? Is the mere fact of difference sufficient to explain, not only the creation of institutions, but equally as significant, the remote *location* of many of these institutions (Scheenrenberger, 1974)? A great many Americans having had little contact with handicapped people, have reached adulthood with no more than fragmentary impressions: the sight of a young child with Down's syndrome, smiling, tongue protruding, as he sits in his mother's grocery cart at the supermarket; the labored, lurching movement of a woman with cerebral palsy; a neatly dressed, middle-aged man expertly moving along a crowded sidewalk with his guide dog or raising his white cane as he reaches a curb.

Most of us, however, have had some more direct, personal experience with exceptionality, experience that in some way has colored our attitudes. For many, associations surrounding these experiences may be intimately bound up with the issue of institutions: nursing homes, hospital wards, correctional facilities, special residential schools—sometimes far away in another state. Some of the images we carry are associated with difficult decisions for families, painful visits, lingering grief.

Contemporary society has inherited, and probably carries on an unconscious level, a *mythology* of exceptionality. Rational justifications for the practice of isolation of the handicapped have been offered. Also, however, there is undoubtedly in this practice some vestige of the primitive fear of the handicapped as people who were marked by supernatural forces, who were considered dangerous, who could bring harm and were therefore avoided or placed in isolation (Wolfensberger, 1969; Wolfensberger and Glenn, 1973). Religious motives led to the provision of caring and humane treatment, and even today there is a popular belief that those who work with the handicapped do so out of martyrlike dedication. Generally, handicapped individuals have been seen as helpless, pitiable, and dependent on the selflessness of "special people" who are willing, with perfect patience and great sacrifice, to care for them.

The compound of mythology, tradition, and personal experience is undoubtedly different with regard to various forms of exceptionality. A tradition of respect has probably been associated more with blindness than with profoundly impaired hearing, but even this respect is colored by beliefs that the blind person has an uncanny sixth sense and by a feeling of being uncomfortable and awkward in his presence. In conversation with a blind person, one may feel foolish to find oneself speaking in an unusually loud voice.

The hearing impaired have had to com-bat a tradition of prejudice and stereotype (Laughton, 1976). The expression "deaf and dumb" is still in use and reflects, not only an erroneous belief, but also an unconscious association with that other use of the word "dumb." Over the centuries, severely and profoundly hearing-impaired persons have had to evolve defensive and adaptive behaviors to avoid physical and psychic harm inflicted by hearing society. There has been a tendency toward voluntary segregation as a means of self-protection and of pursuit of normalcy.

At least three major factors in mid–twentieth century American life have had profound impact on public attitudes toward orthopedic disabilities: the epidemic of poliomyelitis and consequent successful efforts to combat this disease; the return of wounded war veterans; the medical advances leading to the increased survival rate of infants born with birth defects. Media campaigns have succeeded in bringing the public greater awareness of children with physical handicaps. Most American adults today have had some experience in their own families with polio, war injury, or both.

In the case of mental retardation and emotional disturbance, despite both media campaigns (and, in the case of the latter, the high probability of personal experience through one's own problems or those of one or more family members), mythology persists. The retarded are believed by many to be dangerous and therefore must be "put away," isolated. The "moron" is the subject of countless jokes, and words like stupid and dumb pervade the language. "Children can be cruel," it is said. However, children's use of the epithet "re-tard" in name-calling directed toward peers who are different in *any* respect is more of a reflection of adult prejudices and of adult-imposed segregation than of any kind of innate cruelty. The name-calling may not reveal *imitation* of adult behavior so much as *identification* with adult attitudes.

Emotional disturbance is feared perhaps more than any other form of handicap, possibly except terminal illness, and the fear has probably a more personal orientation. Again, popular language contributes to stereotypes of the disturbed individual as "crazy," an object either of great fear or of ridicule. Comic images are associated through "funny" words such as "nutty," "going bananas," and "funny farm," neologisms readily adopted by children. Such images are conveyed through the media with far greater ubiquity and greater impact than the spot messages and occasional serious program or article concerning the needs of the mentally ill or the availability of counseling for problems with alcoholism, drugs, or marital relationships.

Segregation: protective, restrictive, or both?

Perhaps the most compelling reason for urging the integration of handicapped and nonhandicapped children for educational purpose is in the domain of attitude. Segregated instruction at the elementary and secondary levels has the effect of depriving both the special needs student and the one with no outstanding handicap of learning experiences essential for the fullest development of their humanness. Segregated instructional units—whatever the basis for segregation—are restrictive.

For the child with special needs, these attitude-related reasons for integration with nonhandicapped children relate primarily to self-concept, self-esteem, and association with capable models. Ironically, one of the major justifications presented for the self-contained special class approach and for institutional placement (Perske, 1972) has been that the handicapped child will be less inclined to experience failure academically and socially and consequently less likely to suffer damage to his positive sense of self. Conversely, within the special class (or special school), since instruction could there be geared directly to his readiness and special needs, he could more readily experience success in these areas. That particular debate has continued, and research results have been equivocal (Kirk, 1972). It is important to remember, however, that studies comparing the self-concepts and emotional adjustment of handicapped children in regular and special class placement generally have been carried out *in the absence of any full-scale effort to optimize the human relations climate of the regular classroom.*

The special, segregated unit has represented a means of *protecting* the handicapped child. Regular educators have been encouraged to think of these children as someone else's responsibility. Although unintentionally, nonhandicapped children have been encouraged to think of them as *different*—or not to think of them at all.

The resulting social climate—given a child conditioned to dependency and placed in an environment in which he is likely to be regarded with curiosity, fear, or hostility—could not be expected to be conducive to the development of a very positive self-image. Consequently, it seems significant indeed that comparative research of the "efficacy" of special vs. regular class placement has *not* pointed overwhelmingly to the former as superior from the standpoint of the self-concept and emotional well-being of the child with special needs.

The attitudes of adults are certainly greatly influenced by socialization experiences during childhood years. A child's own parents, of course, are most influential. Their values are likely to be internalized by the child on an unconscious level, and he is undoubtedly consciously aware of attitudes reflected in overt behavior and verbal expression. Both the school, as an institution, and specific teachers influence attitudes and values of children, often in unintended ways. Certainly, an important factor that has contributed to the negative, fearful, and hostile attitudes that exist toward the handicapped has been the lack of experience most nonhandicapped individuals have had with them in situations permitting meaningful social contact, communication, and friendship.

The rights of children

At the base of recent attempts to ensure that handicapped individuals are guaranteed their rights, such as the right to an appropriate education, is a far-ranging challenge to attitudes traditionally held toward the handicapped. Our new laws can be described both as reflecting changes in social attitudes in recent years and as intended to have further impact on these attitudes. Basically, the handicapped person is seen not as a *burden* to society, but as a valued, contributing member, no less worthy and no less entitled to rights guaranteed by the American constitution than a person who is not handicapped.

Given the focus of this book, such attitudinal transformation should be discussed in terms of another basic change. The change in the role of the child in society has progressed gradually throughout history—to use Phillipe Aries' phrase, throughout *Centuries of Childhood* (Aries, 1962). One of the most challenging concepts confronting educators, as well as everyone in American society, is the concept of the rights of the child. During the twentieth century, this concept has been explored through increasingly far-reaching and intensive study by such means as the White House Conferences on Children. (Alice Hayden [1974] provides an excellent summary of the goals and accomplishments of these Conferences.)

From a history of neglect and apathy, children would seem finally to have progressed to a point at which their inherent individual value and worth are respected and the benefits due them guaranteed. And this revolution in the conception of the rights of childhood is by no means peculiarly an American phenomenon. In the

Declaration of the Rights of the Child, set forth in 1959 by the General Assembly of the United Nations and unanimously adopted by that body, the following principles were stated:

All children, without any exception whatsoever, shall be entitled to these rights, without distinction or discrimination . . . that he may have a happy childhood and enjoy for his own good and for the good of society the rights and freedoms herein set forth,

1. Every child has the right—from birth —to a name and nationality.
2. . . . the right to adequate prenatal and postnatal care.
3. . . . the right to adequate nutrition.
4. . . . the right to adequate housing.
5. . . . the right to adequate medical care.
6. . . . the right to special care for the child who is handicapped.
7. . . . the right to parental affection, love, and understanding.
8. . . . the right to an education.
9. . . . the right to learn to be a useful member of society.
10. . . . the right to develop abilities.
11. . . . the right to be among the first to receive relief in times of disaster.
12. . . . the right to enjoy fully opportunity for play and recreation (Hayden, 1974, pp. 45-46).

It is tragically obvious two decades later that not all children enjoy these rights. Throughout the world, children continue to be victims, and the ideal of a "happy childhood" is cruelly ironic in light of the tragic suffering and want in which so many millions of children continue to live, deprived even of basic necessities.

Cultural imagery and attitudes toward the handicapped

Attitudes toward groups of people in our culture are transmitted in subtle, often unintentional, and surprising ways. Most important perhaps is the imagery that is used with reference to a particular group, and that comes somehow to be associated with that group. As Wolfensberger (Wolfensberger and Glenn, 1973) notes, one seldom sees magazine or newspaper clothing advertisements depicting old people wearing fashionable clothing. The images of youth, dash, vigor, and sexual attractiveness have become associated in the minds of those who see the advertisements. Older individuals, in contrast, are portrayed in such a way as to suggest feebleness or debility, physical and emotional dependency, and incompetence in the marketplace. In literature and folklore, reinforcement of the images of the crone is found. In such ways as these, Wolfensberger asserts, older people come to be thought of as objects, at best, of pity—at worst, of fear. They are people to be avoided. American culture does not emphasize images found in other cultures associating age with wisdom and leadership. Older citizens are thus devalued.

In a similar fashion, a wide array of uncomplimentary images are associated with the handicapped. In the first place, they are identified with an even broader group comprising all those who are *different* and different in an undesirable way. This group includes all handicapped persons, the aged, the transgressors against law, the racially or ethnically different. Such groups as these comprise all those who are not *we,* but *they.* Reinforcement for such collectivized imagery —and *mutual devaluation by association* —can be seen in the physical locations of agencies for the handicapped, the sick, the aged, the poor, and those who are incarcerated. Wolfensberger speaks of *institutional ghettoes.* With regard to the handicapped, the imagery persists in even more noxious form: we have the images of perpetual childhood of the retarded; the images invoking animalistic pictures that tend to attribute subhuman features to the handicapped; and the images suggesting that the handicapped are potentially dangerous and not to be trusted—large signs saying "danger!" or warning that firearms are not to be brought onto the grounds of institutions. (One does not see such signs, Wolfensberger notes, on the grounds of public schools.)

The mass media continue to perpetuate images of "craziness," villains, or "monsters" who have some physical malformation, comic book characters who look and act "dumb," "silly," or "bad."

TEACHER ATTITUDES TOWARD CHILDREN WITH SPECIAL NEEDS

The problem of attitude change is a pervasive and perennial issue among students of human behavior. Before, during, and even since the major breakthroughs on the part of black Americans achieved through the civil rights movement, there have been many who have insisted that positive attitudes cannot be mandated nor brotherhood brought about by legislation. These individuals say that even *tolerance* —surely a negative rather than a positive virtue—cannot be created by court order or the passage of new laws.

However, there is evidence that seems to contradict this position. Although attitudes undeniably influence behavior toward others, it is also true that our behavior—what we do, whether willingly or even through coercion—inevitably affects our attitudes. Individuals and institutions will often do things, although reluctantly at first, if they are compelled to. Once people adopt new patterns of behavior that are congruent with public policy, court rulings, funding guidelines, or other strictures, more favorable affective responses —or at least a lessening of overt resistance—may develop. But people and institutions are resistant to change in these areas, perhaps in direct proportion to the strength of fears, prejudices, and negative mental associations that are involved.

Professionals can have restrictive attitudes, too

Professionals in the field of special education are very concerned about the attitudes of regular classroom teachers, nonhandicapped children, and others in the school and community, mainly because they believe that negative attitudes can have damaging effects on the self-esteem of the exceptional child. They fear that "regular" educators not only lack knowledge of the unique characteristics of handicapped children and the skills required to teach them, but also that historical-cultural attitudes of apathy, guilt, pity, and fear concerning the handicapped may be shared by regular educators (Harth, 1971; Kingsley, 1967).

These four kinds of attitudes are indeed restrictive. The attitude of *apathy* toward the handicapped is reflected in general education's historical neglect of these children, a neglect that mirrors that of society at large. *Guilt* is a restrictive attitude because of the defenses used to deal with guilt, such as denial, repression, or the attribution of blame to the person whose presence elicits the guilt. *Pity* and *fear,* described by Aristotle in the *Poetics* as products of identification with a tragic protagonist, are restrictive attitudes when applied to the handicapped. The individual who is pitied is not respected as a competent person; the individual who is feared is shunned or attacked.

Special educators are well acquainted with attitudes such as these, which are reflected in the vignettes described, for example, in a parent group meeting. A mother of a handicapped child may tell of her feelings when she takes her child to the supermarket. As others avert their gaze, attempting not to look, she sees in their manner embarrassment or pity or even something very close to disgust.

Special educators have grave concerns about the attitudes of their colleagues. They are concerned that restrictive attitudes in the society at large toward handicapped children are harbored by general education teachers. Parents, too, as well as special educators, may perceive in regular education a structure from which their children have been systematically excluded. Consequently, there is a fear for the well-being of the handicapped child in a hostile environment.

However, it can be argued that such distrust and lack of confidence is itself a restrictive attitude, born of unwarranted protectiveness, that restricts all concerned—but especially the child (Perske, 1972). More specifically, this kind of restrictiveness, sometimes imposed by the advocates for the exceptional child, can be analyzed in terms of several limiting attitudes that may be harbored.

"Smothering" attitudes. The word "smothering," implying excessive "mothering" such that the child's striving for autonomy is restricted, has been used as an apt description of some parent-child relationships. It means overprotectiveness, to the detriment of the child, that is aimed more at meeting the needs of the adult than of the child.

Attitudes of negative expectancy. Originally introduced into the literature of the social sciences by Robert Merton (1967), the *self-fulfilling prophecy* refers to the striking tendency of people to behave as they are expected to behave. Consequently, it is often referred to as the *expectancy phenomenon* (Rosenthal and Jacobsen, 1968). On one hand it is entirely possible that the expectations of the child's advocates may be too low, thus making them overprotective and tending to elicit "handicapped behavior." On the other hand, it must be borne in mind that special educators' beliefs and fears that regular teachers are inordinately responsive to the *handicapped* label a child carries may be exaggerated. Some studies (Fleming and Anttonen, 1970) have implied that most teachers are not nearly as gullible as the idea of a "Rosenthal effect" seems to suggest.

Lack of faith and confidence. When specialists fear for "their" children, they may be expressing a lack of faith, both in their fellow professionals and in the children themselves (Fine, 1967). This, in turn, may be based on quite erroneous beliefs —such as the belief that regular educators have had no contact with the handicapped. Most teachers, and most other adults in the society at large, have indeed had some firsthand experience with handicapped persons. And a basic faith that most persons who have sought a career in the field of education have done so, to a significant degree, out of a need and desire to help others would seem basic to any attempt to "mainstream" the child with special needs.

Preoccupation with control. The phrase "preoccupation with control" was used by Charles Silberman (1970) to describe what he saw as a pervasive problem of schools. The need to control may be inordinately present, also, among some who work with handicapped persons, as Ken Kesey so strikingly portrayed in *One Flew Over the Cuckoo's Nest* (Kesey, 1962). This need is one step beyond overprotection, and it is even more injurious to the human spirit.

Blaming the victim. "Blaming the victim" (Ryan, 1971) is an insidious kind of attitude that has been much discussed in recent years in connection with poverty. The poor and unemployed are collectively portrayed, for example, as "welfare chiselers." The mentality of charity is not far removed from hostility and antipathy.

The notion of blaming the victim has also been related to male attitudes toward rape. Specifically, it suggests that a woman who is violated has somehow "asked for it," and the fault is hers. Such an attitude is also involved in restrictive and limiting programming for handicapped children, implying that the "fault" lies with the child. Perhaps for this reason, Cawley (1975) has pointed out the distinction between *disability* (an objective condition) and *handicap*. A physically disabled child, for example, may have an educational handicap only to the extent that the educational system makes it so. The term "hyperactive" applied to a child may have no meaning whatsoever except in relationship to institutional standards and adult frustration levels. It is submitted that the restrictive attitude toward the handicapped of "blaming the victim" is pervasive in our society and that even advocates for the handicapped are not immune.

Categorical thinking and the "difference orientation." Although categorizing is not only functional and necessary in most spheres of human experience, including the education of handicapped children, it is inherently limiting and erroneous. People simply do not fit into categories! A direct result of categorical thinking concerning the handicapped is what Edward Zigler (1966) has termed a "difference orientation." Special educators and researchers have focused so intensely on those things that are different about handicapped children that the universal characteristics and processes these children have in common with the nonhandicapped are often overlooked. It has also been suggested (Zigler, 1966) that, in the case of the mentally retarded, for example, many of the hypothesized "differences" can be explained on the basis of the ways in which social institutions, including schools, respond to these children and the socialization experiences they provide.

Dichotomous solutions to complex problems. A very restrictive kind of thinking is reflected in polarities, such as normal vs. exceptional or regular vs. special education. Very few important issues in life can be resolved as "either this or that." A personality theorist, George Kelly (1955), has effectively described the limitations of a polarized, dichotomized conceptual set. Applied to recent developments in the education of handicapped children, the restrictiveness of the attitudes that either one of two opposite alternatives must be selected is readily apparent. A "cascade of services" model (Deno, 1970) more adequately fits the reality of a broad range of individual differences in learning styles, needs, and characteristics apparent among any group of children identified as handicapped.

Martyrdom, rescue fantasies, and the "special education mystique." Special educators have undeniably contributed to the reticence many regular classroom teachers have concerning their own abilities to work effectively with children with special needs. It is indeed gratifying to be told, "I don't know how you do it! It must take so much *patience* to teach these children." Consequently, it may be difficult for the specialist to give up the sort of awe in which he or she may be held as the only one with the dedication and the expertise required to teach handicapped children.

Toward least restrictive attitudes

How can special educators, in addition to looking critically at any restrictive attitudes they may harbor, work to bring about positive attitude change regarding the handicapped child within the school? Behavioral and social science concepts suggest a number of considerations and approaches. (See, for example, Kiesler et al., 1969.) Some of these are summarized briefly here.

If ignorance fosters fear and hostility, knowledge can help in combating such restrictive attitudes. Perhaps the first requisite to the involvement of the total educational system in the education of children with special needs is the provision of basic information concerning the characteristics and needs of handicapped children. The research of Barbara Keogh and her co-workers (McGinty and Keogh, 1975) concerning elementary teachers' perceptions of their own abilities to teach handicapped children points conclusively to the readiness of teachers to accommodate exceptional children in the "mainstream" if information and assistance believed essential are provided: What are the characteristics of handicapped children? What is an individual instructional approach and how can it be provided within a group classroom setting? What resources are available? Knowledge about handicapping conditions and how they may affect learning is an important component of attempts to promote positive, receptive attitudes toward children

with special needs (Brooks and Bransford, 1971).

If segregation fosters fear and animosity, exposure to handicapped children can be an effective means of reducing such feelings (Clark, 1976). Fear of the unfamiliar is universal. Contact, association, and especially day-to-day involvement with a handicapped child *as an individual child* can be an effective way to reduce this kind of fear and mistrust (Jaffe, 1967). In the case of the handicapped, beliefs may often be based on cultural imagery (Wolfensberger and Glenn, 1973), rather than personal association. Media-produced images contribute heavily to stereotypes, and these are even more detrimental to the handicapped than the literary images of Barrie's Captain Hook (whose villainy is symbolized by his prosthesis) and Mary Shelley's lurching Frankenstein's monster. Meaningful personal relationships with handicapped children can significantly counteract the "familiarity via imagery" that restricts the attitudes of nonhandicapped adults as well as children.

This is not to say that mere exposure to handicapped children will necessarily positively affect attitudes and expectancies. The nature of the involvement appears to be important, at least with regard to peer attitudes, even with very young children (Guralnick, 1976); random interaction is not sufficient.

Terms and labels used not only reflect, but also influence, attitudes. Euphemisms are transparent, as are the awful words created in an attempt to make palatable the unconscionable horrors of war— words like "body count" and "waste" used with reference to killing. Nevertheless, those who work with handicapped children need to be cognizant of the impact of words used. For example, the word "deaf" may convey an unwarranted generalization of inability to hear; "hearing impaired" is in fact more accurate. A term like "mongoloid" or "mongol" *sounds* callous. Furthermore, it is an abbreviated form of an archaic term: "mongolian idiot." The correct medical designation, "Down's syndrome," does not elicit the negative connotations associated with a word such as "mongoloid."

Regarding social education programming, a term such as "mainstreaming" is replete with misunderstandings; "least restrictive alternative programs," although perhaps flowing less smoothly on the tongue, accurately denotes what is proposed. Furthermore, this phrase makes clear that individualized planning is required, rather than wholesale, indiscriminant "dumping" of handicapped children into regular programs (Martin, 1974).

It is not clear whether "intensive instruction class" (I.I.) is an improvement over "learning disabilities class." However, it does describe what is *done,* and it does not place a collective label on the students served there, each of whom has unique needs.

People tend to behave in ways that bring about consequences that are reinforcing to them. This principle, perhaps the most generally accepted law of human behavior, is applicable to the attitudes of regular educators toward handicapped children in at least two principal ways. First, there has probably existed for some time, at least in some quarters, the notion that "having" to teach special needs students is a kind of penalty, or at least that it does not reflect that a teacher is held in high esteem. This condition, if it exists, can be reversed by means of the reinforcers that are meaningful to teachers and within the power of the educational system to provide (Bradfield, 1976). Such reinforcers include especially the idea of associating high status and prestige with a teacher's work with students with special needs and recognition for the teacher's efforts. Other benefits, such as provision of additional preparation time, may also be warranted and effective. They may also be necessary.

The other dimension of providing for legitimate needs of general educators is suggested by the concept that *mainstreaming is a two-way process.* There are many ways in which the special educator can be enabled to assist his or her colleagues as a resource person, while at the same time being available to work directly or through the teacher in helping those students who do not "qualify" for the label "handicapped," but who nonetheless present specialized learning needs.

A success-oriented approach is an effective avenue toward the development of positive attitudes. This principle, generally accepted in the education of special needs students, is equally applicable to the attitudes of adults toward their integration in regular education programs. The immediate implications would seem to be initial selection of strategies for integration offering the highest probability of success from the standpoint of the receptiveness of the teacher involved, the readiness of the child, and the nature of the integrated experience. Beginning with the most promising combinations of teacher, parent, child, setting, and activity and then proceeding gradually through "successive approximations" would appear to offer the greatest likelihood of success. Each child's program must be thoroughly planned and systematically monitored. Voluntary participation of regular classroom teachers would be sought.

Imitation of and/or identification with models is an effective mode of learning. The applicability of the concept of modeling (Bandura, 1965) to the beneficial effects of integrating handicapped children with nonhandicapped classmates is almost self-evident. The degree to which external *structuring* of the learning situation is necessary for modeling to occur, however, is unclear. Mere "togetherness" appears, in itself, insufficient (Guralnick, 1976). However, some research (Peterson et al., 1977) has shown that handicapped preschoolers are likely to imitate nonhandicapped peers in a nursery setting.

Regarding the willingness of teachers to undertake responsibility for the education of handicapped children, modeling is equally important. Research indicates (Bandura, 1969) that models who are admired or who are perceived as powerful are likely to be imitated. What better reason to enlist the support and involvement of the building principal or program supervisor in any attempt to involve regular classroom teachers in the education of handicapped children?

The teacher and his or her attitudes

Scant research has been done concerning the attitudes of "regular" teachers toward the principle that, insofar as possible, handicapped pupils should be integrated in regular education programs. Teachers do seem, however, to endorse this idea but to feel insecure as to their own abilities to help implement it (Keogh and Levitt, 1976).

In a sense, it may be that special educators have been too successful in convincing their regular education colleagues of the necessity of specialized knowledge and expertise required to teach children with special needs. They have contributed to a widespread feeling of inadequacy among teachers concerning their ability to meet the needs of a child who is "special."

A teacher can take some definite action,

beyond the soul-searching that is certainly necessary, to ensure that he or she is prepared psychologically to accept a young child with special needs. Two specific steps would be to make a point to speak *regularly* (not just a single obligatory contact!) with colleagues who work with exceptional children and to visit classrooms or agencies serving exceptional children. Again, to be effective, the latter cannot be a single "sightseeing" tour. Visits to several settings, involving opportunities to observe and if possible to interact with the children—and to talk with the teachers—can be beneficial. Self-initiated "consciousness raising" can also include the following:

> *Reading,* especially of first-hand accounts written by handicapped persons or by parents or teachers of handicapped children
>
> *Beginning a resource collection or file* of items concerning teaching handicapped children and/or materials that can be directly applied
>
> *Making a conscious study of recent legislation, court cases, and news events* concerning handicapped children and their education, as well as handicapped adults
>
> *Making a study of media reference and portrayal of handicapped persons*
>
> *Making a study of community resources* concerned with the handicapped and what the nature of the services provided is in each case
>
> *Inviting speakers and arranging films or other programs* concerning handicapped children for meetings of school or center staff, professional organizations, or social, church, or community organizations

ATTITUDES OF CHILDREN AND PARENTS

The principle of integrating the exceptional child as much as possible with children who are not handicapped assumes that segregation brings about or increases fear and devaluation. We also have some evidence, however, that placing handicapped and nonhandicapped children together in the same setting, in itself, is not sufficient (Guralnick, 1976).

The child with special needs, like all other children, needs to feel competent and valued. He needs to develop a *success identity* (Glasser, 1969). Probably for most children an optimal degree of association with nonhandicapped age-mates is *a necessary, but not sufficient, condition* for the child to view himself as successful, as capable, and as a person who is valued as an individual. Some programming for success is necessary so that the handicapped child can be seen by his peers in a more favorable light (Snyder et al., 1977).

Affective needs of handicapped children

The need to feel that one is worthy, competent, and valued by others is paramount to a handicapped child, as it is to a child who is not handicapped. For every child, the all-important sense of self is formed to a considerable degree from messages from other people, particularly those people whose judgments are most important, and from the child's own actions themselves. The term "feedback," though overused, satisfactorily conveys the relationships between the "messages" and the way an individual feels about himself.

A handicapped child needs to experience success, as do all children. Having had experiences of failure, however, his needs may be even more acute, and the successes cannot be artificial or contrived; they must be genuine. Interaction with peers in social play situations can be one of the most important sources of success experiences for a young handicapped child (Wylie, 1974).

The reaction of pity that handicapped individuals often elicit in others is not helpful or constructive in that it implies minimal expectations and consequently conveys that the person is not thought to be capable or worthy. It can even be argued that the difference between pity and scorn, rejection, or loathing is not at all very great. Pity is not indicative of respect or love; to pity someone is not necessarily to value him or her as a worthy person in his own right.

It is not unusual for parents, teachers, or other significant adults to set expectations that are too low or to fail to impose limits on behavior, not so much from a lack of regard for the handicapped child as from a preoccupation with one's own needs. A handicapped child may set off a complex response pattern of guilt reactions in others, and there are children who, sensing this, become adroit in playing on the guilt of adults. The anger sometimes seen reflected directly or symbolically by some handicapped children may be both a response to the handicap and a way of reaching out to others for the limits and controls that children demand of their parents and teachers.

Concerns of parents of the child with special needs

The parents of a handicapped child bring with them, as their child enters a nursery school or kindergarten program, a complex set of personal needs, which include their realistic concerns about the well-being of their child. One simply cannot simplify or generalize too freely about the needs of the parents of children with special problems (Safford and Arbitman, 1975). Suffice it to note here that, in many instances, the child's problem represents for them the focal point of a variety of related concerns—worries about family life, the nonhandicapped siblings and their well-being, the spouse, and their own awareness of ambivalent feelings toward the child and consequent guilt. For a family to "adjust" to having a handi-

capped child is not as easy or straightforward a task as might be imagined. On the other hand, just as the child himself is not helped by the pity of others, neither are the parents. If the teacher is truly able to *empathize,* that is, able to feel herself in the position of these parents and respond to them in a way in which she believes would be helpful for her, she will not be uncomfortable in talking with her handicapped pupils' parents. She will be better able to establish with them a warm rapport which will permit open communication, rather than awkward, dishonest, or mutually avoiding conversations.

Preparing the other children

Entrance of a new child into an early education program is always an occasion. Some teachers routinely have "circle discussions" in which various things of importance to the group are talked about. Children have an opportunity to express what seems important to them and to ask questions. A new classmate would probably routinely be an occasion for discussion. That the child has a handicapping condition is not the major emphasis of such discussion. Instead, teacher and children talk about their new friend as a child who likes to do things and to have friends, just as they do. Naturalness and normalcy are better than creating undue concern. Children are quick to pick up and respond to signals that their teacher is a little uneasy.

Jenny Klein (1975) advises the Head Start teacher not to make a "big production" out of such preparation. Often, the teacher may convey personal fears and insecurities to the children rather than alleviate theirs or ensure a smooth entry for the handicapped child. Talks with individual children, rather than a general class discussion, may be a more natural route. But the determination of what kind of preparations should be made depends a great deal on the procedures normally followed by the individual teacher with the class.

The "preparation" will hopefully take the form of an ongoing mode of interaction with the children, a classroom environment, and a curriculum that prepares young children to value others.

Dimensions of a human relations approach

Efforts on the part of teachers to address other important issues involving attitudes and social behavior, such as race prejudice or drug abuse, have indicated the need for a more general and far-reaching approach than simply presenting informational "lessons." Factual information is indeed an important dimension of attitude; however, the experience gained through drug education programs has been that knowledge of facts alone will not influence behavior in that area.

Personal decision making and the importance of an attitude of responsibility for one's own behavior, coupled with an empathetic concern for the well-being of others, are appropriate emphases for educational programs concerned with problems of alcoholism and drug abuse, human sexuality, marriage and family relationships, aggression, and intergroup and intragroup relationships. A number of educational programs developed along the lines of these emphases have been made available in recent years involving *values clarification* (Simon et al., 1972) or other themes of human development and personal-social maturity and responsibility. Ojemann (1963) long advocated that we help children to develop a *causal orientation* toward human behavior. Generally, these programs and materials can all be described as relating to *affective education,* since their focus is primarily on attitudinal rather than purely cognitive areas of learning.

Gearheart and Weishahn (1966, Chapter 9, pp. 192-196) provide excellent summaries of values clarification materials and the age groups for which they are intended. A number of these materials are usable with young children.

In a sense affective education can be more accurately described as a kind of *school environment* than as an area of the curriculum. That is, the themes of responsibility, empathy, social concern, personal development, value decisions, etc. must permeate every facet of learning if they are to have meaningful influence on children's affective development. If such themes are contradicted by the teacher's own model, by tolerance of irresponsible student behavior, or by denial of the affective dimensions of *any* area of human knowledge (Jones, 1968)—or by the continued maintenance of schools that are segregated on the basis of race or other characteristics—their impact will probably be effectively negated.

The term "human relations approach" is used here to convey the interrelatedness of attitudinal areas of education. This term implies also the interrelatedness for children of positive attitudes toward the self and toward others. Although we are concerned here primarily with issues of attitudes relating to the child with special needs, these dimensions are applicable to the even broader issues of responsible social behavior, realistically positive self-concept, and constructive handling of internal and interpersonal conflict.

One of the most important vehicles for affectively focused education is discussion. As described by William Glasser (1969), classroom discussion epitomizes true communication. The contributions of the individual who is speaking are valued, not evaluated, and genuine listening occurs. The adult facilitates and models but does not judge by either rewarding or punishing, that is, by praising or criticizing. Glasser emphasizes that for people to listen to each other and speak to each other, they must be face to face. Therefore a circle format is the only possible way to conduct a discussion.

Supportive materials are available from many sources. Some films portraying handicapped individuals have proved very effective with primary children, especially as springboards for discussion, and an increasing number of excellent children's stories concerning handicaps are available for younger children.

A FINAL WORD ON ATTITUDES

Good learning environments for young children are places where teachers value and believe both in the children they teach and in themselves as competent, caring professionals. A teacher who is receptive and who cares will attempt to seek out whatever technical help may be required to accommodate the special needs of a child. Certainly, "love is not enough," to quote the title of one of Bettelheim's best-known books (Bettelheim, 1950). Neither are "good intentions."

Children with special needs require special help. The mainstreaming movement is not a denial of that principle. Further, providing some forms of special help within a "regular" educational setting is probably far more difficult than it would be to place the child in a separate class or program. Leaving the task to the specialist is easier.

The logic, as well as the inherent justice, of normalizing the lives and learning of exceptional children as much as possible is compelling, however. Individually and collectively, we must make a commitment to the principle of least restrictive education for all children. This means valuing and providing for the uniqueness of each child, as well as recognizing the universality of *all* children's needs. It also means conscientious study, careful planning, hard work, and the risk of failure.

Very special children need very special teachers!

DISCUSSION QUESTIONS

1. What evidences do you see in your community that negative attitudes toward handicapped persons may still persist? What evidences that positive change has occurred have you observed?
2. Why do some professionals, such as Wolfensberger, feel that society's approach to serving the

handicapped has in some ways contributed to perpetuating discrimination and devaluation?

3. As a teacher of young children, what impact may you have on the attitudes toward handicapped persons of the children you teach?

4. Keep a record of references made to handicapped persons in television programs, newspaper articles, or other media in your community for a period of time. How are handicapped persons portrayed in children's entertainment and children's literature?

5. How can you ensure that, as a teacher of young children, your own attitudes toward handicapped children are "least restrictive?"

REFERENCES

Abeson, A. *The impact of P. L. 94-142 on the public school.* Speech presented at the Superintendent's Conference, Lincoln Way Special Education Regional Resource Center, Atwood Lake Lodge, Ohio, February 3, 1977.

Aries, P. *Centuries of childhood.* New York: Alfred A. Knopf, Inc., 1962.

Bandura, A. Behavior modification through modeling procedures. In L. K. Krasner and L. Ullman (Eds.), *Research in behavior modification.* New York: Holt, Rinehart & Winston, Inc., 1965.

Bandura, A. *Principles of behavior modification.* New York: Holt, Rinehart & Winston, Inc., 1969.

Bettelheim, B. *Love is not enough.* New York: The Free Press, 1950.

Bradfield, R. *The North Sacramento Project: a successful failure.* Paper presented at the Conference on Least Restrictive Alternatives in the Education of Handicapped Children, Akron, Ohio, March 12-13, 1976.

Brooks, B. L., and Bransford, L. A. Modification of teachers' attitudes toward exceptional children. *Exceptional Children,* 1971, *38,* 259-260.

Cawley, J. F. Special education: selected issues and innovations. In A. D. Roberts (Ed.), *Educational innovation: alternatives in curriculum and instruction.* Boston: Allyn & Bacon, Inc., 1975.

Clark, E. A. Teacher attitudes toward integration of children with handicaps. *Education and Training of the Mentally Retarded,* 1976, *11*(4), 333-335.

Deno, E. Special education as developmental capital. *Exceptional Children,* 1970, *37,* 229-237.

Fine, M. J. Attitudes of regular and special class teachers toward the educable mentally retarded child. *Exceptional Children,* 1967, *33,* 429-430.

Fleming, E. S., and Anttonnen, R. G. *Teacher expectancy or my fair lady.* Paper presented at the annual meeting of the American Educational Research Association, Minneapolis, 1970.

Gearheart, B. R., and Weishahn, M. W. *The handicapped child in the regular classroom.* St. Louis: The C. V. Mosby Co., 1976.

Glasser, W. *Schools without failure.* New York: Harper & Row, Publishers, 1969.

Guralnick, M. J. The value of integrating handicapped and nonhandicapped preschool children. *American Journal of Orthopsychiatry,* 1976, *46,* 236-245.

Harth, R. Attitudes toward minority groups as a construct in assessing attitudes toward the mentally retarded. *Education and Training of the Mentally Retarded,* 1971, *6,* 142-147.

Hayden, A. Perspectives of early childhood education in special education. In N. G. Haring (Ed.), *Behavior of exceptional children: an introduction to special education.* Columbus, Ohio: Charles E. Merrill Publishing Co., 1974, pp. 37-67.

Hobbs, N. *The futures of children: categories, labels and their consequences.* San Francisco: Jossey-Bass, Inc., Publishers, 1975.

Jaffe, J. Attitudes and interpersonal contact: relationships between contact with the mentally retarded and dimensions of attitudes. *Journal of Counseling Psychology,* 1967, *14,* 482-484.

Jones, R. *Fantasy and feeling in education.* New York: New York University Press, 1968.

Jones, R. L. Labels and stigma in special education. *Exceptional Children,* 1972, *38,* 533-564.

Kelly, G. *The psychology of personal constructs* (Vol. 1). New York: W. W. Norton & Co., Inc., 1955.

Keogh, B., and Levitt, M. L. Special education in the mainstream: a confrontation of limitation. *Focus on Exceptional Children,* 1976, *8*(1), 1-11.

Kesey, K. *One flew over the cuckoo's nest.* New York: The Viking Press, Inc., 1962.

Kiesler, C. A., Collins, B. E., and Miller N. *Attitude changes.* New York: John Wiley & Sons, Inc., 1969.

Kingsley, R. F. Prevailing attitudes toward exceptional children. *Education,* 1967, *87,* 426-430.

Kirk, S. A. *Educating exceptional children.* Boston: Houghton Mifflin Co., 1972.

Klein, J. W. Mainstreaming the preschooler. *Young Children,* 1975, *30,* 317-326.

Laughton, J. *Nonverbal creative thinking abilities as predictors of linguistic abilities of hearing impaired children* (Unpublished doctoral dissertation). Kent, Ohio: Kent State University, College of Education, 1976.

Martin, E. Some thoughts on mainstreaming. *Exceptional Children,* 1974, *41,* 150-153.

McGinty, A. M., and Keogh, B. K. *Needs assessment for inservice training: a first step for mainstreaming exceptional children into regular education.* Technical Report, University of California, Los Angeles, 1975.

Merton, R. *Social structure and social theory.* New York: The Free Press, 1967.

Meyerowitz, J. H. Self-derogatives in young retardates and special class placement. *Child Development,* 1962, *33,* 443-451.

Ogg, E. *Securing the legal rights of handicapped persons.* Public Affairs Pamphlet No. 492, 1973. Reprinted in C. J. Drew, M. L. Hardman, H. P. Bluhm (Eds.), *Mental retardation: social and educational perspectives.* St. Louis: The C. V. Mosby Co., 1977, pp. 103-116.

Ojemann, R. H. The significance of a causal orientation in human development. In *Keeping abreast of the revolution in education.* Report of the Twenty-eighth Educational Conference, 1963, Educational Records Bureau, American Council on Education.

Perske, R. The dignity of risk and the mentally retarded. *Mental Retardation,* 1972, *10*(1), 24-27.

Peterson, C., Peterson, J., and Scriver, G. Peer imitation by nonhandicapped and handicapped preschoolers. *Exceptional Children,* 1977, *43,* 223-224.

Rosenthal, R., and Jacobson, L. *Pygmalion in the classroom.* New York: Holt Rinehart & Winston, Inc., 1968.

Ross, S. L., DeYoung, H. G., and Cohen, J. S. Confrontation: special education placement and the law. *Exceptional Children,* September, 1971, *38,* 5-12.

Ryan, W. *Blaming the victim.* New York: Random House, Inc., 1971.

Safford, P. L., and Arbitman, D. C. *Developmental intervention with young physically handicapped children.* Springfield, Ill.: Charles C Thomas, Publisher, 1975.

Scheenrenberger, R. A. A model for deinstitutionalization. *Mental Retardation,* 1974, *12*(6), 3-7.

Silberman, C. *Crisis in the classroom: The remaking of American Education.* New York: Random House, Inc.

Simon, S. B., Howe, L. W., and Kirschenbaum, H. *Values clarification: a handbook of practical strategies for teachers and students.* New York: Hart Publishing Co., Inc., 1972.

Snyder, L. Apolloni, T., and Cooke, T. P. Integrated settings at the early childhood level: the role of nonretarded peers. *Exceptional Children,* 1977, *43,* 262-266.

Wolfensberger, W. The origin and nature of our institutional models. In R. Kugel and W. Wolfensberger (Eds.), *Changing patterns in residential services for the mentally retarded,* Washington, D.C.: President's Committee on Mental Retardation, 1969, pp. 59-171.

Wolfensberger, W., and Glenn, L. *PASS: a method for the quantitative evaluation of human services: field manual.* Toronto: Canadian Association for the Mentally Retarded, National Institute on Mental Retardation, 1973.

Wylie, R. Integrating handicapped and non-handicapped preschool children: effects on social play. *Childhood Education,* 1974, *50,* 360-374.

Zigler, E. F. Mental retardation: current issues and approaches. In L. W. Hoffman and M. L. Hoffman (Eds.), *Review of Child Development Research* (Vol. 2). New York: Russell Sage Foundation, 1966, pp. 107-168.

Appendices

DEVELOPMENTAL PRESCHOOL ASSESSMENT

Ruth Fisher

Director, Developmental Preschool,
United Services for the Handicapped, Akron, Ohio

The United Services for the Handicapped Developmental Preschool Assessment is an overall evaluation of a child's strengths and weaknesses and is not a standardized testing instrument. The evaluation may indicate need for further assessment; then follow-up and referrals should be made for in-depth evaluation of specific areas (speech and language, hearing, vision, physical or occupational therapy).

Information is gained about the preschool child's motor, language, perceptual, and conceptual ability in addition to general behavior patterns observed during the evaluation. More specific information is learned about the following:

How a child uses the large and small muscles of the body

The child's ability to understand and communicate with others

The child's best modality or combination of modalities for learning or taking in information (tactile, visual, auditory)

The child's ability to understand and organize materials into meaningful units

The child's acquisition of basic concepts

The child's ability to remember and sequentially recall information received

Observation of behavior may indicate specific social and emotional problems. Behavior observed only during specific sections of the assessment can indicate problem areas for the child. An example might be excessive shuffling of feet or chair during auditory tasks. Other behavioral problems noted might include hyperactivity, distractibility, short attention span, perseveration, impulsivity, inconsistency, low frustration tolerance, etc.

Classroom teachers, aides, or other trained adults can administer the evaluation. Scoring is simple and subjective. There is no set sequence in which the evaluation is given. It is dependent on the interest and behavior of the child.

Individual sections can be drawn out and used in isolation. In total, the evaluation takes approximately an hour. Materials used can be easily made, adapted, or found in a classroom. Other than the steps and walking board, all materials can be stored in a square plastic dishpan.

The assessment can be utilized with both normal and handicapped preschool youngsters. For children with physical, language, motor, or other problems interfering with usual presentation of materials, adaptations can and should be made. Insight and ingenuity on the part of the evaluator must be brought to bear. (To illustrate, several examples are included in the activities and material sections. Other methods can be devised for children with visual problems, hearing impairment, etc.)

The main purpose of the USH Developmental Preschool Assessment is not to come up with specific scores or comparisons with the "norm," but to see where a child is and assist in formulating an individual education plan for the child that can be carried out in the preschool classroom or at home.

UNITED SERVICES FOR THE HANDICAPPED DEVELOPMENTAL PRESCHOOL ASSESSMENT

Name _____ Date evaluated _____

Birthdate _____ Evaluated by _____

Age and sex _____ Social worker _____

Diagnosis _____

KEY: 4 = Adequate for age level   NA = Not applicable for child
      3 = Slight inaccuracy or hesitancy NR = No response
      2 = Marked inaccuracy or hesistancy
      1 = Unable to perform

Gross motor	**General comments**	**Score**
Walk _____		
Jump _____		
Hop _____		
Skip _____		
Stairs _____		

Fine motor	**General comments**	**Score**
Grasp _____		
Hold _____		
Dominance _____		
Directionality _____		
Eye focus _____		
Tracking _____		

Visual-motor	**General comments**	**Score**
Ball: catch _____		
throw _____		
kick _____		
Beads _____		
Blocks _____		
Coloring _____		
Cutting _____		
Pegs _____		

Balance	**General comments**	**Score**
In place _____		
Walking board _____		

Communication	**General comments**	**Score**
Reception _____		
Expression _____		
Intelligibility _____		
Commands: (1) _____		
(2) _____		
(3) _____		

UNITED SERVICES FOR THE HANDICAPPED DEVELOPMENTAL PRESCHOOL ASSESSMENT—cont'd

Tactile perception	**General comments** **Score**
Object discrimination:	
(1) _____ (2) _____	_____
(3) _____ (4) _____	_____
(5) _____ (6) _____	_____

Auditory perception	**General comments** **Score**
Object discrimination _____	_____
Digit recall: (2) ____ (3) ____ (4) ____	_____
Sentence recall: 2 syl. _____	_____
6-7 syl. _____	_____
12-13 syl. _____	_____

Visual perception	**General comments** **Score**
Color discrimination _____	_____
Form discrimination _____	_____
Size discrimination _____	_____
Object recall _____	_____
Missing object _____	_____

Perceptual organization	**General comments** **Score**
Copy form: (|) ____ (—) ____ (○) ____	_____
(+) ____ (□) ____ (△) ____	_____
Imitation: (|) ____ (—) ____ (○) ____	_____
(+) ____ (□) ____ (△) ____	_____
Divided forms: (½○) ____ (½□) ____	_____
(¼○) ____ (picture) ____	_____
Block patterns _____	_____

Conceptualization	**General comments** **Score**
Body: locating parts _____	_____
divided person _____	_____
incomplete man _____	_____
Number _____	_____
Size _____	_____
Sorting _____	_____

General observations

Motor _____

Language _____

Perception _____

Continued.

UNITED SERVICES FOR THE HANDICAPPED DEVELOPMENTAL PRESCHOOL ASSESSMENT—cont'd

---

General observations—cont'd

Conceptualization _____

_____

Behavior _____

_____

_____

Recommendations _____

_____

_____

_____

_____

United Services for the Handicapped Developmental Preschool Assessment

Activities and materials utilized*	Observations made	Activities and materials utilized	Observations made
Gross motor		*Dominance*	Note preference for
Walk		Hand—reaching,	right or left side
Forward and backward across room.	Watch for general coordination, control,	holding objects.	in gross motor and
Jump	and smoothness of	Foot—kicking ball, ascending steps.	table activities.
In place.	movement.	Eye—paper tube	Note drooling or lack of control of tongue
Over a chalk line.	Foot used to hop.	"spy glass" held	and lips.
Standing broad jump.	Foot used to ascend stairs.	to eye.	
Across the room.	Alternation of feet on	*Directionality*	*Directionality*
Hop	steps.	Pegboard, drawing of lines, counting	Ability to sequence left to right, top to
In place.	Use of railing.	pennies.	bottom.
Across the room.		*Eye focus*	*Eye focus*
Skip		During all activities.	Eyes on objects, teamed.
Around the room.		*Tracking*	*Tracking*
Stairs		Following finger puppet moving	Head movements rather than eye.
Ascend and descend portable steps three times.		in vertical, horizontal, diagonal,	Smoothness and ability to sustain.
Fine motor		circular motion approximately 18	Jumping of eyes at midline.
		inches from child.	
Grasp	*Grasp, hold, dominance*		
Picking up of small beads and pegs.	During all activities, note how objects are		
Hold	picked up, transferred, and held.		
Use of crayon, pencil, scissors.			

*Illustrations of some materials used are found on pp. 318 to 325.

United Services for the Handicapped Developmental Preschool Assessment—cont'd

Activities and materials utilized	Observations made	Activities and materials utilized	Observations made
Fine motor—cont'd		*Coloring*	*Coloring*
Follow sound of candy wrapper moving in same direction (used as final activity when entire evaluation is done).		Rectangle 4 × 6 inches drawn on 8½ × 5½ inch paper. Child colors within confined area using crayon.	How crayon is held. Ability to stay within confined area. Tracing of outline. Coloring in one area only.
Visual motor		*Cutting*	*Cutting*
Ball	*Ball*	Scissors. 4½ × 6 inch paper. Heavy paper with three lines predrawn. Child opens and shuts scissors. Cuts on straight lines.	Hold of scissors and how used. Ability to snip or series of cuts. Staying on lines.
Use soft 6-inch ball —9 foot distance. Catch—throw ball to child three times. Throw—have child throw ball three times. Kick—place ball between child's feet and let child kick three times.	Catch—preparation of arms for catching. Timing. Throw—use of one or two hands for throwing. Transfer of body weight during throwing. Distance thrown. Direction of ball. Kick—foot used to kick. Speed and direction of ball. Balance.	*Pegs*	*Pegs*
		9½ × 9½ inch pegboard. Ten pegs in bowl placed directly at top center of board. Child asked to place pegs in board across top to form straight row.	Ease of placement of pegs in board. Ability to sequence left to right. Hand used to reach for and place pegs. Direction of removal of pegs. Counting number of pegs removed.
Beads	*Beads*	**Balance**	
Two sets of six small ½-inch beads. Six yellow and six green in small cups. Adult strings three yellow and three green; child copies (third set of red beads is for sorting).	Ease of stringing. Following color pattern used.	*In place*	*In place*
		Four-inch-wide, 8-foot-long walking board. Child stands on preferred leg as long as possible. Child stands on other leg as long as possible.	Need for support. Length of time standing independently on each leg.
Blocks	*Blocks*	*Walking board*	*Walking board*
Ten 1-inch plain cubical blocks. Stack as high as possible—three attempts. Count blocks stacked and as returned to bowl. (Use same blocks for block patterning in block patterns test. [visual organization].)	Hand used. Manner in which placed. Number of blocks stacked. Straightness of column. Speed and accuracy.	Child steps up and crosses board three times.	Foot used to step onto walking board. Ability to cross board without falling. Use of arms to help balance. Size of steps and speed crossing board.

Continued.

United Services for the Handicapped Developmental Preschool Assessment—cont'd

Activities and materials utilized	Observations made	Activities and materials utilized	Observations made
Communication		Utilizing the above, give a series of three three-step commands. (Example: give me the pencil; touch your nose; ring the bell.)	
Reception, expression, intelligibility No specific activities or materials are utilized for this section other than commands. Child's total performance is utilized for evaluation.	*Reception* Does child respond appropriately to questions? Does child respond/and or ask "wh" questions (who, when, what, where, why)? Does child follow verbal directions?		
	Expression Use of gestures, single words, phrases, sentences. Sentence structure, grammatical errors. Vocabulary. Length of sentences. Spontaneous communication and exchange of information.	**Tactile perception**	
		Cloth, drawstring bag. Six common objects: spoon, comb, ball, car, key, toothbrush. Child reaches in bag and removes one object at a time. (Nonverbal or unintelligible child is asked to "find the ball.")	Hand used to reach for and return object. Identification of object before seeing. Ability to gesture or express function of object. Return of objects to bag by oral direction of function of object. (Example: "Give me the one you'd eat ice cream with.")
	Intelligibility Ability to comprehend what child says. Specific articulation errors, initial, medial, or ending distortions, substitutions, omissions.		
		Auditory perception	
Commands Bell, car, pencil. Give child a series of one-step commands: 1. Give me the pencil. 2. Touch your nose. 3. Ring the bell. 4. Clap your hands. 5. Give me the car. Utilizing the above, give a series of three two-step commands. (Example: ring the bell; clap your hands.)	*Commands* Number of commands followed. Order or sequence in which commands were followed.	*Object discrimination* Large cardboard color discrimination card to shield objects making sound. Bell, penny, paper, knock on table. Sight unseen, child identifies objects he hears. If all correct, no need to repeat. If incorrect, child is shown and listens to each sound; objects hidden again and child identifies. (Nonverbal or unintelligible child is asked to "Show me the one you heard.")	*Object discrimination* Observe whether child responds to outside noise during evaluation. Gesturing or naming of objects heard and whether sounds are localized.

United Services for the Handicapped Developmental Preschool Assessment—cont'd

Activities and materials utilized	Observations made	Activities and materials utilized	Observations made
Auditory perception—cont'd		Child names colors (red, yellow, dark blue, light blue, green, orange, brown, purple, pink).	
Digit recall	*Digit recall*	Child returns balls by color named. ("Give me the red ball.")	
Three series of two digits for child to repeat—pause between digits: (Example: 2–8)	Number of digits able to recall. Sequence of digits recalled.	*Form discrimination*	*Form discrimination*
Three series of three digits for child to repeat. (Example: 9–2–6)		Wooden commercial form board with four knobbed parts (circle, two squares, cross).	Hands used to point and place. Self-correction. Identification of shapes expressively and receptively.
Three series of four digits for child to repeat. (Example: 7–1–6–4)		Child points to, places pieces. Cardboard 8½ × 11 inches with five shapes same color pasted on (circle, square, triangle, cross, half circle); five matching individual shapes.	
Sentence recall	*Sentence recall*		
Ask child to repeat the following:	Length of phrase or sentence recalled. Omissions and sequence of words repeated. Articulation problems.		
2 syllables a. hot soup. b. red car. c. nice dog.		Child points to, places pieces, names shapes. Child returns shapes by shape names.	
6-7 syllables a. I have a blue jacket. b. The cat drank all his milk. c. The policeman stopped the car.		*Size discrimination*	*Size discrimination*
		Cardboard with four different size circles pasted on; four matching individual sized circles.	Hand used to point and place. Seld-correction. Placement of circles. Identification of size expressively and receptively.
12-13 syllables a. The little gray cat was playing with the big dog. b. I went to the store with my mother yesterday. c. Last night we had spaghetti and meatballs for dinner.		Child points to, places pieces. Child names and returns circles by size (big, little).	
Visual perception		*Object recall*	*Object recall*
Color discrimination	*Color discrimination*	Washcloth with four objects (toy shoe, bottle, fork, horse).	Ability to unscrew and screw on bottle cap. Naming of function of objects. Associations. Animal sounds. Need to touch hidden objects or look under cloth. Number of objects named.
Large cardboard 14½ × 14½ inches with nine colored balls pasted on; nine matching individual cardboard colored balls.	Hand used to point and place. Ability to self-correct. Identification of colors expressively and receptively. Placement of circles.	Child sees, names objects. Objects covered with cloth; child recalls what was there.	
Child points to, then places matching colored circle.			

Continued.

United Services for the Handicapped Developmental Preschool Assessment—cont'd

Activities and materials utilized	Observations made	Activities and materials utilized	Observations made
Visual perception—cont'd		6-inch cardboard circle divided in quarters. Child asked to make a circle or ball from parts. Child asked to make a square or box from parts. Child asked to make another circle or ball from parts. (Demonstrate if child is unable to form; try again.) Picture of Coke bottle pasted on cardboard 3½ × 8 inches divided into three equal parts. Child is asked to put the bottle together as parts are placed in a horizontal row. Child is asked to point to top, bottom, middle of Coke bottle.	If unable, can it be done following demonstration? Can child identify top, middle, bottom of Coke picture?
Missing object One object at a time is removed and hidden in wash cloth. Child names missing object. (repeat with all four objects).	*Missing object* Understanding concept. Number of missing items named.		
Perceptual organization			
Copy form Six cardboard squares 3½ × 3½ inches individually marked with a vertical line, horizontal line, circle, cross, square, triangle. Plain 8½ × 11 inch paper, pencil. In sequence, cards are shown to child who copies what is drawn.	*Copy form* Hand used and how pencil is held. Direction in which lines and circles are drawn (left to right, top to bottom, counterclockwise). Number of drawings acceptable completed. Placement on paper.		
Imitation Opposite side of paper previously used. Adult utilizing left half of paper separately draws vertical line, horizontal line, circle, cross, square, triangle. Pencil placed in center of paper with point away from child. After each shape is drawn, child imitates on right half of paper.	*Imitation* Manner in which pencil is picked up (wrist rotation) and held. Hand used. Direction in which lines and circles are drawn. Number acceptably completed. Placement. Comparison made between two sides of paper.	*Block patterns* Bowl of ten plain 1-inch cube blocks (used for stacking). Adult makes tower of three blocks; child models. Adult makes train with four blocks; child models. Adult makes bridge with three blocks; child models.	*Block patterns* Ability to follow model. Placement of blocks. Reversals. Imitation of train sound.
Divided forms 6-inch cardboard circle divided in half. 5-inch cardboard square divided in half.	*Divided forms* Ability to form the whole circle or square on verbal direction.		

United Services for the Handicapped Developmental Preschool Assessment—cont'd

Activities and materials utilized	Observations made	Activities and materials utilized	Observations made
Conceptualization		*Number*	*Number*
Body concept	*Body concept*	Ask child to rote count as high as possible.	Ability to sequence numbers.
Finding parts on self; child touches facial and body parts named.	Use of one hand or both.	Ten pennies.	Matching of numbers to object.
	Finding paired parts.	Child counts pennies lined in horizontal row.	Direction used to count (left to right).
Parts include eyes, ears, nose, mouth, head, hair, neck, arms, legs, foot, hands, fingers, shoulders, knees, elbows, wrists, ankles.		Divide pennies into groups.	
		Ask questions about which group has more, less, most, least.	
Divided person	*Divided person*	Ask child to give adult certain number of pennies. (Example: "Give me three pennies.")	
Picture of a lady pasted on 4 × 10 cardboard, cut into five parts.	Awareness of relationship of body parts.		
	Identification of body parts on picture.	*Size*	*Size*
Pieces lined up horizontally.	Ability to form the whole.	Cardboard 4½ × 7½ inches with four different size squares.	Throughout evaluation, concept of size can be determined. (Example: compare big and little balls, toy shoe fitting on child, etc.).
Child asked to put the lady together.	(See divided forms test perceptual organization.)		
Demonstrate if necessary, child repeats.		Child is asked to point to the big, little, biggest, smallest, smaller, bigger square.	
When together, child points to body parts on picture as named.			
Returns pieces by identification of body part named. (Example: "Give me the lady's knees.")		Cardboard 4½ × 6 inches with three different length lines.	
		Child is asked to point to the longest, shortest, line on the top, bottom, middle.	
Incomplete man	*Incomplete man*	*Sorting*	*Sorting*
Line picture of an incomplete man drawn on a 5½ × 8½ inch paper.	Additional features added (such as eyebrows, navel, clothing, etc.).	Three cups of beads (two used for stringing)—six red, six yellow, six green.	Manner in which sorting is done (all one color before proceeding to next, sequencing, etc.).
Pencil.	Location of parts added.	Beads are mixed on table.	Hand used and way beads are picked up.
Missing are one ear, eyes, neck, part of bow tie, one arm and hand, one leg and foot.	Direction of lines drawn.	One of each color is placed in cup.	Compare ability to sort concrete vs. pictorial representations.
	Hand used to draw and pencil hold. (If child's ability to draw is poor, have him point to where parts should be and let adult draw in.)	Child sorts.	Additional information can be obtained by asking child questions about the pictures. (Example: "Which chair is softest?" "Where would
Child is asked what is missing or wrong with picture.		Set of fifteen cards with five pictures of different kinds of trees, tables, chairs.	
After verbalizing missing parts, child is asked to finish the picture.		One of each is placed on table.	

Continued.

United Services for the Handicapped Developmental Preschool Assessment—cont'd

Activities and materials utilized	Observations made	Activities and materials utilized	Observations made
Conceptualization—cont'd		Directional preposition: box 4 × 6 × 2½ inches made into a garage. Toy car. Child is asked to park the car in, beside, next to, and on top of, in front of, behind, in back of the garage.	
Child has to sort cards given to him into three piles. *Color, shape, directional prepositions* Use information gained from using color and shape names expressively and receptively in perception activities.	you find a tree growing like this?" [palm tree]?) *Direction prepositions* Throught the evaluation other directional prepositions are used and should be noted. (Example: "Jump *over* the line"; "hop *across* the room"; "put your chair *under* the table.")		

Finger puppet (felt) for tracking test (fine motor).

Rectangle (actual size, 4 × 6 inches) for coloring test (visual-motor

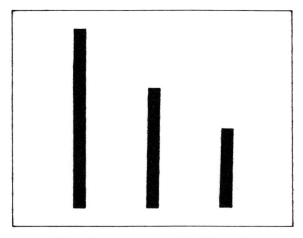

Lines for cutting test (visual-motor).

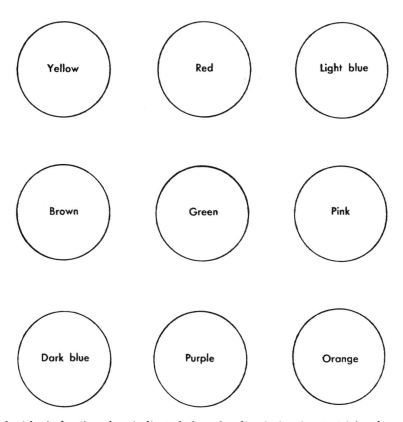

Cardboard with circles (in colors indicated) for color discrimination test (visual perception).

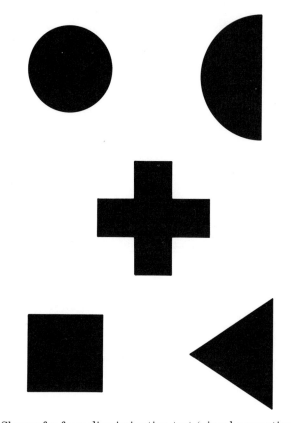

Shapes for form discrimination test (visual perception).

Circles for size discrimination test (visual perception).

Shapes for copy form test (perceptual organization).

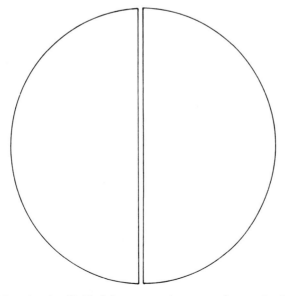

Half circles for divided forms test (perceptual organization).

Half squares for divided forms test (perceptual organization).

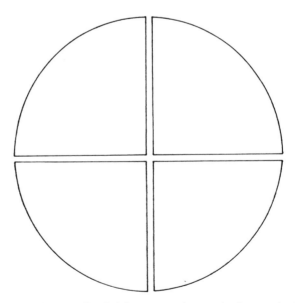

Quarter circles for divided forms test (perceptual organization).

Divided picture for divided forms test (perceptual organization).

Divided picture for divided person test
(conceptualization).

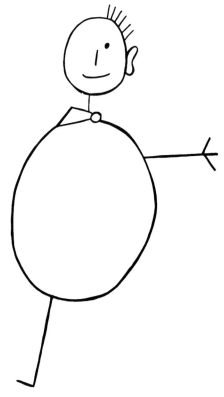

Drawing for incomplete man test
(conceptualization).

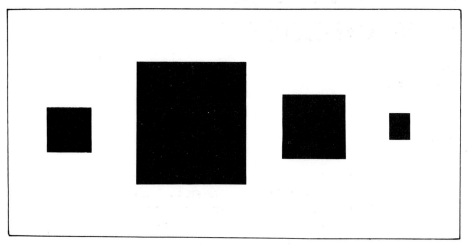

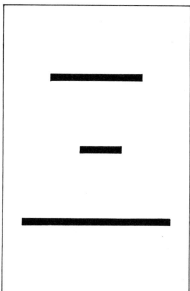

Forms for size test (conceptualization).

NORMATIVE AND DIAGNOSTIC GUIDES FOR WORKING WITH YOUNG CHILDREN

compiled by
Alice Kusmierek

The parent and the professional*

1. You are the primary helper, monitor, coordinator, observer, record keeper, and decision maker for your child. Insist that you be treated as such. It is your right to understand your child's diagnoses and the reasons for treatment recommendations and for educational placement. No changes in his treatment or educational placement should take place without previous consultation with you.

2. Your success in getting as well informed as you will need to be to monitor your child's progress depends on your ability to work with the people who work with your child. You may encounter resistance to the idea of including you in the various diagnostic and decision-making processes. The way you handle that resistance is important. Your best tool is not the angry approach. Some of your job will include the gentler art of persuasion. Stay confident and cool about your own abilities and intuitions. You know your child better than anyone else could. You are, obviously, a vital member of the team of experts.

3. Try to find, from among the many people whom you see, a person who can help you coordinate the various diagnostic visits and results. Pick the person with whom you have the best relationship, someone who understands your role as the principal monitor of your child's progress throughout life and who will help you become a good one.

4. Learn to keep records. As soon as you know that you have a child with a problem, start a notebook. Make entries of names, addresses, phone numbers, dates of visits, the persons present during the visits, and as much of what was said as you can remember. Record the questions you asked and the answers you received. Record any recommendations made. Make records of phone calls too; include the dates, the purpose, the result. It is best to make important requests by letter. Keep a copy for your notebook. Such documentation for every step of your efforts to get your child the service he needs can be the evidence which finally persuades a program director to give him what he needs. Without concise records of whom you spoke to, when you spoke to him, what he promised, how long you waited between the request and the response, you will be handicapped. No one can ever be held accountable for conversations or meetings with persons whose names and titles you do not remember, on dates you cannot recall, about topics which you cannot clearly discuss.

5. Make sure that you understand the terminology used by the professional. Ask him to translate his terms into lay language. Ask him to give examples of what

*From Gorham, K. A., Des Jardines, R. P., Pettis, E., and Scheiber, B. Effect on parents. In N. Hobbs (Ed.), *Issues in the classification of children* (Vol. 2). San Francisco: Jossey-Bass, Inc., Publishers, 1975, pp. 154-188.

he means. Do not leave his office until you are sure you understand what he has said so well that you can carry information to your child's teacher, for instance, and explain it to her in clear, understandable language. (Write down the professional terms too. Knowing them might come in handy some time.)

6. Ask for copies of your child's records. You may or may not get them, but you could ask that a tape recording be made of any "interpretive" conference. It is very hard to remember what was said in such conference.

7. Read. Learn as much as you can about your child's problem. But do not swallow whole what you read. Books are like people. They might be offering only one side of the story.

8. Talk freely and openly with as many professionals as you can. Talk with other parents. Join a parent organization. By talking with people who "have been through it already," you can gain a perspective on your particular problems. Besides, you will receive moral support and will not feel quite so alone. Get informa-tion from parent organizations about services available, about their quality. But bear in mind that a particular program might not help your child even though it has proved helpful to another child. Visit programs if you have the time and energy to do so. There is no substitute for first-hand views.

9. Stay in close touch with your child's teacher. Make sure you know what she is doing in the classroom so that, with her help, you can follow through at home. Share what you have read with her. Ask her for advice and suggestions. Get across the idea that the two of you are a team, working for the same goals. Make your child a part of that team whenever possible. He might have some great ideas.

10. Listen to your child. It is his point of view that he is giving you, and on that he is an expert.

11. Work hard at living the idea that differentness is just fine—not bad. Your child will learn most from your example. Help him to think of problems as things that can be solved if people work at them together.

Normal child development*

Piaget's stage with approximate age			
I. Sensory-motor operations			
1. Reflexive (0-1 month)	Simple reflexive activity, such as kicking	schema (9-13 months)	reaches behind cushion for ball. Distinguishes "me" from "not me." Mental image. Imitates.
2. Primary circular reactions (1-4½ months)	Reflexive behavior becomes elaborated and coordinated, such as eye follows hand movements, begin eye-hand coordination.	5. Tertiary circular reactions (12-18 months)	Discovers new ways to obtain desired goal, i.e., pulls pillow nearer in order to get toy resting on it.
3. Secondary circular reactions (4½-9 months)	Repeats chance actions to reproduce an interesting change or effect; such as kicks crib, doll shakes, so kicks crib again.	6. Invention of new means through mental combination (18-24 months)	Invents new ways and means such as using stick to reach desired object. Engages in thought before doing. Thought precedes language.
4. Coordination of secondary	Acts become clearly intentional, such as		

*From Crain, Jacqueline. *Early childhood education for diversely handicapped children.* Springfield, Ill.: Illinois Office of Education, 1974.

Continued.

Normal child development—cont'd

Piaget's stage with approximate age—cont'd

Child development

Age 1

Motor—Creeps, walks with support, prehension is precise and well developed, transfers objects.

Self-care—Cooperates in dressing, removes clothing.

Communication—5-6 words, listens and repeats words, matches actions to words, "Give it to me."

Adaptive behavior—Solitary play, demonstrates growing sensitivity to emotions of others.

II. Pre-operational

1. Preconceptual (2-4 years)—Capable of verbal expressions, but speech is repetitious, frequent egocentric monologues. Uses word to signify object.

Age 2

Motor—Needs to use two hands for most operations. Interested in finer manipulation of play materials, copies circle, runs well.

Self-care—Helps in dressing, washes and dries hands, eats independently.

Communication—Names of things, persons, actions, and situations greatly predominate. Average 300-word vocabulary, but uses words unequally. Puts 3 words together.

Adaptive behavior—Very self-centered. Infers causes from observing effects and vice versa. Imitates complex, nonhuman, and absent models. Anticipation and memory.

Age 3

Motor—Rides tricycle, copies cross.

Self-care—Takes responsibility for toilet, dresses without help, spoon is grasped between thumb and forefinger.

Communication—Nearly 1000 words; names primary colors; follows 2 or 3 directions; knows age and sex.

Adaptive behavior—Can match simple forms, common fears, beginning of ability to share. Beginning cooperative rather than parallel play.

2. Intuitive (4-7 years)—Speech becomes socialized; reasoning is egocentric; "to the right" has one meaning—to his right.

Age 4

Motor—Draws four-part man, copies square, goes about within block, uses scissors well.

Self-care—Can take own bath with verbal prodding, laces shoes.

Communication—1500-2000-word vocabulary, opposite analogies.

Adaptive behavior—Similarities and differences between pictorial stimuli, considerable rational and even abstract thinking.

Age 5

Motor—Well-developed gross motor, copies triangles, draws six-part man.

Self-care—Plays outdoors safely, blows own nose.

Communication—2200-word vocabulary, language essentially complete in structure and form, defines in terms of use.

Adaptive behavior—Likes supervision, instruction, asks permission. May sit together but work independently, leave at will.

Age 6

Motor—Almost constant activity, draws nine-part man, copies vertical diamond, plays group games.

Self-care—Ties shoes, spreads own bread.

Communication—Usually acquired all of speech forms used by adult. Begins storing factual information. Learning to reason more correctly, great capacity to pretend, but knows reality.

Adaptive behavior—Exasperatingly inconsistent, begins to understand time, past and future, but lives chiefly in the present.

III. Concrete operations (7-11)—Mobile and systematic thought organizes and classifies information; is capable of concrete problem solving. Group, classify objects. Flexibility and reversibility in thought processes.

Age 7

Motor—Grasp releases suddenly, cuts carefully.

Self-care—Cuts meat, tells time, quarter-hour, makes change.

Communication—Similarities and differences between two named things, reads and follows signs, questions "why" of cause and time.

Adaptive behavior—Uses tools to construct idea of good and bad; becoming more abstract, conscientious.

Age 8

Motor—Increase of speed and smoothness in fine motor, beginning to draw in perspective.

Communication—Can verbalize ideas and problems, uses language fluently, almost as adult. Beginning to understand cause-and-effect relationship.

Adaptive behavior—Collects things. Torn between desire to grow up and remain as he is. Interested in evaluating his performance in relationship with others. Interest in money and acquiring it.

Age 9

Motor—Good eye-hand coordination.

Self-care—Self-sufficient.

Communication—Written word more or less established as means of communication.

Adaptive behavior—Relatively well organized, fair, reasonable, dependable, persistent, interest in process and skill.

Normal child development—cont'd

Piaget's stage with approximate age—cont'd

Age 10

Motor—Eyes can take close work with little strain.

Communication—Is eager for factual knowledge and can memorize easily.

Adaptive behavior—Has developed his own individual personality. Is capable of independent action, strong sense of justice, needs active participation in order to learn.

IV. Formal operations (11 years and up)—Can think abstractly, formulate hypotheses, engage in deductive reasoning and check solutions.

Age 11

Self-care—Tests the situation with poor manners.

Communication—Uses it as social tool. Becoming aware of language exploitation but may not grasp irony or sarcasm. Similarities between 3 objects.

Adaptive behavior—Interest in own bodies, sex, reproduction. Fairly well established his learning personality. Start of constant two-somes (first real "capacity to love").

Conceptual development

1 month	Basic sensory motor responses which form the basis for alternatives in future stages.
4-8 months	Intention and means/end relationship are beginning to develop. Child shakes a rattle to hear. Beginnings of object permanence: He looks, for a short time, for object removed from field of vision. Puts "motor meaning" to objects. Shakes head at sight of rattle.
8-12 months	Beginning of symbolic meaning —Actions to represent object. Overpermanence of objects— Child watches you hide an object in one hand and finds it. Watches while hidden in other hand but looks in first hand. First indication of causality. Applies familiar scheme to new situations.
12-18 months	Negation of overpermanence. Development of space perception modifies familiar schema to fit new perceptions. Trial and error processes begin.

	Causality—Child uses string to pull object to him.
18-24 months	Formulates negative judgment. "Spoon is not a fork." Says *no* on high plane of logic. Object permanence—Child looks behind couch for ball that rolled under front.
24-30 months	Understands concepts, *in, under.*
3 years	Understands concepts *in front of, behind, on.* Comparison of lines—Can pick out the longest. Verbs—Can answer, "Show me sitting." Adjectives—Big, little, hard, soft. Can classify objects on the basis of physical attributes.
4 years	Comparison of weights—can find the heaviest. Knows colors. Understands money is for purchasing. Defines objects by their use. Can tell stories without pictures. Can classify on the basis of groups—"These are all animals."
4½ years	Can classify on the basis of function. Can answer "Is it hot in winter?"
5 years	Can make aesthetic comparison. "Which is pretty?" Can make application of "Many-to-one" but not "one-to-many."
5½ years	Can classify by association— rattle goes with baby. Developing right-left concept.

Fine motor development

1 month	Thumb has characteristic curled-in position. Finger movements are not bilateral and simultaneous.
3 months	Disappearance of grasp reflex, no longer are hands tightly closed. Holds rattle voluntarily when it is placed in his hand.
4 months	Thumb doesn't participate in cube prehension. Hands come together as he plays. Plays with rattle placed in hand for prolonged period.
5 months	Approach to objects is two-handed. Grasp is limited to large objects.

Continued.

Normal child development—cont'd

Fine motor development—cont'd	
6 months	Uses hands to reach, grasp, crumple, bang, and splash. Makes scooping motion with hand in grasping pellet. Opposes thumb in grasping cube.
9 months	Transfers objects from one hand to the other. Uses pincer prehension with one hand in picking up object.
10 months	Begins to release object, lets object go deliberately instead of accidentally.
2 years	Palmar grip giving way to extension of radial fingers toward point of writing instrument. Turns door knob, unscrews lids.
3 years	Aligns fingers in anticipation of plucking object from table without touching table top.
4 years	Holds hand above or to one side so as not to obstruct view of what he builds. Independent use of both hands in building. Improved steadiness of hand, timing and release of objects.
5 years	Prehends in adult manner with two ulnar fingers flexed into palm. Prehends and places object in one continuous movement.
Communication	
1 month	Change in pitch—Sign of bodily discomfort.
2 months	Babbling begins, coos, gurgles. Reflex activities produce sounds. Lalling—Repetition of sounds that the child hears for physical pleasure and auditory stimulation. Cry changes with body state.
5 months	Vocal play.
6 months	Directs sounds and gestures to objects. Intonational pattern with jargon.
7 months	Vocalizes emotional state.
8-12 months	Meaningful attempt at conversation. First word. Understands phrases and wholes. Responds by action to command. Echolalia. 1 word sentences (5-6 word vocabulary).

18 months	Jargon directed at people. 1.5-word sentence.
18-24 months	Understands most linguistic units—Not yet separated into word units. Pulls to communicate. Uses one word for many unrelated things—Extension of meaning.
24-30 months	Verbalizes simple experiences and emotions. Speech with pointing. Speech has become a tool as well as warning and safety valve. 1.8-word sentence.
30-36 months	Comprehends time words. Uses compound and complex sentence structure and plurals. Questions begin. 3.1-word sentences.
3 years	Says full name. Final consonants appear, sound begins to include blends. Uses 2-word phrases. Asks questions about persons, things, and processes.
3.6 years	Repetitions are frequent. Relates experiences with understanding of sequence. Asks why but not for knowledge.
4 years	Normally fluent. Advancing sentence structure. Alludes to objects, persons, events outside immediate environment.
4.6 years	Reverses order of sound. Spontaneous grammar correction.
5 years	Relates fanciful tales and present and past events. Language becomes symbolic. Uses all basic sentence structures. 4-5-word sentence length. Counts to 10, knows age, name, primary colors.
Gross motor	
8 weeks	Readily lifts chin in prone position.
12 weeks	Raises head and shoulders with forearms.
16 weeks	Holds head up when sitting supported.
20 weeks	Rolls over on side in supine position. Sits supported in high chair.

Normal child development—cont'd

Gross motor—cont'd		Perceptual development	
32 weeks	Begins to sit unsupported. Can support weight on legs for short period.	1 month	Follows horizontal movement of light or bright object to midline in an arc no greater than 90 degrees. Responds to loud noises by crying or startling (newborn). Quieted and reduced activity level by approaching sounds (1 month).
36 weeks	Sits steadily unsupported for a long time. Raises body to crawling position and may crawl backwards.		
40 weeks	Pulls self to sitting and standing positions.	2 months	Eyes fixate, converge and focus. Long waves (red, orange, yellow) are perceived first. Follows vertical movement. Accepts loud noises as part of environment—doesn't react violently.
44 weeks	Crawls forward with abdomen off the floor.		
48 weeks	Can turn and pick up object while sitting. Walks sideways using support or forward with two hands held. Lowers body from standing to sitting by holding on to support.	4 months	Looks intently at objects in hand or in front of him. Responds massively (head, shoulders and arms) to an object dangling in front of eyes. Lateral head and eye movement in search of sound (beginning of localizing response). Hands together at midline.
13 months	Stands alone.		
15 months	Stands self up without using support. Creeps upstairs.		
Less than 1 year—18 months	Walks alone with immature gait.		
18 months	Climbs stairs holding rail. Goes down stairs creeping backwards. Pulls and pushes toys while walking. Can throw ball without falling.	6 months	Fixates where object disappears. Localizes sound by moving head and eyes laterally and upward.
		7 months	Looks for fallen object. Finds partially hidden object. Localizes sound by moving head and eyes in sweeping arc to source. Unidextrous approach. Transfers object from hand to hand.
21 months	Walks backwards. Begins to run and jump.		
2 years	Walks up and down steps alone, 2 feet per step. Can kick a ball.		
2½ years	Walks on tiptoe. Jumps down with both feet.	9 months	Can pick up string or object the size of a currant between finger and thumb.
3 years	Can stand on one foot for a few seconds. Jumps off floor with feet together. Goes upstairs with one foot per step. Catches large ball with arms out straight. Rides tricycle.	10 months	Looks around corner for object. Imitates gestures (waving bye-bye) and facial expressions.
		1 year	Perceives roundness, puts finger or rod in round hole. Places objects in container. Pincer grasp of small object. Palmar hold of crayon.
4 years	Hops on one foot. Runs, stops, starts, turns. Can carry a cup of water without spilling it. Catches large ball with arms flexed at elbows.	1½ years	Shows interest in pictures and can identify objects in pictures. Can build vertical tower of 2-3 blocks. Matches round block to round hole and either a square or triangle. Imitates vertical stroke.
5 years	Skips with both feet. Marches in time to music. Has body shift when throwing a ball.		

Continued.

Normal child development—cont'd

Perceptual development—cont'd

1½ years—cont'd · Responds to two simple commands.

Can point to own body parts (2-3).

Imitates mother's common chores.

Scribbles spontaneously.

2 years · Increases visual memory span—looks for missing toys, recalls events of previous day.

Can select object named from group of objects or pictures.

Matches mounted colors (red, yellow, green, blue) with 45% right.

Builds vertical tower of 6 blocks.

Builds 3 blocks horizontally.

Imitates horizontal stroke.

Listens to stories.

Repeats 3-4-syllable sentences.

Repeats 2 digits in one of three trials.

3 years · Puts two halves of pictures together even when rotated 180 degrees.

Builds tower of 9-10 blocks with increased command of vertical movements.

Imitates building of bridge, i.e., horizontal and vertical.

Matches forms by inserting circle, square and triangle in cut-out forms even with reversal of position.

Repeats three digits, out of rote sequence, one out of three trials.

Can make a choice of two alternatives.

4 years · Can supply 3 missing parts to a drawing of an incomplete man.

Makes comparative size discriminations consecutively.

Discriminates length of lines regardless of orientation.

Can match eight of ten forms.

Traces diamond shape between 2 parallel lines.

Copies circle more accurately, with ends joining.

Copies cross.

Uses plurals.

Counts, pointing to 3 objects (concepts to 2).

Repeats 12-13 syllable sentences.

Repeats 3 digits, three out of three trials.

Discriminates noisemakers.

Matches sound blocks by loudness.

5 years · Perceives details visually and asks about it.

Puts diagonals together: 2 triangles to make a rectangle.

Matches 10 forms.

Copies square and triangle.

Can insert sequence of nesting cups.

Names four colors.

Carries a melody.

Follows and repeats sequence of a story.

Claps to rhythm of song or drum.

Perceived detail auditorially—selects a word from a sequence and asks about it.

Repeats 4 digits, 3 out of 3 trials.

Can grade sound blocks by loudness.

6 years · Copies diamonds and rectangles.

Repeats five digits.

Social development

12 weeks · Knows mother and recognizes her.

Enjoys evening play with father.

16 weeks · Spontaneous social smile—laughs aloud.

20 weeks · Cries when someone leaves him.

24 weeks · Smiles and vocalizes at mirror image.

Discriminates strangers.

28 weeks · Gravitates towards familiar persons for companionship.

32 weeks · Withdraws from strangers.

40 weeks · Waves bye-bye and pat-a-cakes.

44 weeks · Drops objects deliberately so that they will be retrieved.

52 weeks · Gives object to another on request.

Anticipates body movements when nursery rhyme is being said.

18 months · Hugs and shows affection toward doll or teddy bear.

Plays near other children, not directly with them.

21 months · Mimics household chores.

24 months · Can call himself by his own name.

Calls all men and women *Mommies* and *Daddies*.

Normal child development—cont'd

Social development—cont'd

24 months—cont'd	Cannot play with more than one child without direct supervision.
30 months	Calls women *Women* and men *Man*.
	Knows he is a boy, like father, and that he is different from girls and mothers.
	Says, "I need," "I don't like."
36 months	Can tell difference between boys and girls but makes no distinction in his play.
42 months	Interest in marriage and marrying.
	Imaginary playmates.
	Child plays the role of animals.
48 months	Plays well with 1 child or in supervised group.
	Tendency in play groups for a division along sex lines.
	Beginning of strong feeling for family and home.
54 months	Capable of playing in small groups without supervision.
60 months	Shows ability to delay gratification.
72 months	Beginning of value judgments about his own behavior, setting up standards for himself.

Emotional development

4 weeks	Emotional response of distress begins.
6 weeks	Smiles at mother in response to overtures.
12 weeks	Babbles when spoken to.
16 weeks	Laughs aloud, smiles and sobers.
20 weeks	Emotional responses becoming relative to specific situations.
24 weeks	Stretches arms out to be taken.
	Fear response to loss of support; sudden loud noises.
28 weeks	Plays peek-a-boo with mother.
	Responds to name.
	Pats image of self in mirror.
	Distress differentiates into more specific responses of fear, disgust, anger.
	Delight differentiates into an elation, affection.
9-10 months	Stranger response, shows distrust.
	Accepts new solid food.
	Sleeps through the night.

1 year	Aggressive interaction with environment begins.
	Willfully disobedient.
	Expressions of fear, anger, affection, anxiety and sympathy congruent with situations evoking them.
	Distinguishes between you and me.
2 years	Separates reality from mother when handled properly.
	Curious and busy.
	Uses I, me, you.
	Emotional arousal sudden, intense, brief—temper tantrums.
3 years	Shows sympathy in response to bandages, crying, accidents.
	Develops jealousy toward siblings.
	May rage at difficulties he experiences in dressing.
	Fear of dark, bugs, and strange situations like nursery school.
	Sacrifice immediate satisfaction on promise of later privilege.
4 years	Genital fixation and exploration, likes to go to the bathroom with others to satisfy his curiosity.
	Aware of attitudes of peers.
	Shares possessions.
	Fabricates, alibis, rationalizes.
5 years	Sensitive to social situations, aware of status, feels shame if he doesn't live up to his own expectations or those of others.
	Accomplished in wielding tools and meaningful toys.
	Loyal to playmates and devoted to teacher.
	Proud of school accomplishments, satisfied with artistic production.
	Sparked into increased activity by rivalry.

Developmental sequence
Self-help skills

6 months	Holds bottle.
7 months	Feeds self biscuit.
	Chews food.
15 months	Cooperates in dressing by extending arm or leg.
	Grasps spoon and inserts into dish.

Continued.

Normal child development—cont'd

Developmental sequence—cont'd

15 months—cont'd	Holds cup with digital grasp but apt to tip it too quickly.
	Bowel control with frequent accidents.
	Does not indicate toilet needs but does indicate wet pants.
	Helps turn book pages.
18 months	Fills spoon and feeds self in part; spills much.
	Lifts cup to mouth and drinks well.
	Hands empty cup to mother.
	Toilet regulated in daytime—both bowel and bladder.
	Can take off mittens, hat and socks.
	Can unzip zippers.
	Tries to put on shoes.
21 months	Handles cup with ease, lifting, drinking and replacing.
	Asks for food, toilet, and drink by gesture or word.
2 years	Inhibits turning of spoon, still needs help in feeding.
	Holds small glass in one hand as he drinks.
	Dry at night if taken up at least once.
	Verbalizes toilet needs consistently.
	Pulls on simple garments, finds large armholes and thrusts arms into them.
	Can remove shoes if laces are untied.
2½ years	Little spilling in self-feeding.
	Puts things away.
	Tends toilet without help except for wiping.
3 years	Pours well from a pitcher.
	Puts on shoes.
	Unbuttons front and side buttons by pushing them through buttonholes.
	Washes and dries hands.
3½ years	Puts away toys with some supervision.
	Washes and dries hands and face.
4 years	Brushes teeth.
	Dresses and undresses if lightly supervised.
	Distinguishes front and back of clothes and puts on correctly.
	Laces shoes.
	Likes to serve self at table.
	Rarely needs assistance to complete a meal.
	Goes to bathroom himself and manages clothes without difficulty.
	Puts away toys by himself.
	Goes on errands outside of home.
5 years	Can safely cross street if not too hazardous and can help a younger child to cross street.
6 years	Ties shoe laces.

Appearance and disappearance of reflexes in premature and full-term infants*

Reflexes	How tested	Implications	Gestational age of appearance	Present in full-term infants	Time of postnatal disappearance
Pupillary	Bright light in either eye produces pupillary constriction.	Absent reflex may indicate intra-ocular, optic-nerve or visual pathway abnormality	6-7 fetal months	Yes	Persists
McCarthy	Tapping above the eye produces blinking on the side of the body tapped.	Absent reflex may indicate visual defect. Delayed reflex may indicate retardation.	7-8 fetal months	Yes	2-4 months
Sucking	Placing a finger or nipple in the infant's mouth and then progressively withdrawing it causes flexion of the head of the infant.	Absent or diminished reflex may indicate central nervous system depression due to drugs, anoxia or infection.	2-3 fetal months	Yes	Persists
Rooting	Stroking the corner of the mouth and moving the finger sideways towards the cheek on either side causes the baby to move his tongue, mouth, and often his head towards the stimulated side. Rooting is increased in immature fetuses and a head response can be elicited by touching the chin, eyelids and forehead.	Absent or diminished reflex may indicate central nervous system depression due to drugs, anoxia or infection.	2-3 fetal months	Yes	3-4 months
Palmar grasp	Pressure on the palm by the examiner's finger or a firm object causes flexion of all the infant's fingers and a grasp around the object used for stimulation. In more mature neonates this is followed by flexion of the elbow and shoulder. Pulling an infant upwards while he is grasping is usually sufficient to lift his body off the table.	Weaker reflex may be noted in infants with general central nervous system depression. Absent reflex may indicate spinal cord lesions, injuries to the upper limbs, or paralysis. Persistence of reflex into later childhood may be associated with spastic cerebral palsy.	4-6 fetal months	Yes	5-6 months

*From Hellmuth, Jerome (Ed.). *Exceptional infant; the normal infant.* New York: Brunner/Mazel, Inc., 1967, pp. 79-121.

Continued.

Appearance and disappearance of reflexes in premature and full-term infants—cont'd

Reflexes	How tested	Implications	Gestational age of appearance	Present in full-term infants	Time of postnatal disappearance
Plantar grasp	Pressure on the sole of the foot, just behind the toes, causes flexion of all the toes.	Absent reflex may indicate spinal bifida or spinal cord or nerve	4-6 fetal months	Yes	9-12 months
Crossed extension	Leg of supine infant is extended. Pressure is exerted on the knee of the extended leg, and the sole of the foot of this leg is stimulated with a pin. This results in extension and a slight adduction of the unstimulated limb. An initial flexion movement of the free limb is usually observed prior to the extensor movement. Extension and fanning of the toes may also be observed.	Absent reflex may indicate spinal cord defect. Persistence of reflex may indicate nervous system lesion affecting the lower extremities.	5-6 fetal months	Yes	1-2 months
Doll's eye	Turn the infant's head to the right or the left while the rest of the body is stationary. The eyes stay fixed and do not move with the head. When the head is moved up and down the eyes again do not follow the head.	When good visual fixation is achieved the reflex disappears. Reappearance in older infants may be the result of decerebration. Asymmetrical eye movements may indicate nerve paralysis.	6-7 fetal months	Yes	1 month
Tonic neck	Active or passive turning of the head results in extension of the arm and leg on the jaw side, along with flexion of the limbs on the opposite side. Many normal babies under 6-7 months of age sleep in this position, but when they are awake and actively moving, it may be almost impossible to impose this response.	If the reflex can be produced with ease or if the baby is unable to escape from the imposed position despite active attempts at voluntary movement there may be a central nervous system abnormality. It is abnormal for the response to occur on one side and not the other. Incomplete responses are not	6-7 fetal months	Yes	6-7 months

Appearance and disappearance of reflexes in premature and full-term infants—cont'd

Reflexes	How tested	Implications	Gestational age of appearance	Present in full-term infants	Time of postnatal disappearance
Tonic neck—cont'd		necessarily abnormal. Persistence past 7 months may signify a lack of motor organization which is not necessarily accompanied by mental deficiency.			
Moro	In response to a sudden banging of a hand upon a table, the infant initially abducts, extends and supinates the arms and extends the digits, except for the thumb and index fingers which remain in a "c" position.	Absent reflex in the first 4 months of life may suggest diffuse central nervous system depression. Persistence past 6 months may indicate mental retardation or brain damage. Palsy of the arm or a unilateral fracture of the arm can produce an asymmetrical reflex.	7 fetal months	Yes	4-6 months
Positive supporting	Allow the soles of the baby's feet to touch a solid surface. When the baby is supported in an erect position, the hips and knees extend, and the baby is able to support his weight on his rigid lower extremities. The hips and knees often remain slightly flexed.	Complete extension of the hips and knees or "scissor" which persists after 4 months suggests a neurologic abnormality involving the lower extremities. Presence or absence may not always have value in estimating the maturity of the nervous system.	8-9 fetal months	Yes	2-3 months or variable

Speech sound repertoire*

Age in years at which sound is mastered	Sound	Example
3	(m)	woman made ice cream
3	(n)	hen running nest
3	(p)	puppy rope
3	(h)	had playhouse
3	(w)	wagon sidewalk
4	(b)	baby bathtub (75% final b)
4	(t)	cat table
4	(d)	red Indian doll
4	(k)	black comb pocket
4	(g)	dog green wagon (75% final g)
4	(f)	elephant foot leaf
4	(ou)	house
4	(oi)	boy
5	(ng)	blanket hanging
5	(y)	yellow barnyard
6	(r)	soldier rabbit carrot
6	(l)	lady yellow hall
6	(t)	potato (middle)
6	(v)	violet cover stove
6	(sh)	she washing dish
6	(zh)	measure
6	(ch)	teacher chicken catch
6	(dr)	drum
6	(kl)	clock
6	(bl)	block
6	(gl)	glass
6	(cr)	crayon
7	(th) soft	bath thimble
7	(s)	sister bicycle house
7	(z)	use scissors roses (75% final z)
7	(j)	jump orange juice orange
7	(tr)	train
7	(st)	star (initial)
7	(sl)	slide
7	(sw)	swing
7	(sp)	spoon
7	(wh)	where whistle (not emphasized today)
8	(sk)	scooter desk
8	(sn)	snow
8	(st)	nest (final)
8	(th) harsh	the mother feather this that

*From *Elements of the pediatric screening examination and basic health supervision.* Richmond, Va.: Child Health Services, Virginia State Department of Health, 1975.

Language behavior scale (from REEL scale)*

Age (months)	Receptive language	Expressive language
0-1	Startles to loud, sudden noises. Stops activity when approached by sound.	Frequent crying. Random vocalizing begins.
1-2	Often quieted by a familiar, friendly voice. Appears to listen to speaker. Often looks at speaker and responds by smile.	Vowel-like sounds similar to "e" and "a." Sometimes repeats same syllable while cooing. Develops vocal signs of pleasure.
2-3	Looks directly at speaker's face. Localizes speaker with eyes. Often watches lips and mouth of speaker.	Sometimes responds to sounds by vocalizing. When played with, laughs and uses other vocal expressions of pleasure. Often vocalizes with two or more different syllables.
3-4	Turns head towards speaker. Looks in search of speaker. Usually frightened or disturbed by angry voices.	Often laughs when playing with objects. Repeats series of same sounds. Often uses sounds like "p," "b," or "m."
4-5	Localizes source of voice with accuracy. Recognizes and responds to own name. Usually stops crying when someone talks to him.	Uses vowel-like sounds like "o," and "u." Expresses anger or displeasure by vocal pattern other than crying.
5-6	Appears to recognize words like "daddy," "bye-bye," "mama," etc. Stops in response to "no" half the time.	Takes initiative in vocalizing directly to others. Sometimes uses 4 or more different syllables at one time. Plays at making sounds and noises.
6-7	Recognizes family names even when person not present. Responds with correct gestures to "up," "bye-bye," "come," etc. Gives attentions to music or singing.	Begins two-syllable babbling. Vocalizes when hears name. Appears to be naming some things in own "language."
7-8	Often listens to whole conversations between others. Stops activity when name called. Recognizes names of common objects.	Plays "pat-a-cake," "peek-a-boo." "Sings along" with music.
8-9	Understands simple requests. Looks at pictures as named.	Mimics sounds and number of syllables used by others. Uses some gesture language.
9-10	Enjoys listening to new words. Gives objects to parent on request.	Speaks first words ("dada," "mama," "bye-bye"). Uses jargon.
10-11	Follows simple commands, "Put that down." Understands simple questions. Responds to rhythmic music with body or hand movements.	Initiates games like "pat-a-cake," "peek-a-boo." Tries to imitate new words.

*These portions of the REEL scale are adapted, with permission, from *Assessing Language Skills in Infancy: A Handbook for the Multidimensional Analysis of Emergent Language,* by K. E. Bzoch and R. League, © 1971; reprinted 1978 by University Park Press, Baltimore, Md.

Continued.

Language behavior scale (from REEL scale)—cont'd

Age (months)	Receptive language	Expressive language
11-12	Responds with correct gestures to some verbal requests.	Uses 3 or more words with some consistency.
	Attends and responds to speech intently longer.	"Talks" to toys and people when playing.
12-14	Understands some new words each week.	Uses 5 or more words with some consistency.
	Understands psychological feeling and meanings of most speakers.	Some true words occur in jargon.
	Will look at pictures named for 2 minutes.	Uses voice with gestures to obtain object.
14-16	Carries out verbal request.	Uses 7 or more words with some consistency.
	Recognizes and identifies objects of pictures.	Communicates using true words and gestures.
	Recognizes names of body parts.	
16-18	Can understand and carry out two simple directions with an object.	Uses words without gestures to express needs.
	Can associate new words by category.	Repeats words overheard.
		Gradual increase in speaking vocabulary.
18-20	Responds with gesture to actions, words, body parts, items of clothing.	Imitates 2-3 word sentences.
	Distinguishes personal pronouns, "Give it to her, me."	Imitates environmental sound.
		Speaking vocabulary of 10-20 words.
20-22	Follows series of 2-3 simple commands.	Combines words into simple sentences ("Daddy come").
	Recognizes new words increasingly faster.	Tells experiences using true words and jargon.
	Recognizes and identifies almost all common objects and pictures when named.	
22-24	Selects item from group of 5 or more upon request.	Uses 3-word sentences, "There it is."
	Listens to meaning and reason.	Uses own name to refer to self.
	Understands most complex sentences.	Uses some pronouns but makes errors in syntax.

Identification checklists*
MENTAL RETARDATION

Guidelines: (1) Be a careful observer. (2) Does the child differ markedly in these characteristics when compared to children of like age? (3) If so, check appropriate items. (4) Double check extreme problems.

____ 1. From health history or parent interview determine if any of the following conditions have existed:
  ____ Premature birth.
  ____ Prolonged pregnancy.
  ____ Low birth weight.
  ____ Stressful birth.
  ____ Dehydration.
  ____ Malnutrition.
  ____ Jaundice.
  ____ Rh incompatibility.
  ____ Convulsions.
  ____ Head injury.
  ____ Anoxia.
  ____ Classified as a "very good baby" because of inactivity.
  ____ Mother's age beyond "normal" child bearing.

____ 2. Vocabulary is limited.
____ 3. Immature or slow in attaining developmental landmarks.
____ 4. Exhibits a general lack of response to the environment.
____ 5. Coordination is poor, clumsy.
____ 6. Attention span is short.
____ 7. Has difficulties in concentrating.
____ 8. Is easily distracted.
____ 9. Is hyperactive or hypoactive.
____ 10. Slow to catch on or needs many repetitions.
____ 11. Prefers playmates younger than self.
____ 12. Reaction patterns are slow.
____ 13. Makes no response or inappropriate response.
____ 14. Has frequent or unwarranted emotional outbursts.
____ 15. Is slow in making associations.
____ 16. Tends to become confused easily.
____ 17. Has difficulty in following directions.
____ 18. Transfer of learning is poor, or has difficulty in making generalizations.
____ 19. Demonstrates rigid behavior patterns.
____ 20. Is imitative, not resourceful.
____ 21. Needs much direction and supervision.
____ 22. Dull, lack of general awareness of environment.
____ 23. Needs routine, repetition, and structure.

HEARING HANDICAP

Guidelines: (1) Be a careful observer. (2) Does the child differ markedly in these characteristics when compared to children of like age? (3) If so, check appropriate item. (4) Double check extreme problems.

____ 1. Speech characteristics:
  ____ Any speech impairment, particularly difficulty in pronouncing high frequency sounds such as "s," "sh," "z," "ch," and "h."
  ____ Unusual inflection such as a constant monotone or mumbling.
  ____ Habitually speaking too loudly or too softly.

____ 2. Behavior characteristics:
  ____ Frequent requests to have directions or questions repeated.
  ____ Unusual difficulty in following verbal directions.
  ____ Failure to respond when called on in class.
  ____ Inappropriate or irrelevant answers.
  ____ Less apparent difficulty when facing the speaker.
  ____ Tendency to watch a speaker with unusual intensity.

---

*From Shick, R. L. (Ed.). *Curriculum guide for early education of the handicapped*, Mansfield, Pa.: Mansfield State College, 1974, pp. 27-36.

___ Frequently watches others before beginning a task and a tendency to copy or imitate actions of others.

___ Scholastic achievement below level of apparent ability.

___ Difficulty in locating the direction from which another is speaking.

___ Frequently interrupting others without realizing he is doing so.

___ Disinterest in casual conversation.

___ Appears to be inattentive and bored with what is going on around him.

___ 3. Physical characteristics:

___ Habitual turning, "cocking" or cupping an ear toward the speaker.

___ A strained or bewildered expression on face for no apparent reason.

___ Appearance of being under constant tension and seeming to tire easily.

___ Complains of earaches or buzzing or ringing in ears.

___ Has any discharge from the ear.

___ May be hyperactive and do better in a noisy environment.

___ More than normal use of hands in conversation.

___ Faulty equilibrium—difficulty in maintaining balance, particularly in the dark or when blindfolded.

VISION HANDICAP

Guidelines: (1) Be a careful observer. (2) Does the child differ markedly in these characteristics when compared to children of like age? (3) If so, check appropriate items. (4) Double check extreme problems.

___ 1. Physical problems:
   ___ Red-rimmed, bloodshot, watery eyes.
   ___ Encrusted, swollen eyelids.
   ___ Rolling or rubbing of eyes.
   ___ Excessive blinking.
   ___ Blocked tearducts.

___ 2. Complaints of:
   ___ Dizziness, blurring, double vision.
   ___ Headaches, pains in the eyes, nausea.

___ 3. Strabismus (cross-eyes, lack of alignment of eyes).

___ 4. Nystagmus (rapid, rhythmic, side-to-side movement of the eyes).

___ 5. Frequent sties.

___ 6. Peripheral difficulty.

___ 7. Appears to be daydreaming.

___ 8. Lack of normal curiosity regarding objects visually presented.

___ 9. Lack of response to facial expression of others.

___ 10. Awkwardness with regard to eye-hand coordination activities.

___ 11. Tilting of head to one side.

___ 12. Difficulty estimating distances.

___ 13. Unable to distinguish color differences.

___ 14. Distortion of face when using eyes (frowning, squinting, closes one eye).

___ 15. Holds visual work at abnormal distance.

___ 16. Fails to see, or runs into objects not in his direct line of vision.

___ 17. Walks in overly cautious manner (falters, hesitates, stumbles).

___ 18. Unduly sensitive to variations of light levels.

___ 19. Overly dependent on other senses.

LEARNING DISABILITY

Guidelines: (1) Be a careful observer. (2) Does the child differ markedly in these characteristics when compared to children of like age? (3) If so, check appropriate item. (4) Double check extreme problems.

    ____ 1. Disorders of motor activity:

        ____ Hyperactivity — Restless motor activity such as shuffling the feet, tapping a pencil, twisting and squirming.

        ____ Hypoactivity — Extremely slow in actions.

        ____ Perseveration — Continuous behavior when it is no longer appropriate. The child will have difficulty in shifting from one task to another.

        ____ Uncoordination—The child may appear awkward or clumsy, in both fine motor performance and over-all coordination.

        ____ Mobility—The child may drag his feet or exhibit homolateral walking pattern.

    ____ 2. Emotional disorders:

        ____ Emotional instability—This may be due to the child's perceptual, motor, or symbolization problems.

        ____ Poor self-concept due to repeated failures.

        ____ Instability of performance —A skill that appears to be mastered on one day will be approached as for the first time on the next.

        ____ Impulsivity—The child is unable to control impulses regardless of the situation or possible consequences.

        ____ Low frustration tolerance —If the child does not meet immediate success, he may attack, verbally or physically, the person or situation responsible.

    ____ 3. Perceptual disorders—The inability to recognize and interpret external stimuli either visually, auditorially or tactile-kinesthetically.

        ____ Disorder of body image.

        ____ Poor figure ground perception.

        ____ Dissociation response to pieces of stimulus.

        ____ Reversals.

        ____ Poor eye-hand coordination.

        ____ Lack of fusion while following a moving target with eyes.

    ____ 4. Symbolization disorders:

        ____ Difficulty in dealing with oral instructions.

        ____ Reads slowly and awkwardly—both orally and silently.

        ____ Language may be inappropriate or disjointed.

        ____ Written language may not be concise or meaningful.

    ____ 5. Attention disorders:

        ____ Distractible due to short attention span.

        ____ Excessive attention which is similar to perseveration.

    ____ 6. Memory disorders:

        ____ Poor short-term memory.

        ____ Poor long-term memory.

        ____ Poor sequential memory.

    ____ 7. Miscellaneous characteristics:

        ____ Discrepancy between potential achievement as indicated on standardized tests, and actual performance level of the child in the classroom.

        ____ Unusual discrepancy between verbal and performance scores on standardized IQ test.

SPEECH HANDICAP

Guidelines: (1) Be a careful observer. (2) Does the child differ markedly in these characteristics when compared to children of like age? (3) If so, check appropriate items. (4) Double check extreme problems.

___ 1. Substitutes one letter for another (wabbit for rabbit, thop for stop, etc.)
___ 2. Omits sounds from words (i for is, is for this, etc.).
___ 3. Adds to words (happle for apple, etc.).
___ 4. Lacks distinctness of voice; mumbles.
___ 5. Lacks sufficient volume to be heard.
___ 6. Repeats initial sounds (tttop, cccat, etc.).
___ 7. Tries hard but no sound comes out.
___ 8. Shows excessive eye blinking, gestures, grimaces, and other body motion while talking.
___ 9. Has a lisp.
___ 10. Draws adverse attention to himself because of his speech.
___ 11. Cannot discriminate among various pitches.
___ 12. Cannot produce and duplicate a given pitch.
___ 13. Does not inflect voice appropriately.
___ 14. Has spontaneous change of inflections and pitch.
___ 15. Intensity difficulties, i.e., changes in volume.
___ 16. Voice range, whispering to shouting, is poor.
___ 17. Lowered intelligibility of speech due to misarticulation.
___ 18. Lowered intelligibility of speech due to lapses in grammar and syntax.
___ 19. Speech unpleasant to the listener.

SPECIAL HEALTH PROBLEMS

Guidelines: (1) Be a careful observer. (2) Does the child differ markedly in these characteristics when compared to children of like age? (3) If so, check appropriate items. (4) Double check extreme problems.

___ 1. Appears very easily fatigued.
___ 2. Is abnormal in size to detriment of participation in group; is subject to ridicule.
___ 3. Seems excessively restless and overactive.
___ 4. Is extremely slow and inactive.
___ 5. Is usually breathless after exercise.
___ 6. Is subject to frequent dry cough; complains of chest pains after physical exertion.
___ 7. Flushes easily; has a slightly bluish color to cheeks, lips, and/or fingertips.
___ 8. Is subject to low-grade fevers; frequent colds.
___ 9. Experiences recurrent seizures.
___ 10. Is extremely inattentive.
___ 11. Faints easily.
___ 12. Complains of pains in arms, legs and/or joints.
___ 13. Is excessively hungry and thirsty.
___ 14. Walks with unusual gait.
___ 15. Tilts head.
___ 16. Climbs stairs with difficulty.
___ 17. Stands with unusual posture.
___ 18. Complains of backaches.
___ 19. Falls frequently.

CRIPPLING CONDITIONS

Guidelines: (1) Be a careful observer. (2) Does the child differ markedly in these characteristics when compared to children of like age? (3) If so, check appropriate items. (4) Double check extreme problems.

___ 1. Shows observable physical disability:
   ___ Postural problem.
   ___ Club foot.
   ___ Curvature of spine.
   ___ Motoric (movement) problems.
   ___ Abduction or adduction of feet.
   ___ Scissor-like gait.
   ___ Wears braces.

_____ 2. Has poor motor control or coordination.

_____ 3. Walks with limp or with awkwardness.

_____ 4. Shows signs of pain during exercise.

_____ 5. Has jerky or shaky motions.

_____ 6. Has defects which interfere with normal function of the bones, muscles, or joints.

_____ 7. Inadequate bi-lateral balance.

BEHAVIOR DISORDERS

Guidelines: (1) Be a careful observer. (2) Does the child differ markedly in these characteristics when compared to children of like age? (3) If so, check appropriate items. (4) Double check extreme problems.

_____ 1. Changes in routine are disruptive.

_____ 2. Has tantrums or reacts with explosive anger when disciplined.

_____ 3. Has phobic-like responses.

_____ 4. Has ritualistic behavior patterns.

_____ 5. Enuresis or urinating in inappropriate places.

_____ 6. Is withdrawn or won't participate.

_____ 7. Is irresponsible, defensive, or blames others.

_____ 8. Is overly inhibited, withdrawn, or shy.

_____ 9. Has problems in attending.

_____ 10. Seeks excessive attention.

_____ 11. Has a "me first" attitude.

_____ 12. Has a negativistic "I won't" attitude.

_____ 13. Demonstrates bizarre or eccentric behaviors.

_____ 14. Has difficulty in building and/or maintaining interpersonal relationships.

_____ 15. Has physical symptoms, pains, or fears associated with personal or school problems.

_____ 16. Often has mood swings, is unhappy or depressed without apparent reason.

_____ 17. Isolates self without activity or prefers solitary play.

_____ 18. Is seen negatively by self or peers.

_____ 19. Demonstrates infantile behavior.

_____ 20. Appears preoccupied or is given to daydreaming.

TESTS TO IDENTIFY LEARNING DISABILITIES IN CHILDREN FROM PRESCHOOL TO GRADE 3*

Specific information and/or specimen sets (when available) of the tests described must be obtained directly from the publisher. Refer to the pamphlet *Major U.S. Publishers of Standardized Tests* and the listing of publishers which accompanies this inventory. Please do not write to the Test Collection or the Head Start Test Collection for inspection copies since neither has distribution rights for its holdings. In the case of tests published by Educational Testing Service, please write to the specific office or individual named.

Some of the measures are reviewed or described in the references cited in the bibliography. Reviews which have appeared in the professional literature are referenced in the entry.

Academic Readiness Scale by Harold F. Burks; c1968; Grades K-1; Arden Press.

The scale evaluates the child's capacities in the areas of motor, perceptual-motor, cognitive or intellectual, motivational and interest, and social adjustment. Scale may be used to identify students with potential learning handicaps.

Ahr's Individual Development Survey by Edward Ahr; c1970; Grades K-1; Priority Innovations, Inc.

A screening device designed to identify potential learning or behavior problems in kindergarten and first grade children. Consists of a booklet of forms which are completed by parents and yield developmental, medical, and behavioral information about the child. The Survey covers: The Family, The Child, and The School.

The APELL Test by Eleanor V. Cochran, James L. Shannon; c1969; Ages 4.5-7; EDCO-DYNE.

A system of instructional diagnosis and design which assists the teacher in identifying the individual needs of the child. This criterion-referenced test diagnoses skill levels based on specific performance objectives. Subscores are: Pre-Reading (visual discrimination, auditory discrimination, letter names), Pre-Math (attributes, number concepts, number facts), and Language (nouns, pronouns, verbs, adjectives, plurals, prepositions). A Spanish translation is available.

The Abilities of Babies by Ruth Griffiths; 1954-1967; Age 6⅔ weeks–24 months; The English Universities Press, Limited (U.S. Distributor is Lawrence Verry, Inc.).

A series of tests used in the study, The Abilities of Babies: Locomotor Scale, Personal-Social Scale, Hearing and Speech Scale, Hand and Eye Scale, Performance Scale. Developmental Profiles for deaf children, blind children, and children with inhibited speech are included.

Albert Einstein Scales of Sensori-Motor Development by Sibylle K. Escalona and Harvey Corman; c1969; Age 0-24 months; Child Development Project, Department of Psychiatry, Albert Einstein College of Medicine.

A research device based on Piaget's theory of development. The test includes: Cognitive Scales, Object Permanence Scale, Space Scale, Perhension Scale, and Causality.

Alphabet Writing—From Dictation by Robert M. Wold; c1970; Grades 1-6; Robert M. Wold.*

For children who are unable to write the alphabet spontaneously. As the child completes the task, the following are observed and recorded: body posture, head posture, paper position, paper grasp and posture, vo-

---

*Educational Testing Service, Princeton, N.J.

346

calization or subvocalization, speed, frustra-
tion level, spacing, formation, and fatigue.
*Included in Wold, Robert M. *Screening
Tests To Be Used By The Classroom Teacher.*
San Rafael, California: Academic Therapy
Publications, 1970.

Alphabet Writing—Spontaneous by Robert M.
Wold; c1970; Grades 1-6; Robert M. Wold.*
A test of the ability to reproduce the alphabet, both lower and upper case letters. As the
child writes, the following are observed:
body posture, head posture, paper position,
paper grasp and posture, vocalization or
subvocalization, speed, frustration level,
spacing, formation, and fatigue. *Included
in: Wold, Robert M. *Screening Tests To Be
Used By The Classroom Teacher.* San
Rafael, California: Academic Therapy Publications, 1970.

*The Anton Brenner Developmental Gestalt Test
of School Readiness* by Anton Brenner; c1964;
Ages 4-7; Western Psychological Services.
Evaluates perceptual and conceptual differentiating ability. Subscales are: Number
Producing, Number Recognition, Ten Dot
Gestalt, Sentence Gestalt, Draw-A-Man;
School Readiness Evaluation, Achievement-
Ability Scale, Social Emotional Behavior
Scale. The test may be employed to identify
both gifted and retarded children and can be
effectively used with emotioanlly disturbed,
culturally deprived, and non-English speak-
ing children. Materials are required to administer the test.

*Assessment of Children's Language Compre-
hension: Research Edition* by Carol R. Foster,
Jane J. Giddan and Joel Stark; c1969; Ages
2-12; Consulting Psychologists Press, Inc.
An individually administered measure designed to assign the starting point in training for the child. Assesses core vocabulary
development, comprehension of lexical
items, and consistency of patterns of words
missed within a sequence.

*Auditory Perception Test—Visual Discrimina-
tion:* Not Dated; Grades K-12; The Reading
Clinic, Temple University.
The test covers: Visual Discrimination,
Auditory Perception, and Auditory Word
Discrimination.

Ayres Space Test by A. Jean Ayres; c1962;
Ages 3 years and over; Western Psychological
Corporation.

Developed to identify children with learning
disability due to sensory integrative dysfunction. Evaluates the perceptual dimensions of perceptual speed and space visualization.

Basic Concept Inventory by Siegfried Engel-
mann; c1967; Ages 3-10 years; Follett Educational Corporation.
A criterion-referenced measure designed to
detect deficiencies in basic learning skills. It
is primarily intended for culturally disadvantaged preschool and kindergarten children, slow learners, emotionally disturbed
children, and mentally retarded children.
Covers basic concepts, statement repetition
and comprehension, and pattern awareness.

Behavior Rating Scale by Marion Karl, Russell
Scott, and Vivien Richman; 1969; Ages 6-10;
Learning Research and Development Center,
University of Pittsburgh.
A summated rating scale based on the be-
havioral correlates of learning disabilities.
The scale can be used with mentally re-
tarded and emotionally disturbed children.

Bender Gestalt Test for Young Children by
Elizabeth Munsterberg Koppitz; c1964; Ages
5-10; Grune and Stratton, Inc.
Provides different ways of analyzing Bender
records of young children from a single test
protocol.

Bender Visual Motor Gestalt Test for Children
by Aileen Clawson; c1962-68; Ages 7-11;
Western Psychological Services.
Provides an index of the structural and functional aspects of perceptual-motor development. The test can be administered to
emotionally disturbed and neurologically
handicapped children.

Bingham Button Test by William J. Bingham;
c1967; Ages 3-5; William J. Bingham.
An individually administered test of a
child's knowledge and understanding of concepts and relationships he will encounter in
primary school. The test covers: Sizes and
Comparison, Object/Object Relations, Numbers, and Person/Object Relations, and
Colors. Props are required.

Boehm Test of Basic Concepts by Ann E.
Boehm; c1967, 1969, 1970; Grades K-2; The
Psychological Corporation.
Designed to measure children's mastery of
concepts considered necessary for achieve-

ment in the first years of school. May be used to identify concepts on which children require instruction. The test covers the concepts of space, time, quantity, and miscellaneous. Reviewed in *Professional Psychology* (1:490, Fall '70) *Journal of Educational Measurement* (7:139-140, Summer '70) *Journal of Special Education* (V. 4, No. 2, 1970).

Bzoch-League Receptive-Expressive Emergent Language Scale for the Measurement of Language Skills in Infancy by Kenneth R. Bzoch and Richard League; c1970-71; Birth-3 years; Tree of Life Press.

Designed to accurately reflect the level of decoding (receptive language) and encoding (expressive language) in the first three years of life. The scale may be useful in the differential diagnosis of major disorders affecting language development.

California Preschool Social Competency Scale by Samuel Levine, Freeman F. Elzey, and Mary Lewis; c1969; Ages 2 years, 6 months–5 years, 6 months; Consulting Psychologists Press, Inc.

Designed to measure the adequacy of the child's inter-personal behavior and the degree to which he assumes social responsibility. Norms are based on children participating in preschool or nursery school programs. Child's behavior is rated by the teacher. Percentile norms are presented for children from high and low occupational levels.

Checklist for the Detection of Learning Problems: Experimental Form for Primary Grades, Second Draft by Henrietta Lempert; 1972; Grades K-2; Henrietta Lempert.

A teacher-completed checklist for rating child's development in terms of the class average. Items cover: oral skills, listening skills, number skills, position in space and time, visual skills, movements, handwork, social adjustments, and reading and writing (first and second grade only).

Checklist for the Recognition of Problems in Children by Jacob Schleichkorn; Not Dated; Grades K-3; Jacob Schleichkorn.

A simple checklist designed to assist the teacher in identifying children with problems who may require further study. Areas covered include: coordination and motor activities, behavior, responses (aural), com-

munication (verbal), conceptual ability, and perception.

Child Development Questionnaire by Gertrud L. Wyatt; 1968; Preschool; Wellesley Public Schools

Developed for Title VI Project "Early Identification of Children with Potential Learning Disabilities." Observational questionnaire looking for subtle indications concerning the child's neurological functioning.

Child Screening Interview: Not Dated: Preschool; Institute for Developmental Studies, New York University.

Designed to yield information which may reveal gross developmental abnormalities such as problems with motor skills, delayed speech, or overt signs of disturbed emotional behavior.

Cognitive Abilities Test by Robert L. Thorndike, Elizabeth Hagen and Irving Lorge; c1968; Grades K-3; Houghton Mifflin Company.

Designed to assess child's development of generalized thinking skills. Subtests are: Oral Vocabulary, Relational Concepts, Multi-Mental, Quantitative Concepts. Reviewed in: *Journal of Educational Measurement.* 6:123-124, Summer '69.

Communicative Evaluation Chart From Infancy to Five Years by Ruth M. Anderson, Madeline Miles and Patricia A. Matheny; c1963; Ages 3 months–5 years; Educators Publishing Service, Inc.

Designed for the early detection of communication disabilities by providing a profile of the child's over-all abilities or disabilities in language and performances. Items cover physical well being; normal growth and development; motor coordination; beginning visual-motor-perceptual skills; coordination of speech musculature; development of hearing acuity and auditory perception; the acquisition of the vowels and consonants; and the development of receptive and expressive language.

The Contemporary School Readiness Test by Clara Elbert Sauer; c1970; Grades K-1; Montana Reading Clinic Publications.

Designed to predict the success of children in the first grade. Test is to be administered at the end of kindergarten or the first three weeks of first grade. Test should be given in two sessions. Subtests are: Writing My Name; Colors of the Spectrum; Science, Health, and Social Studies; Numbers; Handwriting Readiness; Reading; Visual Discrimination; Auditory Discrimination; Listening Comprehension.

Dennis Visual Perception Scale by Royce Dennis and Margaret Dennis; c1969; Grades 1-6; Western Psychological Services.

A paper-and-pencil test for screening children for perceptual handicaps sufficiently severe to affect learning. Can be administered individually or to groups.

Denver Developmental Screening Test by William K. Frankenburg and Josiah B. Dodds; c1967; Birth–6 years; Ladoca Project and Publishing Foundation, Inc.

A standardized screening method devised to assist in the early detection of young children with serious developmental delays. Covers four functions: gross motor, language, fine motor-adaptive, and personal-social. Developed for use by people who have not had training in psychological testing.

Developmental Potential of Preschool Children by Else Haeussermann; c1968; Ages 2-6 years; Grune and Stratton, Inc.

May be used for the educational evaluation of children aged 2-6, or functioning at that level, who have handicaps in expression and other difficulties. Covers physical development, sensory intactness, intellectual development, and observation of behavior during the interview.

Developmental Test of Visual-Motor Integration by Keith E. Beery and Norman A. Buktenica; c1967; Ages 2-15; Follett Educational Corporation.

Measures the degree to which a child's visual-motor behavior is integrated. The test is useful in screening children who may need further testing in a specific area. Reviewed in: *Perceptual and Motor Skills.* 27:339, 1968.

Devereux Elementary School Behavior Rating Scale by George Spivack and Marshall Swift; c1966-67; Grades 1-6; The Devereux Foundation.

Subscores are: Classroom Disturbance, Impatience, Disrespect-Defiance, External Blame, Achievement Anxiety, External Reliance, Comprehension, Inattentive-With-drawn, Irrelevant-Responsive, Creative Initiative, Need Closeness to Teacher.

Dyslexia Schedule by John McLeod; c1968; Ages 6-12; Educators Publishing Service, Inc.

A questionnaire to facilitate the systematic collection of relevant social information about children referred to a specialist because of reading disability. The Schedule is completed by the parent.

Early Detection Inventory by F. E. McGahan and Carolyn McGahan; c1967; Ages 3-7; Follett Educational Corporation.

Can be used to identify learning disabilities in the areas of social and emotional development, physical development, and intellectual development. Areas which are evaluated that may be related to learning difficulties are lack of gross motor coordination, lack of fine motor coordination, faulty adjustment to basic life experiences, marked language disorder symptoms, and excessive anxiety or fear. The test covers: School Readiness Tasks, Social-Emotional Behavior Responses, Motor Performance, Overall Readiness Number, Family and Social History.

Elizur Test of Psycho-Organicity: Children and Adults by Abraham Elizure; c1969; Age 6–Adults; Western Psychological Services.

An individually administered test for use with persons suspected of brain damage. Subtests are: Drawing, Digits, and Blocks.

End of First Grade Progress Scale by Harold F. Burks; c1968; Grades 1; Arden Press.

Designed to aid in the evaluation of children at the end of first grade. Useful in identifying children with potential learning handicaps.

Evanston Early Identification Scale by Myril Landsman and Harry Dillard; c1967; Preschool–Grade 3; Follett Educational Corporation.

Designed for the identification of children who can be expected to have learning difficulties. Children are asked to draw a figure of a person. Those who perform poorly may be referred for diagnosis of possible perceptual, emotional, or other problems.

Expressive Vocabulary Inventory for Children by Carolyn Stern; c1968; Preschool-Kindergarten; UCLA Research Project in Early Childhood Learning.

An individually administered test of verbal facility. Test consists of forty items selected after a tabulation of frequencies of words found in primers, word lists, achievement and intelligence tests, also words used are representative of the vocabulary children are expected to possess when they enter kindergarten. The child is required to actually produce the appropriate word. Words used in this test represent a variety of parts of speech.

First Grade Screening Test by John E. Pate and Warren W. Webb; c1966; Grade K-1; American Guidance Service, Inc.

Developed to screen beginning or potential first graders to identify those with learning disabilities and subsequently provide for individual evaluation and planning. Reviewed in: *Journal of Educational Measurement.* 36-37, Spring '69.

Fruit Distraction Test by Sebastiano Santostefano; circa 1964; Ages 6-13; Sebastiano Santostefano.

A measure of constructed-flexible cognitive control—the manner in which a person deals with a stimulus field containing information that potentially distracts from the central task. Subscores are: Reading Time Distractibility, Reading Errors, Distractibility, Number of Intrusive Stimuli Recalled.

Gesell Developmental Kit by Frances L. Ilg and Louise Bates Ames; c1964-65; Ages 5-10; Program for Education.

Subtests are: Name and Address Test; Date; Numbers; Copy Forms; Right and Left Test; Incomplete Man Test; Monroe Visual Test; Naming Animals; Home and School Preferences.

Gesell Developmental Schedules by Arnold Gesell and Associates; 1956; Ages 0-6 yrs; The Psychological Corporation.

The test covers: Postural Behavior, Prehensory Behavior, Perceptual Behavior, Adaptive Behavior, Language-Social Behavior.

Goals for Trainable Pupils—A Record Keeping Instrument; Not Dated; Mentally Retarded Children and Adults; Division of Special Education, Iowa State Department of Public Instruction.

A rating scale designed to aid the teacher in identifying pupil strengths and weaknesses and in assessing individual differences. The items are arranged according to four curricular areas: Social-Emotional (Self Realization Skills, Social Competencies); Academic (Language and Speech Skills, Memory and Reasoning, Reading, Writing, Money and Measures, Number Concepts); Enrichment (Physical Development, Rhythm and Music, Arts and Crafts); Vocational (Personal Management, General Vocational Competencies).

Goldman-Fristoe-Woodcock Test of Auditory Discrimination by Ronald Goldman, Macalyne Fristoe and Richard W. Woodcock; c1970; Ages 4 and over; American Guidance Service, Inc.

Designed to evaluate speech-sound discrimination under both quiet and distracting noise conditions. Requires a pointing response only. Tape recorder is required for administering the test.

Haptic Letter Recognition Test by Robert M. Wold; c1970; Grades 1-6; Robert M. Wold.*

A test to determine whether the child can identify a letter from touch only. *Included in: Wold, Robert M. *Screening Tests to be used by the Classroom Teacher.* San Rafael, California: Academic Therapy Publications, 1970.

Harris Tests of Lateral Dominance by Albert J. Harris; c1947-58; Ages 7 years and over; Albert J. Harris (Distributed by The Psychological Corporation).

An individually administered measure based on the *ABC Vision Test.* The test covers: Knowledge of Right and Left, Hand Preferences, Simultaneous Writing, Handwriting, Tapping, Dealing Cards, Strength of Grip (optional), Monocular Tests (Kaleidoscope, Telescope, Sight Rifle), Binocular Tests (Cone, Hole in Card), Stereoscopic Tests (optional), Foot Dominance (Kicking, Stamping).

Holmgren Color Test; Not Dated; Ages 2 years and over; Graham-Field Surgical Company, Inc.

Tests the ability to discriminate between colors and shades of colors. Used for detecting color blindness. Set consists of three large skeins, light green, rose-purple, and red; and sixty-nine small skeins of confusing colors of various shades.

Informal Evaluations of Thinking Ability by Marjorie Seddon Johnson; Not Dated; Grades

1-12 and Adults; The Reading Clinic, Temple University.

Assesses the ability to understand spoken and written communications. Areas covered are listening, speaking, practical situations, and writing situations.

Initial Learning Assessment by Edward G. Scagliotta; c1970; Ages 4-12; Academic Therapy Publications.

Designed to ascertain the gross acquisition of a child's abilities in order that an individual educational program can be provided. It is an individually administered series of tests in the following areas: peripheral modalities; concept formation; symbolic development; perceptual-motor functions; behavioral and emotional characteristics; academic achievement in reading, spelling, handwriting, and mathematics. Also there is an anecdotal report of the learning assessment. Some of the components of the *Initial Learning Assessment* were drawn from previously existing measures.

Inventory of Language Processes by Joan L. Monaco and Lexa D. Dillon; c1972; Grades K-4 (estimated); Joan L. Monaco.

A comprehensive guide for evaluating children's language abilities including specific problems and strengths. Covers the following areas related to language development: Semantic Level, Syntactic Level, Auditory Skills, Visual Skills, Motor, and Number Concepts.

Inventory of Symptoms: Vision; Not Dated; Preschool–Grade 12; The Reading Clinic, Temple University.

A screening measure in which the child is asked questions which may indicate a visual disorder.

Johns Hopkins Perceptual Test by Leon A. Rosenberg; c1966; Ages 3-9; Leon A. Rosenberg.

An individually administered measure of form discrimination-configurations. The testee is presented with a stimulus picture and is asked to point out the matching stimulus.

Kindergarten Auditory Screening Test by Jack Katz; c1971; Kindergarten; Follett Educational Corporation.

Designed for the early identification of chil-

dren who have auditory perceptual handicaps. The test is group administered. A record player is required. Subtests included are: Speech in Environmental Noise, Phonemic Syntheses and Same/Different (the ability to determine whether words or nonsense words in pairs are the same or different).

Kindergarten Evaluation of Learning Potential by John A. R. Wilson and Mildred C. Robeck; c1963-1966; Kindergarten; Webster Division, McGraw-Hill Book Company.

Designed to identify learning capacities of young children. The test assesses three levels of learning: association, conceptualization, and creative self expression. Subtests are: Skipping, Color Identification, Bead Design, Block Design, Bolt Board, Calendar, Number, Safety Signs, Writing a Name, Auditory Perception, Social Interaction.

Laterality; Not Dated; Kindergarten–Grade 12 and Adults; The Reading Clinic, Temple University.

Covers perceptual dominance, hand preference, eye preference, ear preference, family history of preferences, central dominance (kinaesthetic-kinaesthetic, visual-kinaesthetic, and bi-manual writing).

Leavell Hand-Eye Coordinator Tests by Ullin W. Leavell; c1958-1961; Ages 8-14 years; Keystone View Company.

An individually administered measure consisting of four subtests: Hand-Foot Preference; Eye-Ear Preference; Hand Dexterity Preference; Visual Imagery: Pointed Objects, Incomplete Objects, Moving Objects.

Lincoln-Oseretsky Motor Development Scale by William Sloan; c1954; Ages 6-14 yrs.; Stoelting Company.

A revision of *Oseretsky Tests of Motor Proficiency.*

Lindamood Auditory Conceptualization Test by Charles H. Lindamood and Patricia C. Lindamood; c1971; Grades K-12; Teaching Resources Corporation.

An individually administered measure of the ability to discriminate sameness and difference between speech sounds and perception of the order and number of sounds in sequences of non-syllabic and syllabic patterns. Subscores are: Isolated Sounds in Sequence, Sounds within Syllable Pattern.

Lurcat Test of Graphical Abilities by Lilliane Lurcat and Irene Kostin; c1966; Ages 4-19 yrs.; Educational Testing Service.

Test is designed to test the graphic movements of two hands in copying geometric curves, elongated cycloids and spirals. Three kinds of copying are assessed: simple, simultaneous, and crossed copying.

Marianne Frostig Developmental Test of Visual Perception by Marianne Frostig, Phyllis Maslow, D. Welty Lefever, and John R. B. Whittlesey; c1961-1966; Ages 3-10 yrs.; Follett Educational Corporation.

Designed for use in the identification of children with visual perceptual problems that may cause learning difficulties. Subtests are: Eye-Motor Coordination, Figure Ground, Constancy of Shape, Position in Space, and Spatial Relationships.

Meeting Street School Screening Test by Peter K. Hainsworth, and Marian L. Siqueland; c1969; Grades K-1; Crippled Children and Adults of Rhode Island, Inc.

An individually administered measure of gross-motor, visual-perceptual-motor, and language skills which serve as an aid in identifying children with learning disabilities. The test is based on an information processing model. Emphasis is placed on the child's orientation, integration, and feedback during information processing. Subtests are: Motor Patterning, Visual-Perceptual-Motor, and Language. A Behavior Rating Scale is provided for recording observations of the child's behavior during testing.

Memory-For-Designs Test by Frances K. Graham, Barbara S. Kendall; c1946-60; Ages 8.5-60 yrs.; Psychological Test Specialists.

An individually administered instrument which measures perceptual-motor coordination and may be used to detect brain damage.

Minnesota Percepto-Diagnostic Test: Revised by Gerald B. Fuller; c1962, 1969; Ages 5 yrs.–Adults; Clinical Psychology Publishing Company.

May be used to classify the etiology of reading and learning disorders into primary, secondary, or organic retardation and to classify children who have behavioral problems as having normal, emotionally disturbed, or schizophrenic perception. When testing children, a score is reported for Normal, Primary Reading Retardation, Emotional Disturbance, Schizophrenic Perception, and Maturation Level. When testing adults, scores are reported for Normal Perception, Personality Disturbance and Organic Brain Damage.

Moore Eye-Hand Coordination and Color-Matching Test by Joseph E. Moore; c1949-55; Ages 2 yrs. and over; Joseph E. Moore and Associates.

The test includes: Eye-Hand Coordination, Color Matching (Ages 6 years and over only).

Motor-Free Visual Perception Test by Ronald P. Colarusso and Donald D. Hammill; c1972; Ages 4-8; Academic Therapy Publications.

A test of visual perceptual processing ability which does not require the motor involvement of the examinee. Factors assessed are: spatial relationships, visual discrimination, figure-ground, visual closure, and visual memory.

Naming Test by Robert M. Wold; c1970; Grades 1-6; Robert M. Wold.*

Provides an indication of the developmental level of the child. The tester provides a category (i.e. animals) and asks the child to name as many members of the category as he can in one minute. The examiner can change the category to suit the environment of the child. *Included in: Wold, Robert M. *Screening Tests to be Used by the Classroom Teacher.* San Rafael, California: Academic Therapy Publications, 1970.

Neurological Evaluation by Mark N. Ozer; Not Dated; Ages 4½-8 yrs.; Mark N. Ozer.

An individually administered examination designed for the neurological evaluation of children upon entry to school. Subtests include: Motor Scale: Optokinetic Nystagmus (Ability to fixate on instruction); Tactile Figure-Writing; Visual Figure Ground; Two Point Discrimination; Position Sense Testing; Sound-Touch Test; Face-Hand Test; Rapid Alternating Touching at Fingertips on the Right and Left; Walking Straight Line, Six Feet (Eyes Closed); Walking Backwards, Six Feet (Eyes Open); Tapping Rhythmically with Foot and Ipsilateral Index Finger, Five Seconds (Right and

Left); Walking Straight Line, Six Feet; Standing Heel to Toe; Hopping in Place; Associated Movements; Tapping of Feet; Standing on Foot; Crossing Mid-line; Intelligibility Scoring; Following Directions; Following Directions on Examiner (Testee is asked to point to parts of examiner's body).

Observation of Symptoms That May Indicate a Hearing Problem by Gilbert Schiffman; Not Dated; Preschool-adults; The Reading Clinic, Temple University.

A checklist for use by teachers.

Observation of Symptoms That May Indicate a Visual Problem by Gilbert Schiffman; Not Dated; Preschool-Adults; The Reading Clinic, Temple University.

A checklist for use by teachers.

Oliphant Auditory Discrimination Memory Test by Genevieve G. Oliphant; c1971; Grades 1-6; Educators Publishing Service, Inc.

Designed for screening auditory discrimination ability. Can be administered to entire classes at the second grade and above. It should be administered individually or to very small groups of first-graders.

Oliphant Auditory Synthesizing Test by Genevieve Oliphant; c1971; Grade 1*; Educators Publishing Service, Inc.

An individually administered test of the ability to listen to a spoken word in separate phonemes, to remember these phonemes in the correct sequence, to blend the phonemes mentally and assign them a linguistic meaning. These abilities are essential for successful performance in speech, reading, and spelling. *The test can be used with older children who are suspected of deficiencies in auditory synthesizing ability.

Organic Integrity Test by H. C. Tien; c1960-65; Ages 5 and over; Psychodiagnostic Test Company.

Uses form perception as an indication of brain deficit unrelated to intelligence. Reviewed in: *Perceptual and Motor Skills.* 24:335, 1967.

Oseretsky Tests of Motor Proficiency by Edgar A. Doll; c1946; Ages 4-16 yrs.; American Guidance Service, Inc.

Evaluates the motor capacity of the child and classifies and measures the inadequacies of this functioning. Covers general static coordination, dynamic coordination of the hands, general dynamic coordination, motor speed, simultaneous voluntary movements, and synkinesia.

Parent Readiness Evaluation of Preschoolers by A. Edward Ahr; c1968; Ages 4-6 yrs.; Priority Innovations, Inc.

Designed to enable parents to obtain an objective measure of their child's developmental strengths and weaknesses in various basic skills and abilities. The test consists of a Verbal Section covering General Information, Comprehension, Opposites, Identification, Verbal Associations, Verbal Description, Listening, Language; and a Performance Section which covers Concepts, Motor Coordination, Visual-Motor Association, Visual Interpretation, and Memory.

Parents' Behavior Rating Scale by Gerald A. Strag; Not Dated; Ages 5.5-12 yrs.; Gerald A. Strag.

A rating scale designed to aid teachers in screening for potential learning problems through the observations of parents.

Perceptual Test by Florence E. Suthpin; c1964-1967; Grades K-1; Winter Haven Lions Publication Committee.

Designed to identify potential perceptual disabilities which may interfere with the child's acquisition of basic learning skills. Consists of a Perceptual Forms Procedure and an Incomplete Forms Procedure.

Piaget Right-Left Awareness Test by Lillian Belmont and Herbert G. Birch; 1965; Grades 1-6; Lillian Belmont.*

A measure of the ability to differentiate between right and left, either on oneself or in the mirror position. *Included in: Belmont, Lillian and Birch, Herbert G. "Lateral Dominance, Lateral Awareness and Reading Disability," *Child Development*, Vol. 36, No. 1, 57-71, 1965.

Pre-Reading Screening Procedures to Identify First Grade Academic Needs by Beth H. Slingerland; c1968-69; Grades K-1; Educators Publishing Service, Inc.

A group administered test for the identification of dyslexia or specific language disability in children who have not been introduced to reading and have average or superior intelligence. Subtests are: Visual Discrimination of Letter Forms, Visual Discrimination of Word Forms, Visual Perception Memory, Copying, Auditory Discrimination, and Letter Knowledge. The manual includes *Reproducing A Story* and the *Echolalia Test* for individual auditory screening. An integral part of the screening procedure is a form which can be completed by the first grade or kindergarten teacher. This form, the *Teacher Observation Sheet,* is concerned with the child's mental growth, language skills, writing behaviors, preferred or avoided activities, coordination, and so on.

Preschool and Early Primary Skill Survey by John A. Long, Jr., Morton Morris and George A. W. Stouffer, Jr.; c1971; Ages 3-7; American Test Bureau.

Measures visual recognition, discrimination, and association, cognition of picture story sequences, and perceptual-motor skills. Used as a basis for assigning instructional materials, assigning remedial activities and materials, and in screening to identify children who may need specialized diagnostic procedures. Subscales are: Picture Recognition, Picture Relationship, Picture Sequences, and Form Completion.

Preschool Inventory by Bettye M. Caldwell and Donald Soule; c1967; Ages 3-6 yrs.; Cooperative Tests and Services, Educational Testing Service.

An individually administered measure designed to assess achievement in areas regarded as necessary for success in school. The test covers: Personal-Social Responsiveness, Association Vocabulary, Concept Activation-Numerical, and Concept Activation-Sensory. The test can be used to identify deficiencies in cultural background.

Preschool Inventory Revised Edition—1970 by Bettye M. Caldwell; c1968-70; Ages 3-6 yrs.; Cooperative Tests and Services, Educational Testing Service.

An individually administered screening measure of achievement in areas considered vital to success in school. General factors assessed are: personal-social responsiveness (knowledge about the child's own personal world and his ability to get along with and respond to communications of another person); associative vocabulary (ability to demonstrate awareness of the connotation of a word by carrying out some action or by associating to certain intrinsic qualities of the

underlying verbal concept); concept activation—numerical (the ability to label quantities, to make judgments of more or less, and to recognize seriated positions); and concept activation—sensory (the awareness of certain sensory attributes—shape, size, motion, color—the ability to execute certain visual motor configurations). Some props are necessary.

Pre-tests of Vision, Hearing, and Motor Coordination, Pre-Primary by Elizabeth T. Sullivan, Willis W. Clark and Ernest W. Tiegs; c1951; Grades K-1; CTB/McGraw-Hill.

Helps to screen those who may have difficulty in responding to a group test because of defects in vision, hearing, and motor coordination. Covers: Visual Acuity, Auditory Acuity, and Motor Coordination.

Pre-tests of Vision, Hearing, and Motor Coordination, Primary by Elizabeth T. Sullivan, Willis W. Clark, and Ernest W. Tiegs; c1951; Grades 1-3; CTB/McGraw-Hill.

Helps to screen those who may have difficulty in responding to a group test because of defects in vision, hearing, and motor coordination. Covers: Visual Acuity, Auditory Acuity, and Motor Coordination.

Primary Academic Sentiment Scale by Glen Robbins Thompson; c1968; Ages 4 yrs., 4 months–7 yrs., 3 months; Priority Innovations, Inc.

Designed to obtain objective information regarding a child's motivation for learning and his relative level of maturity and parental independence.

Primary Visual Motor Test by Mary R. Haworth; c1970; Ages 4-8 yrs.; Grune and Stratton, Inc.

Designed to assess visual motor development in the preschool and early primary grades and to evaluate deviations in visual motor functioning during the development process. The test has been standardized on children from various socio-economic strata and can be administered to retarded children up to age 9. Dimensions measured are: Rotation or Reversal; Line Configuration, Linear, Segmentation, Fragmentation, Closure, Omission, Addition, Distortion, Directionality, Alignment, Boundary, No Resemblance, and Gross Signs.

Process for In-School Screening of Children with Emotional Handicaps by Eli M. Bower and Nadine M. Lambert; c1961-62; Grades K-12; The Office of Special Tests, Educational Testing Service.

Experimental screening device designed to identify children with emotional handicaps which may interfere with the learning process. Parts of the test include: Teacher Perception (Behavior Ratings of Pupils), Peer Perception (Class Pictures, Grades K-3; A Class Play, Grades 3-7; Student Survey, Grades 7-12), Self Perception (A Picture Game, Grades K-3; Thinking About Yourself, Grades 3-7; Self Test, Grades 7-12).

A Program for Early Identification of Learning Disabilities—Kit 1: the Educational Evaluation by Wretha Peterson; c1970; Grades K-1*; Special Child Publications, Inc.

Designed for use by special and regular teachers in diagnosing the strengths and weaknesses of the child who has difficulty with a normal academic program. The Kit is individually administered and assesses the child's levels of functioning in the following areas: Information; Language Development; Auditory Discrimination and Perception; Ability to Listen and Follow Directions; Visual Perception, Eye-Hand Coordination and Fine Motor Functioning; Tactile Perception and Kinesthetic Performance; Laterality and Directionality; Spatial and Temporal Relationships; Memory; Ability to Change Set; Organizational Ability; Task Orientation; Manner of Relating to Others; Stamina; Gross Motor Functioning; Body Concept; Recognition and Comprehension of the Printed Word; Number Concepts and Functioning. *With some adaptations, the kit may be used with mentally retarded and elementary grade children.

Psychoeducational Evaluation of the Preschool Child by Eleonora Jedrysek, Lillie Pope, Zelda Klapper, and Joseph Wortis; c1972; Preschool–Grade 1; Grune and Stratton, Inc.

Designed to assess the child's present functions and level of achievement in various areas and identify specific deficits. Curriculum guides are provided. Areas covered: Physical Functioning and Sensory Status, Perceptual Functioning, Competence in Learning for Short-term Retention, Language Competence, and Cognitive Functioning.

Psychoeducational Profile of Basic Learning Abilities by Robert E. Vallett; c1966; Ages 4-8 yrs.; Consulting Psychologists Press, Inc.

An aid in summarizing clinical and standardized test data that are relevant in planning preventive and remedial programs for children with specific learning disabilities. Covers motor integration and physical development, perceptual abilities, language, social-personal adaptivity, and general intellectual functioning.

The Pupil Rating Scale by Helmer R. Myklebust; c1971; Ages 7-10 yrs.; Grune and Stratton, Inc.

Subscales include: Auditory Comprehension (comprehending word meanings, following instructions, comprehending class discussions and retaining information); Spoken Language (vocabulary, grammar, word recall, storytelling, relating experiences and formulating ideas); Orientation (judging time, spatial orientation, judging relationships, and knowing directions); Motor Coordination (general coordination, balance, manual dexterity); Personal-Social Behavior (cooperation, attention, organization, new situations, social acceptance, responsibility, completion of assignments, and tactfulness).

Pupil Record of Educational Behavior by Ruth Cheves; c1971; Preschool–Grade 3; Teaching Resources Corporation.

A diagnostic aid for evaluating a pupil's level and pattern of functioning. Profiles a child's performance along various developmental dimensions. The record is in four sections, each forming a progression of increasingly difficult tasks related to particular pre-academic or academic areas, at various levels: Visual-Motor Perception, Auditory Perception, Language Development, and Mathematical Concepts.

Purdue Perceptual-Motor Survey by Eugene G. Roach and Newell C. Kephart; c1966; Ages 5-10 yrs.; Charles E. Merrill Books, Inc.

Designed to qualitatively assess the perceptual-motor abilities of children in the early grades. Tasks include: Walking Board (Forward, Backward, Sidewise), Jumping, Identification of Body Parts, Imitation of Movements, Obstacle Course, Kraus-Weber Test of Physical Fitness, Angels-in-the-Snow, Chalkboard (Circle, Double Circle, Lateral

Line, Vertical Line), Rhythmic Writing (Rhythm, Reproduction, Orientation), Ocular Pursuits (Both eyes, Right Eye, Left Eye, Convergence), Visual Achievement Forms (Form, Organization).

Riley Preschool Developmental Screening Inventory by Clara M. D. Riley; c1969; Preschool–Grade 1; Western Psychological Services.

Designed to quickly identify children with serious behavioral problems, the Inventory provides an index of the child's developmental age and self-concept. It has been used in Head Start programs in poverty areas.

Rosner Perceptual Survey: Experimental Edition by Jerome Rosner; 1969; Ages 6-10; Learning Research and Development Center, University of Pittsburgh.

A screening measure for the identification of perceptual-motor dysfunction requiring approximately 30 minutes for administration. The Subtests are: General Status, Word Repetition, Near Visual Acuity, Stereopsis, Auditory Organization, Developmental Drawing, Cover, Near Point of Convergence, Ocular Pursuits, Retinoscopy, Motor Skills, Body Image, Rhythmic Hop and Rhythmic Tap, Split-Form Board, Auditory-Visual, Tactual Visual, Rutgers Drawing Test. The test can be used with emotionally disturbed and mentally retarded children.

Rosner-Richman Perceptual Survey: Experimental Edition by Jerome Rosner and Vivien Richman; 1969; Ages 6-10 yrs.; Learning Research and Development Center, University of Pittsburgh.

A screening measure for the identification of perceptual-motor dysfunction requiring 15 minutes for administration. Subtests are: General Status, Word Repetition, Auditory Organization, Developmental Drawing, Near Point of Convergence, Motor Skills, Body Image, Rhythmic Hop and Rhythmic Tap, Auditory-Visual, and Rutgers Drawing Test. The test can be used with emotionally disturbed and mentally retarded children.

The Rutgers Drawing Test by Anna Spiesman Starr; 1952-69; Ages 4-9 yrs.; Anna Spiesman Starr.

A nonverbal copying test which may be used as a performance test of perceptual motor ability, a screening device for detecting visuomotor handicaps, and/or an indicator of a child's method for attacking problems.

School Entrance Check List by John McLeod; c1968; Grades K-1; Educators Publishing Service, Inc.

An aid in screening children for dyslexia and other reading disabilities. The questionnaire is completed by the parent.

The School Readiness Checklist by John J. Austin and J. Clayton Lafferty; c1963-68; Ages 4-6 yrs.; Research Concepts.

A checklist of developmental skill levels covering growth and age, general activity related to growth, practical skills, remembering, understanding, general knowledge, and attitudes and interests. Completed by parents.

School Readiness Survey by F. L. Jordan and James Massey; c1967; Ages 4-6 yrs.; Consulting Psychologists Press, Inc.

Identifies the preschool child's developmental level through the appraisal of skills related to adequate functioning in the school environment. Subtests are: Number Concepts, Discrimination of Form, Color Naming, Symbol Matching, Speaking Vocabulary, Listening Vocabulary, General Information. A General Readiness Checklist is also provided.

Screening Test for the Assignment of Remedial Treatments (START) by A. Edward Ahr; c1968; Ages 4-6 yrs.; Priority Innovations, Inc.

Designed to identify strengths and weaknesses related to visual-auditory-motor discrimination functioning in preschool and kindergarten children. Provides stanine scores in the four subtest areas of Visual Memory, Auditory Memory, Visual Copying, Visual Discrimination.

Screening Test of Academic Readiness by A. Edward Ahr; c1966; Ages 4-6 yrs.; Priority Innovations, Inc.

Designed to aid in identifying a preschooler's learning characteristics, social and emotional difficulties, and developmental and remedial needs. The test covers: Picture Vocabulary, Letters, Picture Completion, Copying, Picture Description, Human Figure Drawing, Relationships, Numbers.

Sentence Writing—From Dictation by Robert M. Wold; c1970; Grades 1-6; Robert M. Wold.*

Assesses the proper formation and orientation of the letters. As the child performs the task, observations are made of the following: posture; vocalization or subvocalization; speed; spacing; sequence; formation; concentration, attention, and fatigue. *Included in: Wold, Robert M. *Screening Tests to be Used by the Classroom Teacher.* San Rafael, California: Academic Therapy Publications, 1970.

Shape-O-Ball Test by Jerry R. Thomas and Brad S. Chissom; 1972; Preschool–Grade 1; Jerry R. Thomas.

A task designed to assess perceptual-motor abilities which are closely related to academic readiness. These skills include: shape recognition, perceptual match, and hand-eye coordination. Task employs a prop (Shape-O-Ball).

Slingerland Screening Tests for Identifying Children with Specific Language Disability, Form A, Revised Edition 1970 by Beth H. Slingerland; c1962-70; Grades 1-2; Educators Publishing Service, Inc.

The nine tests are designed to reveal the relative strengths and weaknesses in perceptual-motor functions, visual, auditory, and kinesthetic functions and to reveal differences in receptive and expressive language performance. The authors define "specific language disability" to refer to children of average or high intelligence whose difficulties in reading, spelling, handwriting, written and sometimes oral expression interfere with academic achievement.

Slingerland Screening Tests for Identifying Children with Specific Language Disability, Form B, Revised Edition 1970 by Beth H. Slingerland; c1962-70; Grades 2-3; Educators Publishing Service, Inc.

The nine tests are designed to reveal the relative strengths and weaknesses in perceptual-motor functions, visual, auditory, and kinesthetic functions and to reveal differences in receptive and expressive language performance.

Slingerland Screening Tests for Identifying Children with Specific Language Disability, Form C, Revised Edition 1970 by Beth H. Slingerland; c1962-70; Grades 3-4; Educators Publishing Service, Inc.

The nine tests are designed to reveal the relative strengths and weaknesses in percep-

tual-motor functions, visual, auditory, and kinesthetic functions and to reveal differences in receptive and expressive language performance.

Slosson Drawing Coordination Test (SDCT) for Children and Adults by Richard L. Slosson; c1962-67; Ages 1 year and over; Slosson Educational Publications.

Used to identify individuals with various forms of brain dysfunction or perceptual disorders where eye-hand coordination is involved.

Southern California Figure-Ground Visual Perception Test by A. Jean Ayres; c1966; Ages 4-10 years; Western Psychological Services.

Designed to facilitate identification of deficits in visual perception which require selection of a foreground figure from a rival background. Reviewed in: *The Journal of Special Education,* Vol. 4, No. 1, 1970.

Southern California Kinesthesia and Tactile Perception Tests by A. Jean Ayres; c1966; Ages 4-8 years; Western Psychological Services.

A battery of six tests used to diagnose disorders of somatic perception. The tests cover: Kinesthesia, Manual Form Perception, Finger Identification, Graphesthesia, Localization of Tactile Stimuli, Double Tactile Stimuli Perception. Reviewed in: *The Journal of Special Education,* Vol. 4, No. 1, 1970.

Southern California Motor Accuracy Test by A. Jean Ayres; c1964; Ages 4-7 years; Western Psychological Services.

Diagnoses severity of perceptual-motor dysfunction. Reviewed in: *The Journal of Special Education,* Vol. 4, No. 1, 1970.

Specific Language Disability Test: Grades Six, Seven and Eight by Nova Malcomesius; c1967; Grades 6-8; Educators Publishing Service, Inc.

Evaluates perception in visual discrimination, visual memory, visual-to-motor coordination, perception in auditory discrimination, auditory-to-visual coordination, auditory-to-motor coordination, and comprehension. All written tests evaluate handwriting and all tests check ability to follow directions.

Standardized Road-Map Test of Direction Sense by John Money, Duane Alexander, and H. T. Walker, Jr.; c1965; Ages 7-18; Johns Hopkins Press.

An individually administered measure of right-left discriminatory ability.

Stanford Early School Achievement Test: Level I by Richard Madden and Eric F. Gardner; c1969; Kindergarten and Beginning of Grade 1; Harcourt Brace Jovanovich, Inc.

Designed to provide a measure of a child's cognitive abilities at various levels. Assesses in the areas of the Environment, Mathematics, Letters and Sounds, and Aural Comprehension.

Symptom Checklist for the Preschool Child by Martin Kohn; circa 1966; Preschool; Martin Kohn.

The test covers: Social Relationships, Emotional Responses, Bodily Functioning, Appearances and Mannerisms, Speech and Voice.

Symptomatology and Identification of a Child with Learning Disabilities: Revised Edition by Lillian K. Vittenson; c1969; Grades K-6; Priority Innovations, Inc.

A checklist covering the following aspects of a child's behavior and performance: specific learning disabilities; physical characteristics; hyper-active; hyper-kinetic; hypo-active; hypo-kinetic; perceptual-motor impairments; coordination; disorders of speech and hearing; vision; aggressive behavior; attention; memory and thinking; impulsivity; social and behavioral characteristics.

Test of Concept Utilization by Richard L. Crager and Ann J. Spriggs; c1972; Ages 4½-18½ years; Western Psychological Services.

Provides for qualitative and quantitative assessment of the use of verbally expressed concepts and a system for the classification of responses. Concept Categories are: Equivalence Scores—Color, Shape, Homogeneous Function, Abstract, Stimulus Bound, and Object Bound; Relational Scores—Relational Function, and Minor Relational; Structure Scores—All Equivalence, All Relational, and All Unilateral; Reality Match Scores—Color, Shape, Homogeneous Function, Abstract, Relational Function, and a Total Reality Match Score; Concept Articulation Scores—Acceptable Mains and Inferior Mains; Qualitative Scores—Action, Object Qualities, Infusions, and Creation; and Negations.

3-D Test for Visualization Skill by Grace Petitclerc; c1972; Ages 3-8 years; Academic Therapy Publications.

Measures 3 levels of visualization skill. At the first skill level, a single fixed image can be held in memory; at the second, a group of images can be recognized and held for observation; and at the third level, the images can be transformed to create new forms (visualization). Tests included are: Shape Identification, Size Perception, Visual Equilibrium, Visual Memory, Operational Imagery, and Image Transformation.

Valett Developmental Survey of Basic Learning Abilities by Robert Valett; c1966; Ages 2-7 years; Consulting Psychologists Press.

Evaluates various developmental abilities and facilitates the planning of individualized learning and remedial programs in accordance with the specific learning disabilities identified by the instrument. Subtests are: Motor Integration and Physical Development, Tactile Discrimination, Auditory Discrimination, Visual-Motor Coordination, Visual Discrimination, Language Development, Verbal Fluency, Conceptual Development. Mainly for use with slow learners.

Van Riper Test of Laterality by C. Van Riper; Not Dated; Grades 1-12 and Adults; The Reading Clinic, Temple University.

Areas covered are visual-kinesthetic and bimanual script.

The Vane Kindergarten Test by Julia R. Vane; c1968; Preschool-Kindergarten; Clinical Psychology Publishing Company, Inc.

Designed to evaluate the intellectual and academic potential and behavior adjustment of young children.

Visual Motor Gestalt Test by Lauretta Bender; c1938-46; Ages 3 years and over; American Orthopsychiatric Association, Inc.

A maturational test of visual motor gestalt junction in children which is used to explore retardation, regression, loss of junction and organic brain defects where there are regressive phenomena.

Visual Retention Test by Arthur L. Benton; c1955-63; Ages 8 years and over; Arthur L. Benton (Distributed by The Psychological Corporation).

A clinical research instrument designed to assess visual perception, visual memory, and visuo-constructive abilities. Subtests are: Omissions (and Additions), Distortions, Perservations, Rotations, Misplacements, Size Errors.

Watson Number Readiness Test by G. Milton Watson; c1961-63; Grades K-1; The Book Society of Canada, Ltd.

Consists of two parts—a Subjective Test which covers social, emotional, and psychological readiness, and an Objective Test. The manual contains a power test to be used a year later to verify prognostication of readiness.

Wetzel Grid Charts: The Baby Grid by Norman C. Wetzel; c1946; Birth to 3 years; NEA Service, Inc.

Wetzel Grid Charts: Grid for Evaluating Physical Fitness by Norman C. Wetzel; c1940-69; Ages 2-11 years; NEA Service, Inc.

The charts cover: Growth, Development, Physique (Body Build), Nutritional Grade, Physical Status, Age Advancement, Maturation, Basal Metabolism, Calorie Needs, Net Progress.

Wold Digit Symbol Test by Robert M. Wold; c1967; Grades 1-6; Robert M. Wold.*

Assesses efficiency in perceptual-motor functioning on the basis of speed. The score can be diagnostic of a visual-motor deficiency. Observations should be made concerning posture, attention and concentration, method of letter or symbol formation, fatigue and frustration. Test is individually administered. *Included in: Wold, Robert M. *Screening Tests to be Used by the Classroom Teacher*. San Rafael, California: Academic Therapy Publications, 1970.

Wold Sentence Copying Test by Robert M. Wold; c1967; Grades 1-6; Robert M. Wold.*

Designed to determine if the child has the ability to rapidly and accurately copy a sentence from the top of a page to the bottom. Observations are made as to posture; the number of fixations (does the child have to look back to the stimulus word after each letter); sparing (figure-ground); vocalization or subvocalization (does he have to say each letter or word to himself before writing it); concentration, attention, fatigue; formation of letters; and frustration level. The test is

timed in order to yield a handwriting rate or copying rate. *Included in: Wold, Robert M. *Screening Tests to be Used by the Classroom Teacher*. San Rafael, California: Academic Therapy Publications, 1970.

Wold Visuo-Motor Test by Robert M. Wold; c1967; Grades 1-6; Robert M. Wold.*

Individually administered measure of hand-eye coordination and/or functioning on the basis of speed and accuracy. Observations should be made concerning the child's posture, directionality, concentration and attention fatigue and frustration, and quality of response. Subtests include: Vertical Directional Coordination Test, Short Horizontal Coordination Test, and Longer Coordination Test. *Included in: Wold, Robert M. *Screening Tests to be Used by the Classroom Teacher*. San Rafael, California: Academic Therapy Publications, 1970.

PUBLISHER ADDRESSES

Academic Therapy Publications
1539 Fourth Street
San Rafael, California 94901

Albert Einstein College of Medicine of Yeshiva University
1300 Morris Park Avenue
Bronx, New york 10461

American Orthopsychiatric Association, Inc.
1790 Broadway
New York, New York 10019

American Test Bureau
459 Grant Street
Room 210
Indiana, Pennsylvania 15701

Arden Press
8331 Alvarado Drive
Huntington Beach, California 93646

Lillian Belmont
33-60 21st Street
Long Island City, New York 11106

William Bingham
Placement Director
Antelope Valley College
3041 West Avenue K
Lancaster, California 93534

Book Society of Canada, Ltd.
4386 Sheppard Avenue
Agincourt, Ontario, Canada

Charles E. Merrill Publishing Company
1300 Alum Creek Drive
Columbus, Ohio 43216

Clinical Psychology Publishing Company
4 Conant Square
Brandon, Vermont 05733

Crippled Children and Adults of Rhode Island, Inc.
Meeting Street School
333 Grotto Avenue
Providence, Rhode Island 02906

The Devereux Foundation Press
208 Old Lancaster Road
Devon, Pennsylvania 19333

EDCODYNE Corporation
Suite 935
One City Boulevard West
Orange, California 92668

Educators Publishing Service, Inc.
75 Moulton Street
Cambridge, Massachusetts 02138

Graham-Field Surgical Company, Inc.
32-56 Sixty Second Street
Woodside, New York 10077

Institute for Developmental Studies
IPS East Building, 3rd Floor
School of Education
New york University
Washington Square
New York, New York 10003

Iowa State Department of Public Instruction
Division of Special Education
Des Moines, Iowa 50319

Johns Hopkins Press
Baltimore, Maryland 21218

Joseph E. Moore and Associates
4406 Jet Road, NW.
Atlanta, Georgia

Keystone View Company
Meadville, Pennsylvania 16335

Martin Kohn
Research Psychologists
William A. White Institute
20 West 74th Street
New York, New York 10023

Ladoca Project and Publishing Foundation, Inc.
East 51st Avenue and Lincoln
Denver, Colorado 80216

Lawrence Verry, Inc.
16 Holmes Street
Mystic, Connecticut 06355

Learning Research and Development Center
University of Pittsburgh
160 North Craig Street
Pittsburgh, Pennsylvania 15213

Henrietta Lempert
South Shore Protestant Regional School Board
6 Desaulniers Boulevard
St. Lambert, Quebec, Canada

Jacob Schleichkorn
Health Sciences Center
State University of New York at Stony Brook
Stony Brook, New York 11790

McGraw-Hill Book Company
330 West 42nd Street
New York, New York 10036

Joan Monaco
Title Vi-A Project
The Joint Special Language Class
Montgomery County Public Schools
850 North Washington Street
Rockville, Maryland 20850

Montana Reading Clinic Publications
517 Rimrock Road
Billings, Montana 59102

NEA Service, Inc.
1200 West Third Street
Cleveland, Ohio 44113

Mark N. Ozer
Associate Neurologist
Childrens Hospital of the D.C.
2125 13th Street, N.W.
Washington, D.C. 20009

Priority Innovations, Inc.
P.O. Box 792
Skokie, Illinois 60076

Programs for Education
Box 85
Lumberville, Pennsylvania 18933

Psychodiagnostic Test Company
Box 528
East Lansing, Michigan 48823

Psychological Test Specialists
Box 1441
Missoula, Montana 59801

The Reading Clinic
Temple University
Broad Street and Montgomery Avenue
Philadelphia, Pennsylvania 19122

Research Concepts
A Division of Test Maker, Inc.
1368 East Airport Road
Muskegon, Michigan 49444

Leon A. Rosenberg
9008 Samoset Road
Randallstown, Maryland 21133

Sebastiano Santostefano
Associate Professor of Psychology
Department of Child Psychiatry
Talbot Building ⅋3
Boston University School of Medicine
82 East Concord Street
Boston, Massachusetts 02118

Slosson Educational Publications
140 Pine Street
East Aurora, New York 14052

Special Child Publications, Inc.
4535 Union Bay Place N.E.
Seattle, Washington 98105

Anna Spiesman Starr
126 Montgomery Street
Highland Park, New Jersey 08904

Gerald A. Strag
Mental Health Institute
Iowa State Department of Social Services
Independence, Iowa 50644

Teaching Resources Corporation
100 Boylston Street
Boston, Massachusetts 02116

Jerry R. Thomas
Georgia Southern College
Statesboro, Georgia 30458

The Tree of Life Press
1309 N.E. 2nd Street
P.O. Box 447
Gainesville, Florida 32601

**UCLA Research Projects in Early
Childhood Education**
1019 Gayley Avenue
Los Angeles, California 90024

Wellesley Public Schools
Wellesley, Massachusetts 02181

**Winter Haven Lions Research
Foundation, Inc.**
P.O. Box 111
Winter Haven, Florida 33880

Robert M. Wold
353 H Street
Chula Vista, California 92010

REFERENCES

Buros, Oscar K., Editor. *The Seventh Mental Measurements Yearbook*. Highland Park, New Jersey: The Gryphon Press, 1972.

Hoepfner, Ralph, Editor. *CSE Elementary School Test Evaluations*. Los Angeles: Center for the Study of Evaluation, UCLA Graduate School of Education, 1970.

Johnson, Orval G., and Bommarito, James W. *Tests and Measurements in Child Development: A Handbook*. San Francisco, California: Jossey-Bass, Inc., Publishers, 1971.

Valett, Robert. *The Remediation of Learning Disabilities: A Handbook of Psychoeducational Resource Programs*. Belmont, California: Fearon Publishers, 1967.

NAME INDEX

SUBJECT INDEX

A

Ability grouping for gifted children, 236
Acceleration
  of behavior, 217
  for gifted children, 236
Accessibility, 185, 253-255
  and physically disabled, 4-5
Accountability and education, 272
Acquired disabilities, 13
Acting out in behaviorally disordered child, 160
Action, role of, in children's learning, 8
Activities of daily living, 202-205
  role of, in children's learning, 113, 114
Adaptation as ego function, 158
Adaptive behavior
  in mental retardation, 104-106
  role of, in assessment, 276
Adaptive Behavior Scale, 105
Affective education, 272, 303-304
Aggression in young children, 176
Aides, 285
Allergy and learning disabilities, 135, 142
Alternatives in special education programming, 272
Amblyopia, 82
American Association for Children in Hospitals, 17
American Foundation for the Blind, 98
Amniocentesis, 26, 29
Amphetamines in treatment of hyperactivity, 142-143
Amputee, 191-192
Anal stage, 162-163
Anoxia, 30
Anxiety, role of, in personality development, 157
Apgar test, 30
Architectural barriers: see Accessibility
Arthrogryposis, 192
Articulation problems, 45; see also Speech disorders
Assessment of handicapped child, 188
Association for Children with Learning Disabilities, 132
Asthma, 193
Ataxia, 188
Athetosis, 188
Attention, role of, in learning, 112, 113
Attentional deficits, 141-143
Attitude(s)
  change in, 298-300
  of teachers, 295-298
  toward handicapped, 4-5, 291-295
  toward physical disability, 198-199

Audiogram, 59
Audiometry, behavioral, 61
Autism, 210, 213-215
Autistic-like behavior in blind infants, 85
Autonomy, 162-163
Autotelic materials, 284
Average, concepts of, related to "normal," 12
Average intelligence, meaning of, 12

B

Barriers, architectural; see Accessibility
Basic trust, 162
Behavior analysis, 278
  in treatment of behavioral disorders, 166
Behavior modification, 166, 173, 214-215
Behavioral approach, 217-221
Behavioral objectives, 277, 281
Behavioral observation methods, 278-280
Behaviorism
  and early education, 6
  scope of, 6
Bilingualism, 49-50
Birth defects, 29
Blaming victim, 297
Blind children, guidelines in teaching, 94
Blindisms, 95
Blindness
  and cognitive development, 83-85
  and emotional development, 84-85
  legal, 81
Bliss symbols, 217-218
Body image
  in blind children, 95-96, 134
  in handicapped children, 201-202
Braces, 200-201
Braille, 81, 93-94
Brain injury and learning disabilities, 134
Brainstorming, 240, 279
British Primary School, 261-263
  family grouping in, 23-24
  goals of, 23

C

Cascade of services, 209, 297
Categorization of children, dangers in, 11
Causality, 196
  concept of, 118-124
Centration in cognitive development, 140-141

Cerebral palsy, 187-188, 210
Channel deficiencies, 140-141
Chemotherapy and hyperactivity, 142-143
Child Development Associate, 17
Child-centered classroom, 273
Children
  attitudes of, 301, 303-304
  at risk, 28
Children's Defense Fund, 155, 178
Class meeting, 243
  Glasser, 279
Class Play, 279
Classification
  of exceptionalities, 11, 12-14
  skills, in teaching mentally retarded child, 112
Classroom, organization of, 258-259, 260-265
Clinical attitude, 273
Clinical method, Piaget's, 197-198, 229, 243
Clubfoot, 192-193
Cognitive approach, 6
Cognitive curriculum for young physically handicapped child, 196-198
Cognitive development
  in blind infants, 83-85
  in retarded children, 116, 118
Cognitive goals for blind children, 97-98
Cognitive skills in curriculum for preschool retarded, 118-124
Commonality of development, 8-9, 11
Communication
  in blind infants, 85-87
  disorders, types of, 42-45
  goals for blind children, 96-97
  interagency, 285
Community Coordinated Child Care, 17
Compensation in blindness, 83
  in infants, 87-88
Competence
  motivation, 239
  sense of, 166, 206
Competencies of teachers of severely or profoundly handicapped, 219-220, 223-224
Concept learning of mentally retarded children, 112
Concrete and abstract thought in mental retardation, 108
Congenital disabilities, 13
Consultant teacher, 286
Contagion of behavior, 170
Contingency management; *see* Behavior modification
Control, preoccupation with, 297
Convulsive disorder, 188, 189-190
Coping mechanisms in young children, 165
Counseling, directive and nondirective methods of, 278-279
Countertheory, 157
Creativity, 231-232
Criterion of ultimate functioning, 221-222
Criterion-referenced assessment, 145, 221, 275, 276-277
Criterion-referenced tests, norm-referenced tests and, 110
Critical incident technique, 278
Cultural differences, 4, 8
  and problems in ability testing, 12, 13
Cultural imagery and attitudes toward handicapped, 294-295

Curriculum
  for preschool retarded children, 116-118
  for severely or profoundly handicapped, 222-223
Cystic fibrosis, 193

D

Day care
  developmental vs. custodial, 16-17
  home vs. center-based, 17
Deaf-blind child, 211-212
Deafness
  and cognitive characteristics, 58-59
  and language ability, 58
  as relative disability, 59
Defect theories of mental retardation, 106
Defense mechanisms, 157
Deficit theories of mental retardation, 107
Denial in handicapped children, 199
Dependency in handicapped child, 202-203
Deprivation
  experimental, 218
  maternal, 107
  sensory, 107
Devaluation
  of deviance, 257
  of handicapped, 295
Developmental delay, 214
Developmental diagnosis, 26-31, 126
Developmental hierarchy, 112-113
Developmental interaction theory, 9-10
  contrasted with behaviorism, 10
Developmental Learning Profile, 128
Developmental milestones; *see* Developmental diagnosis
Developmental orientation, 281
Developmental perspective in teaching severely or profoundly handicapped child, 221-222
Developmental therapy for disturbed children, 169-170
Diabetes, 193
Diagnosis
  developmental, 26-31, 126
  differential, 274
  related to screening, 27
  role of, in education, 273-275
Diagnostic-prescriptive teacher, 286
Diagnostic-prescriptive teaching, 143-145, 175
  of mentally retarded child, 109-111, 125
Diagnostic profile, 110-111, 280, 283-284
Diagnostic teaching, 109-110
Difference orientation, 297
  and mental retardation, 12, 108
Differential diagnosis, 274
Directionality
  in blind infants, 92-93
  and learning problems, 139-140
Disability
  distinguished from handicap, 4
  in relation to handicap, 185
Disadvantaged child, 266-268
Discovery learning, 239-240, 242-243
Discrepancy in identifying learning disabilities, 132
Distinctive features, 141
Distractibility, 141-143
Divergent thinking, 240-242
Dominance, 139-140
Down's syndrome, 26, 29-30, 107

Dramatic play, 168
Drawing as method of child study, 280

E

Early education, scope of, 5, 16-24
Early identification of learning disabilities, 135-143
Early intervention, foundations for, 1-33
Eclecticism in treatment of behavioral problems, 166
Ecological approach in teaching behavior-disordered child, 170
Ecological psychology, 253
Ecosystems, 170
Educable mental retardation, definition of, 105
Education, role of, in development, 6-7
Educational intervention, 14-15
    compensation, 13-14
    need in teaching handicapped, 15
    parallel to medical intervention, 14-15
    primary prevention, 14
    secondary prevention, 14
Educational therapy with behavior-disordered children, 166-170
Ego, 157
Ego identity, 157-158
Ego processes in young children, 165
Ego psychology, 157
Ego strength, 164-165
Egocentricity in retarded children, 121
Egocentrism, 231
Emotional development in blind infants, 86
Emotional needs of handicapped child, 198-200, 301-302, 304
Endogenous vs. exogenous mental retardation, 107
Engineered classroom, 260-261
English Primary School, 239
Enrichment
    for gifted children, 237
    in kindergarten programs, 138
Environment
    and behavior, 6
    dimensions of, 253
    and handicapping conditions, 4
    role of
        in development, 252-253
        in prevention, 266-269
Environmental causes of learning disabilities, 133
Erogenous zones, 161-169
Esthetic appeal of learning environment, 255-256
Etiology, 28-30
Eurythmics, 21
Evaluation of educational programs, 15-16
Exceptionality as distinguished from normal development, 10-11
Exclusion
    in definition of learning disabilities, 133
    of handicapped children from school, 155
Expansion in language learning, 52
Experience, role of, in development, 4-7
Expressive abilities, role of, in teaching retarded, 123
Expressive language, importance of, in teaching mentally retarded children, 114-115
Extinction in behavior modification, 173

F

Facilitation in physical therapy, 187

Failure to thrive, 126, 136
Family grouping in British Primary School, 23-24
Family problems and handicapped child, 199-200
Fantasy, 245
Feeding severely or profoundly handicapped child, 223
Figure-ground disturbance, 134
Fixation, 26, 161
Flexibility in learning environment, 255
Follow through, 5

G

General learning disability as term for retardation, 104
Genetic counseling, 29
Giftedness, 12
    definition of, 230-232
    in disadvantaged children, 235
    in handicapped children, 235
    and psychosocial characteristics, 232
    types of, 232
Gross motor skills in blind infant, 91-93
Grouping in British Primary School, 23-24

H

Head Start, 5, 16, 19-21
    enrollment of handicapped children, 281
    mandate to serve handicapped children, 19
    planned variations in, 21
Hearing aids, 70-72
Hearing impairment
    adventitious, 60
    conductive, 60
    congenital, 60
    degrees of, 60
    incidence, 60-61
    and language ability, 58
    sensory-neural, 60
Hearing-impaired children
    in regular classrooms, 62, 72-75
    and teacher's role, 62
Heart defect, congenital, 193
High-risk infant, 17, 28
Home Start, 18
Home training for hearing-impaired children, 63-64
Home visitor, 85
Homogeneity, assumption of, 272
Hospital programs, 17
    and early identification, 17
Human relations approach, 303-304
Human relations climate of classroom, 293
Hydrocephalus, 191
Hyperactivity, 134, 141-143
Hyperkinecity, 142
Hypoglycemia, 142

I

Identification
    "child-find" program, 29
    of exceptional children
        normative perspective in, 26-27
        perinatal, 30
        prenatal, 26, 29-30
        problems in, 25-26
        purpose, 25-27
        teachers' role in, 23
    of gifted child, 233-235